W9-AAJ-101

COURVOISIER'S®

BOOK *of* THE

BEST

THE INSIDE TRACK
TO EXCELLENCE
AND VALUE AROUND
THE WORLD

EDITED BY
LOYD GROSSMAN

WRITTEN BY AURORA GUNN

EBURY PRESS · LONDON

1 3 5 7 9 10 8 6 4 2

Text copyright © Random House UK Ltd 1996

All rights reserved. No part of this publication may be reproduced, stored
in a retrieval system, or transmitted in any form or by any means, electronic,
mechanical, photocopying or otherwise, without the prior permission of the
copyright owner.

Managing editors	Joanna Sheehan
	Sarah Sutton
Consultant editor	Sue Carpenter
Researchers	Claire Atherton
	Carol Gallacher
	Fiona Hall
	Sue Lanson
	Desley Sherrin
	Mat Waugh
Foreign correspondents	Sandy Charlwood (*Caribbean*)
	Freda Colbourne (*Canada*)
	Claudia Cragg (*America; China; Hong Kong; Indonesia; Japan; Malaysia; Singapore; Thailand*)
	Melissa de Villiers (*South Africa*)
	Michael Gebicki (*Australia; Fiji; New Zealand; Vietnam*)
	Gabriella Kovács (*Hungary*)
	Logan Bentley (*Italy*)
	Martin Lorman (*Spain*)
	Riona MacNamara (*Ireland*)
	Dominique Magada (*Belgium; France*)
	Anne-Elisabeth Moutet (*France*)
	Britta Lee Shain (*West Coast America*)
	Sarah Townsend (*Czech Republic*)
	Evert Van Veen (*The Netherlands*)
	Selina Williams (*Russia*)
Edited by	Alison Wormleighton
Designed by	Harry Green

The information contained in this book was checked as rigorously as possible
before going to press. The publisher accepts no responsibility for any changes
which have occurred since, nor for any other variance of fact from that recorded
here in good faith.

A catalogue record for this title is available from the British Library.

ISBN: 0 09 181299 2

Typeset in Bembo by Textype Typesetters, Cambridge
Printed and bound by Mackays of Chatham plc, Kent

CONTENTS

PREFACE

COURVOISIER
From EMPERORS *to* PRESIDENTS

Although Courvoisier cognac has become a contemporary and rather fashionable base for long drinks in many countries these days, it is a brand that is also long on history.

Emmanuel Courvoisier, the founder of the company, was visited by Napoleon I in 1811 at his Paris-Bercy warehouse. The emperor was so taken with M. Courvoisier's cognacs that he loaded plentiful supplies on board a ship in which he planned to escape to America. In the event, neither he nor the cognac beat the British blockade, but thereafter Courvoisier became known as "Le Cognac de Napoléon".

In 1869 Courvoisier was appointed purveyor to the court of another emperor, Napoleon III, a great anglophile and the visionary who master-minded the rebuilding of Paris. It was in memory of this Napoleonic "double" that the famous silhouette of Napoleon later appeared on all styles of Courvoisier cognac as a symbol of excellence.

The Courvoisier connection with French heads of state has continued ever since. More recently, the former president François Mitterand was buried in his home town of Jarnac, in which the most famous landmark is Château Courvoisier. A museum housing many of the gifts that M. Mitterand received during his presidency now complements the Courvoisier museum as the two main tourist attractions.

The current president, Jacques Chirac, is also linked to Courvoisier, having presented the company with "La Prestige de la France", in recognition of the continued excellence of Courvoisier cognacs and the company's sustained export achievement. On this occasion, France's leader was given a very rare bottle of Courvoisier which he was able to take away without fear of blockade!

INTRODUCTION

Welcome to the latest edition of our biennial attempt at summing up the world's best in a book that remains small enough to travel with.

Each time we begin, we notice that the definition of what's best has changed. When I first contributed to *Courvoisier's Book of the Best*, in 1984, the best was easier to identify – or maybe it would be more accurate to say that what our readers wanted was easier to define. Luxury, excellence and extravagance were all far more closely tied up in those days, before the worldwide recession of the late 80s encouraged people to rethink their lives, priorities and bank balances.

Life around the *Courvoisier's Book of the Best* boardroom table has become a lot more interesting now that people no longer automatically equate the best with the most expensive. I am pleased to say that with the previous edition and this latest one, we have shifted towards a much broader, more accessible and more exciting definition of what the best is.

We live in a world where everything is always available – from the year-round (but often flavourless) asparagus on our supermarket shelves to the instant (but often unaffecting) images on our computer screens. It is a world tending towards bland convenience. I like to think that what we write about in *Courvoisier's Book of the Best* is an antidote to that.

For me the best includes the different, the exciting, the stimulating. Sometimes it involves a startling innovation, at other times a relentless dedication to the way things have always been done. Early editions of this book concentrated more heavily on shopping, restaurants and hotels – all fields where the best was relatively obvious. As we focus more and more on cultural tourism and active travel, it becomes more complicated. As usual for our purposes, the best is what our extensive international network of correspondents enjoy and feel that you will also like.

In this edition we have introduced far more activities than ever before, as we believe that our readers are becoming increasingly interested in active holidays. Indeed, for many people the whole concept of holidaying has changed, from a ring-fenced period of doing nothing to a time for doing something very different – whether that is trekking, fishing, scuba-diving or spending more time going to galleries, museums or concerts. Our new *Courvoisier's Book of the Best* very much reflects this more active approach to travel.

As always, we rely entirely on word of mouth and personal recommendations. All entries are solely on the basis of our contributors' judgement of their merits. This year you will, I hope, find more entertaining writing, and useful as well as inspirational information. By all means put it in your suitcase, but also remember to keep a copy by your bedside to help you dream about your travels.

LOYD GROSSMAN was born in Boston, Massachusetts and graduated from Boston University and the London School of Economics. After working as Design Editor at *Harpers & Queen* and Contributing Editor of the *Sunday Times*, he moved into television devising, writing and presenting some of Britain's top-rated television programmes including *Through the Keyhole*, the award winning *MasterChef* and *Junior MasterChef*. His documentary-making work for the BBC series *The Dog's Tale: A History of Man's Best Friend* and *The World on a Plate: The History and Mystery of the Food We Eat* has taken him around the world many times. He was the inspiration for the Edinburgh Fringe play *Loyd Grossman – Out to Lunch*, described by its author as a tribute to a "cultural icon"! Loyd lives in London with his wife, two children and two dogs. He is a keen fisherman and scuba diver, patron of the National Canine Defence League, vice president of the Sick Children's Trust and Chairman of the Campaign for Museums.

AURORA GUNN'S career started at *Tatler* before she moved to become Commissioning Editor for the relaunch of *Punch*. She is both a journalist and a television commentator.

KEY TO SYMBOLS
☯ The clutch of coins has been used to highlight a place considered to be very good value for the excellent service it provides.

CONTRIBUTORS

SIOBHAN ADAMS Editor of the *Gulf Marketing Review* magazine and has travelled widely throughout the Middle East.

MOHAMED AL FAYED Proprietor of L'Hôtel Ritz, Paris and Chairman of Harrods of Knightsbridge, London.

BONARIA & LUCIO ALIOTTI She is a freelance journalist for prestigious Italian publications, he sells advertising for *The European* and *USA Today*. Both know Milan inside out.

JEFFREY ARCHER Bestselling author and playwright; books include *Kane & Abel, First Among Equals* and, most recently, *The Fourth Estate*. He was made a peer in 1992.

JANE ASHER British actress and writer. Also proprietor of Jane Asher Party Cakes; consultant for Sainsbury's cakes and spokesperson for McVities.

STEPHEN BAYLEY Design expert, Creative Director of Redwood and Bayley consultancy and author of *Taste: The Hidden Meaning of Things*.

FRÉDÉRIC BEIGBEDER A Paris journalist, socialite and novelist.

LOGAN BENTLEY wrote and photographed for leading US publications including *Time* and *People* for 25 years. Now editor and publisher of Made★in★Italy★On★Line which includes the first web about fashion and design on Internet. Two other webs in the series are Italian Wine & Food and Italian Travel & Fun. She has been Italian correspondent for *Courvoisier's Book of the Best* for the last three editions.

JEFF BLYNN is a model turned restaurateur who has travelled all over Italy and loves to introduce cooking from the USA to his young, sophisticated customers in Rome.

JOEL CADBURY A director of Longshot, which owns and runs The King's Club, The Goat in Boots pub, The Andrew Robson Bridge Club and Vingt Quatre, one of London's best 24-hour restaurants. (See page 121.)

SUE CARPENTER Founder author of *Courvoisier's Book of the Best*, she is a freelance writer and journalist on various national newspapers and magazines. Her latest book is *Past Lives: True Stories of Reincarnation*.

JEAN PHILIPPE CHATRIER French actor, screenwriter and biographer of Claude Lelouch, as well as the author of popular crime novels.

FREDA COLBOURNE Director, Corporate Communications at Molson Breweries for the past six years. Has travelled extensively across Canada and throughout the world and has been involved with the book since its first edition.

VICTORIA COLLISON Senior fashion editor at *Vogue Australia* and a regular on the European fashion show circuit.

SIR TERENCE CONRAN Businessman, designer, style leader, restaurateur and owner of the highly acclaimed Quaglino's and Mezzo. (See page 95.)

CLAUDIA CRAGG Journalist and author, Claudia has been Far East correspondent of every single edition of *Courvoisier's Book of the Best*. She is author of the bestselling business book *The New Taipans*, and is correspondent for a number of Japanese glossy publications.

QUENTIN CREWE British writer, restaurateur and traveller, and author of the acclaimed autobiography *Well, I Forget the Rest*. (See page 223.)

ALAIN DE BOTTON A writer

and author of *Essays in Love, The Romantic Movement* and *Kiss and Tell*. His works have been translated into 16 languages. (See page 143.)

MARQUIS DOMINIQUE DE LASTOURS Genealogist and historian, member of the Order of the Cincinnati – the descendants of the French aristocrats who fought with Lafayette for American Independence.

CLEMENCE DE ROCH Novelist, social and royal writer for *Gala* magazine.

MELISSA DE VILLIERS A South African writer and travel journalist, based in London.

STEFANO FABBRI works for the most important Italian news agency, ANSA, has lived in Florence for many years and also publishes a monthly magazine there.

CARLA FENDI is the coordinator and spokeswoman for the five Fendi sisters and the Spoleto Music Festival.

GIANFRANCO FERRE Internationally known Italian fashion designer resident in Milan who designed the Dior high-fashion collection for eight years.

FIORA GANDOLFI An artist, photographer and journalist who lives in a vast loft-apartment near Venice's Rialto bridge. A student of the history of fashion and textiles.

MICHAEL GEBICKI Sydney-based freelance journalist and photographer, and contributor to various national magazines and newspapers including *Gourmet Traveller*.

A A GILL is a writer and journalist, who has recently published his first novel, *Sap Rising*. (See page 213.)

DAVID GOWER Former England

cricket captain turned broadcaster and journalist. Part-time bon viveur.

ROBERTO GUCCI and his wife **DRUSILLA** created the House of Florence specializing in fine leather goods, continuing the tradition of the Gucci family.

JILL HALEY is an American living in Milan, one of Giorgio Armani's favourite models, expert horse-woman and jockey who exercises racehorses for fun.

ROBIN HANBURY-TENISON Explorer and author whose books include *A Ride along the Great Wall*, *Worlds Apart*, *Spanish Pilgrimage* and *The Oxford Book of Exploration*.

MAEVE HARAN Author of *Having It All* and *It Takes Two*, based in London.

SIR JOHN HARVEY-JONES Flamboyant ex-chairman of ICI and *The Economist*. Author, TV presenter and avid traveller.

PAUL HEATHCOTE 'Chef of the Year' 1994 and proprietor of his own restaurant in Preston, Lancashire. Awarded an Honorary Fellowship by the University of Central Lancashire in 1995.

CHARLES-EFFLAM HEID-SIECK Great-great-great-grandson of the original "Champagne Charlie", currently working in the perfume world.

ANOUSKA HEMPEL (LADY WEINBERG) Designer, hotelier, couturier and owner of Blake's Hotel and The Hempel Hotel in London.

PAUL HENDERSON Hotelier who runs the renowned Gidleigh Park hotel in Devon.

JEAN-MICHEL HENRY Hairdresser to the stars and owner of Carita Montaigne salon, whose cus-tomers include actress and Chanel muse Carole Bouquet.

ANNABEL HESELTINE A London-based writer, journalist, TV and radio broadcaster who cannot stop travelling.

GAY HOAR Former Treasury Attaché in Rome who travelled all over Italy and is now an official with the Treasury Department in Washington.

KEN HOM American cookery expert and food consultant based in LA and Hong Kong. Bestselling author of *Ken Hom's Chinese Cookery* and more recently *Ken Hom's Hot Wok*.

JEAN-MICHEL JAUDEL A for-mer international businessman, he is now a full-time artist and has already had two shows at Galerie Henry Bussière on rue Mazarine in Paris.

FRÉDÉRICK JOCHEM French collector, interior decorator and style expert based in New York.

ELIZABETH KING Broadcaster and all-conquering travel writer, who sets the pace for where Australians will go next year.

JUDITH KRANTZ American novelist and francophile, author of megasellers *Scruples*, *Princess Daisy* and *Dazzle*.

SUSAN KUROSAWA Author, travel writer and broadcaster, her incisive column in *The Australian Magazine* dissects the Antipodean psyche.

PIERRE LANSON A former chairman (now retired) of the Lanson champagne house in Reims. International businessman, avid traveller and a world expert on wine.

ALEXANDRE LAZAREFF Author of *Paris Rendez-Vous* and *Guide to Other Cities*, he has also been food adviser to the French Minister of Culture, and is food critic for *Le Figaro*.

ROBIN LEACH American TV host and contributing editor of *Honeymoon* magazine. Co-owner of Carola's, a New York restaurant, and partner of World's Best Chefs Co. Inc.

JULIAN LLOYD WEBBER Internationally acclaimed cellist who has performed with many world-famous orchestras and conductors, and has made numerous major recordings.

MARTIN LORMAN Lives in Barcelona with his Catalan wife and daughter, exporting Catalan products.

MARK MCCORMACK International entrepreneur, founder and chairman of the world's No. 1 sports' management group, IMG. Author of four acclaimed books including *What They Don't Teach You in Harvard Business School*.

LADY MACDONALD OF MACDONALD Journalist and author of many cookery and enter-taining books including *Celebrations* and *Claire MacDonald's Scotland*.

RIONA MACNAMARA Managing editor of the last edition of *Courvoisier's Book of the Best*, now working for Microsoft in Dublin.

DOMINIQUE MAGADA A jour-nalist, currently working for *Bloomberg Business News*. A keen traveller, she has written and writes on art, food and travel.

NICK MASON Longest serving member of Pink Floyd, amateur racing driver and pilot.

NANDO MIGLIO Formerly an editor of Italian *Harper's Bazaar*, he is an image creator *extraordinaire* and an art director.

SHERIDAN MORLEY Author and playwright, he is the drama crit-ic of the *Spectator* and the *International Herald Tribune*. Also, a radio and TV presenter.

ANNE-ELISABETH MOUTET Paris bureau chief for *The European* and French correspondent for the last five editions.

MICHAEL MUSTO Nightlife columnist for *The Village Voice* in New York.

RITA & MARIANO PANE have one of the most beautiful botanical gardens in Italy in Sorrento. She writes about gardens, he writes about Italian food.

DOMINIQUE PIOT Paris-based member of the Société des Gastronomes. Co-chairman of Communication et Développement, a market research and PR company.

UMBERTO PIZZI A veteran photojournalist who has an extensive knowledge of the Roman social and political scene.

JANE PROCTER The editor of *Tatler*, renowned for doubling the circulation by making it the magazine that sets the social, style and fashion agenda.

DAVID PROFUMO is a novelist and fishing columnist, based in London. (See p.227.)

JAMIE PUTNAM is the executive art director for Fantasy Records in Berkeley, Ca.

LIZ REES-JONES British publisher and chairperson of Presse Publishing, she created and launched *Top Santé* magazine in Britain. Formerly publisher of British *Elle* and *Mirabella* magazines.

COUNT LUC REVILLON Famous antiques dealer and patron of the Association des Amis de l'Opera Comique.

HILARY RUBINSTEIN Founder editor of the *Good Hotel Guide* and literary agent.

JEREMY SEAL A British freelance travel writer. His first book *A Fez of the Heart: Travels Around Turkey in Search of a Hat*, is published by Picador. For his second book, he is exploring snake cultures and is in search of survivors of bites from his own 'Big Four': the Australian taipan, the African black Mamba, the Indian cobra and the North American rattlesnake (see page 75.)

SIMON SEBAG MONTEFIORE is an ex-Soviet expert and columnist for the *Sunday Times*. (See p.246.)

BRITTA LEE SHAIN is a freelance novelist and screenwriter whose articles and film reviews have appeared in *Venice* magazine.

NED SHERRIN Film, theatre and TV producer, director and writer. Host of BBC Radio 4's *Loose Ends* and author of *Ned Sherrin's Theatrical Anecdotes* and *Ned Sherrin in His Anecdotage*.

KATE SOLOMON is an LA-based fashion designer who specializes in vintage fabrics.

EDWARD THORPE Former ballet critic for the *Evening Standard*.

JOHN TOVEY Chef-owner of Miller Howe hotel in Cumbria. Makes frequent appearances on TV and radio and his books include *The Miller Howe Cookbook* and *John Tovey's Country Weekends*.

SARAH TOWNSEND A graduate from Sussex University and a qualified solicitor, Sarah lives in Prague with her husband, a British diplomat.

REBECCA TYRREL Editor of the *Sunday Telegraph* magazine. (See p.22.)

CLAUS VON BULOW Barrister-at-Law, Vice President Getty Oil International, investment banker, and retired litigant in the United States. Danish citizen who voted against Maastricht.

STANLEY WEISER An LA screenwriter whose credits include *Wall Street*, *Project X* and *H.B.O.'s Fatherland*.

BEATRICE WELLES An entrepreneur/businesswoman, she's the spokesperson for Oldsmobile (one of the biggest car firms in the US) and works for her father's (Orson Welles) foundation.

SELINA WILLIAMS A freelance journalist who writes for *The European*, *The New York Times* and other publications. She is now based in Tbilisi, Georgia in the Caucasus.

CAROL WRIGHT British journalist specializing in travel; author of over 30 books on travel and food.

Also, special thanks to: Tony Apsler, Claire Barnes, Summer Baye, Raymond Blanc, Karla Bonoff, Sue Avery Brown, Frank Bowling, John Bowman, Richard Branson, Sally Burton, Robert Carrier, Glynn Christian, Richard Compton Miller, Kathleen Cox, Raffaele Curi, Jeffrey Day, Angus Deayton, Lon Diamond, Alain Ducasse, Douglas Fairbanks Jr, Lady Fairfax, Matthew Fort, Marchesa Bona Frescobaldi, Valerie Gibson, Johnny Gold, Shep Gordon, Timothy Greenfield-Saunders, Judith Greer, Sophie Grigson, Lady Hardinge, Marcella Hazan, Lyn Hemmerdinger, Don Hewitson, Caroline Hunt, Pamela Ives, Richard Johnson, Stephen Jones, Barbara Kafka, Kitty Kelley, Michaela Kennedy, Jeremy King, Keith King, Emanuel Lanson, Alastair Little, John McKenna, Jonathan Meades, Hans Meissen, Kate Moss, Jill Mullens, Andrew Neil, Sandy O'Byrne, Elise Pascoe, Steven Podborski, Richard Polo, Andre Previn, Bob Ramsay, Egon Ronay, Albert Roux, Donald Saunders, Claudia Schiffer, Brian Sewell, Rosemary Sexton, Mimi Sheraton, David Shilling, Martin Skan, William Stadiem, Ralph Steadman, Jeffrey Steingarten, Martha Stewart, Daniel Stoffman, Sheila Swerling-Puritt, Sir Peter Ustinov, Ed Victor, Roger Vierge, Faith Willinger, Christopher Winner, Tim Zagat, Jorg Zipprick.

ACKNOWLEDGEMENTS

Loyd Grossman and the publishers would like to thank the following people for their invaluable help in compiling this book: Ivar Braastad, Gillian Delaforce, Harry Green, Carolyn Griffiths of Textype, Ian Jesnick, Roger Jupe, Vicki Robinson, Caroline Staff, Alison Wormleighton.

Aurora Gunn would particularly like to thank Jane Procter, David Gunn, Inigo Wilson and the Studleys for all their help, patience and support.

AMERICA
Boston

ART AND MUSEUMS

BOSTON PUBLIC LIBRARY
666 BOYLSTON ST, COPLEY SQ,
MA 02117
☎ (617) 536 5400
Built in Renaissance palazzo style by Charles
Follen McKim, this is one of the grandest examples of late 19C US architecture, housing the collections of Whitman, Melville and Emerson.
Undergoing restoration for the foreseeable future.

ISABELLA STEWART GARDNER MUSEUM
280 THE FENWAY, MA 02115
☎ (617) 566 1401
Brian Sewell, Lord Gowrie and many of the
natives have a genuine soft spot for Mrs
Gardner's rather outlandish museum. The collection of 2,000 paintings, sculptures and other
works is housed in a fake 15C Venetian palazzo around the corner from the Museum of
Fine Arts. Also *"Its Sunday classical concerts are an
ongoing favourite of Bostonians – the courtyard café
and garden are idyllic and the Caesar salad's delicious"* – SUE AVERY BROWN.

⑩ MUSEUM OF FINE ARTS
465 HUNTINGDON AVE, MA 02115
☎ (617) 267 9300
This is one of America's first-division art
museums, with the largest collection of Monets
outside Paris, a definitive collection of Asian art
and rare 18C silverwork by Paul Revere.
Extensive displays of American fine and decorative art and furniture. Once you've reached sat-
uration point you can withdraw to the café or
restaurant or have a browse in the large gift shop.

BARS AND CAFES

CAFE LOUIS
234 BERKELEY ST, MA 02116
☎ (617) 266 4680
When it comes to coffee, Americans can be
terrible snobs, so when you're told that this
*"boasts one of the best cups of cappuccino outside
Milan"* (SUE AVERY BROWN) take note. It's also
known for being one of the trendiest little eateries in town. You can also dine on the terrace
outside.

CHEERS/BULL & FINCH
84 BEACON ST, MA 02116
☎ (617) 227 9600
This epitomizes the classic American yuppy
bar and is still as popular as ever. As you might
expect, the food mainly consists of burgers and
sandwiches, but just above is the **LIBRARY
GRILL,** which specializes in seafood. On Sun
there's a jazz brunch and at nights dinner is
accompanied by a jazz trio.

CLUBS

THE AVALON
15 LANSDOWNE ST, MA 02215
☎ (617) 262 2424
The biggest club in Boston, set on two floors,
with 12 bars, a VIP room and high-tech lighting systems which flash across the dance floor.
There's a regular, if somewhat eclectic, programme of theme nights and occasional live
music from acts with names like PJ Harvey and
Sonic Youth.

THE ROXY
279 TREMONT ST, MA 02116
☎ (617) 338 7699
Forget minimalism. Converted from an old
theatre space, this is the most opulent club in
town. There are six bars and an unusually large
dance floor. If you want to escape the flash of
photographers' bulbs, there's a little more privacy in the balcony area upstairs.

VENUS DE MILO
11 LANSDOWNE ST, MA 02215
☎ (617) 421 9595
One of Boston's more surreal venues, where
you can pose in elevated cages or weave your
way through Romanesque columns to the
beat. A favourite with the serious dance crowd
– with different styles of music every night,
from techno to hip hop to reggae. Closed Sun.

ZANZIBAR
1 BOYLSTON PL, MA 02116
☎ (617) 351 7000
Upmarket tropicana, all is palm, rattan and
faux-marble. Besuited 30-somethings get
down to favourite 70s and 80s hits on Wed.
On Thurs to Sat the DJs concentrate on the
current top 30 chart, while Tues night is "Ibiza
night", often with live bands. You can always
retreat to the **CRESCENT CLUB** on the 2nd
floor, where you can drink champagne and
play billiards in peace. Closed Sun and Mon.

HOTELS

THE BOSTON HARBOR HOTEL

70 Rowes Wharf, MA 02110

☎ (617) 439 7000

Best views in town. Antique maps in the lobby, generic oil portraits and repro furniture give the place an establishment feel, while you can still rely on your 90s must-haves, such as interactive information channel, CD player and super-luxurious health club. Sunday brunch is Boston's finest. Noted for wonderfully efficient and helpful staff.

THE CHARLES HOTEL

1 Bennett St, Cambridge, MA 02138

☎ (617) 864 1200

Contemporary chic mingles with old America. The patchwork quilts and simple, Shakeresque furniture contrast with the ultra-modern health spa set on three floors and the sophisticated cuisine in **Rarities** restaurant. The USP, though, is the **Regatta** bar, where you can listen to great jazz acts, in comfort.

THE FOUR SEASONS

200 Boylston St, MA 02116

☎ (617) 338 4400

"The most spectacular hotel in Boston," according to Donald Saunders and Frank Bowling. Along with the 19C decor traditionalists will appreciate the relentless attention to detail – even the doorman has been awarded for his services. The restaurant **Aujourd'hui** is still a favourite among the local smart set. Terrific for children: games and videos on tap, milk and cookies grandly provided by room service.

RITZ CARLTON

15 Arlington St, MA 02117

☎ (617) 536 5700

This is the *grande dame* of Boston's hotels. Tight security, the highest staff:guest ratio in town and its rigid formality (ties for gents a must) make it a perfect safe-haven for VIPs, which is why the Prince of Wales, Katharine Hepburn, various Kennedys and European royals have stayed here. The dining room is smart, discreet, if a little bit staid. Guests may use a luxurious health spa around the corner.

MUSIC

BOSTON SYMPHONY ORCHESTRA

Symphony Hall, 301 Massachusetts Ave, MA 02115

☎ (617) 266 1492

World-famous orchestra directed by Seiji Ozawa, who is as keen on playing new works from contemporary composers as he is on maintaining an extensive classical repertoire. The Boston Pops, from May to mid-July, at Tanglewood (west of Boston) are well worth experiencing. It's Boston's equivalent to Glyndebourne: you have a picnic on the lawn surrounding the stage and then listen to the music under the stars.

HANDEL & HAYDN SOCIETY

Horticultural Hall, 300 Massachusetts Ave, MA 02115

☎ (617) 266 3605

Founded in 1815, this is the oldest performing music society in the US. Directed by Christopher Hogwood, the chorus and period instrument orchestra are still considered to be one of America's best. The name, however, is misleading – the group is just as adept at performing the works of Bach, Beethoven, Mozart, Monteverdi along with other baroque and romantic composers.

⊛ TANGLEWOOD MUSIC FESTIVAL

Tanglewood, Lenox, MA 01240

☎ (617) 266 1492

☎ (413) 637 1600 in July/Aug

The outdoor summer retreat of the BSO and venue for the Boston Pops. You'll see and hear artists of the calibre of Jessye Norman, James Galway and John Williams – more interesting though are the regular performances by the country's top music students. Who knows, you might spot the next Maria Callas.

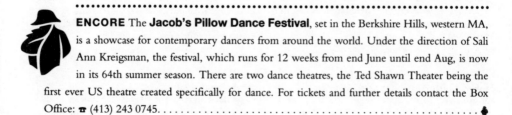

ENCORE The **Jacob's Pillow Dance Festival**, set in the Berkshire Hills, western MA, is a showcase for contemporary dancers from around the world. Under the direction of Sali Ann Kreigsman, the festival, which runs for 12 weeks from end June until end Aug, is now in its 64th summer season. There are two dance theatres, the Ted Shawn Theater being the first ever US theatre created specifically for dance. For tickets and further details contact the Box Office: ☎ (413) 243 0745. . . . . ♦

RESTAURANTS

SEE ALSO HOTELS.

AMBROSIA ON HUNTINGDON

116 HUNTINGDON AVE, MA 02115

☎ (617) 247 2400

"*Breathtaking food*" has been the local verdict on the eponymously named restaurant of Tony Ambrose. Offbeat combinations such as caviare-sprinkled black pearl risotto or quince-stuffed ravioli with John Dory fillets regularly appear on the "fusion" menu.

ANAGO BISTRO

798 MAIN ST, CAMBRIDGE, MA 02139

☎ (617) 876 8444

Chef-owner Bob Calderone has given this place an original flavour – not just with his playful interior consisting of plaster angels and other questionable *objets d'art* but also with an inspired menu. Try the Manila clams and mashed root vegetables. It only seats 40 so booking is advised. Closed Sun/Mon.

BIBA

272 BOYLSTON ST, MA 02116

☎ (617) 426 5684

Still remains one of Boston's most popular restaurants. The diverse nature of the cuisine (inspired by executive chef/owner Lydia Shire) – ranging from bitter broccoli pizza to calves' brains with crisp fried capers – keeps the celeb-heavy clientele happy. Open 7 days, 6 days for lunch. Seats 154.

CAFE BUDAPEST

90 EXETER ST, MA 02116

☎ (617) 734 3388

It's very clearly not a café – but it does, as the name might suggest, serve Hungarian food. The decor is opulent with silk-covered walls, chandeliers and ornate furniture. It's rather like being in one of those period dramas where your co-stars are likely to include GOLDIE HAWN, STEVE MARTIN and KIRK DOUGLAS are regulars. Specialities worth trying include the veal goulash, chicken paprika, and, for pudding, dobos – a multi-layer chocolate mocha cake. Those who've eaten here rate it as one of the best restaurants in America. Owner: Hedda Rev-Kury.

DURGIN-PARK

FANEUIL HALL MARKETPLACE, 30 NORTH MARKET ST, MA 02109

☎ (617) 227 2038

Boston's oldest restaurant, serving authentic, well-cooked New England food. But don't come if you want a relaxing evening for two. The menu and the atmosphere are no-frills 19C, and so is the service. First, you have to queue up, and then sit at long communal dining tables, where you'll be served by feisty, wisecracking waitresses. Chef: Tommy Ryan. Open 7 days.

L'ESPALIER

30 GLOUCESTER ST, MA 02115

☎ (617) 262 3023

One of Boston's more sophisticated restaurants, as well as one of the most expensive. Noted for owner Frank McClelland's modern French cooking and the efficient service. Menu varies each week.

GRILL 23 & BAR

161 BERKELEY ST, MA 02116

☎ (617) 542 2255

This is what proper American grill restaurants are all about – succulent steaks and rôtisserie-cooked fowl along with fresh local seafood. Also worth ordering are the lamb chops – "*the best in the US*" according to DONALD SAUNDERS – and an alternative liquid starter, the oyster shooter, consisting of an oyster squashed into a shot glass of vodka covered in Bloody Mary mix. Dinner only, 7 nights. Bar opens from 4.30 pm. Chef: Robert Fathman.

JIMMY'S HARBORSIDE RESTAURANT

☎ (617) 423 1000

Right-on the water on the historic Boston Fish Pier, this popular restaurant serves New England seafood such as the sublime house-baked stuffed lobster. Very popular with the in-crowd.

⑤ LEGAL SEAFOODS

35 COLUMBUS AVE, MA 02116

☎ (617) 426 4444 AND OTHER LOCATIONS

"*If it ain't fresh, it ain't legal.*" Don't worry, you won't be forced to break the law here – all seafood and fish proffered are so fresh that their next of kin have yet to be informed. ELIZABETH TAYLOR wouldn't be here if it was going to endanger her all too fragile health, nor would other regulars ERIC CLAPTON and ELTON JOHN. No frills but a huge variety of all things from under the New England sea.

LOCKE OBER

3 WINTER PL, MA 02101

☎ (617) 542 1340

The decor is rich, the food is rich and so is the clientele. Downstairs there's a bar, presided over by a huge nude portrait of Madame Yvonne, where many powerbrokers who have dined, retreat to powerbroke. JFK used to come here, but probably didn't stay for long, as it used to be for men only. Favourite fillers include cream-lashed lobster savannah and the hasty pud – an extraordinarily cumbersome mixture of molasses, cream, butter, sugar, nutmeg and ginger – delicious though. Chef: Jam Navaraj.

OLIVE'S

10 CITY SQ, CHARLESTOWN, MA 02116
☎ (617) 242 1999
Slow service and a no-reservations policy might mean that anything would taste good having waited that long. But Chef Todd English's gigantic portions of modern bistro-style food are worth the aggro – especially the wood-grilled swordfish and spit-roasted chicken, followed by falling chocolate cake with warmed raspberry sauce and vanilla ice cream. Located adjacent to the naval yard.

PIGNOLI

79 PARK PLAZA, MA 02116
☎ (617) 338 7690
Pigs, pigs and more pigs, courtesy of designer Adam Tihany. Fortunately the theatrical interior does not detract from extraordinary dishes such as the sea urchin and caviare spaghetti. The food from this particular kitchen of Lydia Shire (of **BIBA** – see entry) and Susan Regis is fast winning local acclaim.

PROVIDENCE

1223 BEACON ST, BROOKLINE, MA 02146
☎ (617) 232 0300
Paul O'Connell's wide-ranging menu includes neo-New England specialities, such as Jonah crab cakes with celery rémoulade and Wellfleet littleneck clams and Maine cod cheeks. The decor is a little harder to pin down.

THE RIALTO

IN THE CHARLES HOTEL (SEE HOTELS)
☎ (617) 661 5050
Chef Jody Adams produces everything from vegetarian dishes like potato gnocchi gratin with a fricassee of wild mushrooms, to lots of tempting meat and fish dishes. The hot chocolate cream with ginger crème anglaise and meringues is irresistible.

RISTORANTE TOSCANO

41/47 CHARLES ST, MA 02116
☎ (617) 723 4090
Recently voted the Best Italian Restaurant in Boston, the food always tastes 100% authentic. The pasta, risotto and bread are all good, as is the veal. Service can be casual.

SALLY LING'S

10 LANGLEY ROAD, NEWTON CENTRE, MA 02159
☎ (617) 332 3600
The most glam Chinese in town. Try the sautéed lobster with ginger and scallions, followed by fresh fruit and ginger ice cream. A range of vegetarian dishes is available and you can always call in advance to give the chef all your do's and don'ts.

SEASONS

BOSTONIAN HOTEL, QUINCY MARKET, NORTH & BLACKSTONE ST, MA 02110
☎ (617) 523 4119
Executive chef Peter McCarthy bases his seasonal menu around lots of fresh local seafood and wild game. Found on the 4th floor of The Bostonian Hotel overlooking Faneuil Hall Marketplace, this is the city's best skyline restaurant. Award-winning selection of wines.

29 NEWBURY STREET

29 NEWBURY ST, MA 02116
☎ (617) 536 0290
Art deco, ultra-chic Back Bay restaurant, which is continually filled with the works of local artists. Christopher Kane's "All American Cuisine" is equally contemporary. The salmon and the beef tenderloin are always reliable as is the home-made fruit tart of the day or the white chocolate and mango mousse.

SHOPPING

NEWBURY STREET is Boston's Bond St, where you'll find all the best shops and art galleries housed in bay-fronted 19C houses. FANEUIL HALL MARKETPLACE (pronounced "fannel" or "fanyool"), ☎ (617) 338 2323, was the old central wholesale market until the late 70s, when it was turned into a wildly popular farrago of fast food and small delicatessens. LE SAUCIER, for example, specializes in fiery seasonings, spices and sauces. For good high-rise shopping, visit COPLEY PLACE's wonderful selection of quality stores. Since the turn of the century, the best place to find antiques has been CHARLES STREET on Beacon Hill, where there are also some very pleasant cafés including COFFEE CONNECTION, 97 Charles St, ☎ (617) 227 3812. But for genuine café culture you must visit HARVARD SQUARE in Cambridge, which is full of bookshops. And you can't go home without visiting the **SOUVENIR STORE** (open 7 days), 19 Yawkey Way, ☎ (617) 421 8686, the largest sports souvenir store in the US. Stocks every baseball cap, warm-up jacket and T-shirt, as well as more arcane American sporting memorabilia.

Chicago

ART AND MUSEUMS

THE ART INSTITUTE OF CHICAGO

MICHIGAN AVE AT ADAMS ST, IL 60603
☎ (312) 443 3600

One of the finest art museums in the US. The collection of over 300,000 works ranges from pre-Renaissance to Post-Impressionist and to architectural drawings, photographs, prints and textiles. There's some impressive Asian art too. *"Superb permanent collection, especially of Impressionist period"* – EDWARD THORPE.

BARS AND CAFES

BUTCH McGUIRE'S

20 W DIVISION ST, IL 60610
☎ (312) 337 9080

These days it's more famous for its OTT Christmas decorations and Bloody Marys but in days gone by this old Irish saloon was among the first singles bars in the country. SYLVESTER STALLONE and WOODY HARRELSON have been spotted there – perhaps they haven't heard that it isn't a pick-up joint anymore.

IGGY'S

700 N MILWAUKEE, IL 60622
☎ (312) 829 4449

This is where cool Chicago kids hang out at all hours and can gorge on Italian food until 4 am. In summer the beer garden provides added appeal.

POPS FOR CHAMPAGNE

2934 N SHEFFIELD AVE, IL 60657
☎ (312) 472 1000

As the name suggests, this is the place to drink champagne, and a lot of it, with a stock of over 100 different kinds. If you're feeling peckish you can order starters and puddings. Although the bar opens at 4.00 pm, the place only really gets going after dinner with the jazz band. Music begins at 8.30 pm during the week, 9.00 pm at weekends.

CLUBS

THE GOLD STAR SARDINE BAR

680 N LAKE SHORE DR, IL 60611
☎ (312) 664 4215

Small building, hip crowd, great jazz.

KABOOM CLUB

747 N GREEN ST, IL 60622
☎ (312) 243 8600

Chicago's celebrity haunt. Set on three floors – there's an unusually large dance floor, cabaret, jazz, pool room and a VIP room for the VIPs, like BILL MURRAY, BOB DE NIRO and JAMES WOODS. Open Thurs–Sat. No food served.

KINGSTON MINES

2548 N HALSTED, IL 60631
☎ (312) 477 4646

Serious jazz fans have been coming here for 28 years to listen to genuine Chicago blues. Pizzas and corn dogs to eat. Book ahead.

THE SHELTER

564 W FULTON ST, IL 60606
☎ (312) 648 5500

Post-modern converted warehouse, sofas covered in white sheets. Five bars and two dance floors: one outside, one in. Outdoors you'll hear rap, and indoors mainly soul and funk. Open Thurs–Sat. No food.

"THE SKYLINE OF CHICAGO IS WONDERFUL – GREAT MODERN BUILDINGS WHICH WE HAVEN'T ACHIEVED IN BRITAIN" –

PETER BLAKE

HOTELS

THE DRAKE

140 E WALTON ST, IL 60611
☎ (312) 787 2200

Renaissance-style hotel which has become a Chicago landmark, with uninterrupted views over the lake. Popular hotel, where BARONESS THATCHER, BOB HOPE and other high-fliers recharge their batteries.

FOUR SEASONS

120 E DELAWARE PL, IL 60611
☎ (312) 280 8800

Set on floors 30–46 of one of Chicago's more

imposing skyscrapers, while the lobby takes up the entire 7th floor. The views over the city and lake are unparalleled. Bedrooms are 18C in style and you can let off steam in the spa – there's also a skylight pool and outdoor jogging track.

RITZ CARLTON

160 E PEARSON ST AT WATER TOWER PL, IL 60611

☎ (312) 266 1000

Located on the "Magnificent Mile", sheer paradise for ladies who shop. Confusingly, it's a Four Seasons property which occupies floors 10–31 of the 74-storey Water Tower Place, a shop/restaurant/theatre complex. The DINING ROOM serves classic French, while the RITZ CAFÉ serves informal Mediterranean fare. There's a spa for winding down too. The CARLTON CLUB is for private dining.

SUTTON PLACE (FORMERLY LE MERIDIEN)

21 E BELLEVUE PL, IL 60611

☎ (312) 266 2100

Chicago's most chic hotel. Award-winning Art Deco interior (granite, glass, metal, Mapplethorpe photos) has lured HARRISON FORD and JOHN MALKOVICH into becoming regulars. BRASSERIE BELLEVUE and bar are usually buzzing.

MUSIC

CHICAGO OPERA THEATER

4140 W FULLERTON, IL 60639

☎ (312) 292 7521

Now entering its 23rd season, the theatre maintains a platform for contemporary American composers, singers, directors and designers, as well as boosting neglected classics. Everything is sung in English.

CHICAGO SYMPHONY ORCHESTRA

ORCHESTRA HALL, 220 S MICHIGAN AVE, IL 60604

☎ (312) 435 6666

The CSO is more than a century old, ancient by US standards. Under the musical direction of Daniel Barenboim, its vitality hasn't diminished. In summer the symphony moves outdoors to Highland Park for the Ravina Festival which runs from end June to early Sept.

LYRIC OPERA OF CHICAGO

20 N WACKER DR, IL 60606

☎ (312) 332 2244

Ranked as one of the top US opera companies.

Under general director Ardis Krainik, and a genius artistic director, Bruno Bartoletti, the old is tempered with the new.

RESTAURANTS

SEE ALSO HOTELS.

AMBRIA

2300 N LINCOLN PK W, IL 60614

☎ (312) 472 5959

Contemporary, international cuisine prepared by chef Takashi Yagishi. Two set menus with special dessert soufflés every night. Try the langoustines with port wine and the roasted sweetbreads. The restaurant's understated style is mirrored by its elegant clientele, which includes ROBERT REDFORD, HARRISON FORD and ALBERT FINNEY. Closed Sun.

CHARLIE TROTTER'S

816 W ARMITAGE ST, IL 60614

☎ (312) 248 6228

Unpredictable. A mixture of American, French and Asian cuisine. Top Chicago chef Charlie Trotter enjoys experimenting – so you never know quite what's going to end up on your plate. If you're very lucky he'll invite you to sit in his kitchen while he improvises his own meal for you, or try one of the two "Tasting" menus. Great for vegetarians. Closed Sun/Mon.

CHEZ PAUL

660 N RUSH ST, IL 60611

☎ (312) 944 6680

Being housed in a 19C mansion might give this traditional French restaurant an unfair advantage, but Chicagoans love it anyway. Guests are wooed with dishes like escalope de veau Normande, sole amandine and the steak au poivre flambé in Armagnac. Piano bar Wed–Sat.

THE ECCENTRIC RESTAURANT

159 W ERIE, IL 60610

☎ (312) 787 8390

Executive chef Jody Denton, trained by Dean Fearing from the Mansion on Turtle Creek in Dallas, is now very much a culinary star in her own right. Denton's eclectic American cuisine represents *"a diversity of cultures, seasons and big bold flavors,"* she says. Highly recommended are Oprah's potatoes with horseradish (OPRAH WINFREY is a part owner). You might see WHITNEY HOUSTON and DAN ACKROYD in there too. Open 7 days. Specials on Thurs.

THE EVEREST ROOM

40TH FL, 440 S LA SALLE, IL 60605

☎ (312) 663 8920

Probably the best French restaurant in town and conveniently set on 40th floor of the Chicago Stock Exchange. John Joho's Alsace-accented cuisine includes treats such as roasted Maine lobster with Gewürztraminer and ginger. Closed Sun/Mon. Parking available.

THE FRONTERA GRILL

445 N CLARK ST, IL 60610

☎ (312) 661 1434

Celebrity author and chef Rick Baylis is always gallivanting off to Oaxaca to brush up and stock up on appropriate Mexican ingredients. Next door is **TOBO PAMPOPO** – a grander menu and a grander bill – produced by the same team. Lunch and dinner Tues–Sat.

GORDON

500 N CLARK ST, IL 60610

☎ (312) 467 9780

Weird and wonderful dishes served in a theatrical setting. *"In many ways the best restaurant in Chicago"* – CLAUDIA CRAGG. The main menu includes grilled red snapper with horseradish, mashed potatoes, lemon dill sauce and asparagus; lamb chops with tabouleh; and baba ganoush (cold eggplant dip, similar to houmus). It's worth leaving room for the strawberry rhubarb tart or warm chocolate and raspberry cake. **CAFÉ GORDON,** 100 E Chestnut St, ☎ (312) 280 2100, is gentler on the senses, offering lighter bistro food in a more laid-back atmosphere.

MORTON'S

1050 N STATE ST, IL 60610

☎ (312) 266 4820

LIZA MINELLI, FRANK SINATRA and MICHAEL JORDAN frequently come to build themselves up on Chicago's biggest and best steaks. Solid, clubby atmosphere. Open 7 days.

PARK AVENUE CAFE

199 E WALTON PL, CORNER OF WALTON ST & MIES VAN DER ROHE AVE, IL 60611

☎ (312) 944 4414

As with its sister restaurant in New York, make sure you're hungry beforehand, otherwise you'll never forgive yourself. The brunch is heaven, especially the "American Dim Sum Brunch", where treat after treat is brought to your table, such as swordfish chops and the Opera in the Park cake.

THE SOUL KITCHEN

2152 W CHICAGO AVE, IL 60622

☎ (312) 342 9742

"Very small, intimate restaurant where all the chefs go," says SHEP GORDON – which speaks for itself. Vibrant New Orleans-style restaurant where chef Monique King creates Southern classics such as pecan-encrusted catfish.

SPIAGGIA

980 N MICHIGAN AVE, IL 60611

☎ (312) 280 2750

Winner of the 1994 James Beard Award for chefs, Paul Bartolotta is still prepared to come out of the kitchen to adapt his menu for those who suggest alternatives. Next door is Bartolotta's lighter version, **CAFÉ SPIAGGIA,** ☎ (312) 980 2764, offering the same regional Italian cuisine but in a casual environment.

SHOPPING

CRATE AND BARREL

646 N MICHIGAN AVE, IL 60611

☎ (312) 787 5900

This is where you can stock up on designer goodies – both the useful and the frivolous kind – from glassware to garden furnishings to lighting.

MARSHALL FIELD

111 N STATE ST, IL 60602

☎ (312) 781 5000

Chicago's Harrods. All familiar designer labels – US and European along with their own "Field Manor" line. Furniture, food, crystal, etc.

ULTIMO

114 E OAK ST, IL 60611

☎ (312) 787 0906

Designer junkies eager to be up-to-the-second in style will be well satisfied with row upon row of the best of Europe, Japan and the US. Ultimo also have their own Sonia Rykiel Boutique at 106 E Oak St and Armani at No. 113.

Dallas

ART AND MUSEUMS

DALLAS MUSEUM OF ART

1717 N HARWOOD ST, TX 75201

☎ (214) 922 1200

Beautiful modern museum building, with a

new wing containing the Museum of the Americas, showcasing Eskimo art and Canadian and American paintings, sculpture and decorative arts. Good pre-Columbian and contemporary Latin American art. The highlight is still the Reves collection. Closed Mon.

KIMBELL ART MUSEUM

3333 CAMP BOWIE BLVD, FORTH WORTH, TX 76107

☎ (817) 332 8451

Louis Kahn's highly acclaimed museum building is a work of art in itself. Wonderful collections of 20C European art and regular guest exhibitions held from all over the world. Closed Mon.

THE SIXTH FLOOR

TEXAS BOOK DEPOSITORY, DEALEY PLACE, TX 75202

☎ (214) 653 6666

Emotive but fascinating museum, set in the place from where Lee Harvey Oswald allegedly shot President Kennedy. Excellent audio-visual exhibition of the Kennedy years.

CLUBS

BILLY BOB'S TEXAS

2520 RODEO PLAZA, FORT WORTH, TX 76106

☎ (817) 624 7117

The best little rodeo in Texas. Built in an old cattle building, there's live entertainment seven nights a week. Don't miss the rodeo on Fri/Sat when the big country-and-western stars play too.

THE CARAVAN OF DREAMS

312 HOUSTON ST, TX 76102

☎ (817) 877 3000

Cabaret-style club, with a rooftop cactus garden and amazing jazz, dance and theatre-based murals. Occasional performances from mavericks like LYLE LOVETT. Regular concerts on Fri/Sat, when simple bar food is available. Reservations recommended. Rooftop bar closed Mon.

HOTELS

HOTEL CRESCENT COURT

400 CRESCENT CT, TX 75201

☎ (214) 871 3200

Part of Caroline Rose Hunt's Rosewood group, and grand centrepiece for the Crescent Complex, which includes shops and a deli-

ciously pampering health club. Two restaurants – **THE CONSERVATORY**, supposedly "*the best little dining room in Texas*" is good for seafood; otherwise, there's **BEAU NASH**, where you can watch the chefs cook in an open kitchen.

MANSION ON TURTLE CREEK

2821 TURTLE CREEK BLVD, TX 75219

☎ (214) 559 2100

The Mansion alone is a very good reason to come to Texas. Now owned by Caroline Rose Hunt's Rosewood group, it is continually lauded for its legendary service (over two staff per guest). Guests include BILL, HILL and CHELSEA CLINTON, ELIZABETH TAYLOR, BARONESS THATCHER and H.M. THE QUEEN. "*It's the most genuinely hospitable place I've ever stayed at. They actually say 'Welcome home' each time you return,*" says GLYNN CHRISTIAN. And chef Dean Fearing is fast becoming one of the most famous chefs in the US – hailed for his wonderfully original Southwestern food. Make sure you try one of his crustacea dishes like the fabulous pan-fried crab cakes.

MUSIC

MORTON H MEYERSON SYMPHONY CENTER

2301 FLORA, TX 75201

☎ (214) 871 4000

Modernist home of the Dallas Symphony Orchestra, designed by I M Pei. "*Very fine hall acoustically and a very unusual building – a square within a circle, all glass and limestone*" – CAROLINE HUNT. Tickets are often scarce. JULIAN LLOYD WEBBER often visits too.

RESTAURANTS

SEE ALSO HOTELS.

BABY ROUTH

2708 ROUTH ST, TX 75201

☎ (214) 871 2345

Southwestern cooking with the odd Asian innovation thrown in, by chef Kevin Rathburne. Neo-trendy decor – all white with splashes of colour – and a young crowd including TOM CRUISE.

CITY CAFE

5757 W LOVERS LN, TX 75209

☎ (214) 351 2233

The Governor of Texas comes here to enjoy warm cabbage salad loaded with melting Roquefort and bacon; or maybe something a little more inventive such as rock shrimp and lobster risotto, with asparagus. All overseen by executive chef Katie Schma – who also does a hearty line in puddings such as warm fresh fruit cobbler with a crunchy topping. Next door, CITY CAFÉ TO GO sells the best take-away food in the area.

DAKOTA'S

600 N AKARD AVE, TX 75201

☎ (214) 740 4001

Not as chic as the Mansion on Turtle Creek but a bit less serious, serving up barbecued shrimp with tomato-horseradish sauce and deep-fried oysters in cornmeal batter. The chicken with pungent pepper and garlic sauce and cranberry relish should be sampled.

THE FRENCH ROOM

IN THE ADOLPHUS HOTEL, 1321 COMMERCE ST, TX 75202

☎ (214) 742 8200

This recently restored Louis XIV-style restaurant may seem rather out of place in the heart of cowboy land. Were Le Roi Soleil still living, even he would have appreciated William Koval's light classic French food. The roast squab with Belgian endive is particularly good. The service and the expansive wine cellar are regal in standard and scale.

NATURA CAFE

2909 MCKINNEY AVE, TX 75204

☎ (214) 855 5483

Healthy but interesting, is the food that chefs Mark Morrow and Larry Bellah produce. Each dish comes with a complete nutritional breakdown, according to the Cooper Clinic. Not to be missed are the goat cheese radicchio pesto or the vegetable tamales with spicy ranchero sauce.

THE RIVIERA

7709 INWOOD RD, TX 75209

☎ (214) 351 0094

This is more coastal/rural than inland/royal France. Chef Michael Weinstein recommends the Dover sole and the rack of lamb. Good international wine list. Open 7 nights.

STAR CANYON

3102 OAKLAWN AVE, TX 75219

☎ (214) 520 7827

Stephan Pyles, who used to be with the Routh Street Café, has said goodbye to minimalism, and gone for vastly OTT rococo instead. Pyles expounds the so-called "New Texas Cuisine": for those with a seasoned palate, the over-stuffed chiles rellenos, the venison with maple-pecan yams and the barbecued chiles are heaven. New cuisine or old, few will refuse the chocolate empanada with dried cherries and whiskey-butter sauce.

SHOPPING

NORTH PARK CENTER, ☎ (214) 363 7441, was America's first indoor mall, designed by art collector Ray Nasher. You can still find some of Dallas's most famous shops there. THE CRESCENT is now the most exclusive mall, with the GALLERIA, ☎ (214) 702 7100, not too far behind.

BOOT TOWN

5909 BELTLINE RD, TX 75240

☎ (214) 385 3052

Boots are serious business in Texas. Here you'll find cowboy boots for everyone from babies to giants, plus jeans, T-shirts, hats and other ranch accessories.

THE GAZEBO

8300 PRESTON RD, TX 75225

☎ (214) 373 6661

Where oil wives get their Karan, Ozbek and Lacroix. Also has frequent "trunk" shows where designers display their collections and customers buy direct. Closed Sun.

LADY PRIMROSE'S SHOPPING ENGLISH COUNTRYSIDE

500 CRESCENT CT, TX 75201

☎ (214) 871 8333

Mirage-like apparition in downtown Dallas – a row of thatched cottages and a baronial hall, filled with antiques and other knick-knacks, all from England. Lady Primrose's also serves real cream teas. Closed Sun.

THE NATURE COMPANY

317 N PARK CENTER, TX 75225

☎ (214) 696 2291

Anyone who loves the great outdoors will love this store, which sells everything from rock collections to camping gear to a beautiful re-creation of Galileo's thermometer. Open 7 days.

NEIMAN MARCUS

1618 MAIN ST, TX 75201

☎ (214) 741 6911

This *"incomparable superstar among department stores"* (HILARY RUBINSTEIN) is also home to America's finest mail-order company. The designer clothes, shoes and bags are almost overshadowed by the extraordinary Christmas catalogue – renowned for deliciously vulgar his-and-hers gifts. Closed Sun.

STANLEY KORSHAK

500 CRESCENT CT, SUITE 100, TX
75201

☎ (214) 871 3600

Caroline Rose Hunt has hit another goldmine
with her highly personalized speciality store.
From designer clothes to designer knick-
knacks for the ranch. Closed Sun.

Hawaii

HOTELS

COLONY SURF HOTEL

2895 KALAKAUA AVE, HONOLULU, HI
96815

☎ (808) 923 5751

Idyllic spot on Waikiki beach at the foot of
Diamond Head, an extinct volcano. Studio-
style accommodation and sickeningly romantic
restaurant where you can hear the waves while
you watch the sun set.

HOTEL HANA-MAUI

MAUI, HI 96713

☎ (808) 248 8211

Resort hotel set in 4,700 acres of ranch on
Maui's east coast. Wooden cottages with private spa tubs all overlooking the sea. Lots to
do: hiking, riding, golf, croquet, and lots not
to do in the Wellness Center, where you'll be
pampered to within an inch of your life.
HILLARY CLINTON, STEVE MARTIN and DANNY
DE VITO regularly recoup here.

KAHALA MANDARIN ORIENTAL (FORMERLY THE KAHALA HILTON)

5000 KAHALA AVE, HONOLULU, HI
96816

☎ (808) 734 2211

Only ten minutes from Waikiki in Oahu's most
prestigious residential area. New ocean-front
restaurant serves (surprise, surprise)
Hawaiian–Californian cuisine. The exotic gardens and its own private lagoon make this one
of Hawaii's most appealing hotels.

KONA VILLAGE RESORT

KAILUA-KONA, HI 96745

☎ (808) 325 5555

Perfect place to relax, swim and play tennis.
Accommodation is in individual thatched huts
on the beach, with verandahs that overlook
black sand and the blue lagoon. HALE SAMOA
restaurant good for dinner.

MAUNA LANI BAY

1 MAUNA LANI DRIVE, KOHALA COAST,
HI 96743

☎ (808) 885 6622

It's not just the local women that are seductive
– so are the lagoons, pools and gorgeous white
beaches surrounding this resort. It might hold
bad memories for KEVIN COSTNER (notably
infidelity and *Waterworld*), but many have
returned, including ROSEANNE BARR and TOM
CRUISE, to play golf or tennis or just watch the
sun set while eating dinner overlooking the
ocean at the CANOE HOUSE (see Restaurants).

RESTAURANTS

SEE ALSO HOTELS.

AVALON

844 FRONT STREET, LAHAINA, MAUI,
HI 96761

☎ (808) 667 5559

Chef/proprietor Mark Ellman's restaurant, set
in a small whaling village, serves a cool combination of Asian and classic French cuisine.
Book well in advance.

THE CAFE KULA

WITHIN THE GRAND WAILEA RESORT
COMPLEX, 3850 WAILEA ALANUI DR,
WAILEA, MAUI, HI 96753

☎ (808) 875 1234

Nutritionally correct spa menus by Kathleen
Daelemans will keep anyone who is on a diet
very happy. The spicy blackbean chilli served
with corn bread and mango salsa, and the
mango, star fruit and kiwi tart feel much
naughtier than they really are.

ENCORE There are all sorts of ways to get around Maui, but one of the most exhilarating
methods of seeing the island is from a bi-plane from **Bi-plane Barnstormers,** Kahului
Airport, Kahului, Maui, ☎ (808) 878 2860. For about $300 an hour, Wayne Wagner can take
you up in his 1935 repro red Waco. And if you're not susceptible to motion sickness you can
go on a loop-the-loop into the Haleakala volcano crater . . . . ♠

THE CANOE HOUSE

IN THE MAUNA LANI BAY HOTEL (SEE HOTELS)

☎ (808) 885 6622

Alan Wong is probably the most versatile of the islands' young chefs. The restaurant overlooks the ocean, so there's a cooling breeze as you dine on dishes such as kalua-pig quesadillas with Hawaiian chilli-pepper sour cream and minted mangos. If you've room finish with the lychee–ginger sorbet.

LA CASCATA

IN THE SHERATON PRINCEVILLE, KAUAI, HI 96722

☎ (808) 826 2761

Splendid resort on the rugged north shore of the island and formerly a home to SYLVESTER STALLONE. The restaurant features memorable fresh fish, and Provençal and Italian specialities.

··

"STILL THE BEST MATCH OF AMERICAN EFFICIENCY AND SOUTH SEAS' HEDONISM" –

SHERIDAN MORLEY ON HAWAII

··

HALIIMAILE GENERAL STORE

900 HALIIMAILE ROAD, MAKAWAO, HI 96768

☎ (808) 572 2666

In the middle of 1,000 acres of pineapple, at the top of Mt Haleakala, is a 65-year-old bungalow housing a superb restaurant. Chef Beverly Gannon offers dishes such as Szechuan salmon topped with caramelized onions, garlic, orange peel and peppercorns. And for a tropical finish go for the chocolate macadamia torte or pina colada cheesecake.

MERRIMAN'S

BOX 2349, KAMUELA, HI 96743

☎ (808) 885 6822

Owner Peter Merriman uses as much native produce as he possibly can at his mountainside restaurant. He serves Pahoa corn from the eastern side of the island, Palani Ranch yearling beef, Kahua Ranch lamb and goats' cheese from Puna. Four years ago, he began "Hawaii Regional Cuisine" with Roy Yamaguchi, Jean-Marie Josselin and other leading chefs, to promote local food and agriculture, way beyond pupu platters. By encouraging local farmers and fishermen, Merriman ensures that a good Hawaiian meal takes advantage of the seasons and the natural bounty of the islands.

A PACIFIC CAFE

KAUAI VILLAGE, KAUAI KAPAA, HI 96746

☎ (808) 822 0013

What looks like a very ordinary shopping centre in Kapaa hides one of the state's best restaurants. 95% of all the produce used by the well-known chef and owner, Jean-Marie Josselin, is local.

ROY'S

6600 KALANIANAOLE HIGHWAY, OAHU, HI 96825

☎ (808) 396 7697

This is the place for creative Pacific Rim and Hawaiian regional cuisine, and while fresh fish is standard throughout the islands, Roy Yamaguchi always offers at least seven or eight varieties in both his Maui and Oahu restaurants. *"I rate it the best restaurant in the islands, very good Pan-Pacific cooking and excellent service headed by the maître d' who is very knowledgeable about wine; they have an excellent selection of Californian 'Rhone Ranger' varieties"* – PAUL HENDERSON.

SAM CHOY'S RESTAURANT

73-5576 KAUHOLA ST, KAILUA-KONA, HI 96745

☎ (808) 326 1545

Weighing in at more than 300 pounds, Sam Choy is the big daddy of Hawaiian cuisine. When working in some of the islands' best resorts, he was renowned for feeding his co-workers even better than his guests, with dishes such as hangover fish soup with sweet potatoes, breadfruit and ginger.

TAHITI NUI

IN HANALEI, KAUAI, HI 96714

☎ (808) 826 6277

No one can visit Hawaii without going to a luau – a local pig-roasting party. The best place to head for is this historic house where you'll be served Tahitian cuisine in an unmistakably Polynesian atmosphere.

Los Angeles

ART AND MUSEUMS

CALIFORNIA MUSEUM OF SCIENCE AND INDUSTRY

700 STATE DR, EXPOSITION PARK, CA 90037

☎ (213) 744 7400

Very 1990s. Interactive exhibits, live broadcasts

from outer space, an Imax theatre with a screen 5 storeys high and 70 ft wide with SurroundSound which can transport you into outer space or simply the neighbouring continent. Museum is currently being updated. Open 7 days; free except **IMAX THEATER**.

GENE AUTRY MUSEUM OF WESTERN HERITAGE

4700 WESTERN HERITAGE WAY,
GRIFFITH PARK, CA 90027
☎ (213) 667 2000
A must-see for anyone wanting a glimpse of the real Wyatt Earp and the real Billy the Kid. Includes weapons and clothing that belonged to the likes of Doc Holliday and Jesse James, as well as old Western movies and costumes, old guns and stage coaches and a playroom with props for children.

THE HUNTINGTON LIBRARY ART COLLECTION AND BOTANICAL GARDENS

1151 OXFORD RD, SAN MARINO, CA 91108
☎ (818) 405 2141
Highbrow cultural centre founded in 1919, by railroad and real-estate developer Henry Edwards Huntington. Over 600,000 books and 3,000,000 manuscripts, a huge collection of 18C and 19C British, French and US art and 130 acres of botanical garden with 15 principal areas including the Japanese, Rose, Jungle and Australian Gardens. English tea served daily in the Rose Garden Café. Closed Mon.

J PAUL GETTY MUSEUM

17985 PACIFIC COAST HIGHWAY,
MALIBU, CA 90265
☎ (310) 459 7611
The most richly endowed museum in the world, established by J P Getty. The building is a re-creation of the Roman Villa dei Papiri in Herculaneum, housing a permanent collection of Greek and Roman antiquities alongside paintings, drawings, illuminated manuscripts, sculpture and photographs. There's an outdoor restaurant and café for light refreshment. Visitors with cars must book. Next year (1997) all exhibits bar the antiquities are due to be moved to the new Getty Center, in West LA. Afterwards, the villa will become the only museum in the US devoted entirely to Greek and Roman antiquities.

LOS ANGELES COUNTY MUSEUM OF ART

5905 WILSHIRE BLVD, CA 90036
☎ (213) 857 6000
Something for everyone. A permanent collection of paintings, sculpture, graphic arts,

costumes, textiles and decorative arts in the Ahmanson Building; big special-loan exhibitions in the Armand Hammer Building; 20C paintings and sculpture in the Robert O Anderson Building; and the renowned Shin'enkan collection of Japanese Edo-period paintings in the Japanese Pavilion along with ceramics, screens, scrolls and prints. The museum also has several sculpture gardens, including the Rodin-rich B Gerald Cantor Garden.

MUSEUM OF CONTEMPORARY ART

250 S GRAND AVE, CA 90012
☎ (213) 626 6222
Forget classical retrospection – MOCA is a showcase for cutting-edge 20C art, in mediums ranging from painting to sculpture to photography. There's a permanent collection of Rothko, Kline, Pollock, Stella and Warhol.

MUSEUM OF NEON ART

501 W OLYMPIC BLVD, CA 90015
☎ (213) 617 1580
An electric tribute to neon, fluorescent and kinetic art, which keeps changing location due to the collection's annual expansion. Now housed in a bigger gallery than ever, but there are sadly no longer flashing exhibits on the building's exterior. Gift shop.

MUSEUM OF TOLERANCE

9786 W PICO BLVD, CA 90035
☎ (310) 553 8403
Interactive exhibits based on the dynamics of racism and prejudice in America, and the history of the Holocaust. Set up by Simon Wiesenthal – an alternative, if rather harrowing, museum experience. Open daily except Sat.

NORTON SIMON MUSEUM OF ART

411 W COLORADO BLVD, PASADENA,
CA 91105
☎ (818) 449 6840
Well-established museum in Pasadena, containing the collection of financier Norton Simon. Noted for its Impressionist and Post-Impressionist paintings. An outstanding collection of sculpture from India and SE Asia spanning 2000 years.

BARS

THE DRESDEN ROOM

1760 N VERMONT AVE, CA 90027
☎ (213) 665 4294
60s-style decor, live jazz and piano. A friendly hang-out popular with both starlets (TORI

A Personal View by Rebecca Tyrrel

The best bit about Las Vegas is the drive there. I had heard about it from an ex-boyfriend who liked to think of himself as a character out of Hunter S Thompson's *Fear and Loathing*. Then I read *Fear and Loathing* – drugs, lost weekends, gambling and sex, sweat and recklessness on a gargantuan scale. Add to this sporadically gleaned information a sprinkling of confused film moments – hot desert nights, bourbon, romance, Frank Sinatra and "the strip" and you start to think (wrongly) that before you die you must go to Vegas.

Die without driving across the desert from Los Angeles and you will have missed out, die without spending any time whatsoever in Las Vegas itself and there will be one less nasty experience flashing before your eyes as you leave this world. The desert is just as you imagine it to be. Sepia-coloured ranges, cacti, rattlesnake warnings and those giant roadside advertising hoardings. The music on the hire-car radio changes as you pass through local wavelengths but it is always just the right kind. Ennio Morricone atmosphere music, heart-bleeding love songs, songs about girls called Mary Lou and chaps called Ray. You can't help yourself, you put your feet up on the dashboard and slug straight from the bottle. After about four hours you cross the state line and there shimmering in the sunset is Vegas. It's all very extra-terrestrial. It looks, looming in the distance, as if it has been dropped out of the sky, womphhhh, into the middle of the desert sand. There is a puce-coloured glow hanging over the skyscrapers and nothing but desert and road between – no left or right turns.

Then it all goes horribly wrong. Within yards of the state line is the first "casino opportunity". A giant Disneyesque steamboat theme palace. You're in Nevada now and nothing exists that wasn't created in the name of gambling. Nothing, from here on in, is real – it's all themed. Poor desert: it just can't compete.

You're in instant-millionaire, get-rich-quick land, you go with it or you turn back to LA.

Las Vegas itself is like a dusty windswept car park. There are no pavements, no street furniture, just dirt and rubbish and ridiculous buildings – built by adults for adults but in childish shapes. Treasure Island has galleons outside in a moat (on the hour, every hour, they start to move: lights flash, automatic waves crash as a pirate battle is acted out). Excalibur is a fairytale castle: turrets, wimples, mullioned windows. There is a giant pyramid – an Egyptian theme; you can take a ride along the Nile in a plastic boat with a guide who tells you about Nefertiti and Tutankhamen. In fact the whole thing looks as if it is made out of plastic, like one of those children's toys, the giant plastic teapot from Fisher Price.

As you approach each themed casino you experience a childish surge of excitement and expectation but inside they are relentlessly identical. The never-ending (24 hours a day, 365 days a year) sound of slot machines; the tumour-inducing flashing lights; the gormless women in storybook outfits with fat thighs, scuffed court shoes and bulging cleavages serving free drinks to seduce the customers; the monotonous whirr of the roulette wheel and the tired pale faces of the punters who look as if they have all been struck by the same devastating disease. It's left them vacant, gawping, stupid. Certainly no one looks like they are winning, even the ones that are. One woman took $400 on a slot machine: her face didn't change, she just scooped the money into her plastic pot and started all over again – coin in, pull the handle, coin in, pull the handle, coin in, pull . . . no smile.

There is nothing smoky, sexy, dangerous or romantic about Las Vegas. As I write I am being coerced by my nearest and dearest to go back – for a heavyweight fight. Boxing and Vegas, a nightmare come true. Take my advice: read *Fear and Loathing* – don't spoil it by going there.

SPELLING) and stars (JULIA ROBERTS, MICHELLE PFEIFFER, NICHOLAS). There's also a restaurant, serving lunch and dinner, and a cocktail lounge/bar.

MOLLY MALONE'S IRISH PUB
575 S FAIRFAX AVE, CA 90036
☎ (213) 935 1577
One of LA's oldest Irish bars – 25 years old last

year. Owned by Dubliner Angela Hanlon, and run by her son Damian, it's especially popular with the Irish – U2 go there – and Irish-Americans. A bastion of Irish culture too, with regular events such as the annual James Joyce festival. Original oil paintings of past patrons line the walls. It's so authentic that it's often been used as a film set, as seen in *Patriot Games*. Popular with the rich and famous but very discreet, good music and friendly.

YAMISHIRO

1999 N SYCAMORE, HOLLYWOOD, CA 90068

☎ (213) 466 5125

Spectacular views over West Beverly Hills from this bar/restaurant nestling in the Hollywood Hills. An exact replica of the Yamishiro Palace in Kyoto, Japan, it was built in 1911 using genuine materials shipped over from Japan. Smashing cocktails and deadly Mai Tais.

CAFES

INSOMNIA

7286 BEVERLY BLVD, CA 90036

☎ (213) 931 4943

JULIA ROBERTS comes here for refuge, so if you're feeling sleepless in Tinseltown you can too. Sink into Victorian velvet sofas, sip speciality coffees, or have breakfast at any hour.

KING'S ROAD CAFE

8361 BEVERLY BLVD, CA 90048

☎ (213) 655 9044

Light, wholesome Italo-American food from vegetable frittata with focaccia for breakfast to goats' cheese pizza with toasted pine nuts for lunch. Ambience reminiscent of San Francisco's North Beach, and proximity to local model agencies explains decorative clientele. Loved by local Brit pack. The coffee, freshly roasted on the premises, is another pull.

MANI'S BAKERY

519 S FAIRFAX AVE, CA 90036

☎ (213) 938 8800

There are now four Mani's in L.A. Hardly surprising with the potent combination of delicious cakes and puddings minus the sugar. "Natural, unrefined" sweeteners such as fruit juice and barley malt are used instead. This, the original store, has a great espresso bar propped up by a mixed bag – including members of the RED HOT CHILLI PEPPERS, KD LANG and ROSEANNE BARR. The other stores

have gift emporiums selling environmentally sensitive' presents.

SWINGERS

8020 BEVERLY BLVD, CA 90048

☎ (213) 653 5858

Comfortable Hollywood diner serving comfort food. Proximity to MADONNA's Maverick Productions no doubt adds to its ever burgeoning street cred.

CLUBS

THE GATE

643 N LA CIENEGA BLVD, CA 90069

☎ (310) 289 8808

A small, cosy supper and dance club; dominated by a 25–30-something singles crowd. Safe music, predominantly 70s and 80s with a dash of 90s. *"A mixture of Tramp and Annabel's; they've tried to make it English country home with a country library setting,"* says JOHNNY GOLD.

THE ROXBURY

8225 SUNSET BLVD, CA 60069

☎ (213) 656 1750

This club is nearly as notorious as its street. Three floors; ground floor is **THE CELLAR**, for alternative live rock; first floor is for dining, and the second is for dancing, with private VIP suite. Some love it – like SHANNEN DOHERTY, KEANU REEVES and ARSENIO HALL.

COMEDY CLUBS

THE COMEDY STORE

8433 SUNSET BLVD, CA 90069

☎ (213) 656 6225

EDDIE MURPHY, STEVE MARTIN, ROBIN WILLIAMS, DAVID LETTERMAN, ROSEANNE BARR, WHOOPI GOLDBERG and JIM CAREY have all performed here. Performances every night. There are three stages, seating 75–400.

THE IMPROV

8162 MELROSE AVE, CA 90046

☎ (213) 651 2583

West Coast version of the renowned East Coast Club; there's one in Santa Monica too. A restaurant and bar have been added at the front, so you can rub shoulders with the comedians who hang out there. BETTE MIDLER, LILY TOMLIN and ROBIN WILLIAMS have performed there while DEBRA WINGER used to be a waitress. Also known for being a *"roaring singles inferno"* – LON DIAMOND.

ONLY IN LA Built in 1923 for $21,000, the **Hollywood Sign** was originally intended as an advertising gimmick for the charming hillside community – Hollywoodland – below. Today, each of its $30,000 restored letters has been donated: sponsors include rock star ALICE COOPER and playboy HUGH HEFNER. No visit to Tinseltown is complete without a glimpse of the sign, so if smog obscures your view, drive to the top of Beachwood Canyon Rd. . . . Fantastic views of the city are offered by **Griffith Park Observatory**, 2800 East Observatory Rd, CA 90027, ☎ (213) 664 1181. Located in Griffith Park, near the Hollywood sign, this beautiful Art Deco building has appeared in countless movies – most famously in *Rebel Without a Cause*. It's open on clear nights. . . . After the OJ trial the cachet of using a gun may have diminished, but LA's rich and famous still want to use them. **The Beverly Hills Gun Club**,12306 W Exposition Blvd, CA 90064, ☎ (310) 826 6411, is the only gun club on the West Side. All gun calibres are available for use in the club's indoor shooting range. Late night is the best time to spot "shooting stars".

FILM

EL CAPITAN THEATER
6838 HOLLYWOOD BLVD, CA 90028
☎ (213) 467 7674
The old Paramount, now taken over and totally refurbished by Disney, showing, predictably, pure unadulterated Disney. Seats 1,000 and during the holiday season they perform live stage shows of their latest release.

SUNSET FIVE
8000 SUNSET BLVD, CA 90046
☎ (213) 848 3505
Five-screen art house cinema housed in Virgin Megastore complex. Pick the right film and you'll be surrounded by a constellation of today's stars. **WOLFGANG PUCK,** ☎ (213) 650 7300 restaurant, also in same complex.

HOTELS

THE ARGYLE (FORMERLY THE ST JAMES'S CLUB)
8358 SUNSET BLVD, CA 90069
☎ (213) 654 7100
Originally home to Marilyn Monroe, Errol Flynn, Clark Gable and the Gabor sisters. Art Deco in style, the Argyle retains its magnificent original features. From most bedrooms, the restaurant and the pool, there's a spectacular view of the city below. It has recently undergone meticulous restoration.

BEVERLY HILLS HOTEL
9641 SUNSET BLVD, CA 90210
☎ (310) 276 2251
After two and a half years and over $100 million investment the Beverly Hills still epitomizes Hollywood glitz. The "Pink Palace" which sits at the top of Rodeo Drive now has larger rooms and five restaurants, including the **POLO LOUNGE**, which MARK MCCORMACK recommends.

FOUR SEASONS
333 S DOHENY, CA 90048
☎ (310) 273 2222
A handsome and homely contrast to LA's inevitable glitz, and you'll still have your workout machines. Plenty of nice touches – the Chelsea Flower show in your bedroom, televisions in the bathroom and free limo service to Beverly Hills. KEVIN KLINE, SIGOURNEY WEAVER and DAVID HOCKNEY all return regularly for more. It's also *"the power hotel for foreign producers,"* says WILLIAM STADIEM.

HOTEL BEL-AIR
701 STONE CANYON RD, CA 90077
☎ (310) 472 1211
Still arguably LA's best hotel, nestling in the deep canyons of LA's most exclusive residential district. Today, as opposed to Kennedys and Rockefellers, you might find the PRINCE OF WALES, SIR ANDREW LLOYD WEBBER, EMMA THOMPSON and AL PACINO enjoying a little

calm in a mad city. *"It's like staying at a country hotel in the city"* – PAUL HENDERSON. A lake with swans and over 11 acres of garden filled with delicious-smelling flowers. Fantastic service – staff:guest ratio is 3:1. Alfresco power breakfasts, as the sunrises are very popular with local movie moguls. *"Individual haciendas set amidst lush semi-tropical foliage – a refuge from urban hustle"* – EDWARD THORPE. Chef Gary Clauson has also created a spa menu to cater for the many special diets that pass through.

●●●●●●●●●●●●●●●●●●●●●●●●●●●●●●●

"ONE OF THE WORLD'S MOST BEAUTIFUL HOTELS" – **EDWARD THORPE** *ON HOTEL BEL-AIR*

●●●●●●●●●●●●●●●●●●●●●●●●●●●●●●●

THE PENINSULA BEVERLY HILLS

9882 LITTLE SANTA MONICA BLVD, BEVERLY HILLS, CA 90212
☎ (310) 273 4888
Anyone who's anyone knows that Friday night is Peninsula night in Beverly Hills. Blockbusting deals take place in the **CLUB BAR**, where you'll see SHARON STONE, SYLVESTER STALLONE and maybe even FRANK SINATRA playing the piano. The office of super-agent MICK OVITZ is conveniently located just opposite. LA's flashiest hotel.

THE REGENT BEVERLY WILSHIRE

9500 WILSHIRE BLVD, BEVERLY HILLS, CA 90212
☎ (310) 275 5200
Very grand old West Coast hotel, currently in tip-top condition following recent renovation. Biggest and best bathrooms in LA. The staff possess an uncanny ability to pick up names – no matter who you are. The swimming pool is a replica of Sophia Loren's, and OPRAH WINFREY works out in the spa. It's also earthquake-proof – which is more important than it may seem. MICHAEL CAINE, ANJELICA HUSTON,

THE AGA KHAN, BOB HOPE and the DALAI LAMA (though not when RICHARD GERE was filming *Pretty Woman* in the hotel), all stay here.

SHUTTERS ON THE BEACH

1 PICO BLVD, SANTA MONICA, CA 90405
☎ (310) 458 0030
A few hundred yards from Santa Monica Pier, the heart of *Baywatch* land, Shutters sits on the sand like a grand, 30s ocean-front beach house. The fresh nautical decor seems rather more East Coast than West – but JAMIE LEE CURTIS, JOAN COLLINS and BILLY JOEL – who sometimes plays the piano in the lobby – love it. All the rooms have jacuzzis, balconies and an unimpaired view of sea. **ONE PICO** is the formal restaurant, whereas **PEDALS** is much more casual – the brunch is to die for.

MUSIC

THE HOLLYWOOD BOWL

2301 N HIGHLAND AVE, CA 90068
☎ (213) 850 2000
All the greats have played here – from PAVAROTTI to KARAJAN to NUREYEV to ELTON JOHN. Since it was built in 1921, this has been the summer home to the Los Angeles Philharmonic. The annual Playboy Jazz festival also takes place here, with performances from HARRY CONNICK, JR. Worth bringing your own champagne and picnic basket with you.

McCABES GUITAR SHOP

3101 PICO BLVD, SANTA MONICA, CA 90405
☎ (310) 828 4497
Well-loved guitar shop that sells all kinds of stringed instruments. Since 1969 they've used the showroom at the back for concerts at weekends (Fri–Sun) – folk, blues and rock bands have all played there. With only about 150 seats, tickets are very hot. Many British acts.

●●

ENCORE The Greek Theater is an open-air concert area nestling into a green, tree-enclosed canyon on a hillside in Griffith Park. There have been legendary performances from NEIL DIAMOND, "Live at the Greek"; ROD STEWART, TINA TURNER, SADE and STING, watched by seated audiences of over 6,000. Legends are given an incentive for unloading 100,000 tickets or more for their performances here – namely, the honour of having their signatures and handprints embedded, true to Hollywood tradition, in cement – in the Greek Theater Wall of Fame. It closes for the winter. For forthcoming shows ring ☎ (213) 665 1927 . . . . ♣

THE ROXY THEATER

9009 SUNSET BLVD, CA 90069

☎ (310) 276 2222

Famous Sunset Strip venue that has always attracted big names, such as DAVID BOWIE and BARRY MANILOW. There is a 750 capacity, which escalates when they remove the seats and often there are very cheap tickets available.

TROUBADOR

9081 SANTA MONICA BLVD, CA 90069

☎ (310) 276 6168

For 35 years stars such as ELTON JOHN, JAMES TAYLOR, VAN MORRISON and GUNS 'N' ROSES have been making their names here. Valet parking.

WILTERN THEATER

3790 WILSHIRE BLVD, CA 90010

☎ (213) 388 1400

Restored 1930s Art Deco movie palace. A mixed bunch come to see everything from dance to comedy to music. Excellent place to see solo artists. Recent performers include SEAL, STING, ELVIS COSTELLO, SINÉAD O'CONNOR, LOS ANGELES OPERA, FRANKFURT BALLET and RITA RUDNER. With about 100 shows a year and a 2,200 capacity you have to be quick off the mark. "*Wonderfully intimate setting*" – STANLEY WEISER.

RESTAURANTS

SEE ALSO HOTELS.

ABIQUIU

1413 5TH ST, SANTA MONICA, CA 90401

☎ (310) 395 8611

Formerly known as **BIKINI**, Abiquiu specializes in modern ethnic cuisine, "*furious, fun food*" says FRANK BOWLING. DUSTIN HOFFMAN and WARREN BEATTY come and eat dishes from tacos and tamales to lobster sushi. Some might find it a little pretentious.

CAFE LA BOHEME

8400 SANTA MONICA BLVD, W HOLLYWOOD, CA 90069

☎ (213) 848 2360

One of LA's best dating spots in the heart of fashionable West Hollywood. Very sexy atmosphere – partly due to the sultry lighting, which makes everyone look wonderful. The food is consistently good, California cuisine with banquet-style portions.

CHAYA BRASSERIE

8741 ALDEN DRIVE, CA 90048

☎ (310) 859 8833

EDDIE MURPHY, MADONNA, and the SCHWARZENEGGERS come here for the exciting

---

WOLFGANG PUCK
Like his fellow Austrian Arnold Schwarzenegger, chef-to-the-stars Wolfgang Puck maintains a regal position in LA. The restless entrepreneur presides over a still-expanding empire of hard-to-get-into restaurants. The new **Spago** in Las Vegas, 3,500 S. Las Vegas Blvd., LV 89109 (in Forum at Caesar's Palace), ☎ (702) 369 6300, is, according to BEATRICE WELLES, "*Wolf's very best – without having to wait a week for a reservation as in LA*". Clear away the inevitable hype about all his joints and you will find eye-catching decor (by Puck's designer wife Barbara Lazaroff), surprisingly reasonable prices and delicious food that's fashionable without being silly. Back in LA, the birthplace of designer pizzas was **Spago**, 1114 Horn Avenue, Los Angeles, CA 90069, ☎ (310) 652 4025, which feeds huge crowds of movie stars, local powerbrokers and delighted tourists wondering who is sitting in the corner with MEG RYAN. You might have better luck getting a table at **Granita**, 23725 W Malibu Rd (in Malibu Colony Plaza), Malibu, CA 90265, ☎ (310) 456 0488. Puck's Gaudiesque shack of a restaurant is a short drive up the coast from Los Angeles, in Malibu (Beverly Hills by the sea). Dishes include grilled vegetable lasagne or grilled free-range chicken with heavenly mashed potatoes and roasted shallots.

SUNSET BOULEVARD Whether it's Billy Wilder's film (that became Andrew

Lloyd Webber's musical), the exploits of Hugh Grant, or the notoriety of the Viper Room, everyone's heard of Sunset Boulevard. It runs for 25 miles through three municipalities – Los Angeles, West Hollywood and Beverly Hills – and where it ends, the United States of America comes to a stop. Working girls aside, however little history there is in LA, much has happened along the Strip. **The Comedy Store** (see Comedy Clubs, page 23) used to be **Ciro's**, a top nightspot from the 30s to the 60s, where PAULETTE GODARD, SAMMY DAVIS and later THE DOORS would party until dawn (and where the stars drank during prohibition). Then there's the very English **Argyle Hotel** (see Hotels, page 24) formerly the St James's Club, on the corner of Kings Road, where TIM ROBBINS goes to meet his stalker in *The Player*. Recent additions include DAN ACKROYD'S back-to-basics-style **House of Blues, ☎** (213) 650 0247, a restaurant and club that looks like a Beverly Hillbilly shack. It's like a Hard Rock Café, only full of Blues memorabilia. It has already become a hotspot, with performers such as TOM JONES and ERIC CLAPTON playing in the music hall. If it's trouble you're looking for, go to **The Viper Room**, 8852 W. Sunset Blvd., CA 90069, ☎ (310) 358 1880, owned by JOHNNY DEPP and MATT DILLON – frequented by the late RIVER PHOENIX; or the **Whiskey Bar** in the Sunset Marquis Hotel, 1200 Alta Loma Rd, CA 90069, ☎ (310) 657 1333 – favoured by the pop and fashion fraternity (JULIAN LENNON, BONO, PATRICK DÉMARCHELIER and supermodels KATE, CINDY and NAOMI). Last but not least there's the **Château Marmont**, 8221 W. Sunset Blvd,, CA 90046, ☎ (213) 656 1010, which is simply groaning with history. The pseudo-Gothic hotel is one of the few places that's remained more or less unchanged over the past 60 years. Regulars included BILLY WILDER, WARREN BEATTY, JOAN COLLINS, LED ZEPPELIN, THE DOORS and HOWARD HUGHES, who would stay for months at a time.

Franco-Italian food, the designer decor of Grinstein-Daniels and the courteous staff. *"Beautiful food, beautiful atmosphere, and beautiful people"* according to KARLA BONOFF. Very popular.

EL CHOLO
1121 S WESTERN AVE N, CA 90006
☎ (213) 734 2773
People have been coming to the Spanish bungalow for the best Mexican food in town since 1927. Ice-cold pitchers of Margaritas go perfectly with heaped platefuls of melted-cheese nachos and carne asada. *"Old LA before the Americans arrived"* – SHEP GORDON.

CITRUS
6703 MELROSE AVE, CA 90038
☎ (213) 857 0034
Best of Californian cooking, with combinations that are clever rather than smart-alec.

Perfectionist chef/owner Michel Richard maintains standards in a cool, clean and minimalist setting.

DRAGO
2628 WILSHIRE BLVD, SANTA MONICA, CA 90403
☎ (310) 828 1585
The huge welcome you receive from the Sicilian patrons can be disconcerting but they put just as much effort into their cooking. The salmon carpaccio and the pasta, especially the tagliatelle with beef ragù, are a lot better than average.

DRAI'S
730 N LA CIENEGA BLVD, CA 90069
☎ (310) 358 8585
Old-fashioned French food updated for the health-conscious Californian clientele – plenty of dairy-free and vegetarian dishes, to feed the

GRAVE-DIGGING

It might be morbid, but in LA they have decided that one interesting way to reminisce about the bygone Hollywood golden era is to go and look at celebrities' graves. Founded in 1899, the 57-acre **Hollywood Memorial Park Cemetery**, 6000 Santa Monica Blvd, Hollywood, CA 90038, ☎ (213) 469 1181, is the epitome of fading Hollywood grandeur. Among the palms and olive trees, visitors will find the graves of RUDOLPH VALENTINO, DOUGLAS FAIRBANKS SR, NELSON EDDY, CECIL B DE MILLE, PETER FINCH, JANET GAYNOR, HARRY COHN, MEL BLANC (the original voice of Bugs Bunny) and many, many others. Alternatively, for something more kitsch, visit **Forest Lawn**, 1712 S Glendale Ave, Glendale, CA 91205, ☎ (213) 254 7251 or tollfree in US ☎ 1 800 204 3131. The inspiration behind Evelyn Waugh's *The Loved One*, the 300-acre cemetery features a collection of marble reproductions of all Michelangelo's major statuary. Or you can go a-hunting for NATALIE WOOD, FRANK ZAPPA, ROY ORBISON, CHARLES MEREDITH, BUDDY RICH, EVE ARDEN, DONNA REED, TRUMAN CAPOTE and MARILYN MONROE in the **Westwood Village Mortuary**, 1218 Glendon Ave, CA 90024 ☎ (310) 474 1579. Finally **Graveline Tours**, ☎ (213) 469 4149, provide what they call "the best tour in LA", visiting the graves of 80 stars in more than 30 miles of movieland covering 100 years of death, sin and scandals. Line up for a seat at the east wall of the Chinese Theater (corner of Hollywood Blvd and Orchid Ave) any day except Mon, at noon.

cream of Hollywood's film and music industries including CHRISTIAN SLATER, GEENA DAVIES, JASON PRIESTLEY, DUSTIN HOFFMAN, QUINCY JONES and SIR ANDREW LLOYD WEBBER. According to WILLIAM STADIEM, it's a *"favourite with the Heidi Fleiss set on paydays"*.

GEORGIA'S

7250 MELROSE AVE, CA 90046
☎ (213) 933 8420
This is where OJ's defence team threw their victory party in 1995. As usual the clientele comes from the small and big screens. JOHN F KENNEDY JR and JACKIE COLLINS eat traditional Southern cooking under palm trees in the courtyard. Can be prohibitively expensive.

THE IVY

113 N ROBERTSON BLVD, CA 90048
☎ (310) 274 8303
ELTON JOHN, JODIE FOSTER, JACK LEMMON, TOM SELLECK and other members of "The Industry" do lunch here in a "Wizard of Oz" cottage, surrounded by a white picket fence. The best grills in town, scrumptious Key lime pie and cappuccinos served from outsize coffee cups.

THE IVY AT THE SHORE

1541 OCEAN AVE, SANTA MONICA, CA 90401
☎ (310) 393 3113
Ideal for Sunday lunch, alfresco. Californian food, with a bit of creole and cajun thrown in – specializing in grilled fish, meat and salads.

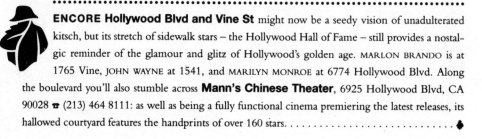

ENCORE Hollywood Blvd and Vine St might now be a seedy vision of unadulterated kitsch, but its stretch of sidewalk stars – the Hollywood Hall of Fame – still provides a nostalgic reminder of the glamour and glitz of Hollywood's golden age. MARLON BRANDO is at 1765 Vine, JOHN WAYNE at 1541, and MARILYN MONROE at 6774 Hollywood Blvd. Along the boulevard you'll also stumble across **Mann's Chinese Theater**, 6925 Hollywood Blvd, CA 90028 ☎ (213) 464 8111: as well as being a fully functional cinema premiering the latest releases, its hallowed courtyard features the handprints of over 160 stars. . . . . ♠

LA FARM

3000 W OLYMPIC BLVD, SANTA
MONICA, CA 90404

☎ (310) 449 4000

Lies in the shadow of George Lucas's office, in
the middle of an "industry" park. Moguls such
as OLIVER STONE are brought back down to
earth with potato waffles smothered in brie,
and other seasonal concoctions oozing with
rusticity. Service is a little slow.

MATSUHISA

129 N LA CIENEGA BLVD, CA 90404

☎ (310) 659 9639

The Disneyland of sushi, and still *"the
hardest reservation in town for fabulous
Peruvian–Japanese–Pacific Rim food"* – WILLIAM
STADIEM.

OPUS

2425 W OLYMPIC BLVD, SANTA
MONICA, CA 90404

☎ (310) 829 2112

Just across from the new MGM offices, and
overlooking a lake and waterfall you're served
contemporary French cuisine with the
inevitable hint of California. Tasty seafood.
TOM SELLECK pops in regularly.

L'ORANGERIE

903 N LA CIENEGA BLVD, CA 90069

☎ (310) 652 9770

Emulates the lush 17C orangery at the palace
of Versailles. A sliding roof, above the diners,
reveals the moon and stars above. Try new chef
Gilles Epie's beignet of foie gras with a
caramelized port wine sauce. Prices might be
wallet-numbing – but it's a romantic place to
take someone on a date and, according to
FRANK BOWLING, *"the most beautiful restaurant in
America"*.

🕸 ORSO

8706 W 3RD ST, CA 90048

☎ (310) 274 7144

Good contemporary Italian food, served on
hand-painted china, at a reasonable price. The
ultra-thin pizzas have become as popular here
as at Orso, London and NYC. Romantic patio
for summer dining.

SADDLE PEAK LODGE

419 COLD CANYON RD, CALABASAS,
CA 91302

☎ (310) 456 7325

Santa Monica mountain getaway – perfect
when avoiding fans/paparazzi. Rustic menu
includes plenty of game.

SCHATZI

3110 MAIN ST, SANTA MONICA, CA
90405

☎ (310) 399 4800

Owned by Hollywood's royal couple –
ARNOLD and MARIA (SCHWARZENEGGER).
Comfortable restaurant in fashionable Main St
serving American and Austrian food. JOHNNY
CARSON lunches here regularly.

72 MARKET STREET

72 MARKET ST, VENICE, CA 90261

☎ (310) 392 8720

TONY BILL and DUDLEY MOORE's restaurant
keeps meat loaf and mashed potatoes firmly on
the map, but a new French chef now influences the once predominantly American
menu. Live music played Thurs–Sun; you
might even catch Dudley at the piano.

TALESAI

9043 SUNSET BLVD, W HOLLYWOOD,
CA 90069

☎ (310) 275 9724

By far and away the best Thai restaurant in the
city. Try the pad tahi, hormock seafood (house
speciality) and coconut chicken soup.

TOSCANA

11633 SAN VINCENTE BLVD,
BRENTWOOD, CA 90049

☎ (310) 820 2448

One of the best trattorias in the city and
arguably the best eatery in Brentwood (OJ and
NICOLE often dined here). Start with a melt-in-

ENCORE If you want to see the bodies beautiful of SHARON STONE, DIANE CANNON, DOLF
LUNDGREN and MAGIC JOHNSON join the **Sports Club LA** (1835 S Sepulveda Blvd, CA
90025, ☎ (310) 473 1447. With two restaurants, a spa, and a full-on beauty salon, this $30
million club ain't your average gym. Membership is limited, though. Currently billing itself
the Mecca of Body building why not try the world-famous **Gold's**, 360 Hampton Dr, Venice
90291, ☎ (310) 392 6004, where ARNIE and HULK HOGAN work out, as well as MEL GIBSON,
MICHELLE PFEIFFER and JANET JACKSON. . . . . ♠

DELUXE DELIS Californians on permo-diets tend not to eat very much, but it doesn't prevent LA from having some wonderful delicatessens for everyone else. **Canters**, 419 N Fairfax Ave, CA 90036, ☎ (213) 651 2030, is an LA institution, where industry Jews gather at Christmas. Popular with ageing comics and young families is **Nate-'N-Al's**, 414 N Beverly Dr, Beverly Hills, CA 90210, ☎ (310) 274 0101. *"The measure of a deli is its chicken soup, and Nate's has the best in town,"* says STANLEY WEISER. For sandwiches big enough to bite back, try **Art's**, 12224 Ventura Blvd, Studio City, CA 91604, ☎ (818) 762 1221, who serve up the best pastrami in LA. **Greenblatt's**, 8017 Sunset Blvd, Hollywood, CA 90046, ☎ (213) 656 0606, is a wine shop/deli. Although it offers table service, it's better to take away. Practically everybody who's been to the Valley has been to **Jerry's Famous Deli,** 12655 Ventura Blvd, Studio City, CA 91604, ☎ (818) 980 4245, a friendly 24-hour joint with an intimidatingly large menu. **Broadway Deli**, 1457 3rd St Promenade, Santa Monica, CA 90401, ☎ (310) 451 0616, is a gourmet food market and wine shop with an airy deli/restaurant. BRUCE WILLIS's office is just upstairs, so DEMI MOORE is a regular, as is MERYL STREEP.

your-mouth Margherita pizza. The risotto is good too.

VERSAILLES

10319 VENICE BLVD, CA 90034
☎ (310) 558 3168
Huge portions of authentic Cuban cuisine, served on red and white checked tablecloths. Great food at great prices, but don't be surprised if you have to queue first.

SHOPPING

Shopping in LA is a very plastic experience. The assistants are plastic, the shops are plastic and you pay with plastic. Make sure you dress up or you might get the same brush off as Julia Roberts did in *Pretty Woman*. Rodeo Drive is lined with international designer boutiques –

which are sometimes appointment only. Above Armani you'll find the **ARMANI CAFÉ**, where many a face-lifted lady does lunch – it's good for light grazing too. For younger, more Bohemian goods try **MELROSE AVE** – often filled by Hollywood kids, making full use of their parents' plastic. The boutiques on **MONTANA AVE** are more cosy, but yuppified. For one stop-shopping try the **BEVERLY CENTER**, in W Hollywood, with over 200 shops. Other chic complexes include **CENTURY CITY** in Beverly Hills, **SUNSET PLAZA** on Sunset Strip and the **BRENTWOOD MART**, which feels more East Coast than West.

FREDERICKS OF HOLLYWOOD

6608 HOLLYWOOD BLVD, CA 90028
☎ (213) 466 8506
So serious about lingerie that it's become a museum for it – MARILYN MONROE's bra is on

ENCORE Only 27 miles from downtown LA is **Disneyland**, 1313 S Harbor Blvd, Anaheim, ☎ (714) 999 4565, where you'll stumble upon the first and best of all the Disney Parks, The Magic Kingdom. A feast of fun and fantasy featuring stomach-churning rides and miles of interactive experiences for kids and adults alike. . . . . ♠ **Universal Studios**, 100 Universal City, ☎ (818) 777 1000, is the biggest in the world, offering elaborate and hair-raising four- to seven-hour tram rides through the back lots includes confrontations with robotic T-Rexes and velociraptors. Not for the fainthearted. . . . .♠

display as are offerings from CHER, MADONNA, MAE WEST and TONY CURTIS. Brilliantly tacky presents like edible undies.

FRED HAYMAN
273 N RODEO DR, BEVERLY HILLS, CA 90210
☎ (310) 271 3000
Designer emporium, including expensive Hayman perfume that no Beverly Hills wife can live without. Also good for accessories and leather goods. Comfort yourself with an extra-frothy cappuccino at the **CAPPUCCINO BAR**. ELIZABETH TAYLOR, BARBRA STREISAND and DIANA ROSS go there.

GALLAY
8711 SUNSET BLVD, W HOLLYWOOD, CA 90069
☎ (310) 858 8711
The sales girls are charming, but that's probably because the clothes are beautiful and the clients with their huge bank balances are even more beautiful. Mere mortals are left pressed to the windows while film stars squash themselves into satin, lycra and silk creations by Alaïa, Gigli, La Perla and Richard Tyler. Good accessories too.

MAXFIELD
8825 MELROSE AVE, CA 90069
☎ (310) 274 8800
Designer delirium at LA's most expensive store – featuring all the biggest designers from the classic couturiers to contemporary trend setters, including Yohji Yamamoto, Gaultier and Dolce & Gabbana. Fab jewellery and fancy repro furniture. *"Still the most fun and most beautiful merchandise this side of Barney's"* – LYN HEMMERDINGER.

Miami

HOTELS

CENTURY HOTEL
140 OCEAN DR, MIAMI BEACH, FL 33139
☎ (305) 674 8855
Not officially in the Deco district, but one of Miami's first and finest Art Deco buildings, the Century is a small, friendly hotel which has recently been refurbished. A mixture of fantasci-inspired and minimalist furnishings with several abstract pieces by Ron Arad.

DELANO
1685 COLLINS AVE, MIAMI BEACH, FL 33139
☎ (305) 672 2000
Another of entrepreneur (remember Club 57?) Ian Shrager's wacky hotels (he was responsible for the Paramount and The Royalton in New York), and where the stars have decided to settle for the time being – MADONNA had her birthday party there recently. The entire place is white and airy with billowing white curtains dividing up the different parts.

PARK CENTRAL
640 OCEAN DR, MIAMI BEACH, FL 33139
☎ (305) 538 1611
Once a favourite with Hollywood stars, the *prêt à porter* set have moved in – models, executives, photographers and all. You can be served Parisian bistro-style food from LE ZÈBRE, either in the lobby restaurant or out on the oceanfront terrace, where you might bump into LAUREN HUTTON.

RESTAURANTS

SEE ALSO HOTELS.

BANG
1516 WASHINGTON AVE, FL 33139
☎ (305) 531 2361
Based on Boom in New York, Geoffrey Murray's wild restaurant is full of top models as well as other SoBe regulars like MADONNA and BRUCE WEBER. The Vietnamese five-spiced quail or the Japanese red snapper with basil, coconut and chilli sauce have to be tasted to be believed. Food aside, it has the best wine list in South Beach. Open evenings only. Closed Mon/Tues throughout the summer.

CHEF ALLEN'S
19088 NE 29TH AVE, N MIAMI BEACH, FL 33180
☎ (305) 935 2900
Whether it is "Miami–American cooking" or "Nuevo Mundo Cuisine" is hard to say, but Allen Susser's food is at the cutting-edge of Miami's gourmet revolution. Meat or fish is often grilled Caribbean style and flavoured with salsas, mojos and adobados, based on local fruits. His most popular dishes include rock-shrimp hash or a seared citrus-crusted yellowfin tuna with a macédoine of papaya, mango and yellow pepper. Open 7 days.

11TH STREET DINER

1065 WASHINGTON AVE, FL 33139
☎ (305) 534 6373
The owners removed a Pennsylvania
Paramount diner, brick by brick, and trans-
ported it to Miami just in time to be greeted
by Hurricane Andrew. It is still very firmly in
place and it's a superb vantage point for
people-watching.

THE GRAND CAFE

IN THE GRAND BAY HOTEL (SEE
HOTELS)
☎ (305) 858 9800
Having left Donald Trump, chef Katsuo
"Suki" Sugiura (French-trained and Japanese-
influenced) lords it over what is now
considered the finest restaurant in Coconut
Grove. Try the Florida shrimp grilled with
Indo-Chinese spices, mango and tropical gin-
ger sauce.

GREEN STREETS CAFE

3110 COMMODORE PLAZA, MIAMI
BEACH, FL 33139
☎ (305) 567 0662
In a street with several cafés spilling onto the
brick pavements, Green Streets is a cut above
the rest. Breakfast is served all day, the Greek
salad is superb and those who want to murder
their waistline can try the chocolate suicide
cake. Open 7 days.

JOE'S STONE CRAB

227 BISCAYNE ST, MIAMI BEACH, FL
33139
☎ (305) 673 0365
Joe's family restaurant is the one place that
Miamians say is a must for out-of-towners.
Patrons wait hungrily, outside or in the jostling
bar, for the legendary local stone crab with
drawn butter, lemon and Joe's mustard sauce,
along with the Key Lime Pie. It's a bit touristy
but one of the city's institutions.

LARIO'S ON THE BEACH

820 OCEAN DR, MIAMI BEACH, FL
33139
☎ (305) 532 9577
Owned by 'Queen' Gloria Estefan, this
colourful and vibrant restaurant serves Cuban
cuisine and celebrates Cuban culture. All the
puddings including natilla custard and cream
cheese and coffee flans are made by an aunt of
the family. MADONNA, DENZEL WASHINGTON,
LENNY KRAVITZ and OPRAH WINFREY are often
in on weekends to listen to the live bands.
Open 7 days.

MARK'S PLACE

2286 NE 123RD ST, N MIAMI, FL
33181
☎ (305) 893 6888
The cool, contemporary, airy restaurant complements Mark Militello's modern and innovative culinary style. Menu changes daily, to
take advantage of the freshest local ingredients.
Open 7 nights – dinner only.

⊛ NEWS CAFE

800 OCEAN DR, MIAMI BEACH, FL
33139
☎ (305) 538 6397
Probably the trendiest 24-hour joint in Miami,
dishing up everything from burgers and bagels
to pâté and pasta. Especially popular for breakfast. There's also a little store selling all major
international newspapers, allowing you to
read, relax and immerse yourself in the Ocean
Drive scene with fellow punters GIANNI VER-
SACE, JFK JR and MADONNA. Open 24 hours a
day, 7 days a week.

VICTOR'S CAFE

2340 SW 32ND AVE, MIAMI, FL 33145
☎ (305) 445 1313
Housed in a stately building modelled on a
colonial Cuban mansion. Chef Arturo
Dudamel excels at traditional dishes, such as
Victor's steak. On weekends the lounge and
the piano bar buzz with energy as patrons
knock back the best "Mojitos" in Miami.
There's live music every night. Open 7 days.

YUCA IN CORAL GABLES

177 GIRALDA AVE, CORAL GABLES, FL
33134
☎ (305) 444 4448
Cuban–American chef Douglas Rodriguez is
so carried away with the "couleur locale" that
guava bark features on his menu. Worth a try
is the yellowtail snapper encrusted with a mix
of avocado, stone-crab meat and crushed
peanuts.

New Orleans

BARS AND CAFES

NAPOLEON HOUSE

500 CHARTRES ST, LA 70130
☎ (504) 524 9752
Drink to the dulcet tones of classical music
courtesy of a jukebox. Only in New Orleans.

OLD ABSINTHE HOUSE

240 BOURBON ST, LA 70130

☎ (504) 523 3181

The building, a French quarter classic, shouldn't be omitted, nor should the Ojen cocktails served here.

PAT O'BRIEN'S

718 ST PETER ST, LA 70116

☎ (504) 525 4823

New Orleans' most celebrated club and home to the "Hurricane" – which you can sup either in the rowdy piano bar or the cool, calm courtyard.

CLUBS

PRESERVATION HALL

726 ST PETER ST, LA 70116

☎ (504) 522 2841

Birthplace of real Delta jazz and blues. Persistently smoky, sweaty and full, but you'll invariably get the city's best sounds.

SNUG HARBOUR

626 FRENCHMEN ST, LA 70130

☎ (504) 895 8477

Lively spot for great jazz and blues in the Faubourg Marigny district. No frills but the pizza's good. Open 7 days, dinner only.

TIPITINA'S

501 NAPOLEON AVE, LA 70115

☎ (504) 895 8477

Whether you're into rock 'n' roll, R & B or Cajun, roll on up to hear the best bands live. You can beer up and chill out, while grazing on grill-style bar snacks. Open Wed–Sun.

FESTIVALS

NEW ORLEANS JAZZ AND HERITAGE FESTIVAL

1204 N RAMPART ST, LA 70116

☎ (504) 522 4786

One of the world's greatest cultural celebrations. It began as a small event in April 1970 when 300 musicians played to an audience half that size. Today over 4,000 musicians, cooks and crafts people converge on the city to share their culture and heritage with over 350,000 onlookers. Filé gumbo, alligator piquante and jambalaya, washed down by terrific jazz, country 'n' western, R & B, gospel, blue grass, Zydeco, Cajun, blues, folk, salsa and ragtime. (Runs from the last weekend in April to the first weekend in May each year.)

HOTELS

THE NEW ORLEANS HILTON RIVERSIDE HOTEL

2 POYDRAS ST, LA 70140

☎ (504) 561 0500

Handy location on the banks of the Mississippi near the French quarter. The bedrooms are large and there are restaurants, shopping and a casino. Jazz enthusiasts may head to PETE FOUNTAIN'S JAZZ CLUB where they play R & B to Dixieland – while sports bores have CABBY'S SPORTS EDITION & GRILLE, featuring non-stop sporting events from around the world on 52 televisions. The RIVERWALK MARKETPLACE, with over 200 stores, is connected to the Hilton.

WINDSOR COURT HOTEL

300 GRAVIER ST, LA 70140

☎ (504) 523 6000

Without doubt one of the finest hotels in the United States (recently voted No. 1 by *Condé Nast Traveler*). Only four blocks from the French quarter, there's $8 million hanging on the walls including works by Gainsborough and Reynolds. Exquisite afternoon tea and a colourful general manager, Hans Jorg Maissen, who's often seen burning around the city on his Harley Davidson.

RESTAURANTS

SEE ALSO HOTELS.

⑤ ACME OYSTER HOUSE

724 IBERVILLE ST, LA 70130

☎ (504) 522 5973

Cheap and understated (read gloomy), but this is more than compensated for by the quality and sheer quantity of oysters at New Orleans' most famous oyster house.

ANTOINE'S

713 ST LOUIS ST, LA 70130

☎ (504) 581 4422

Established in 1840, it's one of America's restaurant legends. Having catered for presidents, royalty and heads of state, it's still a family affair (current owner, Randy Guste, is descended from founder Antoine Alciatore). Many of the world's classic dishes have originated from Antoine's kitchen, including oysters Rockefeller, soufflé potatoes, filet de boeuf marchand de vin, omelette Alaska Antoine and pompano en papillote – which are all still made here according to the original recipes. Wine cellar houses over 25,000 bottles.

BAYONA

430 DAUPHINE ST, LA 70111

☎ (504) 525 4455

The original nouvelle Cajun cuisine, rustled up by Susan Spicer, in a flower-filled 19C Creole cottage, is still as sought after as ever. Try the grilled duck breast with pepper jelly glaze. Closed Sun.

BRENNAN'S

417 ROYAL ST, LA 70130

☎ (504) 525 9713

The eggs benedict and sautéed fish for breakfast are glorious, but they shouldn't eclipse the splendid, fish-rich Creole lunch and dinner menu created by Mike Roussel. Picturesque courtyard with a fountain. Open 7 days for lunch and dinner.

BRIGTSEN'S

723 DANTE ST, LA 70118

☎ (504) 861 7610

A converted town house in uptown New Orleans, where owner-chef Frank Brigtsen (a protégé of local masterchef Paul Prudhomme) serves local fish and poultry dishes. Particularly pleasing crawfish and shrimp dishes, and you must have bananas Foster – a local speciality invented here. Closed Sun/Mon.

COMMANDER'S PALACE

1403 WASHINGTON AVE, LA 70130

☎ (504) 899 8221

Adored by locals and home to the original jazz brunch. Superb haute-Creole food is directed by chef Jamie Shannon and served in a historic Garden District mansion. Stellar turtle soup is the classic dish. Open 7 days.

EMERIL'S

800 TCHOUPITOULAS ST, LA 70130

☎ (504) 528 9393

Nouvelle Creole–American cuisine produced by Emeril Lagasse and his team is all the rage, so reservations are a must. The sautéed crawfish served over jambalaya will have you coming back for more. Closed Sun.

KELSEY'S

3920 GENERAL DE GAULLE DR, LA 70114

☎ (504) 366 6722

Owner Randy Barlow used to cook for PRESIDENT REAGAN at the White House and summit meetings in Williamsburg, but now he's forsaken politics for his hot, young restaurant on the West Bank. He is noted for his fresh seafood served with in-your-face sauces.

Other specialities include eggplant Kelsey and panned rabbit over shrimp and tasso fettuccine.

K-PAUL'S

416 CHARTRES ST, LA 70130

☎ (504) 596 2523

Paul Prudhomme never disappoints. His cooking, which he says is heavily influenced by his mother, is so admired that he became the first American-born chef to receive the coveted Mérite Agricole of the French Republic, which was presented to him by the French Consul General. Need we say more. . .

LOUIS XVI

730 BIENVILLE ST, LA 70130

☎ (504) 581 7000

Chef Agnes Bellet offers a virtuous menu with everything from Caesar salad to filet de boeuf Wellington to crêpe Suzette and bananas Foster.

MIKE'S ON THE AVENUE

628 ST CHARLES AVE, LA 70130

☎ (504) 523 1709

Big, bright and fresh restaurant run by chef/co-owner Michael Fennelley. A creative commingling of Asian, southwestern and southern Louisiana cuisine. Try the grilled filet mignon stuffed with roasted garlic with Fresno chilli–lime butter and country mashed potatoes. Open 5 days for lunch, 7 nights for dinner.

NAPOLI RESTAURANT

1917 RIDGELAKE DR AT W NAPOLEON, MATAIRIE, LA 70001

☎ (504) 837 8463

Owned and operated by Toni, daughter of the most famous fishmonger in town (Deanie of **DEANIE'S SEAFOOD MARKET**), and Patricia, daughter of the most famous publican in town (Billy of **SWEET WILLIAM'S SALOON**). Both brought their mothers' tried and tested seafood recipes into an already successful Italian bistro.

PETRA

541 OAKLAWN DR, OFF VETERANS BLVD, LA 70005

☎ (504) 833 3317

Perhaps it's just the famously romantic booths, but Petra is just as popular as when it opened in November '94. Chef Jonathan Peters has an ambitious culinary agenda, which supposedly covers the entire Mediterranean spectrum, and you can happily order anything from moussaka to baklava to couscous. Hell if you're feeling indecisive.

LA PROVENCE

US HIGHWAY 190 (EXIT 1–12),
MEEDANVILLE (LACOMBE), LA 70445
☎ (504) 626 7662
Very fresh, very fine French food prepared by
chef Chris Kerageorgiou in his inn-style
restaurant overlooking Lake Ponchartrain. The
fish, game and fowl are well worth the hour-
long journey from the city. Closed Mon/Tues.

STRAYA

4517 VETERANS BLVD, LA 70006
☎ (504) 887 8873
Chef Al Copeland, who has cooked for PRES-
IDENT REAGAN and royalty, has now turned his
attention to "Californian Creole". Essentials
include Californian wraps, gourmet pizzas and
rôtisserie chicken. Open 7 days.

VAQUEROS

4938 BRITANNIA ST, LA 70115
☎ (504) 891 6441
Rich Buchsbaum, formerly of La Carabelle in
New York, is executive chef of Vaqueros. Here
you can enjoy good food in a laid-back atmosphere. He also oversees FIGARO'S PIZZERIAS
in Maple Stand in Mandeville St.

VINCENT'S

4411 CHASTANT ST, MATAIRIE, LA
70006
☎ (504) 885 2984
Vincent Catalanotto was born in New
Orleans, started out as a waiter, went to
Hollywood to become an actor but soon
returned to waitering. He opened his own
restaurant over seven years ago. His newest
creation, the corn and crab bisque served in
a unique bread cup, is very flavoursome.

New York

ART AND MUSEUMS

THE CLOISTERS

FORT TYRON PARK, NY 10040
☎ (212) 923 3700
An intriguing branch of the Metropolitan
Museum of Art set in a medieval-style building, is entirely devoted to the art of the Middle
Ages. Regular performances of medieval music
and drama, along with demonstrations of crafts
of the Middle Ages and lectures on medieval life
and arts, take place in the surrounding flower
and herb gardens.

COOPER-HEWITT NATIONAL DESIGN MUSEUM

2 E 91ST ST, NY 10128
☎ (212) 860 6894
The Smithsonian's foremost decorative-arts
collection, housed in the former home of
Andrew Carnegie, has just undergone extensive structural renovation to expand its gallery
space. It is the only museum in the United
States devoted exclusively to historical and
contemporary design. To celebrate the expansion, the "Mixing Messages: Graphic Design in
Contemporary Culture" exhibition will be running until the middle of Jan 1997.

FRICK COLLECTION

1 E 70TH ST, NY 10021
☎ (212) 288 0700
Industrialist and collector Henry Clay Frick's
Beaux Arts mansion is where you'll find his
superb collection of Old Masters, sculpture,
18C French furniture and other works. KEN
HOM describes it as a *"fabulous collection in the
right setting. Mr Frick had obvious good taste."*
Keep an eye out for special exhibitions,
concerts and lectures organized here. Closed
Mon.

METROPOLITAN MUSEUM OF ART

5TH AVE/82ND ST, NY 10028
☎ (212) 879 5500
Dazzlingly large, a tour of the building takes
you through reconstructed rooms, sets and
galleries of the Americas, Africa, Europe,
Asia, Islam and Oceania. Check out the
largest collection of Impressionists and Post-
Impressionists (both paintings and sculpture) in
North America. Recently opened are the
Irving Galleries, featuring South and Southeast
Asian art. There's a celebrated 20C art wing, a
wonderful Costume Institute and a supermar-
ket-sized museum shop which is also good on
jewellery.

MUSEUM OF MODERN ART

11 W 53RD ST, NY 10019
☎ (212) 708 9750
Offers the best and most comprehensive survey
of modern art movements (painting, sculpture,
drawings, prints, architectural models, design,
photography and film) in the world. MICHAEL
MUSTO describes it as a "fine, expansive collection of the world's treasures", while NICK
MASON adds that *"MOMA is still the first culture
stop in New York – it extends beyond 'Art' into
craft, engineering and architecture."* Forthcoming
highlights for the 1996–7 season include:
Screenplays from Broadway to Hollywood;
Piet Mondrian (1872–1944); Picasso and

Portraiture, as well as a Jasper Johns retrospective. Don't forget to have a look at the Abby Aldrich Rockefeller Sculpture Garden.

SOLOMON R GUGGENHEIM MUSEUM
1071 5TH AVE, NY 10218
☎ (212) 523 3500
Remarkable and provocative Frank Lloyd Wright structure. Temporary exhibitions are viewed from a spiral ramp that descends into the museum. In the side galleries you can feast your eyes on Degas, Gauguin, Vuillard, outstanding avant-garde art, Braque and some fine sculpture. *"A great place for modern art with a particularly large collection of Kandinsky"* says JULIAN LLOYD WEBBER. Downtown you'll find the **GUGGENHEIM SOHO**, 575 Broadway, NY 10012, which is housed in a century-old Landmark Building designed by Arata Isosaki, with two floors of innovative and inventive 20C installations.

WHITNEY MUSEUM OF AMERICAN ART
945 MADISON AVE, NY 10021
☎ (212) 570 3676
Founded in 1930 by Gertrude Vanderbilt Whitney, this cult gallery houses 10,000 contemporary, often progressive works of sculpture, painting, print, drawing and photography. Group shows introduce young and relatively unknown artists, and important film and video works are shown.

ARTS CENTRES

LINCOLN CENTER
BROADWAY, BETWEEN 63RD AND 65TH ST, NY 10023
☎ (212) 875 5000
The world's largest arts complex and the hub of New York's cultural life, home to 11 of the world's pre-eminent performing arts organiza-tions – The Metropolitan Opera, the New York Philharmonic, The Juilliard School, New York City Ballet, New York City Opera, The Film Society, The Chamber Music Society, The Lincoln Center Theater, The School of American Ballet and The New York Public Library for the Performing Arts. This year it has started running an annual International Festival, comprising a wide range of dance, music and theatre.

BALLET

AMERICAN BALLET THEATRE
890 BROADWAY, NY 10003
☎ (212) 477 3030
Under the executive directorship of Michael Kaiser and artistic direction of Kevin McKenzie, the ABT continues to maintain and cultivate a dynamic and progressive repertoire, showcasing everything from the classics to the vibrant works of new young choreographers.

NEW YORK CITY BALLET
NEW YORK STATE THEATER, LINCOLN CENTER, NY 10023
☎ (212) 870 5500
Founded by Lincoln Kirstein and George Balanchine, this is the most respected and important company in the US. *"Peter Martins directs the New York's great city ballet; they are absolutely one of the world's greatest companies. Its signature is its huge and definitive repertoire of the legendary George Balanchine"* – EDWARD THORPE.

BARS AND CAFES

🅐 DOJO'S
24-26 ST MARK'S PL, NY 10003
☎ (212) 674 2516
This is the authentic NYC street café, in the

ENCORE Bohemian New York . . . . . the **Chelsea Hotel**, 222 W 23rd St, NY 10011, ☎ (212) 243 3700, is famous for attracting 20C icons of the arts, including DYLAN THOMAS, ARTHUR MILLER, TENNESSEE WILLIAMS and ARTHUR C CLARKE. One room has the distinction of being the set for ANDY WARHOL's *The Chelsea Girls*. Other visitors, who sometimes stay for months at a time, attribute part of its historic charm to its shabbiness. The Chelsea is also the place where SID VICIOUS stabbed his girlfriend, Nancy. **92nd Street Y**, 1395 Lexington Ave, NY, ☎ (212) 415 5440, still presents readings from world-class writers and musical evenings, especially popular with the young people of NYC . . . . . ♣ Media junkies needn't feel deprived, if they are away from home, because **Hotaling's News Agency**, 142 W 42nd St, NY, ☎ (212) 840 1868, sells every type of publication – magazines, papers, journals from over 40 countries . . . . ♣

colourful East Village. You can eat outside, and you can get great vegetarian food for next to nothing. Casual atmosphere.

TIME CAFE

380 LAFAYETTE ST, NY 10003
☎ (212) 533 7000
Where you'll find the typical downtown crowd, ie, young and trendy – BRUCE WEBER hangs out here with lots of beautiful people. It's a bar/nightclub too, attracting rappers and members of the record industry.

TriBeCa GRILL

375 GREENWICH ST, NY 10013
☎ (212) 941 3900
Owners ROBERT DE NIRO and BILL MURRAY have made this one of the most popular and affordable feeding grounds in NYC; good oysters, great desserts and a good choice of Californian wines. The walls are adorned with art by the late Robert De Niro, Sr.

YAFFA CAFE

97 ST MARK'S PL, NY 10009
☎ (212) 674 9302
Open all hours, the Yaffa always entices a lively, somewhat mixed crowd. The food is varied, with an emphasis on continental dishes and a wide choice of vegetarian food.

CLUBS

LIMELIGHT

660 6TH AVE AT 20TH ST, NY 10011
☎ (212) 807 7850
Music and scene vary according to the night, catering for everyone from rock 'n' rollers and ravers to drag queens and suits. Replete with all necessary state-of-the-art video and hi-fi systems. Incongruously housed in a Gothic-style Church of the Holy Communion. RICHARD JOHNSON thinks that *"some people get a lascivious thrill from dancing with wild abandon right in front of where the altar used to be. Since NYC nightlife exemplifies irreverence, where better than a church to party at your most debauched?"* Known for its "Disco 2000" nights.

PALLADIUM

126 E 14TH ST, NY 10003
☎ (212) 473 7171
A former movie palace, this club feels like a never-ending black hole. It's owned by Peter Gatien (who also owns Tunnel, Limelight and Club USA), and is still considered to be an 80s relic. The place to go for hip-hop and rap.

THE SUPPER CLUB

EDISON HOTEL, 240 W 47TH ST, NY 10036
☎ (212) 921 1940
Midtown throwback to a classic 20s nightclub – brainchild of Parisian-born Jean de Noyer. The ballroom of the Edison Hotel used to be the site of big-band radio broadcasts, which de Noyer restored to how it was in its heyday. Everyone loves it. Fri/Sat nights only.

TUNNEL

220 12TH AVE AT 27TH ST, NY 10001
☎ (212) 695 8238
Anything goes in yet another of Peter Gatien's bizarre, gimmick-heavy clubs. The interior, designed by Eric Goode, is like a multi-storey circus, incorporating mad ideas such as a bar in the unisex loo. There's also a wading room, piled three feet high with plastic airballs. Only open Fri/Sat.

WEBSTER HALL

125 E 11TH AVE, NY 10003
☎ (212) 353 1600
New York's most historic nightspot: home of the original bohemians, a venue for wild themed balls and one of NYC's most notorious speakeasies during the Prohibition years. It has also provided ELVIS PRESLEY, FRANK SINATRA and JULIE ANDREWS with a recording studio. Now it's the ultimate Greenwich Village cabaret/entertainment complex, including one of the best stages in NYC. TINA TURNER, GUNS 'N' ROSES and ERIC CLAPTON have all played here.

HOTELS

THE CARLYLE

MADISON AVE AT 76TH ST, NY 10021
☎ (212) 570 7173
The serene, subdued *grande dame* of Manhattan hotels, where the PRINCESS OF WALES and BARONESS THATCHER stay when in New York and where JACKIE O lived briefly following the assassination of JFK. The Aubusson carpets and Gobelin tapestries needn't make you feel as though you're in a time warp. Old-world charm is equalled by 90s efficiency: with state-of-the-art technology in each of the rooms – stereo systems, videos, faxes and dedicated lines and a recently expanded spa–fitness centre. At the hotel's **CAFÉ CARLYLE,** CLAUS VON BULOW enjoys the *"quiet piano and nostalgic crooning by Bobby Short"*, the legendary jazz pianist now in his third decade there.

KIDS If your children are liable to drag their feet while sightseeing in the Big Apple, relief is at hand for all concerned. At the bottom of the Empire State Building you'll find the **New York Skyride**, ☎ (212) 564 2224 – a flight simulator which gives you a bird's-eye view of Manhattan, without having to lift a foot. But it is not for the fainthearted. . . .
. . The dinosaur-packed **American Museum of Natural History,** Central Park W at W 79th St, NY, ☎ (212) 769 5100, will keep children of all ages transfixed. The Jurassic Age aside, there's a planetarium, and Imax cinema screens showing 3D-effect natural adventure films. . . . . . For the ultimate in child-friendliness the **Children's Museum of the Arts**, 72 Spring St, NY 10021, ☎ (212) 274 9198, provides under-10s with an ideal introduction to both the visual and the performing arts. There are regular interactive workshops, and an international gallery displaying works by children from around the world. Children can design computer-generated wall murals and then there's Architects' Alley, where they can learn about geometric shapes, building materials and the principles of design . . . . . For the ultimate toy store, go to **F A O Schwarz**, 767 5th Ave, NY 10153, ☎ (212) 644 9400, in the General Motors Building. Just walking through is an experience. . . . . . . Once you've visited all of the above, go down to **Two Boots (Café)**, 37 Ave A, in the East Village, ☎ (212) 505 2276, for some sustenance. For children the most appealing part of the Italian and Creole menu are the pizzas with faces designed especially for them.

"THE CAFÉ CARLYLE AT THE CARLYLE HOTEL HAS A GREAT ATMOSPHERE, WITH BOBBY SHORT SINGING EVERY NIGHT AND SOMETIMES EARTHA KITT AND DIXIE CARTA" –

DOUGLAS FAIRBANKS, JR.

FOUR SEASONS HOTEL

57 E 57TH ST NY 10022
☎ (212) 758 5700
Whether you're seduced by the monumental lobby, the unparalleled views over Manhattan, or simply the electric curtains in your bedroom, this is New York's hotel of the moment and also its tallest. In the Governor's Suite you can see the crown of the Chrysler Building from the bathtub, while on the other side there's a panoramic view over Central Park. JODIE FOSTER, CLINT EASTWOOD, MICHAEL KEATON and JULIA ORMOND all stay here. (See FOUR SEASONS, under Restaurants.)

THE LOWELL

28 E 63RD ST, NY 10021
☎ (212) 838 1400
It is said that when the very rich in New York get divorced, one partner always moves into the Lowell. It's immensely grand without being showy. Built in 1927 as an apartment hotel, it occupies the smartest location on a tranquil, tree-lined avenue between Park and Madison on the Upper East Side. Financiers and entertainers have often chosen to stay here, including ARNOLD SCHWARZENEGGER and MARIA SHRIVER. The Garden Suite has its own outdoor sitting room with a rose garden and fountain.

THE MARK HOTEL

MADISON AVE AT E 77TH ST, NY 10021
☎ (212) 744 4300
Located at the heart of New York's high-rent district, the Mark is particularly handy for the Met and other Upper East Side galleries,

museums and restaurants. Having undergone a $35 million facelift, it has still retained its intimacy which includes nice touches like having your polished shoes returned carefully wrapped in tissue paper. Another reason for staying there is Giorgio Finocchiaro, the conscientious concierge who is quite capable of arranging the impossible – dinner anywhere or seats at the opera. HARRISON FORD, ISABELLE ADJANI and ANDRÉ AGASSI all stay here. (See also **MARK'S RESTAURANT** under Restaurants.)

THE MAYFAIR HOTEL

610 PARK AVE, NY 10021
☎ (212) 288 0800
The old-world European style and service of this small hotel provides a magnet for Euro-dignitaries and sophisticates. It's also known for its soft and luxurious pillows. However, the two biggest attractions are the manager Dario, *"one of the finest hotel managers in the world"*, according to ED VICTOR, and the world-renowned **LE CIRQUE** restaurant (see Restaurants).

THE PARAMOUNT

235 W 46TH ST, NY 10036
☎ (212) 764 5500
Philippe Starck's theatrical, almost surreal interior has made this one of Manhattan's most publicized hotels and particularly popular with the young and arty. The bedrooms are fairly small but this is compensated for by Starck's humorous touches, such as zebra-striped headboards and lights that reproduce dappled sunlight. The mezzanine **BRASSERIE DES THÉÂTRES** is the most entertaining place to dine as you can see all the goings-on in the lobby below. The **WHISKEY BAR** is quite the New York scene spot, attracting such regulars as CHAKA KHAN, JOHNNY DEPP and MATT DILLON.

THE PENINSULA

700 5TH AVE, NY 10019
☎ (212) 247 2200
About as convenient as you can get when it comes to shopping. The Beaux Arts architecture and Art Nouveau interior, dating from 1902, provide a haven of hushed elegance from the sounds of the city for CATHERINE DENEUVE, DON JOHNSON, RACHEL HUNTER and ROD STEWART, who all stay here. It houses NYC's best pool and spa with an unrivalled view down 5th Ave. The **PEN-TOP BAR AND TERRACE** on the 23rd floor (with great vistas of the Manhattan skyline) is a favourite with the local banking fraternity – and is thought to serve the most expensive drinks in the US. For a drink and light eats, try the **GOTHAM** lounge.

THE PIERRE

5TH AVE AT 61ST ST, NY 10021
☎ (212) 838 8000
Recently renovated to the tune of $45 million, this glamorous and fabled 5th Ave address has lured back a galaxy of stars ranging from MICHAEL CAINE and SEAN CONNERY to MADONNA and TOM CRUISE. In the mornings you'll find the most powerful power breakfasts in town going on in the **CAFÉ PIERRE**, which is used for dinner dancing in the evening, as demonstrated by AL PACINO in *Scent of a Woman*. The muralled **ROTUNDA**, with its *trompe l'oeil* ceiling is a popular setting for high tea, while the vast fitness centre, where each piece of equipment has its own private TV, VCR and stereo, keeps the hotel well up-to-date.

THE RITZ CARLTON

112 CENTRAL PARK S, NY 10019
☎ (212) 757 1900
The $20 million facelift really shows and the former clubby, country-style interior has been replaced with a more traditional look. Chef Craig Henne serves north Italian cuisine in the evenings and American at lunch in the restaurant, **FANTINO**, and the clubby lounge has one of Manhattan's most popular bartenders, Norman Bukofzer. There is also a new fitness centre complete with sauna and spa facilities.

THE ROYALTON

44 W 44TH ST, NY 10036
☎ (212) 869 4400
Ian Schrager's overtly hip design shrine has been a magnet to the rag trade since opening in the 80s. Editors of *Vogue*, Karl Lagerfeld, Calvin Klein and the showbiz jet set hang out here during the collections, a paradise for poseurs. It's worth staying just to see the bathrooms, which are fitted with raw black slate shower stalls and brushed conical steel basins. An efficient and innovatively run hotel. **RESTAURANT 44** is always packed with recognizable faces, including ANNA WINTOUR, TINA BROWN, RICHARD GERE and BIANCA JAGGER.

THE ST REGIS

5TH AVE AT 55TH ST, NY 10022
☎ (212) 767 0525
This Beaux Arts hotel was recently refurbished to the tune of $100 million, which involved the second-largest gold-leafing project ever undertaken in the US. Each room has control panels which can be programmed into six languages. There's good food and good health facilities, and from the famous **ST REGIS** roof ballroom there are spectacular views of mid-

town Manhattan. Equally celebrated is the **KING COLE BAR**.

MUSIC

CARNEGIE HALL

154 W 57TH ST, NY 10019
☎ (212) 247 7800 for guided tours; (212) 903 9629 for museum
Opened in 1891, with Tchaikovsky conducting, Carnegie Hall is still New York's most famous and favourite concert hall, attracting huge names and the best orchestras to the city. According to ANDRÉ PREVIN, it's one of the five best halls on earth.

METROPOLITAN OPERA

METROPOLITAN OPERA HOUSE, LINCOLN CENTER, NY 10023
☎ (212) 362 6000
World-renowned 800-strong company. Here you will find the very best voices, prestigious world premières of new works and musical extravaganzas. Magical free open-air operas in Central Park remain a highlight of the season.

NEW YORK CITY OPERA

LINCOLN CENTER, NY 10023
☎ (212) 870 5570
Dynamic young company representing the best contemporary productions alongside new productions of classics like *The Magic Flute* and *Madam Butterfly*. Known for its superb set and costume design and for nurturing stars in the making – PLACIDO DOMINGO launched his career here. Open Sept–Nov and Mar–Apr.

RESTAURANTS

SEE ALSO HOTELS.

ALISON ON DOMINICK STREET

38 DOMINICK ST, NY 10013
☎ (212) 727 1188
A charming town house restaurant lures diners for Dan Silverman's solid southwestern French food. Local artists and Wall Streeters rub shoulders as they tuck into braised lamb shank with white beans and parsley and roasted garlic sauce.

ARCADIA

21 E 52ND ST, NY 10021
☎ (212) 223 2900
A comfortable and serene setting for Anne Rosenzweig's thoughtful and often inspired New Age American cooking. Kick off with Caesar salad with brioche croûtons, or mini corn cakes topped with crème fraîche and caviare and end with the gooey puddings.

LE BERNARDIN

EQUITABLE CENTER, 155 W 51ST ST, NY 10019
☎ (212) 489 1515
Since the death of the famous chef/co-owner, Gilbert Le Coze, his sister Maguy (who used to run it with him) has almost re-invented the restaurant. It's still probably New York's best seafood restaurant. Notoriously expensive.

BOULEY

165 DUANE ST, NY 10013
☎ (212) 608 3852
Owing to the popularity of chef David Bouley, it's hard to get a reservation here. Best dishes to try include peppered steak; calamari in 100-year-old balsamic vinegar and foie gras roasted in salt with figs, tomatoes and Armagnac. The sorbets are good too. The wine, in particular, is expensive.

THE BOWERY BAR

40 EAST 44TH STREET, NY 10036
☎ (212) 475 2220
Converted gasoline station, with a large garden out back seating up to 80 people. Classic American bistro, serving steak, fish and pasta, but the main attraction is the stars: SYLVESTER STALLONE, ARNOLD SCHWARZENEGGER, ROBERT DE NIRO, KARL LAGERFELD, BRYAN FERRY, to name a few. Hard to get a table at weekends, but easier earlier in the week.

CAFE DES ARTISTES

1 W 67TH ST, NY 10023
☎ (212) 877 3500
Intimate Beaux Arts haven and Chef Thomas Ferlesch's food is as refined as the setting – wonderful pot au feu, fabulous puddings and well-priced champagne. It's also good for Sunday brunch. A favourite haunt of PAUL NEWMAN, KATHLEEN TURNER and executives at the nearby ABC and Lincoln Center. *"Through the years the food has become incredibly good. I go there whenever I can. It's very reasonable, I think, for what it is. Try the hot fudge Napoleon, it's deadly,"* according to MIMI SHERATON.

CHANTERELLE

2 HARRISON ST, NY 10013
☎ (212) 966 6960
The beautifully presented food, especially the

THEMED RESTAURANTS AND CAFES

Bikes . . . . . The **Harley Davidson Café**, 1370 Ave of the Americas, ☎ (212) 245 6000, set in a former bank, is one of the latest eateries to jump onto the themed restaurant bandwagon in NYC. You can eat "gourmet road food" surrounded by Harley Davidson memorabilia and bikes, including the one ridden by Peter Fonda in *Easy Rider*. The service is very cheery and the decor theatrical. **Fashion** . . . . . At the **Fashion Café Restaurant**, 51 Rockefeller Pl, NY, ☎ (212) 765 3131, you probably won't bump into owners NAOMI, CLAUDIA, CHRISTY and ELLE tucking into beefburgers and chips – but you'll certainly see others eating predictable food from a predictable menu. The walls are covered in fashion memorabilia donated by models and designers, from fashion photographs and sketches to couture dresses and shoes. **Rock** . . . . . **Hard Rock Café**, **New York**, 326 W 57th St, NY, ☎ (212) 459 9320, is probably the best and most atmospheric of all the Hard Rocks. Fins of a vintage cadillac mark the frontage to this restaurant, known for its loud rock music and rock star memorabilia. The food is surprisingly good. The hot fudge brownie is fantastic. **Film** . . . . . **Planet Hollywood**, 140 W 57th St, NY, ☎ (212) 333 7827. Owned by BRUCE WILLIS, DEMI MOORE, SYLVESTER STALLONE, KEITH BARISH, ROBERT EARL and ARNOLD SCHWARZENEGGER, it's full of Hollywood kitsch. Always loud – the best dishes are the Mexican ones. **New Yorkers' New York** . . . . . **The Brooklyn Diner USA**, 888 7th Ave, NY 10019, ☎ (212) 977 1957. From the same team as the Trattoria Dell'Arte (see Restaurants) comes this 90-seater diner celebrating Brooklyn past and present. Lots of neon lights, stainless steel and mosaic tiles and you can't miss the All-American 15-foot mural of the Brooklyn Dodgers playing at Ebbets Field. Make sure you order the fabulous cheesecake: it's the best in the district.

signature seafood sausage, excellent puddings including chocolate mille-feuille, and an outstanding selection of cheese and wine, indicate that its *New York Times* four-star status is well earned. This is according to TIMOTHY GREENFIELD-SAUNDERS, *"without question the best restaurant in New York. The design is beautiful because it's simple; the service is flawless."*

LE CIRQUE

IN THE MAYFAIR HOTEL, 58 E 65TH ST, NY 10021
☎ (212) 794 9292
More an event than a mere meal. The most recent regime has lured Sylvain Portay from the stoves of the Louis XV restaurant in Monte Carlo's Hôtel de Paris. Exquisite pastries are produced by pastry chef Jacques Torres. Everyone agrees that the recent changes are really refreshing. *"Le Cirque has a way of re-inventing itself every few years,"* says TIM ZAGAT. Always packed.

COCO PAZZO

23 E 74TH ST, NY 10021
☎ (212) 794 0205
Pino Luongo's hit eatery where renowned chef Cesare Casella produces contemporary Italian food with a strong Tuscan influence. Try his signature insalata di Pontormo, or any of his wonderful fresh pastas. Popular with celebrity couples: WARREN BEATTY with ANNETTE BENING, and MEG RYAN with DENIS QUAID. BARRY DILLER and RON PERELMAN are regulars too. Good wine list heavy on Italian vintages.

DA UMBERTO

107 W 17TH ST, NY 10011
☎ (212) 989 0303
Family-run restaurant serving inventive Tuscan cuisine which includes the best tiramisu in NYC and is currently considered to be New York's best Italian according to MIMI SHERATON who comes for the *"spare and jolly"* decor and *"fabulous antipasto"*.

DAWAT

210 E 58TH ST, NY 10022

☎ (212) 355 7555

Some say this is the best Indian restaurant in the country – it's certainly one of the hippest, though it's often considered to be overpriced. The potato crisp appetizers, the spiced shrimp in curry leaves, the tandoori chicken, the lamb vindaloo and the spinach fritters are especially good. *"The food is wonderfully spiced and beautifully cooked and the decor is not a cliché."* – MIMI SHERATON.

FOUR SEASONS

99 E 57TH ST, NY 10022

☎ (212) 754 9494

Widely regarded as New York's hottest power-lunch spot, the **GRILL ROOM** at the Four Seasons is a NYC institution. For "result" power dinners, the **POOL ROOM** is deeply appropriate with its grand early-Bauhaus decor. Try the crab cakes or the crisp farmhouse duck with a sauce that varies according to the season. *"Every year it gets better. The place to eat in New York"* – ED VICTOR.

GOTHAM BAR AND GRILL

12 E 12TH ST, NY 10003

☎ (212) 620 4020

Over ten years on, this leading contemporary American restaurant is still *"consistently good, catering to a hip publishing and advertising crowd"*, according to TIM ZAGAT. Chef Alfred Portale has brought more sophisticated tastes to the kitchen including his innovative vertical style of food presentation – each plate is an artful edible tower. Good wine list. *"If Michelin had a guide to New York, it would be in its top five, and the service is untypically polite for New York,"* raves PAUL HEATHCOTE.

LA GRENOUILLE

3 E 57TH ST, NY 10022

☎ (212) 752 1495

Classic French *grande dame* that age cannot wither – it's coming up to 30 years old. Known for its beautiful flower arrangements as well as its cuisine. *"New York's most beautiful restaurant"* according to FRANK BOWLING. Wonderful private atelier dining room upstairs.

L'ESPINASSE

2 E 55TH STREET, NY 10022

☎ (212) 339 6719

Signature restaurant of the St Regis Hotel, Swiss chef Gray Kunz blends subtle flavours of the Orient with French cuisine and was awarded the coveted 4 star rating in 1994 by Ruth Reichl in the *New York Times*. Try cassoulet of fresh Perigord truffles, or signature starter fricasse of wild mushrooms and artichoke hearts, with chervil risotto. Reasonably priced, with extensive wine list.

MARK'S RESTAURANT

IN THE MARK HOTEL (SEE HOTELS)

☎ (212) 744 4300

The chef, Christophe Barbier, who has worked in Maxim's and La Grenouille, NYC (see opposite), serves colourful new American cuisine. Mark's is also increasingly popular for afternoon tea, with a new "chocolate buffet" – especially popular among trendy young things.

PATRIA

250 PARK AVE S, NY 10003

☎ (212) 777 6211

Home of Douglas Rodriguez's spectacular-looking and even better-tasting *nuevo latino* cooking. It's New York's cutting-edge food of the moment, with Latin American flavours and ingredients given an inspired twist. Try Honduran Fire and Ice.

RIVER CAFE

1 WATER ST (AT E RIVER), BROOKLYN, NY 11201

☎ (718) 522 5200

Floating restaurant with incredible views of the lower Manhattan skyline, especially at sunset. Rick Laakkonen's contemporary American food includes fruitwood-smoked salmon on johnnycake. Puddings are as dramatic as they are delicious. The prices might be high but the service is excellent.

SPARKS STEAK HOUSE

210 E 46TH ST, NY 10017

☎ (212) 687 4855

"For those who go to the US for steak, this is the place," says BARBARA KAFKA. Co-owner Pat Cetta adds, *"Steak is like sex, you have to have it once in a while."* The shellfish is good too. Best value in NY for carnivores wanting simple dishes done to a T.

TRATTORIA DELL'ARTE

900 7TH AVE, NY 10019

☎ (212) 245 9800

Designed by Milton Glaser, this arty NYC trattoria near Carnegie Hall is full of anatomical sculptures and paintings, while attracting high-energy, arty and beautiful people, including many celebrities. *"Most charming, most 'in' place, a New York must,"* says SUMMER BAYE.

UNION SQUARE CAFE

21 E 16TH ST, NY 10003

☎ (212) 243 4020

This Californian-style restaurant has people clamouring to get in. Insiders spread a white tablecloth on the bar for a spontaneous full meal. They serve great bullshots: order them with garlic chips. Huge portions.

VONG

200 E 54TH STREET, NY 10022

☎ (212) 486 9592

Original restaurant, with sister venue in the Berkeley Hotel in London, offers French-Thai food from Alsatian chef Jean-Georges Vongerichten who has brought a Thai influence through herbs and vegetables. Eclectic crowd at this well established restaurant, corporate at lunch, anybody in the evening, plenty of actors including MATT DILLON and MARISA TOMEI.

SHOPPING

THE ARMY AND NAVY

221 E 59TH ST, NY 10011

☎ (212) 755 1855

The type of casual chic under- and outerwear that you see in all-American movies, for all the family. Calvin Klein T-shirts, Timberland boots, flying jackets and Levis' entire range.

BALDUCCI'S

424 AVENUE OF THE AMERICAS, NY 10011

☎ (212) 673 2600

STEPHEN BAYLEY recommends a visit to Balducci's. Once a vegetable stall, it now sells gourmet food, specializing in Italian cheeses, fresh seafood and delicious breads warm from the oven. JEFFREY STEINGARTEN enthuses: *"Balducci's has the best produce and the best butcher in the city, as well as a very respectable cheese department."*

- -

"GREENWICH VILLAGE IS A COL-LECTOR'S PARADISE. AMAZING SPECIALIST SHOPS, FOR RECORDS, CLOTHES AND EXOTIC IMPORTS"

— JULIAN LLOYD WEBBER

- -

BARNES & NOBLE

105 5TH AVE, NY

☎ (212) 807 0099

Five floors choked with books, records and videos make this emporium fully deserving of the tag 'the world's largest bookstore'. And when you have exhausted your reserves of energy, relax and refresh yourself at the café on the top floor.

BARNEY'S

106 7TH AVE AT 17TH ST, NY 10011

☎ (212) 593 7800

AND 660 MADISON AVE, NY 10021

☎ (212) 826 8900

AND 225 LIBERTY ST, NY 10281

☎ (212) 945 1600

New York's answer to Harvey Nichols. Established over 60 years ago, this is where super-models and the super-chic (male and female) come to stock up on the latest Prada bag and other up-to-the-second clothes, accessories or gifts. The original store on 7th Ave is still regarded as the best of the three New York stores, while the more recent uptown Barney's on Madison attracts people who come to eat at MAD 61, the trendy instore restaurant. The third branch is in the World Financial Center on Liberty St.

- -

"BARNEY'S STILL HAS THE BEST SELECTION OF MEN'S AND WOMEN'S CLOTHES UNDER ONE ROOF" — NICK MASON

- -

BERGDORF—GOODMAN

754 5TH AVE, NY 10019

☎ (212) 753 7300

The most elegant women's- and menswear store in town (the men's store being in the old FAO Schwarz at 745 5th Ave). Part of its success is due to the intimate boutique-style areas allocated to each designer. In contrast to Barney's minimalist chic, the design and decor are more sumptuous. MICHAEL MUSTO is a fan: *"I still enjoy perusing through its rarefied ambience."* Designer goods include the precious costume jewellery and belts of Barry Kieselstein — popular with MICK JAGGER, JACK NICHOLSON and DIANA ROSS.

BIJAN

699 5TH AVE, NY 10022

Exclusive Iranian-run luxury goods store, Bijan's illustrious clientele include KINGS HUSSEIN OF JORDAN and JUAN CARLOS, as well as JACK NICHOLSON, who come to invest in everything from diamond-encrusted rings to the finest custom-made shoes.

MADISON AVENUE

Madison Ave is a striking composite of elegant 19C buildings, reminiscent of a scene from a Henry James novel. The ultra-exlusive, often quirky shops and art galleries make it worth a window-shopping spree, at the very least. **La Maison du Chocolat**, 25 E 73rd St, NY, ☎ (212) 744 7117, sells exquisitely made chocolates, moulded into every shape and form and shipped all over the world. **Dialogica**, 1070 Madison Ave, NY, ☎ (212) 737 7811, provides the interior decor for LISA BONET, NICHOLAS CAGE, LAURA DERN, AL PACINO and RINGO STARR. The shop also supplied furniture for films such as *Boomerang* and *Reality Bites*. **Café Nosidam**, 768 Madison Ave, NY, ☎ (212) 717 5633, (Madison spelt backwards), is a small Italian bistro just around the corner from the Carlyle Hotel. Good for a romantic dinner. Diners include TOM SELLECK, TOM CRUISE, STEVE MARTIN and ELLE MACPHERSON. **Thomas Woodard: American Antiques and Quilts**, 799 Madison Ave, NY, ☎ (212) 988 2906, is where HARRISON FORD and PAUL SIMON come to buy colourful American folk art, antiques, patchwork quilts and choose from a collection of woven carpets. **Pace Wildenstein**, 32 E 57th St, NY, ☎ (212) 421 3292 represents ground-breaking 20C artists including Picasso. (Has a new branch in Beverly Hills now.) HARVEY KEITEL, TOM HANKS, MARY TYLER MOORE and HUGH GRANT come to **Timberland**, 709 Madison Ave, NY, ☎ (212) 754 0434, for casual, environmentally conscious outdoor apparel.

BLOOMINGDALE'S

59TH ST AND LEXINGTON AVE, NY 10022
☎ (212) 705 2000
Bloomingdale's is *"shoppers' paradise"* according to JOHN TOVEY. It's rather like Selfridges only you go away with their signature big brown bag, rather than a plastic yellow one. Keep a lookout for good bargains on designer goods, and other regular special promotions. Good food hall.

DEAN AND DELUCA

560 BROADWAY, NY 10012
☎ (212) 431 1691
Hailed for being one of the greatest food emporia in the US and for changing the way America eats, Dean and Deluca still continue to import foods, including very rare delicacies from all over the world. At 121 Prince St, NY 10012, ☎ (212) 254 8776, there's a skylit **DEAN AND DELUCA CAFÉ** serving a range of original delicacies.

FRED LEIGHTON

773 MADISON AVE, NY 10021
☎ (212) 288 1872
Among the best period jewellers in the world for late 19C and early 20C designs including signed pieces by Cartier, La Cloche and Boucheron and some rare Mogul Indian jewellery – all commanding astronomical prices.

HAMMACHER SCHLEMMER

147 E 57TH ST, NY 10022
☎ (212) 421 9000
Famous for the latest in inventive, though expensive gadgets and gimmicks. Modern sellers range from a desk-top weather station to a soda-fountain CD jukebox – perfect for the man/woman with everything.

HENRI BENDEL

712 5TH AVE, NY 10019
☎ (212) 247 1100
It may have moved to a new premises, but the stock of innovative fashion from rising Euro and American fashion stars in the **NEW CREATORS** boutique is still as intriguing. Delightful café on the 2nd floor.

MACY'S

HERALD SQUARE, BROADWAY AT 34TH ST, NY 10001
☎ (212) 695 4400
Still the world's largest and possibly most famous store. This is where you can buy furniture, kitchenware, clothes and toys ranging

from basics to designer. Known for its regular Christmas extravaganzas and for its Thanksgiving Day Parade.

POLO/RALPH LAUREN

867 MADISON AVE, NY 10021

☎ (212) 606 2100

Flagship for Lauren's creations, stocking ready-to-wear for the whole family, as well as home decorations, and where drinks are served to their customers. POLO SPORT, the more casual, essentially preppy, men's and women's wear line, is across the street at 888 Madison Ave.

SAKS FIFTH AVENUE

611 5TH AVE, NY 10022

☎ (212) 753 4000

Nine floors of stunning international designer-dom – for men, women and children. If you want a makeover to go with that new frock you can have one at the in-store beauty salon and spa, before refuelling in CAFÉ SFA.

SULKA

430 PARK AVE, NY 10022

☎ (212) 980 5200

With almost a century of service behind it, Sulka continues to clothe the sartorially conscious with tailormade everything – from underwear to suits. Each customer is individually fitted and their patterns are kept on file for 50 years. Stores all over the world have kitted out AL CAPONE and JFK along with JOHN TRAVOLTA, GENE HACKMAN and DANNY DE VITO for film roles, and PIERCE BROSNAN who was fitted here for *Goldeneye*.

TAKISHIMAYA

693 5TH AVE, NY 10022

☎ (212) 350 0100

The US branch of Japan's largest department store. Seven floors of the beautiful and unusual provide excellent luxury gifts and accessories. The TEA BOX basement café and gourmet shop provides wonderful cross-cultural cuisine.

TIFFANY

727 5TH AVE, NY 10022

☎ (212) 755 8000

The pride of New Yorkers, immortalized by Audrey Hepburn who gazed wistfully and unforgettably through its hallowed windows. It just isn't the same in any other city. Famous for its Art Deco entrance, its jewellery and other trinkets which are always parcelled up in the famous azure-coloured Tiffany boxes.

ZA BAR'S

2245 BROADWAY, NY 10007

☎ (212) 787 2000

One of the most popular and least pretentious gastrodomes in NYC, with an irresistible fragrance of fresh bread and cheeses. Also sells a wide range of kitchen electricals.

THEATRE

⊛ NEW YORK SHAKESPEARE FESTIVAL

425 LAFAYETTE ST, NY 10003

☎ (212) 539 8500

Excellent summer Shakespeare series, which runs June–Aug at the DELACORTE THEATER in Central Park, which you can watch for free. George Wolfe is the producer. In the past it has attracted such talents as WILLIAM HURT, KEVIN KLINE, MARTIN SHEEN and MERYL STREEP. At all other times of the year, performances take place in any one of five theatres housed in the building on Lafayette St.

San Francisco

BALLET

SAN FRANCISCO BALLET

455 FRANKLIN ST, CA 94102

☎ (415) 861 5600

"The SF ballet under Helgi Tomasson's leadership is one of the spectacular success stories of the arts in America" – New York Times. Undoubtedly one of the finest ballet companies in the country, performing a varied repertoire of full-length neo-classical and contemporary ballet. All performances accompanied by the SF Ballet Orchestra.

BARS AND CAFES

TOSCA CAFE

242 COLUMBUS AVE, CA 94133

☎ (415) 391 1244

Old, established celebrity hang-out with *film noir* atmosphere. Italian standards, Italian flavour, and Italian opera on the jukebox. FRANCIS FORD COPPOLA, SAM SHEPARD, MIKHAIL BARYSHNIKOV are regulars who come to sample coffee from a fantastic old coffee machine.

CLUBS

DNA LOUNGE

375 11TH ST, CA 94103
☎ (415) 626 1409
Long-established club, favoured by insomniacs who want to hear rock, funk and rap. Go upstairs to the smart bar for an espresso or try one of the nightly drink specials at one of the other bars. Live music most nights.

THE GREAT AMERICAN MUSIC HALL

859 O'FARRELL ST, CA
☎ (415) 885 0750
One of America's great nightclubs. First-rate performers of blues, jazz, folk and rock, and the odd comedian too. Colourful dance floor area with marble columns.

LOVES

1500 BROADWAY, CA 84199
☎ (415) 931 6053
At the bottom of Russian Hill, the ever-popular Mr Johnny Love's nightspot is the place to be seen. As the night goes on, the place changes character: live jazz at dinner, then blues, reggae, rockabilly and good old rock 'n' roll right into the early hours.

THE PARADISE LOUNGE

308 11TH ST, CA 94103
☎ (415) 861 6906
Two stages, for dancing and eclectic live music, while off-beat acts perform in the cabaret upstairs. Open 3 pm–2 am.

FILM

SAN FRANCISCO INTERNATIONAL FILM FESTIVAL

1521 EDDY ST, CA 94115
☎ (415) 929 5000.
Fortnight of parties, premières and other special events held every spring, based around international features, documentaries and animated films.

HOTELS

CLIFT GRAND HERITAGE HOTEL

495 GEARY ST, CA 94102
☎ (415) 775 4700
The former **FOUR SEASONS**, now managed by Grand Heritage, still dominates the heartland of San Francisco's theatre quarter. Service is smooth; and high tea and brunch in the Louis XV-style **FRENCH ROOM** still lures in outsiders. You can even choose the colour of your room, which is always filled with plants and flowers.

HUNTINGTON HOTEL

NOB HILL, CA 94108
☎ (415) 474 5400
Red-brick, ivy-covered, family-run hotel, atop prestigious Nob Hill, with spectacular views over the city and bay. It's fiercely protective of the privacy of its more famous guests – such as PAVAROTTI, ARCHBISHOP DESMOND TUTU, ROBERT REDFORD, PALOMA PICASSO and ALISTAIR COOKE, who has been a regular for over 20 years and has had a suite named after

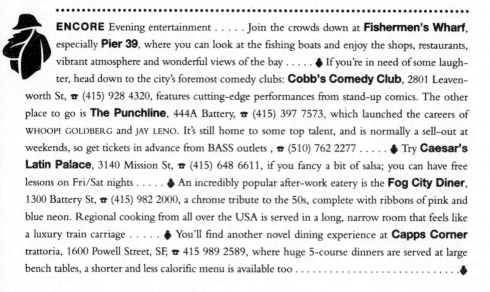

ENCORE Evening entertainment . . . . . Join the crowds down at **Fishermen's Wharf**, especially **Pier 39**, where you can look at the fishing boats and enjoy the shops, restaurants, vibrant atmosphere and wonderful views of the bay . . . . . ♠ If you're in need of some laughter, head down to the city's foremost comedy clubs: **Cobb's Comedy Club**, 2801 Leavenworth St, ☎ (415) 928 4320, features cutting-edge performances from stand-up comics. The other place to go is **The Punchline**, 444A Battery, ☎ (415) 397 7573, which launched the careers of WHOOPI GOLDBERG and JAY LENO. It's still home to some top talent, and is normally a sell-out at weekends, so get tickets in advance from BASS outlets , ☎ (510) 762 2277 . . . . . ♠ Try **Caesar's Latin Palace**, 3140 Mission St, ☎ (415) 648 6611, if you fancy a bit of salsa; you can have free lessons on Fri/Sat nights . . . . . ♠ An incredibly popular after-work eatery is the **Fog City Diner**, 1300 Battery St, ☎ (415) 982 2000, a chrome tribute to the 50s, complete with ribbons of pink and blue neon. Regional cooking from all over the USA is served in a long, narrow room that feels like a luxury train carriage . . . . . ♠ You'll find another novel dining experience at **Capps Corner** trattoria, 1600 Powell Street, SF, ☎ 415 989 2589, where huge 5-course dinners are served at large bench tables, a shorter and less calorific menu is available too . . . .♠

him. All rooms are furnished in a traditionally English style, while the handsome **BIG FOUR RESTAURANT**, named after four famous railroad tycoons, serves award-winning contemporary American food.

MANDARIN ORIENTAL

222 SANSOME ST, CA 94104
☎ (415) 885 0999
Dramatic hotel occupying the top 11 floors of the city's third-tallest building. From the safety of your bubble bath you look out of the huge windows onto all of the city's most famous landmarks. SILKS restaurant serves Californian food with an Oriental twist.

THE SHERMAN HOUSE

2160 GREEN ST, CA 94123
☎ (415) 563 3600
The city's most exclusive hotel is set in an exquisite, white, gabled, 19C town house in Pacific Heights. ROBIN WILLIAMS, KEVIN COSTNER, KATE CAPSHAW AND STEVEN SPIELBERG, KEVIN KLINE and PHOEBE CATES have all been lured by the wood-burning fires with marble mantelpieces, big four-poster beds and lavish window seats.

OPERA

🎭 OPERA IN THE PARK

GOLDEN GATE PARK (OPPOSITE THE DE YOUNG MUSEUM)
☎ (415) 666 7024
Held the Sunday after the opening of the autumn opera season, a free, alfresco concert featuring the San Francisco Opera orchestra and the stars from their opening-night production. Not to be missed.

SAN FRANCISCO OPERA

301 VAN NESS AVE, CA 94102
☎ (415) 861 4008
Artistically the most successful operatic organization in the US outside NY, under the dedicated direction of General Director Lotfi Mansouri and music director Donald Runnicles. During an extended 1996-7 season the company will perform nine productions in the Bill Graham Civic Auditorium and the Orpheum Theatre, while the War Memorial Opera House, the company's usual home, undergoes 18 months of seismic renovations.

SAN FRANCISCO SYMPHONY

DAVIES SYMPHONY HALL, VAN NESS AVE, CA 94102
☎ (415) 431 5400

Michael Tilson Thomas, formerly of the London Symphony Orchestra, has replaced Herbert Blomstedt as conductor. Continues to uphold tradition of sponsoring up-and-coming artists and commissioning new work every season.

RESTAURANTS

SEE ALSO HOTELS.

BOULEVARD

1 MISSION ST, CA 94105 (AT THE CORNER OF MISSION ST & STEWART ST)
☎ (415) 543 6084
This beautiful Parisian-style eatery is a veritable Garden of Eden. It is usually jam-packed, but if you can't get a table you can still order the full menu at the bar.

FLEUR-DE-LYS

777 SUTTER ST, CA 94109
☎ (415) 673 7779
The ruby red decor makes it more like a sheikh's tent than a traditional French restaurant; however, it's quite a romantic spot. You'll find classic French dishes varied with a wide range of vegetarian food.

GORDON BIERSCH

2 HARRISON ST, CA 94105
☎ (415) 243 8246
Bayside brewery restaurant where German-style beers are brewed on the premises in huge tanks imported from Germany. Customers can watch the process through large plate-glass windows. Greg Markey provides a menu that is both international and beer-friendly, including beer-steamed mussels and clams.

GREENS

BUILDING A, FORT MASON, CA 94102
☎ (415) 771 6222
Take-aways: ☎ (415) 771 6330
Open-plan warehouse restaurant, famous for its adventurous haute-vegetarian cooking, owned and operated by the Tassajara Zen Center of Carmel Valley. Spectacular views of the Golden Gate Bridge.

MOOSE'S

1652 STOCKTON ST, CA 94133
☎ (415) 989 7800
Evokes the great old European cafés and dinner houses. Chef Marc Valiani's contemporary American cuisine includes specialities like cumin-crusted sea bass perched on a pile of grilled chayote, onions and chillis. A further

CHEAP EATS Stars Oakville

Café, 500 Van Ness Ave, ☎ (415) 861 4344, has been relocated just around the corner from Jeremiah Towers's famous **Stars restaurant**. At Stars Oakville Café you can relax in simpler surroundings, at the bar or a table. Enjoy some great pizza. **Townsend Restaurant**, 2 Townsend St, ☎ (415) 512 0749, is a lively, family-owned and operated restaurant–café with an in-house bakery and take-out. Especially popular for breakfast and brunch. For more ethnic eating experiences, try **Cha-Cha-Chas**, 1801 Haight St, ☎ (415) 386 5758, which offers a mix of Cajun, Southwest & Caribbean – hot and spicy. No-reservations policy means you will probably have to wait. **Duset Thai**, 3221 Mission St, CA 94110, ☎ (415) 826 4639, is a small family business serving typical Thai cuisine.

attraction is the owner Ed Moose, a local raconteur, who works the tables.

STARS
150 REDWOOD, CA 94102
☎ (415) 861 7827
Jeremiah Tower, self-proclaimed Californian culinary king, continues to do brilliant business – especially after the theatre. But if you can't get a reservation you can always drop in for a light snack or pudding at the bar, the longest in California which overlooks the frenetic activity of the kitchen.

YO YO TSUMANI BISTRO
1611 POST ST, CA 94116
☎ (415) 922 7788
French dishes with a Japanese twist. Upstairs there's a tsumani bar, tsumani being the Japanese equivalent to tapas. Striking interior with arts and crafts displays, while on the upper level there's a small sitting area/gallery featuring the work of Bay Area artists.

Santa Fe

••

"THE MOST FASCINATING TOWN IN THE US, WITH ITS CULTURAL MIXTURE OF NAVAJO INDIAN, SPANISH COLONIAL AND MODERN AMERICA SET AMIDST STUNNING DESERT/MOUNTAIN SCENERY" –
EDWARD THORPE

••

ART AND MUSEUMS

MUSEUM OF THE INSTITUTE OF AMERICAN INDIAN ARTS
108 CATHEDRAL PLACE, NM 87501
☎ (505) 988 6281
Newly expanded premises holds the largest collection of contemporary Native American art in the United States.

NEDRA MATTEUCCI GALLERIES
1075 PASEO DE PERALTA, NM 87501
☎ (505) 982 4631
The gallery features work by artists of the American West, the California regionalist, the early Taos and Santa Fe schools, as well as masters of American Impressionism and Modernism. Also represented are some of the country's leading painters and internationally acclaimed sculptors. Jewellery by Italian artist Buccelati and the timeless designs of Spratling are exhibited.

HOTELS

THE BISHOP'S LODGE
BISHOP'S LODGE RESORT, BISHOP'S LODGE RD, NM 87501
☎ (505) 983 6377
Just five minutes from downtown Santa Fe, this country retreat offers cosy accommodation, good food and a thousand acres to play in. From spring to autumn, guests can ride, play tennis, skeet and trap, go hiking or swim in, supposedly, the prettiest pool in New Mexico.

HOTEL SANTA FE
1501 PASEO DE PERALTA, NM 87501
☎ (505) 982 1200

A few minutes' walk from the plaza, Hotel Santa Fe is the only hotel here owned by Native Americans and also houses a definitive collection of sculpture by the renowned late Native American artist Allan Houser.

INN OF THE ANASAZI

113 WASHINGTON AVE, NM 87501

☎ (505) 988 3030

Set in the heart of the Plaza district, the hotel provides you with your own concierge as well as your own personalized exercise equipment. It also has a library containing books on the folklore of the region and a restaurant (see Anasazi, under Restaurants).

RESTAURANTS

ANASAZI

113 WASHINGTON AVE, NM 87501

☎ (505) 988 3030

Located in the Inn of the Anasazi (see Hotels). Chef Peter Zimmer serves New Mexican and Native American dishes such as Navajo flatbread and fire-roasted sweet peppers. There is a private wine cellar available for parties. Prompt and friendly service.

THE COYOTE CAFE

132 WEST WATER ST, NM 87501

☎ (505) 983 1615

The constantly changing Southwestern menu of the main Coyote dining room is impressive. A typical dinner might include buttermilk corn cakes with chipode shrimp, followed by "the cowboy" rib chop with onion rings and sour lemon bread pudding. Decor is whimsical and there's an open view of the kitchen. Service is friendly and efficient. Open daily for dinner and brunch at weekends. At **COYOTE'S ROOFTOP CANTINA,** the colourful open-air cantina next door, sample a taste of Old Mexico with the barbecued duck quesadilla or Ensenada taco. Good for a quick lunch or cocktail – the house cocktail being Brazilian daiquiri. The **COYOTE CAFÉ GENERAL STORE** is a gourmet store where you can find take-away snacks and sandwiches, and speciality breads.

THE DOUBLE A

331 SANDOVAL ST, NM 87501

☎ (505) 982 8999

Located in the Guadalupe district of the city, the design and furnishing of both the bar and restaurant represent the cultural mix of the area, as does the food – keeping everyone happy.

Seattle

CLUBS

THE BACKSTAGE

2208 N W MARKET ST, WA 98107

☎ (206) 781 2805

One of Seattle's major clubs, set in the basement of an old brick building. An exciting and diverse programme of live music.

THE CROCODILE CAFE

2200 2ND AVE, WA 98121

☎ (206) 441 5611

For a real glimpse of Seattle's very cool alternative rock scene. Funky, makeshift decor complements the thrift-shop crowd.

THE RIVERSIDE INN

14060 INTERURBAN AVE S, TUKWILA, WA 98168

☎ (206) 244 5400

Country music is still alive and well, for both young and old, in this country club just south of Seattle.

HOTELS

THE ALEXIS

1007 1ST AVE, WA 98104

☎ (206) 624 4844

This is where out-of-towners and Seattle sophisticates go to get pampered. When the SULTAN OF BRUNEI visited, he had four suites refurbished and the ceilings decorated with arrows pointing to Mecca. The **PAINTED TABLE** restaurant is known for its decorative plates, while the smaller **CAFÉ ALEXIS** features experimental seasonal American cuisine.

FOUR SEASONS OLYMPIC

411 UNIVERSITY ST, WA 98101

☎ (206) 621 1700

Many will remember this elegant hotel as the setting for the hi-tech cyberspace shenanigans in *Disclosure*, Michael Crichton's bestseller. The **GEORGIAN** restaurant is a favourite spot for special occasions, and the **GARDEN COURT** bar, with its large trees, floor-to-ceiling windows and jazz, serves the most expensive drinks in the city.

SORRENTO

900 MADISON ST, WA 98104

☎ (206) 622 6400

The octagonal lobby, with its mahogany walls, beams and striking marble fireplace, makes it feel like a club and it's become a firm favourite with the smart, young and upwardly mobile set. The **HUNT CLUB**, overseen by Eric Lenard, is noted for its excellent Pacific Northwest cuisine. Superstar chef WOLFGANG PUCK concurs.

RESTAURANTS

SEE ALSO HOTELS.

CHINOOKS

1900 W NICKERSON – SUITE 103, WA 98119
☎ (206) 283 4665
Although Fisherman's Terminal (on the south side of the Lake Washington Ship Canal) has been tarted up beyond recognition, you can still watch the fishermen working on their nets. So, naturally, this is the place to go for the freshest salmon, cod or halibut, prepared any way you choose. Weather permitting, the patio is the best place to sit.

THE DAHLIA LOUNGE

1904 4TH AVE, WA 98101
☎ (206) 682 4142
Tom Douglas's fashionable downtown restaurant embodies what's commonly referred to as Northwest cuisine. The finest and freshest of local ingredients are conjured up into dishes which have an increasingly Asian flavour, reflecting recent changes in the local populace. A typical dish worth trying is thick fillet of king salmon grilled with sesame-cilantro vinaigrette, served over soda noodles.

EMMETT'S OYSTER BAR

IN PIKE PLACE MARKET, 1916 PIKE PLACE, WA 98101
☎ (206) 448 7721
Emmett Watson's bar, set in the middle of an oyster market, offers locally produced molluscs from Puget Sound. All of these go well with local micro-brews such as Pyramid Wheaton Ale or Red Hook. For the best Semi-Ahmoos or Penn Cove oysters, visit in winter.

THE HERBFARM

32804 ISSAQUAH FALL CITY RD, FALL CITY, WA 98024
☎ (206) 784 2222
30 miles E of Seattle in the foothills of the Cascade Mountains, you'll find excellent Northwest cuisine. The fixed-price set menu of nine courses might be wallet-numbing, but it's still wildly popular. Book ahead.

KASPAR'S

2701 1ST AVE, WA 98119
☎ (206) 298 0123
One of Seattle's most peaceful dining spots with magnificient sunset views of the Olympic Mountains and Puget Sound. Swiss-born and trained chef Kaspar Donier offers an innovative menu based on local market produce. His signature vegetable sushi is particularly colourful. Open Tues–Sat, dinner only.

RAY'S BOATHOUSE

6049 SEAVIEW AVE NW, WA 98107
☎ (206) 789 3770
Situated on Shilshole Bay, on an old pier with a stunning view over the bay and the Olympic Mountains beyond – you can feast on steamed smoked black cod and the ubiquitous smoked salmon. The smoking is done at Port Chatham and is unlike anything you have tried before. No sauces required.

ROVERS

2808 E MADISON ST, WA 98104
☎ (206) 325 7442
Set in a dainty little house with a courtyard garden of herbs and flowers, Rovers is perfect for dining outside, while the doting service makes it a troublefree spot for special occasions. All Thierry Rauturau's food tastes good. Open Tues–Sat, dinner only.

SALEH AL LAGO

6804 E GREEN LAKE WAY N, WA 98115
☎ (206) 522 7943
Chef-owner Saleh Joudeh began his career as a cardiologist, then started cooking in a bowling alley and is now widely recognized as a gifted chef. His menus – enjoyed by JEFF BRIDGES and KIEFER SUTHERLAND – are predominantly northern Italian, although he recalls his Syrian background with the occasional Middle Eastern speciality. Friendly service. Closed Sun.

WILD GINGER

1400 WESTERN AVE, WA 98010
☎ (206) 623 4450
Very popular, vibrant and convivial eatery serving all manner of Southeast Asian dishes. You can sip a variety of local beers while watching the food being seasoned and skewered in the sizzling satay bar. Open 7 days. Executive chef: Jeem Han Lock.

Washington

ART AND MUSEUMS

HIRSHHORN MUSEUM & SCULPTURE GARDEN
INDEPENDENCE AVE AT 7TH ST SW, DC 20560

☎ (202) 357 2700

Houses the Smithsonian's extensive collection of modern and contemporary art, particularly famous for the Rodin, Moore and Giacometti sculptures in the garden.

NATIONAL GALLERY OF ART
4TH ST AND CONSTITUTION AVE NW, DC 20565

☎ (202) 737 4215

Outstanding collection of European and American art from the 13C onwards, including Leonardo da Vinci's *Ginevra de' Benci* and Renoir's *A Girl with a Watering Can*. Check out Alexander Calder's giant organically shaped mobile.

PHILLIPS COLLECTION
1600 21ST ST NW, DC 20009

☎ (202) 387 2151

The first permanent museum of modern art in the US. A small, genteel museum housing works by Braque, Cézanne, Klee, Matisse, Renoir and Rothko. Sunday afternoon concerts played in the Music Room are a joy.

SMITHSONIAN INSTITUTION
1000 JEFFERSON DRIVE SW, DC 20560

☎ (202) 357 2700

An impressively large operation – 13 museums in Washington and two in New York, together housing more than 78 million works. At various addresses around town you'll find the NATIONAL MUSEUMS OF AMERICAN ART AND AMERICAN HISTORY (Hollywood memorabilia and the First Ladies' restored gowns), the NATIONAL PORTRAIT GALLERY, the RENWICK GALLERY (US arts and crafts), the FREER GALLERY (19C and 20C American art; Oriental Art), the MUSEUM OF NATURAL HISTORY (containing the Hope Diamond) and the much talked-about NATIONAL AIR AND SPACE MUSEUM.

UNITED STATES HOLOCAUST MEMORIAL MUSEUM
100 RAOUL WALLENBURG PL, DC

☎ (202) 488 0400

Movies, artefacts and pictures telling the story of the 11 million murdered by the Nazis between 1933 and 1945. *"It's all done in an industrial way – you're shuttled in like cattle, no windows, you feel slightly claustrophobic – which gives you a sense of what it must have felt like"* – KITTY KELLEY. Open 7 days. Free entry, but ticket reservation required.

ARTS CENTRES

THE JOHN F KENNEDY CENTER
2700 F ST NW, DC 20566

☎ (202) 416 8000

A concentration of some of the best performing arts in the country. The wood-panelled EISENHOWER THEATER stages major shows, the TERRACE has music, the AMERICAN FILM INSTITUTE THEATER screens films (new and old) and the small THEATER LAB stages cabaret and comedy. The Washington Opera is based in the OPERA HOUSE and the CONCERT HALL is the proud home to the National Symphony Orchestra.

CLUBS

BLUES ALLEY
1073 WISCONSIN AVE NW, DC 20007

☎ (202) 337 4141

America's greatest jazz musicians perform here with surprising regularity.

CLUB ZEI
1415 ZEI ALLEY NW, DC 20005

☎ (202) 842 2445

Very 80s New York – loud, wall-to-wall video monitors; built out of cast iron and concrete with balconies overlooking the dance floor.

FIFTH COLUMN
915 F ST NW, DC 20004

☎ (202) 393 3632

Vibrant club with energetic crowd, generic music. Drinks are expensive.

KILIMANJARO LOUNGE
1724 CALIFORNIA ST NW, DC

☎ (202) 328 3838

Biggest dance club in town, open Thurs–Sun. An astonishing collection of world music.

SPY CLUB
805 15TH ST, DC 20005

☎ (202) 289 1779

Perfect for suits. Good dance floor – try to wangle a billiards table in the members' room. Open Thurs–Sun, nights only. Happy hour 5–8 pm.

HOTELS

HAY ADAMS

1 LAFAYETTE SQ, DC 20006
☎ (202) 638 6600
Worth coming here just to have breakfast – the views from THE ADAMS ROOM over the White House are sensational. Establishment hotel, with three English country-house-style reception rooms and impressive Renaissance-style lobby.

THE MADISON

15TH AND M STS NW, DC 20005
☎ (202) 862 1600
Private, locally owned hotel in the financial district. A favourite with visiting heads of state.

PARK HYATT

24TH AND M STS NW, DC 20037
☎ (202) 789 1234
Abundant fresh flowers, helpful staff and if you're just after 100% privacy you can have that too. Heavy-hitting celebrity clientele from PLACIDO DOMINGO to ZSA ZSA GARBOR to SPIKE LEE.

RITZ-CARLTON

2100 MASSACHUSETTS AVE NW, DC 20008
☎ (202) 293 2100
Smallish, understated high-society hotel beautifully placed for the Phillips Collection and within a few blocks of the World Bank, the US Treasury, the White House and Georgetown. Once called The Fairfax and owned by Vice-President Gore's family, the hotel has always been a networker's dream – it's permanently teeming with politicians, journalists and diplomats. The JOCKEY CLUB is a favourite dining spot for senators – and has been since JACKIE O made it fashionable in the 60s – while the cosy FAIRFAX BAR is a good place for them to meet their secretaries.

THE WILLARD INTERCONTINENTAL

1401 PENNSYLVANIA AVE NW, DC 20004
☎ (202) 628 9100
Beaux Arts-style building, steeped in history – Mark Twain and Charles Dickens stayed here, while Martin Luther King wrote his "I have a dream" speech within its walls. Still a favourite with pre-inaugurated presidents. For formal high-powered dining the WILLARD ROOM serves good American cuisine with a hint of EC flavours. The NEST LOUNGE is good for tea and jazz.

RESTAURANTS

SEE ALSO HOTELS.

BOMBAY CLUB

815 CONNECTICUT AVE NW, DC 20006
☎ (202) 659 3727
PRESIDENT CLINTON's favourite Indian, only one and a half blocks from the White House. Strong echoes of Empire and the traditional Pimms-drinking in the bar.

BUSARA

2340 WISCONSIN AVE NW, DC 20007
☎ (202) 337 2340
Slick neon decor and delicately flavoured food make this the best Thai in town. There's a jazz club upstairs and an Oriental garden with waterfalls and streams.

LE CAPRICE

2348 WISCONSIN AVE NW, DC 20007
☎ (202) 337 3394
Cosy French bistro fronted by Alsatian chef Edmund Foltzenlogel. With no-nonsense specialities such as salmon roulade, and a meringue mushroom covered in chocolate sauce for pudding. Some good vintage port. Open Mon–Fri for lunch, 7 nights for dinner.

CHRISFIELDS

8012 GEORGIA AVE, SILVER SPRINGS, MD 20910
☎ (301) 589 1306
Bustling restaurant, more like a diner in appearance with its beer stains and celebrity snaps but still serves splendid seafood.

CITRONELLE

3000 M ST NW, DC 20007
☎ (202) 625 2150
The light California touch of chef Michel Richard of LA is highly prized by local cognoscenti.

DUKE ZIEBERT'S

1050 CONNECTICUT AVE NW, DC 20036
☎ (202) 466 3730
A Washington institution, which packs in 400 at a time. Famous for designer deli dishes. LARRY KING, who has a favourite table here, is always popping in for a healthy plate of chicken (no skin), broiled fish or tuna salad. Where you are seated denotes your position in the Washington power structure – so don't get upset if you end up behind a potted plant.

LA FERME

7101 BROOKVILLE RD, CHEVY CHASE, MA 20815

☎ (301) 986 5255

Just a few miles north of town and run by Marcel Montagnier, who is known for favouritism. He particularly enjoys catering for the city's power-lunchers, but, in Washington, who doesn't? He'll set aside a particular table and conjure up a special dish in honour of his most favoured guests.

GERARD'S PLACE

915 15TH ST NW, AT MCPHERSON SQUARE, DC 20005

☎ (202) 737 4445

Two Michelin star chef Gerard Panguad offers an ever changing seasonal menu. If you're lucky you might catch his signature dish of steamed lobster with ginger, lime and a sauternes sauce with mango. Be warned: competition for a table is fierce. Book ahead.

THE INN AT LITTLE WASHINGTON

P O BOX 300, WASHINGTON, VA 22747

☎ (703) 675 3800

More than just a restaurant, the Inn consistently ranks with America's very best – for its food, decor and accommodation. It's 67 miles from Washington, at the foot of the Blue Ridge Mountains, but it's well worth the trek. The food is new American borrowing heavily from the French, although by using Virginian ingredients – Smithfield ham rather than prosciutto – it's much lighter. A favourite of GEORGE BUSH. *"Chef O'Connell understands that guests travel there to eat what they can't eat in the city"* – ALAIN DUCASSE. Closed Tues.

JEAN-LOUIS AT WATERGATE

WATERGATE HOTEL, 2650 VIRGINIA AVE, DC 20037

☎ (202) 298 4488

Washington's one remaining hot-shot French chef presides over the capital's finest dining room. Jean-Louis Palladin's multi-course, *prix-fixe* menu enlivens the taste buds of the élite. Impressive wine cellar, indeed Jean-Louis is known for creating special menus around the wine of your choice. Closed Sun/Mon.

MAISON BLANCHE

1725 F ST NW, DC 20006

☎ (202) 842 0070

French taste in food and French taste in decor with a little Mediterranean warmth added by Italian owner Tony Greco. Good view of the White House's executive offices.

THE OCCIDENTAL GRILL

1475 PENNSYLVANIA AVE NW, DC 20014

☎ (202) 783 1475

Historic, if a touch too serious, DC eatery, where Roosevelt and Churchill dined. A very solid gentlemen's club atmosphere and famous for its swordfish club sandwiches. Open 7 days.

PALLADIN

2650 VIRGINIA AVE NW, DC 20037

☎ (202) 298 4455

Though Jean-Louis Palladin is known for his truffle-rich *haute cuisine* at JEAN-LOUIS AT WATERGATE (see opposite), his more modest upstairs bistro is just as powerful a crowd-puller. The veal cheeks in red wine are first-rate.

THE PALM

1225 19TH ST NW, DC 20006

☎ (202) 293 9091

Seems ordinary but its almost mythical reputation has moved with it from New York to Washington. The walls are covered with drawings of the rich, famous, powerful and important. According to owner Ray Jacomo, *"If they're not steady customers, their pictures don't go up, and no one who hasn't been here is on the wall."*

RED HOT AND BLUE

1600 WILSON BLVD, ARLINGTON, VA 22209

☎ (703) 276 7427

Memphis-style barbecue restaurant, full of Memphis memorabilia. Opened by the late Lee Atwater, Bush's chief campaign strategist. Always bursting at the seams with off-duty senators and congressmen.

TIBERIO'S

1915 K ST, DC 20006

☎ (202) 452 1915

Ensuring that they're visible to others is a significant factor when Washingtonians decide where to dine. Tiberio's huge dining room caters for this extremely well. Guests are welcomed into a high-ceilinged foyer dominated by an enormous vase spilling roses, one of which is given to each lady as she leaves.

VIDALIA

1990 M ST, DC 20030

☎ (202) 659 1990

Butter is banished in Vidalia, which is named after the sweet Georgia onion, and replaced by an onion marmalade. In fact almost everything has a trace of onion, even the apple cobbler. Chef–owner Jeffrey Buben celebrates the home-grown, established traditions of American cookery, and the dining rooms contain examples of American folk art, creating the air of an old country manor. Dinner only on Sat. Closed Sun.

SHOPPING

It's difficult to get to and hard to park, but people are still lured to Georgetown's antique, craft and designer shops, including **SAKS JANDEL**, which houses most high-stepping labels. The **METRO CENTER**, 5510 Wisconsin Ave, Chevy Chase, MD 20815, ☎ (301) 652 2250, is where you'll find your Harrods and Selfridges, which in this case are **HECHT'S**, ☎ (202) 628 6661, and **WOODWARD AND LOTHROP**, ☎ (202) 347 5300. It's worth visiting **UNION STATION**, 50 Mass Ave NE, ☎ (202) 371 9441, a beautiful Beaux Arts train station with marble floors and vaulted ceilings. There are three levels, offering everything from trendy clothes to special-interest shops like **POLITICAL AMERICA** (for campaign buttons and memorabilia). **CELEBRATE AMERICA**, National Press Building, 14th and 15th Sts NW, ☎ (202) 347 0830, is the place to go for quality Americana. In the CIA's home town the **SPY SHOP**, 1420 K St NW, ☎ (202) 682 5380, stocks all the latest in surveillance equipment. The homely type should visit **DEAN AND DELUCA**, 3276 M St, Georgetown NW, DC 20007, ☎ (202) 342 2500, for home-made pastas, vegetables and other delicacies such as freshly ground coffee and pastries.

THEATRE

ARENA STAGE
6TH ST AND MAINE AVE SW, DC 20024
☎ (202) 554 9066
One of America's highest-rated regional theatre companies and the first to tour Moscow. A complex of three theatres produce everything from the classics to contemporary American pieces. Closed Mon.

NATIONAL THEATER
1321 PENNSYLVANIA AVE NW, DC 20004
☎ (202) 628 6161
Established in 1835, this is DC's oldest cultural institution, often a pre-Broadway tester. Good on musicals, comedy and drama. Closed Mon.

ARGENTINA
Buenos Aires

CAFES

GRAN CAFE TORTONI
PLAZA DE MAYO AT AVE DE MAYO 892, BUENOS AIRES
☎ (541) 342 4328
The oldest café in town which opened in 1858 is still as crowded as ever. Grand interior. Serves light snacks.

CLUBS

CASA BLANCA
CALLE BALCARCE 668, BUENOS AIRES
☎ (541) 334 5010
The best place to visit for traditional tango, sensual dance and soulful song – and a favourite with PRESIDENT YEMEN. You can learn the steps too. Phone for opening times.

POLO

ASOCIATION ARGENTINA DE POLO
H YRIGOYEN 636, 1ST FLOOR, BUENOS AIRES
☎ (541) 343 0972
Nobody plays better polo than the Argentinians – Jilly Cooper would vouch for that – and Argentina is the place to watch the players at their very best. Canchas Nacionales in Buenos Aires, a 20,000-seater stadium, is where the World Championships are held every Nov. The season is Mar–May and Sept–Dec.

HOTELS

ALVEAR PALACE
AVE ALVEAR 1891, 1129 BUENOS AIRES
☎ (541) 804 4031
A Louis XVI-style palace which was constructed in 1932 from materials shipped in from France. It is conveniently situated in the heart of the fashionable Recoleta district. The bedrooms have great views over the city and river. Two restaurants: **LA BOURGOGNE** for French food and **LA CAVE** for casual French and Argentine food.

IGUAZU NATIONAL PARK One of the wonders of the world set in a bend in the Iguazu River on the Brazilian border, the Iguazu Falls consists of 275 separate waterfalls. The best views are from the Brazilian side where there are some great beaches and you can swim right up to the falls. The hotel in the park – **Internacional Cataratas De Iguazu,** Parque Nacional Iguazu, ☎ 0757 20295 – may not be aesthetically pleasing, but the views from the floor-to-ceiling windows more than compensate. Make sure you specify a view room on the falls side when booking and dine outside on your own balcony and enjoy the most spectacular views at sunset and sunrise.

HOTEL PARK HYATT
POSADAS 1086/88, 1011 BUENOS AIRES
☎ (541) 326 1234
Europe blends with Latin America in this turn-of-the-century French mansion. The rooms are filled with historic artefacts, and the European restaurant is well up to catering for picky VIP visitors.

MARRIOT PLAZA HOTEL
CALLE FLORIDA 1005, BUENOS AIRES
☎ (541) 312 6001
One of Buenos Aires' most gracious hotels, where the President sometimes entertains. Lots of plush red carpets and chandeliers.

RESTAURANTS

SEE ALSO HOTELS.

LA CABANA
AVE ENTRE RIOS 436
☎ (541) 381 2373
When visiting Argentina you've got to have steak, and in Buenos Aires this is where to go. The dark panelling and well-spaced tables make it cosy and private. House specialities are the baby beef (a steak from a young steer) and the baked Alaska.

LAS NAZARENAS
CALLE RECONQUISTA 1132, BUENOS AIRES
☎ (541) 312 5559
A two-storey colonial-style building is a popular parrilla (grill). Popular with Argentine business people.

SHOPPING

The **PATIO BULLRICH**, Ave del Liberador 750, near the Park Hyatt Hotel, is the city's most luxurious shopping arcade. Recently, however, the **ALTO PALERMO**, corner of Ave Santa Fe and Ave Colonel Diaz, has become even more popular. The **SAN TELMO** district in Buenos Aires hosts great flea markets on Sun.

THEATRES

LA PLAZA
AVE CORRIENTES 1660, BUENOS AIRES
☎ (541) 372 6079
An open-air mall and entertainment centre right in the middle of town, including a small amphitheatre and two regular theatres. There are shops and a restaurant here too.

TEATRO COLON (COLUMBUS THEATRE)
CALLE CERRITO 618, CATEDRAL AL SUR, BUENOS AIRES
☎ (541) 355 4146, ext 230 (box office)
World-famous opera house with excellent acoustics where Maria Callas, among others, has performed. The 350 seats are always in demand, especially when an international artist is performing, since most are held by season-ticket holders. The international season runs from Apr to Nov.

AUSTRALIA
Adelaide

ART AND MUSEUMS

ART GALLERY OF SOUTH AUSTRALIA
NORTH TERRACE, SA 5000
☎ (8) 8207 7000
Thanks to the eponymous collection of philanthropist Max Carter, this contains some of

the finest colonial art in the country. The modern Australian art scene is also represented.

SOUTH AUSTRALIAN MARITIME MUSEUM
117 LIPSON ST, PORT ADELAIDE
☎ (8) 8240 0200
Fascinating collection of ships' figureheads, shipwreck relics, scale models, and wooden boats, located in an old stone warehouse. Re-creates experiences such as childhood outings to the beach and life aboard an immigrant ship.

SOUTH AUSTRALIAN MUSEUM
NORTH TERRACE, SA 5000
☎ (8) 8207 7500
Brilliant collection of Central Desert Aboriginal and Melanesian artefacts, plus changing displays of Aboriginal culture.

BARS AND CAFES

BOLTZ CAFE
268 RUNDLE ST, SA 5000
☎ (8) 8232 5234
Has all the subtlety that you might expect from an Australian bistro. Designer pizzas and pasta accompanied by live music until after midnight most nights. Favoured by the laid-back grunge brigade.

THE MECCA
290 RUNDLE ST, SA 5000
☎ (8) 8232 5655
Former butcher's shop, which has taken on a

new lease of life as one of the swishest café/brasseries on Adelaide's café row.

UNIVERSAL WINE BAR
285 RUNDLE ST, SA
☎ (8) 8232 5000
Michael Hill Smith's split-level café-bar, in Adelaide's eat street, is still the toast of the city's café society. Excellent selection of vintage wines and gutsy, honest game and offal dishes.

HOTELS

HYATT REGENCY
NORTH TERRACE, SA 5000
☎ (8) 8231 1234
Glamorous high-rise decked out in ochre and glass, set in a prime location on North Terrace. Dine in, for modern Australian marvels at **BLAKE'S**, ☎ (8) 8238 2381, where the menu makes a fashionable nod towards the Orient, aided by a tandoor oven; also famous for its grills.

RESTAURANTS

SEE ALSO HOTELS.

THE GRANGE RESTAURANT
IN THE HILTON ADELAIDE, VICTORIA SQ, SA 5000
☎ (8) 8217 0711
One of Australia's most important new restau-

ENCORE What's up in Adelaide . . . . . ♠ the **Adelaide Festival of Arts** is a cultural binge held in Feb/Mar every other year ('96, '98, etc), which includes music and other performing arts from home and abroad. The Festival's **Writers' Week** is a heavyweight literary event and you could catch the occasional gem at the **Fringe Festival** . . . . . ♠ In mid-Aug 30 wineries open their cellar doors for the annual **Barossa Classic Gourmet Weekend** when everyone eats, drinks and makes merry. The **Hills Harvest Festival** in March, above Adelaide, is similar but different – there's no music . . . . . ♠ Gourmets gallop to **Central Markets** for Asian veg and groceries from Kuo Chi, for prosciutto and zampone from **Marino**, Providore Central Market for just about everything else . . . . . .♠ **The North Adelaide Heritage Apartments**, 109 Glen Osmond Rd, Eastwood, SA 5061, ☎ (08) 8272 1355 – the creation of antique dealers Rodney and Regina Twiss – are boutique-style apartments with character, a dash of luxury and a bargain-basement price tag, tucked away in converted villas in leafy N Adelaide . . . . . . ♠ Don't leave town without walking around the marvellously manicured **Botanic Gardens**; taking the tram to **Glenelg**; visiting **The Jam Factory**, packed with arts and crafts; having a pie floater from the pie cart outside the Adelaide Casino . . . .

rants, is overseen by superchef Cheong Liew, in the Hilton Hotel. Cheong has stormed the dizzy heights of food fashion, with his East-meets-West cuisine.

NEDIZ TU

170 HUTT ST, SA 5000
☎ (8) 8223 2618
One of the most consistently good and innovative restaurants in the country. Crisp decor and a menu that draws its inspiration from both East and West.

RED OCHRE GRILL

129 GOUGER ST, SA 5000
☎ (8) 8212 7266
Andrew Fielke is the man who has taken bush tucker – now gentrified by the name "Australian native cuisine" – from the campfire to the starched white tablecloth. Emu pâté, kangaroo pepperoni, braised Tasmanian possum with a native pepper glaze.

T-CHOW

47 GOUGER ST, SA 5000
☎ (8) 8410 1413
Proletarian appearance belies an inspired hand in the kitchen. Small, individual, fashionable and named after its own special style of Chinese cuisine.

Rest of South Australia

HOTELS

APPLE TREE COTTAGE

PO BOX 100, OAKBANK, SA 524
☎ (8) 8388 4193
Pure country cliché – a rose trellis above the door, garden brimming full of violets and forget-me-nots, a goat tethered out front and a hammock slung under the walnut tree. The house sleeps five comfortably and the picture-postcard village of Hahndorf is down the road. Adelaide is only 45 minutes away.

COLLINGROVE HOMESTEAD

EDEN VALLEY RD, ANGASTON, SA 5353
☎ (8) 8564 2061
Ancestral Barossa Valley home of one of the state's pioneering dynasties. The guest rooms, in the former servants' quarters at the back of the house, are simple but stylish. Guests have the run of the National Trust house in the evening, and jackeroo-size breakfasts with the currawongs are served on the verandah.

THE LODGE

RSD 120, SEPPELTSFIELD, SA 5355
☎ (85) 628277 (AFTER FEB '97: 8562 8277)
The aristocrat of Barossa Valley hotels was built for one of the 13 children of Joseph Seppelt, founder of the magnificent winery across the road. There's a wine cellar, a library and a formal rose garden at the front, which rambles away into an orchard. Dinner may vary from a formal banquet one night to a barbecue the next.

PADTHAWAY HOMESTEAD

PADTHAWAY, SA 5271
☎ (87) 655039 (AFTER FEB '97: 8765 5039)
A classic two-storey stone homestead with wide verandahs and a tracery of wrought iron, A handful of comfy colonial rooms, plus splendid food and drink served on porcelain, crystal and silver. The Coonawarra vineyards are just down the road.

THORN PARK COUNTRY HOUSE

COLLEGE RD, SEVENHILL, SA 5453
☎ (88) 8843 4304
Stone farmhouse in Clare Valley brought back to life by David Hay, and Michael Speare.

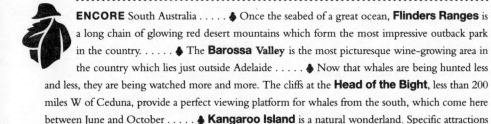

ENCORE South Australia . . . . . ♠ Once the seabed of a great ocean, **Flinders Ranges** is a long chain of glowing red desert mountains which form the most impressive outback park in the country. . . . . . ♠ The **Barossa Valley** is the most picturesque wine-growing area in the country which lies just outside Adelaide . . . . . ♠ Now that whales are being hunted less and less, they are being watched more and more. The cliffs at the **Head of the Bight**, less than 200 miles W of Ceduna, provide a perfect viewing platform for whales from the south, which come here between June and October . . . . . ♠ **Kangaroo Island** is a natural wonderland. Specific attractions are the seal colonies at Seal Bay, the pearly beaches and the rugged seascapes . . . . ♠

Breakfasts are marvellous: pots of home-made jams, fig compote and toast from the Aga, eaten in the slate-floored kitchen.

WARRENDA

MENZEL RD, LYNDOCH, SA 5351

☎ (8) 8524 4507

Family-sized house low down on the bald hills bordering the Barossa Valley. The small house is furnished rustically with mosquito nets and linen sheets in the bedrooms, plus there's a huge, old-fashioned bathroom with its own fireplace. Breakfasts include home-cured bacon and preserves made from fruit grown on the property.

RESTAURANTS

PETALUMA'S BRIDGEWATER MILL

MOUNT BARKER RD, BRIDGEWATER, SA 5155

☎ (8) 8339 3422

The testing ground for wine guru Brian Croser's talents is an 1860s flour mill – perfect for long, lazy, sunny-day lunches. Best to clinch a table on the top deck, where you can hear the water mill sloshing alongside and the bees droning in the garden below. If your plans for the afternoon aren't too ambitious, ask to see the special wine list. Lunch only.

VINTNERS

NURIOOTPA RD, ANGASTON, SA 5353

☎ (85) 642488 (AFTER FEB '97: 8564 2488)

The Barossa's best-loved restaurant. Local trout, lamb, kangaroo and home-made sausages imbued with flavours ranging from Paris to Penang. Fabulous wine list and enthusiastic advice from maître d' Doug Coats.

Brisbane

ART AND MUSEUMS

QUEENSLAND CULTURAL CENTRE

SOUTH BANK, QLD 4000

☎ (7) 3840 7229

A temple to high culture, includes the **QUEENSLAND ART GALLERY**, **QUEENSLAND MUSEUM**, the **STATE LIBRARY**, and the **PERFORMING ARTS COMPLEX**. Downstairs several cafés and restaurants line the sparkling waterfront, including the well-used **FOUNTAIN ROOM** restaurant.

BARS AND CAFES

BAGUETTE BAR AND BISTRO

RACECOURSE RD, ASCOT, QLD 4064

☎ (7) 3268 6168

The Provençal-inspired menu served in a canvas-chaired conservatory is a bit of light relief in contrast to the more heavyweight **BAGUETTE RESTAURANT** (see Restaurants).

GRAND ORBIT

LEVEL 1, EAGLE ST PIER, QLD 4000

☎ (7) 3236 1384

Brisbane's most bubbling new riverside eatery is a restaurant/bistro/bar/library/jazz club rolled into one. The modern Oz-style menu emphasizes light dishes and gourmet pizzas.

LOUIS' RESTAURANT AND JAZZ BAR

CNR CORONATION DR AND PARK RD, MILTON, QLD 4064

☎ (7) 3368 1200

A transparent, goldfish bowl-style upstairs is the alternative to ground-floor **HARRIERS RESTAURANT**, with kitchen handiwork by Louis Pherad, protégé of Anton Mosimann and Hermann Schneider.

HOTELS

BEAUFORT HERITAGE HOTEL

CNR EDWARD AND MARGARET STS, QLD 4000

☎ (7) 3221 1999

Poised on the edge of the Botanical Gardens with impressive river views, where the executive-stress-relieving service is appreciated by all. Eat in at **SIGGI'S** (see Restaurants).

SHERATON BRISBANE HOTEL & TOWERS

249 TURBOT ST, QLD 4000

☎ (7) 3835 3535

From floors 27 to 29, there's the Sheraton Towers, a hotel within a hotel providing added privileges such as use of a private club-style lounge.

RESTAURANTS

ABOUT FACE

252 KELVIN GROVE RD, KELVIN GROVE, QLD 4059

☎ (7) 3356 8605

One of Brisbane's most exciting and sophisticated chefs, Andrew Mirosch oversees a multi-cultural menu that changes every couple of weeks.

AUSTRALIA'S BEST SURFING BEACHES Queensland:

The most consistent wave formation in Queensland is found on headlands. The best spots are Snapper Rocks and Burleigh Heads on the Gold Coast; Alexandra Headlands and Noosa Heads on the Sunshine Coast; **Victoria**: Bells and Jan Juc beaches at Torquay; Airey's inlet on the Great Ocean Rd; and Woolomai on Phillip Island. In **Western Australia,** the best five surf-breaks are: Surfer's Point at Margaret River; North Point at Cowaramup Beach; Strickland Bay at Rottnest Island; Red Bluff (100 miles north of Carnarvon) and Gnarloo between Exmouth and Carnarvon. In **Tasmania** head for Marawah Beach on the northwest coast. In **South Australia** beginners and intermediates can try Waitpinga and Parsons beaches (west of Victor Harbour) and Beachport (SA's south-east). Chinaman's Beach (York Peninsula), Cactus Beach and Streaky Bay on the west coast of the Eyre Peninsula are for advanced surfers only. In **Sydney** there's Bondi (of course), Narrabeen and Cronulla. For the rest of **NSW**: The Pass, Main and Tallows in the Byron Bay area. Steamer beach (Jervis Bay), Rennies Beach (Ulladulla) and Mollymook on South Coast, and Angourie Beach to the north.

PIER NINE OYSTER BAR AND SEAFOOD GRILL

EAGLE ST PIER, BRISBANE, QLD 4000
☎ (7) 3229 2194
Probably the most appropriate place to eat oysters in the country, especially at lunchtime, sitting on the terrace overlooking the river.

RAE'S

179 MARY ST, BRISBANE, QLD 4000
☎ (7) 3229 2271
Vincent Rae's latest creation, is an Oz-style bistro which concentrates on seafood and salsa and has already conquered the hearts and minds of Brisbane's hip bodies beautiful.

SIGGI'S

IN THE BEAUFORT HERITAGE HOTEL
(SEE HOTELS)
☎ (7) 3221 4555
A hot favourite for big-occasion dining, where you can rely on the polished cedar and gold cutlery. International menu big on fish and good on 'roo too. A finely honed wine list.

TABLES OF TOOWONG

85 MISKIN ST, TOOWONG, QLD 4066
☎ (7) 3371 4558
The talk of the town: Russell Armstrong's pretty boathouse-style restaurant with its East–West menu fiercely supports regional produce and his regular dégustation nights have become one of Queensland's gastronomic highlights.

VICTORIA'S

BRISBANE HILTON, 190 ELIZABETH ST, QLD 4000
☎ (7) 3231 3131
Opulent, old-world restaurant, still a favourite for a big night out. Hushed service and a portly international menu.

Rest of Queensland

HOTELS AND RESORTS

BLOOMFIELD WILDERNESS LODGE

P O BOX 966, CAIRNS, QLD 4870
☎ (7) 4035 9166
Plonked in the middle of the wilderness just south of Cooktown at the base of Cape York: good-natured haven of chilled wine, hot showers, clean sheets and waiters who know how to deal with the wild pigs.

COCONUT BEACH RAINFOREST RESORT

P O BOX 6903, CAIRNS, QLD 4870
☎ (7) 4098 0033
Rainforest-swathed resort perfect if you want both worlds – ie, pretend to be Robinson Crusoe but still have your fresh croissants for breakfast. With 40 individual, fan-cooled, timber bungalows.

HAYMAN ISLAND
QLD 4801
☎ (7) 4046 9100
Hayman's impressive natural assets are given the full gloss treatment with sculpted bits of greenery, waterfalls, reflecting ponds, and titanic pools with palmy islands. Good food at LA FONTAINE.

HYATT REGENCY COOLUM
WARRAN RD, COOLUM BEACH, QLD 4573
☎ (7) 5546 1234
A resort for the hyperactive offering tennis, swimming, jogging, golf, squash, plunge baths, massage and aromatherapy.

KINGFISHER BAY RESORT
P O BOX 1122, BRISBANE, QLD 4001
☎ (7) 3221 1811
Eco-sensitive timber and corrugated iron resort wrapped around a wetland reserve on Fraser Island, the largest sand island on the planet. Rooms and facilities are functional rather than fancy.

SHERATON MIRAGE PORT DOUGLAS
PORT DOUGLAS RD, PORT DOUGLAS, QLD 4871
☎ (7) 4099 5888
The ultimate in no-expense-spared luxury. Palm trees border a championship golf course to one side and a beach on the other. The pool is a vast sea with islands, bridges, sand coves, currents and tides of its own. Most rooms have their own jacuzzi.

SILKY OAKS LODGE
C/O P&O RESORTS, P O BOX 5287, SYDNEY, NSW 2001
☎ (7) 4098 1666
Stilt houses are buried in tropical rainforest along the banks of the Mossman River. The resort blends hothouse warmth, unbuttoned living and is polished by Edit Whitelaw's cooking. There are no phones, no televisions and the only wake-up call on offer is the feathered kind.

RESTAURANTS

SEE ALSO HOTELS.

CHILI JAM THAI
195 WEYBA RD, NOOSAVILLE, QLD 4566
☎ (7) 5449 9755

Challenge your tastebuds with dishes such as marinated, free-range quail fried with garlic and peppercorns.

SASSI ISLAND POINT RESTAURANT
ISLAND POINT RD, PORT DOUGLAS, QLD 4871
☎ (7) 4099 5323
Brilliant, gutsy Italian-style seafood. The seafood platter for two is legendary, as is the view of the coast and the distant mountains.

SOLEIL
SUNSHINE BEACH CENTRAL, DUKE ST, SUNSHINE BEACH, QLD 4567
☎ (7) 5474 5533
The latest venture from Noosa chef Patrick Landelle. His beach house-style bistro features an ambitious range of dishes, including Vietnamese soups, sushi, pasta, Indian lamb curries and Moroccan tagines.

Canberra

ART AND MUSEUMS

AUSTRALIAN NATIONAL GALLERY
PARKES PLACE, ACT 2600
☎ (6) 271 2502
National art bunker, with every major Australian and Aboriginal artist represented along with several international 20C icons. Alfresco dining in the sculpture garden, surrounded by Rodins and many pieces of native Australiana.

NATIONAL SCIENCE AND TECHNOLOGY CENTRE
PARKES PL, ACT 2600
☎ (6) 270 2800
Building blocks for the budding astro-physicist with plenty of buttons, levers and things that go whizz and bang. An informative and highly addictive encyclopaedia covering physics, mathematics and human perception.

BARS AND CAFES

BAROCCA CAFE
60 MARCUS CLARKE ST, ACT 2600
☎ (6) 248 0253
Vivacious aquamarine and Art Deco café. Modern Mediterranean dishes are ideal for the calorie-conscious while the puddings are rather more damaging.

CAFE CHAOS
CITY WALK AND AINSLIE AVE, ACT
2600
☎ (6) 248 5522
Modish, clean-cut café offering the capital's best espresso. Lots of pasta and designer pizzas, perfect for a quick bite at any time.

TOSOLINI'S
EAST ROW AND LONDON CIRCUIT, ACT 2600
☎ (6) 247 4042
Italian-style café food. Focaccia sandwiches, pasta, chargrills glistening with olive oil and fresh fruit juices. Good for warm-weather lunches out on the terrace.

HOTELS

PARK HYATT
Commonwealth Ave, Yarralumla, ACT 2601
☎ (6) 270 1234
A calm place which is very popular with besuited ministers and yes-minister mandarins who hob-nob over high tea in the PROMENADE CAFÉ on Sundays.

RESTAURANTS

THE LOBBY
KING GEORGE TERRACE, PARKES, ACT
2600
☎ (6) 273 1563
An enduring institution in the no-man's-land between Parliament House and the Trade/Treasury/Foreign Affairs axis. Savvy Euro/Asian menu with a strong line in salads.

THE OAK ROOM
PARK HYATT HOTEL, COMMONWEALTH AVE, YARRALUMLA, ACT 2601
☎ (6) 270 1234
Good spot for big-occasion dining – discreet, hushed, soft lighting and a menu that will cater for most tastes.

OTTOMAN CUISINE
8 FRANKLIN ST, MANUKA, ACT
☎ (6) 239 6754
A genuine Turkish delight. Imaginative dips, wonderful bread, shellfish and soups prepared with delicacy.

TU TU TANGO
124 BUNDA ST, ACT 2600
☎ (6) 247 1717

Mediterranean menu with Asian undercurrents and a fashionable hint of the bush. Jazz club by night.

Darwin

HOTELS

THE BEAUFORT
THE ESPLANADE, NT 0800
☎ (8) 8981 5322
A stylish base camp for the Northern Territory alias Crocodile Dundee country. Impressive dining room called SIGGI'S (see Restaurants).

RESTAURANTS

HANUMAN THAI
28 MITCHELL ST, NT 0800
☎ (8) 8941 3500
Thai and Nonya fuse, under the expert eye of Jimmy Shu, who fled to these warmer climes from his illustrious Melbourne restaurant ISTHMUS OF KRA. Surroundings are elegant though understated. The oysters in a chilli, lemon grass and basil sauce are a knockout.

LINDSAY STREET CAFE
2 LINDSAY ST, NT 0800
☎ (8) 8981 8631
Unfussy decor. Ex-Mietta's chef Jock Mitchell gives all his attention to dishes such as chargrilled vegetable terrine, green papaya salad, spicy fish cakes and fresh tuna salad. Sunday brunch in the courtyard is invariably a sell-out – especially with Darwin's power munchers.

⊛ MINDIL BEACH SUNSET MARKET
MINDIL BEACH, NT 0800
Finger-food paradise. Darwin's dry-season food-stall market leads you on a gastronomic tour of the Orient. Bring a bottle of wine, sit on the sand and watch the sun go down over the Timor Sea. Open Wed. from 5 pm, April–Oct.

SIGGI'S
IN THE BEAUFORT HOTEL (SEE HOTELS)
☎ (8) 8982 9911
The Beaufort's plush dining room impresses not only with heavyweight French food, but also with a modern Australian menu.

Rest of the Northern Territory

HOTELS

SAILS IN THE DESERT
YULARA DR, NT 0872
☎ (8) 8956 2200
A stone's throw from Ayres Rock, it was designed by Phillip Cox who uses hi-tech sails to cushion the blowtorch desert heat. Serene, splendid and a noble bush tucker menu in the KUNIA ROOM restaurant.

SEVEN SPIRIT BAY
C/O SEVEN SPIRIT WILDERNESS PTY LTD, P O BOX 4721, DARWIN, NT 0801
☎ (8) 8979 0277
At the northern tip of the Cobourg Peninsula surrounded by Aboriginal-controlled Arnhem Land. Seven Spirit Bay is more functional than fanciful. Individual bush cabins are set in the midst of an Attenborough paradise, teeming with wildlife. Asian-inspired fish dishes are some of the best in the Territory.

Hobart

HOTELS

ISLINGTON
321 DAVEY ST, HOBART TAS 7000
☎ (3) 6223 3900
Colonial Georgian-style mansion with only eight guest rooms. There are views of Mt Wellington and hearty country-style breakfasts, all within brisk walking distance of the city.

LENNA OF HOBART
20 RUNNYMEDE ST, BATTERY POINT, TAS 7004
☎ (3) 6223 2911
Italianate villa, which is quite a landmark in Battery Point. The hotel has most of the facilities of a larger hotel, and is also within easy reach of Salamanca Place.

SHERATON HOBART
1 DAVEY ST, HOBART TAS 7000
☎ (3) 6222 2229
The most sophisticated hotel in town. Harbourside rooms have a front-row seat over the classic blue waters of the Sydney–Hobart divide.

RESTAURANTS

ALI AKBAR
321 ELIZABETH ST, N HOBART, TAS 7002
☎ (3) 6231 1770
Genius George Haddad will redefine Lebanese food for you, by whisking you away on a magic carpet ride of new-wave Middle Eastern cooking.

ATLAS
315 ELIZABETH ST, N HOBART, TAS 7002
☎ (3) 6236 9292
Chris Jackman, who used to work for Paul Bocuse in Melbourne, creates lusty French food. George "Ali Akbar" Haddad's latest venture has made a decisive shift from the Middle East to the South of France, inside a handsome Federation shopfront.

BATTERY POINT BRASSERIE
59 HAMPDEN RD, BATTERY POINT, TAS 7004
☎ (3) 6223 3186
At last Graeme Phillips has expanded his tiny shopfront, thus allowing more people to squeeze in and expand their waistlines as a sign of appreciation for Hobart's seminal eating experience. Strong on game and offal.

DEAR FRIENDS
8 BROOKE ST, HOBART TAS 7000
☎ (3) 6223 2646
A converted waterfront flour mill that's been a long-standing favourite on the gourmet map of Oz. Sensational game and fish in a warm and calm atmosphere, Chris Richard's menu features Barilla oysters, Pirate's Bay octopus, local honeys and goats' cheese and other dishes which make inspired use of all things Tasmanian.

MOORILLA WINE CENTRE
MOORILLA ESTATE, 655 MAIN RD, BERRIEDALE, TAS 7011
☎ (3) 6249 2949
Casseroles, smoked salmon from local legend Piers Ranicar, charcuterie, salads and home-made cakes on the Derwent estuary with vinous views of the Moorilla Estate. If the sun is shining, take the ferry from Hobart.

MURE'S FISH CENTRE
VICTORIA DOCK, HOBART, TAS 7000
☎ (3) 6231 1999
Fishy eating on two storeys: upper deck for views and table service, steerage for take-away dining on the dock.

Rest of Tasmania

HOTELS

CRADLE MOUNTAIN LODGE

P O BOX 153, SHEFFIELD, TAS 7306
☎ (3) 6492 1303
Well-appointed lumberjack cabins surrounded by the Marlboro-man country of central Tasmania. Guaranteed to turn jelly-kneed city slickers into either mountaineers, fly fishermen or David Attenborough. Book a spa cabin.

FREYCINET LODGE

FREYCINET NATIONAL PARK, COLES BAY, TAS 7215
☎ (3) 6257 0101
Comfy cottages buried among casuarinas, at the foot of The Hazards. The scenery's spectacular with salty views across Coles Bay and divine sunsets. Made even more worthwhile by the freshest local oysters.

PROSPECT HOUSE

RICHMOND, TAS 7025
☎ (3) 6262 2207
Georgian house in the historic heart of Tasmania, where patrician style and fine food are set against the most marvellously rugged countryside.

RESTAURANTS

FEE AND ME

190 CHARLES ST, LAUNCESTON, TAS 7250
☎ (3) 6231 3195
Still fortifying the reputation they established at the brasserie of the same name, Peter Crowe and Fiona Hoskin's more sophisticated restaurant version continues to boast food made from the best of Tasmania's farms and fields.

Melbourne

ART AND MUSEUMS

NATIONAL GALLERY OF VICTORIA

180 ST KILDA RD, VIC 3000
☎ (3) 9208 0203
Central bank for the Heidelberg school (Roberts, Streeton, McCubbin), whose opalescent canvasses brought light into Australian painting at the turn of the century. Widest collection of contemporary Australian art in the country.

VICTORIAN ARTS CENTRE

100 ST KILDA RD, VIC 3000
☎ (3) 9281 8000
Houses the **NATIONAL GALLERY** and the **MUSEUM OF VICTORIA** while the riverside complex incorporates a **CONCERT HALL**, a performing arts museum, three theatres and an outdoor performance space. Home to The Australian Ballet.

••••••••••••••••••••••••••••••••••••••

"I FOUND THE STANDARD OF ALL SORTS OF THINGS BETTER IN MELBOURNE THAN IN MOST PLACES. I FIND IT A MORE INTEGRATED CITY THAN SYDNEY, BUT SYDNEY'S FASCINATING, OF COURSE, IT'S SO BEAUTIFUL" –

SIR PETER USTINOV

••••••••••••••••••••••••••••••••••••••

BARS AND CAFES

CAFE DI STASIO

31 FITZROY ST, ST KILDA, VIC 3182
☎ (3) 9525 3999
Ronnie di Stasio's very small, very personal and very Italian café in increasingly hip St Kilda has taken Melbourne's café society by storm.

CONTINENTAL CAFE

132A GREVILLE ST, PRAHRAN, VIC 3181
☎ (3) 9510 2788
Brasserie-style Italian food, style, surroundings and service make this a bit more than a mere café.

DOG'S BAR

54 ACKLAND ST, ST KILDA, VIC 3182
☎ (3) 9525 3599
Sunny, beachy café with a light bar/deli/patisserie menu that favours grazing rather than stoking up. Still the place to hang out after a promenade along St Kilda pier.

GLOBE CAFE

218 CHAPEL ST, PRAHRAN, VIC 3181
☎ (3) 9510 8693
Groovy hangout for the Doc Martens crowd by day, super cool lounge bar by night. Global menu from Cajun chicken to Thai to minestrone.

CLUBS

CHASERS

386 Chapel St, Prahran, VIC 3181
☎ (3) 9827 6615
An institution on the Melbourne club scene
and one of the smarter places by virtue of its
location in Melbourne's ritziest suburb.
Adopted by preppy 20-somethings who sport
après-work-out wear, so don't go without your
Hi-techs and tracksuit bottoms.

THE METRO

20–30 Bourke St, VIC 3000
☎ (3) 9663 4288
Natives pump it up in what is supposedly the
biggest disco in the southern hemisphere.
There is a café, eight bars, and three dance
floors where the action is very fast and very
loud.

75TH SQUADRON

Gate 14, Exhibition Reserve,
Rathdowne St, Carlton, VIC 3053
☎ (3) 9663 7575
Unique World War II "bomber" design is a
handy talking point. Melbourne's slick young
things can home in on four bars, a restaurant,
and the dance floor.

SILVERS

445 Toorak Rd, Toorak, VIC 3142
☎ (3) 9827 8244
Aspiring, perspiring groovers and shakers
combined with sensible high-society subur-
banites have fun in toney surroundings.

HOTELS

ADELPHI HOTEL

187 Flinders Ln, VIC 3000
☎ (3) 9650 2709
Clean, cool, functionalist design marks a
radical departure from your average hotel bedroom. Best rooms are at the front, with
numbers ending in "01". The *pièce de résistance,*
though, is the glass-bottomed rooftop pool
that juts out from the edge of the building.

GRAND HYATT

123 Collins St, VIC 3000
☎ (3) 9657 1234
Melbourne's No. 1 hotel for glitz and marble.
Also houses the sparkling **COLLINS CHASE**
shopping galleries, restaurants, nightclubs, a
fabulous health complex and the **REGENCY
CLUB**. Excellent service.

HOTEL COMO

630 Chapel St, South Yarra, VIC
3141
☎ (3) 9824 0400
Sleek, stylish, black and metal boutique hotel,
attracting the young jet set. The well-dressed
shops and snappy cafés of South Yarra/Prahran
are a short walk away.

THE REGENT

25 Collins St, VIC 3000
☎ (3) 9653 0000
The omnipresent I M Pei has got a finger in
the Melbourne pie too. The Regent takes up
the top floors of his Collins Place complex and
has the best views in town. The rooms are
palatial and plush and the service helpful,
which is why the JAGGERS stay here. Easy
access to Melbourne's parks and gardens.

ROCKMAN'S REGENCY

Cnr Exhibition and Lonsdale Sts,
VIC 3000
☎ (3) 9662 3900
Friendly giant-sized rooms, some with private
terraces for outdoor dining. Popular with
smart businessmen who appreciate its proximity to the commercial district, as well as the
snappy service and close attention to detail.

SHERATON TOWERS SOUTHGATE

1 Brown St, VIC 3000
☎ (3) 9696 3100
Latest to join the ranks of Melbourne's five-star
hotels, they'll even give you your own butler.
Situated on the banks of the Yarra, at the hub of
the trendy Southgate arts and shopping centre.

THE WINDSOR

103 Spring St, VIC 3000
☎ (3) 9653 0653
The genuine aristocrat of Melbourne's five-star
brigade, fresh from a recent facelift, Victorian
in splendour and Napoleonic in scale. Even if
you don't stay, come for tea.

RESTAURANTS

See also Hotels.

AKITA

Cnr Courtney and Blackwood Sts,
N Melbourne, VIC 3051
☎ (3) 9326 5766
The decor may not be up to much, but the food
– Japanese – is impressive. Check first to see if
there'll be a sumo performance.

BLAKES

LANDING PROMENADE, SOUTHGATE,
VIC 3000

☎ (3) 9699 4100

Slick riverside brasserie, overseen by Andrew
Blake, ex Chez Oz, whose Mediterranean-
inspired menu includes zucchini flower fritters
with goat ricotta and pizzas from the wood-
fired oven. Tremendous views and swinging
atmosphere seduce pre-concert crowds *en route*
to the Arts Centre.

CAFFE E CUCINA

581 CHAPEL ST, S YARRA, VIC 3141

☎ (3) 9827 4139

The darling of Melbourne bistro eating. More
restaurant than café these days, although the
buzz, the hearty Italian street food and the legendary espresso are all unchanged. Book one
of the upstairs tables.

CHINOIS

176 TOORAK RD, VIC 3000

☎ (3) 9826 3388

West meets the wok. French cooking techniques are balanced with the texture and fresh-
ness of Chinese cuisine by Chef Allen Koh,
who offers a menu keen on fish. Downstairs is
modern and bustling while upstairs is much
more traditional.

FLOWER DRUM

17 MARKET LA, VIC 3000

☎ (3) 9662 3655

Still Melbourne's champion Chinese, where
the steamer and the fast stir-fry are venerated
by scrupulous chef Gilbert Lau, culinary taipan of Melbourne's Chinatown.

FRANCE-SOIR

11 TOORAK RD, S YARRA, VIC 3141

☎ (3) 9866 8569

Butcher-papered tables, a menu that works
from mid-morning till after midnight and fabulous pommes frites.

ISTHMUS OF KRA

50 PARK ST, S MELBOURNE, VIC 3205

☎ (3) 9690 3688

Always inventive and usually outstanding Thai
food, modified by Chinese and Indian cross-
currents. Comfortable surroundings.

JACQUES REYMOND'S RESTAURANT

78 WILLIAMS RD, WINDSOR, VIC 3181

☎ (3) 9525 2178

Formal, French and magnificent. Originally
from Burgundy, eponymous owner Reymond
harnesses his French technique to Australian
flavours and ingredients with flair.

MARCHETTI'S LATIN

55 LONSDALE ST, VIC 3000

☎ (3) 9662 1985

Tremendous style, attentive service and the
squid-ink pasta confirm that this is still the top
Italian in town. The clientele is a form guide
as to who's who in Melbourne society.

PAUL BOCUSE RESTAURANT

LEVEL 4, DAIMARU, VIC 3000

☎ (3) 9660 6600

State winner of *Gourmet Traveller*'s Restaurant
of the Year in 1995. Still overseen, albeit from
afar, by Bocuse, but the true guiding light is
Philippe Mouchel, one of Australia's finest
chefs, who applies his expertise to an ever-
expanding repertoire of local specialities.

STEPHANIE'S

405 TOORONGA RD, HAWTHORN E,
VIC 3123

☎ (3) 9822 8944

A grand Victorian mansion provides a sumptuous showcase for the formidable talents of
Stephanie Alexander. Still Melbourne's ultimate food experience.

TOLARNO BAR AND BISTRO

42 FITZROY ST, ST KILDA, VIC 3182

☎ (3) 9525 5477

Seriously good French food blended with the
flavours of North Africa and Asia despite the
modest monicker. Iain Hewitson has reworked
this long-established 60s bistro, where many
Melburnians first dipped into onion soup, and
has taken it to the culinary front line.

TOOFEY'S

162 ELGIN ST, CARLTON, VIC 3053

☎ (3) 9347 9838

Melbourne's smartest and sharpest seafood
restaurant. Michael Bacash takes the best from
Melbourne's fish markets and serves them with
light, inventive sauces.

SHOPPING

DAIMARU

221 LATROBE ST, VIC 3000

☎ (3) 9660 6666

One-stop fashion shop at the heart of the vast
Melbourne Central complex, and the only
stop for Dolce and Gabbana, Kenzo and
Gianfranco Ferré. Great food hall too.

GABRIEL GATE'S COOKSHOP

549 BURWOOD RD, HAWTHORN, VIC
3122

☎ (3) 9819 9967

The very best of culinary world gadgetry, from daunting high-tech to your old-school, labour-intensive friends. Cooking classes to elevate your technique from Gabriel himself – charming TV chef.

GEORGE'S

162 COLLINS ST, VIC 3000

☎ (3) 9283 5555

Old-world service and genuinely chic. Melbourne's only Chanel boutique, Armani by the armful and more.

HENRY BUCK'S

320 COLLINS ST, VIC 3000

☎ (3) 9670 9951

Melbourne's equivalent to Turnbull and Asser. Snappy dresses will be seduced by the natty headgear and Valentino menswear.

LE LOUVRE

74 COLLINS ST, VIC 3000

☎ (3) 9650 1300

A point of calm in the ever-changing world of fashion. This is where women come for the classic Euro-look.

MAKERS' MARK GALLERY

SHOP 9, 101 COLLINS ST, VIC 3000

☎ (3) 9654 8488

A showcase for the talents of Australia's best jewellery designers.

MINTMAX

5585 MALVERN RD, TOORAK, VIC
3142

☎ (3) 9826 0022

Plate stands, laundry bags, asparagus brushes – clever, practical, stylish solutions to the perennial problems of urban life.

SABA

131 BOURKE ST, VIC 3000

☎ (3) 9654 6176

Fashion for both sexes in a high energy, bop-while-you-shop environment. Oz labels mingle with those from the wider world of style.

TAMASINE DALE

SHOP 1, 94 FLINDERS ST, VIC 3000

☎ (3) 9650 7122

The Philip Treacy of Melbourne millinery – modern miracle head-dresser for the young and beautiful.

WENDY MEAD HATS

SHOP 11, TOORAK RD, TOORAK, VIC
3142

☎ (3) 9240 9093

Lovely traditional hats. Always sets the pace on Melbourne Cup day.

Rest of Victoria

HOTELS

HOWQUA DALE GOURMET RETREAT

HOWQUA DALE RD, MANSFIELD, VIC
3722

☎ (3) 5777 3503

Sarah Stegley and Marieke Brugman have created a foodie paradise at the foothills of the Australian Alps. Ultra-modern Australian cuisine, using fresh local ingredients and gallons of delicious Australian wine. Most people stay for five days and enjoy picnics, brunches and hyper-formal dinners.

KINGBILLI

CATHEDRAL LANE, TAGGERTY, VIC
3714

☎ (3) 5774 7302

A bluestone and corrugated iron, high-country bush cottage has been redesigned, revamped and furnished with flair. There's lots to do on the 500-acre property. You can fish, swim, ride the wild range, play tennis, watch the wallabies or paddle with a platypus. Generally, guests cater for themselves, but Ginny and Michael Beach will provide meals from their home.

LAKE HOUSE

KING ST, DAYLESFORD, VIC 3460

☎ (3) 5348 3329

Smart lakeside pavilion where Allan and Alla Wolf-Tasker dish out some of the most inventive modern Australian meals in spa country. The guest rooms at the back are pretty, breezy and all in white.

QUEENSCLIFF HOTEL

16 GELIBRAND ST, QUEENSCLIFF, VIC
3225

☎ (3) 5252 1066

Flowery, lacy, stained glass Victorian extravaganza where Patricia O'Donnell will organize your room and Xavier Robinson will rustle up good, French-inspired meals. Make sure you book the tower room and always dress for dinner.

Perth

BARS AND CAFES

UNIVERSAL BAR AND GRILL
221 WILLIAM ST, NORTHBRIDGE, WA 6000
☎ (9) 227 6771 (AFTER SEPT '97: (8) 9227 6771)
Still the grooviest combined bar/brasserie in town. Mandy Smith's Mediterranean-style menu scores well too.

CLUBS

METROPOLIS
58 S TERR, FREMANTLE, WA 6160
☎ (9) 336 1511 (AFTER SEPT '97: (8) 9227 6771)
Hottest nightclub in town. Nine bars set on three levels, and a massive dance floor can pack in up to 1500. Live bands, like INXS, play.

HOTELS

HYATT REGENCY
99 ADELAIDE TERRACE, WA 6000
☎ (9) 225 1234 (AFTER SEPT '97: (8) 9225 1234)
Chicest hotel in town, with a 13-storey atrium designed with steel lattice and glass roof. Serious extras if you're staying on the Regency Club floors. Home to **GERSHWIN'S** (see Restaurants).

PARMELA HILTON
MILL ST, WA 6000
☎ (9) 322 3622 (AFTER SEPT '97: (8) 9322 3622)
Strongly individualist hotel with a clubby atmosphere along with some rather bizarre furnishings including Mussolini's mirror. Remains a popular choice for corporate types.

RADISSON OBSERVATION CITY RESORT HOTEL
THE ESPLANADE, SCARBOROUGH BEACH, WA 6019
☎ (9) 245 1000 (AFTER SEPT '97: (8) 9245 1000)
Oceanfront hotel/resort 15 minutes from the centre of Perth. Lavish guest rooms with terraces, from which you can watch the sun melting into the Indian Ocean.

MUSIC

PERTH ENTERTAINMENT CENTRE
WELLINGTON ST, WA 6000
☎ (9) 322 4766 (AFTER SEPT '97: (8) 9322 4766)

The city's main performance venue which is highly regarded by performers, who appreciate the pin-sharp acoustics.

RESTAURANTS

FRASER'S RESTAURANT
FRASER AVE, KINGS PARK, PERTH WA 6000
☎ (9) 481 7100 (AFTER SEPT '97: (8) 9481 7100)
Serene, outdoorsy restaurant set in riverside parklands overlooking the city. Seafood and mostly Med-flavours with a hint of the Orient dominate Chris Taylor's menu.

GERSHWIN'S
IN THE HYATT REGENCY (SEE HOTELS)
☎ (9) 225 1234 (AFTER SEPT '97: (8) 9225 1234)
Big-night-out dining, slick service and an innovative menu that showcases the best of Western Australian ingredients.

THE LOOSE BOX
6825 GREAT EASTERN HWY, MUNDARING, WA 6073
☎ (9) 295 1787 (AFTER SEPT '97: (8) 9295 1787)
Celebrated by food critics and winner of *Gourmet Traveller*'s 1995 Restaurant of the Year award. Alain Fabregues's temple to gastronomy is and always will be doggedly Gallic. His current fixation is the cooking of Renaissance France.

MEAD'S FISH GALLERY
JOHNSON PARADE, MOSMAN PK, WA 6012
☎ (9) 383 3388 (AFTER SEPT '97: (8) 9383 3388)
Fresh from Quaglino's, chef Mark Rogers has brought a bit of slickness to one of Perth's favourite fish restaurants.

PERUGINO
77 OUTRAM ST, WEST PERTH 6005
☎ (9) 321 5420 (AFTER SEPT '97: (8) 9321 5420)
Giuseppe Pagliaricci dishes out the classics from his native Umbria to an ever-appreciative clientele – and there's a charming garden too.

SAN LORENZO
23 VICTORIA AVE, CLAREMONT, WA 6010
☎ (9) 384 0870 (AFTER SEPT '97: (8) 9384 9870)
Winner of *Gourmet Traveller*'s Restaurant of the Year award in 1994. It's a stylish showcase for the prodigious talents of Gary Jones, now replaced by Deborah Whitebread, who has added Asian flavours to Jones' classics such as Kervella goats' cheese soufflé, and black pudding.

AUSTRALIA'S LEAST-KNOWN LANDSCAPES Western

Australia is log-jammed with some truly weird landscapes. **Windjama Gorge**, the world's oldest fossilized reef, offers the chance to experience the Palaeozoic era close up . . . . . Vivid sunsets and spectacular weather are the evocative backdrops for **Broome**'s least-known attraction – **The Stairway to the Moon**. Be there when low tide and full moon coincide. **Cocklebiddy Cave** on the Eyre Highway is the world's largest underground cave, where a world underground diving record was set. In the central-south region of WA, any expedition should include **Mt Augusta**, the world's largest rock (Ayers Rock is not strictly a rock); **Shell Beach**, one of the only two beaches in the world composed entirely of seashells; and the **Zuytdorp Cliffs,** named after the Dutch ship wrecked close by, and easily as spectacular as the Great Australian Bight. In Queensland, the remote Channel Country harbours **Lark Quarry** – the fossilized remains of the only dinosaur stampede ever recorded. The 200,000-year-old **Undara Lava Tubes** in the Gulf Savannah Country are majestic, colossal and overwhelming. **Wilpena Pound**, in South Australia, 250 miles from Adelaide in the Flinders Ranges is the remains of a huge dome of rock pushed up from the ocean bed 350 million years ago. Finally, 60 miles from Ayers Rock, there's the **Petermann Ranges**, the oldest existing landscape on earth.

Rest of Western Australia

HOTELS

CABLE BEACH CLUB
CABLE BEACH RD, BROOME WA 6725
☎ (91) 92 0400 (AFTER MAY '97: (8) 9192 0400
Sun-struck white and tandoori-coloured bungalows and studios surrounded by palmy gardens, with a chain of canals and little arched bridges that run though the middle.

EL QUESTRO
BOX 909, KUNANURRA, WA 6743
☎ (91) 691 777
Former cattle station converted by Englishman Will Burrell into an architect-designed safari camp/dude ranch. The homestead is poised spectacularly on a cliff above the Chamberlain River. Both the accommodation, and food are first-rate, although tented accommodation is available for those who shy away from the rather more expensive homestead.

MUSIC

LEEUWIN CONCERTS
LEEUWIN ESTATE, GNARAWARY RD;
TICKETS: 1ST FLOOR, 1B HIGH ST,
FREMANTLE, WA 6160
☎ (9) 430 4099 (AFTER SEP '97: (8) 9430 4099
The Glyndebourne of down under, held, appropriately, in a vineyard. Estate owner Denis Horgan's outdoor concert series takes place every Feb and Mar and includes the best of the West.

Sydney

ART AND MUSEUMS

ART GALLERY OF NEW SOUTH WALES
ART GALLERY RD, NSW 2000
☎ (2) 9225 1700
An overview of Australian art, from Aboriginal works on bark to pieces by Brett Whitely, under the spirited direction of Edmund Capon. Sumo-class collection of Asian ceramics.

HOGARTH GALLERY

7 WALKER LA, PADDINGTON, NSW
2021

☎ (2) 9360 6839

Serious collectors will love Clive Evatt's private gallery, showcasing the very best in contemporary Aboriginal art.

MUSEUM OF CONTEMPORARY ART

140 GEORGE ST, THE ROCKS, NSW
2000

☎ (2) 9252 4033

Over 3,000 pieces of modern art are housed in an Art Deco style monolithic building on the harbour-front location near Circular Quay. Have lunch at the **MCA CAFÉ** (see Bars and Cafés)

MUSEUM OF SYDNEY

37 PHILLIP ST, NSW 2000

☎ (2) 9251 5988

Fascinating collection of paintings, artefacts and contemporary observations that document the history of the city to 1850. An aesthetic rather than an educational experience.

POWERHOUSE MUSEUM

500 HARRIS ST, ULTIMO, NSW 2000

☎ (2) 9217 0111

Interactive, hands-on assembly of technical, scientific and industrial wizardry. Housed in the electricity station that once powered Sydney's trams – recently converted by architect Lionel Glendinning.

BARS AND CAFES

BAR COLLUZZI

322 VICTORIA ST, DARLINGHURST,
NSW 2010

☎ (2) 9380 5420

Luigi Colluzzi's Lamborghini-sized bar is popular with Lycra-loving cyclists on weekends, and safe enough to take your mother.

BAR PARADISO

7 MACQUARIE PL, NSW 2000

☎ (2) 9241 4141

Slick bar/café brings creamy cappuccino and freshly baked focaccia to a shady piazza at the heart of the city. Fabulous cakes too.

BILL'S

433 LIVERPOOL ST, DARLINGHURST,
NSW 2010

☎ (2) 9360 9631

An unmistakably groovy joint where you can gorge on fresh ricotta hotcakes. But it's very small, so you have to be thin to get in and there's often a queue.

BOGEY-HOLE CAFE

473 BRONTE RD, BRONTE, NSW 2024

☎ (2) 9389 8829

Sunny Sydney at its best. Fresh juices, salads and devil-may-care cakes overlooking Bronte Beach.

CENTENNIAL PARK CAFE

GRAND DRIVE, CENTENNIAL PARK,
NSW 2021

☎ (2) 9360 3355

Housed in a modern glass conservatory in Sydney's favourite jogging and rollerblade park. Healthy, brasserie-style menu, great for brunch.

DOV

252 FORBES ST, DARLINGHURST, NSW
2010

☎ (2) 9360 9594

An interesting mixture of creative professionals, and students from Sydney's academy of all things avant-garde across the road. Good salads, and bargain breakfasts consisting of plates of piping hot toast and caffè latte.

FEZ CAFE

247 VICTORIA ST, DARLINGHURST,
NSW 2010

☎ (2) 9360 9581

Moorish kilims, couscous, flat Turkish bread and the best citron pressé in town.

HYDE PARK BARRACKS CAFE

QUEENS SQ, MACQUARIE ST, NSW
2000

☎ (2) 9223 1155

Convenient city-centre eating in the courtyard beneath Sydney's finest Georgian façade. You couldn't get a stranger mix of patron – politicians and journos from state parliament next door; or white-collar criminals converse with their silks from the law courts across the road. Modern Mediterranean food with a touch of Thai.

MCA CAFE

140 GEORGE ST, THE ROCKS, NSW
2000

☎ (2) 9241 4253

Deco-style café at the waterfront side of the Museum of Contemporary Art where Neil "Rockpool" Perry dishes up Italian dishes against a classic view of Sydney Cove. Book ahead for a terrace table.

SPORTING CHANCES Riverside Oaks PGA National Golf Club,

O'Brien's Rd, Cattai, NSW 2756, ☎ (45) 72 8477, a championship course 90 minutes NW of Sydney, offers spectacular golf in the bush on the banks of the Hawkesbury River. **Jogging tracks**: Bondi Beach to Tamaram via the cliffs. A favourite corporate jog track to work off those fat lunches is through the Royal Botanic Gardens between the Opera House and Mrs Macquarie's Chair. **Rose Bay Windsurfer School**, 1 Vickery Ave, Rose Bay, NSW 2029, ☎ (2) 9371 7036, hires out windsurfers for sailing around Sydney Harbour, along with lessons to steer you away from trouble. **Coopers Park Tennis Courts,** Off Suttie Rd, Coopers Park, Double Bay, NSW 2028, ☎ (2) 9389 9259, comprises eight synthetic grass courts set in a park surrounded by bushland. **Sydney Cricket Ground,** Moore Park, Paddington, NSW 2021, ☎ (2) 9360 6601, is the main Sydney venue for big international matches between Nov and Apr. **Sydney Football Stadium**, Moore Park, Paddington, NSW 2021, ☎ (2) 9360 6601, provides a gladiatorial ring for "real men" eager to indulge in Sydney's winter addiction: rugby league. Season is Apr–Sept. **White City Tennis Club**, 30 Alma St, Paddington, NSW 2021, ☎ (2) 9331 4144, is the venue for the NSW Open, held every January as a prelude to Melbourne's grand slam – the Australian Open. **Homebush**, ☎ (2) 9267 0099 (Olympic Information Centre), is the ever-expanding athletic/swimming/track complex at the hub of the Sydney 2000 Olympics.

THE PIG AND THE OLIVE
71A MACLEAY ST, POTTS POINT, NSW 2011
☎ (2) 9357 3745
You can have anything you want as long as it's on a pizza. Big, brash, chaotic and a constant party, with a clientele that varies from grunge to Zegna.

CLUBS

ANGEL PLACE BRASSERIE
1-10 ANGEL PL, NSW 2000
☎ (2) 9223 2220
Retro specials every Saturday night (wall-to-wall Abba). Dress to mortally wound and party on down with the mascara-heavy crowd.

THE BASEMENT
29 REIBY PL, CIRCULAR QUAY, NSW 2000
☎ (2) 9251 2797
Subterranean and Stygian jazz club. In fact, it's so dark you can't see the ceiling, but it's the best place by far to catch visiting jazz and blues acts.

THE CAULDRON
207 DARLINGHURST RD, DARLINGHURST, NSW 2010
☎ (2) 9331 1523
Fleshy, flashy, smoky, noisy – mid-20-somethings love it. Particularly good for a late-night bop.

KINSELA'S
383 BOURKE ST, DARLINGHURST, NSW 2010
☎ (2) 9331 2699
The former funeral parlour, now risen from the dead, is livelier than ever and is pulling a smarter crowd. With a disco, cabaret and cocktail bar, most nocturnal inclinations will be satisfied.

RIVA
IN THE PARK GRAND HOTEL, 162 ELIZABETH ST, NSW 2000
☎ (2) 9286 6000
Triple chamber nightclub entertains city slickers. The dynamite decor and slinky bathrooms are favoured by a swinging crowd of models, glossy magazine types and *enfants terribles* of the financial world. Keen on playing music by the artist formerly known as Prince.

SKY

LEVEL 3, SKYGARDEN, 77 CASTLEREAGH
ST, NSW 2000

☎ (2) 9223 4211

Sydney's hottest new dance club. High-tech
mood lighting and house music for the
fashion-conscious and bodily-pierced. Fri/Sat
only.

SOHO

171 VICTORIA ST, POTTS POINT, NSW
2011

☎ (2) 9358 4221

Bar and dance club with soul that plays soul along
with funk and R&B. Seriously cool.

DANCE

SYDNEY DANCE COMPANY

PIER 4, HICKSON RD, WALSH BAY,
NSW 2000

☎ (2) 9221 4811

Graeme Murphy has won international acclaim
for his surprisingly innovative company that sets
the pace for contemporary Australian dance.

FASHION

JODIE BOFFA

9A/94 OXFORD ST, DARLINGHURST,
NSW 2010

☎ (2) 9361 5867

Uncomplicated dressing with an edge, by Jodie
Boffa, an ex-pupil of Jasper Conran. The
exquisite fabrics and a visionary sense of style
distinguish each of her designs.

MORRISSEY EDMISTON

(WOMEN) SHOP 68, STRAND ARCADE,
NSW 2000

☎ (2) 9221 4466

(MEN) SHOP 63, STRAND ARCADE,
NSW 2000

☎ (2) 9221 5616

Pumped-up fashion team has won top marks
for creativity from style pundits including
Harpers Bazaar in the US.

SUSAN NURMSALU

DAVID JONES, ELIZABETH ST, NSW
2000

☎ (2) 9266 5544

One of the hottest, new-breed designers: flow-
ing jerseys and knits in beautiful colours and
loose, unstructured styles.

HOTELS

THE OBSERVATORY

89-113 KENT ST, NSW 2000

☎ (2) 9256 2222

The city's most patrician hotel. Part of the
illustrious Orient–Express stable and sister to
the Cipriani in Venice it boasts the chicest
health club of any Sydney hotel.

PARK HYATT

7 HICKSON RD, THE ROCKS, NSW
2000

☎ (2) 9256 1234

Smallish and cosmopolitan with dynamite
views across Sydney Cove to the Opera House.
High on personal attention – butler service, a
check-in on every floor, which keeps CHER,
ELIZABETH TAYLOR and PLACIDO DOMINGO
happy. The food in **NO. 7 AT THE PARK** is as
appealing as the scenery.

THE REGENT

199 GEORGE ST, NSW 2000

☎ (2) 9238 8000

Glossy, glam and still considered one of the
best hotels in the land. Most rooms have
harbour views. Fitness facilities include an outdoor pool, health centre, golf, tennis and
squash. High-quality Australian fodder at
KABLES (see Restaurants).

RITZ-CARLTON

93 MACQUARIE ST, NSW 2000

☎ (2) 9252 4600

A home from home for the travelling sophisticate, who enjoys the old and aristocratic.
Opposite the Royal Botanic Gardens and close
to the Opera House, but sadly no watery views.

SEBEL TOWN HOUSE

23 ELIZABETH BAY RD, ELIZABETH BAY,
NSW 2011

☎ (2) 9358 3244

Cosy, clubby and a showbiz favourite – you
might see ELTON JOHN, BRUCE SPRINGSTEEN,
TINA TURNER or PINK FLOYD in residence. Few
five-star facilities and no view below the 7th
floor, but its proximity to Kings Cross/
Darlinghurst is the attraction for night owls.

MUSIC

SYDNEY OPERA HOUSE

BENNELONG POINT, NSW 2000

☎ (2) 9250 7111

An architectural marvel it's home to the

BEST BUILDINGS Sydney Opera House alone proves that a country with a shortage of history needn't have a shortage of fine, if disparate, architecture. **Elizabeth Bay House,** 7 Onslow Ave, Elizabeth Bay, NSW 2011, ☎ (2) 9358 2344, is one of Australia's finest colonial homes, a patrician mansion built in regency style. At the other end of the spectrum there's Australia's oldest existing farmhouse, **Elizabeth Farm**, 70 Alice St, Granville, NSW 2142, ☎ (2) 9635 9488. **Hyde Park Barracks**, Queens Sq, Macquarie St, NSW 2000, ☎ (2) 9223 8922, is a Georgian masterwork by the colony's first notable builder, convict architect Francis Greenway. **The Mint Museum**, Queens Sq, Macquarie St, NSW 2000, ☎ (2) 9217 0122, was originally the southern wing of the Rum Hospital, now it houses a collection of decorative and fine arts. **Vaucluse House**, Wentworth Rd, Vaucluse, NSW 2030, ☎ (2) 9337 1957, is a Gothic revival mansion built by 19C explorer, publisher and politician, William Wentworth.

Australian Opera Company, the Sydney Symphony Orchestra and the Australian Chamber Orchestra. However, *"the acoustics are not as good as one might expect from the outside"* – JULIAN LLOYD WEBBER.

RESTAURANTS

ARMSTRONG'S NORTH SYDNEY
1 Napier St, N Sydney, NSW 2060
☎ (2) 9955 2066
A modern Australian menu that draws its inspiration from every imaginable culinary source is applied to exotic ingredients like kangaroo loin and Queensland scallops. Favourite hangout for power-lunching ad-men. Chef: Marcia Branson.

BATHER PAVILION
4 The Esplanade, Balmoral, NSW 2088
☎ (2) 9968 1133
From her New Age beach house, Victoria Alexander has orchestrated a light, modern Australian menu with an Oriental twist. With Riviera-style views of Balmoral Beach, it's a popular spot for brunch on the weekend. The new **Refreshment Room** caters for casual, sand-still-in-your-toes dining.

BAYSWATER BRASSERIE
32 Bayswater Rd, Kings Cross, NSW 2011
☎ (2) 9357 2177
Smart, shiny and still Sydney's favourite

brasserie. You can always rely on the modern Mediterranean menu.

BISTRO MONCUR
116 Queen St, Woollahra, NSW 2025
☎ (2) 9363 2782
Damien Pignolet's pub bistro combines exceptional French food with a brisk, fuss-free atmosphere. No reservations, so arrive early or expect a lengthy queue.

BUON RICORDO
108 Boundary St, Paddington, NSW 2021
☎ (2) 9360 6729
Armando Percuoco's gutsy Italian cooking re-invigorates classics. Certainly one of the best (if not *the* best) Italians in town.

CLAUDE'S
10 Oxford St, Woollahra, NSW 2025
☎ (2) 9331 2325
Tom Pak Choy has inherited Damien Pignolet's formidable mantle as Sydney's custodian of the finest French cuisine. Expect a small menu big on game, fish and poultry, light sauces and an air of hushed reverence. Dust off one of your own vintages as it's unlicensed.

DARLEY STREET THAI
30 Bayswater Rd, Kings Cross, NSW 2011
☎ (2) 9358 6530
Still top of the Thais in Sydney, David

Thompson's East–West food continues to enchant people's tastebuds with his precise flavouring.

FORTY ONE

LEVEL 41, CHIFLEY TOWER, 2 CHIFLEY SQ, NSW 2000

☎ (2) 9221 2500

Dietmar Sawyer has created a gastro-temple, in a suitably elevated position on the 41st floor, popular with big-expense-account diners at lunch, though it's much better at night when the city lights up below. The ladies' loo offers mind-blowing views of the harbour. *"It is a superb restaurant, the chef gives food which is manna from heaven. And from it you can see trees, the ocean and distant horizons"* – LADY FAIRFAX.

KABLES

IN THE REGENT (SEE HOTELS)

☎ (2) 9255 0226

In his crusade to redefine Oz cuisine, Serge Dansereau continues to amaze people with his ever-widening sources of raw material – Illabo lamb, Tasmanian salmon, Coffin Bay scallops, – while the wine list offers the very best of Australia. The appropriate choice for a big night out.

MEZZALUNA

123 VICTORIA ST, POTTS POINT, NSW 2011

☎ (2) 9357 1988

A classy, understated, modern Italian restaurant by Marc Polese. Fabulous city views from the terrace ensure that it's jam-packed at lunchtime.

PARAMOUNT

73 MACLEAY ST, POTTS POINT, NSW 2011

☎ (2) 9358 1652

Chris Mansfield and Margie Harris have created a crisp modern cuisine artfully blending the flavours of the Mediterranean and Asia.

ROCKPOOL

107 GEORGE ST, THE ROCKS, NSW 2000

☎ (2) 9252 1888

It might still be the ultimate for Sydney's name-droppers – but it's the Asian flavours of wunder-chef Neil Perry that ordinary mortals clamour after. His fish is especially good. The bold interior and a glitzy crowd may make you feel as though you've just walked into an Academy Awards ceremony.

• •

"WORLD CLASS, THE MOST IMAGINATIVE COOKING OF ANY RESTAURANT IN SYDNEY" –
PAUL HENDERSON ON *TETSUYA'S*

• •

TETSUYA'S

729 DARLING ST, ROZELLE, NSW 2000

☎ (2) 9555 1017

Tetsuya Wakuda's blend of French and Japanese cooking may break some of the culinary rules but the results are invariably pleasing. The

---

AUSTRALIA'S TOP 11 CITY PUBLIC GOLF COURSES

The cities are brimming full of new courses – but because it's sunny Australia you'll rarely need to combat the elements or the diamond-knit tank tops. In **Sydney** head for Camden Lakeside, Hume Hghwy, Narallen, ☎ (46) 46 1203 and Moore Park, Cleveland St, Moore Park, ☎ (2) 9663 3960. **Melbourne**: Sandringham, Wangara Rd, Sandringham, ☎ (3) 9598 3590 and Beacon Hills, Stony Creek Rd, Beaconsfield, ☎ (7) 5544 6222. **Brisbane**: Kooralbyn Valley, Rentley Drive, Kooralbyn, ☎ (7) 5544 6222 and Hope Island, Oxenford-Southport Rd, Hope Island, ☎ (7) 5530 8988. **Perth**: The Vines, Verdelho Drive, Upper Swan, ☎ (9) 297 3000 and Joondalup, Country Club Blvd, Connolly, ☎ (9) 300 1538. **Tasmania**: Richmond Country Club Casino, Richmond Rd, Camden, ☎ (3) 6248 5450. **Adelaide**: North Adelaide, War Memorial Drive, NA ☎ (8) 8267 2171 and Wirrina Cove Resort, Cape Jervis Rd, Second Valley ☎ (85) 98 4001.

menu is probably the most innovative in Sydney. PAUL HENDERSON says it is *"a marriage of diverse influences and is what Australian cuisine should be all about"*. Book well ahead.

UNKAI

LEVEL 36, ANA HOTEL, THE ROCKS, NSW 2000

☎ (2) 9250 6123

Beautiful, exquisitely presented Japanese food that makes no concessions to occidental palates. Stunning views across Sydney Harbour. Kaiseki menus – a modern equivalent of the tea ceremony – are a speciality here.

SHOPPING

ACCOUTREMENT

611 MILITARY RD, MOSMAN, NSW 2088

☎ (2) 9969 1031

The place for stocking up on pots, knives, vinegars and oils, plus cooking classes from Australia's food stars.

ARIEL BOOKSHOP

42 OXFORD ST, PADDINGTON, NSW 2021

☎ (2) 9332 4581

Essential browsing material for the bookish. Sells everything new, art or avant-garde. You can come for a late-night read.

THE CHEESE SHOP

797 MILITARY RD, MOSMAN, NSW 2088

☎ (2) 9969 4469

An astonishing collection of designer cheeses: goats' cheese from Gabriel Kervella, Meredith Sheep's Blue by Richard Thomas, washed rind cheeses from Top Paddock, bocconcini from Paesanella, plus the best from the rest of the world. Range of specialist pâtés, terrines and marinated titbits useful for sprucing up the table.

COUNTRY ROAD

VARIOUS CITY ADDRESSES.

Tailored but sporty clothes for him and her, somewhere between Ralph Lauren and Timberland in design, along with an ever-expanding range of rustic Conran-style soft furnishings.

DAVID JONES FOODHALL

MARKET ST, NSW 2000

☎ (2) 9266 5544

Department store devoted to food: kangaroo prosciutto and pheasant pies from Maggie Beer and the flavours of wild Australia by Andrew Fielke of the Red Ochre Grill in Adelaide.

LA GERBE D'OR

255 GLENMORE RD, PADDINGTON, NSW 2021

☎ (2) 9331 1070

Complete provisions for a picnic: smoked salmon, trout and caviare mousse, tarte citron, tomato and aubergine quiches – all made on the premises, as are the best baguettes in town.

MAKERS' MARK

CHIFLEY PLAZA, 2 CHIFLEY SQ, NSW 2000

☎ (2) 9231 6800

Melbourne's leading art jeweller, now at a smarter Sydney address. Broome pearls, anodized aluminium earrings and collectables from Peter Coombs, who still provides ELTON JOHN with his glittery face-furniture.

PADDY PALLIN

507 KENT ST, NSW 2000

☎ (2) 9264 2685

Actually smelling of adventure – you can find maps, books and mountains of equipment all

SYDNEY MARKETS Ex-hippy urbanites find weekend solace at **Balmain Market**, St Mary's Church, Darling St, Balmain, NSW 2041 (open Sat 9–4). . . . . . New Age meets suburban chic at another, rather more of-the-moment bazaar: The **Paddington Village Bazaar**, St John's Church, Oxford St, Paddington, NSW 2021 (open Sat 9–4), stocks crystals, tribal silver, slinky socks and here you can rebalance your aura. In the historic centre you can go to **The Rocks Market**, Upper George St, The Rocks, NSW 2000 (open weekends 10–5), a big covered bazaar with a multi-cultural collage of music, food, arts, crafts and entertainment.

tailored for the great outdoors here. An essential stop-off for anyone heading for the Amazon, Annapurna or the wilds of Australia.

PARAMOUNT STORES
67–69 MACLEAY ST, POTTS POINT, NSW 2011
☎ (2) 9358 4595
A take-away version of Maggie Harris's and Chris Mansfield's restaurant, Paramount. Everything you need for a gourmet picnic, or a meal to impress your friends, with helpful hints from Barbara Alexander.

LE PATISSIER CHOCOLATIER
SHOP 1, 121–123 MILITARY RD, NEUTRAL BAY, NSW 2089
☎ (2) 9953 8550
An art gallery dedicated to the chocoholic. Superbly presented boxes of fresh chocolates from Belgium and Switzerland.

RM WILLIAMS
389 GEORGE ST, NSW 2000
☎ (2) 9262 2228
The original bushman's outfitter supplying Akubra hats, bandanas and moleskin trousers,

Jeremy Seal on Australian Snakes

When they told me my fellow jackaroo had been bitten by a common brown, I wondered whether this was likely to be worse than an attack from, say, a cabbage white or clouded yellow. Australia's common brown may sound like a butterfly but, as I discovered when working on an Australian sheep station 15 years ago, this fearsome snake bites a great deal worse. The jackaroo collapsed within ten minutes, and only recovered after a fortnight in intensive care.

In most parts of the world, harmless snakes far outnumber their venomous relatives, and the exotic names are reserved for the relatively few dangerous ones like Africa's black mamba and the Far East's king cobra. In Australia, where there are at least 20 species of highly dangerous snake, familiarity allied with that blasé Aussie attitude has spawned innocuous-sounding names such as browns, king browns and blacks. There's a moral here: if you come across an exotically named snake, you can be pretty sure it's really nasty. Such is the case with Queensland's taipan, whose venom has been measured at over seven times the potency of the cobra's. At the same time, its impressive fangs deliver considerably more poison in the course of an attack, which can consist of a whole series of rapidly inflicted bites. The taipan's remote, largely unsettled habitat – coastal Queensland – means it has had less contact with human beings than other species, and thus has caused far fewer deaths. So you are unlikely to come into contact with one, but if you do . . .

Until an anti-venom was developed in the 1950s there was only one known survivor of a taipan bite, a young man who was lucky enough to be bitten through the highly mitigating effects of a thick leather boot, a thick sock and thick, calloused skin. Taipans are shy, but capable of extraordinary ferocity when provoked or startled. They say that most taipan attacks happen so fast that victims do not know what has happened to them until the snake is backing off afterwards. One Queenslander disturbed a taipan during an afternoon walk along a river bank. "I just don't know what hit me," he said. He described being bitten as someone taking a hammer to his knee as he received seven bites in rapid succession. Quite by chance, the attack happened 100 yards from the nearest hospital. Otherwise it is highly unlikely that he would have survived such a concerted attack.

Despite presumptions to the opposite, Australians have a healthy respect for snakes. Their forebears may have put their trust in antidotes such as extreme drunkenness, blowing up the bite site with a small pile of gunpowder or even drinking highly poisonous mercury, but modern Australians are rigorously taught the drill – which is to immobilize the entire length of the bitten limb with splint and bandage, rather than the now discredited tourniquet. Keeping the victim calm is also crucial. Anti-venom is likely to be administered but in most circumstances not until the patient is admitted to hospital, when tests on poison traces around the wound can confirm the identity of the snake, ensuring that the correct anti-venom is administered.

Driza-Bone riding coats, plaited kangaroo-skin belts, string ties and unique stitched boots.

ROX JEWELLERY

31 STRAND ARCADE, NS 2000

☎ (2) 9232 7828

Serious one-offs at the cutting edge of lapidary chic, seen on many a well-dressed wrist, including those of TINA TURNER and ROXETTE.

SIMON JOHNSON'S ENOTECA

181 HARRIS ST, ULTIMO, NSW 2007

☎ (2) 9552 2522

Clearing house for the pick of Australia's gourmet products. Chutneys and pickles by Stephanie Alexander and Tasmanian salmon prepared by Damien Pignolet.

THEATRE

BELVOIR STREET THEATRE

25 BELVOIR ST, SURRY HILLS, NSW 2010

☎ (2) 9699 3444

Often provides innovative and challenging contemporary socio-political drama. Novelties include Theatresports, a more cerebral equivalent to the Gladiators.

SYDNEY THEATRE COMPANY

PIER 4, HICKSON RD, MILLERS POINT, NSW 2000

☎ (2) 9250 1700

Sparkling theatre on the harbour, always at the forefront with new, outstanding Australian drama. Also imports major productions from Broadway and the West End.

Rest of New South Wales

HOTELS

BRINDABELLA

BRINDABELLA, NSW 2611

☎ (6) 236 2121

One of the prettiest and most welcoming homesteads in rural Australia, run by Brian and Guillermina Barlin. You can go trout fishing, canoeing, bushwalking, swimming, mountain biking and horse riding. This mountain valley provided the inspiration for Miles Franklin. Highly recommended.

CLEOPATRA

4 CLEOPATRA ST, BLACKHEATH, NSW 2785

☎ (47) 87 8456 (AFTER AUG '97 (2) 4787 8456)

There's something quite seductive about this old farmhouse. The cottage garden bursts with roses, magnolias, rhododendrons and exotic trees, while ex-film-set designer Trish Mullene has filled the interior with antiques and artistic arrangements of wildflowers. In the kitchen Dany Chouet cooks up sensual feasts that emphasize the robust flavours of her native Dordogne.

THE CONVENT

HALLS RD, POKOLBIN, NSW 2320

☎ (49) 98 7764 (AFTER AUG '97: (2) 4998 7764)

The Convent can provide people with a refuge for body, mind and soul as a five-star hotel. The building now has 17 baroque-style suites. It's also in the middle of **PEPPER TREE COMPLEX**, which includes a winery and **ROBERT'S** restaurant where the superb provincial Italian and French food has won acclaim for chef Robbie Molines.

ECHOES

3 LILIANFELS AVE, ECHO POINT, KATOOMBA, 2780

☎ (47) 82 1966 (AFTER AUG '97: (2) 4782 1966)

Precipitously perched on the edge of the Jamison Valley and Blue Mountains, close to the town of Katoomba, this small hotel has everything you want such as a sauna, underfloor heating and an à la carte menu from chef Claude Corne, formerly of Claude's in Sydney.

HEADLANDS

PRETTY BEACH, NSW 2257

☎ (43) 60 1933 (AFTER AUG '97: (2) 4360 1933)

Small, secluded and within easy reach of Sydney. The house is on the edge of Bouddi National Park, which has idyllic beaches both on the ocean and within the protective arms of the bay. The food is an eclectic fusion of East and West, with the emphasis on seafood.

KIMS

P O BOX 1, TOWOON BAY, NSW 2261

☎ (43) 32 1566 (AFTER AUG '97: (2) 4332 1566)

Individual timber bungalows with large windows overlook a jungle tangled with creepers, banana palms, hibiscus and an avenue of century-old Norfolk Island pines. Legendary, buffet-style meals, a resident masseuse and the sound of the surf and the gentle sea breeze.

LILIANFELS

LILIANFELS AVE, LEURA, NSW 2780
☎ (47) 80 1200 (AFTER AUG '97: (2) 9780 1200)

A stylish rendition of the classic country house hotel – close to the walking trails that lead down into the Jamison Valley. Smart though relaxed and very high on creature comforts with elegant rooms, huge armchairs for curling up in front of the fire, a pampering health club and one of the best restaurants in the mountains.

MILTON PARK

PRIVATE BAG 1, BOWRAL, NSW 2576
☎ (48) 61 1522 (AFTER AUG '97: (2) 4861 1522)

A Southern Highlands mansion offers a taste of Edwardian country living, against a background of English-style gardens classified by The National Trust. One of only two Australian members of Relais & Château.

TAYLOR'S

MCGETTIGAN'S LN, EWINGSDALE, BYRON BAY 2481
☎ (66) 84 7436 (AFTER AUG '97: (2) 6684 7436)

In the hills behind Byron Bay Ross and Wendy Taylor have created a small, country retreat. THE SUMMER HOUSE is particularly striking, decorated in candy-colours with a sheikh-size bed. Dinners tend to be long and mildly debauched while breakfasts rely heavily on fresh fruit and free-range eggs from the property.

Rest of Australia

TOURS AND CHARTERS

AIRCRUISING AUSTRALIA

18 ROSS SMITH AVE, KINGSFORD SMITH AIRPORT, MASCOT, NSW 2020
☎ (2) 9693 2233

See Australia. Cruise with the crocs in Kakadu, barbecue a barramundi in Broome and blunder about in the Bungle Bungles. Passengers travel in style aboard an F27 Fokker that slashes Australia's tyranny of distance in manageable hops. Food and accommodation are first-class all the way.

MARY ROSSI TRAVEL

SUITE 3, THE DENISON, 65 BERRY ST, N SYDNEY, NSW 2060
☎ (2) 9957 4511

The person to see if you want to go ballooning over Africa, press paws with polar bears or just cuddle koalas in the wilds of Australia.

OUTLAND EXPEDITIONS

P O BOX 403, STANFIELD, NSW 21356
☎ (2) 9746 8025

Sydney-based adventure travel outfit with guided tours tailored for the urban adventurer with only a day or two to spare. Abseiling, climbing, kayaking, and whitewater rafting.

P&O RESORTS

LEVEL 18, AIDC TOWER, 201 KENT ST, SYDNEY 2000
☎ 13 2469

A line-up of smart accommodation in some of the best bits of wild Australia.

PEREGRINE ADVENTURES

258 LONSDALE ST, VIC 3000
☎ (3) 9663 8611

The complete Oz adventure specialist, catering to urbanites as well as aspiring Tarzans and Janes.

WALKABOUT GOURMET ADVENTURES

P O BOX 52, DINNER PLAIN, VIC 3898
☎ (3) 5159 6566

Guided rambles through the Snowy Mountains and along the Great Ocean Rd in southern Victoria.

AUSTRIA
Salzburg

FESTIVALS

MOZART WEEK

POSTFACH 34, SCHWARZSTRASSE 26, A-5024
☎ (662) 873154

January's increasingly popular Mozart Week is far more accessible than Salzburg's main music festival in summer. *"Even so, you need to book tickets well in advance because locals tend to flood in for this excellent series of homages to the greatest citizen of Salzburg. There is wonderful opera and also smaller-scale concerts in the Mozart Hall itself, a gorgeous baroque building with fabulous acoustics"* – ED VICTOR.

SALZBURG FESTIVAL

POSTFACH 140, HOFSTALLGASSE 1, A-5010

☎ (662) 844501; TICKET OFFICE FAX (662) 846682 (ATTN DR ANDREAS VRTAL)

Salzburg's annual celebration of music and culture runs from mid-July to end Aug. Tickets should be bought at least six months in advance.

HOTELS

GOLDENER HIRSCH

GETREIDEGASSE 37, A-5020

☎ (662) 8485110

Slap bang in the heart of the old city, a medieval inn complete with vaulted stairs, arched corridors and period antiques. *"The place to stay. Apart from the fact that you can walk from there to all the concert halls, the after-concert suppers are wonderful"* – ED VICTOR. The restaurant is known for its creative cuisine, chic clientele and fluffy soufflés.

HOTEL ÖSTERREICHISCHER HOF

SCHWARZSTRASSE 5, A-5024

☎ (662) 88977

Salzburg's undisputed *grande dame*. Built as the Hotel d'Autriche in 1866 on a quiet bank of the river Salzach, all the rooms face the river and have breathtaking views of the fortress and the old city. The hotel's restaurants are well patronized by the Salzburg establishment.

Vienna

ART AND MUSEUMS

ALBERTINA

AUGUSTINERSTRASSE 1, A-1010

☎ (1) 534830

Home to the world's largest collection of drawings, sketches, engravings and etchings.

KUNSTHISTORISCHES MUSEUM

BURGRING 5, A-1010

☎ (1) 521770

An exceptionally well-run museum and also one of the world's great repositories of European art dating from antiquity to the Post-Impressionist period. The 19C and early 20C works are housed in the Neue Galerie at Stallburg Palace.

BARS AND CAFES

CAFE CENTRAL

HERRENGASSE 14, A-1010

☎ (1) 533 3763

Where Sigmund Freud and Leon Trotsky tucked into the most sublime Viennese apple strudel. Plenty of newspapers to read on old-fashioned cane racks.

DEMEL

KOHLMARKT 14, A-1010

☎ (1) 533 5516

Former Imperial hangout and probably Vienna's most famous café, boasting the most mouthwatering cakes and pastries in the world.

HOTELS

HOTEL IM PALAIS SCHWARZENBERG

SCHWARZENBERGPLATZ 9, A-1030

☎ (1) 7984 5150

Housed in a baroque palace, the luxurious Schwarzenberg is surrounded by 18 acres of private park, providing glorious garden views and an idyllic setting for jogging, croquet, tennis or simply resting. The TERRASSEN-RESTAURANT overlooks the gardens of the palace park and serves classical French and Viennese cuisine – the à la carte menu is particularly good.

HOTEL SACHER WIEN

PHILHARMONIKERSTRASSE 4, A-1015

☎ (1) 514560

The Hotel Sacher belongs to Vienna itself. Founded in 1876 by Eduard Sacher, opposite the State Opera House, it's like a museum but at the same time has a homely air of faded grandeur. Downstairs you can indulge in the world-famous Sachertorte in the Kaffeehaus Sacher where it was invented The piano is played in the lobby during afternoon tea and in the evening. *Third Man*-type zither music is played at the restaurant ROTE BAR.

IMPERIAL

KÄRNTNER RING 16, A-1015

☎ (1) 501100

An original Württemberg Palace inaugurated in 1873 by Emperor Franz Josef I. The hotel embodies old Vienna at its most regal and still manages to attract travelling monarchs (only this time they have to pay). In 1994 readers voted it *Condé Nast Traveler's* "best hotel in the world". ANDRE PREVIN considers it "*an elegant home away from home with exquisite service*". Make sure you try the delicious Imperial cake and other Viennese pastries at the CAFÉ IMPERIAL.

MUSIC

VIENNA FESTIVAL

WIENER FESTWOCHEN,
LEHARGASSTRASSE 11, A-1060
☎ (1) 58 92 20
An annual gathering of well-known orchestras, soloists, and theatre and performance groups, from around the beginning of May to mid-June. Trendies gather around the "Tone und Gegentone" sub-festival of exotic and avant-garde music.

VIENNA STATE OPERA

OPERNRING 2, A-1010
☎ (1) 514440
Built in 1869 and reconstructed after World War II, this is one of the best and most stunning opera houses in the world. Under the new and enthusiastic direction of Joan Holender, Pavarotti, Domingo and Carreras are annual visitors. The February Opera Ball is billed as one of the most beautiful dances in the world.

RESTAURANTS

SEE ALSO HOTELS.

DO & CO

HAAS HAUS, STEPHANSPLATZ 12, A-1010
☎ (1) 535 3969
Housed in the controversial new Haas Haus building, from its roof terrace there's a spectacular view right over the multicoloured roof of St Stephen's Cathedral and beyond. The menu is international but doesn't quite match up to the grand surroundings.

HEDRICH

STUBENRING 2, A-1010
☎ (1) 512 9588
Small restaurant run by chef Richard Hedrich, who is well-known for his modern cooking and generous helpings. Allow room for the puddings.

RESTAURANT DREI HUSAREN

WEIHBURGGASSE 4, A-1010
☎ (1) 512 1092/0
The ultimate spot for a romantic, candlelit, old-fashioned, piano-accompanied Viennese dinner. Kick off with a selection from the hors d'oeuvres trolley; this should be followed by traditional specialities like Tafelspitz saddle of venison and finally a hot pudding like the pancake "Three Hussars". Courtly and impeccable service.

STEIRERECK

RASUMOFSKYGASSE 2, A-1030 VIENNA
☎ (1) 713 3168
Owned and run by the Reitbauer family and widely regarded as the best restaurant in Austria. Traditional Viennese cuisine has been re-invented with dishes such as lamb in red paprika and olive sauce with red cabbage gelée. For those with a sweet tooth, the Bohemian Austrian desserts should not be missed. And you can visit the impeccable wine cellar.

12 APOSTEL KELLER

SONNENFELSGASSE 3, A-1010.
☎ (1) 512 6777
Very famous, typical Viennese wine and beer cellar, in the catacombs of a historic 1561 building, featuring the only Gothic well on public display in the city. Dishes are traditional Austrian.

SHOPPING

ARCADIA

KÄRNTNERSTRASSE 40, A-1015
☎ (1) 513 9568
An unusual shop in the State Opera House arcade, selling a vast range of recordings as well as tumblers, coasters, handkerchiefs, paperweights, posters and postcards, all with an operatic theme.

AUGARTEN

STOCK-IM-EISEN-PLATZ 3-4, A-1010
☎ (1) 512 1494
Makers of fine porcelain and the second-oldest porcelain firm in Europe; each piece is hand-painted. The factory, Schloss Augarten, is open to visitors.

HAAS HAUS

STOCK-IM-EISEN-PLATZ 4, A-1010
Floor upon floor of glamorous and expensive boutiques, set in a modern building right in the heart of Vienna.

MARKETS The Christkindlmarkt is a major part of the build-up to Christmas all over Austria. In Vienna it lasts from the 2nd Sat of Nov until the end of Dec, and is held in front of the town hall (Rathaus). There are stalls galore, selling all manner of gifts, decorations and goodies. And there's usually plenty of Glühwein to keep you going while you browse. The atmosphere is great, especially after the sun's gone down. "*The best Christmas Market in the world*," says SHERIDAN MORLEY, but as it's open-air, "*take a coat*".

MODELLBAHN-ECKE
OLLWEINGASSE 21, A-1051
☎ (1) 893 9909
This sensational retailer of model railways is a must even for the non-enthusiast.

Rest of Austria

HOTELS

HOTEL SCHLOSS FUSCHL
A-5322 HOF BEI SALZBURG
☎ (6229) 224530
A splendid 15C lakeside castle which nestles in the foothills of the Fuschl mountains, half an hour from Salzburg. Plays host to CHANCELLOR KOHL and LIZA MINNELLI. The award-winning **IMPERIAL RESTAURANT** serves classical haute cuisine. "*One of the great hotels of the world. Lunch and breakfast overlooking Lake Fuschl is wonderful*" – SIR JOHN HARVEY-JONES.

SCHLOSS DURNSTEIN
A-3601 DÜRNSTEIN AN DER DONAU, WACHAU
☎ (2711) 212
On the banks of the river Danube, this old castle provides an oasis of calm and luxury. Indeed, the hotel is as renowned for its cuisine and wine cellar as it is for its breathtaking views from the leafy terrace.

MUSIC

BREGENZER FESTSPIELE
FESTSPIEL-UND-KONGRESSHAUS, PLATZ DER WIENER SYMPHONIKER, A-6900 BREGENZ
☎ (5574) 49200/20023
Every July and Aug this medieval town hosts a flamboyant festival on Lake Constance. There is an indoor theatre too, featuring symphony concerts and opera.

BRUCKNERFEST
BRUCKNERHAUS, POSTFACH 57, UNTERE DONAULÄNDE 7, A-4010 LINZ
☎ (732) 76120
A series of recitals and concerts showcasing the work of Austrian composer Anton Bruckner, which takes place in Sept. A highlight is the "Linz Cloud of Sound", which opens the festival, when music played within the Bruckner House is transmitted outside the building and accompanied by lasers, fireworks, water and lighting effects.

BEST OF THE REST

Apart from the tremendously glamorous and relatively expensive ones, there are plenty of other excellent Austrian resorts to choose from, such as **Söll**, **Kitzbühel** and **Mayrhofen**. Further up the valley from Mayrhofen is the less well-known village of **Hintertuch**. Small and idyllic, it has good access to the glacier, where the conditions are fantastic. **Obergurgl** is another Austrian secret – one of the highest resorts in the Tyrol where you can guarantee that there'll be snow. In the Salzburg region, **Zell am See** has access to the glacier at Kaprun. Its lakeside location is good for a summer escape too.

MÖRBISCH LAKE FESTIVAL (Seefestspiele Mörbisch)

FREMDENVERKEHRSAMT DER
GEMEINDE, A-7072 MÖRBISCH AM SEE
☎ (2685) 8430

Throughout July and Aug opera buffs converge on this little town beside Lake Neusiedler for night-time opera performances which take place on a stage that floats on the lake, lit by flaming torches. The finale at the end of Aug features a spectacular firework display. BARBARA TAYLOR BRADFORD highly recommends it.

CARINTHIA or Kärnten, is one of Austria's best-kept secrets. The area's outstanding natural beauty and excellent opportunities for watersports on local lakes, cycling and walking in the mountains make it well worth the visit if you're feeling energetic and out-doorsy. During the summer the towns and villages lining Lake Wörther (Wörthersee), such as Pörtschach, are particularly lively with their bustling restaurants and casinos. The climax is Kirchtag ("church day") in August which essentially gives everyone a good excuse to dress up and drink for 24 hours.

SKI RESORTS

LECH

The wide cul-de-sac valley of Lech is a short drive up through Zürs from neighbouring St Anton. It is favoured by wintering royals including KING HUSSEIN and QUEEN NOOR OF JORDAN, PRINCESS CAROLINE OF MONACO and PRINCESS DIANA. *"The skiing on the Lech-Zürs axis is very reliable as it is high, interesting without being too difficult. I recommend the* **GOLDENER BERG,** ☎ *(5583) 22050, run by Gucky and Franz Pfefferkorn: it is beautifully isolated, very personalized, very relaxing and right on the piste above Oberlech. Excellent food and wine list. Lunch is served on the terrace and is one of the popular spots for skiers as it is just off the main piste"* – MARTIN SKAN.

ST ANTON

The resort for serious skiers and après-skiers, from PRINCE EDWARD to KIM WILDE. Top spot to descend from is Valluga Mountain, while top spots to stay at are the family run **ST ANTONER HOF,** ☎ (5446) 29100, and the **HOTEL NEUE POST** ☎ (5446) 21130. Both are at 6580 St Anton am Arlberg.

ST CHRISTOPH

A relaxed resort. Stay at the luxurious **HOTEL HOSPITZ,** ☎ (5446) 2611, run by Adi Werner. The restaurant faces the slopes – by day sit on the terrace, and by night enjoy the rustic-looking dining room.

BELGIUM
Brussels

BARS

LE CERCUEIL

DE HARINGSTRAAT 10, 1000
☎ (2) 513 3361

A rather macabre bar (the name means "coffin") in a small street just off the Grand Place. The tables are made from old coffins, and beer is served in a skull.

LA CHALOUPE D'OR

GRAND PLACE 24-25, 1000
☎ (2) 511 4161

A cosy Brussels café where one can enjoy good brandy late at night by the fireplace.

HOTELS

CONRAD

AVE LOUISE 71, 1050
☎ (2) 542 4242

A relative newcomer, the city's brightest and probably best hotel has played host to hordes of the city's most powerful visitors, BILL CLINTON included. Business travellers and Eurocrats are made especially welcome – PCs and faxes can be brought to the rooms on request.

HILTON INTERNATIONAL

BLVD DE WATERLOO 38, 1000
☎ (2) 504 1111

Overlooking the parc d'Egmont, as the city's first high-rise, the Hilton provides a distinctive landmark. And in spite of its name, the MAISON DU BOEUF restaurant does some great fish dishes.

SAS ROYAL HOTEL

RUE DU FOSSE-AUX-LOUPS 47, 1000
☎ (2) 223 1818
Fascinating architecture: you can even see part of the old city wall in the atrium. You can have a room to suit your taste – the Art Deco rooms are the most popular. The SEA GRILL is one of the best fish restaurants in town and sports a Michelin star.

STANHOPE HOTEL

RUE DU COMMERCE 9, 1000
☎ (2) 506 9111
The feel of a townhouse with smallish but opulent rooms. Multilingual staff and the city's only caviare bar.

RESTAURANTS

SEE ALSO HOTELS.

AMADEUS

RUE VEYDT 13, 1060
☎ (2) 538 3427
One of the trendiest bar–restaurants in town, based in an old sculpture studio. There are two dining rooms and a bar, all overlooking a courtyard. Very cosy and intimate, and the food is good. Centrally located off the ave Louise, with an entrance that takes you through a courtyard filled with bits of statue. Best in the evenings.

AUBERGE NAPOLEON

BOECHOUTLAAN 1, 1860 MEISE
☎ (2) 269 3078
A classy restaurant in pure Belgian style; deli-

cious food and smart atmosphere. Located just out of town so provides a good excuse to escape the city. Open 7 days.

AU ROY D'ESPAGNE

GRAND PLACE 1, 1000
☎ (2) 513 0807
The oldest café in town, where the city's Bohemian set tend to congregate. The decor and atmosphere may make you feel as though you've walked straight back into the Middle Ages – but it's great for a hot drink on a cold winter afternoon, or a stiff drink last thing at night. Serves food until late too.

AUX ARMES DE BRUXELLES

RUE DES BOUCHERS 13, 1000
☎ (2) 511 2118
Bustling, enthusiastic establishment peddling large helpings of well-cooked Belgian staples including steaks, moules and chips.

COMME CHEZ SOI

PLACE ROUPPE 23, 1000
☎ (2) 512 2921
Long considered the top restaurant in Brussels and possibly the rest of Belgium and a worthy rival to any three-star kitchen in Europe. Chef Pierre Wynants's domain – like his clientele – is grander than grand and reassuringly expensive.

⊛ LE FOU CHANTANT

AVE DU FRÉ, UCCKLE
☎ (2) 374 3315
A quarter of an hour from the centre of Brussels, this atmospheric restaurant has become all the rage for the local trendy young things. Delicious meats are cooked in the fireplace, and there's live music every night – jazz on Thurs and classical on other nights. Very enjoyable and reasonably priced.

ENCORE Where to eat in Brussels. Two minutes' walk from the Grand Place in the heart of Brussels is the **rue des Bouchers**. Very atmospheric, it feels like a Mediterranean street with one restaurant sidling up to the next, serving reasonably priced Belgian and French food. The best-known eaterie is **Chez Leon**, rue des Bouchers 18, ☎ (2) 511 1415, a must for Brussels's best moules et frites . . . . . ♠ The **Place du Grand Sablon**, is an elegant square, surrounded by restaurants and shops. It also adjoins several streets and alleys among which you'll find lots of antique shops and art galleries. Go there on Sunday morning and have a look around the flea market. And don't miss **Wittamer**, Grand Sablon 12, ☎ (2) 512 3742, the best-known patisserie in town . . . . . ♠ The **Place Ste-Catherine** is where true Belgians go – there are around six seafood restaurants bordering the square and they are all good . . . . ♠

LA MAISON DU CYGNE

RUE CHARLES BULS 2, 1000

☎ (2) 511 8244

Prestigious and historic restaurant perched on the edge of one of Europe's most beautiful and impressive squares, the Grand Place. Karl Marx used to be a regular and even in his day it was pricey. Slightly ponderous cooking, but wonderful service.

LA QUINCAILLERIE

RUE DU PAGE 45, 1050

☎ (2) 538 2553

French–Belgian cuisine in an old warehouse. Very stylish decor, with one dining room downstairs and another on the mezzanine upstairs. Just off the place du Chatelain.

RICK'S STEAK HOUSE

AVE LOUISE 344, 1050

☎ (2) 648 1451

The place to find the young international crowd, this American bar was named after Rick's Bar in the film *Casablanca*. Tex-Mex food, great atmosphere (especially late in the evening) and a large garden at the back – nice to sit out in in summer. Well priced.

VILLA LORRAINE

AVE DU VIVIER D'OIE 75, 1180

☎ (2) 374 3163

Another top restaurant and the main rival to Comme Chez Soi (see entry). Tradition is the name of the game in this country-house style restaurant with its glass-covered terrace overlooking the Bois de la Chambre. Anton Mosimann used to work here as a young chef; now the current chef Freddy Vandecasserie rustles up a wonderful combination of *cuisine d'Escoffier* and *cuisine du marché*. Recommended by PAUL HENDERSON.

Rest of Belgium

HOTELS

HOTEL DE ROSIER

ROSIER 23, 2000 ANTWERP

☎ (3) 225 01 40

Just ten minutes' walk from the centre of town, this beautiful 17C mansion is full of antiques, luxury and charm. High-ceilinged rooms overlook a private garden where there is a swimming pool cleverly hidden in its historic structure. Impeccable service.

RESTAURANTS

DE BARBARIE

VAN BREE STRAAT 4, 2018 ANTWERP

☎ (3) 232 8198

One of Antwerp's best-known restaurants, it offers a range of Belgo-French cooking in a chic atmosphere. Renowned for its meat dishes, it's worth coming simply to sample chef Koan Carals's duck baked with acacia honey and red peppers.

DE KERSELAAR

GROTE PIETER POT STRAAT 22, 2000 ANTWERP

☎ (3) 233 5969

Try Yves Michiel's inventive French cuisine, in homely surroundings.

DE MATELOTE

HAARSTRAAT 9, 2000 ANTWERP

☎ (3) 231 3207

Tucked away in a house down a narrow street, this is considered the best fish restaurant in town and so it's packed most nights. Try the matelote, a river-fish stew with white wine.

DE WITTE POORTE

JAN VAN EYCKPLEIN 6, 8000 BRUGES

☎ (50) 330883

Fun family-run restaurant in an old vaulted warehouse. Fresh from the North Sea, the fish is the best in Bruges. Excellent game too.

HET FORNIUS

REYNDERS STRAAT 24, 2000 ANTWERP

☎ (3) 233 0269

Traditional Belgian restaurant offering fresh seasonal cuisine, and particularly good fish. Closed weekends.

HUIS DE COLVENIER

SINT ANTONIUS 8, 2000 ANTWERP

☎ (3) 266 65 73

Well-presented modern international food is served in this small, homely dining room. There are only six tables, so reservations are essential.

LA PEROUSE

PONTON STEEN, ANTWERP

☎ (3) 231 3151

Once the summer pleasure trips are over, *La Perouse* docks at the Steen and becomes, during the winter months, an outstanding gourmet restaurant serving the freshest fish and plenty of meat. Book well in advance. Closed Sun & Mon, and mid-Jun to Sept.

Rio — The Marvellous City

Rio has certainly had its ups and downs over the past few decades. From the golden age of the 1920s–1950s, it was *the* exotic hangout for Hollywood and the international jet set. Rio was immortalized in song and celluloid in "The Girl from Ipanema", "Flying down to Rio" and "Copacabana" and became the romantic destination for eloping lovers. But the city's mythical mask slipped in the 1970s and 80s when the world discovered the Rio where it's too dangerous to stop at a red traffic light for fear of being robbed; the favelas (slums) where nearly 3 million live in grinding poverty, ever fearful of being bumped off by the local drug baron; and the place where all of Europe's most notorious war criminals and train robbers were lying low. In recent years Rio's image has had a good shake-up, though it's worth remembering that it's still a typical high-rise South American city; so don't drop your guard and think you're in St Tropez.

The city enjoys a classic tropical climate: it's always warm and often humid, so you can visit year round. The most hectic and exciting time to visit is during Carnival, which lasts the four days leading up to Ash Wednesday, when all the "Samba schools" emerge from the "Sambadrome", built by Oscar Niemeyer (the architect responsible for Brasilia in the 1950s), and parade around the city in vivid costume. The smartest areas are in the South and include Ipanema, Copacabana and Leblon. Copacabana is probably the most famous and it's now also one of the most densely populated areas of urban real estate in the world — not so appealing. One major reason for going there, however, is James Sherwood's Riviera-style **COPACABANA PALACE**, av Atlantica 1702, ☎ (21) 255 7070. The hotel is pure Hollywood and has been since the 1920s. In the 1940s ORSON WELLES came here to party, and in a fit of jealousy threw his furniture out of the window — setting a precedent years before rock stars started following suit. The hotel where the PRINCESS OF WALES stayed when she came to visit her friend LUCIA FLECHA DA LIMA, overlooks the famous **COPACABANA** beach strip and is a perfect base for watersports or simply lingering by the pool drinking cocktails.

As you fly in along the coast you can make out the famous granite outcrops you've seen so often in travel posters, **PAO DE ACUCAR** (Sugar Loaf) and Corcovado topped by **CRISTO REDENTOR** (Christ the Redeemer) — and, of course, the skyscrapers which shot up in the 1960s. Hidden beneath these are all the old colonial churches and museums. It takes some effort to see these as the city is so vast, hot and not that easy to manoeuvre your way around. Most of the city's cultural interest is towards the north in the old commercial district, where you'll find the best-preserved colonial museums — it's very lively during the week and relatively safe, but should be avoided at weekends, particularly at night.

While there you should try a few local specialities such as churrasco (barbecued meat) and feijoada (a dish made from black beans). And it would be a crime not to have lots of the wonderfully fresh fish, which comes in every shape and size. MADONNA, MICK JAGGER, STING and TRUDI SYLER all travel to Rio for the red snapper baked in rock salt served at **SATYRICON**, ☎ (21) 521 0627, in Ipanema. It's the best fish restaurant in town and even has its own fishing fleet. The assado no sal grosso arrives at the table in a hot sarcophagus of salt, which is split open by the waiter with a mighty blow and served simply with chunks of lemon and thick, thick olive oil.

People forget that Brasilia, rather than Rio, is the capital of Brazil, and it's hardly surprising because in terms of colour, culture and excitement the Cidade Maravilhosa — the marvellous city, as Brazilians call it — will always outshine the rather bland political capital.

BRITAIN
Bath

ART AND MUSEUMS

John Wood and son revolutionized town-planning in Britain with their 18C scheme for Bath. There are 18 museums throughout the city, the most famous being the **ROMAN BATHS MUSEUM** – which is open all year round, but perhaps best visited on an Aug evening when the baths are lit by torches. You can taste the mineral water in the Pump Room, while listening to a chamber orchestra or opt for a Bath bun and a cup of tea at Sally Lunn's instead. Dedicated followers of fashion can visit the **MUSEUM OF COSTUME** in the Assembly Rooms; a fascinating collection of assorted fashions from the late 16C to the present day. At the **VICTORIA ART GALLERY** there's a fine collection including a Gainsborough portrait completed while he lived in Bath. On the outskirts of Bath, the **AMERICAN MUSEUM** is housed in Claverton Manor and contains complete rooms from 17C–19C American homesteads, along with a large collection of patchwork quilts and other American folk art. For further information on all the city attractions, telephone the Bath Tourism Bureau on ☎ (01225) 461111.

HOLBURNE MUSEUM AND CRAFTS STUDY CENTRE
GREAT PULTENEY ST, BA2 4DB
☎ (01225) 466669
Collection of decorative and fine art put together by Sir William Holburne (1793–1874). It includes English and continental silver, porcelain, Italian majolica and bronzes, together with glass, furniture, miniatures and pictures by Turner and Gainsborough. There's a teahouse in the grounds, perfect for a light lunch or afternoon tea with home-made cakes. Open daily Tues–Sat, and Sun afternoons. Closed mid-Dec to mid-Feb.

HOTELS

BATH SPA HOTEL
SYDNEY RD, BA2 6JF
☎ (01225) 444424
Carefully restored Neo-Classical building, set in 7 acres of landscaped garden, with a health spa and a grand restaurant in the original ballroom, while each bedroom has been decorated individually.

THE QUEENSBERRY HOTEL
RUSSELL ST, BA1 2QF
☎ (01225) 447928
Small Georgian townhouse hotel, in a quiet residential street. Very homey, with antiques and plenty of fresh fruit, magazines and books. *"A perfect small hotel with a wonderful restaurant, The Olive Tree, in the basement"* – NED SHERRIN.

ROYAL CRESCENT HOTEL
ROYAL CRESCENT, BA1 2LS
☎ (01225) 739955
It might be a little stuffy, but this is still Bath's grandest hotel, set on the Royal Crescent. Stay in the main house, in the pavilion or even the Beau Nash suite, where you can enjoy your own personal supply of "Bath" water and a balcony overlooking the hotel's beautiful walled garden. The **DOWER HOUSE** restaurant is one of the best in town.

Birmingham

Birmingham is full of well-disguised treasures, both artistic and historic. Birmingham also boasts a culturally rich surrounding area (Stratford-upon-Avon, the Cotswolds, Warwick and the Severn Valley). You can amuse yourself from watching craftsmen make traditional jewellery at the **JEWELLERY QUARTER DISCOVERY CENTRE**, ☎ (0121) 554 3598, to taking the Willy Wonka option and learning about the history of chocolate at **CADBURY WORLD**, ☎ (0121) 451 4180. Tourist Office ☎ (0121) 643 2514.

ART AND MUSEUMS

THE BARBER INSTITUTE OF FINE ARTS
UNIVERSITY OF BIRMINGHAM (EAST GATE), OFF EDGBASTON PARK RD, B15 2TS
☎ (0121) 414 7333
A small picture gallery which counts among the city's greatest cultural assets, comprising an outstanding collection of Old Master and modern paintings, drawings and sculptures, including major works by Bellini, Poussin, Rubens, Monet and Renoir. The Institute also features a regular programme of concerts, lectures and events, all open to the public. Open all day Mon–Sat, and Sun afternoons.

BIRMINGHAM MUSEUM AND ART GALLERY

CHAMBERLAIN SQ, B3 3DH

☎ (0121) 235 2834

Founded in 1885, this spectacular Victorian building houses one of the biggest and best collections of Impressionist and Pre-Raphaelite paintings in Britain. You can journey from ancient cultures to 20C arts and crafts. The more recent GAS HALL GALLERY is a new, high-tech space designed for temporary exhibitions. There's an EDWARDIAN TEA ROOM where you can treat yourself.

BALLET

BIRMINGHAM ROYAL BALLET

BIRMINGHAM HIPPODROME, THORP ST, B5 4AU

☎ (0121) 622 2555

Following the retirement of Sir Peter Wright, David Bintley, considered the most distinguished choreographer of his generation, now directs the company, which is fast making its mark on the world ballet scene.

CLUBS

BOBBY BROWN'S THE CLUB

52 GAS ST, B1 2JP

☎ (0121) 643 2753

Former canalside warehouse stylishly converted into the most original nightclub in town, offering three separate bars, bistro and discotheque. Attracts the over-25s mainly. Open Wed–Sat.

RONNIE SCOTT'S

BROAD ST, B1 2HF

☎ (0121) 643 4525

This internationally acclaimed jazz club invites the world's top artistes on stage every evening. Tables can be reserved to dine. Open Mon–Sat from 7.30 pm, and Sunday from 7 pm.

HOTELS

HYATT REGENCY

2 BRIDGE ST, B1 2JZ

☎ (0121) 643 1234

Imposing 24 storeys of mirrored exterior, with spacious atrium lobby. The Hyatt has three restaurants including Californian cuisine in the Court Café, Brasserie on Broad St and Glassworks pub/restaurant. Easy access from the International Convention Centre, to which it is linked by a glass bridge.

SWALLOW HOTEL

12 HAGLEY RD, FIVE WAYS, EDGBASTON B16 8SJ

☎ (0121) 452 1144

98 rooms' worth of Neo-Edwardian elegance including original mahogany woodwork and crystal chandeliers. Comprehensive fitness facilities, including a swimming pool, in the Egyptian-themed leisure centre. Chef Jonathan Harrison (winner of the 1993 Roux Brothers scholarship) dishes up his inventive brand of French/European cuisine in the SIR EDWARD ELGAR RESTAURANT.

MUSIC

CITY OF BIRMINGHAM SYMPHONY ORCHESTRA

SYMPHONY HALL, INTERNATIONAL CONVENTION CENTRE, BROAD ST, B1 2EA

☎ (0121) 212 3333 (BOX OFFICE)

Outstanding international orchestra under the charismatic leadership of wunderkind Sir Simon Rattle. Its home, Symphony Hall, is one of the finest concert halls in the world.

RESTAURANTS

HENRY'S CANTONESE RESTAURANT

27 ST PAUL'S SQ, B3 1RB

☎ (0121) 200 1136

Birmingham has many Chinese restaurants, but this split-level Cantonese is probably the best. Open for lunch and dinner Mon–Sat.

SLOAN'S

27 CHAD SQUARE, HAWTHORNE RD, EDGBASTON, B15 3TQ

☎ (0121) 455 6697

Laid-back Mediterranean restaurant in a small suburban shopping centre, offering a selection of European dishes under the direction of new chef, Douglas Barker.

Cambridge

Cambridge has been described as one of the most beautiful cities in Britain – home to the famous university, the rival to Oxford. Dating back to 1209, it is only some 40 years Oxford's junior. PETERHOUSE was the oldest college, founded *c.* 1280 – the original hall survives. Among its other notable colleges are **St John's** (which has a spectacular Tudor gateway and its own Bridge of Sighs); **Corpus Christi** (whose Old Court is the oldest in the town); **Trinity** (with the largest court and the prized library designed by Wren). Unmissable is Cambridge's biggest showstopper of all: **King's**. It is worth visiting Cambridge for King's College chapel alone; a high point of Gothic architecture, with spectacular fan-vaulting where the Rubens masterpiece *Adoration of the Magi* hangs above the altar. Who knows, you may be lucky enough to hear the world-famous choir. Visit **Magdalene** for the celebrated Pepys Library (Pepys was an undergrad at Magdalene) complete with his diary. One of the loveliest walks in Britain is along the Backs, where the college lawns meet the river Cam. To get the real Merchant-Ivory Cambridge experience, hire a punt along here for an hour or so. The jewel of Cambridge's gardens is the stone-walled **Fellow's Garden** of Clare College. Cambridge has a wealth of museums and galleries, covering a wide range of interests. **The Corn Exchange**, ☎ (01223) 357851, **The Junction** ☎ (01223) 412600, and other venues provide programmes covering all aspects of entertainment. The **Cambridge Folk Festival** is held on the last weekend in July. For further details contact Tourist Information on ☎ (01223) 322640.

ART AND MUSEUMS

FITZWILLIAM MUSEUM
Trumpington St, CB2 1RB
☎ (01223) 332900
Beautifully displayed prize collection of Renaissance, Dutch and English Old Masters, along with some some Impressionists. There are also illuminated manuscripts, antiques, arms and armour, European and Oriental porcelain, sculpture and some Greek and Roman antiquities.

HOTELS

THE GARDEN HOUSE HOTEL
Granta Place, Mill Ln, CB2 1RT
☎ (01223) 259988
Set in peaceful riverside gardens, the hotel is renowned for its high standard of facilities and attentive service, and boasts a first-class restaurant, **Le Jardin**, together with a riverside lounge and cocktail bar which offer elegant surroundings in which to relax.

THE UNIVERSITY ARMS
Regent St, CB2 1AD
☎ (01223) 351241
Built as a coaching inn in 1834, the recently refurbished University Arms still maintains its Edwardian elegance. The hotel overlooks Parker's Piece, a 25-acre park where cricket is played in summer. You can have tea in the unique **Octagon Lounge**, while good food is served in the majestic oak-panelled restaurant with its fine stained glass windows.

RESTAURANTS

MIDSUMMER HOUSE
Midsummer Common, CB4 1HA
☎ (01223) 369299
Scottish lobster and scallops, or ginger soufflé are just two of chef Jonathan Bishop's most tempting dishes. Though his restaurant, set in a refurbished Victorian house, may not be quite within a student budget, it's worth it if you can afford it. Open for lunch and dinner Tues–Fri, for dinner Sat and lunch Sun.

London

ART AND MUSEUMS

BRITISH MUSEUM
Great Russell St, WC1
☎ (0171) 636 1555
One of the world's greatest and oldest museums contains ancient, medieval and Renaissance works. Plus there are Japanese galleries; well-preserved Egyptian mummies, the even better-preserved 2,200-year-old Lindow Man, and a fine Oriental collection. Major galleries for exhibiting the long-hidden North American collections are due to open shortly.

COURTAULD INSTITUTE GALLERIES
Somerset House, Strand, WC2
☎ (0171) 872 0220
Sir William Chambers' great neo-classical Thames-side building, built between 1775 and 1780, is a fitting home for the important collections of Impressionism and Post-Impressionism it contains including the Princess Gate collection of Flemish and Italian Old Masters. "*It has a very good collection but its exhibiting space is*

minute" – BRIAN SEWELL. The gallery rotates its thousands of prints, watercolours and drawings. Good café and bookshop.

DULWICH PICTURE GALLERY

COLLEGE RD, SE21
☎ (0181) 693 5254
Built by SIR JOHN SOANE, it's England's oldest public art gallery, hosting an extensive collection of 17C and 18C Old Masters. Surrounded by parks and fields, it retains the rural atmosphere that made it so popular with 19C visitors.

••••••••••••••••••••••••••••••••••

"LONDON'S MOST PERFECT GALLERY" – **THE GUARDIAN** ON THE *DULWICH PICTURE GALLERY*

••••••••••••••••••••••••••••••••••

IMPERIAL WAR MUSEUM

LAMBETH RD, SE1
☎ (0171) 416 5000
One of London's most lively and dynamic museums. Besides the standard collection of real war planes, arms, paintings and memorabilia, the latest interactive technology allows you to see, smell and hear the trenches and the Blitz. Much is aimed at children, including a wonderful exhibition called "Biggles, the True Story". On a more sober note, there's a gallery devoted to the liberation of Belsen. *"An incomparable record of Man's destructive ingenuity. Helpful, knowledgeable staff"* – EDWARD THORPE.

MUSEUM OF THE MOVING IMAGE

SOUTH BANK CENTRE, SE1
☎ (0171) 401 2636
"The best movie museum in the world and also the most interactive" – Sheridan Morley. No less than 40 bright and exciting exhibition areas depict the history of the moving image, from ancient Chinese shadow puppets to film, video, satellite and hologram technology, while giving you the opportunity to star alongside Superman, Dr Who and Frankenstein – perfect for children. Next door, the **NATIONAL FILM THEATRE**, ☎ (0171) 928 3232, hosts the London Film Festival every Nov, when 150 films are shown in venues around the capital.

NATIONAL GALLERY

TRAFALGAR SQUARE, WC2
☎ (0171) 839 3321
London's grandest old art institution and probably its most popular. There are collections from all the European schools, and the Sainsbury Wing contains an extensive early Renaissance collection – which includes some of the gallery's oldest and most fragile works. HILARY RUBINSTEIN describes it as *"an awesome setting for great art – and the Miró on the first floor is a technological marvel too"*. The National is also acclaimed for its meticulous and sympathetic picture-hanging, which is always done chronologically. Good brasserie with excellent views of Trafalgar Square. *"In principle, I prefer the smaller museums, like the Wallace or the Courtauld, but if a choice is necessary one must obviously make a 'Desert Island selection' and opt for the one with most of one's personal treasures"*– CLAUS VON BULOW.

NATIONAL MARITIME MUSEUM

ROMNEY ROAD, GREENWICH, SE10
☎ (0181) 858 4422
A treasure house containing paintings, models, maps, globes, sextants, uniforms, and relics of old sea dogs, which all chart Britain's illustrious maritime heritage. Highlights include Britain's biggest refracting telescope and Nelson's blood-stained uniform from the Battle of Trafalgar. Recommended by SIR JOHN HARVEY-JONES.

NATIONAL PORTRAIT GALLERY

TRAFALGAR SQUARE, WC2
☎ (0171) 306 0055
The world's first purpose-built gallery, depicting Britain's history through the portraits of its leading figures. The NPG constantly commissions new works of current notables, and there are often exciting temporary exhibitions to see. Beautifully decorated, with an exhibition space for 20C portraits and a video and photographic gallery. The best place to stock up on postcards.

NATURAL HISTORY MUSEUM

CROMWELL RD, SW7
☎ (0171) 938 9123
The museum is split into the Life Gallery, where you can walk among the huge dinosaur skeletons and life-sized blue whales; and the Earth Gallery, where you learn about natural resources, including fossils and minerals, and see the brilliant collection of gems. Very popular with children.

THE ROYAL ACADEMY OF ARTS

BURLINGTON HOUSE, PICCADILLY, W1
☎ (0171) 439 7438
Exhibitions are varied and carefully put together such as "American Art in the 20th Century" and "Goya: Truth and Fantasy". The

PARKS AND GARDENS

With more than 80 gardens within 10 miles of the city centre, fresh air is never too far away. **Hyde Park**, ☎ (0171) 298 2100, is London's best and most interesting park. From the waters of the Serpentine, where you can hire a rowing boat or pedalo and where London's foolhardy actually swim, to the immaculately maintained and ever-flowering **Flower Walk** behind the Albert Memorial, to the fascinating **Serpentine Gallery**. Adjacent is the more formal Kensington Gardens, ☎ (0171) 298 2100, which, of course, houses **Kensington Palace** – home to the Princess of Wales and several other royals. Attached to the Palace is **The Orangery**, ☎ (0171) 937 9561, where you can reward yourself after a long walk or a strenuous roller-blade with a hearty afternoon tea. Richmond Park, ☎ (0181) 948 3209, and Hampstead Heath, ☎ (0181) 455 5183, are London's wildest (Richmond is also London's largest), offering glimpses of deer and foxes as well as spectacular views of the city. The **Royal Botanic Gardens**, Kew Rd, Richmond, ☎ (0181) 940 1171, features 300 acres of superb botanical gardens and a magnificent curved glass Palm House and other hothouses containing rare tropical plants. But if you are in the centre of the city and don't want to stray too far from the shops, visit **St James's Park**, ☎ (0171) 930 1793, or **Green Park**, next door. St James's has a very Victorian feel, with a bandstand, promenades and weeping willows. Not too far from the centre you'll find one of London's least touristy parks – **Holland Park**, ☎ (0171) 602 9483, which includes 55 acres of themed gardens, woodland and secluded lawns where peacocks wander about freely.

Summer Exhibition (mid-June to mid-Aug) is more socially than artistically challenging.

SOANE MUSEUM

13 Lincoln's Inn Fields, WC2
☎ (0171) 430 0175
An eccentric 1813 house, designed and lived in by architect and collector Sir John Soane, is as he left it. With 30,000 architectural drawings, and 10,000 books not forgetting the violent yellow drawing room, it provides a fascinating and very personal insight into the life of a London gentleman in the early 19C. Admired by Stephen Bayley for its *"unmatchable curiosity"*.

TATE GALLERY

Millbank, SW1
☎ (0171) 887 8000
Widely publicized for its piles of bricks and double-decker buses passing as works of art, people tend to forget that the Tate houses some first-rate national collections of British and international modern art. Basement restaurant graced by beautiful Rex Whistler murals and a good wine list is currently on the

way up, with hipper, better cooking.

VICTORIA & ALBERT MUSEUM

South Kensington, SW7
☎ (0171) 938 8500
While it is best known for its ceramics, glass, textiles and costumes dating from the Middle Ages, it also contains some wonderful paintings (more than the National Gallery), prints, drawings and sculpture. Genuinely interesting giftshop – worth a visit in its own right.

WALLACE COLLECTION

Hertford House, Manchester Square, W1
☎ (0171) 935 0687
A genteel collection set in the sumptuous interiors of Hertford House. On display are Old Masters in abundant supply, the finest collection of arms and armour outside The Tower of London, 18C French paintings, furniture and porcelain, and the 1740 Astronomical Clock, which tells the time anywhere in the northern hemisphere, plus the date, month and sign of the zodiac.

ARTS CENTRES

BARBICAN

BARBICAN CENTRE, EC2

☎ (0171) 638 8891

The architecture may be hideous, but aesthetics aside, the Barbican provides the ROYAL SHAKESPEARE COMPANY with a spacious London home. Shakespeare and other classics are performed in the main theatre, and slightly more avant-garde productions in the Pit. The LONDON SYMPHONY ORCHESTRA regularly performs in the centre's concert hall under the dynamic direction of Michael Tilson Thomas. There are also two cinemas, a public library and a space for exhibitions.

BALLET

ROYAL BALLET COMPANY

ROYAL OPERA HOUSE, COVENT GARDEN, WC2

☎ (0171) 304 4000

The brainchild of Dame Ninette de Valois, the Royal Ballet Company was initially nurtured by the legendary choreographer Sir Frederick Ashton, who introduced its lyrical, dramatic and, some say, distinctively English style. Under the directorship of Sir Anthony Dowell for the last ten years, its recent stars have been the envy of the rest of the ballet world – the most important being Irek Mukhamedov, ex-leader of the Bolshoi, the exquisite Darcey Bussell and the lithe-bodied Sylvie Guillem who defected to the Royal Ballet from Paris. The company shares its home with the ROYAL OPERA (see Music), offering lavish productions throughout the year.

BARS AND CAFES

BAR ITALIA

22 FRITH ST, W1

☎ (0171) 437 4520

At night London tends to die an early death: by 11.30 the pubs are shut and restaurants are grinding to a halt, unless, that is, you're in Soho. Of all its streets, Frith Street is the liveliest – largely thanks to Bar Italia. Since 1949 it has been the place to go for a late-night coffee. Open 24 hours at weekends.

CAFFE E NERO

43 FRITH ST, W1, (AND OTHER BRANCHES)

☎ (0171) 287 3397

The frenetic coffee bar where media types, visiting Italians and other fashion-conscious young things go for good coffee, gutsy sandwiches and very convincing pastries.

FREUD'S

198 SHAFTESBURY AVE, WC1

☎ (0171) 240 9933

Arty basement café, which holds its own exhibitions; popular with painters, designers and photographers.

MILDRED'S

58 GREEK ST, W1

☎ (0171) 494 1634

Hang-out for artists and filmies such as BOY GEORGE and SPIKE LEE, who come for the fine vegetarian food washed down with organic wine.

PRESTO

4–6 OLD COMPTON ST, W1

☎ (0171) 437 4006

• •

ENCORE There is still nothing quite like driving down to Chiswick or Richmond on a warm summer evening to have a quick pint beside the Thames to remind you of what London is genuinely about. And while many pubs are still loved for their 'olde worlde' feel, the face of the traditional London pub has changed over the past few years. Many have adapted to the 1990s attracting a younger clientele by providing more seating, cleaner decor and cheery young staff – rather than the brassy middle-aged barmaid. In Chelsea there are pubs which fall into both camps. **The Phene Arms**, 9 Phene St, ☎ (0171) 352 8391, is a model little town pub, tucked away on a quiet side street in the heart of Chelsea – idyllic on long summer evenings when you can sit outside in the garden with your pint of Pimms. For something a little more upbeat however you could try the **Goat in Boots**, 333 Fulham Road, SW10 ☎ (0171) 352 1384 or the fresh pine-dominated **Cooper's Arms**, 87 Flood St, SW3 ☎ (0171) 376 3120 . . . . ♣

STAR BARS In recent years a new breed of watering hole has sprung up, steering Londoners towards the more comfortable and more civilized European-style bar, many of which do a convincing line in Mediterranean-inspired bar food. For something ultra-cool, **Beach Blanket Babylon**, 45 Ledbury Rd, W11, ☎ (0171) 229 2907, is the place. Here you'll not only be surrounded by Notting Hill trendies, but rich Gaudíesque decor and a good small restaurant downstairs serving dinner in the evening, while you can eat lunch in the bar. **Mwah Mwah Bar**, 241 Fulham Rd, SW3, ☎ (0171) 823 3079, is open throughout the day, offering cocktails, aperitifs and coffee as well as light lunchtime snacks. A bit further up the road, on the corner of Fulham Rd at 4 Sydney St, you'll find **R-Bar** ☎ (0171) 352 3433 – popular with sophisticates and bankers, who come for the fabulous cocktails and general bonhomie of Australian owner Will Ricker. Upstairs there's a restaurant, which belongs to the same establishment. **Bar Central** has two branches: one at 131 Waterloo Rd, SE1, ☎ (0171) 928 5086, and one on Kings Rd. Blue and white are the definitive colours, while each also has the understated look of a New York warehouse. You can eat here too. For a bar on a truly vast scale, go to the **Atlantic Bar & Grill**, 20 Glasshouse St, W1, ☎ (0171) 734 4888. If you can get past the slightly aggressive doormen and women, you go downstairs into a very comfortable and spacious complex. As well as **Dick's** cocktail bar, there's a colossal Art Deco-style bar and restaurant which looks like the sort of American drinking and gambling halls used during Prohibition.

Great atmosphere and surprisingly good Italian food, popular with NIGEL BENN and RIK MAYALL.

RIKI-TIK

23–24 BATEMAN STREET, W1
☎ (0171) 437 1977
Two-levelled bar full of ultimately cool types, great flavoured vodkas (white Toblerone, peppermint cream).

HOTELS

London's grandes dames

With so many large, grand old hotels, location, location, location is often the way people make their choice.

THE BERKELEY

WILTON PLACE, SW1
☎ (0171) 235 6000
Grand, a little dull but discreet like a club, which is why it is so popular with visiting roy-

alty. The top-floor health suite with its rooftop swimming pool has great views over Hyde Park. While on the ground floor there's an exclusive cinema – THE MINEMA – and VONG (see Restaurants), an exquisite new Thai restaurant. Ideally located for shopping at Harrods and Harvey Nichols.

CLARIDGES

BROOK ST, W1
☎ (0171) 629 8860
Considered one of the world's great hotels, it's clearly favoured by royalty and visiting heads of state. The Art Deco interior, the slightly chaotic Hungarian Quartet who play at tea and at cocktails and the handsomely liveried staff make the whole Claridges experience quite unique. Perfectly located for shopping in the boutiques of Bond St and South Molton St.

THE CONNAUGHT

16 CARLOS PLACE, W1
☎ (0171) 499 7070
The standard bearer for old-world dignity and

charm. It might feel a touch sombre, but it's quiet and luxurious and has the most discreet staff in London. Excellent Grill and Restaurant (see Restaurants). Well situated for Annabel's, the American Embassy and Nicky Clarke.

THE DORCHESTER

PARK LANE, W1
☎ (0171) 629 8888
The 6,000 books of gold leaf used during the Dorchester's recent refurbishment have continued to attract visiting film and pop stars on international publicity pushes. The ORIENTAL RESTAURANT is among the most refined Chinese eateries in London. Health freaks will be lured by the DORCHESTER SPA and the hotel is perfectly located for walks in Hyde Park.

FOUR SEASONS INN ON THE PARK

HAMILTON PLACE, PARK LANE, W1
☎ (0171) 499 0888
The monolithic and rather bland exterior belies the typically grand Four Seasons' interior. Immaculate accommodation and seamless service have made this the most popular hotel in London. The food in the restaurant is very good, very French and very rich.

THE HYDE PARK

66 KNIGHTSBRIDGE, SW1
☎ (0171) 235 2000
Edwardian splendour with late 20C comforts. Great public areas, including the restaurant, which has spectacular views overlooking Hyde Park – as do most of the bedrooms. A huge bar is well-positioned for Marco Pierre White's award-winning THE RESTAURANT (see Restaurants) where you can break the bank while eating what is undoubtedly some of the best food in London.

THE LANESBOROUGH

1 LANESBOROUGH PLACE, SW1
☎ (0171) 259 5599
The Lanesborough has settled down nicely after its multi-million pound conversion from hospital to hotel although some might find the wood-panelled rooms a little heavy. However, the service, which includes a personal butler to run your bath and unpack your bags, does have its appeal. Bullet-proof glass, personal safes and a clutch of security cameras ensure the safety of guests such as RACQUEL WELCH. THE CONSERVATORY is worth a visit for family Sunday brunch. Perfect location for the embassies of Belgrave Square.

THE RITZ

PICCADILLY, W1
☎ (0171) 493 8181
The Ritz was the result of César Ritz's 1906 intention to create "the most fashionable hotel in the most fashionable city in the world". In the past it has pleased a disparate group of guests, ranging from the DUKE AND DUCHESS OF WINDSOR to ANDY WARHOL. New owners, the reclusive Barclay brothers, are restoring it to its original Empire glamour. Tea at the Ritz remains an institution. Good location for the galleries of Dover St and Albemarle St as well as the gentleman's outfitters of Jermyn St.

THE SAVOY

1 SAVOY HILL, WC2
☎ (0171) 836 4343
Though Edwardian in style and atmosphere, the Savoy is fully up-to-date, with a pleasant spa and very attentive 1990s service. From the RIVER RESTAURANT and the RIVER SUITE the views over the Embankment Gardens and the Thames are unparalleled. Unusually for London, where locals tend to stay away from hotels, Londoners regularly flock to the AMERICAN BAR and the yew-panelled SAVOY GRILL – very popular with besuited heavyweights including SIR DAVID FROST, RUPERT MURDOCH, MICHAEL PARKINSON and DAME DIANA RIGG, who all come for the rare treat of good, traditional English cooking. Perfectly located for Whitehall, the City or the Royal Opera House.

Townhouse hotels

THE BEAUFORT

38 BEAUFORT GDNS, SW3
☎ (0171) 584 5252
Elegant 5-storey townhouse within striking distance of the South Kensington museums and shopping in Knightsbridge. Guests have their own front-door key and there's none of this mini-bar nonsense: you can help yourself to champagne from the well-stocked, complimentary bar or the brandy provided in your room.

BLAKE'S

33 ROLAND GARDENS, SW7
☎ (0171) 370 6701
A rather Bohemian "boutique hotel", converted from a late-19C building. The glittering array of haute-couture rooms have been tailored by designer Anouska Hempel including, for example, Empress Josephine's day bedroom. Celebrated for its dark, sultry, though notoriously expensive, bar and restaurant.

CAPITAL HOTEL

22 BASIL ST, SW3

☎ (0171) 589 5171

A grand hotel in miniature with a home-from-home atmosphere, thanks to the warm interior designed by Nina Campbell. Its greatest lure though is probably the finely wrought food of Philip Britten (ex Chez Nico) in the Michelin-starred restaurant.

11 CADOGAN GARDENS

11 CADOGAN GARDENS, SLOANE SQUARE, SW3

☎ (0171) 730 3426

One of London's most discreet hotels, very cunningly disguised as a townhouse, which provides a haven for RICHARD GERE, HELENA CHRISTENSEN and GENE WILDER whenever they're in town. Established in 1949 by a Swiss hotelier, Charles Reider, the hotel is clubbish rather than grand and attracts a faithful clientele of models, pop stars, diplomats and businessmen. There's a health club in the basement.

THE GORE

189 QUEEN'S GATE, SW7

☎ (0171) 584 6601

Idiosyncratic, though rather appealing, younger sister of Hazlitt's (see entry) set in a narrow, labyrinthine building near Kensington Gardens. Full of quirky antiques and *objets d'art*. The Tudor Suite has its own minstrel gallery and a mammoth four-poster bed. It also houses two good restaurants – **DOWNSTAIRS AT 190** and **BISTROT 190**.

HALCYON

81 HOLLAND PARK, W11

☎ (0171) 727 7288

A large, old Holland Park house that has been painted pink and turned into one of London's trendiest hotels attracting the likes of JACK NICHOLSON, LAUREN BACALL and sackloads of rock stars. Downstairs you'll find locals having dinner in the restaurant or drinking champagne cocktails in the bar. Guests can use the Vanderbilt tennis club down the road.

THE HALKIN HOTEL

5 HALKIN ST, SW1

☎ (0171) 333 1000

Popular with glossy European and Asian visitors. Sleek, hard-edged minimalist decor, designed by Emporio Armani's creators, Lorenzo Carmellini and Rocco Magnoli. Armani designed the staff uniforms. Like the decor, the designer food in the restaurant is minimalist – don't go if you're feeling ravenous.

HAZLITT'S

6 FRITH ST, W1

☎ (0171) 434 1771

With virtually all its business derived from the film, TV, fashion and music industries, Hazlitt's is invariably hip. The 18C- and 19C-style bedrooms are light and airy, providing an oasis in the frenetic heart of Soho for SUZANNE VEGA, JULIETTE BINOCHE and ISABELLA ROSSELLINI.

THE PELHAM

15 CROMWELL PLACE, SW7

☎ (0171) 589 8288

The flagship of Tim and Kit Kemp's three London hotels. Exceptionally cosy and located 200 yards from the Natural History Museum. The beds are enormous and the period decor very warm and welcoming.

THE PORTOBELLO HOTEL

22 STANLEY GDNS, W11

☎ (0171) 727 2777

Eccentric and informal, attracting familiar faces from the worlds of film, fashion and, in particular, music. VAN MORRISON and CINDY CRAWFORD are regulars. A variety of rooms range from the rather cramped "ship's cabins" to enormous suites with Victorian baths.

THE STAFFORD

ST JAMES'S PLACE, W1

☎ (0171) 493 0111

A hidden treasure that is quite as discreet and charming as ever after its recent renovation. The loyal staff of old are all there including the hotelier's hotelier, Terry Holmes, back in charge after a brief spell at the Ritz. The attractive terrace bar in the cobbled mews is a delight.

22 JERMYN STREET

ST JAMES'S, SW1

☎ (0171) 734 2353

The perfect substitute for having your own flat in St James's – Henry and Suzanne Togna run their hotel along very personal lines. Stock up on shirts and ties from the world-famous gentlemen's outfitters along the street. "*Very comfortable suites*", according to PAUL HENDERSON.

MUSIC

ENGLISH NATIONAL OPERA

LONDON COLISEUM, ST MARTIN'S LANE, WC2

☎ (0171) 836 3161

The company that has brought opera to the people, the ENO continues to uphold its reputation for imaginative and innovative works sung in English. Currently under the general direction of Dennis Marks and the baton of young conductor Sian Edwards.

HENRY WOOD PROMENADE CONCERTS

ROYAL ALBERT HALL, KENSINGTON GORE, SW7

☎ (0171) 589 8212

Since 1898, the Proms (July–Sept) have made top-quality classical concerts available to all, with 67 concerts in 58 days. The Last Night, a beloved, if slightly silly, British tradition, sees the masses swaying in patriotic frenzy to the emotive strains of "Rule Britannia" and "Land of Hope and Glory".

ROYAL FESTIVAL HALL

SOUTH BANK CENTRE, SE1

☎ (0171) 928 3002

Home of the London Philharmonic. Together with the **PURCELL ROOM** and the QUEEN ELIZABETH HALL, it presents more live music than anywhere else in the world.

ROYAL OPERA HOUSE

COVENT GARDEN, WC2

☎ (0171) 304 4000

Prestigious and increasingly expensive (though following recent cash injections from the National Lottery fund, hopefully prices will go down and improvements are about to be made), Covent Garden is home to the **ROYAL OPERA** and the **ROYAL BALLET** (see Ballet).

WIGMORE HALL

36 WIGMORE ST, W1

☎ (0171) 935 2141

Highly acclaimed for its atmosphere as much as for its acoustics, the Wigmore Hall continues to attract top-class artists and musical events.

RESTAURANTS

SEE ALSO HOTELS.

Best new restaurants

COAST

26B ALBEMARLE ST, W1

☎ (0171) 495 5999

Not everyone goes for the 1950s futurist style of Oliver "The Atlantic" Peyton's most recent venture. However, Stephen Terry, formerly of The Canteen, creates food that will soon make you forget that you're sitting in what still resembles a car showroom. The menu has a strong West Coast feel. With all the windows, it's better to be able to look out at lunchtime than be looked in upon at dinner. SIMON and YASMIN LE BON go there.

MEZZO

100 WARDOUR ST, W1

☎ (0171) 314 4000

Terence Conran's latest 700-seater may feel like a hip aircraft hangar or even a factory, but the food doesn't seem to suffer in Europe's largest restaurant. The menu is modern and international and caters for most tastes including those of MELANIE GRIFFITH, ANTONIO BANDERAS and RICHARD E GRANT. The service, however, is swift – each dinner sitting is carefully timed and then you'll be eased out – so it's not the ideal choice if you want a long, lingering evening.

NICOLE'S

158 NEW BOND ST, W1

☎ (0171) 499 8408

The ultimate for ladies who lunch is set in the basement of Nicole Farhi's eponymous store, ideally located for all the best shops in Bond St and Piccadilly. Decor is clean and chic. Head chef Annie Wayte has made quite an impression with her modern British and Mediterranean menu and her grilled fish, poultry and salads.

L'ODEON

65 REGENT ST, W1

☎ (0171) 287 1400

L'Odeon enjoys one of the city's most happening locations overlooking the bright lights of Piccadilly Circus at the bottom of Regent St. The slick and brightly coloured interior, with its huge bar, has provided Bruno Loubet (of BISTRO BRUNO fame, 63 Frith St, ☎ (0171) 734 4545) with his most conspicuous venture to date. An interesting menu, with lots of excellent offal dishes, is both adventurous and unusual.

OLIVETO

49 ELIZABETH ST, SW1

☎ (0171) 730 0074

Young, fun Italian specializing in pizza and appealing to everyone from actors and pop stars in the evening to young families at Sat lunchtime.

VONG

WILTON PLACE, SW1

☎ (0171) 235 1010

At Vong – sister of the acclaimed restaurant of the same name in New York – the chef combines the freshest and best Southeast Asian

SIR TERENCE CONRAN'S TIPS ON EATING WELL AROUND THE WORLD

In London and other major cities around the world, the best restaurants tend to be the busiest and if you want to secure a table at one of these you have to book well ahead. If you haven't, you'll need to resort to rather more desperate measures . . . I'd suggest either pretending to be a food writer when you phone to make the reservation or marrying into the aristocracy (which always helps). Or, if neither of these appears to work, just turn up at the restaurant on the night you wish to eat there and ask, in the friendliest manner, of course, whether there are any "no shows". When you're at home or abroad, there are several tell-tale signs that apply to all good eateries. The menu should be shortish, using fresh, local produce. Unfeasibly long menus indicate that everything comes out of the freezer and goes straight into the microwave. I once had the misfortune to eat at a terribly proper AA-recommended hotel in Devonshire, with a menu longer than my arm. I was served a seven-course meal, each course obviously straight from the deep-freeze and each one inedible – the wine, I swear, was vinegar. Another indication of a good restaurant, particularly when you're abroad, is to see whether the locals eat there. If a restaurant is swarming with tourists, then there's a strong chance that the food will be overpriced and not terribly good. The smell should indicate the quality of the food; if you can smell good stock emanating from the kitchen door, that is a good sign. Every restaurant should be spotlessly clean and tidy, from the menu to the tablecloths to the flower arrangements. All of these demonstrate how much the management cares about its establishment. But even if all of the above apply, never eat at a restaurant if you don't like its atmosphere.

ingredients with French techniques to create the most mouthwatering concoctions. GIORGIO ARMANI, ERIC CLAPTON, LUC BESSON and CATHERINE DENEUVE have feasted here.

ZAFFERANO
15 LOWNDES ST, SW1
☎ (0171) 235 5800
MARCO PIERRE WHITE eats here, which has to be a good sign, as do BARONESS THATCHER and family, JOAN COLLINS and MICHAEL CAINE. The decor is decidedly subtle and so is the exquisitely light, modern Italian food created by Giorgio Locatelli.

Heavyweights

AUBERGINE
11 PARK WALK, SW10
☎ (0171) 352 3449
The standards keep getting higher and higher (as do the prices) and Aubergine is now undoubtedly one of London's top five restaurants. Chef Gordon Ramsay, winner of a well-deserved Michelin star last year, produces classically based French cooking full of the most wonderful flavours. BRYAN FERRY, ROBERT DE NIRO and MICHAEL CAINE come here. French service can be a little pompous. "*Great restaurants often score more on starters and desserts than on the main dishes. Aubergine, by contrast, provides faultless thrilling gastronomy, from amuse-gueules to petits fours*" – HILARY RUBINSTEIN.

CHEZ NICO AT 90 PARK LANE
90 PARK LANE, W1
☎ (0171) 409 1290
Classic French *haut bourgeois* cuisine with a hint of English, executed by perfectionist Nico Ladenis. Recent specialities from Nico include risotto à la crème de cèpes; and lobster with leeks.

THE CONNAUGHT
IN THE CONNAUGHT (SEE HOTELS)
☎ (0171) 499 7070
Cognoscenti are divided over the competing charms of the Grill, which looks like a restaurant, and the Restaurant, with looks like a grill, but the menus are the same in both. Chef Michel Bourdin turns out faultless, perhaps slightly old-fashioned French renditions of English classics and Connaught specialities, all served with smooth and discreet efficiency. "*They can replace the tablecloths in the course of a meal without the diners noticing*" – STEPHEN BAYLEY. Good-value set lunch Mon–Fri. The Restaurant is one of London's leading places for power-breakfasting.

LE GAVROCHE
43 UPPER BROOK ST, W1
☎ (0171) 408 0881
Michel Roux, Jr, who succeeded his father, Albert, has dragged Le Gavroche – one of London's most respected restaurants – from the 1980s very firmly into the 1990s. His classically inspired slightly bourgeois French food is lighter and much more in tune with modern tastes.

LEITH'S
92 KENSINGTON PARK RD, W11
☎ (0171) 229 4481
Leith's is back at the top of modern British cuisine. Alex Floyd (still in his 20s) has now been head chef of this Notting Hill gastrodome for five years and is still producing careful and sophisticated dishes.

LE PONT DE LA TOUR
36D SHAD THAMES, BUTLER'S WHARF, SE1
☎ (0171) 403 8403
Part of the Conran empire, providing the City and the Docklands with its best food in its most elegant restaurant. In summer the Thames-side seats are worth fighting for, while night-time views of Tower Bridge floodlit are a veritable treat too. JOAN COLLINS, SEAN CONNERY, ANNIE LENNOX and ROWAN ATKINSON all come here.

THE RESTAURANT (MARCO PIERRE WHITE)
HYDE PARK HOTEL, KNIGHTSBRIDGE, SW1
☎ (0171) 259 5380
It might be on the expensive side – but "*it's hard to beat Marco Pierre White,*" says NED SHERRIN, and his undoubted genius was made clear last year when he became the youngest ever three-star Michelin chef. But the quality and presentation of the food are what really distinguish The Restaurant.

RIVER CAFE
THAMES WHARF, RAINVILLE RD, W6
☎ (0171) 381 8824
Rustic non-pasta-based Italian food cooked with tremendous finesse, is what makes many consider the River Café to be the best Italian in town. Particularly good fish, seafood and Italian salads. Nothing fancy, but absolute devotion to the best ingredients and the sure palates of cooks Rose Gray and Ruth Rogers. Views over the Thames and a good supply of Italian wines.

LES SAVEURS
37A CURZON ST, W1
☎ (0171) 491 8919
Chef Joel Antunes's cooking is renowned as some of the most brilliant and most original in London. The staunchly French fare is influenced by Antunes's stint as head chef at the Oriental hotel in Bangkok. Weird, wonderful and immaculately presented creations include raviolis of langoustine; and roast sea-bass with sweet red pepper and apricot. Lunchtime set menu under £20 is well worthwhile.

LA TANTE CLAIRE
68 ROYAL HOSPITAL RD, SW3
☎ (0171) 352 6045
London's best French restaurant is overseen by chef Pierre Koffmann, whose inspiration comes from the flavours of southwest France. The lunch menu is amazingly good value.

Fashion-conscious

⑥ THE CANTEEN
UNIT 4G HARBOUR YARD, CHELSEA HARBOUR, SW10
☎ (0171) 351 7330
Large and smart brasserie owned by Michael Caine and cooked by chef Tim Powell. Big views of Chelsea Harbour and impeccable service. "Canteen" used to mean gambling house, hence the card-theme decor but this good value food doesn't break the bank. "*A nice place in a yuppie hell-hole*" – JONATHAN MEADES.

LE CAPRICE
ARLINGTON HOUSE, ARLINGTON ST, SW1
☎ (0171) 629 2239
The Ivy's sister restaurant, where the PRINCESS OF WALES, GEORGE MICHAEL, MICHAEL WINNER, SIR HAROLD PINTER and LADY ANTO-

NIA FRASER sit among the striking black-and-white decor, and David Bailey's photographs. Tim Hughes's simple but delicious fare includes fabulous fish cakes, uncomplicated salads and the best pommes frites outside France – and according to JEFFREY ARCHER it's the best restaurant in England.

DAPHNE'S

112 DRAYCOTT AVE, SW3
☎ (0171) 589 4257

Bursting at the seams with all of London's latest stars and flash-in-the-pans: everyone is vying for attention at Mogens Tholstrup's trendier-than-thou restaurant. There are so many famous people that even ELIZABETH HURLEY has been known to make a din, scraping her chair backwards and forwards, to get her fair share of the limelight. But the light, Italian food is good and there's a garden/conservatory at the back which is particularly pleasant in summer.

• •

"EXCELLENT FOOD, FROM

CAVIARE TO COD AND CHIPS"

– EDWARD THORPE

ON *THE IVY*

• •

THE IVY

1 WEST ST, WC2
☎ (0171) 836 4751

Unless you're SIR TERENCE CONRAN, JEFFREY ARCHER, STEPHEN FRY, MICHAEL WINNER or VIVIENNE WESTWOOD or have just brought out a blockbusting film/novel/TV show, it's impossibly difficult to secure a table here. If you do get in, however, you must try one of Des McDonald's wonderful salads. Service is

impeccable and the decor clubby with lots of green leather upholstery, stained glass and oak panels. *"The best theatre restaurant in the world for late-night star cuisine and loving attention"* – SHERIDAN MORLEY.

QUAGLINO'S

16 BURY ST, SW1
☎ (0171) 839 2566

No London restaurant has generated more controversy than Sir Terence Conran's homage to the great brasseries of Paris. The kitchen expertly turns out huge quantities of mostly well-cooked and well-priced modern food. Everyone and anyone goes there from PRINCESS DIANA, PRINCESS MARGARET, VISCOUNT LINLEY and the DUCHESS OF YORK to your average punter on a quick visit to the West End.

Fun and trendy

L'ALTRO

210 KENSINGTON PARK RD, W11
☎ (0171) 792 1066

Slick, small and young, with a crumbling Italianate setting. Wonderful antipasti and pasta. A hang-out for people from the pop and TV worlds including BRYAN FERRY and ELVIS COSTELLO.

✪ THE COW

89 WESTBOURNE PARK RD, W11
☎ (0171) 221 0021

Tom Conran's stylish pub conversion has certainly captured the imagination of the Notting Hill trendies. The restaurant upstairs serves French and English country food while downstairs Conran (who is also the chef) specializes in easy-priced seafood – which includes the great-value Cow Special: one pint of draught Guinness washed down with half a dozen oysters.

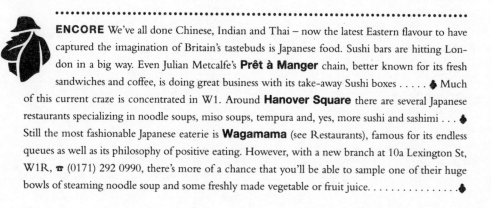

ENCORE We've all done Chinese, Indian and Thai – now the latest Eastern flavour to have captured the imagination of Britain's tastebuds is Japanese food. Sushi bars are hitting London in a big way. Even Julian Metcalfe's **Pret à Manger** chain, better known for its fresh sandwiches and coffee, is doing great business with its take-away Sushi boxes . . . . . ♠ Much of this current craze is concentrated in W1. Around **Hanover Square** there are several Japanese restaurants specializing in noodle soups, miso soups, tempura and, yes, more sushi and sashimi . . . ♠ Still the most fashionable Japanese eaterie is **Wagamama** (see Restaurants), famous for its endless queues as well as its philosophy of positive eating. However, with a new branch at 10a Lexington St, W1R, ☎ (0171) 292 0990, there's more of a chance that you'll be able to sample one of their huge bowls of steaming noodle soup and some freshly made vegetable or fruit juice. . . . . ♠

LOYD GROSSMAN ON THE LONDON RESTAURANT SCENE

For many years the London restaurant scene was celebrated for the glacial pace of its evolution. The fickleness of New Yorkers and Parisians, with their endless search for novel and fashionable restaurants, contrasted sharply with the loyalty and conservatism of London's diners. The great restaurant occasion of 80s London was the opening, and after a slow start the flourishing, of **Le Caprice**, which remains as we reach the second half of the 90s London's see-and-be-seen restaurant *par excellence*. But in spite of Le Caprice's unshakeable eminence, the London restaurant scene has been transformed almost beyond recognition in the four years since Terence Conran opened **Quaglino's**. The huge, high-design and open-late-into-the-night Quaglino's ushered in an era of large-scale, supposedly more democratic dining in London. A herd of mega restaurants have followed, some from Conran's stud – **Mezzo** and next year's **Bluebird Garage** – and others like **L'Odéon** and **The Avenue** from newly ambitious chefs and entrepreneurs. Paradoxically, the giant new restaurants, for the time being at least, are as difficult to get into as their more élite predecessors, leading some people to ask where all the new customers are coming from. In the shadow of the mammoths, smaller predators have flourished too: even a casual observer will have noticed that London restaurant sites are increasingly filled by chains like **Café Rouge** or the many restaurants (eg **Dell' Ugo, Zoe, The Atrium**) associated with chef/tycoon Anthony Worrall Thompson. The new vogue for dining out has also helped the transformation of many pubs into local restaurants (like **The Eagle** or Tom Conran's **The Cow**) as well as encouraging a much higher quality of cooking in many pubs that now see themselves more as restaurants than mere beer shops.

192

192 KENSINGTON PARK RD, W11
☎ (0171) 229 0482
A cliquey, local and very trendy crowd includes the likes of DAVID HOCKNEY, VAN MORRISON, MICK JAGGER, BELLA FREUD and DAVE GILMOUR. Albert Clark's designer salads are no doubt popular with supermodel clients KATE MOSS and NAOMI CAMPBELL. Very modern decor, with a transparent staircase and a fibre-optic bar designed by co-owner Tchaik Chassay.

OSTERIA BASILICO

29 KENSINGTON PARK RD, W11
☎ (0171) 727 9372
Young and fun Italian in the heart of Notting Hill. It is permanently bursting at the seams with models and pop stars including MICHAEL HUTCHENCE, especially in summer when people and tables spill out onto the pavement.

Wonderful rustic Italian food. Make sure you sit upstairs for the best atmosphere.

WAGAMAMA

4 STREATHAM ST, W1
☎ (0171) 323 9223
Hectic, Oriental tuck shop and noodle bar, which is more of a hip refectory than a restaurant. The long benches and decor which is minimalist to the point of invisibility, are designed by John Pawson. Great noodle soups and tempura. Eat well but eat fast.

Safe bets

ALASTAIR LITTLE

49 FRITH ST, W1
☎ (0171) 734 5183
Despite the somewhat stark environment, the faithful keep returning to Little's Soho bistro,

which still provides a good, predominantly Italian menu. And for the people of Notting Hill/Holland Park, a new branch has recently opened in 136a Lancaster Road, ☎ (0171) 243 2220.

BIBENDUM

MICHELIN HOUSE, 81 FULHAM RD, SW3

☎ (0171) 581 5817

The most civilized of Sir Terence Conran's restaurant empire – in terms of food, design, atmosphere and service (you won't be booted out after an hour). Good classic dishes. CLEMENT FREUD recommends **THE OYSTER BAR**, ☎ (0171) 589 1480, downstairs *"for my favourite crab salad. It's underrated and inexpensive with good food and nice staff."* One of the best wine lists in town. NED SHERRIN is a regular.

THE BRACKENBURY

129–31 BRACKENBURY RD, W6

☎ (0171) 748 0107

Adam Robinson's wide-ranging menu travels from the Mediterranean to Asia; returning for the ever-popular British Sunday roast – all served at an exceedingly fair price. *"The best food in London for the money, probably the best food in London for twice the money"* – ALASTAIR LITTLE. Manager Clive Green's wine list is very worthwhile.

CLARKE'S

124 KENSINGTON CHURCH ST, W8

☎ (0171) 221 9225

Streamlined space, decorated by Ken Turner, where Sally Clarke brings Californian inspiration to traditional English cooking. There's a fixed, no-choice dinner menu in the evenings so ring ahead to check.

THE GREEN HOUSE

27A HAY'S MEWS, W1

☎ (0171) 499 3314

Chef Gary Rhodes prepares reliable, tradition-al English food. Sunday supper with bacon and eggs, smoked salmon and scrambled eggs and Caesar salad is also very popular.

KENSINGTON PLACE

201 KENSINGTON CHURCH ST, W8

☎ (0171) 727 3184

Very, very busy, with two or even three sittings per table each night, and this isn't simply because Julian Wyckham's chairs are so famously uncomfortable. People still clamour after Rowley Leigh's deliciously varied and well-priced menu.

LOU PESCADOU

241 OLD BROMPTON RD, SW5

☎ (0171) 370 1057

French fish bistro laden with South of France atmosphere and flavours. Would-be Riviera denizens, including NED SHERRIN, come here for some of the freshest, most authentic French food in London. The menu runs to good salads, pizzas and boeuf bourgignon too.

OLIVO

21 ECCLESTON ST, SW1

☎ (0171) 730 2505

Belgravia and Chelsea crowds jostle with the likes of BEN DE LISI, DARYL HALL, NEIL KINNOCK, RICHARD BRANSON and MAGGIE SMITH in this lively if rather cramped Sardinian bistro.

ORSO

27 WELLINGTON ST, WC2

☎ (0171) 240 5269

Atmosphere and more atmosphere are what you'll get here. The northern Italian food is very popular with actors fresh off stage and with theatre-goers, who come and tuck into great pizza, pasta, grills and salads, all served on brightly coloured, chunky Tuscan pottery. West Londoners go to sister restaurant **ORSINO**, 119 Portland Rd, W11, ☎ (0171) 221 3299.

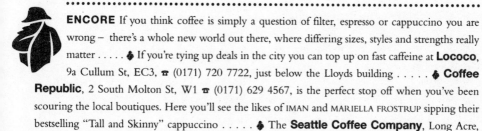

ENCORE If you think coffee is simply a question of filter, espresso or cappuccino you are wrong – there's a whole new world out there, where differing sizes, styles and strengths really matter . . . . . ♠ If you're tying up deals in the city you can top up on fast caffeine at **Lococo**, 9a Cullum St, EC3, ☎ (0171) 720 7722, just below the Lloyds building . . . . . ♠ **Coffee Republic**, 2 South Molton St, W1 ☎ (0171) 629 4567, is the perfect stop off when you've been scouring the local boutiques. Here you'll see the likes of IMAN and MARIELLA FROSTRUP sipping their bestselling "Tall and Skinny" cappuccino . . . . . ♠ The **Seattle Coffee Company**, Long Acre, WC2, ☎ (0171) 836 2100, is where you'll see Covent Garden opera stars, as well as MICHAEL PALIN and JONATHON ROSS, queuing up for their bestselling Tall Latte, flavoured with vanilla . . . . ♠

RIVA
169 CHURCH RD, SW13
☎ (0171) 748 0434
Rather spartan, proper Italian, home to chef
Francesco Zanchetta who cooks food strictly
from northern Italy. Diners may include a
strong pop element – U2, PHIL COLLINS, SIMON
and YASMIN LE BON, LISA STANSFIELD as well as
the likes of AUBERON WAUGH, SUE LAWLEY,
JEFFREY ARCHER and JAMES HERBERT.

SIMPSON'S-IN-THE-STRAND
100 STRAND, WC2
☎ (0171) 836 9112
Established in 1828, Simpson's made its reputation by serving traditionally grand roasts, and
it has held its reputation to this day. A popular
and well-established meeting place for famous
people. Charles Dickens, William Hazlitt and
other literary luminaries were early patrons.

SHOPPING

AMANDA WAKELEY
80 FULHAM RD, SW3
☎ (0171) 584 4009
The elegant beige and lacquer shop matches
the understated luxury of the clothes. Armani-
style tailoring, evening gowns and special
orders such as embroidered wedding dresses
have become her trademark.

ASPREY
165 NEW BOND ST, W1
☎ (0171) 493 6767
A treasure chest of jewellery, silver, leather,
china, clocks, watches, luggage and antiques –
well worth having a browse if you can brave
the uniformed doormen and endure the
pompous atmosphere.

BROWNS
23–7 SOUTH MOLTON ST, W1
☎ (0171) 491 7833
Rapidly taking over South Molton Street, this
designer emporium offers a tightly edited
selection from Jil Sander, Moschino, Sonia
Rykiel, Donna Karan, Romeo Gigli and
Byblos.

BUTLER & WILSON
20 SOUTH MOLTON ST, W1
☎ (0171) 409 2955 (AND BRANCHES)
Long-time No. 1 for fashionable and overtly
ostentatious costume jewellery that adorns the
bodies and lapels of LAUREN BACALL, ALI
MCGRAW, JERRY HALL and ELLE MACPHERSON.

CHELSEA DESIGN COMPANY
65 SYDNEY ST, SW3
☎ (0171) 352 4626
Catherine Walker's elegant dress and suit
designs are much favoured by the PRINCESS OF
WALES among others. And about 300 yards
away on the Fulham Road there's Catherine
Walker's wedding dress shop, where you'll find
many a society belle having a browse.

THE CONRAN SHOP
81 FULHAM RD, SW3
☎ (0171) 589 7401
The famous Art Deco Michelin building, in
which the shop is housed, complements the
designer-desirables inside – from furniture and
furnishings to eatables and sunglasses. "*Still the
best selection of furniture, kitchen and house stuff –
great for presents*" – NICK MASOn.

DAVID LINLEY FURNITURE
60 PIMLICO RD, SW1
☎ (0171) 730 7300
The place to go for beautiful inlaid wood,
hand-crafted one-off pieces. Or if money is no
object, you could, like ELTON JOHN, furnish
your entire house with it.

DINNY HALL LTD
200 WESTBOURNE GROVE, W11
☎ (0171) 792 3913
Dinny's signature pieces are her sandblasted resin
and filigree silver necklaces and earrings, but she
also creates one-off special commissions. Recently
opened a new branch on the Fulham Rd.

EDWARD GREEN & CO
90 JERMYN ST, SW1
☎ (0171) 930 7691
One of Britain's best makers of traditional
ready-to-wear men's shoes. Expensive, but still
only half the price of bespoke shoes.

FLORIS
89 JERMYN ST, SW1
☎ (0171) 930 2885
Scented everything, including soaps, bath oils,
shaving soaps and body milks.

FORTNUM & MASON
181 PICCADILLY, W1
☎ (0171) 734 8040
Britain's finest food emporium where you'll
find a fine selection of traditional English fare,
including mustards, preserves and chocolates as
well as the finest and freshest foie gras and
truffles. Upstairs you'll find a good hat and a
fine stationery departments.

FRANK SMYTHSON
44 NEW BOND ST, W1
☎ (0171) 629 8558
Stationers to everybody. Renowned for their custom-made notepaper and leatherbound address books and diaries, including the innovative international address book.

GENERAL TRADING COMPANY
144 SLOANE ST, SW1
☎ (0171) 730 0411
Indian papier-mâché, grand china, travelling rugs and a solid selection of silly presents provide the traditional British family with eternal amusement.

GEORGINA VON ETZDORF
149 SLOANE ST, SW1
☎ (0171) 823 5638
Famed for her slinky silk and plush velvet scarves, hand-printed with her swirly fantasyland designs.

HACKETT
136–138 SLOANE STREET, SW1
☎ (0171) 730 3331 (AND BRANCHES)
An entire English gentleman's lifestyle catered for. Find formal wear at 117 Harwood Rd; suits at 65A New King's Rd; shirts, shoes and nightwear at 1 Broxholme House, New King's Rd; and casual wear at 65B New King's Rd.

HARRODS
KNIGHTSBRIDGE, SW1
☎ (0171) 730 1234
One of the world's most celebrated stores. It houses acres of the best of British clothes along with the best of Europe and the US for men and women. A multitude of other merchandise, including children's wear, accessories, furniture, fabrics, household linens, books, hi-fi, scent and flowers, as well as vast food halls, restaurants and a champagne and oyster bar, enables the store to live up to its motto of "Omnia, Omnibus, Ubique" (Everything for Everybody Everywhere).

HARVEY NICHOLS
109–125 KNIGHTSBRIDGE, SW1
☎ (0171) 235 5000
This is where all the smart Londoners go. All the best designers such as Calvin Klein, Moschino and Jasper Conran are chosen discriminately and well displayed, over several floors. On the 5th floor there's a very good restaurant, café and bar (also open in the evenings), and a world-class, beautifully designed food market.

HERBERT JOHNSON
30 NEW BOND ST, W1
☎ (0171) 408 1174
Modern designs now sit alongside the more traditional trilbies, caps and panamas. Especially popular for Ascot week.

JOHN LOBB
9 ST JAMES'S STREET, SW1
☎ (0171) 930 3664
Beautiful, handmade, quintessentially British shoes of every description.

JOSEPH
21 SLOANE ST, SW1
☎ (0171) 235 1991 (AND BRANCHES)
The flagship store for Joseph Ettedgui's London empire – which also extends to more specialized stores, cafés and restaurants about town. Joseph mixes his own label with the cream of British design, and a splash of European labels too.

LIBERTY
REGENT ST, W1
☎ (0171) 734 1234
Truly delectable store best known for its wood-panelled rooms full of originally designed scarves and Liberty-print. Once renowned for its English-cum-Oriental style, the shop is now acquiring a name for its distinctive selection of clothes, including the collections by highly-acclaimed designers.

MARKS & SPENCER
MARBLE ARCH, 458 OXFORD ST, W1
☎ (0171) 935 7954 (AND BRANCHES)
Where everybody buys something at some time (especially food for an instant dinner party) even if they won't admit it. It's estimated that at any one time one in three British women is wearing M & S knickers. "*The best value in London for food, underwear and especially cashmere among the clothes*" – HILARY RUBINSTEIN.

NEW & LINGWOOD
53 JERMYN ST, SW1
☎ (0171) 493 6621
Excellent shirts, brogues and braces (which held up MICHAEL DOUGLAS'S trousers in *Wall Street*) sold by helpful staff.

PENHALIGON'S
16 BURLINGTON ARCADE, W1
☎ (0171) 629 1416 (AND BRANCHES)
Old-fashioned smells in old-style bottles and packed in lovely boxes make the perfect gift.

They also do a line in beautiful, brightly coloured enamel trinkets

RIGBY & PELLER
2 HANS RD, SW3
☎ (0171) 589 9293
The court corsetiers.

STEPHEN JONES
29 HEDDON ST, W1
☎ (0171) 734 9666
Open by appointment only, the illustrious milliner and his team lurk in a luxurious basement creating quirky, witty and wearable collections, which now include Model Hats (the couture range), Miss Jones (the diffusion range) and Jones Boy, his range for men. Clients include the PRINCESS OF WALES and AZZEDINE ALAÏA. He also does collections for many of the big fashion houses.

THOMAS GOODE
16 S AUDLEY ST, W1
☎ (0171) 499 4291
Classy goodies for the table and the home – especially china, glass, silver and antiques. Not surprisingly, the recently opened restaurant features splendid place settings.

TIFFANY
25 OLD BOND ST, W1
☎ (0171) 409 2790
Run by Rosa Monckton, the London branch is as full of glamorous gifts and jewellery as its New York counterpart. Upstairs is where you'll find the more affordable silver jewellery.

TRICKER'S
67 JERMYN ST, SW1
☎ (0171) 930 6395
Wonderful step-in-and-go shoes as well as custom-made. The tapestries for their famous slippers can also be made to order.

TURNBULL & ASSER
70/71 JERMYN ST, SW1
☎ (0171) 930 0502
Makers of probably the best bespoke shirts in London, worn by the PRINCE OF WALES. They also make the very highest-quality silk scarves.

WHISTLES
12–14 ST CHRISTOPHER'S PLACE, W1
☎ (0171) 487 4484 (AND BRANCHES)
Designer showcase for the young and the young at heart, Whistles's very witty collection is the starting point for many a successful designer.

THEATRE

SEE ALSO ARTS CENTRES.

OPEN AIR THEATRE
REGENT'S PARK, NW1
☎ (0171) 486 2431/1933 (END MAY TO MID-SEPT); (0171) 935 5884 (ALL YEAR)
The New Shakespeare Company's invariably excellent productions are held each summer in this charming open-air theatre in the park. Matinées and evening performances. On Sunday evenings concerts are held (summer only).

ROYAL NATIONAL THEATRE
SOUTH BANK, SE1
☎ (0171) 928 2252
World-beating national theatre company and standard-bearer for excellent drama. Now under the directorship of Trevor Nunn, it is housed in the South Bank arts complex, near the Royal Festival Hall (see Music).

Manchester

CLUBS

THE HACIENDA
11–13 WHITWORTH ST W, M1 5WG
☎ (0161) 236 5051
Still Manchester's biggest dance venue, squeezing in up to 1,400 at a time, all dancing to hot and thrusting Mancunian house music.

HOTELS

HOTEL PICCADILLY
PICCADILLY PLAZA, M60 1QR
☎ (0161) 236 8414
In the heart of the city, overlooking the Piccadilly Gardens. Bright and airy **VERANDAH RESTAURANT**.

VICTORIA & ALBERT HOTEL
WATER ST, M3 4JQ
☎ (0161) 832 1188
A converted warehouse on the banks of the River Irwell has become a mecca for fans of Granada TV's productions – rooms are themed according to programmes. Try the **SHERLOCK HOLMES RESTAURANT** (with good food by trendy chef John Benson Smith) the **WATSON BAR**, or the **CAFÉ MAIGRET**.

MUSIC

BRIDGEWATER HALL

PETER ST, M2 9DW

☎ (0161) 834 1712

This new £90 million stainless-steel home of the Hallé Orchestra will now regularly play host to the BBC Philharmonic and Camerata Chamber Orchestra, making it one of Britain's more upbeat venues for classical music.

RESTAURANTS

SEE ALSO HOTELS

MARKET RESTAURANT

104 HIGH ST, SMITHFIELD CITY CENTRE, M4 1HQ

☎ (0161) 834 3743

Antique crockery, house wine served from 30s milk bottles, 40s music, and a worldwide menu.

MOSS NOOK

RINGWAY RD, MOSS NOOK, M22 5WD

☎ (0161) 437 4778

Many are prepared to journey to the airport, (it is ½ a mile from it) for formal French cooking in a highly polished room.

YANG SING

34 PRINCESS ST, M1 4JY

☎ (0161) 236 2200

The top Chinese in town constantly teems with hungry punters who come to savour the Cantonese cuisine.

Oxford

The city of dreaming spires and aspiring dreams, Oxford is synonymous with Britain's oldest and most famous university (founded c. 1167). The glorious, golden-stoned colleges include MERTON (whose Mob Quad, the oldest quadrangle in Oxford, contains the oldest library in England), majestic CHRIST CHURCH (with Wren's Tom Tower), NEW COLLEGE (with a magnificent hall and enchanting cloisters), and MAGDALEN (with cloisters, the landmark bell tower and deer park). Don't miss the 15C DIVINITY SCHOOl in Broad St, featuring the oldest lecture room in the city, or Wren's SHELDONIAN THEATRE.

ARTS & MUSEUMS

ASHMOLEAN MUSEUM

BEAUMONT ST, OX1 2PH

☎ (01865) 278000

This is the oldest public museum and includes a superb collection of paintings, prints and drawings by Michelangelo and Raphael, Old Master paintings, Impressionists, Pre-Raphaelites and the museum's prize possession, Uccello's *The Hunt in the Forest*. Other treasures include Eastern art and decorative works, archaeology, 17C and 18C English furniture, sculpture, silver, and the Alfred Jewel. And the newly opened shop and restaurant mean that less lofty needs are catered for too.

GARDENS

BOTANIC GARDENS

ROSE LANE, OX44 7NL

☎ (01865) 276920

Set on the banks of the River Cherwell, the 4-acre gardens (thought to be Britain's oldest) feature a beautiful array of trees, including a yew tree dating from the 1650s, a tropical greenhouse, water-lilies, deep herbaceous borders, a cacti and a palm house.

HOTELS

THE OLD PARSONAGE HOTEL

1 BANBURY RD, OX2 6NN

☎ (01865) 310210

Brought to you by Jeremy Mogford, the man behind Oxford's most famous restaurant, Browns (see Restaurants), this privately owned stone building provides 30 charmingly furnished guest rooms and fine food along with all mod cons.

RESTAURANTS

⑩ BROWNS

5-11 WOODSTOCK RD, OX2 6HA

☎ (01865) 511995

The first in a string of young, fun bar/brasseries set in historic buildings in English university towns (there are Browns in Bristol, Cambridge, Brighton and now London). Hearty English food with a bit of EC flavour thrown in. Excellent game pies with chips, and a variety of salads served with unusual dressings – try the hot chicken salad. An encyclopaedic selection of cocktails is served too.

Rest of England

ART & MUSEUMS

1853 GALLERY

SALTSMILL, VICTORIA RD, SALTAIRE,
W YORKS, BD18 3LB
☎ (01274) 531163
One of Britain's finest private collections of
paintings by David Hockney is housed in this
exquisite mill. Saltsmill also accommodates the
shops "Skopos" (stocking an attractive range of
furnishings) and "The Home" (supplying a
comprehensive range of quality kitchenware).

NATIONAL MUSEUM OF PHOTOGRAPHY, FILM AND TELEVISION

PICTUREVILLE, BRADFORD, BD1 1NQ
☎ (01274) 727488
The most visited British museum outside
London – fantastically popular with young and
old alike. Six floors of displays, interactive features, theatre, educational and special exhibitions. Permanent displays include The Story of
Popular Photography (the Kodak Museum)
but the highlight of the visit must be
the IMAX cinema; at 52 x 64 feet, it is the
largest screen in the UK (the height of a
5-storey building) and provides the ultimate
3-D cinema experience. Allow yourself
plenty of time.

TATE GALLERY

ST IVES, CORNWALL, TR26 1TG
☎ (01736) 796226
This stunning gallery, opened in 1993, was
purpose-built to exhibit work by the St Ives
School of artists. Set into a cliff in the heart of
the small Cornish town, it can be entered
either at the cliff top or at its base on
Porthmeor Beach, even if you're still in your
wetsuit and carrying your surfboard. The
gallery is host to a changing collection of art
and sculpture, much of which reflects the life
and culture of Cornwall. The restaurant is situated on the roof.

HISTORIC BUILDINGS & GARDENS

BLENHEIM PALACE

WOODSTOCK, OXFORDSHIRE, OX20
1PX
☎ (01993) 811325
Built by architect and playwright Sir John
Vanbrugh, this magnificent baroque palace was
the 1st Duke of Marlborough's reward for his
battle victories. Superb collections of 18C furniture, porcelain and bronzes and precious
paintings; while five rooms of memorabilia celebrate the birthplace of Sir Winston Churchill.
The grounds feature wonderful water terraces,
a lake, an arboretum that stretches for over a
mile and the Marlborough Maze, Europe's
largest symbolic hedge maze.

BROUGHTON CASTLE

BANBURY, OXFORDSHIRE, OX15 5EB
☎ (01295) 262624
The family seat of the Lords Saye and Sele
since 1447, a perfect country house. Features
include a 50-acre parkland, with a fine formal
garden, a 3-acre moat and a 14C gatehouse;
17C oak furniture; and, in the Great Hall,
arms and armour used in the Civil War.

BURGHLEY HOUSE

STAMFORD, LINCOLNSHIRE, PE9 3JY
☎ (01780) 52451
Built by William Cecil, this has been the Cecil
family home for over 400 years and is the
largest and finest late-Elizabethan house still in
existence in the UK. Set in deer park by
Capability Brown.

CASTLE HOWARD

YORK, N YORKSHIRE, YO6 7DA
☎ (01653) 648333
Designed for Charles Howard, the 3rd Earl of
Carlisle, by Sir John Vanbrugh at the beginning of the 18C. The breathtaking palace is
instantly recognizable as the setting for
Brideshead Revisited. (Waugh had had it in mind
before he'd even put pen to paper.) The walls

ENCORE Following the recent bout of Bloomsbury mania, one hidden gem which should not be missed is **Charleston Farm House**, Firle, Nr Lewes, E Sussex, ☎ (01323) 811265. Set in the rolling Sussex Downs, it's both a museum and a home, where the artists Duncan Grant and Vanessa Bell used to live – and where her sister Virginia Woolf, and lots of their Bloomsbury friends, including Dora Carrington, would visit. "*A wonderfully evocative place – you can practically smell the paint drying*" – MAEVE HARAN.

are set alight by the works of Gainsborough, Romney, Rubens and Reynolds, while the gardens are still animated by the elaborate Atlas fountain.

CHATSWORTH

BAKEWELL, DERBYSHIRE, DE45 1PP
☎ (01246) 582204
The seat of the Duke and Duchess of Devonshire and one of England's grandest and most important houses. Built in the late 17C and set in parkland, the grounds include 105 acres of garden sprinkled with waterworks and fountains. It's most famous for the splendid interior with its magnificent library and art collection. Characterful shop full of local and home-made produce including delicious honey. The house is open from Easter to end Oct.

HAREWOOD HOUSE

HAREWOOD, LEEDS, W YORKSHIRE, LS17 9LQ
☎ (01132) 886225; FOR INFO CALL (01132) 886331
Marvellous 18C house, with an Adam-designed interior, set in one of Capability Brown's largest and most beautiful parks. Full of Chippendale furniture and Chinese and Sèvres porcelain. Absorb the sounds and smells of the rose and bird gardens, the rhododendrons and Epstein's awe-inspiring sculpture of Adam.

HATFIELD HOUSE

HATFIELD, HERTFORDSHIRE, AL9 5NQ
☎ (01707) 262823
A magnificent example of Jacobean architecture built in the early 1600s by Robert Cecil and now home to the Marquess of Salisbury. Rich collections of rare tapestries, fine furniture, paintings and historic armour. The surviving wing of the old royal palace is where Elizabeth I spent much of her childhood.

HEVER CASTLE

NR EDENBRIDGE, KENT, TN8 7NG
☎ (01732) 865224
Anne Boleyn's childhood home, dating back to 1270 and richly restored by the Astor family. Wonderful woodcarvings and plasterwork, plus marvellous collections of paintings and furniture. The exquisite Italian garden contains sculptures and statues from Roman to Renaissance times.

HOUGHTON HALL

NR KINGS LYNN, NORFOLK, PE31 6UE
☎ (01485) 528569
The home of the Marquess of Cholmondeley and set in beautiful parkland, this is one of the finest examples of Palladian architecture in England. Sumptuous interiors by William Kent. "*Lord Cholmondeley's wonderful house with its regiments of toy soldiers collected by his father. This is the house King Edward VII looked at before buying Sandringham next door*" – MOHAMMED AL FAYED.

LEEDS CASTLE

MAIDSTONE, KENT, ME17 1PL
☎ (01622) 765400
Moated castle, one of the most ancient, romantic and best-preserved buildings in the land. Dating back to 857, when it was a wooden fortress, it was rebuilt in stone in 1119. Magnificent furnishings, tapestries and paintings and delightful parkland, with streams, waterfalls, greenhouses, a maze and vineyard.

LONGLEAT HOUSE

WARMINSTER, WILTSHIRE, BA12 7NN
☎ (01985) 844400
Elizabethan manor, built in 1580. The first stately home to open its doors to the public (in 1949), and the seat of the 7th Marquess of Bath. The tour of the house now includes the former private apartments of the present Marquess. There's a fascinating memorial exhibition for the 6th Marquess, who died in 1992 comprising souvenirs and remnants of the past, including images of Edward VIII, souvenirs of Neville Chamberlain and one of the world's finest collections of Churchill memorabilia. There is also extensive material from the Hitler era. Outside, the Capability Brown parkland contains the world's largest maze, and the world's first safari park – set up in partnership with Jimmy Chipperfield (of circus fame) 30 years ago.

PENSHURST PLACE

PENSHURST, TONBRIDGE, KENT, TN11 8DG
☎ (01892) 870307
Viscount De L'Isle's country home has one of the finest medieval halls in the country, as well as a magnificent 10-acre Tudor walled garden, subdivided by yew hedges.

HOTELS

AMBERLEY CASTLE

NR ARUNDEL, W SUSSEX, BN18 9ND
☎ (01798) 831992
Medieval castle now a small hotel – hailed for its warmth and friendliness. Attentive service and good food in a pretty rural setting.

THE CASTLE HOTEL

CASTLE GREEN, TAUNTON, SOMERSET,
TA1 1NF

☎ (01823) 272671

Although it is in the centre of town, it still manages to compete with proper country-house hotels, in terms of quietness, style and cuisine. The celebrated restaurant is overseen by Phil Vickery, who bases his menus on traditional English flavours and local produce. "*He applies the lessons of nouvelle to an invigorating passion for classic English dishes. Something like the reinvention of English cooking*" – MATTHEW FORT.

CHARINGWORTH MANOR

CHARINGWORTH, NR CHIPPING
CAMPDEN, GLOUCESTERSHIRE,
GL55 6NS

☎ (01386) 593555

Fresh fruit, home-made biscuits and a glass of sherry greet guests when they reach their bedroom at this lovely manor house, where much of the the medieval decor is still intact.

CHESTER GROSVENOR HOTEL

EASTGATE, CHESTER, CHESHIRE,
CH1 1LT

☎ (01244) 324024

A Cheshire landmark. No expense has been spared by the Duke of Westminster on his half Bath stone, half mock-Tudor hotel. Everything is done with absolute attention to detail.

CHEWTON GLEN

NEW MILTON, HAMPSHIRE, BH25 6QS

☎ (01425) 275341

Set in the New Forest, it might be Britain's least rural country-house hotel, but it's easily one of the slickest. Highlights include Lyonnaise chef Pierre Chevillard's classic seasonally based cooking, matched by a wine list spanning 400 bottles; and the spa. "*It's the most fantastic place to recover from jet lag. Book a massage, go to the spa and swim in the world's most beautiful pool*" – ELISE PASCOE.

CLIVEDEN

TAPLOW, BERKSHIRE, SL6 0JF

☎ (01628) 668561

The stateliest of stately homes, originally built for George Villiers, 2nd Duke of Buckingham, in 1666 and now Britain's most aristocratic hotel. (Cliveden is also famous for providing the scene for the Profumo affair.) Stunning black-and-white marble fireplaces, vast reception rooms, 17C tapestries on the walls and access to the 376 acres of National Trust garden and parkland beside the Thames. There's a health and fitness centre too, including Turkish baths, massage, Jacuzzis, and indoor and outdoor tennis. STEPHEN JONES reckons, "*It's like being in Disneyland. Beautiful house and very good restaurant.*"

"THE KIND OF COUNTRY HOUSE GOD WOULD RUN IF HE HAD THE MONEY" –
SHERIDAN MORLEY
ON *CLIVEDEN*

THE FEATHERS HOTEL

MARKET ST, WOODSTOCK,
OXFORDSHIRE, OX20 1SX

☎ (01993) 812291

Within walking distance of Blenheim Palace and situated in the heart of a historic village, this 17C building is much admired for its antiques and uncluttered interior. JONATHAN MEADES comes here for the atmosphere and JULIAN LLOYD WEBBER comes for the restaurant – "*Very good food, relaxed atmosphere.*"

GIDLEIGH PARK

CHAGFORD, DEVON, TQ13 8HH

☎ (01647) 432367

Paul Henderson's country house enjoys a spectacular setting in 40 acres of riverside gardens in Dartmoor National Park. Hunting, shooting, walking, tennis, golf or croquet are invariably followed by tea in front of a blazing fire. You'll also get some of the best restaurant food in Britain, from chef Michael Caines, who trained with Raymond Blanc; choose from a wine list as thick as the Bible. JEREMY KING admires the "*impeccable hotel skills from room to restaurant and beyond*". SIR JOHN HARVEY-JONES appreciates the "*excellent comfort and service in an area of unparalleled beauty*".

GRAVETYE MANOR

VOWELS LN, NR EAST GRINSTEAD,
W SUSSEX, RH19 4LJ

☎ (01342) 810567

Elizabethan manor house, loved by those who appreciate the wonderful gardens. As RICHARD COMPTON MILLER raves: "*The panelled restaurant has a menu to die for – the best of English cooking. It has a beautiful, beautiful garden with wonderful views and surrounded by a thousand-acre forest.*" With over 400 wines from Europe and the New World, it's also been given an "Award for Excellence" by the *Wine Spectator* of America for "*one of the most outstanding Restaurant wine lists in the world*".

HAMBLETON HALL
HAMBLETON, OAKHAM, RUTLAND,
LEICESTERSHIRE, LE15 8TH
☎ (01572) 756991
A comfortable and elegant 19C lakeside hunting lodge – which has even provided the PRINCE OF WALES with a luxury countryside retreat. The rooms, which are filled with freshly cut flowers and period furniture, enjoy panoramic views over the Rutland countryside. There's also an outdoor swimming pool and tennis court. Aaron Patterson is in charge of the kitchen and EGON RONAY says "*Very, very, very complex food in terms of combinations and arrangements – pyrotechnics on a plate.*"

HARTWELL HOUSE
OXFORD RD, AYLESBURY,
BUCKINGHAMSHIRE, HP17 8NL
☎ (01296) 747444
First mentioned in the Domesday Book, and home to a wealth of artistic treasures, Hartwell House has a long and royal history. The house is set in 90 acres of parkland and includes a health spa, a trout-filled lake and a church ruin in the grounds. Could well deserve TERRY HOLMES's commendation for being "*the most beautiful country-house hotel in the country*".

⑥ THE LAMB INN
SHEEP ST, BURFORD, OXFORDSHIRE,
OX18 4LR
☎ (01993) 823155
What the quintessential country inn should be – log fires, flagstones, hearty English food and comfy chairs. "*Burford is the gateway to the Cotswolds and a great town to explore. Time really does seem to stand still in the hotel . . . a tremendously restful place to go,*" says JONATHAN MEADES. Tremendously good value too.

LUCKNAM PARK
COLERNE, WILTSHIRE, SN14 8AZ
☎ (01225) 742777
On the southern edge of the Cotswolds lies this spectacularly luxurious early Georgian manor. Solarium, spa, gym, shooting are all available. And good food from chef Michael Womersley, who concentrates on using the freshest and best local West Country produce.

MILLER HOWE
RAYRIGG ROAD, WINDERMERE,
CUMBRIA, LA23 1EY
☎ (015394) 42536
John Tovey's fine Edwardian house enjoys some of the best views in the Lake District, with grounds that sweep down almost to the edge of Lake Windermere. Comfortable, lived-in feel and the bonus of the much-celebrated 4-course dinner menu, overseen by the owner and prepared by chef Chris Blaydes. "*Really exceptionally good,*" applauds JULIAN LLOYD WEBBER.

SHARROW BAY
HOWTOWN RD, LAKE ULLSWATER,
CUMBRIA, CA10 2LZ
☎ (017684) 86301
Frances Coulson and Brian Sack's hotel is the ultimate country retreat – a great base for hiking, boating and fishing but little else, which makes it the perfect place to relax and enjoy the food. It's one of PAUL HENDERSON's favourites and RICHARD COMPTON MILLER comments: "*It's amazing because it's right on Ullswater with nothing at all but the most romantic view.*" PAUL HEATHCOTE raves: "*47 years at the top – Frances Coulson and Brian Sack are living legends in the hotel world.*"

STAPLEFORD PARK
STAPLEFORD, NR MELTON MOWBRAY,
LEICESTERSHIRE, LE14 2EF
☎ (01572) 7875222
The building reflects a mixture of architectural styles dating back to the 16C. Each of the 42 rooms are vastly different too, having been individually styled by famous interior designers. Lots of local country pursuits to entertain, while Malcolm Jessop's hearty, unpretentious cooking is worth rushing back for.

WOOLLEY GRANGE
WOOLLEY GREEN, BRADFORD ON
AVON, WILTSHIRE, BA15 1TX
☎ (01225) 864705
Homely and picturesque old hotel that combines all the attractions of the country-house hotel – open fires, antiques and dogs – with terrific facilities for families with young children, including an intelligently equipped games room and full-time nanny.

MUSIC

GLYNDEBOURNE OPERA HOUSE
NR LEWES, E SUSSEX, BN8 5UU
☎ (01273) 812321
The first new opera house in Britain since the father of the present chairman, Sir George Christie, built the original over 60 years ago. Glyndebourne continues to be acclaimed as a

highlight of the international Festival scene. Don't forget the hamper for dinner on the lawn.

OPERA NORTH

GRAND THEATRE, NEW BRIGGATE,
LEEDS, LS1 6NU

☎ (0113 2) 439999

Innovative and creative, Opera North produces opera of the highest quality. From behind the scenes to front of house, it is striving to compete with the very best, while *"touching the common psyche"* – RALPH STEADMAN.

RESTAURANTS

SEE ALSO HOTELS.

ANNIE'S

3 OXFORD STREET, MORETON-IN-MARSH, GLOUCESTERSHIRE, GL56 0LA

☎ (01608) 651981

An unpretentious and relaxed country establishment with lots of log fires, flagstones, pewter and really good cooking. Also quite a celebrity haunt; WILLY CARSON, DAVID GOWER and for some bizarre reason the entire CAST OF CORONATION STREET. However, the single greatest recommendation is that PRUE LEITH is a regular and a particular devotee of David Ellis's Cajun Salmon.

THE BAY HORSE INN

CANAL FOOT, ULVERSTON, CUMBRIA,
LA12 9EL

☎ (01229) 583972

More and more praise continues to be heaped on Robert Lyons's traditional English menu, which pays particular attention to local fish, Lakeland lamb and Ashdown smoked meats. Sensational views from the dining room in this 17C inn. Lyons, who was head chef at Miller Howe (see Hotels) for 16 years, also offers cookery demonstrations and one-day courses. The wine list is predominantly New World.

THE FRENCH CONNECTION

EDENFIELD RD, CHEESEDEN, NORDEN
ROCHDALE, MANCHESTER, OL12 7TY

☎ (01706) 50167

Against sweeping views of the Ashworth moors. Savoy-trained Andrew Nutter serves up treats like panaché d'escargots followed by stuffed fillet of sea bass with lobster mousse and champagne sauce. *"The food is just delicious. With its warm colours, its candlelight and its chandeliers, The French Connection is a hit with those of a romantic turn of mind"* – JOHN TOVEY.

HEATHCOTE'S

104 HIGHER RD, LONGRIDGE,
LANCASHIRE, PR3 3SY

☎ (01772) 784 969

Paul Heathcote's ever-popular establishment in a row of cottages in the Ribble Valley still provides innovative modern British dishes. *"Brilliant – classical training allied to deep appreciation of the quality of local ingredients. Barnes is happy to apply his techniques to the most humble of British dishes"* – MATTHEW FORT.

LE MANOIR AUX QUAT' SAISONS

CHURCH RD, GREAT MILTON,
OXFORDSHIRE, OX44 7PD

☎ (01844) 278881

English manor house more famous for Raymond Blanc's world-class restaurant and its seasonally changing menu than for its plush accommodation. Fantastically expensive, but generally worth it, though you should make sure that you stay when Raymond is cooking. Recommended by NICK MASON and PAUL HENDERSON. JULIAN LLOYD WEBBER comments: *"I was very impressed. You go there saying 'show me' and they manage to do it."* RICHARD BRANSON adds: *"Raymond Blanc does such a brilliant job"*. According to MATTHEW FORT, *"Raymond Blanc is the most creative chef working in England. If I had one meal left in the country, I'd be very tempted to go there."*

MARKWICKS

43 CORN ST, BRISTOL BS1 1HT

☎ (0117) 926 2658

This underground restaurant, set in a converted safety deposit vault complete with wood panelling, original marble floors and subdued lighting is probably more suitable for lunch than dinner. *"Peter and Judy Markwick were apprentices many years ago to George Perry-Smith, and the cooking sticks to that style, which pleases me and almost everyone else"* – PAUL HENDERSON. Their French provincial and modern British menu lays emphasis on fresh, seasonal foods, especially the speciality fish menu which changes daily, depending on the fish that comes in, fresh from Cornwall. *"Very diligently done French food with a West Country accent,"* says JONATHAN MEADES, who adds, *"great wine list . . . it's a very cosseting place".*

POPHAMS

CASTLE STREET, WINKLEIGH, DEVON,
EX19 8HU

☎ (01837) 83767

It's 15ft square, squeezed behind a deli, unlicensed and only open for lunch; but to its fans there is no beating the busy atmosphere and imaginative and hearty "baked to order" menu, which is based around simple, fresh and mostly local produce. Especially good are the wide selection of home-made ice creams. *"This has to be seen to be believed. Dennis Hawkes and Melvin Popham try to pretend that they are only amateurs, but they are consummate pros. There is no restaurant in the country where we would rather eat"* – PAUL HENDERSON.

SEAFOOD RESTAURANT

RIVERSIDE, PADSTOW, CORNWALL, PL28 8BY

☎ (01841) 532485

Join the likes of DAVID BOWIE for a true Cornish fishing-village experience: the freshest of fish and modern interpretations of classic dishes. *"Rick and Jill Stein serve the best cooked fish anywhere. Stay and sleep in Room 5 and watch the dawn come up over Betjeman country across the Padstow Estuary"*– ROBIN HANBURY-TENISON. *"This is certainly the best restaurant in Cornwall, and probably the best fish restaurant in Britain. Rick and Jill Stein started this in the mid 70s and it has become a great success. I always have the lobster."* – PAUL HENDERSON.

21 QUEEN STREET

19–21 QUEEN ST, PRINCE'S WHARF, QUAYSIDE, NEWCASTLE UPON TYNE, NE1 3UG

☎ (0191) 222 0755

Geordie owner/chef Terry Laybourne, who trained on the continent, serves a French menu, strongly emphasizing Mediterranean flavours. Having just been refurbished, it's now colourful and light in decor as well as flavour and particularly modern for Newcastle, but fits in well. Recommended by JONATHAN MEADES.

WATERSIDE INN

FERRY ROAD, BRAY, BERKSHIRE, SL6 2AT

☎ (01628) 20691

Bought by the Roux brothers in 1972, and now run to the highest standards by Michel Roux, Waterside Inn is located on the banks of the Thames in the 16C village of Bray. Above the restaurant are a few extremely comfortable bedrooms, some overlooking the river. *"The best restaurant in Britain . . . and you can stay there"* – JONATHAN MEADES. *"It's really quite magical sitting by the Thames on a summer's evening ... it's how one imagines England to be"* – STEPHEN JONES. *"An experience no one can miss. The Roux brothers stand out in setting the standards of English cuisine"* – LADY HARDINGE. Sample aperitifs or coffee in one of the summer houses or on board the river launch.

Scotland
Edinburgh

ART AND MUSEUMS

THE NATIONAL GALLERY OF MODERN ART

BELFORD RD, EH4 3DR

☎ (0131) 556 8921

All the major European and American 20C artists are represented here, from Matisse to Moore, and from Picasso to Paolozzi.

NATIONAL GALLERY OF SCOTLAND

THE MOUND, EH2 2EL

☎ (0131) 556 8921

The National Gallery is an impressive, though manageable, collection of great masters including Raphael, Titian, Rembrandt, Van Dyck, Gainsborough, Degas and Cézanne along with some outstanding works by Scottish masters.

THE NATIONAL PORTRAIT GALLERY

QUEEN ST, EH2 1JD

☎ (0131) 556 8921

Housed in a magnificent neo-Gothic hall, the Portrait Gallery is where you'll see great Scots immortalized on canvas and in stone. The ROYAL MUSEUM OF SCOTLAND, situated in the same building, contains the most comprehensive collection in existence of exhibits telling the story of Scotland and its people.

FESTIVALS

EDINBURGH INTERNATIONAL FESTIVAL

21 MARKET ST, EH1 1BW

☎ (0131) 225 5756 (BOX OFFICE)

Culture vultures flock in their millions to the Athens of the North for a heady August, offering insomnia and a series of festivals: the biennial BOOK FESTIVAL, ☎ (0131) 228 5444; the JAZZ FESTIVAL, ☎ (0131) 557 1642; the FRINGE, ☎ (0131) 226 5257; and the INTERNATIONAL FESTIVAL, ☎ (0131) 226 4001. The last two offer a cornucopia of theatre, comedy, dance, music, opera and ballet ranging from the seriously good to the seriously dreadful. It's a cultural lucky dip, so you'll have to take your chances, though you'll usually find something decent on at the ASSEMBLY ROOMS, 50 George St, ☎ (0131) 226 5992. The round-the-clock party kicks off with the famous military TATTOO, ☎ (0131) 225 1188, at Edinburgh Castle.

HISTORIC BUILDINGS

EDINBURGH CASTLE

☎ (0131) 225 9846

The imposing symbol of Scotland's capital and the nation's martial past dominates the skyline while commanding dramatic views over the city. Features include the 11C ST MARGARET'S CHAPEL, the city's oldest building; the CROWN ROOM, where the Regalia of Scotland are displayed; the OLD PARLIAMENT HALL and QUEEN MARY'S APARTMENTS, where Mary, Queen of Scots gave birth to the future King James VI of Scotland (James I of England).

PALACE OF HOLYROODHOUSE

CANONGATE, THE ROYAL MILE, EH8 8DX

☎ (0131) 556 7371

Founded by King James IV at the end of the 15C and later extensively remodelled by Charles II in the late 17C, this remains the Queen's official Scottish residence. Her summer garden parties are held here. The ancient abbey and the state apartments, with their fine collections of tapestries and paintings, are the only parts that can be visited.

HOTELS

THE BALMORAL

1 PRINCES ST, EH2 2EQ

☎ (0131) 556 2414

Built in 1902 and completely restored to its original glory in 1991, the Balmoral is now also bang up to date – there's even a TV in the sauna. However, Edinburgh's greatest old railway hotel is still seen as one of its most elegant landmarks. The GRILL ROOM is one of Edinburgh's finest restaurants, specializing in a highly creative treatment of Scottish dishes and grills. BRIDGES BRASSERIE is more informal though the food is equally good. "*As slick and professional as the Mandarin, Hong Kong.*" – JOHN TOVEY.

••

"IT HAS FOR MANY YEARS

BEEN MY FAVOURITE HOTEL IN

ONE OF MY FAVOURITE CITIES" –

DOUGLAS HURD ON THE

CALEDONIAN

••

CALEDONIAN HOTEL

PRINCES ST, EH1 2AB

☎ (0131) 459 9988

Popularly known as the "Caley", this 90-year-old institution constantly plays host to visiting heads of state. The POMPADOUR ROOM, with its subtle colours and delicate murals, is a sophisticated affair offering fine French cuisine in the evening, balanced by a more Scottish menu at lunchtime. JULIAN LLOYD WEBBER recommends the bar "*to escape the Princes St crowds at lunchtime*".

ROYAL TERRACE HOTEL

18 ROYAL TERRACE, EH7 5AQ

☎ (0131) 557 3222

Grand, luxurious hotel set in a beautifully preserved Georgian building and surrounded by lovely landscaped gardens. The CONSERVATORY RESTAURANT serves inventive international cuisine and the cosy PEACOCK BAR is used by residents and locals alike. Pamper yourself in its leisure club which includes a swimming pool and steam room.

EDINBURGH'S BEST PUBS These are concentrated around Rose St

(New Town) and around The Royal Mile (Old Town). Try the **Abbotsford**, 3 Rose St, E End, EH2 2PR ☎ (0131) 225 5276 a long-standing favourite with city slickers, featuring a large selection of ales and reasonably priced pub food. For a truly traditional Edinburgh bar, the atmosphere at the **Bow Bar**, 80 West Bow, EH1 2HH ☎ (0131) 226 7667, is difficult to beat; their vast selection of ales include their own Edinburgh Real Ale and over 140 malts; good simple bar snacks are available too. If you're up for the Festival, check out the **Bannerman's Bar**, 212 Cowgate, EH1 1NQ (0131) 556 3254, where the rooms are awash with creative types and boardgame junkies.

SHERATON GRAND HOTEL
1 FESTIVAL SQ, EH3 9SR
☎ (0131) 229 9131
Situated in the heart of the city with views of the castle, minutes from Princes Street. The Scottish baronial style decor inside features specially designed tartans for each room. This is one of Sheraton's international flagships.

MUSIC

USHER HALL
LOTHIAN RD, EH1 2EA
☎ (0131) 228 1155
Home to the Royal Scottish National Orchestra and host to all manner of musical events. *"The Usher Hall is my favourite place in Scotland. It actually has the effect of lifting your performance"* – JULIAN LLOYD WEBBER.

RESTAURANTS

SEE ALSO HOTELS.

ATRIUM
10 CAMBRIDGE ST, EH1 2ED
☎ (0131) 228 8882
Post-modern Gothic punk is one way you could describe the Atrium's interior. Chef/owner Andrew Radford conjures up a menu that is warmly Mediterranean. Good selection of wines, sensible prices. Recommended by JEFFREY DAY and LADY MACDONALD OF MACDONALD.

L'AUBERGE
56–58 ST MARY ST, EH1 1SX
☎ (0131) 556 5888
A warm, elegant, old-fashioned restaurant in the Old Town is currently celebrating its 20th birthday. Renowned French chef Michel Bouyer now heads the kitchen, where he prepares innovative *grande cuisine* with fabulous enthusiasm such as home-smoked breast of duck; or noisette fillets of Scottish border lamb – which can be washed down by a wine from a selection of over 400.

KELLY'S
46 WEST RICHMOND ST, EH8 9DZ
☎ (0131) 668 3847
A former baker's shop, near the Festival Theatre, renowned for its superb though simple, modern British food. Open for dinner only Wed–Sat. Recommended by LADY MACDONALD OF MACDONALD.

MARTIN'S
70 ROSE STREET, NORTH LANE, EH2 3DX
☎ (0131) 225 3106
Charming and comfortable restaurant, great for imaginative vegetarian dishes and seafood. *"Martin Irons also has a peculiar passion for cheeses, so if you want half an hour's rest after your meal, ask him what's on the cheeseboard"* – JEFFREY DAY.

VINTNER'S ROOM
THE VAULTS, 87 GILES ST, LEITH EH6 6BZ
☎ (0131) 554 6767
The magnificence of the ornate 350-year-old Venetian stucco plasterwork, lit entirely by candles, could lead to a particularly romantic evening. Dinner and lunch can also be enjoyed in the Long Room. Chef Tim Cumming, together with his wife, Sue, provides an excellent menu of seasonal dishes, using the freshest of local produce, served in hearty helpings.

THE WITCHERY BY THE CASTLE
352 CASTLEHILL, ROYAL MILE, EH1 2NF
☎ (0131) 225 5613
Once the seat of witchcraft and sorcery in Scotland, this 16C building is now the home of fine Scottish hospitality. Here you can dine by candlelight on chef Andrew Main's exquisite blend of fresh Scottish produce and French cuisine, among surroundings steeped in mystery.

SHOPPING

RAGAMUFFIN
276 CANONGATE, ROYAL MILE, EH8 8AA
☎ (0131) 557 6007
A captivating collection of original garments and knitwear for men, women and children – unique designs, enchanting colours and glorious textures. *"Unique. Quite the best designer of jerseys and hand-knitted jackets in Scotland"* – LADY MACDONALD OF MACDONALD.

VALVONA & CROLLA
19 ELM ROW, EH7 4AA
☎ (0131) 556 6066
Imports the best food and wine from small producers on the Continent, and from Italy in particular. Recently opened is an in-house Café Bar seating 50, and with the newly constructed kitchen they are producing their own

fresh Italian breads. The owners often hold wine tastings, cookery demonstrations and events like mushroom hunts. Having been twice nominated Italian Specialist Wine Merchant of the Year, Valvona & Crolla has an outstanding selection of Italian wine, as well as a large range of olive oil and balsamic vinegar.

THEATRE

PLAYHOUSE THEATRE

18–22 GREENSIDE PL, EH1 3AA
☎ (0131) 557 2590
A direct copy of a Broadway theatre and the largest in Great Britain, seating over 3,000. All of the biggest acts perform here, from stand-up comedians to ballets.

THE ROYAL LYCEUM

30A GRINDLAY ST, EH3 5AX
☎ (0131) 229 9697
The 110-year-old theatre is one of the finest examples of Victorian theatre architecture in Britain; it's also Edinburgh's only rep theatre, performing everything from Greek tragedy to pantomime.

Glasgow

G lasgow enjoys a well-earned reputation as one of Europe's most vibrant cultural capitals. Indeed it is one of the few British cities to emerge from the shadow of greedy, overbearing London, and in spite of Edinburgh's better pedigree and more obvious beauty, it provides Scotland's capital with a serious rival for visitors. There's a dazzling array of galleries and museums including Glasgow University's **HUNTERIAN GALLERY**. Glasgow also enjoys a densely packed calendar of performing arts – it is home to many national arts organizations – **SCOTTISH OPERA, SCOTTISH BALLET** and the **ROYAL SCOTTISH NATIONAL ORCHESTRA**. Visitors also appreciate the city's buzz, which comes from centuries of inventiveness and commercial adventure.

ART AND MUSEUMS

ART GALLERY AND MUSEUM

KELVINGROVE G3 8AG
☎ (0141) 287 2699; education programmes
☎ (0141) 334 1131
The headquarters of Glasgow Museums, this purpose-built red sandstone building opened at the turn of this century. It houses a magnificent collection of great paintings as well as stimulating new work by contemporary artists. Exhibitions also include historic and modern silver, jewellery, glass and ceramics; European armour, swords and firearms; and clothing, tools and weapons from prehistoric times.

BURRELL COLLECTION

2060 POLLOKSHAWS RD, POLLOK COUNTRY PARK, G43 1AT
☎ (0141) 649 7151
A comfortable and cheery home for the vast collection of 19C shipping tycoon William Burrell. With more than 8,000 exhibits from all over the world, highlights include the antiquities, Dutch and French masters, Elizabethan and Georgian furniture, tapestries, silver and Chinese ceramics.

ST MUNGO MUSEUM OF RELIGIOUS LIFE AND ART

2 CASTLE ST, G4 0RH
☎ (0141) 553 2557
A stimulating museum reflecting the central importance of religion in human lives. Masterpieces like Dali's *Christ of St John of the Cross* share space with curiosities like the lantern-slide box used by Glasgow evangelists Bessie and Seth Sykes. Other areas focus on religion in art and in Scottish history. Britain's only authentic Japanese Zen garden contributes its own sense of peace to the place, while the excellent pastries in the café will help you digest it all better.

HOTELS

GLASGOW HILTON

1 WILLIAM ST, G3 8HT
☎ (0141) 204 5555
The bedrooms might be like any other Hilton, however, the rest is not. The New York deli-style food of **MICHEY'S**; the *haute* Scottish dining available at **CAMERONS** and the grand atrium-style reception make it slightly different. You'll know that you're very definitely in Scotland if you drop into the **SCOTCH BAR**, where you can sample an amazing selection of malt whiskies.

⑨ MALMAISON

278 WEST GEORGE STREET, G2 4LL
☎ (0141) 221 6400
The brainchild of Ken McCullouch, owner of the far grander and more expensive *One Devonshire Gardens*, this smart and stylish hotel occupies a former 19C Episcopalian church

CHARLES RENNIE MACKINTOSH

Glasgow is a city of architectural contrast, beginning with the city's medieval roots in the 12C cathedral, leading onto the grandeur of the City Chambers in George Square – and the Art Nouveau style of Glasgow's most celebrated architect, Charles Rennie Mackintosh. Visitors will have been attracted by the **Mackintosh House**, a reconstruction of some of the major rooms from his home. Mackintosh's now global reputation has been well served by Glasgow. His greatest building, the **Glasgow School of Art**, has long been open to architectural pilgrims. Now the **Scotland St School** (also a fascinating museum of public education) has been opened, the **Art Lover's House** first planned in 1901 has been built and you can once again drink tea in one of Mackintosh's most important interiors, the **Willow Tea Rooms**. Much credit goes to the splendid **Charles Rennie Mackintosh Society**, Queen's Cross, 870 Garscube Rd, ☎ (0141) 946 6600, who will provide information and suggested itineraries. In May 1996 Glasgow presented a great Mackintosh exhibition, which was then sent off to New York, Chicago and Los Angeles, and will no doubt raise the current pitch of international Mackintosh fever even higher.

close to the city centre. Services are not provided on tap in a deliberate attempt to keep prices reasonable The vaulted brasserie in the basement provides classic fare at modest prices.

ONE DEVONSHIRE GARDENS
1 DEVONSHIRE GDNS, G12 0UX
☎ (0141) 339 2001
Once the home of wealthy Glaswegian merchants and shipowners, this is Glasgow's, and perhaps Scotland's, chicest hotel. Although it is fully updated, the original stained glass has been retained, as have the rich mahogany and the four-poster beds, all set off by a cunning use of lighting. A butler greets you at the door, and the staff – all dressed in Edwardian uniforms – will look after you impeccably. With fine cuisine and an interesting cellar, One Devonshire Gardens is set in the heart of a tree-lined Victorian terrace..

RESTAURANTS

SEE ALSO HOTELS.

THE BUTTERY
652 ARGYLE ST, G3 8US
☎ (0141) 221 8188
Warm and cosy converted pub where everything is done with exact attention to detail, from the handwritten menus and *objets d'art* to the hearty Scottish food devised by chef Stephen Johnson. Recommended by JULIAN LLOYD WEBBER.

ROGANO
11 EXCHANGE PL, G1 3AN
☎ (0141) 248 4055
With its unique 1930s atmosphere, Rogano is the oldest surviving restaurant in Glasgow. It is particularly famous for its wide selection of seafood; the fresh fish is perfectly cooked and

· ·

ENCORE Glasgow's pubs . . . . . ♣ The **Horseshoe**, 17–21 Drury St, ☎ (0141) 221 3051, is always busy and bustling with a fun, friendly crowd who not only enjoy a drink but appreciate the amazingly cheap food . . . . . ♣ For a trendier, more vibrant atmosphere the **Blackfriars**, 36 Bell St, ☎ (0141) 552 5924, is a friendly bare-boards bar scattered with round tables and chairs and offers a good range of beers and pub grub . . . . ♣

complemented by delicate sauces and butters. Both the ground-floor restaurant and **CAFÉ ROGANO** in the basement boast amazing Art Deco interiors by the same craftsmen who decorated the *Queen Mary*. The café is open throughout the day and is ideal for lunch after a shopping trip or for supper before or after the theatre.

THE UBIQUITOUS CHIP

12 ASHTON LN, G12 8SJ
☎ (0141) 334 5007
Glaswegians call it "the Chip", but the food is much more highbrow than the name might suggest and it offers a wonderful selection of fresh local Scottish produce. It has both an impressive wine list and an off-sales outlet, and is a recent Scottish Wine Merchant of the Year. JEFFREY DAY explains that "*they have the most bizarre combinations on the menu, and they get away with it*". JULIAN LLOYD WEBBER comes here for the real ale that few restaurants do.

SHOPPING

PRINCESS SQUARE, an award-winning shopping area just off Buchannan St, offers the best concentration of high-quality shops in Scotland. Glasgow now also boasts the largest glass-covered shopping centre in Europe, the **ST ENOCH CENTRE**, which incorporates 80 stores in one area. And as all things Italian go down so well in Scotland, Glasgow has an ITALIAN CENTRE, dedicated to Italy's best designers, including, of course, Armani.

Rest of Scotland

HISTORIC BUILDINGS AND GARDENS

CAWDOR CASTLE

NAIRN, HIGHLAND, IV12 5RD
☎ (01667) 404615
Built by the Thane of Cawdor in 1370, with additions in the 17C, this fairy-tale moated and turreted castle was used by Shakespeare as the setting for the murder of Duncan by Macbeth, Thane of Cawdor. It is lived in by the family to this day. Surrounded by one of the oldest woods in Europe. Open May–Oct.

CRATHES CASTLE

CRATHES, BY BANCHORY, KINCARDINESHIRE, AB31 3QJ
☎ (01330) 844525
The ancient seat of the Burnett of Leys family is one of the finest and best preserved examples of Scottish baronial architecture, dating back to the 16C. The castle also contains magnificent painted ceilings and some very fine furniture. Outside you can go for a walk in woodlands filled with roaming deer, or the walled gardens with their overflowing herbaceous borders, endless rose bushes and yew hedges that were planted in 1720. The estate extends to some 600 acres.

HOTELS

AIRDS HOTEL

PORT APPIN, ARGYLL, PA38 4DF
☎ (01631) 730236
Splendid views of Loch Linnie and wonderful cooking from the kitchen of Betty and Graeme Allen characterize this 300-year-old family-run hotel. Oban langoustines, lobster, oysters and turbot are cooked by mother and son, while the father, Eric, looks after the huge wine cellar. MATTHEW FORT says, "*They manage their local ingredients very well – Betty Allen is very particular*," and LADY MACDONALD OF MACDONALD thinks it's "*just the best, the food is marvellous*".

ARISAIG HOTEL

ARISAIG, INVERNESS-SHIRE, PH39 4NR
☎ (01687) 450210
Worth checking in for the views alone, the Arisaig hotel sits on the shores of Loch Nan Ceal. The unfettered views across the bay to the isles of Skye, Muck, Rhum and Eigg are spectacular. It's run by Malcolm and Jacqueline Ross, who provide consistently fresh food made from local produce.

ARISAIG HOUSE

BEASDALE, ARISAIG, INVERNESS-SHIRE, PH39 4NR
☎ (01687) 450622
Tucked away in a park with century-old beeches and crimson-and-mauve rhododendrons, this old manor house surrounded by walled gardens is now a Relais & Châteaux hotel, serving delicious game and seafood. After serious fire damage, the house was reconstructed in 1937, and retains a somewhat 1930s atmosphere. It also has an interesting wartime history, having been requisitioned by the army in 1941.

ABERDEEN Aberdeen has always had to play third fiddle to Glasgow and Edinburgh – but there's more to Scotland's third-largest city than North Sea oil and gas. Aberdeen, standing between the rivers Dee and Don, enjoys a rich heritage, which is displayed in the **Maritime, Marischel** and **City Museums**, and in the much admired **Art Gallery**. It boasts some extremely handsome 18C granite architecture, an ancient university and a wonderful fish market. And there is no better place to discover the once illicit distilling process of whisky-making, which you can do at several distilleries in Speyside. Recommended hotels include **Ardoe House Hotel**, South Deeside Rd, Blairs, AB1 5YP ☎ (01224) 867355, a Scottish baronial mansion with lovely views over Royal Deeside a few minutes from the city centre: and the recently refurbished, family-run **Craighaar Hotel,** Waterton Road, Bucksburn, Aberdeen, AB2 9HS, ☎ (01224) 712275. Both serve good, fresh local Scottish food.

CREGGANS INN
STRACHUR, ARGYLL, PA27 8BX
☎ (01369) 860279
Dating back to the 17C, this traditional inn serves delicious lunches with breathtaking views of Loch Fyne. Local produce and seafood are specialities including the freshest Loch Fyne oysters and smoked salmon. For overnight visitors, the breakfast is superb.

GLENEAGLES
AUCHTERARDER, PERTHSHIRE, PH3 1NF
☎ (01764) 662231
Set in its own 830-acre estate, surrounded by breathtaking Perthshire scenery, Gleneagles is not just for golf buffs; there's riding, clay-pigeon shooting, tennis, squash, fishing and falconry, or you can lock yourself away in the health spa. It's super-luxurious and there's a fantastic choice of food in its three restaurants. "*The best resort hotel in the world*," according to JEFFREY DAY.

INVERLOCHY CASTLE
TORLUNDY, FORT WILLIAM,
INVERNESS-SHIRE, PH33 6BN
☎ (01397) 702177
A magnificent Victorian lochside castle, built by Lord Abinger in 1863, Inverlochy is Scotland's grandest country-house hotel. It is set in 500 acres in the most magnificent part of the West Highlands, of which Queen Victoria herself said, "I never saw a lovelier or more romantic spot." Come here for peace and seclusion or activities ranging from skiing to fishing. In the sumptuous dining room you can enjoy wonderful Angus beef, excellent local grouse and fish; and mouthwatering puddings. According to PAUL HENDERSON, Inverlochy "*still leads the way in showing the rest of us how a country house hotel should be run*".

KINLOCH LODGE
SLEAT, ISLE OF SKYE, HIGHLANDS,
IV43 8QY
☎ (01471) 833333
Lord and Lady Macdonald of Macdonald's home is adorned with ancestral portraits and fine antiques: charming, cosy and shabbily luxurious. Lady Mac does cookery demonstrations as well as feeding her guests with her own wonderful food.

THE OLD COURSE HOTEL
ST ANDREWS, FIFE, KY16 9SP
☎ (01334) 474371
A golfer's paradise. The hotel now has its own brand-new championship-standard course, designed by Peter Thomson (five times open champion) at Craigtoun Park, two miles from the hotel. Golfing widows can enjoy the spa, which is "*absolutely wonderful*" according to SALLY BURTON, and the great views of the town, St Andrew's Bay and the Highlands beyond.

TURNBERRY HOTEL
TURNBERRY, AYRSHIRE, KA26 9LT
☎ (01655) 331000
People flock from all over Britain to revitalize themselves in Turnberry's fabulous spa. There are excellent golfing facilities too – the hotel overlooks two links golf courses. The bed-

rooms are very, very luxurious, and wonderful Scottish/French cuisine is prepared by chef Stewart Cameron.

RESTAURANTS

SEE ALSO HOTELS.

ALTNAHARRIE INN

ULLAPOOL, WESTER ROSS, HIGHLANDS, IV26 2SS

☎ (01854) 633230

Access by private launch only. Some may come here for the stunning waterside views, but most have made the pilgrimage for Gunn Eriksen's stunning no-choice, five-course dinner that uses only the very freshest of ingredients. The area of sea near the inn, which is marked with her red buoys, is her living larder. JEFFREY DAY says, *"When you're on the island you're stuck, but the food is excellent."*

....

"ONE OF THE MOST ROMANTIC RESTAURANT-CUM-HOTELS IN GREAT BRITAIN" – JEFFREY DAY ON THE ALTNAHARRIE INN

....

CELLAR RESTAURANT

24 EAST GREEN, ANSTRUTHER, FIFE, KY10 3AA

☎ (01333) 310378

A small affair in Anstruther harbour. Chef proprietor Peter Jukes offers fish simply cooked and a cellar that runs to 250 bins of the finest French wines. Closed Sun–Mon.

CHAMPANY INN

CHAMPANY CORNER, LINLITHGOW, LOTHIAN, EH49 7LU

☎ (01506) 834532

Dating from the time of Mary, Queen of Scots, this former millhouse offers the best local produce, including lobsters and oysters from the inn's own seawater pool, as well as Shetland

salmon and new-season lamb. The finest locally reared Aberdeen Angus. Now you can extend your evening by staying over. Reservations for both the rooms and the restaurant are recommended.

THE PEAT INN

PEAT INN BY CUPAR, FIFE, KY15 5LH

☎ (01334) 840206

A welcoming gem set in the tiny village of Peat Inn (the village having been named after the Inn) and sparkling with the inventiveness of chef David Wilson. Game and seafood are a speciality. If the outstanding wine list takes its toll, you can always stay in one of its eight suites.

....

"STILL THE ONE RESTAURANT IN BRITAIN IN WHICH I WOULD MOST LIKE TO EAT TOMORROW." PAUL HENDERSON ON LA POTINIÈRE

....

LA POTINIERE

MAIN STREET, GULLANE, LOTHIAN, EH31 2AA

☎ (01620) 843214

Situated just half an hour from Edinburgh, in a pretty seaside village, La Potinière is the creation of David and Hilary Brown and run entirely on their own – Hilary cooking, David waiting on tables and serving the wine. There is only one sitting, and no choice on their four-course menu, but few complain as the ingredients are the freshest (chosen and bought that day) and the cooking displays a rare skill. *"Angelic, divine fare cooked by Hilary and the best winelist I have ever seen done by David"* – JOHN TOVEY.

SEAGULL RESTAURANT

BREAKISH, ISLE OF SKYE, IV42 8PY

☎ (01471) 822001

And for something completely different . . . chef, Vichar Kroehnert specializes in concocting dishes that you won't find anywhere else using

ENCORE Nestling at the foot of the Craigellachie rock in the Spey Valley is the Highland's first purpose-built resort. **Aviemore** is bustling wth restaurants, hotels and sporting facilities and from here there is easy access east into the heart of the Cairngorms, including Glen More Forest Park, Rothiemurchus Estate, and the ski slopes of Cairngorm itself. For further details you can call ☎ (01479) 810363. . . . . ♦

interesting sea creatures such as squat lobsters and Arctic char. LADY MACDONALD OF MAC-DONALD is game: "*Really excellent and you feel quite out of it if you're dressed up to go there. They do wonderful three-course lunches. Try the chocolate and marzipan cake.*"

SHOPPING

BARLEY MILL CLOTHES

GATESIDE MILLS, GATESIDE, FIFE, KY14 7ST
☎ (01337) 860616
Everything from shirts and skirts to wedding dresses, all designed with imagination and loving attention to detail by Wendy Dover. "*Quite amazingly brilliant, yet tucked away there*" – LADY MACDONALD OF MACDONALD. Closed Sun–Mon.

Wales

HISTORIC BUILDINGS AND GARDENS

CASTELL COCH

TONGWYNLAIS, CARDIFF, CF4 7LS
☎ (01222) 810101
Built by William Burges for the Marquess of Bute, this is Victorian neo-gothic romanticism at its best – a fairy-tale castle set in woodland on the side of a mountain.

POWIS CASTLE

NR WELSHPOOL, SY21 8RS
☎ (01938) 554336
Magnificent medieval castle set in stunning 17C gardens featuring hillside terraces, formal parterres and tunnels of immaculately clipped hedges which contrast with areas of wilderness. The castle also houses a unique collection of Indian works of art, brought back by Lord Clive and his son.

HOTELS

BODYSGALLEN HALL

LLANDUDNO, GWYNEDD, LL30 1RS
☎ (01492) 584466
Still the grandest hotel in Wales, Bodysgallen

Hall is an imposing Grade 1 listed 17C mansion that sits in the hills above the Victorian seaside town of Conway. It is set amid 200 acres of parkland in beautifully maintained formal gardens. The panelled public rooms are filled with fresh flowers and have large, roaring open fires in winter. Bedrooms are elegantly furnished, plus there are self-contained cottages for more reclusive guests. This year they have just opened a spa complex with swimming pool, sauna, steam room and whirlpools.

HOTEL PORTMEIRION

PORTMEIRION, GWYNEDD, LL48 6ET
☎ (01766) 770228
A charming, eclectic hotel situated in the heart of Sir Clough Williams-Ellis's "fantasy village" as seen in *The Prisoner*. As the tourists go home, the village is yours to enjoy, as is the hotel. The individually styled rooms are decorated with bright fabrics, carved panels and ornaments from Rajasthan. The Mirror Room, with floor to ceiling gilt-framed mirrors, should not be missed. Welsh culture also has its place, on the menu and in the music and atmosphere. The dining room looks out over the beautiful, tranquil estuary, and the food is equally pleasing, with a broad and imaginative wine list.

LAKE VYRNWY HOTEL

LLANWDDYN, POWYS, SY10 0LY
☎ (01691) 870692
Old-fashioned country-house hotel set in a 24,000-acre estate with sensational views of Lake Vyrnwy. From here you can embark on traditional country pursuits which include shooting, fishing (they have sole rights to the lake), walking and tennis, while the more adventurous can go ballooning, abseiling and white-water rafting. Award-winning cuisine is a big draw with daily changing menus blending traditional, classical and country influences, using the freshest ingredients from the kitchen garden.

LLANGOED HALL

LLYSWEN, BRECON, POWYS, LD3 0YP
☎ (01874) 754525
Set against a backdrop of wooded hills, Llangoed Hall is situated between the Black Mountains and the Brecon Beacons (ideally located for the Hay Festival). Staying here is like being at a private house party – which is owner Sir Bernard Ashley's intention. LAUREN BACALL, IAN HISLOP, EDNA O'BRIEN and DR MIRIAM STOPPARD all stay here. You can admire Sir Bernard's £1.5 million collection of early 20C British art, browse in the library that

dates back to 1632, play croquet on the lawn, get lost in the maze or go for walks along the River Wye or into the hills. There's no reception desk – you are greeted on arrival and taken straight to your room. All the rooms are decorated differently in designs by Laura Ashley (Sir Bernard's late wife). There are plenty of public areas filled with fresh flowers, including a games room and you can even land your helicopter here. Chef Ben Davies's cooking is "modern classical with a Provençal feel", often using produce from the vegetable gardens.

* * * * * * * * * *

"SADLY MY STOMACH IS ONE THING THAT NEVER TRAVELS WELL, SO WHEN I AM ON AN AIRPLANE WHAT I IDEALLY LIKE IS A GOOD SANDWICH" –

ALBERT ROUX

* * * * * * * * * *

MUSIC

BRECON JAZZ FESTIVAL
WATTON CHAMBERS, BRECON, POWYS, LD3 7EF
☎ (01874) 625557
Fizzy little Aug weekend festival which holds its own among its European counterparts. Over 80,000 jazz fiends converge on Brecon for the weekend.

WELSH NATIONAL OPERA
JOHN ST, CARDIFF, CF1 4SP
☎ (01222) 464666
Based in Cardiff when not on tour, the Welsh National Opera has been going for half a century. Regarded as one of Britain's finest companies, it is now winning acclaim internationally too. Has a tremendous Welsh chorus.

RESTAURANTS

SEE ALSO HOTELS.

PLAS BODEGROES
PWLLHELI, GWYNEDD, NORTH WALES LL53 5TH
☎ (0758) 612363
A Georgian house set in fabulous gardens and just half a mile from the sea, this 'restaurant with rooms' offers a timeless tranquillity and

the perfect setting to unwind. By day there are plenty of walks along the Heritage coastline and in the evening you can feast on the freshest seafood and local produce.

WALNUT TREE INN
LLANDEWI SKIRRID, NR ABERGAVENNY, GWENT, NP7 8AW
☎ (01873) 852797
French-trained Italian chef–owner Franco Taruschio turned this bustling little pub in the hills into a foodie shrine, offering up fabulous local produce imbued with a beguiling mixture of Italian (Franco comes from the Marches) with a touch of Eastern exoticism for good measure. The menu is large but invariably fresh.

SHOPPING

VIN SULLIVAN
4 FROGMORE ST, ABERGAVENNY, GWENT, NP7 5AE
☎ (01873) 856989
John Sullivan's gourmet grocery offers an extraordinary array of seafood, including Kenyan and Turkish écrevisses; Cornish and Canadian lobsters; sea urchins and a wonderful variety of local game, fruit and veg, as well as local honey and lava bread. Supplies some of the finest hotels and restaurants in Britain.

Channel Islands

The Channel Islands became part of Britain in 1066, but still maintain their own system of ruling. Jersey is the most frequently visited because of its great beaches (excellent for surfing) and a few good hotels. Guernsey is a more relaxed, more residential island. Both islands make full use of the fresh fish in their restaurants, while Jersey Royal potatoes and the milk and cream from Jersey cows are in great demand throughout the islands and the rest of the UK. Alderney and Sark are the quietest islands, while all share wonderful walking trails along the clifftops with lovely views out to sea.

HOTELS

CHATEAU LA CHAIRE
ROZEL VALLEY, JERSEY, JE3 6AJ
☎ (01534) 863354
A dignified mansion on a secluded street, which sits just above Rozel – one of Jersey's most charming harbours. The hotel is a large building

with a sunny aspect; all 14 bedrooms are comfortable, some with Jacuzzis. Restaurant serves delicious Jersey fish.

HOTEL L'HORIZON

ST BRELADE'S BAY, ST BRELADE, JERSEY, JE3 8EF

☎ (01534) 43101

One of Jersey's most luxurious, upbeat hotels, with big bedrooms and plenty of space to relax. Pool, sauna and spa. Two restaurants serve the same food in different surroundings: there's the formal **CRYSTAL ROOM** or the more relaxed **GRILL**. Great scampi in ginger, honey and lemon sauce.

INCHALLA HOTEL

THE VAL, ST ANNE, ALDERNEY, GY9 3UL

☎ (01481) 823220

A really peaceful place, even for this silent island, set in beautiful grounds on the edge of the town looking out to sea. Simple and elegant, with a great seafood restaurant – try the squid Provençal.

LONGUEVILLE MANOR

LONGUEVILLE RD, ST SAVIOUR, JERSEY JE2 7SA

☎ (01534) 25501

The Channel Islands' only member of the Relais & Châteaux group is set in 15 acres at the foot of a private wooded valley. The old manor, which has stood there since the 13C, is surrounded by beautiful gardens and filled with expensive chintzes and antiques. The food served in the ancient oak-panelled dining room is essentially English; if you're feeling indecisive, go for the 8-course menu *dégustation* where you can try a bit of everything. Much of the food is fresh from the hotel's own walled gardens and hothouses.

MILLBROOK HOUSE

RUE DE TRACHY, MILLBROOK, ST HELIER, JE2 3JN

☎ (01534) 33036

Beautifully restored 18C home, set in secluded surroundings. Most rooms have outstanding views of the sea and over the 10 acres of gardens, park and grounds. Ideal for a tranquil and relaxing getaway. Discreet but efficient service. A good menu with lots of fresh dishes and an extensive wine list.

PLACES TO VISIT

HAUTEVILLE HOUSE

HIGH TOWN, GUERNSEY, GY1 1DG

☎ (01481) 721911

Home of writer Victor Hugo, during his voluntary political exile which lasted 18 years. It is now owned by the City of Paris. From the top floor it is possible to see France, and also directly into a house across the street, which used to be the home of his mistress. Guided tours only, with a limited number of people.

SAUSMAREZ MANOR

GUERNSEY, GY4 6SG

☎ (01481) 35571

Found about two miles south of St Peter Port, this is Guernsey's only stately home open to the public. One of the finest examples of the Queen Anne Colonial style of architecture. Set in lovely gardens, which include woodlands and some wonderful tropical plants.

RESTAURANTS

SEE ALSO HOTELS.

CAFE DU MOULIN

RTE DE QUANTERAINE, ST PETER PORT, GUERNSEY, GY7 9PD

☎ (01481) 65944

A restaurant in a converted watermill set in a peaceful valley on the east side of the island. As with most places in the Channel Islands, fish is the priority. Ultra-fresh and full of flavour, with an East Asian emphasis in some of the dishes. One of the best-stocked bars on the islands.

LA NAUTIQUE

THE QUAI STEPS, ST PETER PORT, GUERNSEY, GY1 1LE

☎ (01481) 721714

One of the best restaurants in the Channel Islands, old-established, serving fish with a huge variety of sauces and using French cooking techniques.

SHOPPING

An undoubted attraction of the Channel Islands is that there is no VAT. The biggest selection of shops is in **ST HELIER** (Jersey) and in **ST PETER PORT** (Guernsey), which are especially good for cosmetics and alcohol. St Helier also has several exclusive small boutiques. Jewellery is duty-free too, which is why it's worth popping into **JERSEY PEARL**, La

Route des Issues, St John, Jersey,☎ (01534) 862137. Here you'll find the largest collection of pearl jewellery on the island and you can watch pearl workers creating new pieces. The selection of goods on display isn't always that discerning, however. The main shopping area on Guernsey, beginning at the QUEEN ELIZABETH MARINA in St Peter Port, is not as glitzy as St Helier. The pedestrian shopping area is a maze of lanes with speciality shops, especially jewellers; and it's particularly good for watches.

CANADA
Montreal

ART AND MUSEUMS

MUSEE DES BEAUX ARTS

1380 RUE SHERBROOKE OUEST
☎ (514) 285 1600
Well worth a visit, if only to see the Pavilion Jean-Noel-Desmarais, a 1991 addition which has doubled its size. The buildings are connected by an underground tunnel, and both house an impressive collection of European and North American fine and decorative art. During the summer the museum usually hosts a world-class touring exhibition.

BARS AND CAFES

CAFE CINE LUMIERE

5163 ST LAURENT BLVD
☎ (514) 285 1600
Cool art-house café, where bohemian late-20 to early-30-somethings go for the great-value French food, low lighting and old movies.

SANTROPOL

3990 ST URBAIN
☎ (514) 842 3110
A corner café famous for its gardens and gold-fish ponds. It has its own private roof garden and speciality sandwiches are served in the café. There's no alcohol, but popular with students, locals and out-of-towners.

THE SHED CAFE

3515 ST LAURENT BLVD
☎ (514) 842 0220
Warehouse-style café is covered with impres-

sive murals by Montreal artist Pierre Raby. There's a DJ at weekends. Try the popular homemade beer known as "Belle Guele". Stays open 'til 3am.

WILENSKY'S LIGHT LUNCH

34 RUE FAIRMOUNT OUEST
☎ (514) 271 1247
Owned by the Wilensky family since 1932, a well-known deli where the service is swift and prices are good.

CLUBS

L'AIR DU TEMPS

191 RUE ST-PAUL OUEST
☎ (514) 842 2003
Best known of Montreal's thriving jazz clubs, small and smoky with 90 per cent local talent and a few international acts. Stays open into the night. There's a cover charge at weekends.

FESTIVALS

BENSON AND HEDGES INTERNATIONAL FIREWORKS COMPETITION

NOTRE DAME ISLAND, ABOVE ST LAURENT RIVER
☎ (514) 872 6120
Every May/June the most spectacular displays of fireworks that you'll ever see, all set to music, shower down over the St Laurent river.

JUST FOR LAUGHS

2101 ST LAURENT BLVD
☎ (514) 845 3155
Held each July, this world-famous laugh fest features classic comedy and comedians from all over the world. Events are performed in both English and French.

MONTREAL JAZZ FESTIVAL

822 SHERBROOKE ST
☎ (514) 871 1881
A cosmopolitan celebration of jazz held every June/July. Dixie, swing, blues, bebop and others all ring out across the city, from restaurant cellars, hotel lounges and vast outdoor stages.

MONTREAL WORLD FILM FESTIVAL

1432 BLEURY ST
☎ (514) 848 3883 (OR 1888 515 0515 TOLL-FREE IN US AND CANADA)
The largest public film festival in the world takes place in Aug/Sept. There are at least 12

Joel Cadbury on pubs, clubs and bars

It's very hard to know what a club is going to be like until you actually get inside. You cannot tell if it's going to be overcrowded or whether it's going to take the rest of your life to reach the bar – but there are a few basic signs that will give you a good idea as to what you're in for, many of which are pure common sense.

1 Doormen . . . You never get a second chance at a first impression, which is why the doorman to a club is the key to a good first impression. All clubs, whether night-clubs, gentlemen's clubs or dining clubs, go in and out of fashion – this type of business by its very nature is cyclical. In the 80s it was cool to have rude doormen, rude chefs, rude everything; manners were as instantly disposable as money. With the recession the whole industry has had to be streamlined. Customer care has returned. But whether business is booming or not, door policy is vital – you should never be made to feel unwelcome or unworthy. The doormen at gentlemen's clubs know this, which is why they are among some of London's great unsung heroes. Whether you're in London, New York or Hong Kong, you should always expect courtesy from doormen. But you won't always get it.

2 Drinks . . . Always look at what pouring brands are being served. Bottles of Absolut may be lining the walls – but is that, or an inferior brand, ending up in your glass? If you're being given inferior vodka or gin to go with your tonic, on the assumption that you, the customer, can't tell the difference, don't go back. The benchmark of a good bar is a good Bloody Mary. A good barman will always take particular pride in his Bloody Mary.

3 Clientele . . . Look at the people who are going in. Do you want to spend the evening with that particular crowd of people? If you don't, avoid. Clubs are confined, often claustrophobic spaces – so the last thing you want is to be thrust against a group of people you can't stand.

4 Loos . . . Clean loos – always a good sign.

5 Staff . . . Staff should never be sitting around as there's always something they can be doing. Similarly, in a good club or bar the staff should be on the same wave-length as their regular clientele. While your average publican might be a 50-something fat drunk with his elbows permanently propped up on the bar, he is not going to cater for the needs of a vibrant young crowd who would be better served by more youthful and energetic staff.

6 Cleanliness . . . There's never an excuse for a lack of it.

7 Atmosphere . . . Alex Langlands Pearse believes that the secret of a good pub or bar, other than the location, is its atmos-phere. A good atmosphere should be there even when the place is empty, having already been created by appealing decor and welcoming staff, before the first cus-tomer has arrived.

8 Flexible service . . . The sign of a good restaurant, club or bar is flexibility – giving you what you want, not excuses.

9 Be wary of venues . . . There's a difference between venues, hired out to different out-fits on different evenings, and regular nightclubs. At a venue there's no personal standard on admission, service or music, whereas in a nightclub the staff remain the same and there's interaction between the staff and customer. Good clubs should also return the loyalty of regular clients by catering for their every need – making them feel at home, knowing their names and being utterly reliable.

10 Admissions . . . If pretty girls automatical-ly jump the queue, that in itself is not always a good sign. However, don't say you know the owner or, worse, make out that he's your best friend – he could well be standing by the door.

While many of these tenets are specifically rel-evant to London, they should apply universally (even though when you're in Paris or New York you will notice that the locals seem to have a slight problem with politeness). But wherever you are, always be nice to doormen and you'll go far.

venues in downtown Montreal showing films ranging from international features to documentaries to short films. Each year the cinematography of a country is celebrated; while a particular interest is taken in Latin American cinema and the work of new young filmmakers. Stars include JANE FONDA, CLINT EASTWOOD and GERARD DEPARDIEU.

HOTELS

HOTEL DE LA MONTAGNE

1430 RUE DE LA MONTAGNE
☎ (514) 288 5656
This hotel is characterized by its striking Early American/neo-rococo decor featuring a remarkable lobby complete with naked, butterflied nymph which rises out of a fountain to greet you. LUTETIA is one of Montreal's most respected restaurants, while the main attraction next door is still the famous singles bar LES BEAUX JEUDIS, populated by a mixture of bilingual locals and business-persons from Toronto.

HOTEL VOGUE

1425 RUE DE LA MONTAGNE
☎ (514) 285 5555
Transformed into a swan of a hotel complete with striking granite façade in 1990, it lies in the heart of Downtown, with a great view over the trendy rue de la Montagne from L'OPÉRA BAR. A genuine comfort hotel. The SOCIETY CAFÉ serves Euro-Asiatic cuisine.

LES QUATRE SAISONS

1050 SHERBROOKE ST W
☎ (514) 284 1110
Contemporary glass high-rise hotel, renowned for luxury and slick service. The 3rd-floor health club has a heated outdoor pool connected by a tunnel to the indoor one. The ZEN Szechuan/ Chinese restaurant is a major Montreal attraction.

RITZ-CARLTON KEMPINSKI

1228 RUE SHERBROOKE OUEST
☎ (514) 842 4212
Montreal's *grande dame*, often used by screen stars to shoot a film scene or use as a pit stop when they're in town. It's also famous for being the venue for Elizabeth Taylor and Richard Burton's first marriage. Tremendous attention to detail. The 1912 courtyard, where you can have afternoon tea by the duck pond, is a Montreal summertime institution for residents and locals alike. LE CAFÉ DE PARIS is the spot for government officials' power breakfasts.

LE WESTIN MONT-ROYAL

1050 RUE SHERBROOKE OUEST
☎ (514) 284 1110
Outstanding in terms of service and hospitality; the concierge will arrange anything and everything. Very much a business hotel with a well-equipped health club and excellent facilities.

MUSIC

MONTREAL SYMPHONY ORCHESTRA

SALLE WILFRID-PELLETIER, PLACE DES ARTS
☎ (514) 842 9951
World-famous orchestra under the guidance of talented conductor Charles Dutoit. When not on tour, the MSO plays at home in the Place des Arts, providing ever-popular free summer concerts in Olympic Park and its wonderful Christmas and Summer concerts in the Basilique Notre-Dame.

RESTAURANTS

SEE ALSO HOTELS.

AUX ANCIENS CANADIENS

34 RUE ST-LOUIS, QUEBEC CITY
☎ (418) 692 1627
This out-of-town restaurant is the place for truly authentic French–Canadian cuisine. The patrons also serve the best caribou – a local speciality made of red wine and whiskey. The house dates from 1675 and has four individually decorated dining rooms.

BEAVER CLUB

AT LA REINE ELIZABETH HOTEL, 900 BLVD RENÉ-LEVESQUE OUEST
☎ (514) 861 3511
Famous French restaurant founded by fur traders in colonial times, and later a social club for Montreal's business and political élite. Although membership is no longer required, reservations are recommended, as chef John Cordeaux has a very keen following.

CHEZ DELMO

211-215 RUE NOTRE-DAME OUEST
☎ (514) 849 4061
Founded in 1910, Chez Delmo is a top-notch seafood restaurant halfway between the courts and the stock exchange. It has two dining rooms – one is great if you're in a hurry, while the other is a lot more leisurely. Prices vary according to the fishmarket.

L'EXPRESS

3927 RUE ST-DENIS

☎ (514) 845 5333

Parisian-style bistro which opened in the mid 80s is where media types go to see and be seen. It's smoky and loud at weekends, but the service is efficient and the food well priced. One of the best and most original wine cellars in the city, with many wines and champagnes available by the glass too.

GIBBY'S

298 PLACE D'YOUVILLE

☎ (514) 282 1837

Housed in a 19C building with thick stone walls and fireplaces that date back to 1825, and considered by many to be the finest steak restaurant in the city. If you're off beef, you can always have Cajun-blackened grouper instead.

LES HALLES

1450 RUE CRESCENT

☎ (514) 844 3438

Lively restaurant named after the famous market in Paris and decorated accordingly. An exceptional wine cellar features over 250 choices, ranging from $20 to $540 a bottle. The menu is a combination of the classic and the imaginative, with the odd foray into nouvelle cuisine.

NUANCES

1 AVE DE CASINO

☎ (514) 392 2708

The Casino de Montréal's main restaurant is befitting the unusually good government-owned casino. The view of the city is spectacular both by day and night. Mainly contemporary food.

TOQUE

3842 RUE ST-DENIS

☎ (514) 499 2084

One of the quirkiest restaurants in Montreal. The decor is a funky mix of red velvet, grey and yellow; the food is equally arty. Normand Laprise, the owner is now one of the city's best chefs. A must, but book ahead.

LES TROIS TILLEULS

290 RUE RICHELIEU, SAINT MARC SUR RICHELIEU

☎ (514) 584 2231

About 30 minutes southwest of downtown Montreal lies this prestigious Relais & Châteaux restaurant beside the Richelieu river. A small, romantic inn, it has a light, airy dining room with a terrace. There are also 24 guest rooms and a grand palatial suite.

SHOPPING

For fashion, head for Sherbrooke St. For a bit of Bohemia go to St Laurent Blvd, where you'll come across the hip clubs, artists' studios and avant-garde boutiques nestling between kosher butcher shops, Hungarian bakeries and bric-à-brac. Lined with luxury and designer shops, rue St-Denis and ave Laurier are Montreal's Bond Street, while Notre-Dame St W in Old Montreal is the spot for antique lovers. Mount-Royal St E is where you can pick up secondhand clothing and furniture bargains.

EATONS

677 RUE STE-CATHERINE OUEST

☎ (514) 284 8411

The city's leading department store, famous for selling absolutely everything except tobacco. Its founder was Methodist and his descendants honour his anti-tobacco principles even today.

HOLT RENFREW

130 RUE SHERBROOKE OUEST

☎ (514) 842 5111

Canada's oldest and most prestigious designer store stocking all the top labels. It's particularly well known for its furs, which it used to supply to members of the British Royal family.

OGILVY'S

1307 RUE STE-CATHERINE OUEST

☎ (514) 842 7711

A kilted piper greets customers at noon outside this Montreal institution. Now it stocks more traditional wear such as Aquascutum and Jaeger.

Toronto

ART AND MUSEUMS

THE ART GALLERY OF ONTARIO

317 DUNDAS ST

☎ (416) 979 6648

Since a dramatic renovation in 1992, this gallery has won international acclaim with a collection including works by Van Gogh, Turner, Chagall and many others. There is also a strong emphasis on contemporary Canadian art and sculpture; and there's a Henry Moore Sculpture Centre. Plenty of hands-on displays for children.

DX (Design Exchange)

234 BAY ST

☎ (416) 363 6121

North America's first design exchange, housed in the city's old stock exchange and designed by one of Toronto's top architectural firms – Kuwabara, Payne, McKenna, Blumberg. The space is breathtakingly simple; it even has a suspended staircase.

BALLET

NATIONAL BALLET OF CANADA

O'KEEFE CENTRE

☎ (416) 362 1041

The company is going from strength to strength, under the direction of Reid Anderson. Their Christmas performance of *The Nutcracker* is a Toronto institution. "*There is no question that they are the top company in Canada*" – EDWARD THORPE.

BARS AND CAFES

HEMINGWAY'S

142 CUMBERLAND ST

☎ (416) 968 2828

One of the city's most popular singles bars, full of middle-class professionals, but much more laid back and homely than most of Toronto's bars. There is live music at the weekends.

REMY'S

115 YORKVILLE AVE, TORONTO

☎ (416) 968 9429

This elegant bar next to the Four Seasons hotel is used by the likes of JANE FONDA or other celebrity guests who regularly pop in from next door. Remy's also has an outdoor patio and Italian-style restaurant.

SENATOR DINER

249 VICTORIA ST

☎ (416) 364 7517

Beautifully restored 40s diner with authentic green leather booths serving great burgers and fishcakes. It's just off the main theatre and shopping street, making it the perfect stop-off for a milkshake, cappuccino or breakfast.

TERRONI

720 QUEEN ST W

☎ (416) 504 0320

A tiny sliver of a café which has recently spawned several other Terronis around the city. Authentic Italian pizza and panini.

CLUBS

THE BAMBOO

312 QUEEN ST W

☎ (416) 593 5771

All kinds of music, from calypso and reggae to jazz, is played in this crazy-looking old laundry, which is better suited to frenetic dancing than quiet conversation. "*It's somewhat iconoclastic and we like that*," says STEVE PODBORSKI, especially with its heady mix of funky music, Thai cooking (some of the best in the city) and Christmas lights. Serves Caribbean food too.

••

"*THE BEST JAZZ IN TORONTO*" –

TONY APSLER ON TOP O'

THE SENATOR

••

TOP O' THE SENATOR

249 VICTORIA ST

☎ (416) 364 7517

Just above the Senator Diner (see Bars and Cafés) is the city's first dedicated jazz venue – a kind of Canadian Ronnie Scott's with the feel of a between-the-wars jazz lounge.

YUK YUK'S COMEDY KABARET

5165 DIXIE AVE

☎ (416) 967 6425

Long-established as the centre of the Toronto comedy scene, this was one of Jim Carrey's first major venues; and other top names, such as Robin Williams, have played here too. It's part of the ever-expanding emporium of Mark Breslin (who used to write for Joan Rivers). There are new talent shows each Tues. "*Very highly recommended, a great evening*" – STEVE PODBORSKI.

FILM

TORONTO INTERNATIONAL FILM FESTIVAL

☎ (416) 967 7371

A serious celebration of film, held every Sept. More than 250 movies from around the world, from blockbusters to obscure art-house, are shown in all the downtown cinemas. There are big parties, big premières and heaps of stars. In addition there's always a retrospective of a prominent figure from the film world – like Marguerite Duras, Martin Scorsese or Robert Duval.

HOTELS

FOUR SEASONS

21 AVENUE RD

☎ (416) 964 0411

The flagship hotel for one of the world's best hotel chains sits on the edge of Yorkville. Check out the indoor and outdoor swimming pools, the original artworks adorning the walls and each of its fab restaurants: the STUDIO CAFÉ – the place to be seen; the LOBBY BAR; LA SERRE; and, last but not least, TRUFFLES, the formal French dining room that is the favourite *haute* haunt of Toronto socialites.

KING EDWARD HOTEL

37 KING ST E

☎ (416) 824 5471

Grande dame of Toronto's hotels, the King Edward was built in 1903 and remodelled in the early 80s, when it became part of the Forte chain. With its vaulted ceilings and marble pillars, it still retains its Edwardian elegance. Guests have included MARGARET THATCHER, CHARLES DE GAULLE and the DUKE OF EDINBURGH. The hotel's culinary highlight is the CHEF'S TABLE, when you can watch executive chef John Higgins prepare an 8-course meal for you in his kitchen, followed by a full kitchen tour. "*A fabulous hotel with wonderful old-styling; excellent renovations have continued to keep it up to the mark*," says STEVE PODBORSKI.

SUTTON PLACE

955 BAY ST

☎ (416) 924 9221

Lobbyists, the business-oriented set and the few celebrities not at the Four Seasons gather here for some serious luxury. Complimentary limos ensure a smooth journey from Toronto's business centre.

RESTAURANTS

SEE ALSO HOTELS.

BISTRO 990

990 BAY ST

☎ (416) 921 9990

Informal but the food is so good it's worth dressing up. Decor is quite simple with Cocteau-style stencils lining the stone walls, a tiled floor and sturdy chairs – all very 90s. BOB RAMSAY comes here for the "*wonderful comfort food*", and ROSEMARY SEXTON for the "*interesting people and the vivacious patron, Alfred Caron*".

CENTRO

2472 YONGE ST

☎ (416) 483 2211

Regarded by some as Toronto's best restaurant. Every detail is overseen by owner Franco Prevedello (who has lavished $2 million on his beautiful dining room), right down to the variety of home-made breads and valet parking. On the outside it may seem a little too hard and trendy but it's a lot more accessible inside, with a clever use of lighting and columns, beautiful furniture and plenty of squashy banquettes. "*An outstanding restaurant, very popular and trendy, with an eclectic menu and good wine list*" – DANIEL STOFFMAN. "*It has probably taken over from Splendido* [see entry] *as the place to be seen – all the stars come here*," says VALERIE GIBSON.

GRANO

2035 YONGE ST

☎ (416) 440 1986

Authentic Italian food in a very lively atmosphere. Lots of freshly baked ciabatta and focaccia bread; delicious antipasti and some very original pasta dishes. You can either wait at the espresso bar for your table or take away. The menu is vast, with 40 vegetarian dishes alone. "*It's almost as much fun as eating in Italy*" – SHEILA SWERLING-PURITT.

JOSO'S

202 DAVENPORT ST

☎ (416) 925 1903

This old Victorian house, decorated with the proprietor's quirky collection of busts and breasts, happens to serve the best seafood in town. Popular with Hollywood types.

NORTH 44

2537 YONGE ST

☎ (416) 487 4897

Still highly acclaimed as much for the visually arresting decor as for the spectacular food. Brushed steel, mirrors and marbled floor, and exotic flowers like fresh ginger and lilies provide the backdrop. Chef Mark McEwan's inventive menu is essentially Southwestern with the odd Asian undertone. There is a private dining room at the back seating 12–15 with a hand-painted mural depicting the view from a Venetian canal. "*I admire Mark McEwan for his unpretentious cooking, which he evidently takes very seriously. He always seems to catch the public mood*" – DANIEL STOFFMAN.

IL POSTO

148 YORKVILLE AVE

☎ (416) 968 0469

Toronto's San Lorenzo or Daphne's – popular

CANADIAN FASHION Visit any of Canada's major cities these days and you'll find lots of talented designers creating eminently wearable frocks. In Toronto there's **Alfred Sung**, 55 Avenue Rd, ☎ (416) 515 8625, who provides loosely cut but beautifully tailored classic suits for working girls. For figure-hugging street gear along the lines of Jean-Paul Gaultier go to **Comrags**, 410 Adelaide St W, ☎ (416) 504 7175. **Deborah Kuchme**, 380 Queen St E, ☎ (416) 360 1600, is renowned for her beautifully feminine clothes. For something a bit more dressy, **Stephen Caras**, 720 King St W, Suite 801, ☎ (416) 703 6929, will provide you with glamorous evening and day wear. Toronto's Mr Haute Couture is **Winston Kong**, 10 Irwin St, ☎ (416) 924 8837. His outfits are an occasion in themselves – he'll knock up something for everything from a charity gala to a wedding. In Vancouver **Catherine Regehr**, Suite 1, 2245 Trafalgar St, ☎ (604) 734 9339 is the great fashion hope, specializing in eye-catching, elegant evening wear, including fabulously long and lean black numbers. However, it is Montreal that has appointed itself Canada's fashion capital (no doubt playing on its French – hence Parisian – associations to the full). "La Cité de la mode" combines Canada's world-famous technology with French flair, resulting in clothing that is quite unique. **Hélène Barbeau**, 3416 Park Ave, Montreal, ☎ (514) 849 4010, is owned and run by the designer herself. This high-ceilinged, airy store caters for young professionals and media types. Her main objective is to transform and tailor the latest styles into more comfortable working clothes. Alterations can be made on the premises for customers. **Marie Saint Pierre**, 4455 rue St-Denis, Montreal, ☎ (514) 281 5547, offers styling for those with artistic tastes – *prêt à porter* fashion for career women – making everything from dresses to trousers to coats. **Muse**, 4467 rue St-Denis, Montreal, ☎ (514) 281 5547, specializes in career wear, but is more avant-garde than that might suggest. Designer Christian Chenall designs a *prêt à porter* collection and individual pieces, ranging from the nostalgic to the novel, for artists and special customers.

with socialites and business types who come for lunch for the simple but excellent Italian food, and in summer, for the flower-lined patio. "*The rich and famous eat here and it's excellent; elegant yet very cosy. Nella knows everyone*," says ROSEMARY SEXTON. BOB RAMSAY is also a fan: "*You can always rely on it – it weathers all fads and is always full.*"

SPLENDIDO BAR AND GRILL
88 HARBORD ST
☎ (416) 929 7788
One of a new generation of slick Italian restaurants, popular with film and media types – from the King of Toronto restaurateurs, Franco Prevedello. Californian/Italian contemporary menu. The bar is a popular stop-off for nightcaps.

SHOPPING

DAVID'S
66 BLOOR ST
☎ (416) 920 1000
One of Toronto's most popular designer stores, specializing in the highest-quality footwear at the highest prices. VALERIE GIBSON recommends the lower-priced line in the **CAPE DAVID** boutique.

F/X
116 CUMBERLAND
☎ (416) 975 5511
The trendy Queen St fashion house offers tons of party dresses that involve miles of tulle and rainbow colours, created by Betsey Johnson, Anna Sui and others.

SPORTING LIFE

2665 YONGE ST

☎ (416) 485 1611

A staggering range of sports equipment and clothing from the hippest sports ranges. "*A terrific store with a great selection of ski-wear and informal type clothes*" – DANIEL STOFFMAN. Excellent service but can get horrendously over-crowded.

WILLIAM ASHLEY

55 BLOOR ST W

☎ (416) 964 2900

Where every bride in Toronto should be registered, it features all the best china, crystal and silver gifts in the country.

YUSHI

162 CUMBERLAND ST, RENAISSANCE CT

☎ (416) 923 9874

A carefully chosen collection of Japan's foremost designers.

THEATRE

PANTAGES THEATRE

263 YONGE ST

☎ (416) 872 2222

A beautiful old vaudeville theatre full of gilding and mirrors. It's currently home to the Canadian production of *The Phantom of the Opera*.

PRINCESS OF WALES THEATRE

300 KING ST W

☎ (416) 872 1212

Entirely new theatre built by Ed and David Mirvish, owners of Toronto's Royal Alexander and London's Old Vic, to house *Miss Saigon*.

ROYAL ALEXANDRA THEATRE

260 KING ST

☎ (416) 872 3333

The place to be seen at in Toronto ever since it was first built in 1907. For the best view of the stage and the rest of the theatre, book the first row of the stalls circle.

Vancouver

CLUBS

RICHARD'S ON RICHARDS

1036 RICHARDS ST

☎ (604) 687 6794

Ever popular trendy disco playing current chart music affectionately known as "Dick's on Dicks". "*An iconoclastic icon, it's been there for ever*" – STEVE PODBORSKI.

HOTELS

FOUR SEASONS

791 W GEORGIA ST

☎ (604) 689 9333

Bustling 28-storey hotel, next to the Vancouver Stock Exchange and attached to Pacific Centre shopping mall. Stylish and tasteful, with outstanding service and all the usual Four Seasons perks plus a huge sun deck and an indoor–outdoor pool. The club-like formal dining room, the CHARTWELL, is one of the city's finest eateries.

PAN PACIFIC HOTEL

300–999 CANADA PL

☎ (604) 662 8111

The dramatic and modern Pan Pacific (built for Expo 86) has unbelievable views of the mountains and harbour. Rooms are decorated in earth tones and have a minimalist Japanese feel. The FIVE SAILS dining room has one of the best panoramic views in the city and serves an imaginative menu to match it. Wonderful health club. "*You want it, you got it. It really stands out in a class of its own*" – STEVE PODBORSKI.

WEDGEWOOD HOTEL

845 HORNBY ST

☎ (604) 689 7777

Small, elegant property, owned and run by a very caring proprietress, Eleni Skalbania. A real treasure – no tour groups or conventions stay here. The bar is a fun place for star-spotting. "*Beautifully run, immaculate. Like a little English oasis in the middle of Vancouver*," raves ROSEMARY SEXTON.

ENCORE Anyone who is anyone in Vancouver will know that Yaletown is fast becoming the area to hang out. For a little refreshment while you're down there, go to the **Yaletown Pub**, 1111 Mainland Ave, ☎ (604) 681 2739, owned by well-known Vancouverite Mark James, or to one of the many local cafés and pool halls that line the area, including the **Bar None**, 1222 Hamilton St, ☎(604) 689 7000 . . . . ◗

MUSEUMS

MUSEUM OF ANTHROPOLOGY

6393 N W MARINE DR, UNIVERSITY
OF BRITISH COLUMBIA
☎ (604) 822 5087
Designed by internationally acclaimed
Canadian architect Arthur Erickson, the muse-
um houses a collection of Northwest Coast
Indian art built on Point Grey cliffs. Displays
totem poles, war canoes and carved works.

OMNIMAX AND SCIENCE WORLD

1455 QUEBEC ST
☎ (604) 268 6363
Commissioned for Expo 86, this is the world's
largest dome screen (more than seven regular
screens' high) featuring mostly travel and nature
films. Science World next door is a hands-on
museum with performance demonstrations and
a special "Search Gallery" for children.

VANCOUVER PUBLIC AQUARIUM

STANLEY PARK
☎ (604) 682 1118
This is one of the best and most exciting
aquariums in the world, home to killer whales,
sharks and a myriad of other marvellous underwater creatures. The humid Amazon rain-
forest gallery, complete with assorted alligators,
giant cockroaches, piranhas, tropical birds and
jungle vegetation, is a big attraction too.

RESTAURANTS

SEE ALSO HOTELS.

BISHOP'S

2183 W 4TH AVE, KITSILANO
☎ (604) 738 2025
Here owner–chef John Bishop effectively
blends West Coast and Continental cuisine,
while concentrating on local seafood. The
restaurant is made up of several small rooms,
each decorated in white with a large
Expressionist painting. A favourite of ROBERT
DE NIRO when he's in Vancouver.

CHARTWELL

AT THE FOUR SEASONS (SEE HOTELS)
☎ (604) 884 6715
The flagship restaurant of the Four Seasons
hotel and the perfect place for powerbroking.
It has the air of a smart St James's club. Robust
but inventive Continental cuisine is served and
there is a good choice of low-fat and low-
calorie alternatives.

LE CROCODILE

100–109 BURRARD ST
☎ (604) 669 4298
Famed for serving superb simple food, chef
Michael Jacob's Alsatian background is evident
in his rather romantic little French bistro.
Prices are very reasonable.

IL GIARDINO DI UMBERTO

1382 HORNBY ST
☎ (604) 687 6316
Built by Umberto Menghi (who also owns the
original Umberto Florentine Restaurant down
the road), this is considered the city's best
Italian. It's popular with a wealthy crowd who
want to be seen out and about. "*Whenever
Umberto Menghi opens a restaurant there's a stampede. I love his menus, they have a unique character*"
– STEVE PODBORSKI.

LOLA'S

432 RICHARDS ST
☎ (604) 684 5652
Having closed Delilah's, the same team have
now opened up Lola's in a renovated old building in downtown Vancouver. The menu is
more upmarket – superb food with theatrical
presentation – as is the extremely fashionable
crowd. The best martinis in town.

STAR ANISE

1485 W 12TH AVE
☎ (604) 737 1485
A beautiful little arty restaurant in the increasingly fashionable 12th and Granville neighbourhood. Overseen by maître d' Sam Lalji and
chef Adam Busby, who is praised for his consistent, imaginative and not overhandled food.

SHOPPING

LEONE

757 W HASTINGS ST
☎ (604) 683 1133
Ultra-chic boutique selling all the designer
gear, notably DKNY and Giorgio Armani. Set
in an award-winning heritage building. They
also do a good line in shoes, handbags, fragrances and costume jewellery, not to mention
the cosy in-house cappuccino bar. Celebrities
flock there including ERIC CLAPTON, MEL GIB-
SON, BRUCE WILLIS and GOLDIE HAWN.

VERSUS

1008 W GEORGIA ST
☎ (604) 688 8938
Architecturally stunning boutique where the

ultra-hip and rather rich sip espressos while browsing through potential purchases from Versace's ready-to-wear range.

Rest of Canada

ART AND MUSEUMS

NATIONAL GALLERY OF OTTOWA

380 SUSSEX DR, OTTOWA
☎ (613) 990 1985
Inside one of Ottawa's main attractions you'll find the reconstructed Rideau Convent Chapel – a 19C piece of French Canadian architecture – and a comprehensive collection of Canadian art. There are several restaurants and cafés and a large bookshop.

HOTELS

HASTINGS HOUSE

PO BOX 1110, GANGES, BC
☎ (604) 537 2362
Romantic inn-type retreat right on the water at Salt Spring Island. It's very English in atmosphere – comfortable rooms and impeccable service and food. Visit the local artists' studios, and the arts and crafts on sale at the Saturday market.

THE MILLCROFT INN

P O BOX 89, JOHN ST, ALTON, ONTARIO
☎ (519) 941 8111
After an hour's drive from Toronto you can sit out on the patio of this restored 19C knitting mill and manor house and listen to the sound of falling water, while in the kitchen exquisite French food will be cooked up for you by head chef Reinhard Scheer-Hennings. Unsurprisingly, this is one of Canada's finest hotels

THE SHERWOOD INN

PORT CARLING, MUSKOKA, ONTARIO
☎ (705) 765 3131
Set on stunning Muskoka Lake, the New England style Sherwood Inn offers a holiday home to Canada's richest. It effectively combines health and hedonism with its spa, lake sports and other outdoor pursuits, which are invariably followed by huge six-course dinners.

SOOKE HARBOUR HOUSE

1528 WHIFFEN SPIT RD, RR4, BC
☎ (604) 642 3421
Rustic California-style rooms with hot tubs, lots of wood, big windows and Indian blankets. Rooms face either the ocean or the wide panorama of the mountains. There's easy access to the 3,500-acre national park.

RESTAURANTS

GRANNAN'S

MARKET SQ, ST JOHN, NEW BRUNSWICK
☎ (506) 634 1555
Nautically decorated old warehouse serving serious quantities of seafood such as the "Captain's Platter" for two. There are also three lively bars connected to the restaurant, which spills out onto the pavement in summer.

SKI RESORTS

BANFF, ALBERTA

Half the fun of Banff is getting there. If you catch the train from Vancouver or take a car from British Columbia, you'll pass through the most awe-inspiring part of one of the world's most dramatic mountain ranges – the Rockies. Once there, you'll find skiing aplenty, with 11 lift-service ski areas and abundant opportunities for cross-country skiing. But remember to

TOUR DE FORCE For the strong skier, a heli-skiing holiday with **Canadian Mountain Holidays**, P O Box 1660, Banff, Alberta, ☎ (403) 762 7100, is *"the ultimate ski vacation – there's absolutely nothing like it in the world,"* according to STEVE PODBORSKI. You'll be dropped off in the freshest powder and stay in the company's own mountain lodges in a wild and otherwise inaccessible part of the mountains. In summer you can go heli-hiking too and stay at one of the company's private luxury hiking lodges in the Cariboo and Purcell mountain ranges. But book well in advance.

take your thermals – skiing in Canada is usually a lot chillier than it is in the Alps. The expert should head for **MOUNT NORQUAY**, ☎ (403) 762 4421 (information service), where there are lots of notoriously steep runs. At **LAKE LOUISE**, ☎ (403) 522 3555, the terrain is larger and more varied with a good spread of runs for all standards. Similarly, **SUNSHINE VILLAGE**, ☎ (403) 762 6500, which is quite high up, offers lots of intermediate runs. The best hotels in Banff are old and stately and situated in breathtaking spots. The **BANFF SPRINGS HOTEL**, Spray Ave, P O Box 960, Banff, ☎ (403) 762 2211, looks like a beautiful old castle and is one of the resort's main attractions. The **RIMROCK**, Mountain Ave, P O Box 1110, Banff, ☎ (403) 762 3356, is perched on top of Sulphur Mountain, which is surrounded by hot pools. It has a fantastic view over the Rockies. For good food, eat at **RISTORANTE CLASSICO** at the Rimrock, ☎ (403) 762 3356 a very cosy restaurant where you can sit in grand armchairs and gorge on chef Hans Sauter's crespelle con porcini served with various fine wines from an extensive list. For more Gallic flavours go to **LE BEAUJOLAIS**, 212 Buffalo St at Banff Ave, ☎ (403) 762 2712. Elegantly decorated in sumptuous neo-classical style with lots of heavy tapestries on the walls, it seems strikingly out of place in casual Banff.

WHISTLER AND BLACKCOMB, BC

Probably the finest resort in Canada, offering the two biggest ski mountains in North America and the most advanced ski-lift system in the world. In the winter, the main attractions are the skiing and the hot-tubbing, while in summer tennis, golf and mountain biking predominate. The one constant seems to be the nightlife, which keeps going throughout the year. The best hotel is **CHATEAU WHISTLER**, 4599 Château Blvd, P O Box 100, Whistler, ☎ (604) 938 8000, a large and friendly-looking fortress just outside the village. The floor-to-ceiling windows have a dramatic view over the foot of Blackcomb Mountain. The suites, with their specially commissioned quilts and antique furnishings, are fit for a king. *"You can practically fall out of bed and on to the ski lift and ski right into the hot tub. Several fine restaurants also,"* reports STEVE PODBORSKI. When you're eating out, don't miss **LES DEUX GROS**, 1200 Alta Lake Rd, Whistler, ☎ (604) 932 4611. The trusty French cuisine tastes superb and is well presented, with good but unobtrusive service. Great spot for a cosy romantic dinner – ask to sit by the huge stone fireplace.

CARIBBEAN
Anguilla

CAP JULUCA
MAUNDAY'S BAY
☎ 497 6666
Cap Juluca is a secluded resort set in its own 179-acre private estate, where JANET JACKSON and MICHAEL J FOX come to relax. Accommodation, whether room, suite or pool-villa, is set in whitewashed Moorish-style buildings stretching out across the magical mile-long white sand beachfront of Maunday's Bay. The gardens are filled with palms, orchids and frangipani, while the rooms have their own ice-machines, sunken baths and private walled gardens. The villas even have their own swimming pool. The food is exceptional by Caribbean standards and if you get bored with lying around on the beach, you can be as active as you like with everything from croquet and tennis to waterskiing and sailing. *"I love Anguilla – the weather, the service, the food, the little bungalows, the quality of the sand, like walking on satin sheets"* – DOUGLAS FAIRBANKS JR.

COVECASTLES
P O BOX 248, SHOAL BAY
☎ 497 6801
Small beach-house resort with simply decorated private villas commanding spectacular views of the sea. Treats include Roux brothers' cuisine in the French restaurant, lots of fishing, snorkelling and windsurfing from the hotel. Complimentary Dom Perignon and caviare for those on their third visit.

MALLIOUHANA HOTEL
P O BOX 173, MAIDS BAY
☎ 497 6111
Probably Anguilla's most sophisticated resort, Malliouhana sits on a promontory commanding views of a secluded cove and two miles of white sand. The rooms are large and Michel Rostang's French restaurant offers exceptional seafood and the finest selection of wine in the Caribbean – indeed, with a wine cellar containing 25,000 bottles, this has to be *the* most prized Caribbean port of call for the food and wine connoisseur. And for the sporty, outside there are two swimming pools, an outdoor Jacuzzi, four tennis courts and some lovely landscaped gardens.

Antigua

COPPER & LUMBER STORE

P O Box 184, St John's

☎ 460 1058

A former warehouse in the English Harbour which has prime dockfront views and pretty Georgian-style suites. Eat fish and chips out of the *Sunday Times* with a pint of English beer in the **MAINBRACE BAR**, which becomes the focal point of the Antigua Race Week madness at the end of April. Or try some of Angella Jackson's West Indian cuisine in the **WARDROOM RESTAURANT**.

CURTAIN BLUFF HOTEL

P O Box 288, Old Rd, Curtain Bluff Peninsula, St John's

☎ 462 8400

The super-smart Curtain Bluff provides the perfect stop-off for yachties. Swiss chef Rendy Portmann produces good food, and if yachting isn't your thing, you can play tennis, squash, any water sport or opt for a bit of putting.

JUMBY BAY CLUB

P O Box 243, St John's

☎ 462 6000

The reclusive's exclusive, all-inclusive resort, set in 300 acres of peace and quiet, a mile or so off the north coast of Antigua. A private island where SIR PETER USTINOV, PAUL McCARTNEY and THE EX-KING AND QUEEN OF GREECE come to flop – there are no radios, no telephones and no televisions. Transport around the island is by bicycle only and water sports are non-motorized. You can eat in your suite or at the Estate House.

ST JAMES' CLUB

Mamoray Bay, P O Box 63, St John's

☎ 460 5000

St James' Club is one of the Caribbean's most action-packed resorts. There are two beaches (ideal launching pads for all kinds of water sport), three swimming pools, a gymnasium, riding and seven tennis courts. In the evening you can wind down in one of three restaurants and a casino.

Barbados

COBBLER'S COVE HOTEL

Road View, St Peter Parish

☎ 422 2291

This rather grand, old-style hotel offers newly revamped bathrooms and several fresh new suites designed by Pru Lane Fox, complete with four-poster beds, private roof terraces, Jacuzzis and enough reading matter to satisfy the most voracious bookworm. Chef Leslie Alexander uses the freshest of ingredients in the Continental menu and there's plenty of waterskiing, sailing, windsurfing and golf.

THE COLONY CLUB HOTEL

Porters, St James

☎ 422 2335

The Colony Club's 77 colonial-style private apartments are scattered around 7 acres of tropical gardens overlooking St James Bay. Relax or bomb around the bay on waterskis, windsurfers, sailboats or flippers.

ROYAL PAVILION

Porters, St James

☎ 422 5555

One of the Caribbean's finest hotels and the more glamorous, upstart sister of neighbouring Glitter Bay. The colonial-style hotel offers stunning ocean-front suites, set in lovely tropical gardens. While breakfast and lunch is best on the beach, dinner is in the **PALM TERRACE** or the less grand bistro café. There are boutiques selling designer gear, lots of health and fitness facilities, an outdoor swimming pool and a couple of floodlit tennis courts. Water sports are complimentary as are transfers to the champion golf course nearby.

SANDY LANE

St James

☎ 432 1311

This is where MICHAEL WINNER, DES O'CONNOR, ANDREW NEIL, assorted babes and the occasional lottery winner all come to have a good time. Everything is done on a grand scale – whether you're being met off Concorde by

ENCORE The Antigua Classic Yacht Regatta followed by Antigua Sailing Week is the Caribbean's equivalent to Cowes. The sight of classic sloops, yawls, ketches and gaffers all sailing along the same course at the same time is a breathtaking spectacle. A week later (usually on the last Sunday in April), the Sailing or Race Week begins. With over 250 international yachts competing, it eventually culminates in the spectacular Nelson's Ball, when the prizes are awarded . . .

one of the hotel's shining white Rolls-Royces, dousing yourself in complimentary Floris or drinking champagne at breakfast. There are five tennis courts, the hotel's own 18-hole championship golf course, extensive water sports and a fitness centre – all with expert tuition. Deep sea fishing and scuba diving including certification are also available. The cuisine is prepared by top international chefs including Hans Schweitzer, and there is an excellent cellar.

Barbuda

"I HEARD BARBUDA IS PARADISE ON EARTH, BUT I STILL WASN'T PREPARED FOR THE BREATHTAKING VIEWS WHEN I ARRIVED" –

CLAUDIA SCHIFFER

THE K CLUB
BARBUDA
☎ 460 0300
The K Club is owned by Mariuccia Mandelli – mastermind of the Krizia empire. You stay in private cottages, all of which sit on the Caribbean's most beautiful private beach, the showers are outside and if you wish, someone will come and cook breakfast for you in your own private kitchen. The central clubhouse is vast and is where you can tuck into delicious home-made pastas, breads and pastries. If you want to keep busy, you can go deep sea fishing, play golf, tennis, swim in a heated swimming pool. Or just be pampered by the resident masseur. *"The architecture, the decoration and the atmosphere are excellent; the location is idyllic, with such a natural calm. Cuisine and service are excellent and the wine cellar is well chosen,"* advises ROGER VERGE. CLAUDIA SCHIFFER adds, *"At the resort I lived amidst beauty and comfort, from soft armchairs with a wondrous view of the ocean to freshly baked bread."*

Bermuda

CAMBRIDGE BEACHES
MANGROVE BAY, SANDY'S PARISH
☎ 234 0331
Set on a peninsula with a bay of its own, Cambridge Beaches dates back to the 17C,

when it was a cottage colony. These days it's a modern resort, with a fully equipped spa, a marina, croquet lawn and putting green.

Grenada

THE CALABASH
BOX 382, L'ANSE AUX EPINES BEACH, ST GEORGE'S
☎ 444 4334
Set in a natural cove with 8 acres of shady tropical gardens and a fine beach, the Calabash has 30 suites – all with garden and sea views and some with their own plunge pools. The hotel has a good reputation for its food, wine and general hospitality. You can have a casual lunch at **JEFFERSON'S BEACH BAR** and dinner at the slightly more formal **CICELY'S RESTAURANT**. Fitness facilities include a secluded freshwater pool, floodlit tennis and a gym.

SECRET HARBOUR
BOX 11, ST GEORGE'S
☎ 444 4439
Grenada's most romantic resort, hidden away in lush tropical gardens on the slopes of Mount Harman. There are 20 deluxe suites, all of which have huge verandahs with superb views.

Grenadines

BASIL'S BAR
BRITANNIA BAY, MUSTIQUE
☎ 458 4621
Built out into the water on stilts, this is the best – and most infamous – bar on Mustique where you can sample the very best lobster that the Caribbean has to offer. Wednesday night is barbecue buffet night, which is followed by an excellent "jump up" (the Caribbean term for a dance), usually accompanied by live music from great Caribbean bands.

THE COTTON HOUSE
P O BOX 349, MUSTIQUE
☎ 456 4777
Mustique's only hotel is a lovingly restored 18C house built of stone and coral. The rooms have private balconies and views to die for. The dining verandah is the place to eat in the evening and is a hang-out for the locals – which include MICK JAGGER and JERRY HALL, PRINCESS MARGARET and VISCOUNT and VISCOUNTESS LINLEY as well as the occasional Hollywood star.

BEST PLACE FOR NEW YEAR'S EVE

There's nothing like escaping the soggy British winter for a dry, warm and sunny Christmas and New Year in the Caribbean. But where do you spend Old Year's Night (as it is known here)? Basil's Bar on Mustique is one of the hot favourites. After a sumptuous feast you dance the night away to live bands under a star-spangled blanket of a sky. If you're really lucky, you might even get an invitation to a private party given by one of the many illustrious islanders. And on New Year's Day you can join Mick Jagger's Educational Trust Charity party on Macaroni Beach.

PALM ISLAND BEACH HOTEL
PALM ISLAND, ST VINCENT
☎ 458 8824
Quintessential tropical island, half a mile long offering a scattering of stone cottages and its own 52-foot yacht. Deep sea fishing, scuba diving and great Créole cuisine.

PETIT ST VINCENT RESORT
PETIT ST VINCENT
☎ 458 8801
A small, privately owned island hideaway, almost totally surrounded by white sand beaches. The 22 spacious cottages are scattered over 113 acres of variable terrain and all have complete privacy. Personal service is provided by staff in Mini Mokes who respond to flags hoisted outside each cottage. There's a fitness trail (with hammocks lining the route), various water sports, snorkelling, deep sea fishing, tennis and kayaking.

Jamaica

THE HALF MOON CLUB
P O BOX 80, MONTEGO BAY
☎ 953 2211
Set on a mile-long stretch of white-sand beach and 400 acres of tropical garden, each of its villas has its own swimming pool, cook, maid and gardener. There is also an 18-hole golf course, several tennis and squash courts, water sports and some of the best riding in Jamaica. Famous guests have included QUEEN ELIZABETH II and GEORGE BUSH.

JAMAICA INN
OCHO RIOS
☎ 974 2514
You can swim in freshwater pools, snorkel, kayak and dine under the stars in this intimate, colonial-style, family-run affair where people come not to show off, but to genuinely relax.

SANS SOUCI LIDO
P O BOX 103, OCHO RIOS
☎ 974 2353
Pastel-pink fantasy land tucked between two headlands, complete with gazebos and grottoes. Pampering at the spring-fed health spa includes massage, body scrubs and facials. Oceanside pool, golf, tennis club, and water sports.

STRAWBERRY HILL
IRISHTOWN, JAMAICA
☎ 944 8400
Created by music mogul Chris Blackwell and set in a remote part of the Blue Mountains (accessibility isn't a problem – it's got its own helipad), Strawberry Hill is the ultimate bolt-hole for the hip at heart. It may look like your typical whitewashed 19C planter's house, complete with ceiling fans, four-posters and hammocks, but you'll find enough technology in each room to keep the gadget-conscious happy. The food – new Jamaican cuisine – is good.

TRYALL GOLF, TENNIS AND BEACH CLUB
P O BOX 1206, MONTEGO BAY
☎ 956 5660
This is the golf or tennis junkie's dream, where CLINT EASTWOOD and BILL MURRAY come to play and BORIS BECKER to practise. There are nine tennis courts and a championship golf course. You stay in super-serviced seaside or hillside apartments, each with its own cook, chambermaid, laundress, gardener and swimming pool.

St Barthélemy

HOTEL LE TOINY
ANSE DE TOINY
☎ 278888
Totally private and with spectacular views, all

the villas are tastefully appointed with Italian fabrics, mahogany and all mod-cons and a private swimming pool.

St Kitts and Nevis

THE GOLDEN LEMON INN
DIEPPE BAY, ST KITTS
☎ 465 7260
Set in a grand 17C house, on a black-sand beach beneath the spectacular volcanic peak of St Kitts. There are no televisions, no children, no entertainments – so it's perfect for a serious flop or a serious read. Lots of people come here either to get married or to honeymoon. You can, however, go hiking, mountain climbing, riding, do some water sports, or play tennis.

MONTPELIER PLANTATION INN
P O BOX 474, NEVIS
☎ 469 3462
Definitely the Caribbean's most characterful hotel, owned by old Etonian James Milnes Gaskell. Located on a hillside overlooking the sea, this is where SAM NEILL comes to relax. The Inn was rebuilt when the Gaskell's bought it in the late 60s and returned it to its 18C glory (this is where Lord Nelson got married in 1787). There's a private beach, tennis court and a large freshwater pool set in a tropical garden, with its own pool bar. Wonderful local produce is served in the restaurant.

St Lucia

THE BISTRO
RODNEY BAY
☎ 452 9494
A charming and cheerful little restaurant, with its own marina, on the waterfront. Run by Nick and Pat Bowden, the atmosphere is friendly and the cooking French, with a varied menu which makes good use of local seafood.

JALOUSIE PLANTATION
P O BOX 251, SOUFRIÈRE
☎ 459 7666
An ever-popular luxury complex regularly attracts royalty and celebrity. Good food, a full range of water sports plus an unusual adventure playground are set among the 18C sugar-plantation ruins.

St Martin

LA SAMANNA
BP4077, 97064 ST MARTIN, FRENCH WEST INDIES
☎ 876 400
ROBERT DE NIRO, DIANA ROSS, TED TURNER and JANE FONDA, and SIR DAVID and LADY CARINA FROST all come to this ultra-discreet resort. You can certainly feel the French influence on the food – which is ultra-fresh – and the excellent wine list. There is a fitness pavilion, windsurfing, waterskiing and tennis. Each room has a huge fridge filled with ice-cold drinks and its own kitchen.

"I GET COMPLETELY AWAY FROM WORK IN THE CARIBBEAN – IT'S PEACEFUL, BEAUTIFUL AND HOT"
– KATE MOSS

Virgin Islands

LITTLE DIX BAY
PO BOX 70, VIRGIN GORDA, BRITISH VIRGIN ISLANDS
☎ 495 5555
Originally developed by Laurence S Rockefeller, a keen conservationist, each room has its own private path leading down to the beach, and guests are given their own rubber

ENCORE Every May **St Lucia** hosts a week-long jazz festival where international artists, such as George Benson, perform all over the island. It culminates in a finale on the breathtaking setting of Pigeon Island . . . . . ♦ The best time to visit **Barbados** is March – the apogee of the Barbadian social season. The weather is ideal and it's time for cricket, polo, gold cup racing and opera under the stars at Holders Hill (a house belonging to John Kidd, father of supermodel JODIE KIDD). . . . . ♦

sunbeds which double up as lilos. Try the wonderful tropical cocktails, which are brought to you on the beach; as well as the delicious freshly grilled lobster.

PETER ISLAND RESORT AND YACHT HARBOUR

P O BOX 211, ROAD TOWN, TORTOLA
☎ 494 2561
Island-sized resort with acres of breathtaking gardens. Tennis courts, mountain bikes, fitness trail, dive shop, big-game fishing. The best villa is the hilltop Crow's Nest. Go swimming in Dead Man's Bay.

CHILE
Santiago

CLUBS

THE OZ

CHUCRE MANSUR 6
☎ (2) 737 7066
Of the smarter clubs, this is one of the best, offering a good mix of current music. It's great for people-watching as there's a huge staircase sweeping down from the bar to the dance floor.

CRUISES

For an unforgettable 800-mile trip through fjords running the length of Chile, a cruise is your answer. The Skorpios cruise, past the SAN RAFAEL GLACIER with its 230 ft-high spires of 30,000-year-old ice, is probably the most dramatic. You can go on *Skorpios II*, a luxury cruise ship with indoor and outdoor thermal pools where each cabin suite has its own bathroom. For details contact the head office at Augusto Leguia Norte 118, Las Condes, ☎ (2) 231 1030. In southern Chile you can go for a

cruise around the TIERRA DEL FUEGO and PATAGONIA CHANNELS and visit the exotic and historic city of Puerto Williams, the most southern city in the world. For details on a luxury cruise here contact Cruceros Australis, Ave El Bosque Norte 0440, ☎ (2) 203 5030.

HOTELS

CARRERA

TEATINOS 180
☎ (2) 698 2011
Santiago's oldest hotel, which, though traditional in style, has been updated recently for business travellers – it has set aside an entire floor, complete with butler service and a private bar for executives. On the roof there's a pool as well as the ROOF GARDEN restaurant while downstairs you can indulge in the gastronomic delights of the COPPER ROOM. Full health and fitness facilities available.

HOTEL KENNEDY

AVE KENNEDY 4570
☎ (2) 219 4000
A tall glass structure, which opened in 1994, provides mainly business travellers with all mod cons: telephones in the bathrooms, bilingual secretaries, full conference facilities and a beauty salon. Try the 5-star AQUARIUM restaurant, which serves international cuisine by a first-rate French chef and has access to an excellent cellar of Chilean export wines.

HYATT REGENCY

AVE KENNEDY 4601, LAS CONDES
☎ (2) 218 1234
Situated in an affluent area of Santiago – don't worry about being a bit out of the centre – the hotel offers its own transport services to and from downtown. The architecturally striking building is designed so that each room has a spectacular view; most have private terraces too. The 4-storey executive suites have private dining and games areas. There's a large health club and a pool with a waterfall.

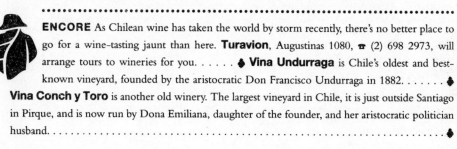

ENCORE As Chilean wine has taken the world by storm recently, there's no better place to go for a wine-tasting jaunt than here. **Turavion**, Augustinas 1080, ☎ (2) 698 2973, will arrange tours to wineries for you. . . . . . ♦ **Vina Undurraga** is Chile's oldest and best-known vineyard, founded by the aristocratic Don Francisco Undurraga in 1882. . . . . . . ♦ **Vina Conch y Toro** is another old winery. The largest vineyard in Chile, it is just outside Santiago in Pirque, and is now run by Dona Emiliana, daughter of the founder, and her aristocratic politician husband. . . . . ♦

RESTAURANTS

SEE ALSO HOTELS.

AQUI ESTA COCO
LA CONCEPCIÓN 236, PROVIDENCIA
☎ (2) 205 5985
The best fish and shellfish restaurant in
Santiago, where the decor is suitably nautical
and the waiters know what the freshest and
best fish catches are each day. Closed Sun.

BALTHAZAR
AVE LAS CONDES 10690
☎ (2) 215 1090
A carefully restored adobe stable now serving
excellent, often unusual, Chilean-style *nouvelle
cuisine*. The owners might prefer to think of it as
French, but there are distinct shades of Japanese,
Indonesian, Chinese and Arab in the cooking.

METRO
AVE LAS CONDES 10690
☎ (2) 217 3130
Two restaurants in one – a highly regarded
sushi bar upstairs and a wider menu downstairs, serving everything from ribs to Asian-
inspired dishes. Set in a former nightclub.

SHOPPING

THE WINE HOUSE
AVE EL BOSQUE NORTE 0500
☎ (2) 232 7257
Having tasted all the wines at the vineyards, you
can buy most of the export range at this speciality wine shop. The Chileans usually prefer
the old traditional-style wines, which are likely
to have sat in beech barrels for far too long, so
it is vital that you go for the export stuff.

SKIING

For clean air during the Chilean winter (last-
ing from June to Oct), head for the Andes,
where you'll find some of the finest skiing in
the Southern hemisphere. Most of the best
resorts are easily accessible from Santiago, but
none is as highly developed as resorts in
Europe or the US, so don't be surprised if
roads are blocked even after a relatively light
snowfall. Only 25 miles east of the capital is
FARELLONES – EL COLORADO, which has 18
lifts connecting up with pistes of varying difficulty and offers night-time skiing Fri–Sat. In

the same skiing area, 34 miles from Santiago, is
LA PARVA, a slightly more upmarket resort with
pistes for all standards and ample opportunity for
snowboarding and heli-skiing. For specialized
instruction on heli-skiing and heli-surfing,
VALLE NEVADO is the place to go, where you'll
find plenty of decent hotels. The smartest choice,
however, is 90 miles northeast of Santiago –
PORTILLO (no relation) is where Olympic skiers
go to train off-season. It offers the best accommodation in the whole of the Andes, including
the colonial-style **HOTEL PORTILLO**. There's
expert avalanche control, and new snow-making
machinery means that the pistes are always well
covered. Portillo, with its legendary 9-mile run
from the statue of Christ of the Andes, is particularly well suited to the serious skier. Facilities
such as heated swimming pools and massage parlours are the rule rather than the exception. For
further details contact Sernatur, National
Tourism Board, Ave Providencia 1550, ☎ (2) 236
1416. Or for Portillo contact Americas in Britain
on ☎ (0181) 673 9222.

CHINA
Beijing

HOTELS

JIANGUO
5 JIANGUOMENWAI RD
☎ (10) 500 2233
One of Beijing's most reliable hotels, with a
good, central location and all necessary mod-
cons, making it perfect if you're there on business. **CHARLIE'S COCKTAIL LOUNGE** is a
popular evening meeting spot. "*My favourite,
the nicest hotel in Beijing; it's as cosmopolitan as you
get in China,*" says ROBIN HANBURY-TENISON.

PALACE HOTEL
WANG FUJING ST
☎ (10) 512 8899
This grand 15-storey hotel is superbly situated
in the heart of town. With a dozen-plus
restaurants you can eat whatever you want,
while businessmen can use the full business
services of **THE PALACE CLUB**.

SHANGRI-LA
29 ZIZHUYUAN RD
☎ (10) 831 2211
The flagship for the Shangri-La chain and

HOTEL RESTAURANTS IN BEIJING It is as well to remember that in China poor hygiene is rife, so unless you have a cast-iron stomach, avoid street stalls. A much safer bet is to eat in the restaurant of a reputable hotel. **The Kunlun Hotel**, 2 Xin Yuan Nan Lu, Chao Yang District, ☎ (10) 500 3388, has one of the city's best Shanghainese restaurants. Excellent Sichuan food can be found in **The Palace Hotel** (see Hotels), which also has surprisingly good Western food to offer. Another alternative, if you're really desperate, is McDonald's, currently in Wangfujing St, where international standards of hygiene should apply; in the next few years a further 600 are due to open throughout the country. Or head for the **Great Wall Sheraton Hotel** where there's a new **Hard Rock Café**.

about 30 minutes outside Beijing, it is the preferred choice for visiting tycoons. Sumptuous accommodation, Cantonese or Continental food, a pool, gymnasium and a health centre. "*An exquisite level of service*" – CLAUDIA CRAGG.

TRADERS HOTEL
1 JIANGUOMENWAI AVE
☎ (10) 505 2277
Situated in the China World Trade Centre, an utterly European, if quite flash, hotel with huge, well-furnished rooms and speedy room service.

RESTAURANTS

SEE ALSO HOTELS.

BEIJING KAOROUJI
14 QIANHAIDONGYAN SHISHAHAI
☎ (10) 401 2170
When you have finished your tour of the Forbidden City, pop into this restaurant next to it, set in a 140-year-old building, for a delicate feast.

FANG SHAN RESTAURANT
BEIHAI PARK
☎ (10) 404 2573
Dishes from imperial chefs continue the traditions of the Forbidden City. Their combination of unusual ingredients and intricate presentation is traditionally supposed to endow recipients with health, wealth and sexual prowes.

FENGZEYUAN
XINFUSANCUN, CHAOYAN DISTRICT
☎ (10) 401 7508
The best place in Beijing for visitors to try out Shandong cuisine – not something you're likely to find easily back home. Be sure to try the particularly good snowflake prawns, the duck marrow soup and the braised asparagus.

KAMOGAWA
CHINA WORLD HOTEL, JIANGUOMENWAI AVE
☎ (10) 505 2266
One of the city's best Japanese restaurants, serving expertly prepared sushi.

QIAN MEN QUAN JE DE ROAST DUCK RESTAURANT
32 QIANMEN ST
☎ (10) 701 6321/3687
"*The direct descendant of the street stall on which Peking Duck was invented last century. Real Peking Duck is surprisingly simple, no marinade, no basting, just a special breed, roasted in front of a wood fire: the skin is separated from the flesh by compressed air to encourage crispness. Served with pancakes and small sesame buns – you remove the centre to make room for the duck – and they told me never to include spring onion AND cucumber, just one or the other,*" explains GLYNN CHRISTIAN.

SICHUAN FANDIAN
RONGXIAN HUTONG, NO 51
☎ (10) 303 6356
A beautifully decorated old mansion containing nine courtyards where you can sample excellent hot, peppery Sichuan dishes including lantern chicken and hot sauce noodles.

TINGLI GUAN
SUMMER PALACE
☎ (10) 208 1276
This restaurant is worth visiting for the location alone. The former private theatre of the Dowager Empress Ci Xi, it has a stunning location on the shore near the Marble Boat.

NOSTALGIA IN SHANGHAI

Today Shanghai is a sprawling metropolitan area where 13 million people live, betwixt and between miles of subway and freeway. But in spite of this, it is the last place in China where you can witness the unmistakable decadence of the early 1900s, when Shanghai was known as the "Paris of the Orient". Sadly, as the city undergoes its current feverish building boom, the last vestiges of the colonial era and its Art Deco monuments are finally beginning to vanish, so go now. Take a nostalgic walk starting at Nanjing Road (across from the Park Hotel) through the area that used to be the **International Settlement**, where you can still see some of the grand colonial mansions. There's also the former **Shanghai Race Club**, which is now the municipal library. Going east towards the Huangpu River, the **Cathay Hotel** is an Art Deco classic. Part of this building used to be contained in what was formerly **Sassoon House**, owned by a wealthy Iraqi–Jewish tycoon, in old Shanghai and where Noël Coward wrote *Private Lives* in 1930. Walk north across Suzhou Creek on Waibaidu Bridge and take the elevator to the roof of Shanghai Mansions, which is now a hotel but used to be **Broadway Mansions**, a well-known homebase for expats in Shanghai. Also close by are the former **Astor House Hotel** (now housing the Shanghai Securities Exchange) and the Russian Consulate. What used to be the **French Concession** is separated from the British quarters by Yanan Road (formerly Avenue Edward VII). In the circular Old Town, visit **Yu Gardens**, which dates from the 16C and is a tranquil, classical Chinese garden.

Shanghai

HOTELS

SHANGHAI HILTON INTERNATIONAL
250 HUASHAN RD
☎ (21) 248 0000
Modern international hotel for travelling execs. Facilities galore – gymnasium, tennis and squash courts, billiards, swimming pool, and a rooftop bar where you can have aperitifs before dinner in one of four restaurants.

RESTAURANTS

SEE ALSO HOTELS.

OLD TOWN RESTAURANT
242 FU YOU LU, SHANGHAI
☎ (21) 328 2782
Old-world establishment offering both Shanghainese and Huaiyangese cuisine as it was served in Shanghai's glory days.

Rest of China

HOTELS

GOLDEN FLOWER HOTEL
8 WEST CHANGLE RD, XIAN, SHAANXI PROVINCE
☎ (29) 332981
Next to the archaeological site of the Terracotta Army, this is one of the best hotels in China, renowned for its efficient staff. There is both a Chinese and an international restaurant, piano bar, health club and pool. "*Very unusual to find such personal management, quite a spectacularly different standard from anywhere else in China*" – ROBIN HANBURY-TENISON.

WHITE SWAN HOTEL
SHAMIAN ISLAND, GUANGZHOU, GUANGDONG PROVINCE
☎ (20) 888 2288
Spectacular spot on historic Shamian Island encircled by the Pearl River. Countless restau-

---

EXOTIC FOOD IN CHINA
If you're a hardy culinary adventurer, you may want to pay a visit to the **Shang Chi ("Victory") Seafood and Wild Delicacies Restaurant** in Guangzhou province. Here you'll find delicacies that you are unlikely to find anywhere else on earth, let alone Europe. Even the "ordinary" menu consists of pheasants, guinea hens, cats, sea snails and eels. The 6 ft Cobra meal, for a mere $600, is, let's face it, rather special. It even includes a soup based on the fragrant bouquet of snake bladder liqueur. The house speciality is mushrooms and bamboo sprouts with rats.

---

rants, tennis courts, swimming pools, a health and beauty club and beautiful **BANYAN GARDENS**. CLAUDIA CRAGG recommends it: *"An old tried and true favourite, largely responsible for setting the standard in this part of the mainland. They serve up a mean bacon and eggs, otherwise hard to find in edible form."*

CZECH REPUBLIC
Prague

....

"PRAGUE IS THE LEFT BANK OF THE 90S" – ALAN LEVY,
EDITOR-IN-CHIEF,
PRAGUE POST

....

ART AND MUSEUMS

NATIONAL GALLERY
HRADCANSKE NAM 15
☎ (2) 24 51 0594
This cannot be missed. Housed in the 18C Sternberg Palace, it includes icons and religious art from the 3C to 14C; works by Holbein, Van Dyck, Canaletto and modern masters. And so far it's been blissfully free from tourists.

THE STATE JEWISH MUSEUM
U STAREHO HRBITOVA 1
☎ (2) 24 81 0099 (CEREMONIAL HALL)
Adolf Hitler had planned to open a museum here documenting the life of what he anticipated would be an "extinct" people. Today's museum is made up of the old Jewish cemetery and Prague's collection of synagogues. The names of those who died under the Nazi regime are listed in the Pinkas Synagogue. A combined ticket for the cemetery and the synagogues is available from the office at the Ceremonial Hall or at the High Synagogue.

BARS AND CAFES

CAFE MILENA
STAROMESTKE NAMESTI 22, PRAGUE 1
☎ (2) 26 08 43
The Café Milena is the best place to take a good look at the famous Astronomical Clock over a strong coffee, away from all the crowds in the square below.

LOBKOVICKA
VLASSKA 17, MALA STRANA
☎ (2) 53 01 85
A wine hall, set inside a 17C palace, it's known for some of the most imaginative food in town. Wine will be brought up from a musty cellar as required.

U ZLATEHO TYGRA
HUSOVA 17, STARE MESTO
☎ (2) 24 22 90 20
One of the last surviving authentic Czech beer halls, great to go to for a quick half-pint. Doors open at 3 pm.

HOTELS

DIPLOMAT
EVROPSKA 15, PRAGUE 6
☎ (2) 24 39 41 11
Rather lacking in character but regarded as the best business hotel in town. Convenient for both the airport and the city centre. Bilingual staff, and full fitness and conference facilities.

FORUM

KONGRESOVÁ 1, PRAGUE 4

☎ (2) 61 19 11 11

A towering new hotel near the Palace of Culture. Worth staying at for the splendid views across Prague from the top-floor gym.

PALACE PRAHA

PANSKA UL 12, PRAGUE 1

☎ (2) 24 09 31 11

Set in a renovated Art Nouveau palace which Franz Kafka used to frequent, the Palace has well-furnished bedrooms with large, white marble bathrooms. The ground floor houses the city's best casino.

PRAGUE HILTON ATRIUM

POBREZNI 1, 1800, PRAGUE 8

☎ (2) 24 84 11 11

One of Prague's newest, it has an impressive atrium-style interior, a choice of bars and restaurants, two indoor tennis courts and full spa facilities.

U PAVA

U LUZICKEHO SEMINARE 34, MALA STRANA

☎ (2) 24 51 09 22

Set on a quiet street which is still lit by gas, this neo-classical inn offers unparalleled views of Prague Castle from its top-floor suites and is reputed for its discreet and courteous staff.

MUSIC

CZECH PHILHARMONIC

RUDOLFINUM, NAM JANA PALACHA

☎ (2) 24 89 33 52

If they are playing in town (a rare event, as they spend most of their time on the road), catch them if you can.

PRAGUE SPRING MUSIC FESTIVAL

BOX OFFICE: HELLICHOVA 18, PRAGUE 1

☎ (2) 24 51 04 22/24 53 34 73

The annual Prague Spring Festival attracts international names to the city each May. Concerts and recitals take place in glorious settings such as the Rudolfinum and St Vitus Cathedral. Book early for the major events.

OPERA

NARODNI DIVADLO (National Theatre)

NARODNI TRIDA 2

☎ (2) 24 91 34 37/24 21 50 01 (Box Office)

STATNI OPERA PRAHA (State Opera House)

WILSONOVA 4

☎ (2) 26 53 53 (Box Office)

There is a strong operatic tradition in Prague and some truly excellent productions are staged. Usually sung in Czech, they often feature national composers such as Dvořák and Smetana.

RESTAURANTS

SEE ALSO HOTELS.

U MALIRU

MALTEZSKE NAMESTI 11, PRAGUE 1

☎ (2) 24 51 02 69

This French restaurant is reputedly the city's most expensive, but it's worth eating here for the lovely setting – a medieval building in Maltese Square.

U MECENASE

MALOSTRANSKE NAMESTI 10, PRAGUE 1

☎ (2) 53 38 81

For a real taste of traditional Czech hospitality and food this is your place – a 17C inn, with dark, high-backed benches in the front and comfy sofas at the back. Book a table in the old room. Great steaks.

U MODRE KACHNICKY (The Blue Duckling)

NEBOVIDSKA 6, PRAGUE 1

☎ (2) 24 51 02 17

A rather appealing Czech restaurant, enhanced by exotic murals on the walls, where game and duck are the specialities. Extremely popular, so book ahead.

OPERA GRILL

KAROLINY SUETLE 35, PRAGUE 1

☎ (2) 24 26 55 08

A cosy restaurant with Meissen candelabras and a menu that includes the best steaks in the city. Book early and take a taxi – it is as popular as it is tricky to find.

PARNAS

SMETANOVO NABREZI 2, NOVE MESTO

☎ (2) 24 22 76 14

A comfortable 1920s-style restaurant, popular with visiting dignitaries, who come for the great views of Prague Castle across the river (make sure you request a window seat) and the food. The menu is international but includes some Czech specialities and a predominantly Czech wine list. Book ahead.

PENGUIN'S

ZBOROVSKA 5, PRAGUE 5

☎ (2) 54 56 60

Classic Czech cuisine. Good for steak, and some of the freshest vegetables in town. The name refers to the owner's favourite hockey team – the Pittsburgh Penguins.

U ZLATE HRUSKY
NOVY SVET 3, HRADCANY
☎ (2) 53 11 33
The "Magic Pear" is set in an 18C building in the magical heart of old Prague. The service may be a little pompous, but you'll find the best in traditional East European food, such as duck served with cranberries or cabbage and sliced dumplings.

SHOPPING

MOSER
NA PRIKOPE 12, PRAGUE 1
☎ (2) 24 21 12 93/4
The biggest and best selection of Bohemian glassware at its central Prague showroom.

PAVILION
VINOHRADSKA 50, PRAGUE 2
☎ (2) 242 331 251
A smart new indoor shopping centre with specialist shops and boutiques stocking international brand names.

DENMARK
Copenhagen

BALLET

ROYAL DANISH BALLET
THE ROYAL THEATRE, KONGENS NYTORV, P O BOX 2185, DK-1017
☎ 3314 1002
World-class ballet under the direction of Peter Schaufuss. Renowned for its large repertoire of classical and modern productions, including the works of Denmark's great choreographer August Bournville.

BELOW STAIRS Look out for those small, atmospheric cellar restaurants on either side of Strøget (the pedestrian street), between Rådhus Pladsen (the Town Hall square) and Kongens Nytorv. **Kanal-Kaféen**, on Frederiksholms Kanal, has a view of the canal and Christiansborg; while the paintings at **Husmanns Vinstue** will give you a better idea of how old Copenhagen was. In this type of restaurant, seasonal dishes are served – for example, lumpfish roe and the first garfish in early spring, and new asparagus and hand-peeled shrimps a bit later.

HOTELS

HOTEL D'ANGLETERRE
KONGENS NYTORV 34, DK-1050
☎ 3312 0095
Copenhagen's best hotel with an unbeatable location on the city's largest square. This classically decorated and antique-crammed neo-Georgian mansion now enjoys a new health club with a swimming pool, Jacuzzi, fitness centre, sauna, Turkish bath, solarium and massage facilities.

PHOENIX COPENHAGEN
BREDGADE 37, DK-1260
☎ 3395 9500
A Louis XVI-inspired hotel characterized by bright, elegantly furnished rooms and fabulous Italian-marble bathrooms. Set in the midst of Copenhagen's financial district, it's got all the modern facilities that one needs. You can eat at

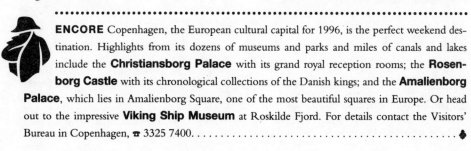

ENCORE Copenhagen, the European cultural capital for 1996, is the perfect weekend destination. Highlights from its dozens of museums and parks and miles of canals and lakes include the **Christiansborg Palace** with its grand royal reception rooms; the **Rosenborg Castle** with its chronological collections of the Danish kings; and the **Amalienborg Palace**, which lies in Amalienborg Square, one of the most beautiful squares in Europe. Or head out to the impressive **Viking Ship Museum** at Roskilde Fjord. For details contact the Visitors' Bureau in Copenhagen, ☎ 3325 7400. . . . . ◆

either **MURDOCH'S BOOKS AND ALE** (a Scottish-style pub) or **VON PLESSEN**, which offers French cuisine.

SKOVSHOVED HOTEL

STRANDVEGEN 267, DK-2920, CHARLOTTENLUND
☎ 3164 0028
In the charming village of Skovshoved, a couple of miles from the city centre, this hotel with its wonderful sea views provides a great escape. The bar, restaurant and tap rooms feature Danish and French cuisine.

RESTAURANTS

SEE ALSO HOTELS.

CAFE LUMSKEBUGTEN

ESPLANADEN 21, DK-1263
☎ 3315 6029
Old port-authority building oozing 1850s splendour. Chef Knud Wolmuth's cuisine is traditional Danish with a modern French twist. There's an extensive wine list, and 39 brands of cigar on offer. They also have a famous "green mobile" which will deliver meals wherever you want. Closed Sun.

KONG HANS KAELDER

VINGÅRDSTRAEDE 6, DK-1070
☎ 3311 6868
A magnificent vaulted Gothic cellar, this is the first Michelin-starred restaurant in Denmark, thanks to the wonderful French food of Alsatian chef Daniel Letz. There's also a daily market menu and an impressive list of French wines. Closed Sun.

RESTAURANT KOMMANDANTEN

NY ADELGADE 7, DK-1104
☎ 3312 0990
Once the residence of the city's military governor in the 16C, this is now the showcase for Francis Cardenau's artful blend of traditional Danish and French flavours.

DUBAI

Dubai is where East meets West, where the mystique of the Arab world combine with a modern city on the edge of the Arabian Gulf. Its progress from a sleepy trading port in the 1950s to the commercial, shopping and sports capital of the Middle East is due to the vision of the late Sheikh Rashid Bin Saeed al-Maktoum, who, mindful of Dubai's limited oil reserves, set out to build upon its trading traditions and create a commercial and service-oriented hub open to the outside world. Today his sons uphold their father's tradition of accessibility.

In the hotels and restaurants, the menus offer a variety of international food and drink, including alcohol. Sporting facilities are extremely varied, with golf and polo, along with rather more original pastimes including camel racing, falconry, wadi-bashing (desert forays in a four-wheel drive vehicle) or sailing in the Creek on the ancient dhows.

For shoppers, Dubai is a tax-free haven, and that extends well beyond the airport. The traditional souks (markets) compete with the air-conditioned modern malls. Gold (24 carat) is the cheapest to be found anywhere. The best time to visit is during the six-week Shopping Festival. Prices are slashed, shops are open all hours and there are cultural events such as the heritage and diving villages, folk dancing and international singing stars.

The most prestigious event, however, is the Dubai World Cup, the richest horse race in the world bringing together the best thoroughbred horses from across the globe.

But remember that, despite the easy atmosphere, it is an Islamic country, and so what you wear and what you do should be tempered accordingly.

SIOBHAN ADAMS

FIJI ISLANDS

CASTAWAY ISLAND RESORT

MALOLO ISLAND
☎ 611 233
Set on a rocky point this fully refurbished, large and luxurious resort is perfect for a water-sports holiday or simply for sitting by the pool and sipping cocktails. Listen out for the local band.

THE REGENT, FIJI

P O BOX 908, NADI
☎ 780 700
The most luxurious resort on the main island, set in lush tropical gardens near the beach. Western whims are catered for, from extensive tennis facilities to hairdressers, while in the evening you can immerse yourself in pure Polynesia and watch fire-walkers and singers.

Alain de Botton on Egypt

Those who hate to follow a crowd are soon forced to realize that going to Egypt is hardly an original thing to do. The country is the world's oldest tourist destination. When Antony met Cleopatra, she offered to take him on a tour of Upper Egypt in order to see what she was already referring to as "the Ancient Monuments". And that was in 42 BC, with the monuments of Thebes, Kom Ombo and Abu Simbel dating back 2,000 years, which is about what separates *us* from Cleopatra.

There may be a huge gulf of time between us and Ancient Egypt, but uniquely it hardly seems that way to someone walking around the halls of the Egyptian Museum in Cairo or the annexes to the temple at Luxor. Everything is astoundingly well preserved, so well preserved that my impulse was to believe that a group of canny decorators from the Egyptian tourist board had been at work adding bright paint to some of the friezes on the ancient stones. But no: it is merely the climate, which is so dry that paintwork has survived on many a temple exactly as it was left by an Egyptian craftsman after a hard morning's work one sunny hot Monday 4,000 years ago. It is also the result of a culture obsessed with preserving itself for the next world, an obsession which, ironically, has in actuality turned out to mean preserving itself for *this* world, complete with Nikon cameras and Hilton hotels.

A danger of any trip to Egypt is to develop what might be termed "Date-guilt" – nothing romantic in this case, simply a nagging feeling, which can strike at any time, but most particularly in a bus on the way to a monument, that one has forgotten how the pharaonic dynasties work, that Rameses II's dates have become a blur and that one has no clue what the god Amun was up to in the spirit world. Having returned from a trip to Egypt four months ago, but now remembering precious few dates, gods and dynasties, my only advice would be to ignore the pressure to know facts. Simply spend time dreamily looking at sunsets, at the colour of stones, at the pillars of temples – for these are the things which will stick in the mind.

Inevitably, the tourist in Egypt has to work hard at not being turned into the docile, miniature-pyramid-buying sheep that the tourist industry relishes. Particularly dangerous are cruises down the Nile. These take place on rectangular floating hotels packed with ghastly groups of people betraying their worst national characteristics, and enthusiasically responding to the announcement of an evening's entertainment with a belly dancer. The boat I travelled on threatened to drive me to murder or suicide, for over the Tannoy, it manifested a singular fondness for Chris de Burgh. What should have been aesthetic peaceful moments gliding down the Nile had, in the background, permanent imbecilic droning about the lady in red and fire on the water. Far more appropriate are the two great hotels along the Nile, the Old Cataract at Aswan and the Old Winter Palace in Luxor. These are places that transport guests back to the days of Edwardian ladies who used to escape the cold English winters, and who introduced the very civilized habit of sandwiches and tea on the terrace at five.

Slightly off the beaten track in Aswan is a stone-quarry with a reminder of the human effort that went into building the huge monuments of Egypt: it is an unfinished obelisk, which the craftsmen had been carving out for Luxor temple, but which broke mid-way through the process and had to be abandoned. You can imagine the frustration of the workmen and the difficulty of their task – and it goes to make this beautiful ancient world seem all the more immediate and human.

Take a picnic to the secluded island of Akuilau – exclusive to Regent guests.

TOBERUA ISLAND

P O Box 567, Suva
☎ 302 356 (OFFICE); ☎ 479 177 (ISLAND)
A tiny island paradise, with only 14 private thatched bures (cottages). Go day-tripping to

the uninhabited islands nearby and by night feast under the stars.

TURTLE ISLAND

Level 38, Rialto South Tower, 525 Collins St, Melbourne, Australia
☎ 3000 008 816 717 OR 9629 4200
Great food, wine and comfortable accommo-

dation overseen by a wonderfully good-natured cast of islanders. The 500-acre island is ringed by 14 private beaches – one per couple. Water sports dominate the activities list and the diving is sensational.

VATULELE ISLAND RESORT
P O Box 470 Woollahra, NSW 2025, Australia
☎ 326 1055
TOM CRUISE and NICOLE KIDMAN come here to get away from it all,. Not even their agents can contact them – there are no telephones, no papers and no televisions. It's run by the energetic producer-turned-hotelier Henry Crawford who has created 12 rather theatrical villas beside the beach using thatch, terracotta and tree trunks. Meals are eaten together on the terrace, overlooking the lagoon, but if you prefer you can either have your meal served at your beach-house or go and have your own private dinner party on nearby Nooki-Nooki Island. The food is Thai, Indian or Japanese.

THE WAKAYA CLUB
P O Box 15424, Suva
☎ 440 128
Eight authentic looking private "huts" with hand-woven bamboo walls overlooking a white-hot beach. Each hut has a proper bathroom, a fully stocked bar and a fridge. There are lots of sports: scuba diving, nine-hole golf, floodlit tennis, croquet and deep sea fishing.

YASAWA ISLAND LODGE
P O Box 10128, Nadi Airport
☎ 663 364
The paradise island of Yasawa consists of over 12,000 acres of rain forest and coconut palm, a handful of smiling villagers and just one resort. The food is cosmopolitan and the 16 thatch-roofed huts are a luxury version of your average traditional Fijian house.

FINLAND
Helsinki

ACTIVITIES

SAMPO ICE BREAKER TOURS
Runeberginkatu 40, FIN-00260 Helsinki
☎ (0) 440 326
The hardy can join the ice breaker *Sampo* as it

carves its way through the frozen sea off Lapland. The cruise can also be combined with fishing on the ice, riding on snowmobiles, reindeer driving, and immersing oneself in the ice-cold sea wearing special survival suits.

ART AND MUSEUMS

SEURASAARI PARK & OPEN AIR MUSEUM
Seurasaari
☎ (0) 484 712
A forested island about 3 miles from the centre of Helsinki, which has been transformed into an open-air museum. There are buildings covering Finnish folk heritage and a beautifully preserved 17C church. During the summer you can watch folk dancing, concerts and the traditional midsummer celebration. In winter you can go skiing or sleigh riding in the area.

HOTELS

HOTEL KALASTAJATORPPA
Kalastajatorpantie 1, 00330 Helsinki
☎ (0) 45811
Based on the coast in a quiet garden suburb of Helsinki (2½ miles from the centre), this hotel enjoys its own beach and cross-country skiing trails. The hotel is made up of several buildings which are linked by underground halls. There are various cafés and restaurants offering good traditional fishy Finnish food or a full international menu.

LORD HOTEL
Lönnrotinkatu 29, 00180 Helsinki
☎ (0) 6801680
A centrally located castle hotel which looks rather severe from the outside but is warm and beautifully decorated, Art Deco style, within. Many of the rooms are housed in a modern wing leading off the central courtyard.

⊛ OMAPOHJA TEATTERIMAJATOLO
Itä Teatterikuja 3, 00100 Helsinki
☎ (0) 666 211
An inn dating from 1906, which used to accommodate actors from the National Theatre. The rooms are large, atmospheric and old-fashioned with big windows.

HOTEL GRAND MARINA
Katajanokanlaituri 7, 00160 Helsinki
☎ (0) 16 661
An old customs house built at the beginning of

the century and now converted into a luxury hotel. The rooms are decorated simply and stylishly and most modern needs are catered for, from rooms specially equipped for allergy sufferers to heated parking.

KAIVO

PUISTOTIE, HELSINKI

☎ (0) 17 7881

This is where all the super-cool students of Helsinki go to relax, eat and drink. Friendly atmosphere and regular live music.

Rest of Finland

FESTIVALS

PORI JAZZ FESTIVAL

PORI JAZZ 66 RY, ETELARANTA 6, 28100 PORI

☎ (39) 550 5550

This festival features some of the best musicians from Europe, performing in big open-air concerts and jam sessions during July.

SAVONLINNA OPERA FESTIVAL

OLAVINKATU 35, SAVONLINNA

☎ (57) 576 750

This festival, which has been going since 1912, involves a series of operatic performances, art exhibitions and concerts which are held in and around the main courtyard of the medieval **OLAVINLINNA CASTLE**. Another venue is the **RETRETTI ART CENTRE**, the largest manmade cave in Europe. The festival takes place each July and the easiest way to get there is via the regular "opera flights" from Helsinki.

FRANCE
Paris

ART AND MUSEUMS

CENTRE GEORGES POMPIDOU

PLACE BEAUBUORG, 75004

☎ (1) 44 78 12 33

Designed by architects Richard Rogers and Renzo Piano, it stands in the heart of old Paris; is home of the Musée National d'Art Moderne, containing both French and international 20C art; and is host to a whole range of contemporary art, design and photography exhibitions. There's a good reading library and it's a great place to pick up lots of funky posters, postcards and design objects. Lively piazza with trendy cafés and tuneful buskers. Closed Tues.

CITE DES SCIENCES ET DE L'INDUSTRIE

PARC DE LA VILLETTE, 30 AVE CORENTIN CARIOU, 75019

☎ (1) 40 05 70 00

Understand the latest developments in science and technology. Explora covers the Earth and the universe, while La Géode is a state-of-the-art panoramic cinema. There's also a planetarium and Inventorium with the latest scientific inventions. Closed Mon.

GALERIES NATIONALES DE JEU DE PAUME

PLACE DE LA CONCORDE, 75001

☎ (1) 42 60 69 69

Unique gallery for post-1960 art housed in a restored pavilion looking on to the Jardin des Tuileries. Excellent video room. Closed Mon.

THE GRAND PALAIS

3 AVE DU GÉNÉRAL EISENHOWER, 75008

☎ (1) 44 13 17 17

The top venue for all the major international touring exhibitions, it usually hosts the FIAC (Foire International d'Art Contemporain) each Oct, where all the main international art galleries have stands – however, this is currently being held at the Espace Tour Eiffel, Quai Branly, until repair work is completed at the Grand Palais in 1998. Closed Tues. The **PETIT PALAIS** opposite, at ave Winston-Churchill, ☎ (1) 42 65 12 73, houses a permanent collection ranging from antiquities to 19C art. Closed Mon.

INSTITUT DU MONDE ARABE

1 RUE DES FOSSÉS-ST-BERNARD, 75005

☎ (1) 40 51 38 38

A celebration of Arabic culture and civilization, using books, film, art and architecture, all housed in French architect Jean Nouvel's extraordinary 1987 building. There's also a museum full of scripts, rugs, ceramics, silver and brass. Stop off in the top-floor café, which has beautiful views of the Seine and the Ile St Louis especially on sunny days. Closed Mon.

MUSEE CARNAVALET

23 RUE DE SÉVIGNÉ, 75003

☎ (1) 42 72 21 13

Follow the history of Paris through art, memorabilia, maps and a series of splendid reconstructed Louis XIV, Louis XV and 18C

SPECIALIST MUSEUMS ..

As you're in the birthplace of *haute couture*, not to be missed is the **Musée Palais Galliéra**, 10 Ave Pierre ler de Serbie, 75115, ☎ (1) 47 20 85 23 for a history of the fashion industry . . . . .
For stunning Asian art, visit the **Musée Guimet**, 6 Place d'Iéna, ☎ (1) 47 23 61 65 . . . . . The **Musée Nissim de Camondo**, 63 rue de Monceau, 75008, ☎ (1) 45 63 26 32, is a townhouse on Parc Monceau filled with exquisite 18C furniture, paintings and china. The **Musée Bourdelle**, 16 rue Antoine Bourdelle, ☎ (1) 45 48 67 27, is the house and studio of Rodin's contemporary and fellow sculptor Emile Bourdelle; and the **Musée des Arts Africains et Océaniens**, 293 Ave Daumesnil, 75012, ☎ (1) 43 46 51 61, contains the best primitive art to be found in Paris, as well as Marshall Lyautey's splendid Ruhlmann Art Deco study. JEAN-MICHEL JAUDEL loves the slightly old-fashioned atmosphere: "*It's off the beaten track, but their collection of Océaniens art is unequalled in this hemisphere.*"

rooms. Also housed in the 17C **HÔTEL CARNAVALET** and the neighbouring **HÔTEL LE PELETIER DE ST-FARGEAU** is art from the Revolution. Closed Mon.

MUSEE D'ORSAY

I RUE DE BELLECHASSE, 75007
☎ (I) 40 49 48 14
A temple to the golden era of French art – the Impressionists and their predecessors. Join the queues to see Manets and Monets galore. Its latest most controversial acquisition is Gustave Courbet's scandalous *L'Origine du Monde*. Superb collections of sculpture and decorative arts (especially Art Nouveau) plus a smart restaurant and chic café behind the glass clockface. The revamped bookstore is brilliant for art books in all languages. Closed Mon.

MUSEE DU LOUVRE

34 QUAI DU LOUVRE, 75001
☎ (I) 40 20 53 17
The Louvre is now the third-largest museum in the world (after the Metropolitan, New York, and the National Gallery, Washington). "*It's a great institution for getting your teeth into the whole of European culture – the only trouble is, people go to see the dreary things like the Mona Lisa whereas they should be wandering around the antiquities*" – BRIAN SEWELL. The awesome collection covers Egyptian, Greek (Venus de Milo, etc), Roman and Oriental antiquities; objects and furniture; and countless master works of sculpture and painting from European schools. The best place to rest is the trendy **CAFÉ MARLY** in the Aile Richelieu, overlooking the sculpture courtyard. Other features are a new shopping centre (if you need a pair of glasses, don't miss **MIKISSIME**, where computer screens will help you choose the most flattering frames) and the best multilingual bookshop in town. "*If I had to choose only one gallery, I would have to be greedy and choose the Louvre*" – CLAUS VON BULOW. Closed Tues.

MUSEE PICASSO

HÔTEL SALÉ, 5 RUE DE THORIGNY, 75003
☎ (I) 42 71 25 21
Delightful museum based in a lovely 17C hotel in the heart of the Marais district. Follow Picasso's life through his paintings, statues, ceramics, book illustrations, manuscripts and sketches. Closed Tues.

MUSEE RODIN

HÔTEL BIRON, 77 RUE DE VARENNE, 75007
☎ (I) 47 05 01 34
The Kiss, The Thinker and *The Bourgeois de Calais* are all represented amid the calm of this very grand 18C house and garden next to Les Invalides. You can see many of Rodin's preparatory works: drawings, sketches and plastercasts.

PALAIS DE TOKYO

AVE DU PRÉSIDENT WILSON, 75116
☎ (I) 47 23 36 53
One of the top modern-art venues in Paris. The wing to the right is the **MUSÉE D'ART MODERNE DE LA VILLE DE PARIS**, ☎ (1) 47 23 61 27; it has no permanent collection but

hosts temporary exhibitions, such as the recent Giacometti retrospective. The wing to the left is a national centre for photography (the largest exhibition/archive space in the world) and for cinema (four projection rooms with the last word in modern technology, archives and a training school). There's also a library, brasserie and bookshop with views over the Seine. Closed Mon.

BALLET

L'OPERA DE PARIS

PALAIS GARNIER, 8 RUE SCRIBE, 75009
☎ (1) 47 42 53 71
One of the largest opera houses in the world, designed by the architect Charles Garnier, it houses the world's oldest ballet company, originally developed from the Académie Royale de Musique founded in 1669 by Louis XIV. Now under the direction of Hugues Gall, it once more produces opera as well as ballet.

BARS AND CAFES

ANGELINA

226 RUE DE RIVOLI, 75001
☎ (1) 42 60 82 00
"*An elegant, old-fashioned café which does the most marvellous Mont Blanc – rich and delicious. A place to go if you've been doing hard shopping or sightseeing and want a little rest in elegant circumstances*" – SOPHIE GRIGSON. Great place to collapse with a cup of rich and thick hot chocolate too.

AUX DEUX MAGOTS

170 BLVD ST-GERMAIN, 75006
☎ (1) 45 48 55 25
Famous Left Bank arty meeting place, firmly on the tourist trail, but don't be put off. Just get there early in the morning for a croissant and a petit noir.

✺ LE CAFE BLEU

15 RUE DU FAUBOURG ST-HONORÉ, 75008
☎ (1) 44 71 32 32
Recently opened in the basement of the Lanvin shop, it's the perfect stop-off for busy shoppers hungry for good, quick and easy meals – good value.

CAFE DE FLORE

172 BLVD ST-GERMAIN, 75006
☎ (1) 45 48 55 26

Former talking shop for Rive Gauche intelligentsia – Sartre, Simone de Beauvoir, Camus and Picasso – next door to the Deux Magots. "*For me the best breakfast café . . . scrambled eggs and good coffee*" – ALEXANDRE LAZAREFF.

L'ECLUSE

15 QUAI DES GRANDES-AUGUSTINS, 75006 AND BRANCHES
☎ (1) 46 33 58 74
The best of a chain of wine-bars – devour an assiette autour de l'oie and a glass of sauternes – in unfussy, minimalist surroundings.

WILLI'S

13 RUE DES PETITS-CHAMPS, 75001
☎ (1) 42 61 05 09
Trendy wine bar owned by Englishman Mark Williamson, with a splendid list of more than

NIGHT TRIPS AND DAY TRIPS . . . . . Don't

be put off by the kitsch connotations, but you really haven't "done" Paris until you've been for an evening boat ride along the Seine and seen the floodlit flying buttresses of Notre-Dame and spectacular views hidden from the streets. There's an over-whelming number from which to choose. One of the best companies is Bateaux Parisiens, port La Bourdonnais, 75007, ☎ (1) 44 11 33 44, based on the Left Bank, just off the esplanade des Invalides. Their *bateaux mouches* are better than most – more up-to-date, with on-board restutants and special lights to illuminate the monuments better. Their trips also last longer . . . . . .
A day trip to Burgundy from Paris, in order to do some serious wine-tasting, is quite feasible. Catch the TGV to Dijon, hire a car and visit the most famous vineyards: Chassagne Montrachet, Nuits St-Georges or Pommard.

100 wines, particularly strong on Côtes du Rhône. The French may sigh in disbelief but the food is good too.

CLUBS

LES BAINS

7 RUE DU BOURG-L'ABBÉ, 75003
☎ (1) 48 87 01 80
The absolute No. 1 spot for a wild night in Paris. You can meet anyone here from JEAN-PAUL GAULTIER to CINDY CRAWFORD; it's also a favourite with rich Russian mafia.

LE BAL DU MOULIN ROUGE

82 BLVD DE CLICHY, 75009
☎ (1) 46 06 00 19
Come to the birthplace of the can-can and the famous haunt of Toulouse-Lautrec for the most authentic cabaret.

LE BARFLY

49 AVE GEORGES V, 75008
☎ (1) 53 67 84 60
A huge bar–restaurant–music place filled with beautiful girls. A steady crowd will meet here for pre-theatre drinks; a wilder crowd comes for dinner before moving off; and finally by 11 pm it becomes a hip watering hole. Supermodels NADJA AUERMANN and KAREN MULDER are habituées.

CAVEAU DE LA HUCHETTE

5 RUE DE LA HUCHETTE, 75005
☎ (1) 43 26 65 05
The most famous of the jazz clubs. Laid-back and great music.

LE KEUR SAMBA

79 RUE LA BOÉTIE, 75008
☎ (1) 43 59 03 10
Black beat and dry heat. The place to be in the 90s.

LE LIDO

116 BIS AVE DES CHAMPS-ELYSÉES, 75008
☎ (1) 40 76 56 10
A more modern cabaret act than the Moulin Rouge with some fabulous dancers.

LA LOCOMOTIVE

90 BLVD CLICHY, 75018
☎ (1) 42 57 37 37
Hip club right next to the Moulin Rouge. All types of music on three levels with half an hour of pure 70s every evening.

LE NEW BACK

6 RUE ARSÈNE HOUSSAYE, 75008
☎ (1) 53 76 17 71
A new Beur (French–Arab) place that specializes in the rock-inspired North African music called "rai". AZZEDINE ALAÏA, anti-racist leader HARLEM DÉSIR, the model FARIDA and other North African luminaries often drop by.

NEW MORNING

7–9 RUE DES PETITES-ECURIES, 75010
☎ (1) 45 23 51 41
Paris's answer to a Soho jazz club in London. Some of the biggest names in jazz, Latin and soul music perform here. Cool but friendly.

REGINE'S

49 RUE DE PONTHIEU, 75008
☎ (1) 43 59 21 60
One of the greats of the club world, regularly featured in the pages of *Paris-Match*.

LE TANGO

11 RUE AU MAIRE, 75003
☎ (1) 42 72 17 78
A small, slightly dingy Afro–Latino place just behind the Centre Georges Pompidou with a surprisingly electric atmosphere. Younger people show up between 11 pm and midnight, while the older, more sophisticated crowd shows up around 4 am for a last Cuba Libre. A favourite with socialite novelist FRÉDÉRIC BEIGBEDER.

HOTELS

HOTEL LE BRISTOL

112 RUE DU FAUBOURG ST-HONORÉ, 75008
☎ (1) 53 43 43 00
The Bristol provides a quietly glamorous stop-off for heads of state and high-flying diplomats. Superb Louis XV and XVI furnishings and a charming rooftop swimming pool designed by César Pinnau, the naval architect responsible for the yachts of Onassis and Niarchos.

HOTEL DE CRILLON

10 PLACE DE LA CONCORDE, 75008
☎ (1) 44 71 15 00
One of the world's great hotels in one of the world's most celebrated squares. Inside the exquisite 18C exterior you'll find lavish decor. The best rooms have terraces overlooking the Place de la Concorde. LES AMBASSADEURS restaurant (see box under Restaurants), which is positively glittering with Baccarat glass and

HOTEL RESTAURANTS

For years the French wouldn't have dreamt of eating in a hotel restaurant unless absolutely necessary – it was for tourists. But Parisians are beginning to come to terms with their hotel chefs, and they have also realized that hotels are rich enough to afford some of the best cellars in town. Dinner at L'ESPADON at the Ritz, 1 place Vendôme, 75001, ☎ (1) 43 16 30 80, matches anything Taillevent or Lucas Carton can offer. Chef Guy Legay manages to offer a dazzling variety of 3-star dishes. Other remarkable hotel restaurants include the newcomer LES ELYSÉES DU VERNET at Hôtel Vernet, 25 rue Vernet, 75008, ☎ (1) 44 31 98 98, where young chef Alain Solivérès cooks up inventive seafood dishes and regional specialities. LE MEURICE at Hôtel Meurice, 228 rue de Rivoli, 75001, ☎ (1) 44 58 10 50, is just as inventive, if a little grander, under chef Marc Marchand – this is where ANNA WINTOUR, editor of American *Vogue*, eats. LES PRINCES, at Hôtel Georges V, 31 ave Georges V, 75008, ☎ (1) 47 20 40 00, is a favourite with ALEXANDRE LAZAREFF, who likes to dine in the flowered open-air courtyard in summer and swears by chef Jacky Joyeaux's cooking: *"He pays attention to everything, the simplest dishes like a consommé or a simple salad and, of course, his more elaborate stuff is splendid."*

acres of marble, upholds its reputation as one of the best and easily the most beautiful dining room in Paris. Recommended by MARK MCCORMACK.

HOTEL DE VIGNY

9 RUE BALZAC, 75008
☎ (1) 40 75 04 39
This small, intimate newcomer has already built a reputation for style and service. Handsome with mahogany furniture, and luxurious bathrooms. Decorated by Nina Campbell. Popular with the discerning businessman.

HOTEL LANCASTER

7 RUE DE BERRI, 75008
☎ (1) 40 76 40 76
A member of the Savoy group, with the atmosphere of a quaint private house. Persian rugs, fine ornaments, marble fireplaces and a charming courtyard garden where you can enjoy inventive *nouvelle cuisine* in summer.

HOTEL MONTALEMBERT

3 RUE DE MONTALEMBERT, 75007
☎ (1) 45 49 68 68
Revamped by design darling Christian Liagre, this 1926 hotel, just off the blvd St Germain, has become a haunt for style-setters including KARL LAGERFELD and ROY LICHTENSTEIN. The BAR MONTALEMBERT attracts an equally with-it clientele.

HOTEL LE PARC VICTOR HUGO

55 AVE RAYMOND POINCARÉ, 75116
☎ (1) 44 05 66 10
A solid stone, turn-of-the-century apartment building, transformed by Nina Campbell into a charming townhouse hotel a few years ago. A style shrine for the likes of SHERYL CROW, OLIVER STONE, CHRIS ISAAK and CYNDI LAUPER, who all stay here. The hotel's restaurant, LE RELAIS DU PARC, is overseen by Paris's premier chef, Joël Robuchon, whose three-Michelin-rosetted restaurant is next door at number 59 and is about to be taken over by Alan Ducasse. British publisher, LIZ REES-JONES, is enthusiastic: *"For one-third of the price, one can enjoy a meal with some of Robuchon's best dishes, including his heavenly purée de pommes de terre. And they do room service!"*

HOTEL PLAZA ATHENEE

25 AVE MONTAIGNE, 75008
☎ (1) 47 23 78 33
Grand hotel whose bright red awnings have been a feature of the ave Montaigne for almost a century. The acclaimed RÉGENCE restaurant is great for a classic French dinner; while the RELAIS-PLAZA grill room remains a popular spot for power lunching.

BISTROS These provide some of the best food in the city and the emphasis is on atmosphere rather than decor. **Chez Géraud**, 31 rue Vital, 75016, ☎ (1) 45 20 33 00, is a favourite of DOMINIQUE PIOT: "*They are quiet, almost bourgeois, but they show inventiveness and style. Their canette à l'ail is a marvel and so, of course, is their foie gras. And they have Admiral de Beychevelle and Clos du Marquis wines, which almost no restaurant offers because they're so cheap for the quality.*" For visitors, **Le Vieux Bistrot**, 14 rue du Cloître, Notre-Dame, ☎ (1) 43 54 18 95, is worth the wait. Don't be put off by the tourist location opposite the cathedral – it is charming and very authentic. JEAN-MICHEL JAUDEL swears by it. Another great bistro is **Pierre Vedel**, 19 rue Duranton, 75015, ☎ (1) 45 58 43 17, especially favoured by its most famous habitué, Président Chirac.

HOTEL RAPHAEL
17 AVE KLÉBER, 75016
☎ (I) 44 28 00 28
Intimate hotel near the Etoile, a favourite rendezvous for Parisians, but also notorious as the place where the stars carry on their love affairs. Lots of dark wood and leather and an original Turner in the English-style bar.

HOTEL RITZ
15 PLACE VENDÔME, 75001
☎ (I) 43 16 30 30
Unashamed extravagance in Paris's most ostentatious square. The Imperiale suite remains one of the world's most sought-after bedrooms. Sip champagne before dinner in the famous **HEMINGWAY BAR**, where Coco Chanel, Proust and Scott Fitzgerald used to come. Then dine at the excellent **L'ESPADON** restaurant (see box under Restaurants). "*The spirit of César Ritz, history's most renowned hote-*

lier, lives on here" – MOHAMED AL FAYED. Regular habituées include MICK JAGGER, WOODY ALLEN and COUNTESS RAINE DE CHAMBRUN.

RELAIS CHRISTINE
3 RUE CHRISTINE, 75006
☎ (I) 43 26 71 80
Located in the middle of the Latin Quarter, this 16C former monastery with its beautiful walled garden and elegant rooms attracts an arty crowd.

LA VILLA
29 RUE JACOB, 75006
☎ (I) 43 26 60 00
In the heart of St-Germain, this chic little hotel by Marie-Christine Dorner is a hot spot for the design-conscious. The split-level bar/jazz cellar is a hang-out for fat cats from the city.

MUSIC

CENTRE DE MUSIQUE BAROQUE
16 RUE STE-VICTOIRE, 78000 VERSAILLES
☎ (I) 39 49 48 24
Responsible for 17C and 18C music which echoes throughout Versailles as concerts, operas and ballets are performed in the château, the park and throughout the town.

FESTIVAL D' OPERA DE VERSAILLES
C/O SYNDICAT D'INITIATIVE, 7 RUE DES RÉSERVOIRS, 78000 VERSAILLES
☎ (I) 39 50 36 22
A summer gem – a week of opera and concerts during May/June. The climax is the baroque opera performed in its original setting, the opera house in the Château, originally built by Louis XV to celebrate the marriage of the future Louis XVI to Marie-Antoinette.

L'OPERA BASTILLE
120 RUE DE LYON, 75012
☎ (I) 44 73 13 00
Carlos Ott's controversial modern building is now established as the home of the Paris Opéra. Productions are monumental in comparison to those of the smaller Garnier (see L'Opéra de Paris).

OPERA COMIQUE or SALLE FAVART
RUE FAVART, 75002
☎ (I) 42 60 04 99
Belle-époque productions of classics like

Offenbach's *Tales of Hoffmann* and Lehár's *Merry Widow*.

PALAIS OMNISPORT DE PARIS BERCY

8 BLVD DE BERCY, 75012

☎ (I) 44 68 44 68

Huge auditorium for everything from pop concerts to grand operas, such as *Aïda* and *Nabucco*. It's worth checking the programme regularly.

SALLE PLEYEL

252 BLVD ST-HONORÉ, 75008

☎ (I) 45 61 53 00

Where the Orchestre Philharmonique de Radio-France often performs. One of the best places to hear classical music in Paris.

THEATRE DES CHAMPS-ELYSEES

15 AVE MONTAIGNE, 75008

☎ (I) 49 52 50 50

Considered Paris's best concert hall, it hosts opera, ballet, music and mime performances; it also doubles as an auction house (an offshoot of Drouot).

THEATRE MUSICAL DE PARIS

2 RUE EDOUARD COLONNE, 75001

☎ (I) 42 33 00 00

The former Théâtre du Châtelet, now highly regarded hall for recitals, musicals and opera, with a resident orchestra as well as guest orchestras from around the world.

THEATRE DE LA VILLE

2 PLACE DU CHÂTELET, 75004

☎ (I) 42 74 22 77

Formerly called the Théâtre Sarah Bernhardt, this is the home of popular theatre. It shows plays as well as the occasional concert (classical, modern or pop) and is well known for its international theatre festival.

RESTAURANTS

SEE ALSO HOTELS.

L'AMBROISIE

9 PLACE DES VOSGES, 75004

☎ (I) 42 78 51 45

Former 16C goldsmith's shop, and now one of the city's most elegant eateries. Master chef Bernard Pacaud serves meticulously prepared *nouvelle classique cuisine*. PAUL HENDERSON is full of admiration: "*Absolutely wonderful cooking in a beautiful building in Paris's most beautiful square.*" "*It is the restaurant in Paris that most deserves its 3*

Michelin stars," agrees CHARLES EFFLAM HEID-SIECK.

L'AMI LOUIS

32 RUE DU VERTBOIS, 75003

☎ (I) 48 87 77 48

Still going strong since its heyday under the late, great Antoine Magnin (1899–1987). The dizzy atmosphere – and prices – have attracted a stellar clientele, including Marlene Dietrich and Judy Garland in the past, and more recently BARBRA STREISAND and ROBERT DE NIRO

L'ARPEGE

84 RUE DE VARENNE, 75007

☎ (I) 47 05 09 06

A warm, if minimalist, setting for young master chef Alain Passard's original cooking. JEREMY KING is impressed by "*such innovation in both food and surroundings*", while DOMINIQUE PIOT says, "*It is very rare to see somebody who's consistently inventive and retains the original taste of the ingredients.*"

AU PETIT MONTMORENCY

5 RUE RABELAIS, 75008

☎ (I) 42 25 11 19

Much-vaunted dining spot created by chef/proprietor Daniel Bouché together with his wife, Nicole, who tends the wonderful cellar.

CARRE DES FEUILLANTS

14 RUE DE CASTIGLIONE, 75001

☎ (I) 42 86 82 82

Alain Dutournier has inspired Paris with his Southwestern cuisine. His Gascon specialities include pressed duck bathed in a foie gras sauce.

CAVIAR KASPIA

17 PLACE DE LA MADELEINE, 75008

☎ (I) 42 65 33 52

Originally a gourmet deli, Kaspia is where you can feast on caviare and blinis, washed down with champagne or rare grain vodkas, surrounded by Tsarist memorabilia. "*The best place for a romantic dinner à deux*" – JEAN-MICHEL JAUDEL.

CHEZ PAULINE

5 RUE VILLEDO, 75001

☎ (I) 42 96 20 70

This is one of Paris's best bistros. André Génin, who took over from his father 20 years ago, serves perfectly cooked traditional food using the best raw materials. The wine list is impressive, with good Bordeaux and an exceptional selection of red Burgundies.

LE CHIBERTA

3 RUE ARSÈNE HOUSSAYE, 75008

☎ (1) 45 63 72 44

The new chef, Christophe Milcent, is quickly winning this restaurant a great reputation. The decor is modern as is the emphasis on the essentially Southwestern cuisine. A great favourite with JEAN-MICHEL JAUDEL: "*It looks like a serious place for a sober business lunch and, in fact, you can enjoy some of the most sybaritic food in town.*"

LES COLONIES

10 RUE ST-JULIEN-LE PAUVRE, 75005

☎ (1) 43 54 31 33

Delightful little restaurant on the Left Bank serving classic French colonial cuisine using exotic flavours and spices to good effect. "*Tiny and lovely, it never ceases to amaze,*" says ANNE-ELISABETH MOUTET.

LE DIVELLEC

107 RUE DE L'UNIVERSITÉ, 75007

☎ (1) 45 51 91 96

One of the finest fish restaurants in Paris, with a wine list and service to match. Jacques Le Divellec's loyal patrons include former PM EDOUARD BALLADUR.

LE DUC

243 BLVD RASPAIL, 75014

☎ (1) 43 20 96 30

INÈS DE LA FRESSANGE regularly eats here and PIERRE BERGÉ swears that this is the best fish restaurant in Paris. The fish is exceptionally fresh and rarely disguised by over-fancy sauces.

FAUGERON

52 RUE DE LONGCHAMP, 75116

☎ (1) 47 04 24 53

"*A very individual restaurant. Monsieur Faugeron often comes out and suggests alternatives to the menu depending on what he has in the kitchen. I take French people there and they are amazed,*" raves SIR PETER USTINOV. It serves classic food and attracts a very loyal clientele.

GERARD BESSON

5 RUE DU COQ-HÉRON, 75001

☎ (1) 42 33 14 74

A small restaurant where Monsieur Besson creates wonderfully subtle flavours. Besson is probably one of Paris's most underrated chefs at the moment.

LE GRAND VEFOUR

17 RUE DE BEAUJOLAIS, 75001

☎ (1) 42 96 56 27

A lavishly decorated 18C treasure in the grounds of the Palais Royal. Savour Guy Martin's light, classic Southwestern cuisine. "*Uniquely combines haute cuisine, a fine wine list and a decor of great beauty with many historical associations,*" concurs CLAUS VON BULOW.

GUY SAVOY

18 RUE TROYON, 75017

☎ (1) 43 80 40 61

The setting is attractive; the service swanky and it's great for creative *cuisine rustique* at a reasonable price. Guy Savoy has also opened the **BISTRO DE L'ETOILE** next door.

LE JULES VERNE

TOUR EIFFEL, CHAMP DE MARS, 75007

☎ (1) 45 55 61 44

High-society high spot, several hundred feet up with breathtaking views of the city (on a clear day). Arrive by private glass lift and enter one of the most striking dining rooms in Paris. Fine, light classic cuisine. A favourite of the COMTESSE DE CHAMBRUN.

LAURENT

41 AVE GABRIEL, 75008

☎ (1) 42 25 00 39

Set in the gardens of the Champs-Elysées, SIR JAMES GOLDSMITH'S distinguished establishment is ideal for special-occasion dining. Philippe Braun, a disciple of Joel Robuchon, is on his way to becoming one of Paris's top chefs with his classic French cuisine. The exceptional wine list is directed by Philippe Bourguignon, one of France's top sommeliers.

LEDOYEN

CARRÉ DES CHAMPS-ELYSÉES, 75008

☎ (1) 47 42 35 98

The chef is Ghislaine Arabian, the only woman to run a 3-rosette restaurant, assisted by her husband Jean-Paul, the maître d' and administrator. It's an old-world restaurant with a beautifully preserved 18C frescoed interior. You can also try **LE CERCLE LEDOYEN**, decorated by YSL's Jacques Grange. This is an elegant, modern, 50s-style brasserie serving up-market bistro food.

LUCAS CARTON

9 PLACE DE LA MADELEINE, 75008

☎ (1) 42 65 22 90

Flash food, flash surroundings (including listed Art Nouveau decor by Majorelle) and flash prices. At his best, chef Alain Senderens is in league with Bocuse and Robuchon. "*It's got everything. Senderens is an incredibly imaginative chef. Even his mistakes are more interesting to taste than other people's dishes. They also have a wonderful cellar"* – CHARLES EFFLAM HEIDSIECK.

LE PRE CATELAN

ROUTE DE SURESNES, BOIS DE
BOULOGNE, 75016
☎ (1) 45 24 55 58
A gourmet gem – a small château in the heart of the Bois de Boulogne with a beautiful belle-époque dining room. Chef Roland Durand's creative flair is reflected in dishes like gratin de macaroni au foie gras. Surrounded by heavenly gardens, it's one of the loveliest al fresco dining spots in summer.

....

"THE BEST RESTAURANT IN THE WORLD: BEST FOOD, BEST SERVICE AND DECOR" –
ANNE-ELISABETH MOUTET ON
TAILLEVENT

....

TAILLEVENT

15 RUE LAMENNAIS, 75008
☎ (1) 45 61 12 90
Splendid setting in a grand two-storey townhouse always buzzing with its chic clientele, who come for Jean-Claude Vrinat's creative menu. One of ANNE-ELISABETH MOUTET'S favourites: *"The oeufs brouillés aux truffes sur un risotto au jus de truffes is absolutely marvellous."* PAUL HENDERSON adds: *"Classically as good as the first time I ate there 20 years ago."*

LA TOUR D'ARGENT

15 QUAI DE LA TOURNELLE, 75005
☎ (1) 43 54 23 31
Love it or loathe it, this is one of Paris's grandest old gourmet institutions, with a string of bests to its credit: the best view over Notre-Dame and the Seine, the best wine cellar in Paris, if not the world, and a fabulous menu created by veteran chef Manuel Martinez. Peruse the walls for autographs of famous diners – Churchill, de Gaulle, Roosevelt, Khrushchev, Fred Astaire, Woody Allen, Robert de Niro and Edward VIII.

LE VAL D'ISERE

2 RUE DE BERRI, 75008
☎ (1) 43 59 12 66
Charming authentic bistro frozen in the 60s. The walls are covered in autographed photographs of Brigitte Bardot, Sophia Loren and other European icons and it serves feisty bistro food. It's a great place to go before or after a show. *"It's like the people have just walked off a Roger Vadim set. Great atmosphere,"* enthuses CHARLES EFFLAM HEIDSIECK.

SHOPPING

ANDREA PFISTER

4 RUE CAMBON, 75001
☎ (1) 42 96 55 28
A new, luxurious and very feminine shoe shop, an earring's throw from Chanel. The shoes can be made to order in any material or fabric you choose so that they can exactly match an outfit. A favourite with INÈS DE LA FRESSANGE and PALOMA PICASSO.

BARRIER ET FILS

20 AVE FRANKLIN AND ELEANOR
ROOSEVELT, 75008
☎ (1) 42 89 05 29
Beautiful jewellery made to order with your own stones or you can simply buy "off the peg". Very friendly, welcoming service.

BOUCHERON

26 PLACE VENDÔME, 75001
☎ (1) 42 60 32 82
Grandest of jewellers whose patrons have included the Empress Josephine. There's an 18C panelled 1st floor apartment for personal service.

LES CAVES TAILLEVENT

199 RUE DU FAUBOURG ST-HONORÉ,
75008
☎ (1) 45 61 14 09
A stone's throw away from his Taillevent restaurant, Jean-Claude Vrinat's daughter Valérie presides over a wonderful selection of wines. Regular tastings.

CHARVET

28 PLACE VENDÔME, 75001
☎ (1) 42 60 30 70
De Gaulle regarded it as a piece of France's heritage. Classic suits and shirts for men and women; chic shoes and slippers in supple leathers and every colour of the rainbow. Noël Coward used to buy his ascots here, politicians adore it and so does JUDITH KRANTZ.

DALLOYAU

99 RUE DU FAUBOURG ST-HONORÉ,
75008
☎ (1) 43 59 18 10
Now at five addresses, this elegant foodies'

BARGE CAFES Anchored

in every available waterway in the city are "barge cafés", ie, cafés on barges. As most are heated, they can be enjoyed in all seasons. Try **Le New Opus Café**, 167 quai de Valmy, 75010, ☎ (1) 40 34 70 00, on Canal St-Martin for jazz and classical concerts. **Le Bateau Blues Café** on quai de la Tournelle, 75005, ☎ (1) 43 25 55 55, is just behind Notre-Dame, and is open until late. At **Bateau Six/Huit**, 2 quai Malaquais, 75006, ☎ (1) 43 80 74 54, you can look at the temporary art shows before dinner and then dance afterwards. In the Bois de Boulogne, on a small, idyllic wooded island in the middle of the Lac du Bois, **Le Chalet des Iles**, ☎ (1) 42 88 04 69 or ☎ (1) 45 25 16 73 is almost a barge café, as you have to take a little shuttle boat to get there and back.

favourite is a feast for all the senses. Make up a picnic or come for their marvellous macaroons. Upstairs there's a pleasantly un-chic *salon de thé* which has been going since 1801.

DEHILLERIN

18 RUE COQUILLÈRE, 75001
☎ (1) 42 36 53 13
A professionals' store, dedicated to the culinary arts. Knives, pots, heavy copper pans and all manner of utensils for cooking, serving and eating food – they look great and are built to last.

DINERS EN VILLE

27 RUE DE VARENNE, 75007
☎ (1) 42 22 78 33
Everything for the perfect hostess: antiques and gems that look as if they came from your grandmother's garret; new and old china; silverware; a wonderful array of damask table-cloths and a marvellous collection of old St Louis coloured cut glass.

GALERIES LAFAYETTE

40 BLVD HAUSSMANN, 75009
☎ (1) 42 82 34 56 AND BRANCHES
Art Nouveau building – complete with stained glass roof – containing ultra-chic *petites boutiques*. Don't overlook the in-house labels and accessories.

GIORGIO ARMANI

149 BLVD ST-GERMAIN, 75006
☎ (1) 42 22 92 50
This newly opened shop replacing the old drugstore on the corner of rue de Rennes and the blvd St-Germain-des-Prés, is the largest Armani outlet in Europe. It is set on three storeys and sells men's and women's fashions and accessories. Come here for Emporio and made-to-measure; linens and tableware and there's a café too. With regular art shows on the walls, it is fast becoming one of the coolest stores in town.

HERMES

24 RUE DU FAUBOURG ST-HONORÉ, 75008
☎ (1) 40 17 47 17
Magnificent, traditional family-run emporium that began as a saddler before finding fame with the silk square and Kelly bag. Superb luxury leather goods, from bags to diaries, which can be made to order in any kind of leather and colour. They can upholster on request – from private planes to boats, even a Renault 5 in pigskin. Their regular *prêt à porter* line for men and women now competes with Paris's best, as do their beautiful made-to-measure shoes. Pop into the museum of original designs and see Napoleon's overnight case.

· ·

JANE PROCTER *ON INÈS DE LA FRESSANGE: "INDIVIDUAL STYLE, CLOTHES THAT ARE BEYOND FASHION"*

· ·

INES DE LA FRESSANGE

14 AVE MONTAIGNE, 75008
☎ (1) 47 23 08 94
Now at two addresses, the former Chanel muse continues her ever-successful line of no-label classics. Accessible prices; great and original accessories; the best navy blazer; perfect pumps and slippers. PRINCESS CAROLINE OF MONACO and other royal figures shop here regularly.

LIONEL POILANE

8 RUE DU CHERCHE-MIDI, 75006
☎ (I) 45 48 42 59
Prepare to join the queue. This celebrated boulangerie has been filmed regularly by Soviet TV to prove that even in the West people have to queue for bread. As hot as ever, especially the world-beating sourdough. Eat it fresh and steaming from the wood-fired ovens.

LOUIS VUITTON

54 AVE MONTAIGNE, 75008
☎ (I) 45 62 47 00 (BOUTIQUE)
78B AVE MARCEAU, 75008
☎ (I) 47 20 47 00 (LUGGAGE)
Vuitton's monogrammed range might seem a bit old hat, but the fine *cuir epi* bags still retain their appeal. They are made to order in sensational colours – from deep azure to screaming pink – as are the steamer trunks and writing desks. Now you can complete the luxury look with accessories – watches, pens, wallets, keyrings – designed by architects and designers including Philippe Starck and Gae Allenti.

MARCEL BUR

138 RUE DU FAUBOURG ST-HONORÉ, 75008
☎ (I) 42 56 03 89
Where diplomats and politicians come for beautiful, though conservative suits. One of Paris's last great tailors to cut his own cloth. Sadly, prices are now comparable to Savile Row.

MARCEL LASSANCE

17 RUE DU VIEUX COLOMBIER, 75006
21 RUE MARBEUF, 75008
☎ (I) 45 48 29 28
Top quality sportswear and suits – dynamic but no frills – plus own-name luggage, briefcases, belts and ties. Popular with politicians.

MAUD FRIZON

83 RUE DES SAINTS PÈRES, 75006
☎ (I) 42 22 06 93
Fabulous footwear for *femmes fatales* – including CATHERINE DENEUVE and ISABELLE ADJANI. Exquisite and delicate shoes crafted from the finest leathers – calf, pig, patent – and finished with handmade soles. Bags at 7 rue de Grenelle, 75006.

DECOR HEAVEN

Paris is Mecca for those who want to have their antiques, paintings, or any other decorative piece, properly upholstered, framed, restored and/or lit. The best decorating fabrics are to be found in the narrow streets of the St-Germain des Prés area. Try **Nobilis**, 29 rue Bonaparte, ☎ (1) 43 29 21 50; **Simrane**, 23 rue Bonaparte, ☎ (1) 43 54 90 73; **Pierre Frey**, 5 rue Jacob, ☎ (1) 46 33 73 00; **Canovas**, 7 place de Furstenburg, ☎ (1) 43 25 75 98; or **Rubelli**, 6 bis de l'Abbaye, ☎ (1) 43 54 27 77. **Tissus Colony**, 28 rue Jacob, ☎ (1) 43 29 61 70, sells wondrously thick brocaded silks manufactured in Italy, using 18C drawings. For good, fast-working upholsterers, no one beats **Apa Tani**, 40 rue de la Réunion, 75020, ☎ (1) 40 24 24 99; they are also classically trained furniture makers and will restore furniture and frame pictures. Otherwise, you can go to Paris's most inventive frame-maker, **Christian de Beaumont,** who frames works for the Musée de l'Orangerie and the Galerie Claude Bernard, based at 11 rue Frédéric-Sauton, 75005, ☎ (1) 43 29 88 75. JEAN-MICHEL JAUDEL says he cannot praise him too highly: "*He will study a picture and create an individual frame that is an extension of the artwork. For one of my contemporary paintings he devised an extraordinary asymmetrical frame that looked as if it grew out of the wall where it hung. But he can equally make a faux-tortoiseshell and ebony frame worthy of a Rembrandt.*" Both Jaudel and FRÉDÉRIC JOCHEM swear by **Casa Lopez**, 58 ave Paul Doumer, 75016, ☎ (1) 45 03 42 75, a versatile decorating shop for lighting, specially woven carpets and textiles, ranging from seagrass mats to fake zebra throws.

Loyd Grossman on le weekend

Although it's only an hour by air, the London-to-Paris journey has been completely and irrevocably transformed by the through-the-channel rail link, ☎ (0345) 881881. Nicholas Grimshaw's elegantly space-age Waterloo International terminal and the sleek Eurostar trains themselves are a slightly misleading introduction to a decidedly low-tech crawl through the unlovely suburbs of southeast London; but once in the Tunnel and on to the surer rails of France, it's foot-on-the-floor time for the engine driver. Although there have been delays and horror stories, my trip ran like clockwork, with the exception of chaos at the Waterloo end of the return journey. Service on board is solicitous. The breakfast (Continental or cooked) is hardly great but no worse than many hotels dish up. And swift security checks, no queues for passport control, no admonitions about tray tables or seatbelts and none of the endless kerfuffle about getting on and off planes all add up to a pretty blissful journey. Best of all is the arrival in Paris, seemingly without having travelled at all, out the door and on to the platform at the Gare du Nord. If you do as I did and stay at the Terminus Nord Hôtel (a biggish 19C joint recently very well done up, with good staff and rather painless prices), you will have the added comfort of a porter meeting you off the train. Getting the 7.10 from Waterloo meant being able to check in, change and travel across town to one of my Paris favourites (yes, it really is called Chez Georges, 1 rue du Mail, ☎ 42 60 07 11) and be eating my first mouthful of celeriac remoulade at 1.00 pm. The Eurostar certainly ain't cheap (that is, if you travel first-class) but I found myself saying that it would mean being able to go to Paris more often than I already do. And I must confess that I rather enjoyed the slightly grubby neighbourhood of the Gare du Nord, an easy Métro or cab journey to the main attractions of shopping and culture that all lie to the south. The Paris Weekend, which has become an increasingly expensive and rather hassled feature for many British visitors, is, alas, never going to become any less expensive. It remains to be seen whether the recent initiative by the French government to encourage les Parisiens to be more visitor-friendly has much effect. I confess to finding Paris easy and charming, but then again I'm not English and so am pretty lacking in historical enmity. It is impossible to recommend what to do in a city that has so much on tap, but a fairly good weekend formula (and by weekend I mean leaving London on Friday morning and returning from Paris on Sunday afternoon) probably runs something like this: Friday: travel – lunch – shopping – cinema – dinner. Saturday: culture – lunch – shopping – dinner. Sunday: culture – lunch – travel. Consult the relevant listings in these pages for the restaurants, shops and museums that might engage you.

PALOMA PICASSO
5 RUE DE LA PAIX, 75008
☎ (1) 46 40 58 14
A showcase for Paloma Picasso's beautiful and distinctive accessories. Eminently stylish, but barely affordable.

PETROSSIAN
18 BLVD DE LA TOUR MAUBOURG, 75007
☎ (1) 44 11 32 22
Disciples come from far and wide for the top-quality caviare in the classic blue tin – a treasure in itself. Also very fine smoked salmon, foie gras, truffles, fresh blinis and delectable Russian pastries.

ROBERT CLERGERIE
5 RUE DU CHERCHE-MIDI, 75006
☎ (1) 45 48 75 47
Footwear designer who's usually one step ahead of the rest – he brought the platform back two years before they hit the high street. His work is both modern and original.

SOULEIADO
78 RUE DE SEINE, 75006
☎ (1) 43 54 62 25
Sheets, fabrics, curtains, bedcovers, are ready-made or made to order using reworked Provençal designs by Charles Demery and Nina Campbell.

WALTER STEIGER

83 RUE DU FAUBOURG ST-HONORÉ, 75008
☎ (I) 42 66 65 08
5 RUE DE TOURNON, 75006
☎ (I) 46 33 01 45
Classic, elegant pumps, shoes and boots for the high-society set. Made to order to match any outfit.

YVES ST LAURENT ACCESSOIRES

32 RUE DU FAUBOURG ST-HONORÉ, 75008
☎ (I) 42 65 01 15
Magnificent shop, designed and decorated by Jacques Grange, housing the fabulous designs of Loulou de la Falaise. Couture accessories and an extraordinary collection of costume jewellery – chunky rock crystal necklaces and earrings made to order, one-off original watch pieces and handbags to complement any outfit.

REST OF FRANCE
Alsace

ART AND MUSEUMS

MUSEE ALSACIEN

23 QUAI ST NICHOLAS, 67000 STRASBOURG
☎ 88 35 55 36
A lovely little museum concentrating on the popular arts and traditions in Alsace, including reconstructions of a typical Alsatian farmhouse complete with period furniture; wonderful costumes and ceramics.

CHAMPAGNE Within a cork's pop of Paris is Champagne, a region that's worth visiting not just to get unbelievably inebriated – although it's good for that too – but to visit its lovely towns and cities, which include **Reims** and **Epernay**. One of the oldest cities in France, Reims is home to a magnificent 13C Gothic cathedral (open daily, 7.30 am–7.30 pm). Next to the cathedral is the **Palais du Tau**, ☎ 26 47 81 79, the former Archbishop's palace, housing a colourful display of tapestries and coronation robes. For fine art followers, the **Musée des Beaux Arts**, 8 rue Chanzy, ☎ 26 47 28 44 (closed Tues), contains a collection of works dating from the Renaissance, including drawings by Cranach and paintings by Corot and by 19C landscape artists. When hunger strikes, head for Gérard Boyer's restaurant at **Château des Crayères**, 64 blvd Henri Vanier, ☎ 26 82 80 80 – ideal if money is no object. Or go to **Le Cheval Blanc**, 2 rue Moulin, 51400 Sept-Saulx, ☎ 26 03 90 27, one of Champagne's oldest restaurants to the southeast of Reims. For beautiful food in beautiful surroundings try the **Royal Champagne**, 51160 Champillon Bellvue, ☎ 26 52 87 11, about 5 miles outside Epernay. For traditional cuisine the locals favour **L'Assiette Champenoise**, 40 ave P Vaillant-Couturier, 51430 Tinqueux, ☎ 26 04 15 56. The best time to visit the region is undeniably during the Vendange, or harvest, when all the grapes are picked by hand. Many Champagne houses, who together oversee more than 62,000 acres of vines, offer guided tours of their underground cellars. These include **Dom Pérignon**, ☎ 26 51 20 00, **Lanson**, ☎ 26 78 50 50, **Laurent-Perrier**, ☎ 26 58 91 22, **Moët et Chandon**, ☎ 26 51 20 00, **Mumm**, ☎ 26 49 59 70, **Piper Heidsieck**, ☎ 26 84 43 44, **Pommery**, ☎ 26 61 62 55, **Ponsardin**, ☎ 26 40 25 42, **Ruinart**, ☎ 26 85 40 29, **Taittinger**, ☎ 26 85 45 35, and **Veuve Clicquot**. For more details contact Tourist Information in Reims, ☎ 26 47 45 25, or Epernay, ☎ 26 53 33 00.

MUSEE NATIONAL DE L'AUTOMOBILE

192 AVE DE COLMAR, 68100 MULHOUSE

☎ 89 42 29 17

The Schlumpf brothers built up this amazing collection of classic and vintage cars but to repay a debt, the entire collection was given to the town and turned into a public museum. It's a must for car enthusiasts.

FESTIVALS

FESTIVAL DE MUSIQUE DE STRASBOURG

9 AVE DE LA LIBERTÉ, 67000 STRASBOURG

☎ 88 35 64 00

A major music festival which takes place each June and has great jazz and classical music.

HOTELS AND RESTAURANTS

L'ATELIER

RUE DU MARÉCHAL FOCH, 67390 MARCKOLSHEIM

☎ 88 74 92 74

Up-and-coming chef Michel Magada recently left the Quisiana in Capri to open his own, extremely promising restaurant in the heart of Alsace. His menu combines top-class Italian and French cooking with lots of added local flavour. There are rooms available too if you wish to stay the night after dinner. Worth the trip.

AUBERGE DE L'ILL

RUE DE COLLONGES, ILLHAEUSERN, 68970 RIBEAUVILLÉ

☎ 89 71 83 23

The Haeberlin brothers have transformed traditional Alsatian cooking into a gastronomic treat, in what is probably the best restaurant in Alsace. Go in summer and sit in the lovely riverside garden.

CHEZ YVONNE

RUE DU SANGLIER, 67000 STRASBOURG

☎ 88 32 84 15

Everyone who is anyone in Strasbourg knows Yvonne – and that includes the entire membership of the European Parliament. Simple food, beautifully cooked.

HOSTELLERIE DU CERF

ROUTE DU GÉNÉRAL DE GAULLE, 67520 MARLENHEIM

☎ 88 87 73 73

Well-established restaurant offering modern and classic Alsatian cuisine. Famous for its range of fresh, local produce. Closed Tues–Wed.

MAISON KAMMERZELL

PLACE DE LA CATHÉDRALE, 67000 STRASBOURG

☎ 88 32 42 14

One of the city's oldest restaurants, in a beautiful old Alsatian house, well known for its good traditional food.

RESTAURANT BUEREHEISEL

PARC DE L'ORANGERIE, 67000 STRASBOURG

☎ 88 61 62 24

Located in the middle of the Parc de l'Orangerie, it is especially lovely in summer. Chef Westerman's inventive cooking is, however, good throughout the year.

RESTAURANT LA CHARRUE

30 RUE DE LA RÉPUBLIQUE, 67720 HOERDT

☎ 88 51 31 11

For the great regional speciality, visit this rustic auberge in spring, when they serve wonderful asparagus, freshly picked that morning. La Charrue is only 6 miles from Strasbourg, and each May members of the European Parliament come for an evening of asparagus in the village.

Brittany and Normandy

FESTIVALS

FESTIVAL DU CINEMA AMERICAIN DE DEAUVILLE

C/O PROMO 2000, 36 RUE PIERRET, 75017 PARIS

☎ 46 40 55 00

OFFICE DU TOURISME, 14800 DEAUVILLE

☎ 31 88 21 43

Seems like a long way for ELIZABETH TAYLOR, ROBERT DE NIRO and SHIRLEY MACLAINE to come but the Deauville Festival – a minor affair compared to Cannes – has managed to retain its rather indefinable appeal. The best hangouts are: **CHEZ MIOQUE** for good food, street cred and the wonderful Monsieur Mioque; and **LES VAPEURS** in nearby Trouville for *cuisine normande* and the more exalted company of ANOUK AIMÉE or SABINE AZÉMA. After dinner everyone heads for the hotel bars.

FINE WINE AND FINE ART The annual wine sale at **Hospices de Beaune**, held on the third Sunday of Nov, is an occasion to pick up some of the finest primeur Burgundy alongside professional buyers. While you're in Beaune, look round the 15C hospital known as the Hôtel-Dieu; this is where the wine auction used to be held and it contains some fine tapestries and Van der Weyden's *Last Judgement*. Nearby is Dijon which was a leading art centre in the 15C and the capital of the Dukes of Burgundy. Visit their fabulous collection of paintings at the **Musée des Beaux-Arts** in the Palais des Ducs, regarded as one of the finest museums outside Paris. Useful addresses: Office de Tourisme, rue de l'Hôtel-Dieu, 21200 Beaune, ☎ (1) 80 26 21 30; Office de Tourisme, 29 place Darcy, 21000 Dijon, ☎ (1) 80 44 11 44; Bureau Interprofessional des Vins de Bourgogne, rue Henry Dunant, 21200 Beaune, ☎ (1) 80 22 21 35.

HOTELS AND RESTAURANTS

LES GRANDS FOSSES
PLACE DU GÉNÉRAL-LECLERC, 35000 DINAN
☎ 96 39 21 50
One of the new generation of chefs, Alain Colas, adds a particularly subtle touch to local produce, doing wonders with fresh fish.

HOTEL ROYAL
BLVD CORNUCHE, 14800 DEAUVILLE
☎ 31 98 66 33
One of the two hotels where one simply has to stay when in Deauville for the American Film Festival. This is where Hollywood stars are snapped lounging around the kidney-shaped pool.

MAISON DE BRICOURT
1 RUE DUGUESCLIN, 35260 CANCALE
☎ 99 89 64 76
Locally known as 'Mr Sea' for the fact that he puts seaweed everywhere (even in the bread), chef Olivier Roellinger is also considered *the* chef of Brittany.

LE NORMANDIE
38 RUE JEAN MERMOZ, 14800 DEAUVILLE
☎ 31 98 66 22
The other favourite for the film festival run by Lucien Barrière, who also oversees the Majestic in Cannes. This has a stronger French feel – chic Parisians often come here to rest at weekends. It faces the sea and is impeccably run.

Burgundy

FESTIVALS

FESTIVAL DE MUSIQUE BAROQUE DE BEAUNE
RUE DE HÔTEL-DIEU, 21200 BEAUNE
☎ 80 26 21 30
In one of Burgundy's most famous towns in the heart of its wine region, this month-long July festival features 18C composers including Handel, Bach and others that are less well known. The perfect excuse to combine culture and gastronomy.

HOTELS AND RESTAURANTS

LA COTE D'OR
2 RUE D'ARGENTINE, 21210 SAULIEU
☎ 80 64 07 66
Thanks to his innovative *cuisine légère* and vegetarian food, chef Bernard Loiseau now has three Michelin stars at his restaurant. A former roadside stop, good it's got some great guest accommodation too. "*Wonderful hotel and lovely food,*" according to QUENTIN CREWE.

L'ESPERANCE
89450 ST-PÈRE-SOUS-VÉZELAY
☎ 86 33 20 45
One of France's superstars, Marc Meneau's signature "sexual cuisine" continues to seduce the most distinguished of palates. However some might find it a little on the rich side.

Provence

FESTIVALS

CHOREGIES

BP 205, 84107 ORANGE

☎ 90 34 24 24

A three-week season of magnificent one-off operas, recitals and concerts, all held in the Théâtre Antique, a Roman amphitheatre, every July.

FESTIVAL D'AVIGNON

BUREAU DU FESTIVAL, BP 92, 84006 AVIGNON

☎ 90 82 67 08

Vibrant, important midsummer festival of drama (July–Aug) created by Jean Vilar, who was the French equivalent to Laurence Olivier. Offers experimental, comic, all-night and ethnic theatre, sketches, mime, dance, lectures and exhibitions.

HOTELS AND RESTAURANTS

AUBERGE DE NOVES

DOMAIN DU DEVÈS, RTE DE CHÂTEAU-RENARD, 13550 NOVES

☎ 90 94 19 21

Timber and stone farmhouse set amidst pines and cypresses. Much celebrated traditional cooking from chef Robert Lalleman. "*Absolutely divine*," according to KITTY KELLEY.

LA BASTIDE DE MOUSTIERS

LA GRISOLIÈRE, QUARTIER ST-MICHEL, 04360 MOUSTIERS-STE-MARIE

☎ 92 70 47 47

Alain Ducasse's latest venture, set in its own private parkland on the edge of the Verdon Gorge. The food is exceptional, emphatically rustic.

LA BONNE ETAPE

CHEMIN DU LAC, 04160 CHÂTEAU ARNOUX

☎ 92 64 00 09

Quiet, picturesque Provençal château run by the Gleize family. The award-winning restaurant is a favourite with politicians and heads of state. "*It is run by a father and son celebrity team, Pierre Gleize and his son Jany. They cook wonderful game, hare and boar, and Pierre is also a great pudding man. A wonderful place,*" reports QUENTIN CREWE.

CHATEAU DE LA CHEVRE D'OR

06360 EZE VILLAGE

☎ 93 41 12 12

Medieval stone house perched 1,200ft above the Med, with 14 sea-facing rooms and a tiny swimming-pool terrace. Fine cuisine from Bruno Ingold. Closed during the winter months.

CHRISTIAN ETIENNE

10 RUE MONS, 84000 AVIGNON

☎ 90 86 16 50

Etienne is one of France's rising stars. He specializes in using fresh local produce to create typical country dishes.

LA COLOMBE D'OR

06570 ST-PAUL-DE-VENCE

☎ 93 32 80 02

Delightful hotel on the edge of a perfect medieval hill town, where the Roux family continues to maintain its high standards. Once a legendary artists' hideaway, now every surface bears testimony to their work. Dining on the terrace is a joy. "*A wonderful old hotel, great food and wonderful art,*" reports RICHARD POLO, with a "*perfect club privée atmosphere*" according to STEPHEN BAYLEY.

HOSTELLERIE DE CRILLON-LE-BRAVE

PLACE DE L'EGLISE, 84410 CRILLON-LE-BRAVE

☎ 90 65 61 61

Delightfully simple hotel set in a small village about an hour from Avignon, with a pretty ter-

ENCORE Les Fêtes d'Arles was created by Frédéric Mistral, who was determined that Paris fashion should not take over and dominate the region's language and culture. Come for the period costumes (works of art in themselves), the food and the dancing. And the festival, which usually takes place in the first weekend of July, is free . . . . . ♣ **Bastille Day** celebrations last for about two days from around the evening of 13 July. The whole of France enjoys street parties and balls, but you'll find the best atmosphere in the smaller villages, where dances take place in the main square to the accompaniment of local bands. . . . . ♣

raced garden looking out across the vineyards of the Rhône Valley. "*Unpretentious and rustic. Simple and honest cooking served in a very attractive basement cellar with a roaring log fire. The owner is an American who is totally dedicated and very innovative; a charming person and a charming place*" is MARTIN SKAN'S verdict.

L'ISLE SONNANTE RESTAURANT

7 RUE RACINE, 84000 AVIGNON
☎ 90 82 56 01
A charming and unpretentious restaurant. MARTIN SKAN reports: "*Very small, perhaps 20 covers; immaculate cooking by chef-patron Monsieur Gradassi and well backed up by his charming wife at the front of house. Very original and the very best type of restaurant in every way.*"

LE MAS DE CHASTELAS

CHEMIN DE CHASTELAS, 83580 GASSIN, ST TROPEZ
☎ 94 56 71 71
Beautiful 18C *mas* (farmhouse) set among vineyards. Elegant little villas with private gardens ensure complete privacy. The restaurant is one of St Tropez's best.

LA MIRANDE

4 PLACE DE LA MIRANDE, 84000 AVIGNON
☎ 90 85 93 93
An old palace formerly belonging to a cardinal and now converted into a 20-bedroom hotel. "*One of the most beautiful city hotels I have ever seen, with an outstanding restaurant. A very special experience that is worth a great detour,*" enthuses MARTIN SKAN. SIR PETER USTINOV agrees: "*La Mirande – superb hotel, superb conversion and superb food.*"

LE MOULIN DE MOUGINS

QUARTIER NOTRE-DAME DE VIE, 434 CHEMIN DE MOULINS, 06250 MOUGINS
☎ 93 75 78 24
Roger Vergé's restaurant, with its shady terrace and pretty gardens, continues to draw the style-conscious from all along the coast for his signature *cuisine du soleil*. There is a hotel and cookery school here for those who want to emulate Monsieur Vergé's food. "*The ultimate dining experience in the world that I know.*" – SHEP GORDON.

OUSTAU DE BAUMANIERE

LE VALLON, 13520 LES-BAUX-DE-PROVENCE
☎ 90 54 33 07
Beautiful 16C mountain farmhouse where some of the rocks have been carved by artists.

An oasis of calm and tranquillity, impeccable service and a Michelin-starred restaurant. "*An absolutely ravishing spot in an abstract wild white rock village with marvellous food and a great shop selling beautiful linen*" – BARBARA KAFKA.

LA VILLA GALLICI

AVE DE LA VIOLETTE, 13100 AIX-EN-PROVENCE
☎ 42 23 29 23
A small hotel decorated in authentic Aixois style. Outside there's a light sun-dappled courtyard and swimming pool. "*It's so good it can't remain a secret much longer. Eat next door at the RESTAURANT LE CLOS DE LA VIOLETTE – great food, grown-up prices,*" advises JILL MULLENS.

Rhône

HOTELS AND RESTAURANTS

ALAIN CHAPEL

83 ROUTE NATIONALE, 01390 MIONNAY
☎ 78 91 82 02
The memory of Alain Chapel, one of the late great chefs, continues with chef Philippe Jousse producing traditional French *haute cuisine*.

AUBERGE DE L'ERIDAN

13 VIELLE ROUTE DES PANSIÈRES, 74290 VEYRIER-DU-LAC
☎ 50 60 24 00
Chef Marc Veyrat has made a name for himself (and won three Michelin stars) via his creative use of forgotten herbs which he picks each day at dawn. Closed on Wed and Sun evenings. It's also a small hotel.

CHATEAU DE BAGNOLS

69620 BAGNOLS
☎ 74 71 40 00
Over £4 million was spent on turning this 700-year-old castle into one of the most beautiful country hotels in the world. Owners Paul and Helen Hamlyn have thought of everything, from the electrically heated floors to the 17C sofas covered in silk brocade, and Limoges plates at dinner.

GEORGES BLANC

01540 VONNAS
☎ 74 50 90 90
Georges Blanc's restaurant with its masterly 3-

star cuisine and idyllic flower-filled garden is still considered one of the most romantic eateries in France. "*He seems to own half the village now, but this is one of the best restaurants in France offering his speciality 'poulet de Bresse' in that lovely rich creamy sauce,*" says QUENTIN CREWE. BARBARA KAFKA adds, "*It remains wonderful. He even owns a winery now, making fine Mâcon wine.*"

PAUL BOCUSE

50 QUAI DE LA PLAGNE, 69660 COLLONGES-AU-MONT-D'OR, LYON
☎ 72 42 90 90
These days legendary chef Paul Bocuse spends virtually no time in his kitchen but his extraordinary culinary legacy lives on through several of his chosen disciples. Landmark dishes and wines still make it worth a detour.

PIC

285 AVE VICTOR HUGO, 26000 VALENCE
☎ 75 44 15 32
Still teeming with gastronomes eager for Jacques Pic's flavourful fine food.

LA PYRAMIDE

14 BLVD FERNAND POINT, 38200 VIENNE
☎ 74 53 01 96
The restaurant, which used to be run by top chef Fernand Point, is now run by chef Patrick Henriroux, who maintains his predecessor's high culinary standards.

LA TERRASSE

PLACE DE L'EGLISE, 01360 LOYETTES
☎ 78 32 70 13
Chef Gérard Antonin, currently one of France's most creative chefs, offers a delicious choice of game and fish dishes as well as his very own foie gras. Serves bucketfuls of the most exquisite truffles in season.

LA TOUR ROSE

22 RUE DU BOEUF, 69005 LYON
☎ 78 37 25 90
A highly praised restaurant, under the skilful hands of chef Philippe Chavent. Also a select, chicly decorated hotel.

TROISGROS

PLACE JEAN TROISGROS, 42300 ROANNE
☎ 77 71 66 97
Legendary family-run hotel–restaurant set in immaculate gardens. The Troisgros brothers offer unpretentious, bourgeois cooking at its very finest. Plenty of refreshingly affordable fine wines.

Riviera

ART AND MUSEUMS

ATELIER CEZANNE

9 AVE PAUL CÉZANNE, 13100 AIX-EN-PROVENCE
☎ 42 21 06 53
Cézanne's tiny studio, which nestles in an overgrown garden complete with cherub statue and the descendants of his oft-painted apples.

FONDATION MAEGHT

06570 ST-PAUL-DE-VENCE
☎ 93 32 81 63
One of the best modern galleries in the South of France, featuring stained-glass windows by Ubac and Braque, a Braque mosaic, sculpture by Alberto Giacometti and the vividly coloured works of former locals such as Chagall, Miró and Matisse.

MUSEE D'ART CONTEMPORAIN

LE PAVILLON, 06000 NICE
☎ 93 62 61 62
Impressive modern building built to house principally 20C artists, including César and Arman.

MUSEE JEAN COCTEAU

QUAI MOLÉON, 06500 MENTON
☎ 93 57 72 30
Fine collection covering Cocteau's career as a painter, film-maker and poet, plus photographs.

MUSEE MARC CHAGALL

AVE DU DOCTEUR MENARD, 06000 NICE
☎ 93 53 87 20
Opened in 1973 to exhibit Chagall's huge biblical series. Some of his smaller works are now also on show.

MUSEE MATISSE

164 AVE DES ARÈNES-DE-CIMIEZ, 06000 NICE
☎ 93 81 08 08
This museum, in the beautiful old Roman part of town, is well worth visiting to see some of the artist's finest work.

MUSEE PICASSO

CHÂTEAU GRIMALDI, PLACE DU CHÂTEAU, 06600 ANTIBES
☎ 93 34 71 07
Picasso donated his prolific output from the second half of 1946 to this museum.

MUSEE RENOIR

LES COLLETTES, 13100 CAGNES-SUR-
MER

☎ 93 20 61 07

The house, studio and gardens where Renoir
lived with his family from 1907 to his death in
1919 have been preserved just as he left them.

VILLA EPHRUSSI DE ROTHSCHILD

AVE DENIS SEMERIA, 06230 ST-JEAN-
CAP-FERRAT

☎ 93 01 33 09

Turn-of-the-century Italianate villa housing an
eclectic collection of 18C art assembled by
Baroness de Rothschild. Important examples
of Sèvres and Meissen porcelain, French rococo paintings, Savonnerie carpets and Oriental
decorative arts. "*Enchantingly offbeat ornate viewing, full of superb collections amid wonderful gardens
(very exotic). Good tea room*" – CAROL WRIGHT.

CASINOS

CASINO DE MONTE CARLO

PLACE DU CASINO, 98007 MONACO

☎ 92 16 21 21

The world's best and most famous casino,
designed by Charles Garnier. The first salon is
for European roulette, and slot machines; the
private salon, where there is no betting limit, is
for British roulette, blackjack and craps. The
public casino is now at the teeming, touristy
CAFÉ DE PARIS, opposite. Best in the spring.

CLUBS

BEACH CLUB

MONTE CARLO BEACH HOTEL, ROUTE
DU BORD DE MER, 06190
ROQUEBRUNE-CAP-MARTIN

☎ 93 28 66 66

Daytime club at the Monte Carlo Beach Hotel
that offers jet-skiing, paragliding, waterskiing
or swimming out to a raft. Or just languish by
the swimming pool and feast on a buffet lunch
– delicious salads, antipasti and sorbets.

JIMMY'Z D'HIVER (winter)

PLACE DU CASINO, 98007 MONTE
CARLO

☎ 92 16 22 77

JIMMY'Z D'ETE (summer) or PARADY'Z

MONTE CARLO SPORTING CLUB, AVE
PRINCESSE GRACE, 98000

☎ 93 30 61 61

The best nightclub in Monaco, catering for the
musical tastes of all age groups. The summer
home has a motorized sliding roof that opens
to reveal the sparkling night sky.

FESTIVALS

FESTIVAL MONDIAL DE JAZZ D'ANTIBES

MAISON DU TOURISME D'ANTIBES,
PLACE CHARLES DE GAULLE, 06600
ANTIBES

☎ 93 33 95 64

This great jazz festival for a couple of weeks
each July is held as a result of American jazz
players' love affair with France.

FILM

CANNES INTERNATIONAL FILM FESTIVAL

C/O 71 RUE DU FAUBOURG ST-
HONORÉ, 75008 PARIS

☎ (1) 48 06 16 66

The world's most prestigious and important
film festival where every kind of film is shown.
The most exciting actors – STONE, DE NIRO,
PITT – adorn what in reality ends up as a
round-the-clock social whirl. The hottest invi-
tations are to the **HÔTEL DU CAP-EDEN-ROC**
(see Hotels) and to Cannes President, PIERRE
VIOT's infamous matchmaking dinners. The
only places to be seen having lunch are at the
MAJESTIC (see Hotels), **LA PALME D'OR** at
the Hôtel Martinez or **LA PLAGE SPORTIVE**,
the beach. And if you've nothing to do in the
small hours, go to the café-bar, **LE PETIT
CARLTON**, rue d'Antibes.

HOTELS

CARLTON INTER-CONTINENTAL

58 LA CROISETTE, 06406 CANNES

☎ 93 06 40 06

A belle-époque-style luxury hotel, constantly
being revamped and upgraded – was seen in
the film *French Kiss*. There's nothing quite like
the 13-room penthouse suite which has its
own private limousine and butler. Good food
in **LA CÔTE**, plus a great fitness centre.

GRAND HOTEL DU CAP FERRAT

BLVD DU GÉNÉRAL DE GAULLE, 06290
ST-JEAN-CAP-FERRAT

☎ 93 76 50 50

A traditional Riviera palace hidden away in

14 acres of garden by the sea. The recently renovated rooms and suites have huge marble bathrooms and wonderful views along the coastline. There are several tennis courts, offering one of the best tennis pros in the region. But the unique selling point has to be the exquisite swimming pool, which is like a mirage shimmering beside the sea. Here you can learn from legendary swimming instructor PIERRE GRUNEBERG, who taught Charlie Chaplin and Picasso. Ask to have a look at his famous book containing notes and photographs from all the celebs he has taught. The **CLUB DAUPHIN**, next to the pool, is a wonderful place to have lunch. The food created by Jean-Claude Guillon at the restaurant **LE CAP** is truly mouthwatering – very light and delicate.

HOTEL DE PARIS

PLACE DU CASINO, BP 2309, 98007 MONTE CARLO
☎ 92 16 30 00
One of Europe's last really grand hotels, Monte Carlo's lavish landmark continues to play host to the world's richest jetsetters. Harbourside suites, luxury shops, wonderful pool and a new health spa, but most notably home of Alain Ducasse's **LOUIS XV** restaurant.

HOTEL DU CAP-EDEN-ROC

BLVD J F KENNEDY, CAP D'ANTIBES, 06602 ANTIBES
☎ 93 61 39 01
One of the world's most glamorous, romantic hotels, with stratospheric prices to match. Walk through the immense marble-floored lobby to the beautiful gardens that give out on to the sea. A glittering guest list that has included all the stars, from Noël Coward to HARRISON FORD. No cheques or credit cards accepted so bring sacks of cash.

HOTEL MAJESTIC

14 LA CROISETTE, 06407 CANNES
☎ 93 68 91 00
Conveniently located by the Palais du Festival, this sparkling white hotel is where things really happen in Cannes. Star-spot over lunch on the poolside terrace and bask in reflected glory.

HOTEL NEGRESCO

37 PROMENADE DES ANGLAIS, 06007 NICE
☎ 93 16 64 00
A Nice landmark, as much a museum as a hotel, oozing opulence. "*Its belle-époque architecture is a veritable treasure*" – ROBERT CARRIER.

RESTAURANTS

SEE ALSO HOTELS.

CHANTECLER

AT THE HOTEL NEGRESCO, NICE (SEE HOTELS)
☎ 93 16 64 00
Here young chef Dominique le Stanc serves up delectable Provençal cuisine. "*Perhaps the most creative cook on the coast and perhaps the best ice-cream I have ever had – glace miel au safran,*" reports ROBERT CARRIER.

CHEZ BRUNO

ROUTE DE VIDAUBAN, 83510 LORGUES
☎ 94 73 92 19
There is no written menu, no wine list, everything depends on what Clément Bruno decides to buy at the market that day. Gourmets from all over France, and beyond, make the trip to sample this very personal cooking. According to ROBERT CARRIER, "*Clément Bruno is a generous giant of a man. A born cook who loves the back-country products of his native Provence: truffles, wild asparagus, wild mushrooms and wild game.*"

DON CAMILLO

5 RUE DES PONCHETTES, 06300 NICE
☎ 93 85 67 95
A small restaurant where chef–proprietor Frank Cerutti, who trained with Ducasse and Maximin, continues to seduce with his cuisine, based in Provence with a touch of the Italian hills thrown in. Recommended by ROBERT CARRIER.

LOUIS XV

AT THE HÔTEL DE PARIS, MONTE CARLO (SEE HOTELS)
☎ 92 16 30 00
Alain Ducasse was one of the youngest chefs to earn a third Michelin star and the only hotel chef ever to have won three such stars. His showpiece, the Louis XV, is the apogee of opulence, with beautiful porcelain, glass, knives and forks – and beside each chair there's even a little upholstered stool for your handbag or your peke. According to the maestro, "What appears to be the most simple is also the most dangerous and complicated." But Ducasse's "simple" cuisine has turned Monaco into a destination for serious eaters.

LE PROVENCAL

2 AVE DENIS SEMERIA, 06230 ST-JEAN-CAP-FERRAT
☎ 93 76 03 97

Elegant little restaurant with a terrace overlooking the port of Saint-Jean-Cap-Ferrat, offering smiling service and wonderful food. "*Jean-Jacques Jouteaux is certainly one of the most charming and inventive chefs on the coast,*" advises ROBERT CARRIER.

TETOU
AVE DE ROUSTRAN, 06220 GOLFE GUANS
☎ 93 63 71 16
Fabulous family-run waterside fish restaurant, especially popular for Sunday lunch and dinner. According to HANS MEISSEN, "*Their speciality – bouillabaisse – is excellent.*"

Southwest of France

FESTIVALS

FESTIVAL MUSICAL DU PERIGORD NOIR
53 RUE DU GÉNÉRAL FOY, 24290 MONTIGNAC
☎ 53 51 95 17
The largest music festival in the Southwest of France is held from mid-July until end Aug, in the region's Romanesque churches.

HOTELS AND RESTAURANTS

L'AUBERGADE
52 RUE ROYALE, 47270 PUYMIROL
☎ 53 95 31 46
Gastronomes continue to gather at Michel Trama's beautiful medieval hillside restaurant set in a wonderful terraced garden. High-class French cooking also includes amazing breakfasts and legendary nibbles using local charcuterie.

CHATEAU CORDEILLAN-BAGES
ROUTE DES CHÂTEAUX, 33250 PAUILLAC
☎ 56 59 24 24
Elegant château with wonderfully airy rooms. "*A class Napoleon III château in its own vineyards, owned and run by the Lynch-Bages winemakers. They also run a wine school and have a 42-page wine list to accompany the fine classical French cuisine which is served in the courtyard*" – CAROL WRIGHT.

GRAND HOTEL DU LYON D'OR
69 RUE CLEMENCEAU, 41200 ROMORANTIN-GEORGES
☎ 54 76 00 28
Chef Didier Clement is startling his contemporaries with his unusual use of ingredients such as soy sauce, poppy seeds and Coca-Cola.

LE GRAND LARGE
BAIE DE LA REMIGÉASSE, 17550 ILE D'OLERON
☎ 46 75 37 89
Comfortable modern hotel facing the ocean. "*It is kept by very warm-hearted, welcoming people who provide excellent French food. It is very beautiful there and makes a perfect place for a quiet holiday or a honeymoon*" – DAME BARBARA CARTLAND.

HOTEL DU PALAIS
1 AVE DE L'IMPÉRATRICE, 64200 BIARRITZ
☎ 59 41 64 00
Right on the Atlantic Ocean, this splendid summer palace was built under the direction of Napoleon III. Original period style and grandeur are evident in the formal gardens (which contain an immaculate putting green), the huge bedrooms and LE GRAND SIÈCLE restaurant which is in the palace's original old ballroom.

MICHEL BRAS
ROUTE DE L'AUBRAC, 12210 LAGUIOLE
☎ 65 44 32 24
The ultimate forum for Michel Bras to display his culinary talents and an imaginative collection of wine. "*An innovative chef of genius in a restaurant/hotel of his own creation, in tune with the romantic environment of the Aubrac mountains,*" enthuses HILARY RUBINSTEIN. QUENTIN CREWE adds, "*Very lovely, very modern hotel. Michel is a superb chef and serves some wonderful Aubrac beef from rather wonderful bison-like cattle and he uses lots of fresh vegetables, herbs and seeds in such an imaginative way.*"

LES PRES ET LES SOURCES D'EUGENIE
40320 EUGÉNIE-LES-BAINS
☎ 58 05 06 07
Only a Frenchman – Michel Guérard – would attempt to combine a health spa with a 3-star restaurant and make it work. The Empress Eugénie and much of the French aristocracy used to come here for the waters. Today distinguished foodies and health fiends still make the pilgrimage to dine, (on either the *gourmande* or *minceur* menu) take the waters or simply go for a walk in the enchanting gardens full of tulip trees, orange blossom and magnolias.

GERMANY
Berlin

FILM

BERLIN INTERNATIONAL FILM FESTIVAL
BUDAPESTER STRASSE 50, 10787
☎ (30) 254890
After Cannes, this is Europe's best film festival. Each Feb, Eastern European films vie with Western European and American offerings for the prestigious Golden Bear Award.

HOTELS

BRISTOL HOTEL KEMPINSKI
KURFÜRSTENDAMM 27, 10719
☎ (30) 884340
This hotel, otherwise known as the "Kempi", sits in the heart of the city, with all of the best shopping at its doorstep. Lots of creature comforts – big bedrooms, marble bathrooms, cable TV, three restaurants, an indoor pool and a gym.

HOTEL INTER-CONTINENTAL
BUDAPESTER STRASSE 2, 10787
☎ (30) 26020
Standards at one of Berlin's largest hotels have soared following its recent makeover. This is where the film world comes to let its hair down after the festival (see Film). Anyone missing Hollywood can go to the newly opened LA CAFÉ, which serves Californian cuisine.

MARITIM GRAND HOTEL
FRIEDRICHSTRASSE 158–64, 10117
☎ (30) 20270
It's difficult to imagine how this grand turn-of-the-century hotel in Berlin's historical centre ever quite fitted into socialist East Berlin. There are specially designed suites named after Schinkel, Goethe, Lessing and Tokyo. Gourmet cuisine is served in the Art Deco restaurant SILHOUETTE. There's an exotic Wintergarten (a conservatory) and a summer garden with an orchid conservatory – great for cocktails. Extensive fitness and pampering potential, along with excellent service.

MARITIM PRO-ARTE HOTEL
FRIEDRICHSTRASSE 150–153, 10117
☎ (30) 20335
Originally the Hotel Metropol, this hotel has been totally updated by French designer Philippe Starck and filled with modern art. Great for business travellers (desks, phones, fax and PC connections are installed in each room).

SCHLOSSHOTEL VIER JAHRESZEITEN
BRAHMSSTRASSE 10, 14193
☎ (30) 895840
The exclusive Wilmersdorf home of art collector Walter von Pannwitz has been transformed into the most sought-after hotel in Berlin. Couturier Karl Lagerfeld chose the colour schemes and designed the stationery, porcelain and staff uniforms. And if he is out of town ask to stay in his private suite.

MUSIC

PHILHARMONIE
MATTHÄIKIRCHSTRASSE 1, 10785
☎ (30) 254880
Much lauded and respected modern home of the Berlin Philharmonic, directed by the great Claudio Abbado.

RESTAURANTS

Until recently, East Berlin, when compared with West, was very much the poor relation when it came to restaurants. Today the old Eastern side of town more than matches the West, with many of the best (and most expensive) restaurants in the city.

SEE ALSO HOTELS.

BAMBERGER REITER
REGENSBURGERSTRASSE 7, 10777
☎ (30) 244282

 ENCORE Not to be missed, owing to Berlin's world-class reputation for music, the **Berlin Festival Weeks**, Festspiele GmbH, Kärtenbüro, Budapester Strasse 50, 10787 Berlin, takes place every Aug–Sept. There are concerts, theatre, art exhibitions, operas, and ballet . . . . . ♠

Warm, rustic, oak-beamed restaurant, filled with fresh flowers, complements chef Franz Raneburger's excellent menu. Based on the freshest market produce available, it changes every day. The **BAMBERGER BISTRO** next door offers a more affordable version of the same. Open for dinner only and closed Sun–Mon.

BORCHARDT
FRANZÖSISCHESTRASSE 47
☎ (30) 229 3144
A fashionable East Berlin restaurant that has emerged since unification, Borchardt is evocative of the Art Nouveau cafés of 1920s Paris. Sunday brunch is very popular so book ahead.

PARIS BAR
KANTSTRASSE 152, 10623
☎ (30) 313 8052
Top-class, central restaurant just off the Ku'damm, the Paris Bar serves high-quality French fare and is a magnet for film stars, artists and the rich. Reservations are recommended.

ROCKENDORF'S RESTAURANT
DÜSTERHAUPSTRASSE 1, 13469
☎ (30) 402 3099
One of Germany's most outstanding restaurants, set in a luxurious Art Nouveau villa just outside Berlin. Upstairs in the dining room there are lovely views over the gardens, while the superb cellar contains over 600 different wines. Siegfried Rockendorf's elegant *haute* French style uses the best of German products as part of a fixed-price menu. Closed Sun–Mon.

TURMSTUBEN
AM GENDARMENMARKT 5, 10117
☎ (30) 229 9313
Tucked under the cupola of the French Cathedral on the Gendarmenmarkt, this restaurant is not for the vertigo-sufferer as it can only be reached via a long and winding staircase. Not a vast selection of food, but a decent wine list. Reserve if you want a table at the weekend.

SHOPPING

Berlin's most popular shopping district is the long and imposing **KURFÜRSTENDAMM** and the streets that feed off it, all of which are lively with cafés, bars and shops. The area between Breitscheidplatz and Olivaer Platz is especially busy. At Breitscheidplatz the massive **EUROPA-CENTER** encompasses more than 100 shops, restaurants and bars, including one of several

very popular Irish bars. **THE KÖNIGLICHE PORZELLAN MANUFACTUR (KPM)**, the former Royal Prussian Porcelain Factory, is at Kurfürstendamm 26A, ☎ (30) 8811802, while you can pick up some seconds from the factory salesroom at Wegelystrasse 1. **KADEWE** (short for Kaufhaus des Westens, or Department Store of the West), Tauentzienstrasse 21, 789 Berlin, ☎ (30) 21210, is the largest department store in Continental Europe. In East Berlin, **FRIEDRICHSTRASSE** has the most elegant shops, while the chicest and most expensive boutiques will be found on the famous street **UNTER DEN LINDEN**. Around **ALEXANDERPLATZ**, in the centre of East Berlin, you'll find things that are a bit cheaper.

Munich

ART AND MUSEUMS

ALTE PINAKOTHEK
BARER STRASSE 27
This magnificent gallery, commissioned by Ludwig I and dating from 1827, is currently closed for renovation until the end of 1997–8. Its outstanding collection of Old Masters and early Renaissance German painting has been temporarily moved to the Neue Pinakothek (see entry) across the lawn.

BMW MUSEUM
PETUELRING 130, 80788
☎ (89) 3820
Munich is the home of BMW, so this futuristic museum is the best place to have a look at the full range, old and new, of this thoroughbred car manufacturer.

DEUTSCHES MUSEUM
GERMAN MUSEUM OF SCIENCE AND TECHNOLOGY, MUSEUMINSEL, 80538
☎ (89) 217 9369
You need a full day to explore this vast museum with its 12 miles of corridor and six floors of exhibits. Special attractions include a new planetarium and an IMAX theatre – a kind of 3-D cinema.

NEUE PINAKOTHEK
BARER STRASSE 29, 80799
☎ (89) 2380 5195
Another project of Ludwig I, originally built to house his 19C European collections, but destroyed during World War II and rebuilt in

1980. Skylights provide excellent viewing conditions for this collection which includes French Impressionist and 19C paintings.

STAATSGALERIE MODERNER KUNST

PRINZREGENTENSTRASSE 1 (HAUS DER KUNST), 80538

☎ (89) 211270

Situated at the south end of the Englischer Garten, this building stems from the Hitler era and has been beautifully restored. It houses an impressive range of 20C works including Picasso, Beckmann, Burri, Klee and de Chirico.

FILM

MUNICH INTERNATIONAL FILM FESTIVAL

KAISERSTRASSE 39, 80801

☎ (89) 381 9040

Week-long June showcase for both mainstream and avant-garde pictures not seen in Germany before. Russian, Asian and Latin American films line up alongside top Western European and US releases.

HOTELS

ADMIRAL

KOHLSTRASSE 9, 80469

☎ (89) 226 6414

Located in the city centre on a peaceful side-street near the Deutsches Museum, this small hotel has a pleasant garden overlooked by balconies. Service is friendly and cosy. Highly recommended.

BAYERISCHER HOF

PROMENADEPLATZ 2–6, 88333

☎ (89) 21200

A luxury hotel filled with fine paintings, antiques and painted wood, that has a palatial all-suite wing, once patronized by King Ludwig I. Things have changed since his day. These days there's the slightly incongruous

TRADER VIC Polynesian restaurant famous for its exotic cocktails, a comedy theatre, a nightclub featuring international bands, and a rooftop swimming pool with views over Munich. SIR PETER USTINOV says, "*It's like a railway station with enormous bustle and full of vigour, lots of very useful amenities, with restaurants staying open till 2am.*"

RAFAEL

NEUTURMSTRASSE 1, 89331

☎ (89) 290980

The two great conductors, SIR GEORG SOLTI and ZUBIN MEHTA, always stay at the flagship hotel of Georg Rafael's renowned group. The hotel is set in a neo-classical building in the heart of the old town. The rooms ooze style with their extravagant marble bathrooms and there's great attention to detail – including an unpacking service for each guest. The rooftop pool has postcard views of historic Munich, while **MARK'S** gourmet restaurant will ensure that the inner-you is happy as well. "*Decorated in the most elegant way; very private and exclusive and the restaurant is superb*" – ROBERTO GUCCI.

SPLENDID

MAXIMILIANSTRASSE 54, 80548

☎ (89) 296606

A small hotel filled with imposing chandeliers and Oriental rugs. There's no restaurant to speak of, although in fine weather you can have breakfast in the courtyard, but the shops and restaurants of Maximilianstrasse are only a few minutes away. Smooth service.

VIER JAHRESZEITEN KEMPINSKI

MAXIMILIANSTRASSE 17, 80539

☎ (89) 21250

Munich's most elegant hotel, built in 1858 for Bavaria's high society and in a great location on Munich's best shopping street. Legendary for once having handled the King of Siam's 1,320 pieces of luggage, it is still noted for the gracious service of the staff.

ENCORE Munich boasts the usual array of good-quality department stores – like **Hertie, Kaufhof,** and **Karstadt** – in the centre, but look out for some of its superb one-off stores. **Alois Dallmayr** is a fabulous delicatessen, on Dienerstrasse just off Marienplatz, famous for fresh coffee, including its own brand (it offers 50 types altogether) . . . . . ♣ Make sure you visit the **Schwabing** area, north of the centre, which is not only home to Munich University, but also has a great selection of expensive boutiques . . . . . ♣ Once you've shopped until you've dropped, visit the beautiful **Englischer Garten** where you can refresh yourself with delicious cold Bavarian beer and salty pretzels. . . . . ♣

MUSIC

Munich's principal orchestras are the **MUNICH PHILHARMONIC** (housed in the Gasteig centre), the **BAVARIAN STATE ORCHESTRA** (housed in the Nationaltheater) and the **KURT GRAUNKE SYMPHONY ORCHESTRA** which performs at the Gärtnertheater. You may find both impromptu and planned jazz sessions in the city's bars and cafés on a Sunday afternoon. However, if it's Lederhosen, traditional Bavarian Volksmusik, busty barmaids and beer that you're interested in, you really can't omit the annual 16-day **OKTOBERFEST**, held at the end Sept. Or visit Munich's oldest beer garden, the famous 16C **HOFBRÄUHAUS**, just off Marienplatz.

BAVARIAN STATE OPERA

NATIONALTHEATER, MAX-JOSEPH-PLATZ 9, 80539
☎ (89) 218501
World-class opera company renowned for its gilded opera house and sumptuous sets. The evening ticket office opens an hour before curtain up.

MUNICH OPERA FESTIVAL

FESTSPIELKASSE, BAYERISCHE STAATSOPER, MAXIMILIANSTRASSE 11, 80539
☎ (89) 221316
Opera buffs converge on this annual feast of music, which lasts throughout July. Book far, far in advance.

RESTAURANTS

SEE ALSO HOTELS.

BOETTNERS

THEATINERSTRASSE 8, 80333
☎ (89) 221210
The oldest city-centre restaurant (open since 1905) feels like an intimate club with its dark wood-panelled interior and grand old bar. Munich's business élite savour the predominantly seafood-based menu. SIR PETER USTINOV says it is "*very old, very charming and with a great atmosphere*".

TANTRIS

JOHANN-FICHTE-STRASSE 7, 80805
☎ (89) 362061
As famous for its tasteless 70s decor as for the artful, top-class *nouvelle cuisine* dished up by Hans Haas (voted the nation's top chef in 1994

by Germany's critics). Not to be missed. Open Tues–Sat.

SPATENHAUS

RESIDENZSTRASSE 12, 80333
☎ (89) 290 7060
This is your stereotypical Bavarian restaurant: wood-panelled walls, beams and, of course, Bavarian specialities to match. There's an international menu too.

Rest of Germany

ART AND MUSEUMS

RÖMISCH-GERMANISCHES MUSEUM

RONCALLIPLATZ 4, 50678 COLOGNE
☎ (221) 221 4438
Located opposite the cathedral, this museum was built in the 70s around the famous Dionysus mosaic – at one time the floor of a wealthy Roman trader's house – and exhibits Roman sarcophagi, memorial tablets and tombs.

STAATSGALERIE

KONRAD-ADENAUER-STRASSE 30–32, 70182 STUTTGART
☎ (711) 212 4050
British architect James Stirling's influential postmodern building, housing an impressive collection of 19C and 20C art, from Impressionism to the present day. Strong on German Expressionists (Grosz, Beckmann, *et al*) and Bauhausers.

WALLRAF-RICHARTZ-MUSEUM/MUSEUM LUDWIG

BISCHOFSGARTENSTRASSE 1, 50667 COLOGNE
☎ (221) 221 3491
The Rhineland's largest gallery, featuring two major collections. The first covers European works from 1300 to 1900. The second part, the Museum Ludwig, is devoted to 20C art. The Picasso series is a main attraction; indeed, a new museum is due to be built to house these alone.

HOTELS

ATLANTIC HOTEL KEMPINSKI

AN DER ALSTER 72–79, 20099 HAMBURG
☎ (40) 28880
This is one of Germany's most sumptuous hotels, set on the shores of the Alster lake. Miles of thick-pile carpets, acres of marble and

glitzy bedrooms which have appealed to visiting pop stars including MICHAEL JACKSON. Service is good, as is the food in the striking, post-modern **ATLANTIC RESTAURANT** which is all black pillars and inlaid marble.

BREIDENBACHER HOF
HEINRICH-HEINE-ALLEE 36, 40213 DÜSSELDORF
☎ (211) 13030
Düsseldorf's oldest and most elegant hotel still continues to be a 180-year-old standard-bearer for luxury living, from the thick marble baths to the gilt-mirrored drawing rooms. "*Terribly well run, spotless and extremely friendly*," reports SIR PETER USTINOV.

BRENNER'S PARK
AN DER LICHTENTALER ALLEE, SCHILLERSTRASSE 6, 76530 BADEN-BADEN
☎ (7221) 9000
Palatial turn-of-the-century hotel, set in a large private park facing the famous Lichtentaler Allee. Complete with spa and beauty farm, it is the place to come for indulgent pampering.

DOM-HOTEL
DOMKLOSTER 2A, 50667 COLOGNE
☎ (221) 20240
This old-fashioned hotel has bags of charm. Elegantly furnished with lots of antiques. Service is personal and efficient and there's a great view of the towering cathedral.

••••••••••••••••••••••••••••••••••

"THE RESTAURANT IS TINY, ONLY SIX TABLES, BUT THE FOOD IS ABOUT AS GOOD AS ANY RESTAURANT IN HAMBURG" –

PAUL HENDERSON ON

HOTEL ABTEI

••••••••••••••••••••••••••••••••••

HOTEL ABTEI
ABTEISTRASSE 14, 20149 HAMBURG
☎ (40) 442905
Set in a smart residential district near the centre of Hamburg, where the bourgeoisie built superb houses for themselves in the 19C, the Abtei was one such residence. Now a charming hotel with only nine rooms, it retains a cosy period atmosphere, with richly decorated lounges and an exquisite landscaped garden. Friendly and personal, it's ideal for the independent traveller.

HOTEL COLOMBI
AM COLOMBI PARK/ROTTECKRING, 7098 FREIBURG
☎ (761) 21060
This central though quiet family hotel, which was extended in 1995, is still best-known for its award-winning **COLOMBI RESTAURANT**. Overseen by Herr Klink, it serves fine French and German *nouvelle cuisine*. Also has a swimming pool with sauna and steam baths.

HOTEL IM WASSERTURM
KAYGASSE 2, 50676 COLOGNE
☎ (221) 20080
Formerly Europe's tallest water tower, this unique 11-storey brick hotel is a place you'll either love or hate. Completely designed and decorated by French designer Andrée Putnam, it offers the strangest of conveniences (including dog-sitters, should you need them). Fine French and German cuisine is served in the 11th-floor restaurant and there's a roof terrace for eating out in summer. "*The decor is wonderful. Because the building is round, the rooms are constructed like pieces of cake*" – JORG ZIPPRICK.

KASTENS HOTEL LUISENHOF
LUISENSTRASSE 1–3, 30159 HANNOVER
☎ (511) 30440
Run by the Kastens family since 1856, this top-drawer hotel is noted for its luxurious rooms and impeccable service. Have your aperitif in the **LUISENPUB** before dining in **LUISENSTUBE**.

SCHLOSS CECILIENHOF
NEUER GARTEN, 14469 POTSDAM
☎ (331) 37050
Where Churchill, Stalin and Truman met at the end of World War II. Only 45 minutes outside Berlin, this splendid Prussian version of an English country house is half museum, half hotel. Rooms are ravishingly pretty – ask for Princess Cecilia's bedroom.

SCHLOSSHOTEL KRONBERG
HAINSTRASSE 25, 61476 KRONBERG IM TAUNUS
☎ (61) 73 70101
Fairy-tale medieval castle surrounded by a forest. Walls are hung with tapestries and there's a wood-panelled dining room.

VIER JAHRESZEITEN
NEUER JUNGFERNSTIEG 9–14, 20354 HAMBURG
☎ (40) 34940
Although taken over by the Japanese in 1989, this still ranks as one of the best hotels in

Germany, with its wood panelling, tapestries and antiques. Royalty and heads of state have been coming here for nearly a century. Recommended by SIR PETER USTINOV.

MUSIC

BAYREUTH FESTIVAL

POSTFACH 100262, 95402 BAYREUTH
☎ (921) 78780
A festival devoted to Wagner: performances of his music are held in an opera house he designed, while everything is run by his descendants and listened to by his devotees. Tickets are virtually impossible to obtain but you might succeed if you get a programme at the end of Oct and apply for tickets by mid-Nov. Festival runs from the end July–end Aug.

RESTAURANTS

SEE ALSO HOTELS.

BAD DÜRKENHEIMER RIESENFASS

AM WURSTMARKTGELÄNDE, BAD DÜRKHEIM
☎ (6322) 2143
Located inside the world's biggest wine barrel, this exceptional restaurant can seat 420 people inside and a further 230 on the terrace. The atmosphere is fun and the food reasonable.

LE CANARD

ELBCHAUSSÉE 139, 22763 HAMBURG
☎ (40) 880 5057
Small, slightly strait-laced restaurant, in a beautiful setting overlooking the river Elbe, presided over by the much-lauded Austrian chef Josef Viehhauser, who conjures up superb seafood dishes.

DIETER MÜLLER IM SCHLOSSHOTEL LERBACH

LERBACHER WEG, 51465 BERGISCH GLADBACH
☎ (2202) 2040
Grand old castle hotel with fine dining room in the style of "*jardin d'hiver*" sets the stage for Dieter Müller's culinary genius.

GOLDENER PFLUG

OLPENER STRASSE 421, 51109 COLOGNE
☎ (221) 895509
A former tavern with golden chairs and curtains serving a fine mix of German and French cuisine – ideal for a special occasion.

JORG MÜLLER

SÜDERSTRASSE 8, 25980 WESTERLAND
☎ (4651) 27788
Brother of the great Dieter Müller (see entry for his eponymous restaurant), Jorg Müller is famous not only for his cooking but also for his remarkable moustache. He serves inventive German *nouvelle cuisine*, using the finest and freshest regional ingredients.

LANDHAUS SCHERRER

ELBCHAUSSÉE 130, 22763 HAMBURG
☎ (40) 880 1325
Although it is very central, the park-like setting distances this classic Hamburg restaurant from the city. PAUL HENDERSON rates it "*very highly for food, wine, decor and service. The Canard Restaurant is only 50 yards away and more highly rated by the food guides, but it wasn't even close to this in quality. There is a very amusing collection of erotic art hanging on the walls.*"

SÄUMERHOF

STEINBERG 32, 94481 GRAFENAU
☎ (8552) 2401
A surprisingly good restaurant buried in the heart of the Bavarian forest, the Säumerhof is part of a family-run hotel. Head of the clan, Herr Endl, the chef, creates imaginative and delicious food.

SCHWARZER HAHN

AM MARKTPLATZ, 67146 DEIDESHEIM
☎ (6326) 1811
Stylish cellar restaurant of a hotel, where Helmut Kohl dined with Gorbachev, Thatcher and Mitterrand. Very good German *haute cuisine* from Manfred Schwarz.

SCHWARZWALDSTUBE

HOTEL TRAUBE, TONBACHSTRASSE 237, 72270 BAIERSBRONN
☎ (7442) 492665
Part of a luxurious mountain hotel, this Black Forest-style restaurant has beamed ceilings and spectacular views. The service is excellent as is the creative cooking of young chef Harald Wohlfahrt. There is a wonderful wine list to match.

ZUR TRAUBE

BAHNHOFSTRASSE 47, 41515 GREVENBROICH
☎ (2181) 68767
Home to Dieter Kaufmann, one of Germany's best – and most modest – chefs. (He doesn't like critics to talk about him.) Try the variations de foie gras or pigeon aux cèpes, but don't forget pudding (Kaufmann started his career as a

pâtissier). All complemented by one of the best wine lists in the country. Closed Sun–Mon.

GREECE
Athens

FESTIVALS

THE ATHENS FESTIVAL
BOX OFFICE: STADIOU 4
☎ (1) 322 1459
Best known for staging ancient-Greek plays in their original theatres, the Athens Festival presents not only drama but a broad spectrum of music and dance too. The festival takes place from early June till mid Sept; tickets are available a few days before each performance.

HOTELS

APHRODITE ASTIR PALACE AT VOUGLIAMENI
PO BOX 1226
☎ (1) 896 0211
Complex of hotels, 30 minutes from Athens, situated on the very tip of the mainland jutting into Vougliameni Bay. Check out **NAFISKA**, the premier playground for Greece's playboys and ladies of leisure, where there's a nightclub, three swimming pools, tennis courts, private beaches and helipads.

HOTEL GRANDE BRETAGNE
SYNTAGMA SQ
☎ (1) 331 4444
Built in 1862, this grand old pile sits right in the centre of Athens, across from the Greek Parliament and the National Gardens. It's particularly famous for its colourful history and its guest list, which has included Eisenhower and Richard Strauss. Book a suite with views of the Acropolis and away from the traffic at the front.

RESTAURANTS

AGLAMIR
AKTI KOUMOUNDOUROU 52–54, MIKROLIMANO
☎ (1) 411 5511
The most expensive fish restaurant in Mikrolimano harbour, on the water's edge, and one of the best in Athens. Watch the lights shimmer across the bay while dining.

BAJAZZO
ANAPAFSEOS 14, METS
☎ (1) 921 3013
If you are only going to have one meal in Greece, make sure you eat it here. Although the restaurant has recently moved, the original chef is still in charge, serving exquisitely presented food.

VASILENAS
ETOLIKOU 72, AGIA SOFIA, PIRAEUS
☎ (1) 461 2457
The place to come with a group of friends in order to try the 16-dish set menu. Zesty shrimp yiouversi and prawn croquettes are particularly good. Also try a pudding called tiganites: a kind of fried bread filled with walnuts.

Rest of Greece

HOTELS

ACROPOLE
FILELLINON 13, DELPHI
☎ (265) 82675
Friendly family-run hotel with a spectacular view of the mountainside and a sea of olive groves. Secluded gardens.

AKTI MYRINA HOTEL
MYRINA, LIMNOS
☎ (254) 226815
A complex of individual stone-built bungalows, each with its own private garden. The grounds lead straight on to a private sandy beach where you can indulge in various watersports. JULIAN LLOYD WEBBER says, "*It really is an excellent establishment, perfect for my young child. Very good food and lots to do.*"

CANDIDA HOUSE
CANDIDA-IRION, 21100, NAUPLION (THE PELOPONNESE)
☎ (752) 94060
Beautifully decorated hotel, combining good taste with comfort and located to the south of the town centre on beautiful Candida beach.

HOTEL VOUZAS
VAS. PAVLOU AND FRIDERKIS 13, DELPHI
☎ (265) 82232
Set on the edge of a gorge, this hotel has fan-

tastic views from every room. Vouzas is popular with Athenians who come to ski on Mount Parnassus at the weekends.

RESTAURANTS

CAMILLE STEFANI
MAIN STREET, THIRA, SANTORINI
☎ (286) 22265
One of the island's best restaurants, serving seafood and both Greek and international cuisine with good local wines.

HONG KONG

ART AND MUSEUMS

HONG KONG MUSEUM OF ART
10 SALISBURY RD, TSIMSHATSUI
☎ 2734 2167
An ever-growing collection of excellent Chinese art and antiquities, including fine ceramics and paintings, as well as a pictorial record of Sino–British relations. The displays are superb.

ARTS CENTRES

HONG KONG CULTURAL CENTRE
10 SALISBURY RD, TSIMSHATSUI
☎ 2734 9011
An eyesore nicknamed the ski-jump building, this ultra-modern structure on the Kowloon side of the city has superb acoustics and three auditoria, making it Hong Kong's top venue for theatre, opera and exhibitions.

BARS AND CAFES

THE CAPTAIN'S BAR
AT THE MANDARIN ORIENTAL (SEE HOTELS)
☎ 2522 0111
This is the hotel bar to be seen in, especially if you're in town on business.

THE CHAMPAGNE BAR
AT THE GRAND HYATT (SEE HOTELS)
☎ 2861 1234
An Art Deco piano-bar, with lots of black lacquer, serving the largest selection of champagnes in Hong Kong, available by the glass or bottle. Fun atmosphere.

THE GODOWN
ADMIRALTY TOWER II, HARCOURT RD, CENTRAL
☎ 2866 1166
Funky bar/restaurant, celebrated for its style and atmosphere rather than the food.

THE REGENT
AT THE REGENT HOTEL (SEE HOTELS)
☎ 2721 1211
The lobby of the Regent hotel, with its polished granite floor and 40-ft-high windows has fantastic views of the harbour. The best place to have a pre-theatre drink, it also offers an innovative snacks menu.

CASINOS – MACAO

MACAO CASINO
AT THE LISBOA HOTEL, AVENIDA DA AMIZADE, MACAO
☎ 375111
In-your-face gambling – so don't expect suave croupiers and sophisticates – you'll find all sorts, from factory workers to students. Staggering amounts of money are placed on all of the usual games like pontoon and roulette.

MANDARIN ORIENTAL CASINO
AVENIDA DA AMIZADE, MACAO 56
☎ 7888
The only casino in Macao where James Bond would feel at home. The minimum stakes are very grown-up as is the hushed atmosphere.

CLUBS

SEE ALSO BARS AND CAFÉS.

BOSS NIGHT CLUB
14 SCIENCE MUSEUM RD, TSIMSHATSUI
☎ 2369 2883
More akin to some sort of military operation than an evening's entertainment. Rolls-Royces ferry guests to their tables or private rooms, while 400 European and Asian babes dressed in bright pink eveningwear and fur shawls scurry about with walkie-talkies.

CALIFORNIA BAR AND GRILL
30–2 D'AGUILAR ST, CENTRAL
☎ 2521 1345
Heaving with Hong Kong's fashion victims;

models and yuppies get it together over cocktails and West Coast cuisine. In the separate disco dancing goes on till dawn.

CATWALK
18F, NEW WORLD HOTEL,
22 SALISBURY WORLD, KOWLOON
☎ 2369 4111
All-nighters flock to this high-tech combination of live bands, karaoke rooms and dance floor encircled by a catwalk for wannabe models to strut their stuff.

JJ's
AT THE GRAND HYATT (SEE HOTELS)
☎ 2861 1234
This cavernous, glamorous venue with its in-house R&B band still attracts trendy crowds.

JOE BANANAS
23 LUARD RD, WANCHAI
☎ 2529 1811
High-ceilinged American-style disco-café, specializing in sounds from the 50s and onwards. It gets swinging especially when there's a fleet in town.

NEW TONNOCHY NIGHTCLUB
1–5 TONNOCHY RD, WANCHAI
☎ 2575 4376
An audience largely made up of Asian businessmen comes for the bands, singers and elegant hostesses.

NINETEEN 97
9 LAN KWAI FONG
☎ 2810 0613
This melting-pot of styles and music has been going strong since the 80s. Its Lan Kwai Fong location is a great bonus – being Hong Kong's foremost nightlife strip.

FESTIVALS

DRAGON BOAT FESTIVAL
Held in June, this festival commemorates the suicide by drowning of Chu Yuan in 221 BC in protest against corrupt government. Lots of noisy drums and processions with colourful dragons' heads.

HONG KONG ARTS FESTIVAL
C/O 13F, HK ARTS CENTRE,
2 HARBOUR RD, WANCHAI
☎ 2529 5555
This world-class event dominates Hong Kong's theatres and halls from Jan to Feb, offering opera, dance, symphony concerts, mime and Asian arts – don't miss Chinese theatre. Ask your concierge to book the tickets.

HONG KONG FOOD FESTIVAL
35F, JARDINE HOUSE, 1 CONNAUGHT PL, CENTRAL
☎ 2801 7111
Hong Kong's kitchens great and small go crazy towards end Mar and beginning Apr, highlighting the island's position as the crossroads of the world and, more importantly, the culinary heart of Asia.

HOTELS

GRAND HYATT
1 HARBOUR RD, WANCHAI
☎ 2861 1234
Hyatt's flagship hotel, which in recent years has poached several of the Mandarin's old guests as well as staff. The quality of service in Hong Kong, and especially here, is quite unlike anywhere else in the world. The rooms are fabulous. Limber up on the rooftop tennis courts, or in the outdoor swimming pool ("*best in Hong Kong*," according to DAVID SHILLING). Two excellent restaurants, **ONE HARBOUR ROAD** and **GRISSINI'S** (see Restaurants).

MANDARIN ORIENTAL
5 CONNAUGHT RD, CENTRAL
☎ 2522 0111
The unquestioned leader of the colony's small army of hotels. It has the best hotel shopping arcade (see Shopping) and connection by walkways to the Central district's fashionable and expensive boutiques. There's a genuine sense of cool calm and seamless room service is provided by a team of white-jacketed floor butlers. If you care to emerge from your Floris-perfumed bedroom, you can try the pool and health club. You'll see guests ranging from pop stars to IAN BOTHAM, DAME KIRI TE KANAWA or JEAN CLAUDE VAN DAMME. LADY HARDINGE remains loyal: "*Beautiful old colonial hotel with big ceiling fans. Very, very superbly run.*" Several of the hotel's many bars and restaurants – like the **CAPTAIN'S BAR** (see Bars and Cafés), the **CHINNERY BAR**, the **CLIPPER LOUNGE**, **MAN WAH** (see Restaurants) and **PIERROT** (see Restaurants) – have become Hong Kong institutions. For an OTT caviare feast, go to the hotel's **HARLEQUIN BAR** and eat with gold-plated cutlery. The more puritannical can go for the etched-glass, split-level **CHESA GRILL** for Welsh lamb, Scottish steaks

and huge breakfasts. CAROL WRIGHT recommends the Cigar Divan "*for those who still smoke – Cuban cigars, Cuban food and Cuban music are all on offer.*" DAVID SHILLING adds, "*The sushi buffet is wonderful for lunch, small and cosy.*"

THE PENINSULA
SALISBURY RD, KOWLOON
☎ 2366 6251
Built in 1928 as the final destination of the Orient Express, "the Pen" is one of the city's most historic hotels (the British Governor surrendered to the Japanese here in 1941). The attention to detail is wonderful, from the fleet of Rolls-Royces to the twin helicopter pads on the roof, to the Hermés soap in the Portuguese marble bathrooms. LADY HARDINGE loves it: "*It's an absolute institution, so well run and so elegant, with violins over tea and a staff second to none in the world.*" But even if you choose not to stay here, it is definitely worth a visit, if only to see the spectacular lobby; to lunch at **GADDI'S** or to dine with the beautiful people in **FELIX**, one of the hottest nightspots in town.

....

"*THE HARBOUR VIEW SUITES ARE AMONG THE BEST HOTEL ROOMS I HAVE EVER SEEN; A CONSTANTLY CHANGING VIEW OF BOATS IN THE HARBOUR AND HONG KONG BEYOND*" – PAUL HENDERSON ON THE REGENT

....

THE REGENT
SALISBURY RD, KOWLOON
☎ 2721 1211
The Regent is a firm favourite with the fashion crowd – the elegant ballroom was designed with photographic shoots in mind. It also offers some of the most stunning views in Hong Kong, from the 40-ft-high windows of the cocktail lounge to the rooms with private Jacuzzis on terraces overlooking Hong Kong harbour. The hotel has a fine display of Oriental art, a huge outdoor pool and a health-club with saunas, steambaths and whirlpools. **YU** (which is Cantonese for "fish") is its high-design, highly rated fish restaurant. They also serve great oysters. "*No matter who you are, they pamper you. Great service, excellent food and fabulous views*" – LADY HARDINGE.

SHANGRI-LA
PACIFIC PLACE, 2188 QUEENSWAY
☎ 2877 3838
Set between the 39th and 56th floors of the Pacific Place tower, this is a perennial favourite among business travellers. All mod cons, from jet-controlled pools to remote-control curtains. In the evening you can watch a cabaret at **CYANO**, or just flop in **PETRUS**, which is a bit like a European club. If you're after crystal glasses, a deep wine-cellar and imaginative nouvelle-inspired Western cooking, book a table at **MARGAUX**. You'll also find fine Japanese food at **NADAMAN** and Chinese at **SHANG PALACE**. "*If you're six to eight people and really celebrating, book the wine cellar, a smart, private room, and start sampling the selection. Don't arrange appointments for the following day*" – CLAIRE BARNES.

RESTAURANTS

SEE ALSO HOTELS.

CHILI CLUB
88 LOCKHART RD, WANCHAI
☎ 2527 2872
The contemporary surroundings, interesting clientele and New York-like buzz make this a fun and popular institution. The prawns with garlic and ginger are a firm favourite.

THE CHINESE RESTAURANT
AT THE HYATT REGENCY, 67 NATHAN RD, TSIMSHATSUI, KOWLOON
☎ 2723 6226
Similar to a traditional Chinese teahouse of the 20s, the Chinese Restaurant goes in for adventurous renditions of traditional Cantonese food. Chef Chow Chung makes use of food from the West and the rest of Asia.

CITY CHIU CHOW RESTAURANT
EAST OCEAN CENTRE, 98 GRANVILLE RD, TSIMSHATSUI E, KOWLOON
☎ 2723 6226
A great opportunity to try a unique form of Chinese cooking at its best. Chiu Chow food is more eclectic, more subtle and more spicy.

FOOK LAM MOON
459 LOCKHART RD, CAUSEWAY BAY
☎ 2891 2639
Ever-popular Cantonese restaurant, still the best for non-hotel Chinese dining, attracting the most elevated of locals who love the chef's abalone masterpieces.

GRISSINI'S

AT THE GRAND HYATT (SEE HOTELS)
☎ 2588 1234
Decorated with magnificent wood panelling and wrought iron, it serves Northern Italian food with a heavy Tuscan accent. The aroma of the freshly baked bread provides a potent appetizer.

HUNAN GARDEN

THE FORUM, EXCHANGE SQUARE, CENTRAL
☎ 2868 2880
With its hotter, more delicate dishes, Hunan is fast taking over from Sichuan cooking. This rather elegant restaurant has led the way with its style and first-class food, which by Hong Kong standards isn't outrageously expensive. Recommended by PAUL HENDERSON.

JOYCE CAFE

1F THE GALLERIA, 9 QUEEN'S RD, CENTRAL
☎ 2810 1335
Simple but mesmerisingly chic, Joyce attracts the most sophisticated end of the affluent HK market. Flash ladies who lunch in head-to-toe labels can't keep away from the largely vegetarian, health-conscious menu featuring the best meatless club sandwich in the world.

••

"IT IS QUITE SIMPLY THE BEST CHINESE RESTAURANT I HAVE EATEN IN ANYWHERE IN THE WORLD" – **PAUL HENDERSON** ON *LAI CHING HEEN AT THE REGENT HOTEL*

••

LAI CHING HEEN

AT THE REGENT (SEE HOTELS)
☎ 2721 1211
Smart basement restaurant (where you eat with ivory chopsticks and jade spoons) serving Cantonese food. Dishes are geared around the lunar calendar.

MAN WAH

AT THE MANDARIN ORIENTAL (SEE HOTELS)
☎ 2522 0111
One of Hong Kong's premier Chinese eateries, where chef Fok Kam Tong presents Cantonese spectaculars by digging down into China's Imperial past.

MICHELLE'S

ICE HOUSE ST, CENTRAL
☎ 2877 4000
Slightly quirky (watch out for the perilous three-legged chairs), it's a refreshing change from the formality of Hong Kong's hotel restaurants. Melbourne-born owner Michel Garnaut concentrates all his energy on a small but delicious French menu.

ONE HARBOUR ROAD

AT THE GRAND HYATT (SEE HOTELS)
☎ 2861 1234
An elegant harbour-view hotel dining room, where the cuisine is classic Cantonese. Try the seafood, all of which is kept alive in the kitchen until the minute it is cooked.

THE PEAK CAFE

121 PEAK RD, CENTRAL
☎ 2849 7868
Vaguely rustic, with an open kitchen, tandoor oven and dining on the terrace under a thick bower of trees with views over the Lamma Channel. *"Great for a pre-dinner drink, or a private party, extremely good food, splendid views and a marvellous terrace – being able to do anything outside is rare in Hong Kong"* – CLAIRE BARNES.

PIERROT

AT THE MANDARIN ORIENTAL (SEE HOTELS)
☎ 2522 0111
Top French chefs make regular guest appearances in the kitchen at Pierrot, while the cellars boast lots of rare vintages.

STANLEY'S FRENCH RESTAURANT

86–88 STANLEY MAIN ST, STANLEY
☎ 2813 9721
A comfortable, quiet and romantic restaurant, overlooking Stanley Bay, perfect for a quiet *tête-à-tête* away from the bustle of Central.

STANLEY'S ORIENTAL

90B STANLEY MAIN ST, STANLEY
☎ 2813 9988
Spicy foods from all over South and Southeast Asia are served up by Felicia Sorensen, who does particularly good Thai and Indian food. Beautiful Stanley Bay setting.

VA BENE

58–62 D'AGUILAR ST, CENTRAL
☎ 2845 5577
If you're looking for sanctuary in the chaos of Lan Kwai Fong, dive into this Italian. The food is terrific.

VICTORIA CITY

2F SUN HUNG KAI CENTRE,
30 HARBOUR RD, WANCHAI
☎ 2827 9938
Sophisticated restaurant serving the best dim sum in Hong Kong. Indeed, super foodies such as KEN HOM get misty-eyed about house specialities including the lobster dumplings.

🦀 YUNG KEE

32–40 WELLINGTON ST, CENTRAL
☎ 2523 1562
Right in the centre of Central, this is exceptional value for a take-away, boxed lunch. Try the famous "one-dish meal" – roast goose and rice. To find it, look out for the rows of broken-necked geese hanging at the shopfront. Packed with locals night after night.

ZEN CHINESE CUISINE

LG/1 THE MALL, PACIFIC PLACE,
88 QUEENSWAY, CENTRAL
☎ 2845 4555
One of the new wave of contemporary Chinese restaurants; a muted, modern space – the perfect surroundings for Cantonese *nouvelle cuisine*.

SHOPPING

Hong Kong is a tax-free heaven where you can pick up just about anything, from antiques to art; jewellery to jade; silks to suits; and rugs to radios. But don't get too excited – bargain-hunters should check out the prices back home before embarking on a spree. To be safe it is also advisable to shop only where the HKTA sticker is displayed. On the Island, the **MANDARIN** arcade contains some of Hong Kong's local bests (see separate entries) along with some foreign glamour (Chaumet, Fendi, Ferragamo). A network of walkways leads to the smartest, shiniest shopping complexes: **THE LANDMARK** (Ralph Lauren, Buccellati, Bulgari, Ungaro, Vuitton, Loewe, Joyce Ma, The Swank Shop); **PRINCE'S BUILDING** (Chanel, Cartier, Church's shoes, Alfred Dunhill menswear, Gieves & Hawkes); and **SWIRE HOUSE** (which contains the pick of Japan). Kowloon is home to the swish arcades of the **REGENT** (Diane Freis, Basile, Lanvin, Nina Ricci) and **PENINSULA** (Marguerite Lee, Hermès, Gucci), and impressive mega-centres like **OCEAN TERMINAL**, **HARBOUR CITY**, **OCEAN CENTRE** (the best lines from around the globe), **PACIFIC PLACE** (home to every major designer, plus Lane Crawford and Seibu,

which now houses Garrard's), and **TIMES SQUARE**, Hong Kong's newest (with 9 floors of shops including Ferragamo, Fratelli Rossetti and Durban). The best Chinese goods can be found at department stores such as **CHINESE MERCHANDISE EMPORIUM**, **CHINA PRODUCTS** or **YE HWA CHINESE PRODUCTS EMPORIUM**. On HK Island, Pedder Building is a must for knockdown-priced young designer wear. The newly renovated **WESTERN MARKET**, HK's answer to Covent Garden, is home to many of the old "Cloth Alley" salesmen; prices, however, have rocketed recently. Tiny **SPRING GARDEN LANE** is in a maze of streets in Wanchai and is becoming well known to locals and ex-pats alike for its bargains. **STANLEY MARKET** remains a ritual Gweilo haunt on a Sunday (shop then lunch at Stanley's shop). On Kowloon, Nathan Road (or the "Golden Mile") and all roads off to the east are bursting with jewellery, cosmetics, fashion and electronic goods. **GRANVILLE ROAD** is the best place for bargains – look out for Gap, DKNY and Next seconds, plus lots of very affordable silks and linens. **KAISER ESTATE**, Phase I-III, Hung Hom, contains factory outlets for dependable and cheap silk, linen and sportswear. **TEMPLE ST MARKET**, known as the Night Market, runs from 9ish till late and gives you Kowloon's funkiest and funniest shopping: "designer" fakes, cheap wristwatches and sundry souvenirs in a mile-long stretch punctuated by Chinese street opera and fortune tellers.

A-MAN HING CHEONG

MANDARIN ORIENTAL, CENTRAL
☎ 2522 3336
Since 1898, classic men's clothes, tailored to Savile Row standards.

BON BON

PRINCE'S BLDG, CHATER RD, CENTRAL
☎ 2845 7164
Everything for the elegant professional. CLAIRE BARNES is full of praise: "*spot-on designer style for business women. A small but fast-changing collection with quick tailoring for the exact fit and very helpful staff. The only place I buy clothes in Hong Kong.*"

CHINESE ARTS & CRAFTS

STAR HOUSE, KOWLOON
☎ 2367 4061
SILVERCORD BLDG, 30 CANTON RD;
AND BRANCHES
Intricate silk embroidered clothing, Oriental jewellery (jade, lapis lazuli), carpets and affordable *objets d'art*. Good quality and government-controlled prices.

DAVID'S SHIRTS

M7, MANDARIN ORIENTAL, CENTRAL
☎ 2524 2979
GF, 33 KIMBERLEY RD, TSIMSHATSUI
☎ 2367 9556
Quality city shirts for Gweilos who are after something a little different – your initials embroidered in Chinese characters on the breast pocket.

DORFIT'S

SANDS BLDG, 17 HANKOW RD, TSIMSHATSUI
☎ 2721 3938
The best value in town for top-quality angora and cashmere sweaters; available in all colours and sizes.

FASHIONS OF SEVENTH AVENUE

KAISER ESTATE, BLOCK M, HOK YUEN ST, HUNG HOM, KOWLOON
☎ 2365 9061
12A SING PAO BLDG, 8 QUEEN'S RD, CENTRAL
☎ 2868 4208
Can often get hold of Donna Karan silks and knits, and other designer bargains, which arrive from time to time with the labels cut out.

KAI-YIN LO

M1, MANDARIN ORIENTAL, CENTRAL
☎ 2524 8238
THE PENINSULA; PACIFIC PLACE
Glittering, modern designs encrusted with semi-precious stones, pearls, shards of antique bone, and carved beads. With an equally glittering client list – HANAE MORI, British royals, ARIANNA HUFFINGTON, NATALIE MAKAROVA. Surprisingly affordable.

K S SZE & SONS

M6, MANDARIN ORIENTAL, CENTRAL
☎ 2524 2803
The establishment jeweller, where Mr Sze custom-makes virtually everything – take advantage of his fine inlay work.

MARGUERITE LEE

SHOP 210–11, GLOUCESTER TOWER, THE LANDMARK, CENTRAL
☎ 2525 6565
AND BRANCHES (THE PENINSULA, PRINCE'S BLDG)
Lingerie by Anne Lewin, La Perla, *et al*, is as enticing as the swimwear and hosiery.

MAYER SHOES

M16, MANDARIN ORIENTAL, CENTRAL
☎ 2524 3317
Choose your own design and your own skins, leathers and dyes. Wait for about a week, and expect the best handmade shoes Hong Kong has to offer. It's expensive, though.

OLIVER'S

PRINCE'S BLDG, CHATER RD, CENTRAL
☎ 2810 7710
Prestigious chain of international delis, stocking the finest wines, the best cheeses and a cornucopia of things you wouldn't expect to find in Hong Kong, such as Bath Oliver biscuits.

ORANGE-ROOM

SHOP 66, B1, NEW WORLD CNTR, TSIMSHATSUI
☎ 2368 8051
High-quality, well-designed footwear and nifty leather accessories, produced completely in Hong Kong. Relatively affordable.

PARIS SHOES AND LEATHERWEAR

SHOP D5/6, SHERATON HOTEL, KOWLOON
☎ 2723 7170
Still faster than most and a treat for convenience freaks – shoes, bags, briefcases and clothes are made to measure in 10 hours. You sacrifice quality for the convenience of speed.

RONALD ABRAM

SHOP 128, PRINCE'S BLDG, CHATER RD, CENTRAL
☎ 2845 2279
Repository for beautiful examples of antique Cartier, Van Cleef and Arpels – an irresistible Aladdin's cave.

SAM'S TAILOR

BURLINGTON ARCADE, 92–4 NATHAN RD, KOWLOON
☎ 2367 9423
A long-established, world-famous tailor, offering speed, value for money and an impressive corps of well-dressed and satisfied customers – PRINCE CHARLES, THE DUKE OF KENT, SIR CLEMENT FREUD, SIR DENIS THATCHER and members of the services.

SIBA

GF, 22 QUEEN'S RD, CENTRAL
☎ 2525 1234
A dazzling selection of extremely large diamonds.

TEQUILLA KOLA

PRINCE'S BLDG, CHATER RD, CENTRAL
☎ 2877 3295
An eclectic, eccentric mix of furniture and decorations from all over Asia.

THE WORLD OF JOYCE
THE GALLERIA, 9 QUEEN'S RD,
CENTRAL
☎ 2524 6534
Joyce Ma has immortalized herself with a New
Age superstore of franchised designer-wear and
designer-ware. There's also a health-food café,
apothecary and organic florist.

HUNGARY
Budapest

BARS AND CAFES

CAFE NEW YORK
VII, ERZSEBÉT KÖRÚT 9–11
☎ (I) 122 3849
A Budapest institution since 1895, where the
literary world gathers to read, discuss and
debate. (Until quite recently, certain tables
were reserved for writers.) Grand turn-of-the-
century coffee house with cakes as rich as the
surroundings.

GERBREAUD
V, VÖRÖSMARTY TÉR 7
☎ (I) 118 1311
Founded in 1857, Gerbreaud has been a fashionable meeting place ever since. Both locals
and tourists alike still flock here for the infamous chocolate cake (dobos torta), the elegant
imperial interior complete with gilded ceilings.

PIAF
VI, NAGYMEZO ÚT 20
☎ (I) 112 3823
Very trendy, if not slightly pretentious, late-
night bar, with plush red seating and candlelit
tables. You have to ring a bell to get in but after
that you can drink through till 6 or 7 am, if
you choose.

HOTELS

BUDAPEST HILTON
I, HESS ANDRÁS TÉR 1–3
☎ (I) 175 1000
Built around the ruins of a 13C monastery –
modern facilities and a casino do not detract
from its charms, which include wonderful
views over the Danube and, in summer, open-
air concerts in the courtyard.

GRAND HOTEL CORVINUS KEMPINSKI
V, ERZSÉBET TÉR 7–8
☎ (I) 266 1000
This new hotel has acted as a magnet to the
rich and famous visiting the city, despite the
lack of views over the Danube. The design,
while modern, is tasteful.

HOTEL GELLERT
XI, GELLERT TÉR I
☎ (I) 185 2200
This *grande dame* of a city hotel is best known
for its splendid and sumptuous thermal spa
baths, with direct access from the bedroom
floors. You descend into a cathedral-sized
chamber devoted to steam and hot water. What
it lacks in the creature comforts of a modern
hotel it makes up for in character and ambience.

RESTAURANTS

GUNDEL
XIV, ALLATKERTI ÚT 2
☎ (I) 321 3550
Legendary Hungarian restaurant set in a splendid turn-of-the-century palazzo, . Reopened
by New York restaurateur George Lang, it
offers food that is Hungarian in essence but is
cooked with American sensibilities firmly in
mind – ie, less fat and salt than you'd find in a
tavern. A cheaper and simpler bistro menu is
served in the picturesque garden in the summer. Jacket and tie. Highly recommended.

KEHLI
III, MÓKUS ÚT 22
☎ (I) 188 6938
Traditional tavern off the beaten track in old
Buda, buzzing with the friendly, local clientele.
Sit back, relax and tuck into the old-fashioned,
traditional Hungarian fare for a fraction of the
tourist-trap prices found elsewhere.

KISBUDA GYONGYE
III, KENYERES ÚT 34
☎ (I) 168 6402
Renowned restaurant serving excellent cuisine
in pretty surroundings, accompanied by a
pianist playing Mozart in the evening. In the
summer the diners can overflow into a garden
at the back.

MUZEUM
VIII, MÚZEUM KÖRÚT 12
☎ (I) 267 0375
This restaurant has a very loyal following in
Budapest; the service is swift and the candlelit

surroundings elegant. The food will satisfy most palates, with a balance between Hungarian and international food and wine.

INDIA
Bombay

HOTELS

THE OBEROI

NARIMAN POINT, 400021

☎ (22) 202 5757

A blend of both European and Indian-style accommodation and fabulous views over the Arabian Sea. The **RÔTISSERIE** is one of Bombay's leading restaurants, while the **BAYVIEW BAR** provides the best Happy Hour in town. The sparkling swimming pool is an ideal place to escape the heat of the city. SUE CARPENTER reports that "*The Oberoi is still tops for service and reliability at every level.*"

TAJ MAHAL INTER-CONTINENTAL

APOLLO BUNDER COLABA, COLABA 400039

☎ (22) 202 3366

The hotel sits on the waterfront in the heart of the commercial sector opposite the "Gateway to India" (an arch built in 1927 to celebrate George V's 1911 visit). It commands magnificent views of the bay and hills. Make sure you stay in the older, traditional part of the hotel with its intricate alcoves and arches and its cool, high ceilings. Take afternoon tea out on the verandah on wicker chairs. Restaurants include **ZODIAC**, which serves French cuisine, and the more traditional **TANJORE**, which puts on music and dancing every evening. Full fitness facilities available.

RESTAURANTS

SEE ALSO HOTELS.

INDIAN SUMMER

CHURCHGATE, VEER NARIMAN RD

☎ (22) 283 5445

A popular vegetarian restaurant where you can still get quality food in quality surroundings. Sip cocktails amid the stunning glasswork.

THE VENUE

VIKAS CNTR, 106 SV RD

☎ (22) 400 0054

Elegantly furnished to re-create the British Raj, this refined eaterie serves the best Indian cuisine.

Calcutta

HOTELS

OBEROI GRAND

15 JAWAHARLAL NEHRU RD, 700013

☎ (33) 249 2323

AUCTION HOUSES Anyone looking for a bit of excitement and/or an unusual souvenir shouldn't miss a visit to one of Calcutta's auction houses, on either Russell St or Park St. All manner of knick-knacks and trinkets are bought and sold with lots of enthusiasm and lots of noise. You won't find anything of great value, but everything you could possibly imagine is for sale: paintings, glassware, jewellery, furniture, televisions, clocks, even wigs. Without having to raise a finger, you could soon find yourself staggering away under the weight of items you never even knew you wanted. The main auction houses are: **Suman's Exchange**, 2/1 Russell St, ☎ (33) 249 7572; **The Russell Exchange** (Calcutta's oldest), 12C Russell St, ☎ (33) 249 8974; **Modern Exchange**, 12B Russell St, ☎ (33) 249 0756; **Dalhousie Exchange**, 13F Russell St, ☎ (33) 249 9309, and **Chowringhee Sales Bureau**, 24B Park St, ☎ (33) 249 8676.

Located in central Calcutta, this charming hotel is full of Victorian character. "*A shimmer of white in this faded city and a really special place – they haven't stopped polishing it since the old times,*" enthuses KATHLEEN COX. Suites have giant four-posters, and the best rooms overlook a swimming pool and courtyard. Try the low-seating Mughal Room for dinner. Service is very attentive.

TAJ BENGAL
34B BELVEDERE RD, ALIPORE
☎ (33) 248 3939
Built on a grand scale complete with huge planted atrium, this newish hotel is set in one of the quieter, more congenial residential areas of Calcutta. Suites have unique works of modern art and one of its restaurants, **THE GOLDEN VILLAGE**, is a recreation of a Bengali village, right down to the walls. Cutlery is optional, which will enable you to experience the full-on native experience. Close to the Calcutta race course and zoo, Taj Bengal also boasts a shopping arcade, business centre and swimming pool. "*The best of old and new brought together – it feels very peaceful and away from the chaos of Calcutta,*" according to KATHLEEN COX.

ART AND MUSEUMS

VICTORIA MEMORIAL
☎ (33) 285142
Calcutta's greatest museum, inaugurated in 1921 (having taken 15 years to build). An impressive marble monument, it contains 25 galleries filled with regalia and relics from the Raj era. An evocative collection of paintings, manuscripts, firearms, statues, lithographs and furniture is to be found here too. The dome of St Paul's Cathedral (Indian version) is mirrored in the still waters of the lake, while tree-lined walks and tranquil parks create a very peaceful atmosphere. "*Lord Curzon's vast monument to Queen Victoria and its glorious treasures – especially the pictures, which are being lovingly restored by Rupert Featherstone and his team*" – ROBIN HANBURY-TENISON.

Delhi

HOTELS

HOLIDAY INN CROWN PLAZA
BARAKHAMBA AVE, CONNAUGHT PL, NEW DELHI 110001
☎ (11) 332 0101
Delhi's most high-tech hotel is great if you're in town on business. There's a special executive floor, and a private club for those staying in the Presidential Tower part of the hotel. Excellent Indian food at **BALUCHI**.

OBEROI MAIDENS
7 SHAM NATH MARG, OLD DELHI 110054
☎ (11) 252 5464
Built at the turn of the century, the hotel has been dragged into the 1990s in terms of service and facilities but thankfully the quaint old-world atmosphere has remained. About as colonial in style as they come. It's set in cooling gardens in the heart of the old city, so you can flop by the swimming pool insulated from the heat and dust of the world outside.

OBEROI NEW DELHI
DR ZAKIR HUSSAIN MARG, NEW DELHI 110003
☎ (11) 436 3030
Still one of Delhi's most elegant hotels. There's a top-class Thai restaurant, the **BAAN THAI**, a rooftop lounge serving free tea all day and 24-hour business facilities if you need them. Impeccably run, it is on a par with the best Oriental hotels in terms of slick professionalism.

TAJ MAHAL
1 MANSINGH RD, NEW DELHI 110011
☎ (11) 301 6162
Close to Delhi's commercial and shopping districts, the Taj Mahal has a slightly glitzy, European feel to it. The five restaurants are fronted by the **SICHUAN HOUSE OF MING**, and the health facilities include swimming pool, sauna, massage and yoga.

ENCORE If you've had enough of palaces and monuments, get that adrenalin really pumping with **Himalaya River Runners**, F5 Hauz Khas Enclave, New Delhi 110016, ☎ (11) 685 2602, fax ☎ (11) 686 5604, who now offer treks and rafting trips in and around the Himalayas, according to the season. They provide seasoned guides who are committed to the outdoors and the environment and who have done virgin descents on several Himalayan rivers – real *Indiana Jones* stuff . . . . ♦

TAJ PALACE INTER-CONTINENTAL

2 SARDAR PATEL MARG, NEW DELHI
110021

☎ (11) 301 0404

Located in the diplomatic enclave, this is the ultimate corporate hang-out, with the biggest, most high-tech business rooms in Delhi. The French *nouvelle* ORIENT EXPRESS is said to be one of India's top ten restaurants. Chinese and Indian food available too.

WELCOMEGROUP MAURYA SHERATON HOTEL & TOWERS

SARDAR PATEL MARG, DIPLOMATIC
ENCLAVE, NEW DELHI 110021

☎ (11) 301 0101

Another marble monolith, but a popular choice – excellent restaurants, friendly and efficient staff and 24-hour business service.

RESTAURANTS

SEE ALSO HOTELS.

BUKHARA

AT THE WELCOMEGROUP MAURYA
SHERATON (SEE HOTELS)

☎ (11) 301 0101

The food here is Mughal cuisine, slow-cooked in tandoors (clay ovens). Bukhara is well known for its efforts to revive traditional recipes, with great success.

CHOR BAZARRE

HOTEL BROADWAY, 4/15A ASIF ALI RD

☎ (11) 327 3821

Based on the theme of the "Thieves' Market", this is an amalgamation of mismatched furnishings from India's Chor Bazaars. The restaurant also offers walking tours of Old Delhi – a leisurely stroll which naturally ends back at the restaurant for a lunch of the finest Kashmiri and tandoori dishes.

Jaipur

HOTELS

JAI MAHAL PALACE

JACOB RD, CIVIL LINES, RAJASTHAN
302006

☎ (141) 371616

A development built around the Maharajah Mawai Mansingh's former palace, which also

---

RAJASTHAN HERITAGE HOTELS There are three types of

Heritage hotel – palaces, which are the ex-residences of Maharajahs; forts and castles, which are often remote and family-run by the descendants of the original owners; and havelis, which are the homes of merchant communities and local grandees like Samode Haveli (see Jaipur Hotels). **Samode Palace**, Samode, District Jaipur, Rajasthan, ☎ (142) 34114, is owned by the same family as the eponymous **Haveli**. Built into a hill, this building provided the dramatic backdrop for the TV series *The Far Pavilions*. There's a wonderful airy courtyard with big fountains where you can sip your evening cocktail. **Fort Chanwa**, Luni, District Jodhpur, Rajasthan, ☎ (291) 32460, is a recently restored desert outpost, built of red sandstone with latticework balconies and verandahs. It is a friendly place, with light and airy rooms. **Castle Mandawa**, Contact 9, Sardar Patel Marg, C-Scheme, Jaipur 302001, Rajasthan, ☎ (141) 381906, was founded as a defensive outpost in 1755, and has remained family-owned since 1790. An informal oasis in the desert, dinner is heralded by a fire dancer (as it always used to be in the days of the kingship). **Bissau Palace**, Outside Chandpole Gate, Jaipur 302016, ☎ (141) 74191, was founded in 1919 by Rawal Raghubir Singh. He surrounded himself with the finest paintings, furniture and books, which today give the whole place a truly aristocratic feel.

used to be the home of the Prime Minister of Jaipur. The garden was built by Emperor Babur, and features a giant chessboard. Offers a wide range of facilities from tennis and riding, to the health club and yoga lessons.

RAMBAGH PALACE

BHAWANI SINGH RD, RAJASTHAN 302005

☎ (141) 381919

The former home to Jaipur's royal family is now a luxury hotel. The Princess suite has its own fountain and garden while the Maharajah's suite, which was decorated in honour of the Maharajah of Jaipur's third marriage, in 1940, has an extraordinary black marble bath. The rest of the hotel enjoys large verandahs for taking tea, and gardens complete with parading peacocks and fountains by Lalique.

SAMODE HAVELI

SAMOD HOUSE, GANGAPOLE 302002

☎ (141) 42407

A bargain townhouse hotel (and sister of the Samode Palace). There are immaculately preserved frescoes on the walls, beautiful courtyards and jewels set into the walls. KATHLEEN COX describes it as "*exquisite, fastidiously maintained and right on the edge of the old city*".

Rest of India

HOTELS AND RESORTS

....

"*AFTER A FEW HOURS OF SIT-TING ON THE PEARL SAND, WATCHING THE WATER WHICH IS A PALATE OF DIFFERENT SHADES, YOU ARE SUDDENLY IN HEAVEN*" – KATHLEEN COX ON BANGARAM ISLAND RESORT

....

BANGARAM ISLAND RESORT

LAKSHADWEEP, COCHIN, KERALA

☎ (484) 340221

A luxury resort set on Lakshadweep, the only island open to tourists in this small, stunning and remote archipelago of coral atolls. Relax

on the verandah of your thatched cottage in the shade of the coconut grove and the cooking is fantastic. And there's plenty to do, from high-energy watersports to viewing shoals of brightly coloured fish amidst the coral.

NEEMRANA FORT PALACE

OFF NATIONAL HIGHWAY 8, POST NEEMRANA, DISTRICT ALWAR, RAJASTHAN 301705

☎ (11) 494 6005

The first truly restored fort/palace in India, conveniently placed midway between Delhi and Jaipur. Established in 1464, "*it retains an authentic shabbiness, in a genuinely charming way. Tranquil and lovely,*" according to SUE CARPENTER. The rooms are decorated individually and each has its own private terrace and courtyard. Rooms range from the palatial Sheesh Mahal to the Shikar Mahal, a luxury hunting tent on the roof. French and Italian food is available by candlelight. One of the most popular of the "heritage hotels", it also has its own library.

SHIV NIWAS PALACE

UDAIPUR, RAJASTHAN 313001

☎ (294) 28239

Shiv Niwas is part of the magnificent City Palace, on the shores of Lake Pichola. This is the place to stay in Udaipur, but make sure you get one of the deluxe rooms overlooking the lake. Extraordinarily opulent inside with its bright Belgian cut-glass armchairs and tables and an oval carved marble swimming pool lined with mosaic. The most OTT suite is the Imperial.

TAJ HOLIDAY VILLAGE

SINQUERIM, BARDEZ, GOA 403519

☎ (832) 276201

Set back from the Sinquerim beach with its long lawns, under the cooling shade of palm trees, this ritzy Goan resort offers tile-roofed, village-style living – at a high price. "*Politicians hang out here with their armed guards*" – KATHLEEN COX

UMAID BHAWAN PALACE

JODHPUR, RAJASTHAN 342006

☎ (291) 3316

This spectacularly appointed and labyrinthine Maharajah's palace is still partly occupied by an Indian royal family. There are acres of marble corridor, a great skylit dome and fine collections of miniatures, armour and old clocks. Dine at Jodhpur's best restaurant, the **MARWAR HALL** or on the terrace. Sports available include squash, badminton, billiards, golf and croquet. SAM NEILL and JOHN CLEESE have both stayed here. SUE CARPENTER reports that "*the cool swimming pool with its mosaic floors is blissful*". The Maharajah will take guests at his other princely residences too, including a hunting lodge, Sadar Samand, and his orchard retreat, **MAHARANI BAGH**.

WELCOMEGROUP MUGHAL SHERATON

TAJ GANJ, AGRA 282001
☎ (562) 361701
The stunning architecture in brick and marble and the fabulous views over the Taj Mahal make this the best place to stay in Agra. When you're not gawping at the Taj Mahal you can go swimming, play croquet or mini golf, or go for a camel or elephant ride.

INDONESIA
Bali

HOTELS

AMANRESORTS

The Amanresorts were the brainchild of hotelier Adrian Zecha. "Aman" means "peaceful", and each Amanresort is exactly that – a tranquil, self-contained environment combining sophistication with simplicity, while keeping all the aggro of the outside world very firmly outside its parameters. The first Amanresort was the **AMANPURI**, on the Thai island of Phuket (see Thailand). Today there are Amanresorts in eight countries, ranging from Burma to Chile. Much of the appeal lies in the fact that each resort is so understated; there are few guests and the decoration is minimal, usually using local materials. A signature feature of all the resorts is the lipless blue-black pool where you can't quite see where the pool ends and terra firma begins. At **AMANKILA** this mirage effect is particularly breathtaking as the pool seems to merge with the sea beyond. If you're staying in Indonesia, you would ideally stay at all three resorts on Bali (**AMANKILA**, **AMANDARI** and **AMANUSA**) and the **AMANWANA** on Moyo. Each resort is quite distinctive and the hassle of moving on every couple of nights is worth it. Anyway, if you do, all your luggage will be packed into one big leather-and-canvas "Amanbali Bag".

AMANDARI

PO BOX 33, KENDEWATAN, UBUD
☎ (361) 975333
The Amandari is a hilltop rain-forest resort, built on an escarpment, in the middle of Bali above the Ayung River gorge. It is like a recreated Balinese village, blending local custom with modern luxury. "*Sensitivity to local customs is what makes Amandari so special,*" explains ALAIN DUCASSE. As Ubud's most discreet and most luxurious resting place, it is patronized by the likes of HARRISON FORD and KERRY PACKER. If you're feeling adventurous you can go trekking and white-water rafting around the gorge.

AMANKILA

MANGGIS, PO BOX 133, KLUNGKUNG
☎ (363) 41555
Amankila is on one of the quieter parts of the Balinese coast and thanks to its stunning ocean views is the most dramatic of the Amanresorts. Here there are 35 luxury suites constructed out of terrazzo, timber and mirrored glass. The Amankila Pavilion even has its own large private swimming pool. Amankila is accessible by Merpati Airlines from Denpasar followed by either a 20-minute helicopter ride or a two-hour drive.

AMANUSA

PO BOX 33, NUSA DUA
☎ (361) 772335
A manicured rural beach resort built between a golf course and beach, near the city of Denpasar. French windows open onto a private dining area covered in bougainvillea. Several suites have their own private swimming pool.

AMANWANA

MOYO ISLAND, WEST SUMBAWA, PROVINCE OF WEST NUSA TENGARRA
☎ (371) 22233
Moyo is about as remote as you can get – 120 miles east of Bali (and eight degrees, 15 feet south of the equator) – which is probably why the PRINCESS OF WALES escaped here for a holiday with her girlfriends, the HON MRS LAWSON and LUCIA FLECHA DA LIMA. Amanwana is situated on a deserted game-preserve, in splendid isolation – all you have for company are buffalo, turtles, monkeys and the gentle noise of crystal-clear waterfalls. The rooms aren't rooms at all; they are, in fact, big tents with 360-degree windowed sides that filter the sunlight. There are 20 in total and you can choose between having one in the jungle or one with an ocean view.

FOUR SEASONS

JIMBARAN, DENPASAR 80361

☎ (361) 701010

Spread over 35 acres of terraced hillside which gracefully descends to the white sand of Jimbaran Bay, the villas are clustered around a village square (each little cluster has its own "village chief" and private staff) and have every conceivable mod con from satellite TV to CD collections. Each ethnically decorated room has its own warm plunge pool while the royal villas have a cold plunge pool, 280 sq ft swimming pool and sauna. The spa offers fabulous Indonesian treatments from Balinese massage to body scrubs. "*You have your own eating pavilion and your own swimming pool; if you want to go anywhere they send you a buggy; it's a bit like being in* The Prisoner" – ANGUS DEAYTON.

KUPU KUPU BARONG

PO BOX 7, KEDEWATAN, UBUD

☎ (361) 35663

A delightful Balinese country hideaway, precariously poised on the side of a canyon. Go easy on the champagne in the superb restaurant, as it's a bit of a hike back to your private thatched bungalow.

OBEROI

PO BOX 451, DENPASAR 80001

☎ (361) 51061

33 acres of tranquillity on the far western side of Legian Beach, well away from the crowds of tourists. "*The rooms are decorated with carved Indonesian gods, and have bathrooms with huge sunken baths, which have walls around them but no roof, and huge video libraries – truly a place to snuggle up. You eat your dinner and breakfast in the trees looking down on the swimming pool,*" reports CAROL WRIGHT.

TANDJUNG SARI

PO BOX 25, DENPASAR

☎ (361) 88441

Extremely romantic, tranquil, family-run retreat on Sanur beach. Built in a village style with temple-filled grounds. The management supports local artisans and traditional dance.

Jakarta

GRAND HYATT

JALAN M H TAMRIN, 10230

☎ (21) 390 1234

Shiny marble hotel boasting a dramatic conservatory-style lobby complete with waterfall and

"THE WORLD'S MOST SPECTACULAR HOTEL LOBBY – A WONDERFUL CONSERVATORY WITH PLANTS AND WATERFALLS" – CLAIRE BARNES *ON THE GRAND HYATT*

a 5th-floor pool garden and patio restaurant. Excellent sporting facilities include six floodlit tennis courts, two squash courts, a jogging track and a fitness centre. Below the hotel is the Plaza Indonesia, filled with nightclubs and hundreds of shops.

HOTEL BOROBUDUR INTERCONTINENTAL

JALAN LAPANGAN, BANTENG SELATAN

☎ (21) 370333

Set in 23 acres of landscaped tropical gardens, this is one of Jakarta's largest hotels, with equally wide-ranging sporting facilities.

HYATT ARYADUTA

JALAN PRAPATAN 44–48

☎ (21) 376008

Ideally located for VIPs as it is close to the Presidential Palace, government offices and embassies. Smart rooms (all suites) and smart service. Facilities include a jogging track, six tennis courts and the Club Olympus fitness centre.

MANDARIN ORIENTAL

JALAN M H TAMRIN, PO BOX 3392

☎ (21) 321307

Grand hotel with enormous suites, while every normal room enjoys butler service. Eat at the SPICE GARDEN, which serves Chinese food. Superb service and good sporting facilities.

Lombok

SENGGIGI BEACH HOTEL

PO BOX 2, MATARAN 83125

☎ (364) 23430

Lombok, as yet unspoilt, is tipped to become the next Bali. This hotel, consisting of a group of thatched bungalows, is exquisitely located on a small peninsula jutting into the Lombok Strait, with 25 acres of lawn and coconut trees, surrounded by a white beach. Recommended by CAROL WRIGHT.

IRELAND
Dublin

ART AND MUSEUMS

THE ARK
EUSTACE ST, DUBLIN 2
☎ (1) 670 7788
The first cultural centre in Europe built especially for children. The stunningly decorated theatre offers storytelling sessions, exhibitions, and music from all over the world, all of which are aimed at children from four years old upwards. Individuals can visit on Thurs and weekends while other days are devoted to school groups and tours.

IRISH MUSEUM OF MODERN ART
ROYAL HOSPITAL KILMAINHAM,
DUBLIN 8
☎ (1) 671 8666
Splendid 17C Carolean building, constructed around an arcaded courtyard, originally designed to house retired and disabled soldiers. Now it's a spectacular space for displaying contemporary art as well as being a venue for performance art, including musical, theatrical and operatic events.

KILMAINHAM JAIL
DUBLIN 8
☎ (1) 453 5984
Other than being used as a backdrop for the film *In the Name of the Father*, this jail is best known for being the home to many Irish rebels including the leaders of the 1916 rebellion. Rather than being gung-ho, the exhibition is a thoughtful, well-researched depiction of Ireland's past tragedies. Whether you are Irish or not, it is both fascinating and disturbing. New interactive displays allow visitors to vote on matters such as capital punishment. Not to be missed.

NATIONAL GALLERY OF IRELAND
MERRION SQUARE W, DUBLIN 2
☎ (1) 661 5133
Ireland's foremost gallery, now fully restored, houses a fine collection of European masters, as well as a strong representation of Irish painters. Among the gallery's treasures are an extraordinary Caravaggio, discovered only when some priests removed the painting from a school wall and sent it off to be cleaned. Gallery café FITZERS is a popular spot for lunch. Jolly bookshop with a good selection of prints and reproductions.

BARS AND CAFES

BEWLEY'S COFFEE HOUSE
12 WESTMORELAND ST AND 78–79 GRAFTON ST, DUBLIN 2
☎ (1) 677 6761
A Dublin institution since 1842 for coffee, tea, buns and a banter. But go to the waitress-service area upstairs rather than queuing downstairs. Good for families during the day. The Grafton St branch is now open until 5 am on Sun & Sat mornings, attracting a great crowd of clubbers and others. It also has a café theatre and live music performances.

CAFE EN SEINE
40 DAWSON ST, DUBLIN 2
☎ (1) 677 4369
This trendy café is housed in an old church hall and is generally known as Café Insane. Where Dublin trendies come for a cocktail or a cup of tea, Sunday brunch or a light meal. Best

ENCORE Take a wander through the atmospheric cobbled grounds of **Trinity College**, College Green. It was founded by Elizabeth I in 1591 and its illustrious alumni include Oscar Wilde, Bram Stoker and Samuel Beckett . . . . . ♣ **Trinity College Library** houses Ireland's largest collection of books and manuscripts, including its principal treasure, *The Book of Kells*, an illuminated manuscript of the Gospels dating from the 8C . . . . . ♣ Stop off at the **Kilkenny Kitchen**, on the first floor of The Kilkenny Shop, 6 Nassau St, ☎ (1) 677 7066, to enjoy delicious home-made food and bread . . . . . ♣ If the weather is fine visit **Phoenix Park** (one of Europe's largest parks, with almost 1,800 acres of greenery and flowers). It is home to the President, Mary Robinson, and the American ambassador – not to mention a racecourse and the zoo. Take a picnic and watch cricket, polo, hurling and hockey or just laze the day away. . . . . ♣

DUBLIN'S PUBS You can't go to Dublin and not go to the pub, so if you want a taste of Dublin's authentic old-town spirit, drop in for a pint or two of stout. Among the most characterful pubs is **Mulligan's**, 8 Poolbeg St, Dublin 2, ☎ (1) 677 5582. The old **Palace Bar**, 21 Fleet St, Dublin 2, ☎ (1) 677 9290, is traditionally a journos' haunt, where the likes of Patrick Kavanagh and Flann O'Brien used to seek inspiration. For a smokier, noisier scene, **Doheny and Nesbitt's**, 5 Lower Baggot St, Dublin 2, ☎ (1) 676 2945, an old Victorian wood-panelled corner, is as authentic as you'll find. **The Long Hall**, S Great George's St, Dublin 2, ☎ (1) 475 1590, is a spectacular pub where you can nurse a pint and bask in the old-world interior and ambience. If it's music you're after, **O'Donoghue's**, Merrion Row, Dublin 2, ☎ (1) 676 2807, is your place. For those with stamina and a thirst for literary enlightenment as well as the more physical kind, **The Dublin Literary Pub Crawl** runs every Fri and Sat night (as well as some afternoons) and provides an unforgettable and spirited tour of Dublin's most famous literary drinking dens. Book the Pub Crawl on ☎ (1) 454 0228.

during the week and on Sun – too crowded on Fri nights.

CAFE JAVA
145 UPPER LEESON ST, DUBLIN 4
☎ (1) 660 0675
Hip and comfy with a great selection of coffees and good simple food.

THE CHOCOLATE BAR
OLD HARCOURT ST STATION,
HARCOURT ST, DUBLIN 8
☎ (1) 478 0166
New, stylish venue which has eclipsed Café en Seine as the place to be seen. This cool, futuristic bar – which is part of POD (see Clubs) – is popular for its cocktail evenings and simple but delicious food served at lunchtime.

THE GLOBE
11 S GEORGE'S ST, DUBLIN 2
☎ (1) 671 1220
Fab, jumping, jazzy café bar with bare wood and brick interior and rotating displays of local art; attracts cool, classy crowd. Savoury snacks and tapas available. Live jazz 5–8 pm Sun.

HOGAN'S
35–36 S GREAT GEORGE'S ST, DUBLIN 2
☎ (1) 677 5904
Spacious and airy European-style bar, all dark wood and forest green, for those who want a change from the traditional Dublin pub scene.

✪ THE MEAN FIDDLER
26 WEXFORD ST, DUBLIN 2
☎ (1) 475 8555.
Stunningly designed, very bare and cool with great lighting. At lunchtime it does really good international food at excellent prices. A great place to spend the afternoon poring over the papers; not so good at night.

THOMAS READ'S
1, 2 AND 3 PARLIAMENT ST, DUBLIN 2
☎ (1) 677 1487
A favourite trendy bar with lots of space and several nooks and crannies. Good food at lunchtime.

CLUBS

THE GAIETY
S KING ST, DUBLIN 2
☎ (1) 677 1717
Provides the best fun in Dublin on a Friday night with its Club Mambo evenings. Chill out in **JOHN B's** bar, dance to live Latin bands.

THE KITCHEN
AT THE CLARENCE HOTEL (SEE HOTELS)
☎ (1) 677 6178
U2's own nightclub, underneath their hotel, attracting a hip and varied crowd of clubbers and VIPs. Nights vary; always worth a visit.

LILLIE'S BORDELLO

ADAM COURT, GRAFTON ST, DUBLIN 2

☎ (1) 679 9204

Swag-red elegant (though a little brothelesque) and laid back, this is where the stars hang out. MEL GIBSON "lived" here during the making of *Braveheart*; DANIEL DAY LEWIS, JULIA ROBERTS, JOHNNY DEPP and VAN MORRISON are all regulars. Holding its own against Renard's (see entry).

POD

OLD HARCOURT ST STATION, DUBLIN 8

☎ (1) 478 0166

A beautiful "Place of Dance" – set in an old railway vault. A unique hip and happening dance space, attracting the likes of SINEAD O'CONNOR, CHRISTY TURLINGTON and JOHNNY DEPP. Very strict door policy. The equally cool Chocolate Bar (see Bars and Cafés) is here too.

RENARD'S

S FREDERICK ST, DUBLIN 2

☎ (1) 677 5876

Threatening Lillie's Bordello (see entry) as the bar for celebs. It was set up by one-time owner of Lillie's, Robbie Fox, with a long tradition of knowing how to cater for stars. Comfy and laid back with regular jazz on Sun.

RI-RA

DAME COURT, DUBLIN 2

☎ (1) 671 1220

This stark, stylish designer dance space, in the basement of The Globe (see Bars and Cafés), packs in all manner of punters. Especially popular are the Funk Off nights on Thurs and, on Sun, Go to Sleep night where everyone is given hot chocolate and marshmallows.

THE RIVER CLUB

48 WELLINGTON QUAY, DUBLIN 2

☎ (1) 677 2382

Set up as Dublin's answer to London's Groucho club, non-members can come here for classy, modern eating at fairly reasonable prices. It bristles with the famous at night.

HOTELS

THE CLARENCE

WELLINGTON QUAY, DUBLIN 2

☎ (1) 670 9000

Recently acquired by U2's Bono and the Edge, this small, suite-heavy hotel has just undergone a dramatic renovation. It's definitely the hippest hotel in town.

THE SHELBOURNE HOTEL

27 ST STEPHEN'S GREEN, DUBLIN 2

☎ (1) 676 6471

A Dublin landmark, where the Irish Constitution was drafted in 1922. Today Joyce and Thackeray have been replaced by the likes of LIAM NEESON, TIMOTHY DALTON and BRAD PITT who are often seen in the famous **HORSESHOE BAR**. All the bedrooms and public areas have been exquisitely decorated and furnished by Olga Polizzi. Afternoon cream tea in the **LORD MAYOR ROOM** is an institution. The food is delicious, as is the chef Kevin Dundon – or so JULIA ROBERTS thought when she was staying there.

THE WESTBURY

GRAFTON ST, DUBLIN 2

☎ (1) 679 1122

Known for its great service, luxury and good food – especially the atmospheric **SANDBANK SEAFOOD BAR**, a favourite business lunch spot. "*A very engaging hotel. They're awfully nice to me. Last time they put me in the Presidential Suite which is enormous,*" says SIR PETER USTINOV.

MUSIC AND FESTIVALS

Musical activities in Dublin tend to gravitate towards the **NATIONAL CONCERT HALL**, ☎ (1) 671 1533, home of the National Symphony Orchestra and a venue for visiting international artists. The programme is full and varied, with a series of lively lunchtime and teatime concerts throughout the summer. (Comprehensive listings can be found in *The Irish Times*.) Special Dublin events to keep an eye out for include chamber concerts organized by the Limerick Music Association; recitals in the House of Lords and in the Bank of Ireland; and events in the city's art galleries. As for opera, the two short seasons of the **DGOS** (Dublin Grand Opera Society) **OPERA IRELAND** take place at Easter and Christmas in Gaiety Theatre. **OPERA THEATRE COMPANY**, ☎ (1) 661 4884, Ireland's touring opera, also gives regular performances in Dublin. For lovers of church music, the cathedral churches of St Patrick's and Christchurch, Dublin 8, ☎ (1) 677 8099, as well as the Roman Catholic Pro-Cathedral, offer regular song services.

DUBLIN THEATRE FESTIVAL

FESTIVAL OFFICES: ☎ (1) 874 8525
A must. During the first two weeks of Oct, a
vibrant fringe that includes music, drama,
street theatre, circus and puppetry, converges
on the capital from all over the world.

RESTAURANTS

SEE ALSO HOTELS.

BRUBECK'S

SWEEPSTAKES, BALLSBRIDGE, DUBLIN 4
☎ (1) 660 1525
Manager Gerry Doyle, who managed
Quaglino's for several years, aims to bring something of its style and buzz to one of Dublin's
newest restaurants which is already a hot
favourite with politicians and lunching ladies.
The emphasis is on Irish-influenced international cuisine. Strong on seafood. The menu
varies from the eminently affordable to the
more extravagant: you can spend anything from
a tenner on a set lunch to a couple of hundred
pounds or punts. Good and varied wine list.

CANALETTO'S

69 MESPIL RD, DUBLIN 4
☎ (1) 678 5084
Well-cooked food, including pasta and other
Italian-influenced dishes served by friendly
staff in vivid chilli-coloured surroundings.

THE COMMONS RESTAURANT

85–6 ST STEPHEN'S GREEN, DUBLIN 2
☎ (1) 475 2597
Chef Gerard Kirwan serves classic international
cuisine in this elegant and grand restaurant in
the basement of 18C Newman House. Idyllic
location overlooking a sheltered courtyard and
the 5 acres of Iveagh Gardens convenient for a
post-prandial stroll. "*Very good environment for
business lunches and dinners, as well as a lovely place
to take out-of-towners*" – SANDY O'BYRNE.

⬤ COOKE'S CAFE

14 S WILLIAM ST, DUBLIN 2
☎ (1) 679 0536
A fun, fashionable Dublin eaterie that dishes up
Cal-Ital food in a small, minimalist space. Upstairs
there's now a brasserie/café, offering good-value
light meals plus excellent coffee and fresh cakes.
The perfect Dublin venue for brunch.

L'ECRIVAIN

109 LOWER BAGGOT ST, DUBLIN 2
☎ (1) 661 1919
Having recently moved, it still has first-rate

food and traditional decor, though a bit
smarter than before. Check out their Brendan
Behan sculpture – sitting over a pint.
Chef–patron Derry Clarke continues to cook
up his own creative brand of cosmopolitan cuisine. "*His food is very characterful, cuisine with per-
sonality, you can always tell he enjoys cooking and
the staff are great*," enthuses JOHN MCKENNA.

⬤ EXPRESSO BAR

47 SHELBOURNE RD, DUBLIN 4
☎ (1) 660 8632
In the increasingly hip Ballsbridge area, this new
place does a great range of coffees, wine and
good simple Cal-Ital style food, set in a stripped-
bare, stylish setting. VAN MORRISON comes here
to relax. Very good and well priced – about
£3.50 for starters and £7 for a main course.
Very cool.

FITZERS at the RDS

24 UPPER BAGGOT ST, DUBLIN 4
☎ (1) 660 0644
The newest of the Fitzers chain (the others are
at Baggot St and Dawson St), set in part of the
famous Royal Dublin Society. The chef has
brought the successful Fitzers formula here,
with the same laid-back, buzzy atmosphere that
attracts media types and visiting celebs such as
JULIA ROBERTS and MATT DILLON. Although
this one is pricier than the other branches, the
fresh, inventive Cal-Ital food is worth it.

FXB'S

1A LOWER PEMBROKE ST, DUBLIN 2
☎ (1) 676 7721
A carnivore's paradise, known particularly for
the best steaks in Dublin. Chic but relaxed.

⬤ GOTHAM CITY CAFE

8 S ANNE ST, DUBLIN 2
☎ (1) 679 5266
Chilled-out café serving impressive Californian-
style pizza and salads. Great Sunday brunch is
accompanied by softly played jazz. Very good
value.

KING SITRIC

EAST PIER, HOWTH, CO DUBLIN
☎ (1) 832 5235
Situated in a picturesque fishing village just a
few miles north of the city, this is the longest-
established and best fish restaurant in Dublin.
It's run by chef-proprietor Aidan MacManus,
who produces delectable dishes using daily
catches from the harbour. "*King Sitric is a marvellous restaurant, fearfully authentic: I always look
forward to going back there*" – SIR PETER USTINOV.

PATRICK GUILBAUD

46 JAMES PLACE, LOWER BAGGOT ST,
DUBLIN 4

☎ (1) 676 4192

Ultra-chic French restaurant complete with imported waiters. Still considered Ireland's best. "*In a country where so many kitchens have French pretensions, this is the real thing. A classic restaurant, professional, consistent, impeccable standards*" – JOHN BOWMAN.

PIERRE'S

2 CROWE ST, TEMPLE BAR, DUBLIN 2

☎ (1) 671 1248

Traditional homely French cuisine, consistently interesting, put together with care and served without fuss at a competitive price. Wine list is limited but always good value, and the house recommendations are to be trusted. Hard to beat for the best value in Dublin.

ROLY'S BISTRO

7 BALLSBRIDGE TERR, DUBLIN 4

☎ (1) 668 2611

A cheerful and bustling split-level brasserie serving all manner of quality French continental fare. Roly's is still the chattering classes' favourite eaterie – especially for Sunday lunch. "*Excellent value, friendly service, strong varied wine list with low mark-ups. But with the buzz that comes with this restaurant's popularity, they might consider softening the acoustics,*" considers JOHN BOWMAN.

....

*"CERTAINLY THE NICEST DINING
ROOM IN THE CITY AND POSSIBLY
THE MOST BEAUTIFUL IN
THE COUNTRY"* – JOHN MCKENNA
ON *LA STAMPA*

....

LA STAMPA

35 DAWSON ST, DUBLIN 2

☎ (1) 677 8611

One of Dublin's most stylish restaurants, known as much for its lovely interior as for chef Paul Flynn's eclectic menu, where French cuisine sits alongside Irish specialities.

TANTE ZOE'S

1 CROWE ST, TEMPLE BAR, DUBLIN 2

☎ (1) 679 4407

Cajun food at reasonable prices. Attracts a young, hip crowd in the evenings, and office types at lunchtime. Attractive place, if slightly limited wine list.

TOSCA'S

20 SUFFOLK ST, DUBLIN 2

☎ (1) 679 6744

Hip and laid-back restaurant with extremely good-looking staff, who might seem a little bit above the job at times. The food is modern Italian/Irish, and the wine list simple but reliable. Good value.

THE UNICORN

12B MERRION CT, ON MERRION ROW,
DUBLIN 2

☎ (1) 668 8552

Stylish, modern Italian cooking, reasonable prices, good atmosphere and great for lunch. Also a café and wine bar.

SHOPPING

A-WEAR

26 GRAFTON ST, DUBLIN 2

☎ (1) 671 7200

Owned by Brown Thomas (see entry), A-Wear is an interesting chain, which visitors might easily miss. Upstairs it's like your average chainstore but downstairs the designer section features the cream of Irish commercial designers, some of whom are very good such as Quinn & Donnelly and Marc O'Neil. But sadly there's no more John Rocha, but his flagship store is due to open soon on Grafton St.

BASIC INSTINCT

56 S WILLIAM ST, DUBLIN 2

☎ (1) 671 2223

Funky men's clothes. Known for the best underwear (CK, etc) in town.

THE BIG CHEESE COMPANY

ANDREW'S LANE, DUBLIN 2

☎ (1) 671 1399

Every Irish farmhouse cheese is available here, plus a good selection of continental cheeses. They buy in bulk, so prices are kept low. They also do a yummy sideline in American junk food (like Oreos and Peanut Butter Cups) plus French and English delicacies such as foie gras, caviare and specialist vinegars. Great hampers too. A must for value and choice.

BROWN THOMAS

92 GRAFTON ST, DUBLIN 2

☎ (1) 679 5666

Coolly elegant and a delight to shop in the designer section offers the best of international fashion, and the men's fashions are wonderfully laid out. Admire your purchases over croissants, thick and frothy cappuccinos or a sandwich in the stylish **BROWN'S CAFÉ**. There's a terrific beauty room for men and women, and a new department, Bottom Drawer, dedicated to the bedroom sybarite.

DESIGN ASSOCIATES
144 FRANCIS ST, DUBLIN 2
☎ (1) 453 7767
A beautiful, self-styled lifestyle showroom featuring fine furniture and furnishings and a unique collection of one-off fashion garments made by international artists and craftsmen.

⊗ DESIGN CENTRE
POWERSCOURT SHOPPING CNTR,
S WILLIAM ST, DUBLIN 2
☎ (1) 855 0088
One of the most fascinating places to browse. Established designers such as Mairead Whisker rub shoulders with the cream of recent art-school graduates. There's an emphasis on natural fabrics, the prices are surprisingly low, and you can pick up some wonderful pieces.

FIRENZE
WESTBURY CENTRE, BALFE ST,
DUBLIN 2
☎ (1) 679 1600
One of the most stylish women's shops, with all the major labels. Very cool, with helpful staff.

KILKENNY DESIGN WORKSHOP
NASSAU ST, DUBLIN 2
☎ (1) 677 7066
Wonderful ceramics, especially the simple range by Stephen Pearce, and some lovely clothes.

MICHAEL BARRIE
20 DUKE ST, DUBLIN 2
☎ (1) 671 5265
Quality men's clothes for all occasions. They stock all the major designers, and the staff are helpful. Speedy alterations service.

Rest of Ireland

HOTELS

ARBUTUS LODGE HOTEL
MIDDLE GLANMIRE RD, MONTENOTTE,
CORK
☎ (21) 501237
The 18C former home of the Lord Mayor, this hotel houses a fine collection of modern Irish painting and a restaurant that is nationally renowned for its mixture of Irish and French cuisine. The garden suites are best, overlooking beautifully kept gardens where you can eat during the summer. "*Strong on game, innovative with Irish traditional dishes – the tasting menu is a tour de force. Truly outstanding wine list, in depth, breadth and well-chosen house selections,*" raves JOHN BOWMAN.

BALLYMALOE HOUSE
SHANAGARRY, CO CORK
☎ (21) 652 531
Internationally acclaimed country-house hotel, lovingly run by the Allen clan. Myrtle Allen oversees the hotel while Darina Allen, her daughter-in-law, runs the equally respected in-house cookery school. Another extension of the Ballymaloe kitchen is the excellent café/restaurant in the Crawford Gallery in Cork city.

BANTRY HOUSE
BANTRY, CO CORK
☎ (27) 50047
Set in the lush countryside, this 8-bedroomed 18C mansion, overlooking gardens to Bantry Bay beyond, is a showpiece. The hearty full Irish breakfasts at this B&B provide fuel for a day of fresh country walks.

THE BLUE HAVEN
3 PIERCE STREET, KINSALE, CO CORK
☎ (21) 72209; FAX (21) 774268
Set in a picturesque location with the traditional comforts of an Irish country style hotel, the Blue Haven also boasts an excellent award-winning restaurant. Or, if you are just passing through, have a snack in the old style country bar.

⊗ DELPHI ESTATE AND FISHERY
DELPHI LODGE, LEENANE, CO GALWAY
☎ (95) 42211
Set in one of the most unspoilt valleys in Europe this one-time sporting playground of the Marquess of Sligo offers first-class fishing. You can either stay in one of four restored cottages or enjoy the splendours of the private house, Delphi Lodge, where meals are served around a big table, presided over by the person who's caught the day's largest salmon. The food is first-rate, the fishing splendid and the atmosphere warm and welcoming. Truly excellent value. Also known for its wine cellar.

DROMOLAND CASTLE
NEWMARKET-ON-FERGUS, CO CLARE
☎ (61) 368144; FAX (61) 363355

Situated in 350 acres of woodland and parks, DEMI MOORE and BRUCE WILLIS come here to fish, shoot, ride, use the 18-hole golf course or simply to savour the fine food. The large rooms combine splendour with modern convenience.

HILTON PARK

CLONES, CO MONAGHAN
☎ (47) 56007
Owned and run by the eighth generation of the Madden family, this magnificent country-house estate is set at the head of the Erne basin and provides wonderful woodland walks, trout and pike fishing, golf, croquet, lake swimming and boating. *"Beautiful house and the best country-house cooking. Johnny and Lucy Madden are the most creative husband and wife team working in Ireland,"* claims JOHN MCKENNA.

LONGUEVILLE COUNTRY HOUSE AND PRESIDENT'S RESTAURANT

MALLOW, CO CORK
☎ (22) 47156
Splendid Georgian mansion, historic home to the Callaghan family, set in the centre of a 560-acre wooded estate. The kitchen is almost entirely self-sufficient, with a 3-acre kitchen garden and their own lamb, suckling pig, beef and fish from the farm. Weather permitting, they even produce their own wine. *"William Callaghan is a wizard"* – JOHN MCKENNA.

NEWPORT HOUSE

NEWPORT, CO MAYO
☎ (98) 41222
Charming, warm and elegant country-house hotel with splendid interior and just 20 bedrooms. A haven for fishing enthusiasts, as well as comfort seekers. The kitchen will even cook your catch on request.

....

"STILL THE BEST HOTEL IN IRELAND. OWNER FRANCIS BRENNAN IS THE BEST HOTELIER IN IRELAND, HE RUNS THINGS WITH A SIXTH SENSE, QUITE BRILLIANT" – JOHN MCKENNA ON PARK HOTEL KENMARE

....

PARK HOTEL KENMARE

KENMARE, CO KERRY
☎ (64) 41200
Enchanting country hotel with superb views

GO WEST Much maligned but recently revitalized by its inhabitants, Limerick, on the majestic River Shannon, is the perfect base for touring the charming West and Southwest of Ireland – just fly to Shannon Airport. The city was important historically; indeed, it got its charter before London did. Evidence of its strategic importance includes the 12C King John's Castle and St Mary's Cathedral (one of Ireland's most interesting cathedrals), the Treaty Stone (on which the Treaty of Limerick is said to have been signed in the 17C), and the elegant late-Regency Pery's Square.

---

over Kenmare Bay to the mountains beyond. Don't miss breakfast, as chef Bruno Schmidt won the Galtee Irish Breakfast Awards '95 – all the main ingredients are produced in Kerry.

TEMPLE HOUSE

BALLYMOTE, CO SLIGO
☎ (71) 83329
Gorgeous Victorian mansion with five large bedrooms set in terraced gardens and 1,000 acres of farm and woodland. The old-style elegance and atmosphere continue to be upheld by Sandy and Deb Perceval, with turf and log fires and delicious traditional cooking using mostly organically grown produce.

MUSEUMS

⊛ BUNRATTY CASTLE AND FOLK PARK

BUNRATTY, CO CLARE
☎ (61) 360788 (RESERVATIONS) OR
☎ (61) 361511 (GENERAL ENQUIRIES)
This late-15C castle, originally the chief seat of the O'Briens, the rulers of Co Clare, has also been restored. A great trip for visitors, and a fun, educational day out for children. Access to the castle is included. Be sure to have a jar in the famous DURTY NELLIE'S just outside – it's jammed but can be good fun.

THE FAMINE MUSEUM

STROKESTOWN, CO ROSCOMMON
☎ (78) 33710
The first museum dedicated to the national tragedy which halved the population and almost destroyed the language. A must-see for anyone with any interest in Irish history and culture. Closed Mon.

MUSIC AND FESTIVALS

THE CAT LAUGHS COMEDY FESTIVAL

KILKENNY
☎ (56) 512254
In 1996 this attracted some of the very best comics in the world to Kilkenny.

GALWAY ARTS FESTIVAL

GALWAY, CO GALWAY
☎ (91) 583800
Home of the wonderful Macnas Street Theatre Group who are receiving widespread acclaim. Includes travelling theatre, music, film, comedy. . .

GUINNESS JAZZ FESTIVAL

TICKETS: CORK OPERA HOUSE, EMMET PLACE, CORK
☎ (21) 270022
One of Europe's biggest and best jumping jazz festivals, which takes place every Oct bank holiday. Over 150,000 fans and fanatics descend upon Cork city to see top international names. Greats perform in the Opera House, while other acts pack out every pub, hotel and street corner in town. Tickets available in the two weeks preceding the event.

THE MATCHMAKING FESTIVAL

LISDOONVARNA, CO CLARE
☎ (72) 51103
This institution runs from 1st Sept until 8th Oct, with dances all day, every day, starting at 11 am.

WEXFORD FESTIVAL OPERA

THEATRE ROYAL, HIGH ST, WEXFORD
☎ (53) 22240
The Glyndebourne of Ireland. A three-week Oct festival when a loyal following of European and international opera buffs packs out the Theatre Royal: a formal dress code marks the final long weekend. Recitals, fringe events and bands spill out into the streets, while some pubs stay open till 3 am.

PUBS

DE BARRA'S

MAIN ST, CLONAKILTY, CO CORK
☎ (23) 33381
Clonakilty is a wonderful little West Cork town, where you'll find some of the best music in the country, and this pub is where you'll hear it. NOEL REDDING, ex-Jimi Hendrix band, hangs out and plays here, and so has DAVID BOWIE. Possibly the best pub in Ireland. Highly recommended.

FOX'S PUB

GLENCULLEN, CO DUBLIN
☎ (1) 295 5647
The highest pub in Co Dublin and associated with Constance Markiewicz, the Irish patriot. There's music and dancing every night. The views are spectacular.

ENCORE Anyone interested in the Gaelic culture and language gravitates to the West of Ireland, especially to Co Clare, the home of Irish traditional music. The summer schools – an Irish institution – are a huge draw for visitors, and while some are very learned, the emphasis is on the *craic* – ie, fun . . . . . ♠**The Merriman Summer School**, Ballyvaughan, Co Clare, ☎ (1) 286 9305, is the oldest of the lot. It's named after Brian Merriman, famous for *The Midnight Court*, the bawdy, erotic, 18C Irish epic poem. Held in the last two weeks of Aug, some of the lectures and seminars are given in the Irish language. But it's not just about scholarship: there's lots of drinking and dancing too . . . . . ♠If you're a Riverdance convert, **The Willie Clancy Summer School** is irresistible. For the first week or so of July, the little Co Clare town of Milltown Malbay sees its population grow from 800 to 8,000, with visitors soaking up the very best of Irish music and dance . . . . ♠

GOOSER'S
BALLINA, CO TIPPERARY
☎ (61) 376791
A charming pub which embodies the best of Irish: comfort, good pints and excellent food at a decent price. Children are welcome in the afternoons. Outdoor seating is available for you to catch any odd glimpse of sunshine. The locals love it so it can be highly recommended.

LANGTONS
JOHN ST, KILKENNY
☎ (56) 21917
Behind the unprepossessing façade of this pub is what must be one of Ireland's most comfortable eating houses. While you can have pub food in the bar, the dining room, housed in a stained-glass garden room is well worth a visit.

RESTAURANTS

SEE ALSO HOTELS.

ANNIE'S
MAIN ST, BALLYDEHOB, CO CORK
☎ (28) 37292
Renowned locally for the *craic* (Irish for good times) and cosiness. Always welcoming, Annie Barry dishes up exuberant helpings of rustic food, which often includes large amounts of excellent local fish. Decent wine list and wicked puddings.

THE BOLEY HOUSE
KEEL, ACHILL ISLAND, CO MAYO
☎ (98) 43147
Homely Irish food, especially smoked salmon and brown bread, served up in this traditional building (a boley is a labourer's shack). Comfortable and undemanding, this is the best place for holidaymakers on this spectacularly beautiful island, which is one of the westernmost spots in Europe. Ask Tom or Una McNamara for directions to the deserted village, abandoned almost overnight during the Famine.

CLIFFORD'S
18 DYKE PARADE, CORK
☎ (21) 275333
An old, wonderfully atmospheric former library is the backdrop for this well-lauded and well-loved restaurant. Michael Clifford, who is "*truly inventive and creative*" according to JOHN MCKENNA, reworks Irish classics using his French background to produce culinary creations.

DRIMCONG HOUSE
MOYCULLEN, CO GALWAY
☎ (91) 85115
Owners Gerry and Marie Galvin open the doors of their lakeland home to offer a wonderfully warm, cheery atmosphere in which to sample some of the most creative and exciting Irish cooking in the country.

ⓈⒹ ISAAC'S RESTAURANT
MACCURTAIN ST, CORK
☎ (21) 503805
Set in a small part of a converted warehouse, this busy restaurant still manages to seat 100. The short menu suits all tastes, while the keen prices keep the place full from 10.30 to 10.30.

ITALY
Amalfi Coast

HOTELS

HOTEL PALUMBO
VIA SAN GIOVANNI DEL TORO 16, 84010 RAVELLO
☎ (89) 857244
Delightful spot perched high above the Gulf of Salerno, which combines a charming mix of early Moorish, Mediterranean and contemporary styles. Fine Italian and international food.

SAN PIETRO
VIA LAURITO 2, 84017 POSITANO
☎ (89) 875455; FAX (89) 811449
Fabulously glamorous hotel spilling down a cliff face to a tiny private beach. Wonderful seafood and spacious guest rooms. (Also has a direct boat service to Capri.)

LE SIRENUSE
VIA CRISTOFORO COLOMBO 30, 84017 POSITANO
☎ (89) 875066; FAX (89) 811798
Enchanting small hotel high on the cliffside overlooking the picturesque village of Positano and the Gulf of Salerno. It used to be the Sersale family's summer home and still maintains the feel of a private house, with characterful antiques and furnishings. Good traditional Neapolitan cuisine is prepared by chef Alfredo Mazzacano. Recommended by MARTIN SKAN.

Capri

In AD 26 Emperor Tiberius decided to leave Rome and move to Capri, where he built his fantastic residence. He spent most of his time in Villa Jovis, perched on the precipitous northeast tip of the island. Suetonius tells us that "persons who incurred his disfavour were cast to their death from what is called *Il Salto* (the leap)". Today the island still has a hedonistic air.

ART AND MUSEUMS

CERTOSA DI SAN GIACOMO
Built by Queen Anna I of Anjou, this was burned by the Turkish Pasha Dragut when the island was invaded in 1535. It was rebuilt by the monks.

BARS AND CAFES

The main gathering place in Capri is the central piazza, where everybody goes in the morning to buy their newspapers and have coffee. *"Both large cafés serve iced tea with a kind of lemon slush, refreshing during the hot summer months,"* reports LOGAN BENTLEY.

HOTELS

GRAND HOTEL QUISISANA
VIA CAMERELLE 2, 80073
☎ (81) 837 0788; FAX ☎ 837 6080
An impressive, neo-classical sprawl of a hotel, with airy, tiled rooms overlooking beautiful gardens. Fine, imaginative cooking from new chef David Oldani. *"Right smack in the middle of Capri, this is the place to stay. Soak up the atmosphere by having a late-afternoon drink on the terrace overlooking the intersection of the two main shopping drags,"* advises LOGAN BENTLEY.

EUROPA PALACE (CAPRI BEAUTY FARM)
VIA CAPODIMONTE 2, 8007, ANACAPRI
☎ (81) 837 3800; FAX (81) 8378191
An elegant hotel where you can relax by the stunning outdoor pool or indulge in the personalised treatment and diet programme. Distractions include the shops of nearby Capri and the natural beauty of the surrounding countryside.

SHOPPING

CANFORA
VIA CAMERELLE 3, 80073
☎ (81) 837 0487
The moccasins here are unique, and if you have the patience, Signora Canfora will make a pair of leather espadrilles to order.

CARTHUSIA PROFUMI DI CAPRI
VIA CAMERELLE 10, 80073
☎ (81) 837 0529
The Carthusian monks provided the "recipes" for the unique perfumes you can buy here.

LA CAMPANINA
VIA VITTORIO EMANUELE 18/20, 80073
☎ (81) 837 643
Aristotle Onassis kept Jackie happy by buying her baubles here. Wide range, from reasonably priced small charms all the way up to big important pieces. LOGAN BENTLEY is a fan: *"I always indulge in at least one goodie here."*

Florence

ART AND MUSEUMS

GALLERIA DEGLI UFFIZI
LOGGIATO DEGLI UFFIZI 6, 50122
☎ (55) 218341
Incomparable collection of Florentine and Sienese art from the 13C to the Renaissance, housed in Vasari's grand riverside palazzo. Highlights include Titian's glowing *Venus of Urbino*, and Leonardo's unfinished *Adoration of the Magi* – plus a superb collection of prints, drawings and the unrivalled gallery of artists' self-portraits.

GALLERIE DELL' ACCADEMIA
VIA RICASOLI 60, 50122
☎ (55) 214375
Europe's first fine arts academy, founded in 1563 and now a museum, most famous for housing works by Michelangelo including his masterpiece, *David*. Also a picture gallery of 13C–15C Tuscan masters.

MUSEO ARCHEOLOGICO
VIA DEL COLONNA 36, 50121
☎ (55) 247641
Must-sees include the Etruscan bronze *Chimera* and a treasure trove of Medici jewellery, revealed after being hidden for 70 years.

MUSEO DEL BARGELLO
PALAZZO PITTI, VIA DEL PROCONSOLO
4, 50122
☎ (55) 210801
Medieval building once home to the Governor
and later the Constable (Bargello) of Florence,
now dedicated to the celebration of sculpture
and decorative arts. Exceptional pieces, including Michelangelo's *Drunken Bacchus*. Also an
extensive collection of arms and armour.

MUSEO DELL' OPERA DEL DUOMO
PIAZZA DEL DUOMO 9, 50122
☎ (55) 230 2885
Cathedral museum displaying items from the
Duomo, including Michelangelo's famous
Pietà.

MUSEO DI STORIA DELLA FOTOGRAFIA FRATELLI ALINARI
VIA DELLA VIGNA NUOVA 16R, 50123
☎ (55) 234 5458
Private museum of photography in one of the
oldest buildings in Florence, mostly showing
the work of the pioneering Alinari brothers.

MUSEO FRA ANGELICO
PIAZZA SAN MARCO, 50121
☎ (55) 210741
An oasis of peace, the former Dominican
monastery where Fra Angelico – Ruskin's
"inspired saint" – painted his most famous
works, the frescoes that decorate the friars'
cells.

PALAZZO PITTI
PIAZZA DEI PITTI, 50125
☎ (55) 213440
Imposing architectural landmark dating from
1460 and now housing four museums: lavish
state apartments, the exceptional Silver
Museum (fine and decorative arts), the
Modern Art Gallery (19C–20C Tuscan art)
and the fabulously gaudy Palatine Gallery. If all
this leaves you exhausted, relax behind the
palace in the delightful Bóboli Gardens,
designed in 1549 and full of antique and
Renaissance statues.

OPIFICIO DELLE PIETRE DURE
VIA DEGLI ALFANI 78, 50121
☎ (55) 294115
This is more of a restoration studio than a
museum, specializing in "scaglola", which is
work in semi-precious stone such as marble,
malachite and lapis lazuli, used in tables, altars
and other objects. Open 9 am – 7 pm, holidays
9 am – 2 pm. Closed Tues.

BARS AND CAFES

CAFFE ITALIANO
VIA CONDOTTA 56R, 50122
☎ (55) 281082
Recently opened behind the Piazza Signoria,
this has already become one of the most pop-
ular cafés in Florence. Created by the owner of
Alle Murate (see Restaurants), it has a truly
Florentine atmosphere.

DOLCE VITA
PIAZZA DEL CARMINE, 50124
☎ (55) 284595
Located in one of the most beautiful piazzas on
the other side of the Arno (which is sadly also
used by locals as a car park), this has become
one of Florence's most fashionable bars.
Popular with artists and young professionals,
it's open until late. Closed Sun.

DOLCI E DOLCEZZE
PIAZZA BECCARIA 8R, 50123
☎ (55) 234 5458
Long-established high-society café, where all
the smartest Florentines buy their torte. "*Just
by tasting one of the delightful desserts, such as rich
chocolate cake, lemon tart or Bavarian cream, one
can easily understand why Dolci e Dolcezze is one
of the most popular pastry shops and cafés in
Florence*" – MARCHESA BONA FRESCOBALDI.

GIACOSA
VIA TORNABUONI 83, 50123
☎ (55) 239 6206
Lively café/bar where the Campari-based
Negroni was invented and now a meeting
place for Florentine high society, who come to
indulge in hand-made chocolates and pastries.

GILLI
PIAZZA DELLA REPUBBLICA 39R, 50123
☎ (55) 239 6310
Centrally located café near the Cathedral
where you can either sit out on the square or
in the elegant old-world interior. Visit it at
Easter to see the wonderful displays of chocolate in the window.

GIUBBE ROSSE
PIAZZA DELLA REPUBBLICA 13–14R,
50213
☎ (55) 212280
Properly dubbed "The Big Historical Literary
Red Jackets Café", this was the meeting place
for intellectuals and artists at the beginning of
the century. "*Thanks to the influence of such
clients as Giovanni Papini and Ardengo Soffici, the*

café has recently rediscovered its history and now sponsors meetings and exhibits" – STEFANO FABBRI. More popular for drinks and cocktails, but also serves light lunches and dinner until late.

MARAMAO
VIA DEI MACCI 79R, 50122
☎ (55) 234341
The latest of a new generation of places where Florentines like to hang out, near Piazza Santa Croce. Maramao resembles a ship, with its disco-bar surrounded by polished wood and portholes. It also has a small restaurant. Open until 2 am.

RIVOIRE
VIA VACCHERECCIA 4R, 50122
☎ (55) 213312
Grandly old-fashioned café in an imposing spot on the corner of the Piazza della Signoria, overshadowed by the towering bell tower of the Palazzo Vecchio. Famous for its pralines, chocolates and speedy waiters.

CLUBS

MECCANO
VIALE DEGLI OLMI 1, 50144
(55) 331381
A large complex with a disco that features theme evenings and a restaurant, **LA PICCIONAIA**. Trendy and fun.

TENAX
VIA PRATESE 46, 50145
☎ (55) 308160
Long-standing cult for Florentine insomniacs where the young and beautiful thrash around to the latest sounds.

VILLA KASAR
LUNGARNO COLOMBO 23, 50129
☎ (55) 676912
A villa on the right bank of the River Arno. Various rooms include a soothing piano bar, the not-so-soothing disco and the **COCO BLU** restaurant. According to STEFANO FABBRI. *"Most VIPs passing through Florence make at least one stop here."*

YAB YUM
VIA SASSETTI 5R, 50100
☎ (55) 282018
Despite several metamorphoses, this buzzing disco bar in the heart of Florence is still an old favourite. Live jazz bands feature on Tues.

HOTELS

BEACCI TORNABUONI
VIA TORNABUONI 3, 50100
☎ (55) 212645
Upmarket *pensione* on the top three floors of a palazzo in Florence's smartest shopping street. Comfort, convenience and oodles of slightly faded charm. Book ahead.

HOTEL BRUNELLESCHI
PIAZZA SANTA ELISABETTA 3, 50122
☎ (55) 562068; FAX (55) 219653
A unique, though not especially chic hotel, set in one of the smallest and quietest piazzas of Renaissance Florence. Once a prison during the old Florentine Republic, sections of the ancient stone walls and brick arches have been artfully integrated into the modern architecture. Small and comfortable.

HOTEL HELVETIA AND BRISTOL
VIA DEI PESCIONI 2, 50123
☎ (55) 287814; FAX (55) 288353
One of Florence's finest hotels, now fully restored to its original 19C splendour. Exquisite antique furnishings and fine Florentine/Tuscan dining in **THE BRISTOL**.

HOTEL KRAFT
VIA SOLFERINO 2, 50123
☎ (55) 284273; FAX (55) 2398267
A pleasant family-run hotel on a quiet tree-filled square close to the centre of town. There's a swimming pool on the roof, serviced by a bar.

HOTEL REGENCY
PIAZZA M D'AZEGLIO 3, 50121
☎ (55) 245247; FAX (55) 2346735
Two converted 19C villas set in a peaceful residential square provide a luxury haven away from the hassle of the moped-heavy city centre. Fine regional cuisine from chef Paolo Bisogno at the **RELAIS LE JARDIN**.

···

"PROBABLY THE BEST LOCATED HOTEL IN FLORENCE" – **LOGAN BENTLEY** ON THE HOTEL SAVOY

···

HOTEL SAVOY
PIAZZA DELLA REPUBBLICA 7, 50123
☎ (55) 283313; FAX (55) 284840
"Old-fashioned comfort in the heart of the sightsee-

ing and shopping district. Rooms overlooking the Piazza are fun, in fact, you could spend all day just watching the people in the cafés around the square," reports LOGAN BENTLEY.

HOTEL VILLA MEDICI
VIA IL PRATO 42, 50123
☎ (55) 2381331; FAX (55) 2381336
Beautiful hotel not far from the main station, with a garden and swimming pool – a good place to stay during the summer months.

LOGGIATO DEI SERVITI
PIAZZA SS ANNUNZIATA 3, 50122
☎ (55) 239 8280
Delightful small hotel with its twin building, Brunelleschi's Ospedale degli Innocenti (children's hospital) on the other side of the piazza. Terracotta floors and high vaulted ceilings give it an atmosphere of quiet calm. No restaurant.

VILLA SAN MICHELE
VIA DOCCIA 4, 50014 FIESOLE
☎ (55) 59451; FAX (55) 598734
One of the greatest and most romantic hotels in the world – not just Tuscany. A former Franciscan monastery whose façade was designed by Michelangelo. The converted cells, however, are far from monastic: all have Jacuzzis and look either onto a charming courtyard or over a sea of olive trees and cypresses to Florence, which is only 15 minutes away. *"Magnificent view of Florence from the hotel's windows and loggia, where meals are served during the summer. Surrounded by a beautiful garden with a swimming pool, great for the summer,"* raves LOGAN BENTLEY.

RESTAURANTS

SEE ALSO CLUBS AND HOTELS.

ALLE MURATE
VIA GHIBELLINA 52R, 50122
☎ (55) 240617
Modern, informal restaurant serving innovative, southern-based cuisine. Slip into the jazz club next door for after-dinner drinks.

LA BARAONDA
VIA GHIBELLINA 67, 50122
☎ (55) 234 1171; FAX (55) 234 1171
Home-style food, tiled decor and a three-tiered dining room. *"They have a wonderful butcher's counter when you come in,"* says FAITH WILLINGER.

IL BARETTO
VIA DEI PARIONE 50R, 50123
☎ (55) 294122
Intimate, unpretentious restaurant/piano bar with the atmosphere of a private club. Good, simple food and good value. Open evenings.

BUCA DELL' ORAFO
VOLTA DEI GIROLAMI 28R, 50122
☎ (55) 213619
Unpretentious basement trattoria serving traditional, no-fuss Florentine food. *"I still love this restaurant, it's so convenient, located at the foot of the Ponte Vecchio, the service is friendly and the food is good and simple"* – LOGAN BENTLEY.

CAFE DU MONDE
VIA SAN NICCOLÒ 103R, 50125
☎ (55) 234 4953
According to STEFANO FABBRI, *"It's the only restaurant and wine bar where the kitchen is open until 4 am – the place closes an hour later. The cooking is done with great care and as the evening progresses it goes from quiet music to live jazz. Not to be missed."* Closed Mon.

CANTINETTA ANTINORI
PIAZZA ANTINORI 3, 50123
☎ (55) 292234
Wine bar hidden away behind heavy wooden doors on the ground floor of a Renaissance palace. Sample the Antinori family's own vintages from their well-stocked wine cellar. Soak it up with good, reasonably priced fare.

IL CIBREO
VIA DEI MACCI 118R, 50100
☎ (55) 234 1100
Upmarket trattoria where the service is formal and the food is revamped Tuscan. **CIBREO TRATTORIA** round the corner at Piazza Ghiberti 35 serves the same food with less fuss and for less money.

COCO LEZZONE
VIA PARIONCINO 26R, 50123
☎ (55) 287178
Just off fashionable Via Tornabuoni, a trendy trattoria attracting a lively crowd for its working class Tuscan food and rustic atmosphere.

DULCAMARA
VIA DANTE DA CASTIGLIONI 2, 50019
CERCINA – SESTO F.HO
☎ (55) 425 5021
Charming restaurant in an old farmhouse just a few minutes' drive from Florence. *"It's a great place for a candlelit dinner, and on Sundays*

Florentines drive out for lunch with their children, who play in the large garden," reports STEFANO FABBRI.

ENOTECA PINCHIORRI
VIA GHIBELLINA 87, 50122
☎ (55) 242777; FAX (55) 244983
Famous Florentine restaurant with a vast cellar run by Giorgio Pinchiorri, his wife, Annie Feolde, and their two children. *"Wonderful, superb cellars, very chic and very expensive"* – MARCHESA BONA FRESCOBALDI. *"The desserts are to die for,"* adds LOGAN BENTLEY.

GARGA
VIA DEL MORO 48R, 50123
☎ (55) 239 8898
Wonderfully atmospheric and very popular eatery, serving original Tuscan food. *"The owner is a butcher so they feature weird cuts of meat. Frescoes and paintings on the walls – and the food is wonderful"* – FAITH WILLINGER.

OMERO
VIA PIAN DEI GIULLARI 11R, 50125
☎ (55) 220053
Authentic, atmospheric, family-run Florentine trattoria located at the back of a grocery shop where you can enjoy delicious and authentic home-style Tuscan food.

SHOPPING

Head along **VIA TORNABUONI** for the best designer clothes or to **VIA CALZAIOLI**, for more, though not quite as expensive, men's and women's fashion. **VIA MAGGIO**, on the other side of the Arno, is the best for antiques; but for real bargains – especially leather – try the daily market at **SANTA CROCE**. **MERCATO DELLE CASCINE** near the Ponte della Vittoria (Tues am) is the place for second-hand clothes and bric-à-brac.

ANGELA CAPUTI
BORGO SAN JACOPO 82R–78R, 50100
☎ (55) 212972
The place to go for imaginative costume jewellery at the right price. Next door, Angela has a boutique selling simply designed, well-made clothes that go with her accessories.

BELTRAMI
VIA TORNABUONI 48R, 50123
☎ (55) 287779
Top-quality leatherwear, from shoes, coats, bags and belts to super-stylish separates, cashmere and silk scarves.

COLE-HAHN
VIA DELLA NUOVA 77R, 50134
☎ (55) 499940
The biggest selection of the Cole-Hahn line, including wonderfully soft moccasins and the best shoes anywhere for outsize feet.

EMILIO PUCCI
VIA DE' PUCCI 6, 50122
☎ (55) 283061
Brightly coloured, boldly patterned designs that have adorned the rich and famous for decades (Marilyn Monroe asked to be buried in her favourite Pucci dress).

ENRICO COVERI
27/29 VIA DELLA VIGNA NUOVA, 50123
☎ (55) 238 1769
Colourful designs from one of Florence's best known couturiers, the late Enrico Coveri, whose sister carries on the tradition with great success.

FARAONE-SETTEPASSI
VIA TORNABUONI 24R, 50123
☎ (55) 215506
Jewellers whose pieces have adorned Florentine and foreign nobility since 1860. Expertly crafted gems, antique silver and classic settings are sold alongside more modern designs.

FARMACIA DI SANTA MARIA NOVELLA
VIA DEL ESCALA 16, 50123
☎ (55) 216276
Former church, now a temple to fragrances. A unique old-fashioned store where you can buy all kinds of perfumes, essences, soaps and talcum powders. FAITH WILLINGER loves it: *"When you walk in you get an immaculate scent of pot-pourri and essences. It's been here for hundreds of years."* JEREMIAH TOWERS likes their acqua di rose, while LOGAN BENTLEY goes there for *"the very pungent wet pot-pourri and the best lily-of-the-valley essence I've ever found"*.

FRATELLI PICCINI
PONTE VECCHIO 23, 50125
☎ (55) 294768
Carriage-trade jeweller on the Ponte Vecchio. Here you'll find the finest rubies, emeralds, diamonds and sapphires, set to order.

GARBO
BORGO OGNISSANTI 2R, 50123
☎ (55) 295338
Delicate hand-worked silk, linen and lacewear for women. Also unique are the individually designed wedding and christening gowns.

HOUSE OF FLORENCE

Via Tornabuoni 6, 50123

☎ (55) 230 2610

The grandson of the original Signor Gucci continues the family business in this, its main store. "*Ironically, the shop is located across the street from the flagship Gucci store, but Roberto Gucci is on his own here, with a classic, beautifully crafted line of leather goods designed by his wife, Drusilla. Don't miss the delicious line of elephant bags,*" advises LOGAN BENTLEY.

MATUCCI

Via del Corso 46 (women) and 71 (men), 50100

☎ (55) 212018

Everything for the snappy dresser, from jodhpurs and sheepskin jackets to stylish but practical separates. For more of her designs, pop up the road to **BEBA MATUCCI** at number 36.

MOSCARDI

Lungarno Corsini 36r, 50123

☎ (55) 214414

Traditional Florentine craftsmanship at its best. Signore Moscardi carves, paints and gilds the most beautiful picture and mirror frames in town.

QUELLE TRE

Via de' Pucci 43, 50122

☎ (55) 293284

Three sisters, Luciana, Cecilia and Cristiana, run this boutique for women featuring fun, colourful clothes and accessories designed and produced in-house. Suitable for all ages.

SALVATORE FERRAGAMO

Via Tornabuoni 12–16r, 50123

☎ (55) 43951

The flagship store of the Ferragamo family empire, set on the ground floor of a medieval palazzo beside the Arno. Sells a large selection of shoes, handbags, briefcases, belts and leatherware, as well as men's and women's clothes and the most elegant ties. Call ahead to make an appointment to visit the **FERRAGAMO MUSEUM**, a tribute to the artistic creation of the great Florentine shoemaker. Open Mon, Wed and Fri, 9 am–1 pm and 2 pm–6 pm. Closed Aug and Dec 25–Jan 7.

VENNARI

Via della Vigna Nuova 65, 50123

☎ (55) 216558

Exquisite jewellery ranging from priceless diamond necklaces to cufflinks. All of Vennari's jewellery is hand-crafted by their own designers.

Milan

ART AND MUSEUMS

CASTELLO SFORZESCO

Piazza Castello 1, 20121

☎ (2) 870926

This enormous fairy-tale Renaissance castle is now the seat of the Municipal Museum of Art. Worth visiting just to see Michelangelo's last work, his wonderful unfinished *Rondanini Pietà* – but don't miss out on the works by Lippi, Mantegna, Bellini and the Venetians, plus a good collection of Lombard oils.

MUSEO POLDI PEZZOLDI

Via Manzoni 12, 20121

☎ (2) 794889

Charming museum in a 19C villa with a small but select collection of masters – plus antique watches, clocks and armoury.

•••

"IT HOUSES THE MOST WONDERFUL MASTERPIECES OF OUR ART. A PERFECT PLACE TO SPEND A FEW HOURS ON A SUNDAY, AWAY FROM EVERYONE AND EVERYTHING" –

NANDO MIGLIO *ON THE PINACOTECA DI BRERA*

•••

PINACOTECA DI BRERA

Via Brera 28, 20121

☎ (2) 8646 1924

Milan's main picture gallery and one of Italy's best, featuring Mantegna's famously moving *Dead Christ*.

SANTA MARIA DELLE GRAZIE

Piazza Santa Maria delle Grazie 2, 20123

☎ (2) 498 7588

The church is most famous for its refectory, which houses Leonardo da Vinci's super-famous fresco, *The Last Supper*. Despite having been restored many times (it is Leonardo's experimental technique that has caused it to deteriorate so fast), the fresco is in a bad state and restoration continues at a slow pace – so visitors are restricted in both time and number. Choose off-peak hours and avoid weekends. Open 8 am–2 pm. Closed Mon.

BARS AND CAFES

IL BARETTO
Via Sant'adrea 3, 20121
☎ (2) 781255
An intimate bar which also serves tasty food at lunch. Run with tremendous flair by Emanno.

BOCCON DI VINO
Via Carducci 17, 20123
☎ (2) 866040
Buzzing authentic Italian café/bar where locals and strays congregate for a natter and something to eat. "*They serve pasta, cheese, salami, wine − it's a great place to grab a quick bite,*" advises JILL HALEY.

IL CIGNO NERO
Via della Spiga 33, 20121
☎ (2) 7602 2620
The only bar on Milan's most fashionable designer row and the perfect pit stop during a hectic shopping spree.

CLUBS

LA BODEGUITA DEL MEDLO
Via Col di Lana 3, 20136
☎ (2) 8940 0560
Always full, offers interesting food, but best to come here for drinks. Named after the bar Hemingway loved with great live music, and not too expensive. Open 9.30 pm−2 am. Closed Sun.

LA BOLGIA UMANA
Via Santa Maria Segreta 7−9, 20123
☎ (2) 878230
A great club created by popular song-writer−singer (and doctor) Enzo Janacci. There's a restaurant, a theatre for concerts and a cabaret. JILL HALEY says, "*The bar is great − you'll find a varied crowd and music goes from rock to swing to South American.*" Open 8 pm−2 am. Closed Mon.

CAFE DELL' ATLANTIQUE
Viale Umbria 42, 20135
☎ (2) 5519 3925
New and very trendy. American Sunday brunch is served here.

CRAZY BULL
Piazzetta Pattari 2, 20122
☎ (2) 7202 3715
Great beer, American-style food in the evening, and crazy music. Lots of fun and inexpensive. Open every day 6 pm−3 am.

GRAND CAFE FASHION
Corso di Porta Ticinese, corner Via Vetere, 20123
☎ (2) 8940 0709
The original Fashion Café, belonging to the owner of one of Milan's biggest model agencies. The club is set on two floors, and the music is termed acid-jazz. Happy hour is 6.30 pm−9 pm, and you can always order delicious snacks. Open 6.30 pm−3 am.

MAGAZZINI GENERALI
Via Pietrasanta 14, 20141
☎ (2) 5521 1313
The latest hot spot and the newest place to launch books, albums and magazines such as *Vibe* from the US. Set on two floors. Open 10 pm−3 am. Closed Mon−Tues.

PROPAGANDA
Via Castelbarco 11, 20136
☎ (2) 5831 0682
This place is media cyberspace heaven. Look and you'll find TV monitors, computers connected to the Internet, and newspapers from all over the world. Theme nights include Caribbean and revival rock. A very varied crowd. Open 10 am−3 pm.

ZELIG
Viale Monza 140, 20127
☎ (2) 255 1774
Great bar with wonderful snacks and plenty of live entertainment. Famous Italian comedians like Vinicio Capossela, Paolo Rossi, Gene Gnocchi, Gino & Michele head here.

HOTELS

EXCELSIOR HOTEL GALLIA
Piazza Duca d'Aosta 9, 20124
☎ (2) 6785
Grande dame hotel restored to its original Art Nouveau style and fitted out with state-of-the-art health club and a fine Mediterranean restaurant.

GRAND HOTEL ET DE MILAN
Via Manzoni 29, 20121
☎ (2) 723141
Grand hotel where Verdi died and despite recent improvements has retained its turn-of-the-century charm. The restaurant **DON CARLOS** is a popular place to go after a night at La Scala. "*I stayed here once for a year when I worked as a model in Milan; the staff are great, and I love the atmosphere and the period Biedermeier furniture,*" says JEFF BLYNN.

HOTEL FOUR SEASONS

VIA DEL GESÙ 8, 20121

☎ (2) 77088

One of Milan's best hotels, set in a converted 15C monastery only 50 yards from the Via Montenapoleone. Outside there is a large garden featuring the CAFÉ DONEY. "*The restaurant Il Teatro is excellent, with super bread, muffins and brioche. They also have a wonderful concierge, Mauro Delvai,*" reports LOGAN BENTLEY. MARTIN SKAN adds, "*Brilliant. Beautifully decorated – the service is impeccable, as is the restaurant.*"

HOTEL PRINCIPE DI SAVOIA

PIAZZA DELLA REPUBBLICA 17, 20124

☎ (2) 6230

A hotel of *belle-époque* elegance and charm it is still renowned for the fabulous food in the GALLERIA restaurant – great for both lunch and dinner – and the superb service.

MUSIC

TEATRO ALLA SCALA

VIA FILODRAMMATICI 2, 20121

☎ (2) 887 9211

The most famous opera house, it has provided a stage for some of the world's most spectacular performers and performances. The season opens with much fanfare on 7 Dec, feast day of Sant' Ambrogio, and runs through to May. There is a concert season (May–June, Sept–Nov) and a brief ballet season (Sept). Don't forget to check out the new MUSEO LA SCALA, which showcases the history of theatre and music.

RESTAURANTS

SEE ALSO HOTELS.

AIMO E NADIA

VIA MONTECUCCOLI 6, 20147

☎ (2) 416886

Once a simple trattoria, now a rather chic restaurant. "*Always popular with Italy's celebrities and political figures. Lots of space, creative but traditional cooking. Expensive in the evening, but try the fixed-price lunch,*" advises JILL HALEY.

ALFREDO GRAN SAN BERNARDO

VIA BORGHESE 14, 20154

☎ (2) 331 9000

Overseen by Alfredo Valli, one of the greatest cooks specializing in Milanese cuisine. Elegant but warm atmosphere.

ANTICA OSTERIA DEL PONTE

PIAZZA NEGRI 9, CASSINETTA DI LUGAGNANO, 20081 (25 KM FROM MILAN)

☎ (2) 942 0034

"*An obligatory stop for food-lovers. Directed by the Santin family, this is absolutely one of the best places to eat in Milan,*" raves JILL HALEY.

CASANOVA

AT THE PALACE HOTEL, PIAZZA DELLA REPUBBLICA 20, 20124

☎ (2) 6336

Top-class restaurant for big-occasion dining. "*The service is fantastic and the food is excellent, as is their international wine list.*" reports NANDO MIGLIO.

••

"NO. 1 IN MILAN. YOU'RE ALWAYS SURE TO HAVE A GOOD MEAL THERE. IT'S LIKE BEING AT HOME – I SOMETIMES EAT IN THE KITCHEN WHEN THE RESTAURANT IS FULL" – NANDO MIGLIO *ON DA BICE.*

••

DA BICE

VIA BORGOSPESSO 12, 20121

☎ (2) 795528

There's now a Da Bice in Paris, NY and LA, but this is the original and best. BONARIA and LUCIO ALIOTTI are fans: "*The best mix for quality and price.*"

DON LISANDER

VIA MANZONI 12A, 20121

☎ (2) 7602 0130

Overseen by the dedicated Luigi, the cooking is classical, and the wine cellar stretches to an impressive 20,000 bottles. "*A classic restaurant in the Milanese tradition, especially nice in the summer when you can eat outside in the huge courtyard*" – LOGAN BENTLEY.

JOIA

VIA PANFILO CASTALDI 18, 20124

☎ (2) 204 9244

Great food, with some particularly good vegetarian dishes and a vast selection of puddings. Good presentation and excellent wine list.

MASUELLI TRATTORIA SAN MARCO

VIALE UMBRIA 80, 20135

☎ (2) 5518 4138

A temple to Milanese and Torinese cuisine. The atmosphere is bright and breezy while the dishes prepared by Signora Pina are simple and tasty, according to natives LUCIO and BONARIA ALIOTTI.

OSTERIA DEL BINARI

VIA TORTONA 7, 20144

☎ (2) 8940 7428

A good place for after-theatre dinner, with traditional Northern Italian dishes. Open late.

⑨ PAPER MOON

VIA BAGUTTA 1, 20121

☎ (2) 796083

Pio Magrini's widow continues the tradition of this ever-popular pizzeria, which still attracts Milan's most notable (and notorious) style-setters; GIANNI VERSACE even has his own special table. It always has a queue. "*A great place to eat well and cheaply, if you're in a hurry,*" reckons NANDO MIGLIO.

PECK

VIA VICTOR HUGO 4, 20123

☎ (2) 876774

Blond-wood restaurant behind the famous deli, specializing in traditional Northern Italian food. Now overseen by popular French chef Daniel Drovadaine. "*Folks have gone back to Peck lately because of his tasty delights. I think it's much nicer at lunchtime than dinner. Peck also has several retail stores selling gastronomic delicacies in the Duomo area,*" says JILL HALEY.

IL SAMBUCO

AT THE HOTEL HERMITAGE, VIA MESSINA 10, 20154

☎ (2) 3361 0333

Angelo Fioravanti runs this restaurant, which is as elegant as the hotel. Simple and light food.

SAVINI

GALLERIA VITTORIO EMANUELE II, VIA UGO FOSCOLO, 20121

☎ (2) 8646 0535

Offers mouthwatering freshly made pasta and a perfect example of the famous Milanese breaded veal cutlet. Members of the AGNELLI and PIRELLI families all come here to revitalize their jaded palates.

⑨ TORRE DI PISA

VIA FIORI CHIARI 21, 20121

☎ (2) 804483

Popular and homely Tuscan trattoria run by three Pisan brothers who celebrate their culinary heritage.

SHOPPING

The best starting point is **VIA SANT'ANDREA**, where you'll find top of the range creations by Missoni, Chanel and others. Then head for **VIA MONTENAPOLEONE, VIA DELLA SPIGA, VIA VERRI** – all first-rate for fashion shopping. Together, these four streets form Milan's "Golden Rectangle".

ANGELA PINTALDI

VIA SAN PIETRO ALL'ORTO 9, 20121

☎ (2) 781778

Imaginative jewellery that will go with anything from jeans to ballgowns. This Sicilian designer will use any stones you desire, antique or otherwise. Lots of fantasy at high prices.

CARACENI

VIA FATEBENEFRATELLI 16, 20121

☎ (2) 655 1972

First-rate suits and a standard-bearer for Latin tailoring. GIANNI AGNELLI and KARL LAGERFELD are among Caraceni's clientele.

DIEGO DELLA VALLE

VIA DELLA SPIGA 22, 20121

☎ (2) 760 2423

Classic shoes for men and women: everything from cool summer slip-ons to lace-up suede boots. VIPs favouring his white summer canvas "Hogan" shoe include SHARON STONE and TOM CRUISE.

ETRO

VIA MONTENAPOLEONE 5, 20121

☎ (2) 600 5094

A treasure trove of beautifully designed paisley prints, silks, luggage, shirts, coats, scarves and shawls – "*the ultimate status symbols,*" says LOGAN BENTLEY.

FIORUCCI

GALLERIA PASSARELLA 2, 20122

☎ (2) 794 437

Elio Fiorucci's 3-storey fashion emporium is worth checking simply to see the Italian view of the latest in the outrageous.

FORNASETTI

VIA MANZONI 45, 20121

☎ (2) 266 3498

During the late 50s and early 60s, designer Piero Fornasetti designed and made objects such as screens, wastebaskets, lamps, plates and *trompe-l'oeil* decorations based upon turn-of-the-century designs. His son, Barnaba, has now reopened the shop. "*You should not leave Milan without at least one item from Fornasetti – don't miss it!*" advises LOGAN BENTLEY.

FRATELLI ROSSETTI
VIA MONTENAPOLEONE 1, 20121
☎ (2) 7602 1650
Outstanding shoes in the most competitive territory in the world.

LA PERLA AT VALENTINA
VIA MANZONI 44, 20121
☎ (2) 7602 6028
The finest lingerie which has adorned some of the world's most celebrated women, such as CATHERINE DENEUVE and SOPHIA LOREN.

MERU
VIA SOLFERINO 3, 20121
☎ (2) 86460700
According to LOGAN BENTLEY, this is "*the smallest shop in the arty Brera district, featuring clocks, jewellery, and other* objets d'art *designed and made by the Merù brothers. Very special things.*"

L'ORO DEI FARLOCCHI
VIA MADONNINA 5, 20121
☎ (2) 860589
A veritable Aladdin's cave of antiques, unusual *objets d'art*, knick-knacks and precious gifts.

PAPIC
VIALE S. MICHELE DEL CARSO, 20144
☎ (2) 459 4602
Tiny, reasonably priced jewellery store next to the attractive Corso Vercelli. For tailor-made creations be sure to make an appointment.

PAPIER
VIA SAN MAURILIO 4, 20123
☎ (2) 856221
Everything from natural, undyed, recycled paper to paper using coconut, rice, banana bark, corn, cotton and silk, plus wonderful desk accessories.

PRADA FRATELLI
GALLERIA VITTORIO EMANUELE II 63, 20121
☎ (2) 876979
One of the top names in leather – bags, baggage and boots.

FLEA MARKETS
Over the last few years many more flea markets have appeared in Milan. Although they contain a lot of rubbish, it's still worth having a stroll through them to see what the local Italians are buying and selling. FIERA DI SENEGALLIA takes place each Sat along the north side of the Canal. It dates back to the 17C fair and is "*full of new and used valuables and junk. Absolutely crowded*" – JILL HALEY. Often the last Sun of the month is when you'll find the best bargains, especially in summer at markets such as **MERCATONE** at the Naviglio Grande. You'll find antiques at **BOLLATE**, every Sunday and who knows what you'll discover at **VIA LAMBRATE** (near Piazza Loreto).

Naples

In the last century, Naples was an obligatory stop-off for the well-bred youth of Europe and America on their Grand Tour. But for the last two decades Naples has been largely ignored by travellers. However, thanks to the energy of a very active mayor, Bassolino (who hosted the 1995 Economic Summit in Naples), things are rapidly improving again. It was originally founded by Hellenic immigrants in the 6C BC. Since then, Naples has absorbed culture from the peoples of Greece, Rome, Normandy, Anjou, Aragon, France, Spain and North Africa, all of whom have ruled the city at one time. (And don't forget that the entire world is indebted to Naples for inventing the pizza.)

ART & MUSEUMS

CHURCH OF SAN GIOVANNI A CARBONARA
VIA CARBONARA 5, 80139
☎ (81) 295873
An extraordinary building, redecorated in the 18C and containing the statue of King Ladislao of Anjou. The **CARACCIOLO CHAPEL** has beautiful sculptures by two Spaniards, Diego de Siloe and B. Ordones.

CHURCH OF SAN LORENZO MAGGIORE
VIA TRIBUNALI 316, 80145
☎ (81) 454948
The poet Boccaccio met his beloved Fiammetta in this Franciscan church, which dates from the 13C. Inside, the impressive remains will give you an idea of the original Roman city that once stood where modern Naples is today. Open daily.

CHURCH OF SANTA CHIARA
VIA SANTA CHIARA 49/C, 80134
☎ (81) 552 6280
Built in 1328 by rulers from Anjou, this church was transformed into an unusual garden in the 18C by the architect Vaccaro.

MUSEO ARCHEOLOGICO NAZIONALE

PIAZZA MUSEO NAZIONALE 19, 80135

☎ (81) 440166

Here you'll find a rich collection of statues, frescoes, mosaics, vases, papyri, coins and relics from classical Greece and Rome. Many of the artefacts originated from the settlements at nearby Pompeii and Herculaneum. Originally constructed in the 16C as a residence for knights, it became a university between 1616 and 1777 and later a museum under King Charles of Bourbon.

MUSEO NAZIONALE DI S. MARTINO

LARGO SAN MARTINO, 80129

☎ (81) 578 1769

The museum contains important examples of 17C paintings by Ribera, Caracciolo, Reni, and Giordano; old Neapolitan cribs from the 17C; and beautiful inlaid furniture. It was built in the 14C by Charles of Anjou and restored, in a baroque style, by the 17C architect Franzago. There's an impressive view of the Bay of Naples. Open Tues–Sun, 9 am–2 pm.

PALAZZO REALE DI CAPODIMONTE

VIA DI CAPODIMONTE, 80137

☎ (81) 741 5299

Surrounded by a landscaped garden built by the Bourbon King Charles III in the 18C, the Royal Palace holds a precious collection of Renaissance paintings.

PALAZZO REALE DI CASERTA

☎ (823) 321400

The Royal Palace of Caserta, a couple of miles north of Naples, was built in the beginning of the 18C by the extraordinary architect Vanvitelli and is considered by many to be more beautiful than Versailles. The interior was recently reopened, and extensive formal gardens feature a series of connecting fountains and other waterworks. Gardens open 9 am–8 pm in summer, 9 am–3 pm in winter, while the apartments open 9 am–1 pm year round.

VILLA FLORIDIANA

VIA D. CIMAROSA 77, 80127

☎ (81) 578 8418 AND 578 1776

Famous for its camellia trees, this beautiful garden was built by King Ferdinandi I for the Duchess of Floridia. The villa itself houses the MUSEO NAZIONALE DELLA CERAMICA (National Ceramics Museum). Open Tue–Sat, 9 am–2 pm, and Sun 9 am–1 pm.

HOTELS

GRANDE ALBERGO VESUVIO

VIA PARTENOPE 45, 80121

☎ (81) 764 0044; FAX (81) 764 0044

Caruso and de Maupassant slept here, as well as BILL CLINTON. *"A truly grand hotel with excellent service, and a roof-garden restaurant with a view of the gulf,"* RITA AND MARIANO PANE.

GRAND HOTEL SANTA LUCIA

VIA PARTENOPE 46, 80121

☎ (81) 764 0666; FAX (81) 764 8580

Located on the waterfront, this hotel has many rooms with a splendid view.

RESTAURANTS

SEE ALSO HOTELS.

BRANDI

VIA SANTA ANNA DI PALAZZO 1, 80132

☎ (81) 416928

Probably Naples's most famous pizzeria. This is where, over a century ago, they invented the pizza margherita. They also serve pasta. Friendly atmosphere.

LA CANTINELLA

VIA CUMA 42, 80132

☎ (81) 764 8684

For celebrated Neapolitan cuisine, make a pil-

ENCORE To see Naples properly, try walking. Starting from **Via Partenope**, walk along the harbour to Via Caracciolo through the gardens of the Villa Comunale and the Aquarium then continue on to Mergellina, Posillipo and Marechiaro . . . . . ♠ Begin at **Piazza Plebiscito**, the historic centre of Naples with its Palazzo Reale, built in the 17C and enlarged in the 18C, and then head towards the opera house, Teatro San Carlo (1737) . . . . . ♠ Head to the **Via Toledo**, built in the 16C by Pedro Alvarez de Toledo. The most famous street in the city, it has the Galleria Umberto at one end where intellectuals and artists meet . . . . . ♠ Visit the **Via dei Mille** and the surrounding streets, the most elegant shopping area of the city. . . . . . ♠

grimage to this restaurant with its view of the harbour.

MIMI ALLA FERROVIA
VIA ALFONSO D'ARAGONA 19–21, 80139

☎ (81) 553 8525

Considered a temple to local, traditional food. Fresh seafood is brought in every day by private boat and patrons can feast on such specialities as fried zucchini flowers and charcoal-grilled squid. Closed Sunday and for 2 weeks in August.

SHOPPING

BOWINKEL
PIAZZA DEI MARTIRI 24, 80121

☎ (81) 764 4344

This shop, over 100 years old, is the place to buy antique prints from a large selection.

GUIDA
VIA PORTALBA 20–23, 80134

☎ (81) 446477

The most important book store in town, where you can also exchange ideas with Naples's literati.

KNIGHT
PIAZZA DEI MARTIRI 52, 80121

☎ (81) 763 3837

Beautiful jewels, which can be made to order at your request.

MARINELLA
RIVIERA DI CHIAIA 287, 80121

☎ (81) 7644214

Marinella make ties to order, using age-old techniques. Their ties are considered to be among the most beautiful in the world.

TRAMONTANO
SALITA DI CHIAIA 149E

☎ (81) 414758

Exquisite leather articles.

Rome

Rome is one city which really should be enjoyed on foot. Go up to the Pincio at dusk on the edge of the Villa Borghese for the best, most romantic view of the city. Visit Michelangelo's colossal marble *Moses* in the hidden-away church of San Pietro in Vincoli (St Peter in Chains). Go and see the vast Roman baths of Caracalla and the Circus Maximus. Or visit Trastevere, the bohemian quarter on the other side of the Tiber, and enjoy the winding cobbled streets and wonderful little tucked-away restaurants.

ART AND MUSEUMS

BIBLIOTECA NAZIONALE
VIALE CASTRO PRETORIO 105, 00185

☎ (6) 445 7635

Built as an exact replica of the library in Alexandria. Often overlooked but worth a visit.

GALLERIA DORIA PAMPHILI
PIAZZA DEL COLLEGIO ROMANO 1, 00186

☎ (6) 679 4365

One of Italy's finest collections of masters collected by the Doria family and hung in their beautiful 17C palazzo.

MUSEI VATICANI
VIALE VATICANO, 00165

☎ (6) 988 3333

The popes' treasures consist of an extraordinarily rich collection which has been steadily built up over centuries through donations and commissions. In total there are 4½ miles of works including Michelangelo's frescoes in the **SISTINE CHAPEL**, Raphael's **LOGGIA**, the tiny **CHAPEL OF NICHOLAS V** frescoed by Fra Angelico, works by Leonardo da Vinci and the largest collection of antique art in the world. And while you're in the area, you must visit **ST PETER'S BASILICA** to see one of Michelangelo's most moving masterpieces, his marble *Pietà*.

MUSEO BORGHESE
VILLA BORGHESE, VIALE UCCELLERIA 5, 00198

☎ (6) 854 8577

Set in Rome's best-known park, this fresco-filled villa houses an important collection of Renaissance painting and sculpture. Open from 9 am–2 pm; Sun 9 am–1 pm; closed Monday.

MUSEO CAPITOLINO
PIAZZA DEL CAMPIDOGLIO, 00186

☎ (6) 678 2862

Europe's first public art collection, set up in the 15C by Pope Sixtus V in what was then the centre of Rome. Classical Roman and Greek sculpture is its greatest strength.

MUSEO NAZIONALE DI VALLE GIULIA
PIAZZA DI VALLE GIULIA 9, 00197

☎ (6) 320 1951

Renaissance mansion now a museum with a

surprising full-scale Etruscan temple in the garden and a lovely collection of antique sculptures and terracotta and bronze figures.

BARS AND CAFES

ANTICO CAFFE GRECO
VIA CONDOTTI 86, 00187
☎ (6) 679 1700
Founded in 1760, a grand, old-fashioned café whose walls are adorned with pictures of its famous literary, intellectual and political habitués.

BAR DELLA PACE
VIA DELLA PACE 4, 00186
☎ (6) 686 1216
An old-fashioned bar, near Piazza Navona but hidden away from the tourists. A hang-out for artists, intellectuals and gilded youth. Slightly reminiscent of a 1930s Parisian café.

BAR HUNGARIA
VIALE LIEGI 55, 00198
☎ (6) 854 1430
Bustling café/bar usually teeming until the early hours. Serves some of the best hamburgers in Rome.

LE CORNACCHIE
PIAZZA RONDANINI 53, 00186
☎ (6) 686 4485
A fun, if rather frenetic, place to have a drink or snack and enjoy authentic Roman atmosphere.

HEMINGWAY
PIAZZA DELLE COPPELLE 10, 00186
☎ (6) 654 4135
Chic all-night bar favoured by fashionable Romans with three themed rooms to choose from. "*Soft lighting, the kind of bar to go to for a quiet chat among friends. Light snacks are served and in the summer the crowd goes out to the tables in front,*" reports UMBERTO PIZZI.

IL TARTARUGHINO
VIA DELLA SCROFA 2, 00186
☎ (6) 678 6037
Quiet piano bar serving light suppers. Favoured by jacket-and-tied politicos and personalities. In summer, patrons are to be found in the owner's other home, the Country Club in Porto Rotondo, Sardinia.

TRIMANI WINE BAR
VIA CERNAIA 37B, 00185
☎ (6) 446 9630
This is the best place to sample champagnes,

wines and liquors from all over the world. UMBERTO PIZZI says that "*Mr Trimani is a walking encyclopaedia of wine. You can buy by the glass or the bottle and he serves cold snacks to go with the drinks.*"

CLUBS

ALIBI
VIA MONTE TESTACCIO 39, 00153
☎ (6) 574 3448
Behind the former Rome slaughterhouse in a gentrified district of old Rome, this disco plays house and 70's revivial music and is set over three levels and a large terrace. Predominantly gay and trendy.

ALIEN
VIA VELLETRI 13, 00198
☎ (6) 841 2212
A 50s-themed club where a mix of youth and those who remember the days when rock was young, is healthy rather than sad.

GILDA
VIA MARIO DE' FIORI 97, 00183,
☎ (6) 678 4838
A favourite with ageing movie folk such as OLIVER STONE, URSULA ANDRESS and JACQUELINE BISSET. This former *café chantant* has been turned into an elegant disco/restaurant, but still has live shows once in a while. Everybody dresses up.

PANTHEON CLUB
VIA POZZO DELLE CORNACCHIE 36, 00186
☎ (6) 6880 3431
High energy and loud music mean this place is for dancers rather than poseurs.

HOTELS

LE GRAND HOTEL
VIA V E ORLANDO 3, 00185
☎ (6) 4709; FAX (6) 474 7307
Despite its less-than-grand location near the station, this hotel lives up to its name in atmosphere and service, with its hand-painted walls, tapestries and chandeliers and an impressive guest list. Don't miss out on afternoon tea.

HOTEL EDEN
VIA LUDOVISI 49, 00187
☎ (6) 4743551; FAX (6) 482 1584
The Eden is once again Rome's most important hotel, as it was during its *Dolce Vita* heyday. Assets include its unrivalled location near

the Spanish Steps and the gardens of the Villa Borghese; and the puddings of chef Enrico Derflingher (who has worked for both the Princess of Wales and George Bush). Fabulous views from the rooftop bar.

HOTEL HASSLER
PIAZZA DELLA TRINITÀ DEI MONTI 6, 00187
☎ (6) 679 2651; FAX (6) 678 9991
Grand hotel overlooking the Spanish Steps. Complete with glass-roofed lounge with gold and marble walls, and a ritzy rooftop restaurant with views across the city. Rooms are decorated in a variety of styles – some feature frescoed walls, while others are filled with Venetian mirrors and have huge marble bathrooms. Faultless and friendly service.

HOTEL D'INGHILTERRA
VIA BOCCA DI LEONE 14, 00187
☎ (6) 69981; FAX (6) 992 2243
Charming small hotel where Henry James used to stay. Its location in the heart of the shopping district makes it especially popular with visiting fashion folk.

HOTEL LOCARNO
VIA DELLA PENNA 22, 00186
☎ (6) 361 0841
Charming 1920s hotel run by mother-and-daughter team Maria Teresa Celli and Caterina Valente. Attractions include original Art Nouveau furnishings and decorations, a magnificent roof terrace for alfresco summer breakfasts and in winter a welcoming fire in the bar. Within walking distance of most things.

HOTEL LORD BYRON
VIA G DE NOTARIS 5, 00197
☎ (6) 322 0404; FAX (6) 322 0405
This small villa in the smart, peaceful suburb of Parioli is one of Rome's most elegant hotels. The rooms designed by Luigi Sturchio are incredibly stylish with splendid views from the suites on the top two floors. The food is good too, from the freshly baked croissants and brioches at breakfast to dinner in the Michelin-starred **RELAIS LE JARDIN** restaurant.

HOTEL MAJESTIC
VIA VENETO 50, 00187
☎ (6) 482 8014; FAX (6) 488 0984
The Majestic is a favourite with visiting stars such as PAVAROTTI, MADONNA and WHITNEY HOUSTON, who appreciate the opulent, old-world atmosphere. Fine Italian and Mediterranean cuisine from the restaurant.

RESTAURANTS

SEE ALSO HOTELS.

••

"THE OWNER OF THIS TYPICAL ROMAN RESTAURANT PLAYED TRIMALCHION IN FELLINI'S SATYRICON AND HAS ONE OF THE MOST INCREDIBLE FACES YOU'LL EVER SEE" – UMBERTO PIZZI ON AL MORO

••

AL MORO
VICOLO DELLE BOLLETTE 13, 00187
☎ (6) 678 3495
Wonderfully authentic Roman joint attracting a stellar clientele. *"A very homey atmosphere. The fish is especially good,"* says UMBERTO PIZZI.

ANDREA
VIA SARDEGNA 26, 00187
☎ (6) 482 1891
Intimate clubby restaurant where both Hemingway and King Farouk used to eat and now a popular spot for power lunches. Cooking is classic Italian. *"Consistently excellent. It has the most extraordinary salad made up of tomatoes, lobster and potatoes called the salata catalana"* – SIR PETER USTINOV.

BELTRAME
VIA DELLA CROCE 39, 00187
(NO TELEPHONE)
Comfortable Roman restaurant with wonderful food. Don't phone – you just turn up and they'll squeeze you in. *"Unique and simple. Lone diners eat at a communal table. Regulars include many intellectuals,"* promises CARLA FENDI.

CAMINETTO
VIALE PARIOLI 89, 00197
☎ (6) 808 3946
Refined and exotic cuisine frequented by the madding crowd of wannabe models and wannabe film stars. *"Worth it just to watch the parade,"* says CHRISTOPHER WINNER.

DAL BOLOGNESE
PIAZZA DEL POPOLO 1–2, 00186
☎ (6) 361 1426
A popular spot for more than 25 years and frequented by MARCELLO MASTROIANNI, FRANCIS FORD COPPOLA or ROBERT DE NIRO. They all

come for good Bolognese cooking in a large, inviting dining room decorated with paintings donated over the years by hungry artists. In the summer, tables are set outside. *"For those who want a break from Italian food, order the thinly sliced rare roast beef and mashed potatoes. The semi-freddo with hot chocolate sauce is a delight,"* UMBERTO PIZZI advises.

IL MATRICIANO
VIA DEI GRACCHI 55, 00192
☎ (6) 321 2327
Simple, homely trattoria serving unpretentious Roman cooking which has been enjoyed by everyone from MICK HUCKNALL, RICHARD GERE and MARCELLO MASTROIANNI to impoverished local artists. UMBERTO PIZZI loves it: *"It's my favourite place to eat outside in the summer."*

NINO
VIA BORGOGNONA 11, 00187
☎ (6) 679 5676
Homely trattoria in an upmarket area. Fashion folk (EILEEN FORD always eats here) drop in for good simple cooking and wonderful service. *"The waiters are fabulous, they remember you after 10 years. The food is plain but of the highest quality"* – CARLA FENDI.

PAPA GIOVANNI
VIA DEI SEDIARI 5, 00186
☎ (6) 686 5308
Softly lit restaurant where the *cucina* leans towards the *nuova* and the atmosphere towards the romantic. Perhaps overly so, say those who object to the rose petals strewn around their spaghetti al caffè (pasta with a ground coffee-bean sauce). Expensive, formal and highly rated – but justifiably, with the intricate attention to detail from Renato, the owner.

PIPERNO
MONTE DE' CENCI 9, 00186
☎ (6) 6880 6629
Colourful and much loved eatery in the old Jewish quarter, next to the Palazzo Cenci, open for over 100 years. *"I love taking an evening off and enjoying a relaxing dinner"* – BEATRICE REBECCHINI.

LA ROSETTA
VIA DELLA ROSETTA 9, 00186
☎ (6) 686 1002
First-class fish restaurant with a light, breezy atmosphere. *"Without a doubt the best fish in Rome. It's expensive, though. Everything they do is just exquisite, like the scallops with their little blue eggs attached. Wonderful, wonderful food,"* enthuses FAITH WILLINGER.

LA SCALA
VIA PARIOLI 79, 00197
☎ (6) 808 3968
Splendid, dignified food in an utterly Roman atmosphere. *"All can eat in style; no one is picked out, be he a prince or a pauper. Don't miss asking for olive all' ascolana as appetizers,"* CHRISTOPHER WINNER advises.

TAVERNA FLAVIA
VIA FLAVIA 9, 00187
☎ (6) 474 5214
Owner Mimmo Caviccia counts ELIZABETH TAYLOR as well as several other Hollywood stars among her close personal friends – see the autographed photos covering the walls. Surprisingly, the food is simple and unpretentious – unlike the general theme.

IL VALENTINO
VIA DELLA FONTANELLA 15, 00187
☎ (6) 361 0880
Situated in the Hotel Valadier, this slightly flash restaurant is a major meeting place for the city's élite. Chef Michele Rossi serves fine international, Roman and Neapolitan cuisine.

SHOPPING

VIA CONDOTTI and **VIA BORGOGNONA** are the best places to find high fashion, while the offbeat boutiques around **TRASTEVERE** yield younger, more innovative items. For bargains try the flea market at **PORTA PORTESE**.

ANGEL STATION
VIA PANISPERNA 244, 00184
☎ (6) 482 0675
The owner has lovingly collected all kinds of antiques that feature angels all displayed against a sky-blue background.

IL BAGNO
CORSO VITTORIO EMMANUELE 191, 00187
☎ (6) 686 1896
Washbasins by Philippe Starck in stainless steel, taps by Arne Jacobsen and every other component for the ultimate designer bathroom.

BERTONATI
VIA DEI PASTINI 18A, 00186
☎ (6) 678 1893
The place for cameos, new and old; coral necklaces and turquoise. Imaginative work from mother and daughter team who also do their own stringing and repairs.

BULGARI
VIA CONDOTTI 10, 00187
☎ (6) 679 3876
The great jewellery designer. Extravagant pieces with a historical bent as well as bold modern designs.

CAMICIAIA
VIA FRATTINA 38, 00187
☎ (6) 679 2304
High-quality made-to-measure shirts. "*This is the only store that knows how to make a shirt with a Battistoni collar better than Battistoni*," reckons RAFFAELE CURI.

CURIOSITA ANTICHE
VIA DEI PETTINARI 74, 00186
☎ (6) 654 3856
The address for collectors of antique jewellery of all prices.

DAL CO
VIA VITTORIA 65, 00187
☎ (6) 678 6536
Divinely non-workaday shoes: gem-encrusted and embroidered silk slippers for night and the finest snakeskin for day.

FEDERICO BUCCELLATI
VIA CONDOTTI 31, 00187
☎ (6) 679 0329
One of the world's best silversmiths and jewellers, admired for his intricate and delicate craftsmanship.

FENDI
VIA BORGOGNONA 39, 00187
☎ (6) 679 7641
Fendi's furs are the ultimate status symbol. They offer everything from classic capes to dramatic swing coats, all designed by Karl Lagerfeld. There's also a lavish selection of accessories. Also try **FENDISSIME**, at 4L, accessories at 4E, 36A and 38, and clothes at 40.

GUCCI
VIA CONDOTTI 8, 00187
☎ (6) 678 9340
Gucci's flagship, where the famous double Gs rampage over everything from keyrings and wallets to handbags and suitcases. Now includes the most fabulous collection of clothes. ERICA JONG's favourite store.

LOUISE MCDERMOTT
VIA DEI GIUBBONARI 30, 00186
☎ (6) 6880 5285
For bibliophiles who love Italy and anything written about Italy, this is quite a find. Louise stocks over 2,000 secondhand books and receives clients on Thurs or by appointment. There's an incredible variety but if Mrs McDermott doesn't have it, she'll more often than not know where you can find it.

RADICONCINI
VIA DEL CORSO 139, 00186
☎ (6) 679 1807
Italy's oldest men's milliner (run by the grandson of the founder), known especially for fine Montecristo Panama hats.

Venice

ART AND MUSEUMS

CA' D'ORO
GALLERIA GRANCHETTI, CANNAREGIO, 30121
☎ (41) 523 8790
Wonderfully ornate Gothic palazzo on the Grand Canal houses works of art from the Venetian Renaissance as well as temporary shows.

CA' REZZONICO – MUSEO DEL SETTECENTO VENEZIANO
DORSODURO 3136 (CAPO SAN BARNABA), 20123
☎ (41) 410 100
This baroque palazzo, recently under restoration, houses paintings, furniture and a beautiful display of original Tiepolo frescoes.

COLLEZIONE D'ARTE MODERNA PEGGY GUGGENHEIM
PALAZZO VENIER DEI LEONI, SAN GREGORIO 701, DORSODURO, 30123
☎ (41) 520 6288
Peggy Guggenheim's former home, this grand 18C palazzo features an extraordinary collection of modern painting from Cubism, Expressionism and Surrealism to the completely abstract. Contemporary sculpture too. An iron gate and pieces of coloured glass lead to the garden, which is now used as a café and where you'll find the marble "throne" that Peggy used at her parties.

GALLERIA DELL' ACCADEMIA
CAMPO DELLA CARITÀ, DORSODURO 30123
☎ (41) 522 2247
The city's finest picture gallery, containing a remarkable collection of Venetian art from the 14C onwards.

MUSEO QUERINI STAMPALIA

CASTELLO 4778, SANTA MARIA
FORMOSA, 20122
☎ (41) 271 1411
The old palace of the noble Querini family,
restored 30 years ago by the famous architect
Carlo Scarpa, is worth visiting to see the
famous library (which is open in the evenings),
where one can study sitting under lamps from
Murano. The art gallery contains curious
paintings from the 1700s, with folk art showing daily life in Venice at the time.

ORIENTAL MUSEUM

SAN STAE (SANTA CROCE), 20125
☎ (41) 524 975
The top floor of this palazzo holds a fascinating collection of Oriental art put together by
Prince Enrico di Borbone. The main part of
the palazzo is dedicated to relativaly modern
art (ie up to the beginning of the 20th C).

PALAZZO DUCALE

PIAZZETTA SAN MARCO 1, 31024
☎ (41) 522 4951
Former residence of the doges and symbol of
Venetian power and glory during the Republic's
golden age. Magnificently decorated halls, state
apartments, and paintings by Venice's best,
including Tintoretto, Veronese and Bellini.

BARS AND CAFES

ACCINGHETA

CASTELLO 4357, CAMPO SAN FILIPPO E
GIACOMO, 30122
☎ (41) 522 4292
A very typical place beloved by Venetians, who
drop by for a quick drink and snack. "*You stand
at the bar to munch on tiny fried fish, bits of anchovy
rolled around capers or strips of green pepper and bac-
calà manterato (salt cod mousse),*" explains FIORA
GANDOLFI.

BAR PASTICCERIA PONTE DELLE PASTE

CASTELLO 5991 (SAN LIO), 30122
☎ (41) 522 2889
An old pastry shop and bar which has recently
been restored. "*Try the cream-filled masks,
flavoured with vanilla, lemon, orange; and the typical Venetian cookies, zaleti di mais (made from cornmeal)*" recommends FIORA GANDOLFI.

CAFFE FLORIAN

PIAZZA SAN MARCO 56, 30124
☎ (41) 528 5338; FAX (41) 522 4409
In this old bar-restaurant loaded with gilded

mirrors and 19C paintings, clients sip coffee and
hot chocolate with whipped cream in fragile
glasses with silver holders. "*During the summer an
orchestra plays outside for those admiring Piazza San
Marco as they sip their drinks,*" says FIORA GANDOLFI.

CANTINA DO MORI

SAN POLO 429 (RIALTO), 30125
☎ (41) 522 5401
Here you eat standing at the bar (or at a table
if you prefer), surrounded by copper buckets
and cooking pans that hang from the ceiling.
PAUL HENDERSON says it's "*brilliant for sandwiches
and wine at midday*".

••

*"ALWAYS RIDICULOUSLY
EXPENSIVE, BUT ALWAYS VERY
GOOD AND WE WOULD NOT
CONSIDER A TRIP TO VENICE
WITHOUT GOING THERE"* –
PAUL HENDERSON ON HARRY'S BAR

••

HARRY'S BAR

SAN MARCO 1323, CALLE VALLARESSO,
30124
☎ (41) 528 5777; FAX (41) 520 6822
World-famous bar, home of the equally
renowned Bellini cocktail, and adored by the
rich and famous. Go at midday for a drink and
snack downstairs. While you are there, book a
table for dinner. EDWARD THORPE enthuses:
"*Famous rendezvous for international clientele, but
never disappoints for marvellous bar service and
relaxed atmosphere.*" CLAUS BON BULOW adds,
"*Where else but Harry's Bar can you eat squid-ink
risotto at the bar with a perfect Martini?*"

HARRY'S DOLCI

GIUDECCA 773, 30133
☎ (41) 522 4844
"*Run by Harry's, same quality grub at half the
price. Outside tables are nice in the summer, with a
great view across the lagoon to the Zàttere*" – PAUL
HENDERSON. And you can take away the
chocolate cake. Open late Mar–7th Nov.

NICO GELATERIA

DORSODURO 922 (ZÀTTERE, ON THE
GIUDECCA CANAL), 30123
☎ (41) 522 5293
Eating a sherbet or ice cream in the summer
on a floating raft on the canal of the Giudecca
is an unforgettable experience.

HOTELS

AGLI ALBORETTI

DORSODURO 884, RIO TERI ANTONIO
FOSCARI 30123
☎ (41) 523 0058; FAX (41)521 0158
Just 25 rooms and all very quiet in this small, comfortable hotel. There's a charming garden and a good restaurant.

GRITTI PALACE

SAN MARCO 2467, CAMPO SANTA
MARIA DEL GIGLIO, 30124
☎ (41) 794611; FAX (41) 5200942
On the banks of the Grand Canal, a 15C palace with its own traghetto stop (for the cross-canal gondola). Hard to better in terms of hospitality, superb service and splendour. Have dinner at **CLUB DEL DOGE** or a drink on the terrace overlooking the Grand Canal and the church of La Salute. Expensive but worth it. "*A wonderful old hotel*"- RICHARD POLO.

HOTEL CIPRIANI

GIUDECCA 10, 30133
☎ (41) 520 7744; FAX (41) 520 3930
Heavenly hotel impeccably run with enormous flair by Natale Rusconi. Here super-smart, super-rich guests lounge and lunch beside the Olympic-sized pool (unique for Venice). Don't miss the wonderful breakfast/brunch. A 24-hour motor-boat service is available to Piazza San Marco. "*In the centre of Venice this is the only hotel which, during the warm summer months, will allow you to spend half your day with intensive sightseeing and the remainder in sybaritic repose next to the swimming pool and the wonderful restaurant,*" explains CLAUS VON BULOW. You can also sign up for a course at the Cipriani cookery school. The hotel is closed Nov–Mar.

....

"*A GOTHIC HOTEL, FROZEN IN
TIME. GEORGES SAND AND
CHOPIN HAD PASSIONATE
ARGUMENTS HERE. FABULOUS
VIEW OF THE ISOLA DI SAN
GIORGIO*" – FIORA GANDOLFI ON
THE HOTEL DANIELI

....

HOTEL DANIELI

RIVA DEGLI SCHIAVONI 4196, CASTELLO
30122
☎ (41) 522 6480; FAX (41) 520 0208
Landmark seafront hotel, a stone's throw from Piazza San Marco. Despite the more modern annexes, its style and service remain as grand as ever. If you're in Venice during a feast day, eat on the rooftop terrace, overlooking the Grand Canal, and the incredible fireworks.

HOTEL MESSNER

DORSODURO 216, 30124
☎ (41) 522 7443; FAX (41) 522 7266
This hotel, in a Gothic palazzo dating from 1500, has just 20 rooms and a garden where you can eat with a view of the Canale della Salute. "*Here and there, just like in an old relative's house, you'll find collections of glass and other trinkets,*" says FIORA GANDOLFI.

METROPOLE

RIVA DEGLI SCHIAVONI 4149, 30122
☎ (41) 520 5044; FAX (41) 522 3679
Gold mosaics welcome you at the entrance, while inside you'll find over 2,000 antique furnishings in the 70 unique rooms.

⊛ PAUSANIA

DORSODURO 2824 (FONDAMENTA
GHERARDINI), 30123
☎ (41) 522 2083; FAX (41) 522 2989
This charming Gothic-style hotel has a beautiful staircase and includes many writers and artists among its clients. Good value.

PENSIONE ACCADEMIA

DORSODURO 1058, FONDAMENTA
BOLLANI PONTE DELLE MARVECE
☎ (41) 523 7846; FAX (41) 523 9152
It's difficult to find a room, but worth trying for the wonderful ambience and the beautiful garden overlooking the Grand Canal.

MUSIC

CHIESA DI SANTA MARIA DELLA PIETÀ

RIVA DEGLI SCHIAVONI, 30122
The church where Vivaldi used to play. Regular concerts celebrate his masterpieces and other baroque music.

RESTAURANTS

SEE ALSO HOTELS.

ANTICA LOCANDA MONTIN

DORSODURO 1147 (FONDAMENTA
EREMITE) 30123
☎ (41) 522 7131 AND (41) 522 3307
An old traditional restaurant with an inner gar-

AA Gill on Venice

Really chic people hate Venice. Truly tasteful people think it's gaudy, badly made, a confused hotchpotch, nothing more than a theatrical backdrop.

There has always been a type of rigorous, puritanical academic who has looked at Venice as a sort of baroque, Italian version of Coney Island. They are the sort of people who when they die will point out to St Peter that the pearly gates have the wrong sorts of pilasters and that there are just too many pearls. But for you and me – travellers – Venice is as close to being the vision of God's hometown on earth as we are ever likely to see.

Yet Venice is far from godly. In one small square of recycled marsh there is corruption, vice, usury and greed hidden under the most lustrously beautiful covering of art and architecture ever made. If a Martian stopped by on a tour of the galaxy and said he only had a day to understand humanity, I'd tell him to spend it in Venice – all human life is represented there.

If you are not arriving by flying saucer or yacht, then the best way to arrive is by plane and take a water taxi to the city. Venice is a city that was built and paid for by the sea, by trade founded, so the loyal legend goes, by the original Romans escaping the Visigoths and Huns after the collapse of empire. They hid in the reeds and creeks on the northern Italian coast and started to fish and then to trade. Venice's first fortune was made from the east when it traded with Constantinople.

The domes and cupolas swim out of the mist, familiar yet astonishing. There are those who think that the greatest sights in the world are made by wind, rain and small seeds, and then there are those who think that there isn't a mountain or canyon in the world that can compare with a late Renaissance city putting on its best face. Venice is the greatest of all works of nature because it is human nature.

But then there's the smell in the summer. Venice has a uniquely corrupt decomposing smell, an ancient, elaborate, diseased odour which constantly reminds you of the essential contradiction at the heart of the place. It is unsurpassed beauty built on sin.

There are two things to bear in mind when in Venice: one, you won't see everything, and

two, you'll get lost. It's best to get lost as soon as possible because that's when you'll come across the things that you weren't going to see, because you can't see everything. Although Venice is built on water you spend most of your time walking and it's best not to go in large groups. Leave the Mongol hordes being collected by umbrella-wielding guides in St Mark's Square. But don't go on your own – you simply have to have someone to say "My God, look at that" to. Venice, of course, is one of those earmarked, ringed, asterisked spots in the world that are designated for couples. A city for lovers – perhaps not so much honeymoons as illicit affairs: Venice is for mistresses. Indeed, it once had the most highly organized leagues of prostitutes and courtesans in Europe.

Assuming that you bring your own live pleasure, don't expect too much libidinous help from the food. Venetian cooking is Italy's poor relation. That said, it is still Italian and you'll eat better than in 90 per cent of the rest of the world. The grand hotels all have good restaurants. Try the roof of the **DANIELI** and the garden of the **CIPRIANI** and, of course, there's **HARRY'S BAR**, home of the Bellini. People have mixed feelings about Harry's Bar – it does have the rudest waiters west of Hong Kong – but they can also be utterly charming. Eat simply – some of the best food is stuffed bread and cakes from the little bakers in side streets.

Recommending things is like trying to go through your address book picking friends for a life raft. See what you can. First, from the Grand Canal take a vaporetto from the Bridge of Sighs to the Rialto and St Mark's because you have to. Of the rest, the Carpaccios, the Bellini altar, Canova's tomb and Tintoretto's extraordianry St Rocco, and the outer islands are, in my opinion, highlights.

Venice is now a tourist city; the harbour no longer welcomes the wealth of the East. Tourists are like most things in Venice, good and bad, they pay for it and they wear it out and you will be one of them. Apart from a lot of art and a load of people, what you see most in Venice are masks and caricatures of the Commedia dell'Arte. In a city that makes you look for an allegory in everything, they are strangely disturbing and appropriate.

den full of character where you eat classic Venetian fish and pasta dishes.

CARAMPANE

SAN POLO 1991 (RIO TERRÀ CARAMPANE), 30125

☎ (41) 524 0165

This old *osteria* is famous for its roast fish, vongole alla savonarda (clams with grated cheese) and traditional small puddings.

CORTE SCONTA

CASTELLO 3886 (CALLE DEL PESTRIN, ARSENALE), 30122

☎ (41) 522 7024

Fresh, flavourful fish from the lagoon cooked in the simplest way.

DA FIORE

CALLE DEL SCALETER 2202, (SAN POLO) 30125

☎ (41) 721308; FAX (41) 721343

A Venetian institution, serving fresh fish, great risotto and rich puddings, such as warm chocolate cake. You need to book at least a week in advance. PAUL HENDERSON is a fan: "*All things considered, our favourite restaurant in Venice. One of the best wine lists in town.*"

FIASCHETTERIA TOSCANA

CAMPO SAN GIOVANNI CRISOSTOMO 5719, CANNAREGIO 30131

☎ (41) 528 5281; FAX (41) 528 5521

One of the city's best and most charming restaurants, with a strong local clientele. "*Wonderful fish dishes,*" reports MARCELLA HAZAN.

LOCANDA CIPRIANI

PIAZZA SANTA FOSCA 29 ISLAND OF TORCELLO, 30012

☎ (41) 730150; FAX (41) 735433

Homely and tranquil island atmosphere and deliciously simple cooking continues to be intensely appealing. Ernest Hemingway wrote *Across the River and Into The Trees* while a guest in one of the Locanda's few rooms. The cooking is based on flavours and what's in season. "*Also associated with Harry's, great dining in the garden,*" says PAUL HENDERSON. "*A wonderfully romantic place. The setting is unique and the food very good*" – JULIAN LLOYD WEBBER. Open Mar–Nov.

RISTORANTE AI DUE VESCOVI

CALLE FIUBERA 812, SAN MARCO 20124

☎ (41) 523 6990

Rather grand Venetian *ristorante*, serving fine Italian and international fare. There is also an excellent vegetarian menu.

🖐 RISTORANTE DA IVO

SAN MARCO 1809 (CALLE DEI FUSERI), 30124

☎ (41) 528 5004; FAX (41) 520 5889

Small, unassuming, homely restaurant, serving simple Venetian cooking. "*We've only eaten here once, when they were generous with tartufi bianchi, which makes me want to go back. I'm also happy that Michael Winner doesn't like it,*" comments PAUL HENDERSON.

🖐 RISTORANTE VINI AL COVO

CAMPIELLO DELLA PESCARIA, CASTELLO 3968, 30122

☎ (41) 522 3812

Atmospheric restaurant serving traditional Venetian food and a great wine list. Three generations of the same family have worked here. The cooking is very healthy – no MSG, no animal fats, nothing canned and the fish is always fresh. Particularly good value at lunch.

TRATTORIA ALLA MADONNA

SAN POLO 594 (RIALTO), 30125

☎ (41) 522 3824

They've never heard of *nouvelle cuisine* at Alla Madonna. The place is crowded and bustling and serves classic middle-class dishes. "*It's a very Venetian experience to eat here,*" comments FIORA GANDOLFI.

TAVERNA LA FENICE

SAN MARCO 1939 (CAMPO SAN FANTIN), 30124

☎ (41) 522 3856; FAX (41) 523 7866

Located next to the remaining ashes of the recently burned-down Teatro La Fenice and serving traditional Italian dishes. Soft lighting and pink tablecloths give it a very romantic atmosphere.

SHOPPING

BARBARIA DELLE TOLLE

CASTELLO 6657, 30122

☎ (41) 522 3110

Masks in papier-mâché and leather are perfect reproductions of the masks of the commedia dell'arte.

BOTTEGA VENETA

SAN MARCO 1337, (CALLE VALLARESSO), 30124

☎ (41) 522 0409

"*We all know and love the beautifully made leather items from Bottega Veneta, distinguished not only by their initials but often by the woven work. You'll find a good selection here* – LOGAN BENTLEY.

CENERENTOLA
Rio Terrà Nomboli, San Polo
2600/A, 30125
☎ (41) 523 2006
The lampshades here are all made from precious antique fabrics or embroidered bed linens from the 19C.

CODOGNATO
San Marco 1295 (Calle dell' Ascensione), 30124
☎ (41) 522 5042
A prestigious jeweller. Jackie Kennedy Onassis loved this shop, especially its collection of 20s Art Deco pieces.

LIBRERIA FILIPPI
Castello 5284, (Calle Casselleria), 30122
☎ (41) 523 6916
Specializes in books about Venice, ranging from history and art to curiosities and secrets.

LIVIO DE MARCHI
San Samuele 3157/A (near Palazzo Grassi) 30124
☎ (41) 528 5694
This witty and inventive sculptor has made everything including a sculpted wooden shirt for the Emporio Armani window in London. It's the shop *"for those who love to bring back something special and unusual from their trip, even if it won't fit in the suitcase,"* suggests LOGAN BENTLEY.

LUCIO BUBACCO
San Polo 1077A, 30125
☎ (41) 522 5981; FAX (41) 522 5562
Galleria Bubacco, Calle Frutaroli, San Marco 1845, 30124
☎ (41) 423 9494
Works of art in glass made by Lucio Bubacco where human figures, devils, and representatives of mythology twist around the form.

NORE'LENE
Calle della Chiesa, San Vio 727, (Dorsoduro) 30123
☎ (41) 523 7605
Silks and velvets printed or painted by hand and made into capes, jackets, hats and shoes.

PANIFICIO VOLPE
Cannaregio 1143, Calle Ghetto Vecchio, 30123
☎ (41) 715178
Traditional Jewish pastries (made by Christians). You'll find gazelle horns full of almond paste, and tiny sugar candies like solar disks.

TESSUTI MANFROTTO
Via Andrea Gritti 36 (near Piazza Erbe), 35122
☎ (49) 655435
Three brothers – Egidio, Alberto and Francesco – along with their mother, Adele – sell samples of silk, linen, velvet and brocade, including *haute couture*, sold at fixed sale prices.

••

*"IF YOU CAN'T STOP
ANYWHERE ELSE, DON'T MISS
THIS SHOP"* – LOGAN BENTLEY ON
VENETIUM STUDIUM

••

VENETIA STUDIUM
San Marco 2425, Calle Larga 22 Marzo 2403, 30122
☎ (41) 522 9281
Here you'll find the fascinating, minutely pleated Fortuny silks and lampshades meticulously reproduced. Classics that will last for a lifetime.

VITTORIO COSTANTINI
San Polo 2603 (Ai Frari), 30125
☎ (41) 717719
Ultra-realistic scarabs, dragonflies, flies, ants, butterflies of all colours, set in glass. *"Perfect gifts for the hard-to-surprise,"* thinks FIORA GANDOLFI.

Rest of Italy

FESTIVALS

ARENA DI VERONA
Ente Arena, Piazza Brà 28, 37121 Verona
☎ (45) 590 109 AND (45) 596 517; INFORMATION AND CREDIT CARD RESERVATIONS ☎ (45) 800 5151
One of the largest and best preserved of the Roman amphitheatres, dating from the 1C AD, the Arena is host to the annual July–Aug festival season of opera and ballet. Bring a cushion, a picnic, lots of drinks and binoculars.

BATIGNANO MUSICA NEL CHIOSTRO
Santa Croce, 58041 Batignano Grosseto
☎ (564) 38096
Late July–Aug festival of forgotten or rarely aired operas, revived in the cloisters of a semi-ruined convent.

FESTIVAL DEI DUE MONDI

Via del Duomo 7, Spoleto
Box office ☎ (743) 44097; information ☎ (743) 44097
Tickets/information also from Via
Margutta 17, 00187 Rome
☎ (6) 321 0288
Italy's best performing-arts festival, founded by
composer Gian Carlo Menotti. Crowds gather
in late June–July as Spoleto rings with the
sounds of concerts, drama, opera and ballet.

ROSSINI OPERA FESTIVAL

Via Rossini 37, 61100 Pesaro
☎ (721) 697360; information ☎ (721)
30161; fax (721) 30979
A celebration of Rossini's work, held during
Aug in his birthplace. First-class productions,
particularly of his lesser-known operas.

STRESA MUSICAL WEEKS

Settimane Musicali, Palazzo dei
Congressi, Via R Bonghi 4, 28049
Stresa
☎ (323) 31095
Month-long festival (Aug–Sept) of classical music
set in a picturesque lakeside town, featuring international as well as up-and-coming local artists.

HOTELS

IL BACCHINO

Via Bobolino Torreone 126, 52044
Cortona, Arezzo
☎ (575) 603284
Beautiful 17C villa with only four bedrooms,
each of which overlooks the flower-filled gardens. Lovely swimming pool and exceptionally
well-stocked wine cellar and delicious food.

BORGO SAN FELICE

San Felice, 53019 Castelnuovo
Berardenga
☎ (577) 359260
Charming holiday village set in the peaceful
and picturesque wine-producing hamlet of San
Felice near Siena. The russet-roofed medieval
buildings have been restored to form the main
hotel.

CASTELLO DI SPALTENNA

Spaltenna, Gaiole in Chianti, 53013
Siena
☎ (577) 749483
Medieval fortified monastery with Romanesque
chapel attached, beautifully converted into an
ultra-comfortable hotel. Here you can try some
of the most interesting, if unorthodox, food in

this part of Italy. Nice pool and convenient location for visiting the local vineyards.

CERTOSA DI MAGGIANO

Strada di Certosa 82, 53100 Siena
☎ (577) 288180
A mile outside the city walls, a small hotel built
around the 14C cloisters and tower of Tuscany's
oldest Carthusian monastery. Beautiful reception rooms decorated with fresh flowers and
frescoes are quite the place for afternoon tea.
Nice swimming pool and fine Italian food.

HOTEL IL PELLICANO

Calei dei Santi, 58018 Porto
Ercole
☎ (564) 833801
The hotel includes a series of individual bungalows hidden among the olive trees and lush landscape. Enjoy breathtaking views from the pool or
walk down to the sea and the mattress-covered
rocks via steps cut into the cliff. There is also a spa.

HOTEL PITRIZZA

Porto Cervo, Costa Smeralda,
07020 Sardinia
☎ (789) 91500
Luxury villas with a private beach and a superb
salt-water pool carved into the rocks. Take a
boat to the nearby private island of Mortorio.

HOTEL POSTA MARCUCCI

Bagno Vignone, 53027 Siena
☎ (577) 887112
Small, family-run hotel with its good home
cooking and hilltop position. "*Nothing beats
floating in the naturally heated swimming pool (98°
F) especially in the evening with the stars overhead,*"
reminisces LOGAN BENTLEY. Stock up on the
excellent local wine.

HOTEL SPLENDIDO

Viale Baratta 13, 16034 Portofino
☎ (185) 269551
Rose-pink villa with green shutters, once a
monastery and later a private home, and now
the Italian Riviera's finest and most romantic
hotel. Dreamy views from the bedroom terraces. There's also a saltwater swimming pool
built into the hillside, several tennis courts and
excellent traditional Ligurian cuisine.

HOTEL VILLA CIMBRONE

Via Santa Chiara 26, 84010 Ravello
☎ (89) 857459
The beautiful grounds, the breathtaking coastal
views and the villa created by Lord
Grimthorpe, are three good reasons to stay

here. In the past, Bloomsburys, musicians, writers, royals have all been guests.

HOTEL VILLA CIPRIANI

VIA CANOVA 298, ASOLO, 31011
TREVISO
☎ (423) 952166
In the medieval walled town of Asolo, set in the foothills of the Dolomites, this hotel – a peaceful and luxurious 16C villa once the home of Robert Browning – is immaculately run by Giuseppe Kimenir. Fabulous service, wonderful cooking using fresh vegetables from the garden, and beautiful views.

••••••••••••••••••••••••••••••••••••••

"THE MOST WONDERFUL RESORT IN THE WHOLE OF APULIA, IF NOT ITALY. IT'S BETTER THAN OWNING A PIECE OF PROPERTY HERE" – FAITH WILLINGER ON *IL MELOGRANO*

••••••••••••••••••••••••••••••••••••••

IL MELOGRANO

CONTRADA TORRICELLA 343,
MONOPOLI, APULIA 70043
☎ (80) 690 9030
Beautiful old farmhouse lovingly restored by antique dealer Camillo Guara and now a lavish resort and spa. Fine cuisine for dieters and foodies alike in the Michelin-starred restaurant. Tennis and other sporting pursuits are well catered for.

SPA DEUS GRAND HOTEL IL CLUB

VIA LE PIANE 35, CHIANCIANO TERME,
53042
☎ (578) 63232; FAX (578) 64329
One of the best known spa hotels. Run by Hungarian-born Christina Newburgh, it offers special diets, an indoor swimming pool, beauty treatments, a gym and lots of pampering.

VILLA D'ESTE

VIA REGINA 40, 22010 CERNOBBIO,
LAKE COMO
☎ (31) 511471
Old-fashioned luxury and grandeur in a 16C cardinal's palazzo set in large rambling gardens full of temples and follies. Previous owners have included the estranged wife of George IV and a Russian tsarina. Make sure you have a room with a balcony overlooking the lake. Endless opportunities for water sports on the lake, and there's an indoor pool too.

RESTAURANTS

SEE ALSO HOTELS.

FALCHETTO

VIA BARTOLO 20, PERUGIA 06100
☎ (75) 731775
Perugia is an ideal one-day car trip from Rome, and this is the perfect place to stop for lunch or dinner. Simple but delicious food. *"A popular restaurant. The risotto foglio, with tartufo and porcini mushrooms, was delicious and the house wine is great"* – GAY HOAR.

⊛ FONTE DEI FRATI

LOCALITÀ CASE SPARSE 294, 52044
CORTONA
☎ (575) 601370
Just outside Cortona, this unassuming restaurant sits by itself in the middle of the countryside and serves typical Tuscan fare. *"We stumbled across this place completely by accident; I couldn't believe it, I had one of the best meals ever in Italy, and at a very reasonable price. The presentation of each plate was beautiful and the house wine from Montepulciano was delicious,"* raves GAY HOAR.

SAN DOMENICO

VIA SACCHI 1, 40026 IMOLA
☎ (524) 29000
A contender for the best restaurant in Italy. Chef Valentino, who was taught by the chef of the last king of Italy, produces regal food at majestic prices.

TRATTORIA LA BUCA

VIA GHIZZI 3, 43020 ZIBELLO (PARMA)
☎ (524) 99214
Miriam Leonardi follows on from several generations of fine chefs and this particular trattoria is a fine advertisement for the food of Parma.

VIPORE

PIEVE SANTA STEFANO, LUCCA 55100
☎ (583) 59245
It's hard to find, so ring for directions. It is on the hilltop above the city, and has a big herb garden, so you can eat outside. *"I'm absolutely wild about it – the best Tuscan trattoria, period. The adjacent **Piano Bar**, which is open until 3 am, is much cheaper and is one of my favourite places,"* enthuses FAITH WILLINGER.

VISSANI

CIVITELLA DEL LAGO, STRADA STATALE
448, BASCHITODI
☎ (744) 950396
Creative cuisine in a cool classic setting. ALAIN

DUCASSE describes it as "*an incredible restaurant where the very Italian chef, Gianfranco Vissani, serves you delicious, crazy and original cuisine*".

SKI RESORTS

CORTINA D'AMPEZZO
DOLOMITES
Swankiest of the Italian resorts. All the first families of Italy ski here: former royals, the PIRELLIS, BUITONIS, CIGOGNAS and COLONNAS. The best hotels are the MIRAMONTI MAJESTIC and CRISTALLO HOTEL DE LA POSTE (whose bar and terrace is the place to hang out pre-dinner). Best restaurants are EL TOULA, EL CAMINETTO, the tiny IL MELONCINO and the lakeside MELONCINO AL LAGO.

JAPAN
Kyoto

HOTELS

IRAGIYA RYOKAN N
FUYACHO-ANEYAKOJI-AGARU, NAKAGYO-KU
☎ (75) 221 1136
Lovely, typical Japanese *ryokan* (traditional inn) established in 1818. Delightful rooms overlooking Japanese gardens.

TAWARA-YA
NAKAGYO-KU, FUYACHO, OIKE-SAGARU
☎ (75) 211 5566
Kyoto's most famous traditional inn, founded over 300 years ago. Zen-like simplicity throughout – the rooms have screens, tatami mats and futons, as well as unfettered views over peaceful private gardens – along with all modern comforts and good food.

RESTAURANTS

CHIHANA
NAWATE-HIGASHI-IRU, SHIJO-DORI, HIGASHIYAMA-KU
☎ (75) 561 2741
Small but superior *kappo* (good, authentic restaurant). Book ahead.

TEMPLES AND GARDENS

⊛ ENRYAKU-JI TEMPLE
MOUNT HIEI
An ancient centre of Buddhism, it is also the site of the Inextinguishable Dharma Light, which has been glowing for more than 1,200 years. Take the local bus from Kyoto station and get off at Shimeidake.

⊛ HEIAN SHRINE
Renowned for its gardens filled with cherry blossom.

⊛ KINKAKUJI TEMPLE
Replica of the early 15C Golden Pavilion sitting in peaceful water gardens. Don't miss the RYOANJI TEMPLE nearby.

⊛ KIYOMIZU TEMPLE
Very beautiful temple in the hills outside the city, hidden away (well, almost) by trees.

Osaka

HOTELS

HOTEL NEW OTANI OSAKA
4-1 SHIROMI, 1-CHROME, CHUO-KU
☎ (6) 941 1111
Great location next to Osakajo Castle Park and the Neyagawa River, where well-heeled Japanese and Westerners stay. A luxury hotel which caters for most whims with several restaurants, bars, swimming pools, tennis courts and a health club.

RESTAURANTS

CHAMBORD
AT THE ROYAL HOTEL, 5-3-68 NAKANOSHIMA, KITA-KU
☎ (6) 448 1121
First-rate French restaurant located on the 29th floor of the Royal Hotel, with panoramic views of the city and river.

KICCHO
2-6-7 KORAIBASHI, CHUO-KU
☎ (6) 231 1937
The most prestigious restaurant in Osaka, offering delicious food served amid beautiful *objets* and other treasures.

Tokyo

ART AND MUSEUMS

HARA MUSEUM
4-7-25 KITASHINAGAWA, SHINAGAWA-KU
☎ (3) 3445 0651
Owner–director Toshio Hara is a world authority on contemporary Japanese art, and his museum showcases the very best of it alongside works by most major Western artists.

HATAKEYMA COLLECTION
2-20-12 SHIROGANEDAI, MINATO-KU
☎ (3) 3447 5787
A private collection featuring paintings, calligraphy and sculpture, all of which celebrate the Japanese tea ceremony. Set in a traditional building with beautiful gardens.

NIHON MINKA-EN
7-1-1 MASUGATA, TAMA-KU, KAWASAKI-SHI
☎ (44) 922 2181
A showcase of homes that were brought here to save them from ruin. See how merchants, village chieftains and horse-traders once lived.

SUNTORY MUSEUM OF ART
SUNTORY BLDG, 11F, 1-2-3 AKASAKA, MINATO-KU
☎ (3) 3470 1073
Japanese *objets d'art* – the finest textiles, kimonos, lacquered objects, porcelain and paintings.

TOKYO NATIONAL MUSEUM
13-9 UENO KOEN, TAITO-KU
☎ (3) 3822 1111
Unsurpassed collection of Japanese and Asian art housed in four buildings.

BARS AND CAFES

BAMBOO
5-8-8 JINGUMAI, SHIBUYA-KU
☎ (3) 3407 8427
Off the main drag of fashionable Omote-Sando, have a café au lait and a sandwich on the terrace.

CAFE DE ROPE
6-1-8 JINGUMAE, SHIBYA-KU
☎ (3) 3406 6845
The original see-and-be-seen café on the Omote-Sando fashion strip.

GIGER BAR
5-14-19 SHIROGANEDAI, MINATO-KU
☎ (3) 3440 5751
Entertain your ghoulish side in Swiss artist H R Giger's macabre courtyard sipping horrifically named drinks such as Carcass and Cocoon of Sacrifice while sitting in a chair shaped like a skull.

RED THUNDER CAFE
SARUGAKU OHO 24-1, SHIBUYA-KU
☎ (3) 3462 4750
Restaurateur Junichi Matsumoto's café is the hang-out for Tokyo trendies. American-Indian decor, a well-stocked bar and Tex-Mex food prepared by two Romanian chefs.

SPIRAL CAFE
6F, SPIRAL BLDG, 5-6 MINAMI AOYAMA, MINATO-KU
☎ (3) 3498 5791
A real hotspot also renowned for its regular cutting-edge exhibitions. Afterwards, go for a wander through the Spiral Market on the 2nd floor.

CLUBS

ROPPONGI, AKASAKA and HARAJUKU are the trendy areas to go at night. (SHINJUKU and GINZA are filled with endless gaudy gay and transvestite clubs and hostess bars.)

THE BREAKFAST CLUB
MOTO-AZABU 3-12-32, CREST BIRU 1F, MINATO-KU
☎ (3) 3479 3032
For serious, all-night dancers. Opens at 4 am and rocks through breakfast until about 10 am.

ENDMAX
3-4-18 HIGASHI AZABU, MINATO-KU
☎ (3) 3586 0639
Major dance venue. Large floor, several bars and a hip-hop crowd.

JAVA JIVE
B2, ROPPONGI SQUARE BLDG, 3-10-3 ROPPONGI, MINATO-KU
☎ (3) 3478 0087
Live reggae/salsa/calypso music with traditional disco rhythms in between. Caribbean and Thai food upstairs. Highly recommended.

LEXINGTON QUEEN
B1, 3RD GOTO BLDG, 3-13-14 ROPPONGI, MINATO-KU
☎ (3) 3401 1661
Proprietor and society columnist Bill Hersey's

stellar club. If there's a big name in town, you can bet they'll wind up here. Unless you're a superstar it's strictly couples only.

HOTELS

AKASAKA PRINCE

1-2 KIOI-CHO, CHIYODA-KU, 102

☎ (3) 3234 1111

Modern 40-storey building designed by Kenzo Tange, providing cool, comfortable and crisp accommodation. Sip cocktails and absorb the Tokyo skyline in the **TOP OF AKASAKA** bar.

CAPITOL TOKYU

2-10-3 NAGATA-CHO, CHIYODA-KU

☎ (3) 3581 4511

Popular with foreign executives and visiting stars. Comfortable, though slightly austere rooms, nice outdoor swimming pool. Have breakfast in the **ORIGAMI CAFÉ**.

HOTEL OKURA

2-10-4 TORANOMON, MINATO-KU

☎ (3) 3582 0111

Top Tokyo hotel with everything from shops and bars to a couple of swimming pools, a photo studio and a tea-ceremony room. Visit the **OKURA ART MUSEUM** within the hotel grounds with exhibits of antique porcelain, mother-of-pearl and ceramics. "*It is so completely comfortable. They also have tatami rooms – more cerebral, but less comfortable,*" advises STEPHEN JONES. Wonderfully efficient service.

HOTEL SEIYO

1-11-2 GINZA, CHUO-KU

☎ (3) 3535 1111

Boutique hotel with 80 luxury suites and supremely attentive staff. Proper English and American breakfasts. Dine in one of the superb restaurants which includes a branch of Osaka's **KICCHO**. "*Hotel Seiyo is the best in the world – immaculate service, wonderful rooms,*" reckons JEFFREY ARCHER.

IMPERIAL HOTEL

1-1-1 UCHISAIWAICHO, CHIYODA-KU

☎ (3) 3504 1111

The ultimate hotel for top foreign financiers, particularly the younger European set, who hang out at the **OLD IMPERIAL BAR**.

MUSIC

OJI HALL

4-7-5 GINZA, CHUO-KU

☎ (3) 3564 0200

Great concert hall in central Ginza. Top classical acts.

SUNTORY MUSIC HALL

1-13-1 AKASAKA, MINATO-KU

☎ (3) 3505 1001

The world's most technologically advanced concert hall, with astounding acoustics.

RESTAURANTS

SEE ALSO HOTELS.

IL BOCCALONE

1-15-9 EBISU, SHIBUYA-KU

☎ (3) 3449 1430

Rustic Roman trattoria that's popular for its traditional country cuisine cooked by Italians.

CAY

5-6-23 MINAMI AOYAMA, MINATO-KU

☎ (3) 3498 5790

Located in the basement of the Spiral Building, this Thai restaurant/bar is also a performance space. SADE has eaten and sung here.

DAIGO

2-4-2 ATAGO, MINATO-KU

☎ (3) 3431 0811

Small traditional Japanese house in the gardens of a Buddhist temple, where traditional vegetarian cuisine is served in private tatami rooms.

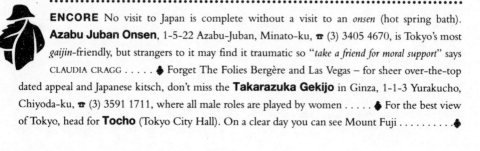

ENCORE No visit to Japan is complete without a visit to an *onsen* (hot spring bath). **Azabu Juban Onsen**, 1-5-22 Azabu-Juban, Minato-ku, ☎ (3) 3405 4670, is Tokyo's most *gaijin*-friendly, but strangers to it may find it traumatic so "*take a friend for moral support*" says CLAUDIA CRAGG . . . . . ♦ Forget The Folies Bergère and Las Vegas – for sheer over-the-top dated appeal and Japanese kitsch, don't miss the **Takarazuka Gekijo** in Ginza, 1-1-3 Yurakucho, Chiyoda-ku, ☎ (3) 3591 1711, where all male roles are played by women . . . . . ♦ For the best view of Tokyo, head for **Tocho** (Tokyo City Hall). On a clear day you can see Mount Fuji . . . . ♦

DAINI'S TABLE

6-3-14 MINAMI AOYAMA, MINATO-KU
☎ (3) 3407 0363
Elegant Chinese restaurant with dark green contemporary Chinese decor. "*Great service, great food. There's always someone interesting eating there*" – JUDITH GREER.

FUKUZUSHI

5-7-8 ROPPONGI, MINATO-KU
☎ (3) 3402 4116
The ultimate Japanese restaurant for power-brokering big-wigs. Tempura, chirashizushi (rice with raw fish) and a marvellous traditional sushi bar where you can roll your own. "*Those jaded by sushi will still be thrilled by this*," believes CLAUDIA CRAGG.

INAKAYA

784 ROPPONGI, MINATO-KU
☎ (3) 3405 9866
"*When you walk in, everyone screams at you. Everyone – diners, chefs and staff – lets their hair down. You order the 'robatayaki' – grilled fish, vegetable, etc – and it is passed to you on paddles by smiling, headband-wearing waiters. A crazy, noisy, delicious restaurant*" – CLAUDIA CRAGG.

ISSHIN

4-21-29 OMOTESANDA
☎ (3) 3401 7991
On the 4th floor of a building in Tokyo's Champs Elysées, is this *nouvelle cuisine* establishment that offers 5- and 7-course (almost) authentic French meals. The set lunch is a bargain.

KATSU KICHI

1-21-12 CHINYOKO-DORI
☎ (3) 3841 2277
This establishment fries up everything from fish roe to chocolate. Some combinations take a strong stomach. Not cheap but very exciting and high-tech.

KIHACHI

4-18-10 MINAMI AOYAMA, MINATO-KU
☎ (3) 3403 7477
Brasserie-style eatery, specializing in seafood.

KISSO

BASEMENT, AXIS BLDG, 5-17-1
ROPPONGI, MINATO-KU
☎ (3) 3582 4191
The best deal for kaiseki cuisine. "*Your best bet is to trust what seasonal specialities the chef serves you*," advises MICHAELA KENNEDY. CLAUDIA CRAGG adds, "*Exquisite Japanese food in a relaxed laid-back environment.*"

L'ORANGERIE

HANAE MORI BLDG, OMOTESANDO,
3-6-1 KITA AOYAMA
☎ (3) 3407 7461
Still popular, elegant dining room on the 5th floor of fashion designer Hanae Mori's building. Delicious Sunday buffet brunch.

⊛ SHINODA SUSHI

SHIN SAKAE-DORI
☎ (3) 3597 9140
One way to avoid the often inflated price of the best sushi is to go to Shinoda Sushi. This delightful sushi-ya offers everything from a cheap set-lunch special to an equally inexpensive evening meal.

SHUNJU-NO-HIBIKI

4-7-10 NISHI AZABU, MINATO-KU
☎ (3) 5485 0020
Eat at the bar or sit down to a light meal of Korean/Japanese food with some Western twists. "*Represents Tokyo of the 90s; not brash or high-tech, but returning to a more traditional feel, yet still chic*," says JUDITH GREER.

SUSHISEI

1F SMOKESTONE BLDG, 7-14-15
ROPPONGI, MINATO-KU
☎ (3) 3403 5680
Expensive institution. "*The best sushi. Japanese 'talento' – young starlets et al. – love to be seen here because they know it's such a big hit with trendy and rich foreigners*," explains CLAUDIA CRAGG.

VOLGA

3-5-14 SHIBA KOEN, ROPPONGI,
MINATO-KU
☎ (3) 3433 1766
If you're all sushied out, hit the vodka and caviare in true ethnic style, served by Russian waitresses.

⊛ ZAKURO

B1, NIHON JITENSHA KAIKAN 1-9-15
AKASAKA, MINATO-KU
☎ (3) 3582 2661
This shabu-shabu restaurant is part of a chain that offers great food and good prices. Various fondue-style all-you-can-eat specials.

SHOPPING

While the major stores are scattered here and there, **NIREKE-NO-TORI** is where you'll find designer darlings Yohji, Comme des Garçons, Issey Miyake, Chantal Thomas and Emporio Armani. In the **SONET AOYAMA BUILDING** there's Ferré, Sonia Rykiel and Missoni, and if you stroll down **KILLER DORI** in Aoyama you'll find some of the best Japanese, as well as Western, designer fashion. In the **COLEZIONE BUILDING** there's Gianni Versace, Cassina furniture and Verry, but if it's funky young fashion you're after, head down to the Jinnan 1-chome section of **SHIBUYA**.

ADAM ET ROPE

4-6-4 SHIROKANEDAI, MINATO-KU
☎ (3) 3444 2421
The best fashion from around the world. Stop off at **STUDIO CAFÉ** on the 3rd floor for a light lunch on the balcony.

AXIS

5-17-1 ROPPONGI, MINATO-KU
☎ (3) 3587 2781
Living/design/concept store. The best in minimalist furniture.

FROM 1ST BLDG

5-3-10 MINAMI AOYAMA, SHIBUYA-KU
One of the best examples of Tokyo's up-scale vertical malls, housing a collection of top Japanese designer boutiques. Take a break at the trendy **CAFÉ FIGARO**.

LAFORET

1-11-6 JINGUMAE, SHIBUYA-KU
☎ (3) 3475 0411
One of the first boutique buildings, showcasing Japanese designers and reasonably priced young fashion. Check out the avant-garde **LAFORET MUSEUM** on the 5th floor.

NUNO

B1, BLDG AXIS, 5-17-1 ROPPONGI, MINATO-KU
☎ (3) 3582 7997
The best and most beautiful traditional fabrics. Hand-painted and silkscreen-printed kimono silk, cut in lengths.

PARCO

15-1 UDAGAWA-CHO, SHIBUYA-KU
☎ (3) 3464 5111
The place for committed style-seekers, a chic consumer paradise of one-stop designer boutiques. It even has its own exhibition space for big international shows, and a cinema and theatre.

SEIBU (GINZA)

2-1 YURAKUCHO, CHIYODA-KU
☎ (3) 3286 0111 AND BRANCHES
Top department store, with an English-language help service: ☎ (3) 3286 5482.

WAVE

6-2-21 ROPPONGI, MINATO-KU
☎ (3) 3408 0111
State-of-the-art hi-fi, music and designer store. Has expanded its 1st floor to include essential oils, incense, dolphin music and other New Age musts.

Rest of Japan

ART AND MUSEUMS

HAKONE OPEN AIR MUSEUM

KANAGAWA-KEN
☎ (460) 21161
Gorgeous galleries and gardens with the finest sculpture from Japan and around the world. Take the **ROMANCE CAR**, an open-top train, from Shinjuku in Tokyo.

HOTELS

FUJIYA HOTEL

359 MIYANOSHITA, HAKONE
☎ (460) 22211
The first Western-style hotel in Japan near Mount Fuji. For more traditional accommodation, the annexe, a former imperial villa, is now run as a *ryokan* (inn). The gardens are exquisite in May when the azaleas are in full bloom.

MIYAJIMA LODGE

MIYAJIMA
☎ (829) 442233
Set on a little island in Japan's inland sea outside Hiroshima, a beautiful country inn where PRINCE CHARLES has enjoyed the full Japanese experience. Visit Empress Suiko's 6C **ITSUKUSHIMA SHRINE** nearby.

SKI RESORTS

Ski like crazy at **NAEBA**, then bathe away the aches and pains in a steam bath. Fabulous pistes and hot water springs make the trip to **SAPPORO**, the north island of Hokkaido, worthwhile. The famous brewery is here (open to the public), and so is the celebrated annual Snow Festival. Great skiing and beautiful scenery are features of **ZAO**, in one of Japan's most spectacular natural parks.

Quentin Crewe on safaris in Kenya

The game parks of East Africa are now inclined to have more tourists than animals. The only moving things you can see in them are cars. The Mara, once the most rewarding area in Kenya, may at any one moment have as many as 2,000 tourists milling around. If anyone spots a lion, within minutes there are 40 Combi vans swarming around it. There is, however, a whole new way of visiting Kenya. I know three hotels of a private, almost secret kind, at any of which you may recapture that feeling of wildness that has all but vanished elsewhere.

First, at KIWAYU SAFARI VILLAGE, near Lamu, PO Box 55343, Nairobi, ☎ (2(503030, Fax (2) 503149, the emphasis of the place is on simplicity, an endeavour to create what one might call a comfortable Robinson Crusoe atmosphere. There are 18 large cabins with huge double beds, and they are totally private. The floors everywhere are covered with coconut matting. No one wears shoes. The sitting area beside the driftwood mahogany bar has tables but few chairs, merely piles and piles of colourful cushions. The food is as simple as everything else, but excellent: glorious lobsters and crabs and delicious fish, and the salads are superb. Despite the desert-island ambience, there is plenty to do: sailing, fishing, canoeing gently along the hushed and eerie channels through the mangrove swamps. But for many, the two long white beaches with no one on them are the greatest pleasure. Glorious picnics are organized on the island opposite – indeed, the hotel would be a perfect place for a honeymoon, for it is solitary without being lonely.

Inland in an area known as Laikipia is BORANA, c/o Tandala, PO Box 24397, Nairobi, ☎ (2) 568804, Fax (2) 564945, which is really a cattle ranch, though several thousand acres are left untouched for conservation purposes. Michael Dyer (whose family have owned land in Kenya since World War I) and his wife, Nikky, have built a small hotel in the middle of their land. It consists of six cottages and a communal area all sharing the wonderful view down to the plain with Mount Kenya beyond. There are interesting touches of Kenyan history woven into the place: many of the doors come from the old Castle Hotel in Mombasa; there are various traditional windows, also brought from the coast, and Arab-inspired brass bolts, handles and latches. There is a glazed verandah, furnished with vast leather chairs and sofas, with a wide view for armchair game and bird watching. At meals everyone eats at the same table and all the fresh supplies come from local farms. The real magic of Borana lies in the opportunity to wander freely, whether on foot, on horseback or by car, guided by unintrusive, knowledgeable people who ensure that you see as many as possible of the 40 or 50 kinds of animal, big and small, that are found here, and who can identify several hundred different birds.

Last, but far from least, is OL ARI NYIRO, c/o The Gallmann Memorial Foundation, PO Box 45593, Nairobi, ☎ (2) 520048, Fax (2) 521220, the 100,000-acre ranch belonging to Kuki Gallmann. After the violent deaths of her husband and of her only son, she created a foundation as a memorial to them. The first object of this foundation is to preserve the ranch as an ecological haven for wildlife and as a place for research. The second object is to educate. In a hidden corner of the ranch, hanging above the Mukutan Gorge, Kuki Gallmann has built three secluded rondavels. On arriving at the ranch by air or car, guests are encouraged either to walk or to ride by camel to the Retreat, as the hotel is known. The idea is to allow people to unwind. Each rondavel is built round a central chimney. The rooms are mostly open to the wild, including the bathrooms and loos, where you may look down and see animals at the salt lick without fear of being seen yourself. There are no locks on the doors, yet privacy is complete, as the ranch is limited to only one party at a time, however small. Again there is a pervading impression of simplicity, with so much varnished living rock, no curtains and a scattering of many local artefacts. But the real charm of the place lies in the certainty of seeing wildlife in total privacy, far removed from any modern distractions. The ranch is a sanctuary for black rhinos, though they are hard to see because of the thick bush in which they hide. But you cannot fail to see elephants, of which there are some 300 at any one time, and there is an abundance of other game. There is so much to do that it is hardly worth staying for fewer than four days.

Seoul

Seoul is a modern metropolis, but it is also the repository of over 600 years of Korean culture, reflecting the nation's proud, vast and vibrant heritage. As a result, some of the most interesting sites are the superb, ancient royal residences. TOKSUGUNG PALACE, now surrounded by a public park, is maintained as it was when the royal family lived there. THE NATIONAL MUSEUM OF KOREA, located in Kyonbbokkung Palace, houses great big bronze Buddhas, fantastic murals transplanted from ancient tombs, splendid gold artefacts and superb paintings, as well as the finest collection of Koryo celadon. And CH'ANGDOKKUNG PALACE contains royal costumes and weaponry from the last Korean dynasty.

If you want to get a feeling for Korea's more recent history, you can always go up to the demilitarized zone along the North Korean border, where American MPs and North Korean soldiers glare at each other across a narrow no-man's-land. It's a 45-minute drive from Seoul, past occasional bridges and the odd tank trap designed to slow down an invasion from the North. A glimpse of the DMZ will help you understand the driven nature of the Koreans. This is a country still technically at war. And if North and South Korea decide to merge again, like Germany, you'll always be able to say that you were there before they took down the barbed wire fence. Most hotels should be able to arrange a tour for you.

While you're in Seoul there is one thing you should eat, one thing you should drink and one place you should dance.

EAT: when in Seoul there's one thing you won't be able to avoid and that's Kimchi – the national dish. If your eyes water from tear gas, that will be nothing compared with what a mouthful of this stuff will do to you. Kimchi is a fiery pickled side dish and in its simplest form it is made of sliced Chinese cabbage, white radishes, garlic, salt and hot red peppers. It is also supposed to have amazing medicinal qualities, curing everything from cholesterol-clogged arteries to impotence. It's even said to give athletes a quick burst of energy like a sudden shot of caffeine.

DANCE: To get to the SEOUL CLUB you drive from Itaewon to the south side of the Han River, which is a newly fashionable part of Seoul built over the reclaimed river flats. The Seoul Club is a marvellous mix of kitsch, glamour and decadence that wouldn't have looked out of place in 30s Havana or Berlin. There is usually a band playing what was once called swing and a master of ceremonies almost as cadaverous as Joel Gray in *Cabaret*. He introduces a variety of torch singers, crooners and belters who perform in spangles and tuxedos from a spotlighted stage above a blue-lighted dance floor. A must see.

DRINK: When you do business in Seoul, be prepared to lift your glass. Known as the Irish of Asia, Koreans consume more alcohol per capita than any other nation (except the Russians, of course). Soju is what you should sip. It's a harsh, 90-proof rice liquor, but the local beer, OB, is better suited to Western tastes.

As far as the shopping goes, you'll find a lot more than plastic bits of rubbish so commonly exported to the West from South Korea. Among the infinite number of things you can buy at the NAMDAEMUN MARKET are silk, sunglasses and the great Oriental restorative root, in all its forms. There are folk medicines for whatever might be ailing you: dried chrysanthemum roots for headaches, rheumania root for heartburn, dried tortoise meat for lumbago and snake wine for impotence. There are also live turtles, eels, snakes and puppies – which can be purchased either as pets or for supper. (Eating dog is not illegal in Seoul, but the authorities have forbidden restaurateurs to serve dogmeat, in order to avoid offending tourists – it doesn't do anything for their soul.)

LAOS

The rush has started to get to Laos before it is "discovered". Just one hour's flying time from Bangkok, the place is, for the moment, still completely uncontaminated by capitalism. Fly into Vientiane's airport (on Thai International, please, not any of the other relics of Communism's attempts at aviation). You'll find everyone still getting around on bikes. As late as 1990, the country still had only one international telephone line. Vientiane itself is full of once-majestic French-colonial buildings. The main hotel, the **LANE-XANG HOTEL**, is the place to stay and a good base camp to visit the Buddhist wats (temples) and other holy shrines, such as the **PHA THAT LOUANG** (Great Sacred Stupa).

Outside Vientiane, you could take a boat trip up the Mekong, to **LOUANG PRABANG**, the old royal capital, 140 miles to the north. It has 30 or so wats (including **XIENG THONG**, the magnificent **GOLDEN CITY TEMPLE**, built in the mid 16C) and envelops **PHOU SI**, a steep hill with a shrine built during the 14C. Many of the older generation can still speak French and you can even buy baguettes in the markets. The place to stay without a doubt is the colonial-style **VILLA DE LA PRINCESSE**. Once the home of Crown Prince Khampha, but now returned to the rightful owners, it has been transformed into a lovely small hotel with only 11 rooms and an open-air restaurant which serves the very best Laotian food. Alternatively, try the **PHOU VAO HOTEL**, a Swiss–Laotian joint venture.

MALAYSIA

HOTELS AND RESORTS

CARCOSA SERI NEGRA
TASIK PERDANA, 50480 KUALA LUMPUR
☎ (3) 282 1888
Heavenly creation of Adrian Zecha, housed in a former British Governor's mansion. THE QUEEN stayed here on her last state visit. Wonderful curries are served on the terrace at weekends, and make use of the extremely skilled barman.

THE DATAI
0700 PULAU LANGKAWI ISLAND
☎ (4) 959 2500
The Datai lies on an isolated stretch of beach between the deep blue of the Andaman sea and 1,800 acres of luxuriant rain forest. Wonderful food – from Malaysian to Western – and consistently warm and attentive service.

EASTERN & ORIENTAL HOTEL
10 FARQUHAR ST, 10200 PENANG
☎ (4) 375322
Old colonial-style hotel once frequented by

Somerset Maugham and Noël Coward. Have a good dinner in the **1885 GRILL**.

RASA SAYANG HOTEL
BATU FERRINGHI BEACH, PENANG
☎ (4) 811811
Traditional Malay-style resort hotel with great leisure facilities and an excellent health centre.

REGENT OF KUALA LUMPUR
160 JALAN BUKIT BINTANG, 55100 KUALA LUMPUR
☎ (3) 241 8000
A favourite address in Kuala Lumpur, with big rooms and big suites. Every desirable health and exercise facility and every type of food.

SHANGRI-LA
11 JALAN SULTAN ISMAIL, 50250 KUALA LUMPUR
☎ (3) 232 2388
Glitziest and biggest hotel, with fine Japanese and Cantonese restaurants within. Great sports facilities. "*All around, it is the best hotel in KL with very fine restaurants too*" – CLAIRE BARNES.

TIOMAN ISLAND RESORT
TIOMAN ISLAND
☎ (4) 44544
Small, scenic island which provided the setting for *South Pacific*. Very accessible, with hopper flights from Singapore and Kuala Lumpur. Private bungalows by the beach offer you every comfort, while the hyperactive can have a round or two of tennis and enjoy the pool, hotel bicycles and several restaurants.

RESTAURANTS

DONDANG SAYANG
28 JALAN TELAWI LIMA, BANGSAR BARU
☎ (3) 254 9388
The place for *nyonya* cuisine – a local variation on Chinese and Malay food which uses traditional Chinese ingredients and local spices like chillies and coconut cream.

KAM LUN TAI
12–14 JALAN SULTAN, KUALA LUMPUR
☎ (3) 238 0845
The friendliest but noisiest *dim sum* restaurant in Kuala Lumpur – truly Chinese.

RIB CAGE
18 MODAN SETIA DUJA, DAMANSARA HEIGHTS, KUALA LUMPUR
☎ (3) 254 5435
This restaurant has good but uncomplicated

food, great grills and near-perfect steaks.

UNICORN SHARKIN SEAFOOD
1ST FL, LOT 10, JALAN SULTAN ISMAIL, KUALA LUMPUR
☎ (3) 244 1695
Serves the best shark's fin in town and is KL's most popular smart Chinese restaurant.

MAURITIUS

HOTELS

DOMAINE DU CHASSEUR
ANSE JONCHÉE, VIEUX GRAND PORT
☎ 631 9261; FAX 631 9261
300-acre sporting estate and nature reserve, offering deer stalking, deep-sea fishing, paragliding and various other adventurous activities. Rustic accommodation in the form of 10 thatched cabins and a truly excellent reataurant where everything on the menu, including the coffee, is produced on the property.

LA PIROGUE SUN HOTEL
WOLMAR, FLIC-EN-FLAC
☎ 453 8441; FAX 453 8449
Sparkling, spacious resort hotel offering all manner of watersports. "*Simple thatched bungalows in acres of tropical garden*" – GLYNN CHRISTIAN.

THE ROYAL PALM
GRAND BAIE, MAURITIUS
☎ 263 8353; FAX 263 8455
JACQUES CHIRAC and the KING AND QUEEN OF SWEDEN have all been seduced by the very exclusive and very discreet Royal Palm, with its white-gloved attendants who provide guests with freshly cut fruit and cool towels by the poolside. Big bedrooms, each with its own private terrace and filled with East Indian mahogany and wicker.

LE SAINT GERAN HOTEL
BELLE MARE
☎ 415 1825; FAX 415 1983
Grande dame of luxury Mauritian hotels. The public areas are vast, and the bedrooms rather smaller. Activities galore – every water sport under the sun, a miniclub for children and a casino. Some of the very finest cooking on the island.

SANDRANI HOTEL
BLUE BAY
☎ 637 3511; FAX 637 4313
Located right on the beach overlooking Blue Bay. Some find this friendler and cosier than its grander sister hotel, the Royal Palm.

NATURE PARKS

DOMAINE LES PAILLES
PAILLES
☎ 212 4225; FAX 212 4226
Situated at the foot of a mountain range, it includes beautiful gardens and the re-creation of a beautiful verandahed plantation house, a sugar cane mill, a rum factory and an equestrian centre. Visitors can use the swimming pool, mini-golf, the casino, and five different restaurants. These offer a diverse selection of local and European cuisine.

MEXICO

HOTELS

LAS BRISAS
CARRETERA ESCÉNICA 5255, ACAPULCO
☎ (74) 841580
Set high on a hillside across Acapulco Bay, Las Brisas is a secluded haven consisting of a luxury

ENCORE Because you will be facing not only exceptional heat but also saltwater, which is very corrosive, you will need to be fully equipped for your fishing trip. The following checklist will guide you:

● A four-piece travel rod, which can be broken down to carry-on size for air travel ● A high-tech fly-reel, together with a spare spinning outfit ● Special flies ● Strong lines ● A long peaked hat (a "flat-cap" with flaps to protect ears and neck), long-zippable trousers (doubling as shorts), flat wading boots ● Sunglasses, with sidepieces to protect your eyes from UV rays (these also help to spot fish) . . . . ♠

David Profumo on Fishing in Mexico

As more new destinations are opened up each year, marine flyfishing for exotic species has become something of an open secret among discerning anglers. They appreciate the unrivalled variety of sporting opportunities on offer when saltwater fly fishing. Over the past five years one particular area has become my favourite part of the world to go fishing, namely Ascension Bay, located in the Sian Ka'an Biosphere Reserve.

Set in the Yucatán Peninsua, the Sian Ka'an Biosphere Reserve covers 1,300,000 acres of tropical forest, savannahs, mangrove swamps, flats, keys, springs and coral reefs. Within the reserve, 296,000 acreas are oceanic, offering some of the finest light-tackle fishing in the Caribbean. Operated by the Mexican government, the Biosphere's stringent regulations restrict commercial angling. This includes a "catch and release" type policy, which will doubtless ensure great fishing for years to come.

There are two types of fishing to be found here. The first is blue-water, or offshore fishing, which is the quintessential Hemingway experience, floating in a big gin-palace style boat, behind which you trail lures for fish such as Striped Marlin, Blue Marlin, Dorado (or Dolphin Fish, also known as "the yellow-and-green fighting machine") or various species of tuna. To do this successfully you have to go a long way offshore, where you find the drop-offs into the marine trenches. The second type of fishing, developed since World War II and pioneered by many North American anglers, is called flats-fishing. When anglers refer to "fishing the salt", they tend to mean fly-fishing or very light-tackle bait fishing. This is done in shallow or "skinny" water, where you wade or get poled by a native guide in a special custom-built skiff. He will take you along the tidal saltwater flats, which lie usually between mangrove islands and off the coral reefs in the Caribbean.

In the Sian Ka'an Biosphere Reserve, there are three main places developed specifically for anglers of all ability. First there's **BOCA PAILA**, a diverse tropical sportfishing paradise. Beginners find Boca Paila one of the best places in the world to take their first bonefish on a fly, an elusive quarry which, for its size, is one of the most powerful fish in the world. Other species commonly caught include tarpon, snook and barracuda. Guests stay in comfortable cottages, each with a private bath, set among miles of palm trees beside the sandy beach. Non-angling guests are well-catered for, with snorkelling and scuba diving on the Palancar Reef, the home of more than 200 varieties of tropical fish. The lodge is owned by Paly Gonzalez and her family and is open all year round, but springtime offers the best angling.

CASA BLANCA is a secluded oasis, a hundred feet from the sea on Punta Pajaros at the southern end of Ascension Bay, offering fishing for the more experienced angler. Ascension Bay is particularly famous for its prolific bonefishing. Under the watchful eye of a local guide, explore the labyrinth of mangrove-rimmed lagoons or the Palancar Reef with its numerous species of exotic fish, including wahoo, dolphin and Spanish mackerel. American-owned and well located, the hotel has nine spacious, very comfortable bedrooms and in the evening you can wind down in the thatched-roofed lanai bar. The best fishing here occurs in June and July.

Finally, just four miles off Punta Allen on the Mexican Yucatán is **THE SEACLUSION**. Perched on a sand dune, the villa offers convenient access to protected lagoons, ocean flats and exciting offshore fisheries in specially designed flat skiffs manned by eagle-eyed local guides. The picturesque surroundings include your own private, tastefully decorated hacienda – indeed because The Seaclusion is self-contained it is only available to parties of four friends or a family. The delicious cuisine includes mouthwatering Mexican food, tropical fruits and seafood platters. The weekly package runs Sun–Sun throughout the year and provides a choice of fishing or just relaxing on the beach in a hammock.

For further details contact Frontiers International, ☎ (0171) 493 0798, Fax (0171) 491 9177. (Also see ENCORE opposite).

complex of small apartments and private *casitas*, each with its own swimming pool. Fresh hibiscus blossoms are floated on the surface of the pools each day.

FIESTA AMERICANA

CARRETERA AEROPUERTO, PUERTO VALLARTA

☎ (322) 42010

Tropical holiday resort. The pool encircles bridges, palm oases and palapa restaurants set on platforms over the water. Excellent food, especially the breakfast buffet by the pool. Every kind of water sport imaginable is laid on here.

HOTEL CANINO REAL OAXACA

CINO DE MAYO 300, OAXACA

☎ (951) 66666

Beautifully restored 16C convent, now a designated National Monument. The hotel is part of the Camino Real chain and has three courtyards, one of which, La Lavandería (the laundry), still has its original stone basin.

HOTEL LAS MANANITAS

RICARDO LINARES 107, CUERNAVACA

☎ (73) 141466

One of the finest hotels in Mexico, in a town 43 miles south of Mexico City. Much of the town is privately owned by the Mexican jet set, who come to their mansions here to get away from it all. Like the town itself, the hotel has a sumptuous, relaxed feel.

RESTAURANTS

EL CENTENARIO

REPUBLICA DE CUBA 79, MEXICO CITY

☎ (5) 521 2934

The talk of the town since it opened in 1993. Situated in the heart of the historic area downtown, a 17C mansion where you'll be served great Mexican food. In the lively street-level cantina you can enjoy drinks, *botanas* and old-time piano music.

FONDA EL REFUGIO

LIVERPOOL 166, ZONA ROSA, MEXICO CITY

☎ (5) 207 2732

Mexico City's most popular venue for genuine Mexican cuisine. The best dishes from each region are featured as is a mouthwatering display of home-made cream puddings which greets you. The menu varies daily. Ask for a table downstairs in the dining salon – this is the prettiest spot. Relaxed atmosphere.

MOROCCO

ART AND MUSEUMS

MUSEUM OF MOROCCAN ARTS

DAR BARTHA PALACE, PLACE DE L'ISTIQUAL, FEZ

Good collection of ancient Moroccan pottery, gold-thread embroidery from Fez, traditional rugs and carpets. Worth a visit.

THE OLD AMERICAN LEGATION

JUST INSIDE RUE DU PORTUGAL WALL OF THE MEDINA

America's very first ambassadorial residence, established in 1777 when Morocco recognized the newly independent United States. Inside this fascinating building is a broad sweep of exhibits covering the history of the city.

CHURCHES

ST ANDREW'S ANGLICAN CHURCH

RUE D'ANGLETERRE, TANGIER

An intriguing mix of Moorish and English culture. Inside, the Lord's Prayer is inscribed in

---

FEELING PEAKY In the summer months, any moderately fit person should experience the thrill of ascending the highest peak in North Africa, Djebel Toubkal in the High Atlas mountains. At 13,676 feet, altitude sickness is a distinct possibility, but with an official guide, a mule and stout shoes, the most you're likely to get is stiff calves and an enormous sense of achievement. Short and long treks can be organized from any travel agent, either before you go or after you've arrived in the High Atlas.

Arabic above the altar. The caretaker is usually happy to show people around.

HOTELS

••••••••••••••••••••••••••••••••••••••

*"A MAGICAL WALLED GARDEN
WHERE THE CARES OF THE
WORLD DISAPPEAR"* – ED VICTOR
ON *LA GAZELLE D'OR*

••••••••••••••••••••••••••••••••••••••

LA GAZELLE D'OR
PO Box 260, TAROUDANT
☎ (8) 852039
Morocco's most exclusive hotel where Northern Europeans seek sanctuary in the winter sunshine. The sprinkling of flower-clad bungalows and tented restaurants all share a panoramic view of the High Atlas Mountains. *"The owner, Rita Bennis, runs the hotel as though it were a country house party, and the group that assembles around the pool every morning is a kind of who's who of London life. It is not, incidentally, the place to be if you want to spend your holiday in more or less solitary confinement,"* says ED VICTOR.

HOTEL PALAIS SALAM
TAROUDANT
☎ (8) 852130
A quiet retreat for anyone who wants to remain at the heart of Taroudant. You may choose a room in one of the majestic towers, or perhaps in one of the garden pavilions.

HOTEL RIAD SALAM
RUE MOHAMMED DIOURI, OUARZAZATE
☎ (4) 882206
On the edge of the Sahara, this little town is a jewel: the heat is not too stifling, the people are welcoming and the surroundings are picturesque. The Riad Salam is built in the shape of a *riad* (an old Moroccan house). Great rooms, a beautiful garden with a large pool as its centrepiece, and delicious food in the traditional Moroccan restaurant.

HOTEL ROYAL MANSOUR
27 AVE DES F.A.R., CASABLANCA
☎ (2) 313011
A hotel with style, tradition and great amenities. French and Moroccan food are well represented, and keen golfers can join the trips organized by staff to courses throughout Morocco.

LA MAMOUNIA
AVE BAB JDID, MARRAKECH
☎ (4) 448981
La Mamounia wasn't Churchill's favourite hotel for nothing. The whole place is magnificent – as are the prices. Each room has a private terrace overlooking the hotel's exquisite gardens. There are several excellent restaurants, serving Moroccan, Italian, French and international food. The hotel also has a sauna, health club, *hammam*, casino, chic night club and exclusive shops. A real oasis.

••••••••••••••••••••••••••••••••••••••

*"OLD, PALATIAL – THEY SPOIL
YOU ROTTEN. GET A ROOM
OVERLOOKING THE POOL – THE
POOL IS THE BEST OF ANY
HOTEL"* – BEATRICE WELLES ON
LA MAMOUNIA

••••••••••••••••••••••••••••••••••••••

EL MINZAH
85 RUE DE LA LIBERTÉ, TANGIER
☎ (9) 935885
Universally acclaimed as Tangier's finest hotel, this is where Matisse painted his Morocco series. Once a private home, El Minzah is a refreshing antidote to the anonymous 5-star hotels everywhere else.

PALAIS JAMAI
BAB-EL-GUISSA, FEZ
☎ (5) 634787
A palace built in 1879, it has tranquil Spanish-style gardens, stunning views of Fez and fine architecture. The restaurant is known for its superb Moroccan cuisine and its belly dancers. Ask for a room with a view of the Medina.

RESTAURANTS

SEE ALSO HOTELS.

L'ANMBRA
47 ROUTE D'IMMOUZER, FEZ
☎ (5) 25177
A restaurant with an international reputation for serving some of the finest food Morocco has to offer.

LA MAISON ARABE
5 DERB FERRANE, MARRAKECH
☎ (4) 22604

Yakout's main rival, open Nov–Mar for food that is renowned throughout the city. The French patron uses the best local ingredients.

YAKOUT

79 SIDI AHMED SOUISSI, MARRAKECH
☎ (4) 441903
Undoubtedly one of the most fashionable restaurants in town. Sit on silk cushions and await a banquet of classic Moroccan food. "*You go down this alley and the restaurant is up on the roof where musicians are playing; the dining room is around a swimming pool with rose petals scattered everywhere. Absolutely incredible*" – SHEP GORDON.

THE NETHERLANDS
Amsterdam

ART AND MUSEUMS

AMSTELKRING MUSEUM

OZ VOORBURGWAL 40, 1012 GE
☎ (20) 624 6604
"Our Dear Lord in the Attic" is a hidden

TREKKING ON THE SUB-CONTINENT

The Indian sub-continent boasts some of the richest cultures and most majestic scenery to be found anywhere in the world. While some of the well-trodden routes have become rather spoilt with hordes of visitors invading them year after year, governments in the region have enforced various safeguards, restricting tourism. For example, in Mustang in **NEPAL**, which has only been open to foreign travellers since 1991, the Nepalese government has tried to protect the local people and environment by imposing strict rules and high trekking fees. This is one of Nepal's most exciting and undiscovered trekking areas (and will hopefully remain so for many years to come). Here you can follow the Kali Gandaki river via villages such as Tangbe – where you'll see black, white and red *chortens*, which typify the upper Mustang region – to the remote city of Lo Manthong.

BHUTAN is another country whose government has intelligently managed to keep out the masses by imposing restrictions on tourism. The best treks will take you through the most staggering scenery, such as the Chomolhari in the western reaches of Bhutan. This is one of the most pristine and ecologically untouched regions of the country. Bears, takin and sheep roam undisturbed and the semi-nomadic people of Tibeto–Burmese origin live in the high summer pastures tending their herds of yak. On the way you can visit wonders such as the fabled Tiger's Nest Monastery at Taktsang. The trekking in this area is tough going, so for something a little gentler head for the Gangtey Valley.

The tiny former kingdom of **SIKKIM**, nestled between Bhutan in the east and Nepal in the west, combines towering mountains, mystical monasteries, fluttering prayer flags and some of the best trekking in the world. Birdlife is prolific and in spring the valleys are covered in wild alpine flowers, from orchids and magnolias to forests of rhododendrons. If you go trekking here you'll also see Mount Kanchenjunga, the world's third highest mountain. For details on exclusive, tailor-made journeys to the Indian sub-continent, contact Steppes East Ltd, Castle Eaton, Cricklade, Wiltshire, SN6 6JU, England, ☎ (01285) 810267.

Roman Catholic chapel extending across the attics of three 17C canal houses. Figure out one of the many different ways to approach the "secret" chapel.

AMSTERDAM HISTORISCH MUSEUM

KALVERSTRAAT 92

☎ (20) 523 1822

Once a convent and later an orphanage, this building now houses a museum showing the historic development of the city. Charming entrance and courtyard, with a pleasant restaurant.

ANNE FRANKHUIS

PRINSENGRACHT 263

☎ (20) 556 7100

Here Anne Frank wrote her famous diary. Features a permanent exhibition on the continuing struggle against anti-Semitism. Open every day.

HEINEKEN BREWERY

STADHOUDERSKADE 78, 1071 ZD

☎ (20) 523 9436

Don't leave Amsterdam without visiting the original brewery of the world-famous Dutch beer Heineken.

JOODS HISTORISCH MUSEUM

JONAS DANIËL MEIJERPLEIN 2–4, 1011 RH

☎ (20) 626 9945

A complex of four synagogues built in the 17C and 18C, showing Jewish culture and the history of Judaism in the Netherlands from the 17C.

MUSEUM HET REMBRANDTHUIS

JODENBREESTRAAT 4–6, 1011 NK

☎ (20) 624 9486

Rembrandt lived here for 20 years during his most lucrative period. Old Masters galore fill this master's house, along with more than 250 etchings. Open daily.

NEDERLANDS SCHEEPVAART MUSEUM

KATTENBURGPLEIN 1

☎ (20) 523 2222

The largest collection of boats and maritime objects anywhere in the world, while a replica of the 17C Dutch East India ship *Amsterdam* is docked at the quay in front of the museum.

RIJKSMUSEUM

STADHOUDERSKADE 42, 1071 ZD

☎ (20) 673 2121

Here you will find the most complete collection of Dutch paintings from the 15C to the 19C, and the best collection anywhere of 17C Dutch painting. Leave time for the sculpture and some outstanding Delft pottery, ceramics, silver, glassware, lace and furniture. Open Tues–Sat 10 am–5 pm; Sun and holidays 1 pm–5 pm.

RIJKSMUSEUM VINCENT VAN GOGH

PAULUS POTTERSTRAAT 7, 1071 CX

☎ (20) 570 5200

The collection has been donated by Van Gogh's family and contains over 200 works including many sketches and early paintings, and some of his most famous works ever. Good shop stocking books, prints and cards relating to the exhibits. Open Tues–Sat 10 am–5 pm, Sun 1 pm–5 pm, Mon 10 am–5 pm, Easter to Sept.

STEDELIJK MUSEUM

PAULUS POTTERSTRAAT 13, 1071 CX

☎ (20) 573 2911

A collection of international paintings and sculptures dating from 1850 to the present day. "*Very good pieces by Kandinsky and Cézanne*," reports JULIAN LLOYD WEBBER. Open daily 11 am–5 pm.

VAN LOON MUSEUM

KEIZERSGRACHT 672

☎ (20) 624 5255

17–18C canal house with period furnishings, portraits and a formal French-style garden reveals how a wealthy Amsterdam family lived during the Dutch golden age. Open Mon 10 am–5 pm, Sun 1 pm–5 pm.

CLUBS

BOSTON CLUB

KATTEGAT 1, 1012 SZ

☎ (20) 624 5561

An exclusive, expensive nightclub for Amsterdam's 30-somethings at the Renaissance Hotel. Famed for its cocktails.

CLUB JULIANA

HILTON HOTEL, APOLLOLAAN 138, 1077 BG

☎ (20) 673 7313

Named after a former Queen of Holland, this is a more traditional discothèque attracting an older clientele.

IT DISCOTHEEK

AMSTELSTRAAT 24, IS

☎ (20) 625 0111

Probably the largest and most popular club in town, especially with the local trendies.

LIDO
MAX EUWEPLEIN 62
☎ (20) 620 1006
Slightly Bond-esque discothèque located downstairs from the Casino in Amsterdam. Evening dress required.

MAZZO
ROZENGRACHT 114
☎ (20) 626 7500
Small and intimate for the young and trendy, who want to dance all night to the latest music.

⊙⊙ ODEON
SINGEL 460
☎ (20) 624 9711
Large club in an old house by one of the canals, featuring an amiable mix of all kinds of dance music. Very popular with the young.

OP DE SCHAAL VAN RICHTER
REGULIERSDWARSSTRAAT 36
☎ (20) 626 1573
Small and cosy club on two floors with three bars and lots of space to sit and chat. Officially members only but unofficially smartly dressed people stand a chance of getting in.

SEYMOUR LIKELY 2
NZ VOORBURGWAL 161
☎ (20) 420 5062
Club set up by a group of artists, hence very strange, arty decor and atmosphere.

HOTELS

⊛ AMBASSADE HOTEL
HERENGRACHT 335–353, 1016 AZ
☎ (20) 626 2333
Set in 17C canal houses, this hotel is popular for its warm, authentically Dutch atmosphere and decor and its surprisingly good value. Best to book in advance.

AMERICAN HOTEL
LEIDSEKADE 97, 1017 PN
☎ (20) 624 5322
This is one of Amsterdam's most popular stopovers. The hotel's Art Nouveau-style CAFÉ AMERICA is now the trendy hangout for visiting and local glamorati.

AMSTEL INTER-CONTINENTAL HOTEL
PROFESSOR TULPPLEIN 1, 1018 GX
☎ (20) 622 6660
Built in 1866, this impressive-looking building is a favourite of KING JUAN CARLOS, JEREMY IRONS and WHITNEY HOUSTON. Wonderful food in LA RIVE restaurant overlooking the water and in summer you can sometimes have dinner in the chef's herb garden. Use the hotel's antique saloon boat to wend your way through the canals.

CANAL HOUSE
KEIZERSGRACHT 148, 1015 CX
☎ (20) 624 5182
Charming and elegant hotel with stunning views over the canal and an atmospheric bar. Great service. No children.

THE GRAND AMSTERDAM
OUDEZIJDS VOORBURGWAL 197, 1012 EX
☎ (20) 555 3111
A deluxe hotel based in the former city hall, between two canals. Recently renovated, it's now very exclusive, featuring a first-rate health spa and restaurants CAFÉ ROUX and THE ADMIRALTY overseen by Albert Roux.

HOTEL DE L'EUROPE
NIEUWE DOELENSTRAAT 208, 1012 CP
☎ (20) 623 4836
Amstel-side hotel, semi-encircled by a canal. The celebrated EXCELSIOR restaurant overlooking the Amstel offers top-quality French cooking.

ENCORE Amsterdam is a relatively small city laced with a fanlike pattern of 15–17C canals. Most points of interest lie within its central district. As a point of reference, begin each day in front of Centraal Station, where most trams and buses start their journey. The Amsterdam Tourist Office or VVV, Stationsplein 10, ☎ (6) 340 34066, fax (20) 625 2869, is also found here. The best way to start your visit is to take a canal-boat cruise. You'll find numerous excursion boats lined up in the inner harbour in front of Centraal Station. They leave every 15 minutes or so and the trips last from an hour to an hour and a half, weaving along the canals to various locations in and around the city . . . . ♦

HOTEL PULITZER

PRINSENGRACHT 315–331, 1016 GZ

☎ (20) 523 5235

This was converted from 24 narrow 17–18C gabled canal houses and has retained the character of a private house. Very charming.

HOTEL WASHINGTON

FRANS VAN MIERISSTRAAT 10, 1071 RS

☎ (20) 623 3373 (RECEPTION); ☎ (20) 679 6754 (RESERVATIONS)

"*Very, very useful to know . . . It is three town houses put together, only very slightly out of the city centre. You get your own key – it feels like you've got an apartment to yourself. The price is reasonable for anyone planning to spend some time there*" – JULIAN LLOYD WEBBER.

SEVEN BRIDGES

REGULIERSGRACHT 31, 1017 LK

☎ (20) 623 1329

Situated on one of the quiet little side canals, the interior is very stylish, with antique furniture in every bedroom. There are no public areas. Breakfast is served in your bedroom.

TORO

KONINGSLAAN 64, 1075 AG

☎ (20) 673 7223

A stylish and tasteful mansion next to Vondelpark. Beautifully decorated and with the feel of a country house. Reasonable room rates.

MUSIC

BEURS VAN BERLAGE

DAMRAK 62A

☎ (20) 627 0466

Formerly the city's stock and commodities exchange, it now houses the Netherlands Philharmonic Symphony Orchestra.

BIMHUIS

OUDE SCHANS 73–77

☎ (20) 623 1361/623 3373

The BIM House is a favourite venue for jazz. Concerts are performed in the amphitheatre Thurs–Sat.

CONCERTGEBOUW

CONCERTGEBOUWPLEIN 2–6, 1017 LN

☎ (20) 675 4411 (24 HR RECORDED INFO); ☎ (20) 671 8345 (BOX OFFICE)

Renowned for its fine architecture, high-quality acoustics and world-class orchestra under the baton of the gifted Riccardo Chailly.

HET MUZIEKTHEATER

WATERLOOPLEIN 22

☎ (20) 625 5455

Opened officially in 1986, it houses the Dutch National Ballet directed by Wayne Eagling, the Netherlands Opera and the foundation Het Muziektheater. Great night-time view of the river through the glass walls.

MELKWEG

LIJNBAANSGRACHT 234A

☎ (20) 624 1777

A well-thought out multimedia venue featuring concerts, dance, theatre, cinema and live music at least four times a week.

PARADISO

WETERINGSCHANS 6–8

☎ (20) 623 7348

Formerly a church, it is now the most prestigious house for rock, pop and rap music concerts in the Netherlands.

RESTAURANTS

SEE ALSO HOTELS.

BEDDINGTON'S

ROELOF HARTSTRAAT 6–8

☎ (20) 676 5201

All white, modern and minimalist interior, providing the backdrop for British chef Jean Beddington's unusual Japanese-influenced Franco–British cooking. Good service too.

BISTRO KLEIN PAARDENBURG

AMSTELZIJDE 59, OUDERKERK AAN DE AMSTEL

☎ (20) 963 1335

Excellent, well-established bistro – just over a mile outside Amsterdam. The French-influenced food is sophisticated and the atmosphere relaxed. Closed Sun and bank holidays.

CHRISTOPHE

L'ELIEGRACHT 46

☎ (20) 625 0807

A modern, stylish but intimate restaurant where chef Christophe Royer offers *nouvelle cuisine* at its best.

LE CIEL BLEU
at the Hotel Okura

FERDINAND BOLSTRAAT 333

☎ (20) 678 7111

Exquisite though expensive food served in this restaurant on the hotel's 23rd floor. Or, eat downstairs in the Japanese restaurant which contains a special sushi/sashimi room and a teppan yaki steak house.

LE GARAGE
RUYSDAELSTRAAT 54–56
☎ (20) 679 7176
Popular with the Amsterdam jet-set: fashion shows and other events are often held here.

LUCIUS
SPUISTRAAT 247
☎ (20) 624 1831
The most celebrated fish restaurant in Amsterdam.

MOLEN DE DIKKERT
AMSTERDAMSEWEG, 104A
☎ (20) 641 1378
A restaurant in an old windmill, in a lovely setting a bit out of town. Classic but very good French cooking carefully prepared by chef Didier Besnard.

THE SUPPERCLUB
JONGE ROELENSTEEG 21
☎ (20) 638 0513
Trendy place for lovers of experimental food and drink and for the cultural avant-garde.

DE TRECHTER
HOBBEMAKADE 63, 1071 XL
☎ (20) 671 1263
Book weeks ahead to nab one of the eight tables at this wonder of Amsterdam's gastronomic scene conducted by chef/owner Jan de Wit. The wine list is as long and distinguished as the waiting list. "*Trechter exceeded our expectations and it should have a distinction – the endive soup was wonderful,*" raves PAUL HENDERSON.

DE VIJF VLIEGHEN
SPUISTRAAT 294
☎ (20) 624 8369
The best place for traditional Dutch cooking. Good food and friendly atmosphere.

SHOPPING

First head to **DAM SQUARE**. Numerous streets lead away from this 12C square, which is also home to two of Amsterdam's main department stores, De Bijenkorf and Vroom & Dreesman. **KALVERSTRAAT** is the city's main pedestrian-only shopping street, where you'll find a variety of fashion, household and jewellery shops. For bric-à-brac and secondhand clothes, **WATERLOOPLEIN**

flea market is a must for all bargain-hunters (open Mon–Sat 9.30 am–5 pm). For plants and flowers, **BLOEMENMARKT**, on the Singel Canal (between Koningsplein and Muntplein), is definitely worth a visit – (open Mon–Sat 9.30 am–6 pm). Antique buffs should make their way to the **SPIEGEL QUARTER**, Nieuwe Spiegelstraat (this runs into Spiegelgracht, which makes up the main thoroughfare of the quarter), where over 150 antique shops can be found.

Rest of the Netherlands

ART AND MUSEUMS

FRANS HALS MUSEUM
GROOT HEILIGLAND, HAARLEM
☎ (23) 319180
Authoritative collection of 17C portraiture, still lifes, landscapes and decorative art. The highlight is, of course, Hals's eight group portraits of militia companies and regiments. There are modern works too, from the Dutch Impressionists to local working artists.

GEMEENTE MUSEUM
STADHOUDERSLAAN 41, THE HAGUE
☎ (70) 338111
Municipal museum with a world-famous collection of musical instruments and paintings by Mondrian.

MAURITSHUIS
KORTE VIJVERBERG 8, 2513 AB, THE HAGUE
☎ (70) 346 9244; fax (70) 365 3819
The Dutch Royal Picture Gallery was originally a nine-room palace, a small but perfect example of Dutch Palladianism built in 1636. It now houses a collection of outstanding paintings including some very important 15-16C Flemish masters, such as Rubens and Van Dyck.

RIJKSMUSEUM KROLLER-MULLER
HOUTKAMPWEG 6, 6731 AW OTTERLO
☎ (838) 21041
Based in the national park, De Hoge Velvive, but worth the trip. Particularly known for its fine collection of over 200 Van Gogh paintings, including *The Sunflowers*, *The Weaver* and *The Potato Eaters*, and French Impressionists. The sculpture garden includes pieces by Rodin, Moore and Hepworth.

CLUBS

CLUB EXPOSURE
WESTDUINWEG 232, THE HAGUE
☎ (70) 356 1289
The most popular club in The Hague, with special theme nights once a month.

NIGHTTOWN
WEST KRUISKADE 28, ROTTERDAM
☎ (10) 436 4020
Large band venue and *the* place in Rotterdam. Basement for private parties.

HOTELS

HOTEL DES INDES
LANGE VOORHOUT 54–56, 2514 EG
THE HAGUE
☎ (70) 346 9553
Grand, former baronial 19C palace, a favourite with diplomats visiting the nearby embassies. LE BAR, with its club-like atmosphere is a good place for quiet conversation. Classic French cuisine at LE RESTAURANT.

KASTEEL WITTEM
WITTEMER ALLÉE 3, 6286 AA
WITTEM-ZUID LIMBURG
☎ (4450) 1208
Historic medieval castle, 8 miles from Maastricht, and once a strategic site in the 80 Years War (16–17C), has more recently been used as a venue for discussing European issues such as the Maastricht Treaty. Twelve raftered bedrooms, including a suite in the tower.

RESTAURANTS

SEE ALSO HOTELS.

CHEZ PIERETTE
FREDERIKSTRAAT 56, THE HAGUE
☎ (70) 360 6167
The small and plain setting, complete with wooden tables, belies the exceptional food. The produce is fresh from France.

LE COQ D'OR
VAN VOLLENHOVENSTRAAT 25,
3016 BG, ROTTERDAM
☎ (10) 436 6405
Still going strong after well over 30 years, a highly regarded, if expensive, restaurant serving classic French cooking.

NEW ZEALAND
Auckland

HOTELS

HOTEL DU VIN
MANGATAWHIRI VALLEY
☎ (9) 233 6314
Only 40 minutes from Auckland, this rather glamorous hotel is set on the floor of a deep green valley and comprises several palatial suites that are scattered through the woodland. The central restaurant and reception areas glow with honey-coloured wood and rough stone fireplaces.

STAMFORD PLAZA
ALBERT ST
☎ (9) 309 8888
Following its refurbishment in 1995, the Plaza has an altogether warmer atmosphere and even nicer rooms with big pampering bathrooms. DON HEWITSON insists, "*It is the only place to stay. Great views of the harbour from the suites. A high standard of room service not evident in other New Zealand hotels.*" Wonderful marble rooftop pool.

SHERATON AUCKLAND HOTEL AND TOWERS
83 SYMONDS ST
☎ (9) 795132
A modern and smooth-running hotel. All rooms have terrific views. The service is friendly, and there's an excellent health club.

RESTAURANTS

SEE ALSO HOTELS.

ANTOINE'S
333 PARNELL RD, PARNELL 1
☎ (9) 798756
Auckland's finest restaurant, housed in an early colonial house, where chef-proprietor Tony Astle combines traditional food with a fantastic wine list.

BIKINI
55 TAMAKI DR, MISSION BAY
☎ (9) 521 9924
Chefs Warren Wood and Kami O'Brien apply their talents to a broad palette of Pacific Rim ingredients to create complex and startlingly

original dishes. Big windows frame watery views across to Rangitoto Island.

CIN CIN ON QUAY
AUCKLAND FERRY BLDG, 99 QUAY ST
☎ (9) 307 6966
Bold, bright and bustly bar/bistro on the waterfront with a menu and lively ambience that runs tirelessly from breakfast to past midnight.

THE FRENCH CAFE
210B SYMONDS ST
☎ (9) 771911
Fun dining room overlooking the street where you can get great tapas, and a more formal restaurant at the back serving simple, well-cooked food.

HARBOURSIDE RESTAURANT
AUCKLAND FERRY BLDG, 99 QUAY ST
☎ (9) 307 0556
Big and bustling, this restaurant overlooks the water and is the place to sample New Zealand seafood accompanied by exciting New Zealand wines. Also seating outside.

IGUACU
269 PARNELL RD, PARNELL
☎ (9) 309 4124
Like the decor, the menu grazes the globe with a long list of surefire crowd pleasers, although no distinctive style emerges.

VINNIES
166 JERVOIS RD, HERNE BAY
☎ (9) 376 5597
Minimalist decor disguises a gutsy, passionate menu that revels in Franco–Italian provincial cooking. Carpaccio of salmon with vanilla and olive oil and braised ox tongue with baby leeks

are typical of the menu which is also strong on game.

Wellington

HOTELS

PARKROYAL WELLINGTON
FEATHERSTON AND GREY ST
☎ (4) 472 2722
Best bet in the capital. Glossy, glamorous, newish hotel with an Art Deco flavour. Go for a room on the harbour side. Perfectly positioned for business and pleasure. The **PANAMA STREET BRASSERIE** is a favourite breakfast hangout.

PLAZA INTERNATIONAL
148–76 WAKEFIELD ST
☎ (4) 473 3900
Modern, elegant hotel offering more great harbour views. Good restaurant, **BURBURY'S**.

RESTAURANTS

SEE ALSO HOTELS.

BRASSERIE FLIP
RSA BUILDING, 103 GHUNZEE ST
☎ (4) 385 9493
Cosmopolitan food, ambience and slick decor attract a sophisticated crowd who come to sample food and wines from all over the world.

LE PETIT LYON
8 VIVIAN ST
☎ (4) 384 9402

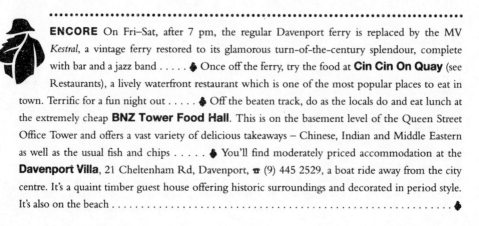

ENCORE On Fri–Sat, after 7 pm, the regular Davenport ferry is replaced by the MV *Kestral*, a vintage ferry restored to its glamorous turn-of-the-century splendour, complete with bar and a jazz band . . . . . ♣ Once off the ferry, try the food at **Cin Cin On Quay** (see Restaurants), a lively waterfront restaurant which is one of the most popular places to eat in town. Terrific for a fun night out . . . . . ♣ Off the beaten track, do as the locals do and eat lunch at the extremely cheap **BNZ Tower Food Hall**. This is on the basement level of the Queen Street Office Tower and offers a vast variety of delicious takeaways – Chinese, Indian and Middle Eastern as well as the usual fish and chips . . . . . ♣ You'll find moderately priced accommodation at the **Davenport Villa**, 21 Cheltenham Rd, Davenport, ☎ (9) 445 2529, a boat ride away from the city centre. It's a quaint timber guest house offering historic surroundings and decorated in period style. It's also on the beach . . . . ♣

Behind the anonymous brick façade is what many regard as the finest epicurean restaurant in the country. Inside, classical French cuisine is presented with all the necessary accoutrements: silver, crystal, plush furniture and faultless service.

Rest of New Zealand

HOTELS

HUKA LODGE
HUKA FALLS RD, PO BOX 95, TAUPO, NORTH ISLAND
☎ (7) 378 5791
The country's only member of Relais & Château sets the standard for New Zealand's sporting lodges. It's buried in parklike grounds close to Lake Taupo, the navel of NZ's North Island. No phones or televisions, but communal dinners in a gentrified Scottish Highlands-style fishing lodge. There's whitewater rafting, deer hunting and trout fishing on your doorstep. TERRY HOLME enthuses: "*Rooms look onto a raging river. Your day's catch is served up by their excellent chef.*"

"*HUKA LODGE RATES VERY HIGHLY ON OUR LIST OF FAVOURITE HOTELS IN THE WORLD*" –
PAUL HENDERSON

LAKE BRUNNER SPORTING LODGE
MITCHELLS, RD1, KUMARA, WESTLAND, SOUTH ISLAND
☎ (3) 738 0163
Set on Lake Brunner, this adventure lodge offers a wide variety of activities. Guest rooms are large, comfortable and well equipped but the emphasis is on comfort rather than opulence. Hunting, hiking, fishing, boating, mountain biking and birdwatching are available. Children are welcome.

MILLBROOK RESORT
MALAGHANS RD, ARROWTOWN
☎ (3) 442 1563
Bespoke accommodation for golfers amid the broom-covered mountain slopes just outside

Queenstown. Designed by professional Bob Charles, the par-72 course is rated among the country's top five. At the nucleus of the resort is **THE INN AT MILLBROOK**, an elevated cluster of big, comfortable 2-storey villas decorated in country style. Each has a fully equipped kitchen, laundry, a large lounge/dining room, ski closet and two bedrooms, both with *en suite* bathrooms.

MOTEUKA RIVER LODGE
HWY 61, NGATIMOTI, MOTEUKA
☎ (3) 526 8668
A luxurious mix of tranquillity, marvellous scenery and superb accommodation. Inside, the rustic flavour of the house is accented with folk art pieces collected from around the world and there are no telephones or televisions. The lodge offers a range of activities such as walking, river rafting, golf and tennis; however, its speciality is dry fly fishing for brown trout in the wild river country which can only be reached by helicopter. Activities are restricted outside the fishing season, which runs from 1 Oct to 31 Apr.

PARKROYAL CHRISTCHURCH
CNR OF KILMORE AND DURHAM STS, CHRISTCHURCH
☎ (3) 365 7799
Glamorous hotel overlooking Victoria Sq and the river. The views are terrific as are the suites. It also houses many restaurants and bars, including the Japanese restaurant **YAMAGEN**, one of the city's finest.

PUKA PARK LODGE
PAUANUI BEACH, COROMANDEL
☎ (7) 864 8088
Two dozen smart timber chalets buried in bushland on the ocean side of the wild, craggy Coromandel Peninsula. Stylishly done up with black cane tables, wooden blinds, mosquito nets and treetop balconies. Glorious beaches and rainforest walks are close by.

SOLITAIRE LODGE
LAKE TARAWERA, ROTORUA, NORTH ISLAND
☎ (7) 362 8208
Probably the most spectacular setting of any lodge. Trout fishing on the doorstep, sublime accommodation, wonderful food and postcard views. Best room in the house is the Tarawera Suite. There's only room for a few guests so it is quite exclusive but the mood is informal and friendly. Other activities include nature bush walks, climbs up Mount Tarawera, waterskiing, white-water rafting and sailing.

TIMARA LODGE

RD 2 BLENHEIM, MARLBOROUGH
☎ (57) 28276

Perfect for wine-lovers as it is in the middle of the Marlborough wine region. The food is excellent too, with plenty of fresh ingredients. There's also a tennis court, a pool and a man-made lake. Cruise down the coast to Kaikoura to spot the whales.

SKI RESORTS

New Zealand has 27 peaks that top 10,000 ft and you can ski here from June–Oct. The New Zealand resorts tend to be in the valleys, way below the snow fields, so you can fly up to the piste every morning. South Island's vast expanses of untouched snow mean that there's great off-piste skiing.

MOUNT COOK

Mount Cook National Park offers 22 of New Zealand's peaks over 10,000 ft and the scenery is spectacular. Heli-skiing is extremely popular. The ultimate skiing experience is the 8 mile run down the Tasman Glacier at Mount Cook. The swish place to stay is THE HERMITAGE, Mount Cook National Park, ☎ (3) 435 1879.

MOUNT RUAPEHU

The Whakapapa ski area on the north side of Mount Ruapehu is New Zealand's largest, with the best springtime snow in the country. Stay at the CHÂTEAU TONGARIRO, Mount Ruapehu, North Island, ☎ (7) 892 3809.

QUEENSTOWN

Queenstown is the most popular resort on South Island and a top retreat for skiers. Jet-boat rides, white-water rafting and riding are also available. And for the more daring, there are two bungy jumps nearby. Lots of good places to stay, the best of which is NUGGET POINT, a stylish, expensive retreat set high in the mountains. Rooms are massive and the service and food terrific. The main advantage is that it's near CORONET PEAK.

PHENOMENAL FJORDS The Norwegian fjords were formed thousands

of years ago when ice settled on river beds and carved deep, steep-sided valleys. When the ice masses finally retreated 14,000 years ago, they left empty valleys in their wake. These were filled by the sea, so creating Norway's most famous natural phenomena.

Fjords can be found along the entire length of the Norwegian coastline, from **Oslo Fjord** to **Varanger Fjord**. The best and most beautiful are found in the west of Norway; glide along the perfectly calm water of **Hardangerfjord** when the fruit trees are beginning to blossom. Some of the largest and most powerful waterfalls are also to be found in this part of the country. They emerge from ledges far above your head and cascade down into the emerald green water. The best way to see all of this is by boat. Norwegian Coastal Voyages Ltd, 15 Berghem Mews, Blyth Road, London, W14 OHN, ☎ (0171) 371 4011, have steamers that sail daily from Bergen, going north past the fjords of western Norway, across the Arctic Circle and via the North Cape to the very northernmost tip of the country. Apart from taking in the picturesque scenery, there's lots more to do, such as fishing for cod in the mouth of the fjord, hiking on a glacier or perhaps even skiing in your shorts in Stryejell.

The towns of the fjordal districts have a tremendous amount of street life. There are music festivals in the old Hanseatic capital, **Bergen**, which also has a wonderful fish market; jazz festivals in **Haugesund** and **Molde**; and a fish festival at **Stavanger**. But don't even think about going at any time other than the summer – if you do, you won't see a thing, as the country is steeped in darkness for most of the year.

POLAND
Warsaw

ART AND MUSEUMS

⊛ CHOPIN MUSEUM
ZAMEK OSTROGSKICH, ULICA OKOLNIK 1
☎ (22) 265935
Here you will find two unmissable exhibitions dedicated to the composer, while just ten minutes' walk away in the Warsaw Academy of Fine Arts (Krakowskie Przedmiescie 5) is a reconstruction of Chopin's drawing room. No visit to Warsaw is complete without seeing his birthplace in Zelazowa Wola, some 45 kms west of the city. In the summer, free Chopin concerts are organised in the old manor house and grounds, as well as by his monument in the beautiful Lazienki park in Warsaw itself.

NATIONAL MUSEUM
ALEJE JEROZOLIMSKIE 3
☎ (22) 6211031
Concentrating on 19th and 20th C Polish art, the museum houses a diverse collection of fine art. Other branches of the museum include the Lazienki Park (ulica Agrykoli 1, ☎ (22) 6216241), a vast landscape garden of old trees, picturesque ponds and remarkable sculptures, and the Wilanow Palace (ulica Wiertnicza 1, ☎ (22) 428101) which is one of the most beautiful baroque monuments in Poland.

CLUBS

AKWARIUM JAZZ CLUB
ULICA EMILII PLATER 49
☎ (22) 6205072
Popular jazz club. Visited regularly by top Polish and international jazz musicians.

TANGO
ULICA SMOLNA 15
☎ (22) 6221919
Located just opposite the National Museum, this is the first Parisian-style cabaret to establish itself in postwar Warsaw.

GROUND ZERO
ULICA WSPOLNA 62
☎ (22) 6255280
One of Warsaw's most popular discos.

HOTELS

BRISTOL
KRAKOWSKIE PRZEDMIESCIE 42–44
☎ (2) 625 2525
As Warsaw's most famous hotel and closest to the Presidental Palace and the Old Town, it is at the heart of the city's social life. Ideal combination of splendid rooms with every modern facility. As MARTHA STEWART says, "*The Bristol is sophisticated, very clean, very chic, it has great service and everything works.*"

MARRIOTT
ALEJE JEROZOLIMSKIE 65
☎ (2) 630 6306
Extremely luxurious and efficient American-run hotel, most popular among foreign businessmen.

SHERATON
ULICA PRUSA 2
☎ (22) 6576100
The newest hotel in the city, it is close to the Council of Ministers, Parliament, the Stock Exchange and many embassies.

MUSIC

TEATR WIELKI
PLAC TEATRALNY 1
☎ (22) 265019
Home of the Grand Theatre of Opera and Ballet, Poland's national opera and ballet groups, this is one of the greatest and best equipped theatres in Europe.

WARSAW CHAMBER OPERA
ALEJA SOLIDARNOSCI 76B
☎ (22) 312240
The repertoire of the Warsaw Chamber Opera includes a variety of plays and musical performances although recently, as home of the well-known Mozart Festival, it has naturally been dominated by Mozart.

RESTAURANTS

SEE ALSO HOTELS.

BAZYLISZEK
RYNEK STAREGO MIASTA 3/9
☎ (22) 311841
The place to go for genuine Polish ambience. Located in a 17C house on the Old Town square, it specializes in traditional Polish cook-

ing – try the excellent wild boar and venison, or blinis and caviare.

BELVEDERE

THE LAZIENKI PARK ORANGERY

☎ (22) 6216241

Located in the elegant setting of an antique orangery, it serves a mixture of old-style Polish and elegant French cuisine.

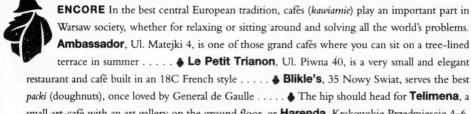 FLIK

ULICA PULAWSKA 43

☎ (22) 494334

Light and spacious featuring a terrace overlooking the Morskie Oko Park. Good food with a touch of the *nouvelle cuisine*, which is fortunately not as expensive as Belvedere.

FUKIER

RYNEK STAREGO MIASTA 27

☎ (22) 311013

Said by some to be the most beautiful restaurant, it revives the tradition of pre--war Polish cuisine.

ODEON

ULICA MARSZALKOWSKA 55/73

☎ (22) 6224594

The first music restaurant in Warsaw, this very popular meeting place combines 50s and 60s music with modern Polish and continental cuisine.

PORTUGAL
Lisbon

ART AND MUSEUMS

CALOUSTE GULBENKIAN FOUNDATION

AVE DE BERNA 45A

☎ (I) 795 0236

This treasure trove contains over 6,000 pieces from Ancient Egypt to early 20C – over 4,500 years' worth of treasures. As well as Old Masters and European sculpture, there's tapestry, Chinese porcelain, ivory and the famous collection of René Lalique's Art Nouveau jewellery.

MUSEUNACIONAL DE ARTE ANTIGA

RUA DAS JANELAS VERDES 95, LAPA
(TRAM 19 FROM PRAÇA DO COMERCIO)

☎ (I) 396 4151

This excellent collection is housed in the former palace of Pombal (a Prime Minister of the 18C), high above the city in the wealthy Lapa district. Highlights include the porcelain, sculpture, furniture, carpets, silver and gold work, old glazed earthenware and the world's best collection of silverware by the French Germain brothers. However, many go merely to see the paintings, which include early work by the Flemish and German schools as well as early Portuguese work, notably the multi-panelled altarpiece by Nuno Gonçalves (1460).

HOTELS

ALTIS

RUA CASTILHO 11

☎ (I) 314 2496

Big modern hotel with good facilities (indoor pool, health club) and dining. The rooftop restaurant is exceptional.

RITZ LISBOA

RUA RODRIGO DA FONSECA 88

☎ (I) 383 2020

One of Europe's and certainly Portugal's grandest hotels, featuring beautiful stately rooms furnished with antiques, each with a terrace. Excellent old-fashioned service and good food.

ENCORE In the best central European tradition, cafés (*kawiarnie*) play an important part in Warsaw society, whether for relaxing or sitting around and solving all the world's problems. **Ambassador**, Ul. Matejki 4, is one of those grand cafés where you can sit on a tree-lined terrace in summer . . . . . ♦ **Le Petit Trianon**, Ul. Piwna 40, is a very small and elegant restaurant and café built in an 18C French style . . . . . ♦ **Blikle's**, 35 Nowy Swiat, serves the best *packi* (doughnuts), once loved by General de Gaulle . . . . . ♦ The hip should head for **Telimena**, a small art-café with an art gallery on the ground floor, or **Harenda**, Krakowskie Przedmiescie 4–6, which has a big terrace and is open all night. **Gwiazdecka**, Piwna 42, is the latest place for chic young Poles . . . . . ♦ Or you can try **Nowe Miasto**, Rynek Nowego Miasta 13–15, a pleasant vegetarian restaurant/café where a harpist accompanies your meal. . . . . ♦

TIVOLI LISBOA

AVENIDA DA LIBERDADE 185
☎ (I) 353 0181
A big, family-run hotel, luxury standards but not exorbitant rates.

RESTAURANTS

Remember that the Portuguese prefer to do their eating at home, so sometimes eating-out can be rather hit-and-miss. However, Portuguese house wine (vinho da casa) is often both reasonably priced and a lot more palatable than you'd expect.

ALCANTARA CAFE

RUA MARIA LUISA HOLSTEIN 15
☎ (I) 362 1036
Ever-popular, trendy, modern restaurant serving traditional Portuguese specialities and a good selection of wine.

AVIZ

AMOREIRAS SHOPPING CENTER, LOJA 2058
☎ (I) 385 1888
Lisbon's smartest French restaurant was saved from the ruins of the old Aviz hotel by staff.

CASA DA COMIDA

TRAVESSA DAS AMOREIRAS I
☎ (I) 388 5376
Imaginative food is served around a flower-filled courtyard garden. Great service and very fashionable, so book ahead.

CERVEJARIA TRINIDADE

RUA NOVA DA TRINDADE 20C
☎ (I) 346 3506
Buzzy, echoey tiled cavern, where politicians, architects and intellectuals get animated over plates piled high with bacalão (salt cod), hefty steaks or steaming garlicky seafood. Beer (try the local Sagres) is served in a stein.

O TERRACO

AT THE TIVOLI LISBOA, AVENIDA DA LIBERDADE 185
☎ (I) 353 0182
Located on the top floor of the Tivoli hotel, this restaurant offers superlative cuisine coupled with an unsurpassable view of Lisbon.

PAP'ACORDA

RUA DA ATALAIA 57
☎ (I) 346 4811
In the bustling Bairro Alto (old quarter), this fashionable, fun and teeming restaurant is where the trendy crowd go to eat.

SUA EXCELENCIA

RUA DO CONDE 34
☎ (I) 603614
The eating-out experience of Lisbon. There's no printed menu; instead the owner describes the entire menu to you in the appropriate language. The food is mouthwatering and reservations are essential.

TAVARES RICO

RUA DE MISERICÓRDIA 35/37
☎ (I) 342 1112
One of Lisbon's most famous grand restaurants, offering the best Portuguese fare in man-size platefuls and some superb wines.

Rest of Portugal

HOTELS

GOLFE DA PENINA

APARTADO 146, 8500 PORTIMÃO
☎ (82) 415415
Impressive golf hotel situated in the heart of a huge golfing area, with excellent courses designed by Henry Cotton. Bedrooms are very pleasant and most have a balcony with a view. Great if you like golf.

ENCORE Despite extensive fire damage in 1988 the **Chiado** remains the best shopping centre in Lisbon, especially around the Rua Garrett. It's also a centre for Bohemian coffee shops. The most popular is the literary **Brasileira**, Rua Garrett 120, ☎ (1) 346 9541, which features a full-size statue of Fernando Pessoa, the national poet of Portugal . . . . . ♠ **Rossio**, the area around the station of that name, is the lively heart of Lisbon, even after midnight when the cafés have closed . . . . . ♠ Flea markets (*feira da ladra*) are held on Tues morning and the whole of Sat in the **Largo de Santa Clara**, which is close to the Alfama district . . . . ♠

PALACIO DE SETEAIS

LAVENIDA BARBOSA DO BOCAGE 8,
SINTRA

☎ (1) 923 3200

Just outside Sintra is this former palace, set in substantial grounds and housing 30 luxurious guest rooms and an excellent restaurant.

POUSADA DO CASTELO DE ALVITO

APARTADO 9, 7595 ALVITO

☎ (84) 48383

On the way from Lisbon to the Algarve in the wild Alentejo, stay at one of Portugal's best historic hotels, or *pousadas*, set in an old castle, luckily surrounded by restaurants. Highly recommended.

POUSADA SAN MIGUEL

SERRA DE SÃO MIGUEL, 7470 SOUSEL

☎ (68) 551160

A comfortable hotel set in a 10,000-acre nature and hunting reserve stocked with wild boar. Staff can arrange hunting expeditions.

QUINTA DEL LAGO

8135 AMANCIL

☎ (89) 396666

Golf resort hotel in the Algarve, 20 minutes from Faro airport. "*Very nice hotel overlooking the Algarve coast and near a famous bird sanctuary. Great place for golf lovers, with four nine-hole courses, two good restaurants and very relaxing and comfortable rooms,*" reports MARTIN SKAN.

RUSSIA

St Petersburg

ART AND MUSEUMS

HERMITAGE

34 DVORTSOVAYA NABEREZHNAYA

☎ (812) 212 9525

The world's largest museum, with 3 million exhibits, housed in Peter the Great's beautiful 18C Winter Palace and boasting stunning views across the Neva River. The Hermitage collection is more than comprehensive, spanning early and primitive art, classical, the Renaissance, Impressionism and modern art. No famous painter is left out. The rooms themselves are part of the permanent exhibit filled with sculptures, jewels, *objets d'art*, antique furniture and silver.

RUSSIAN MUSEUM

1 PLOSHCHAD ISSKUSTV

Another palace museum, housing one of the oldest and largest collections of Russian art.

BALLET AND OPERA

MARIINSKY THEATRE

1 TEATRALNAYA PLOSHCHAD

☎ (812) 114 1244

Formerly called the Kirov Theatre it was built in 1860 in honour of Alexander II's wife. Famous as the training ground for such stars as Anna Pavlova and Rudolf Nureyev it has retained its reputation with its classical performances, impeccable style and perfect technique.

CLUBS

St Petersburg's nightlife is constantly growing and changing, but always entertaining. Check the St Petersburg Press for updates on nightclub addresses.

FISH FACTORY

10 PUSHKINSKAYA ULITSA, FLAT 15,
4TH FLOOR

Contemporary rock and pop music is played in the unlikely setting of an unadorned, bare two-room flat. Cheap drinks, great dancing and very peaceful and friendly clinetele.

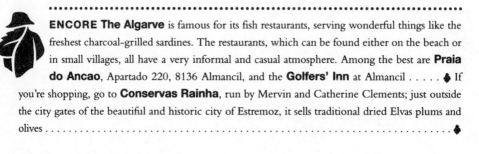

ENCORE The Algarve is famous for its fish restaurants, serving wonderful things like the freshest charcoal-grilled sardines. The restaurants, which can be found either on the beach or in small villages, all have a very informal and casual atmosphere. Among the best are **Praia do Ancao**, Apartado 220, 8136 Almancil, and the **Golfers' Inn** at Almancil . . . . . ♣ If you're shopping, go to **Conservas Rainha**, run by Mervin and Catherine Clements; just outside the city gates of the beautiful and historic city of Estremoz, it sells traditional dried Elvas plums and olives . . . . ♣

FIGHTING THE COLD WAR

St Petersburgers value their health so much that they take a dip in the freezing cold Neva river a couple of times a year. They have to break the ice first before plunging in and then they leap straight out. They say it's good for their hearts. The days are short and extremely cold in the winter so wrap up well. The compensation comes in the summer with long Arctic days, gorgeous sunsets and a huge music festival in June called the White Nights. Lovers stroll along the river embankments, and groups of young people gather to play live music outside. But take care not to get stranded on one of the many islands where the bridges are inaccessible for a few hours in the early morning.

KVADRAT JAZZ CLUB
10 ULITSA PRAVDY
Traditional and mainstream jazz. Good atmosphere.

ROITERDAM CLUB
69 PROSPEKT VETERANOV
Good dance music. Reggae and rock 'n' roll.

HOTELS

ASTORIA
ULITSA GERTSENA 39
☎ (812) 315 9678
Grand hotel in a good central location. It dates from 1912, but has been updated since then and now has four restaurants, a health club plus every other civilized facility.

GRAND HOTEL EUROPE
1-7 MIKHAILOVSKAYA ULITSA
☎ (812) 312 0072
A 5-star hotel where you can stay in rooms that were used by Turgenev, Debussy and Shostakovich. Now completely modernized, it has a swimming pool, sauna and four restaurants. Try the hotel's excellent RESTAURANT EUROPE, ☎ (812) 113 8071, for good Russian dishes or a Sunday jazz brunch in a sumptuous Art Nouveau dining room, or THE BRASSERIE, which is cheaper but just as good.

MARCO POLO NEVSKY PALACE HOTEL
57 NEVSKY PROSPEKT
☎ (812) 850 1500
Another luxury hotel conveniently located on the city's most famous street in the centre and has all mod cons.

MUSIC

SEE ALSO BALLET AND OPERA.

JAZZ PHILHARMONIC HALL
27 ZAHORODNY PROSPEKT
☎ (812) 164 8565
Traditional, mainstream and modern jazz.

RESTAURANTS

SEE ALSO HOTELS.

CHAIKA
14 GRIBOYEDOVA NABEREZHNAYA
☎ (812) 312 2120
Marine Russian restaurant serving good goulash and herring. Open till late.

DEMYANOVA UKHA
53 KRONVERSKY PROSPEKT
☎ (812) 232 8090
This former state restaurant has recently undergone renovation, but prices are still reasonable and booking is strongly recommended.

KAFE LITERATURNOYE
18 NEVSKY PROSPEKT
☎ (812) 312 8536
Famous literary restaurant favoured by Tolstoy and Dostoyevsky, and still the scene of the odd poetry recital or literary reading.

✆ KAFE TBILISI
10 SYNINSKAYA ULITSA
☎ (812) 232 9391
Serves great Georgian food with great service at a good price.

ST PETERSBURG

5 GRIBOYEDOVA NABEREZHNAYA

☎ (812) 314 4947

This very traditional Russian restaurant is worth visiting more for the folky candlelight and musicians than for the food. Good music and lots of rowdy energy and loud fun.

Moscow

ART AND MUSEUMS

ARMOURY PALACE

KREMLIN

☎ (95) 221 4720

Ostentatious collection of armoury, fabulous Fabergé eggs and jewels, Russian gold and silver, rare 16–17C English Silver and diplomatic gifts from courts all over Europe.

NEW TRETYAKOV GALLERY

10 KRYMSKY VAL

☎ (95) 230 1116

20C Soviet and Russian art including famous works by Kandinsky and Malevich. The gallery features a display of Soviet statues that were torn down in Moscow after the August 1991 coup.

OLD TRETYAKOV GALLERY

12 LAVRUSHINSKY PEREULOK

☎ (95) 233 3223

Recently reopened after being closed for ten years for major renovation work, the main exhibit halls feature masterpieces of Russian icon art, paintings by 18C masters and some famous 19C and early 20C paintings.

PUSHKIN FINE ART MUSEUM

12 ULITSA VOLKHONKA

☎ (95) 203 7998

Not long ago the Pushkin hit the headlines for its world-famous exhibition of the "Helen of Troy" treasure. This museum is second only to the Hermitage for its comprehensive collection which includes the ancients, Impressionists and Post-Impressionists.

BALLET AND OPERA

BOLSHOI THEATRE

1 TEATRALNAYA PLOSHCHAD

☎ (95) 292 9986

Having hit rock bottom, the Bolshoi seems to be regaining some of its past magic. In the past year or so Vladimir Vasiliev has been installed and now plans are afoot to revive classical productions. But the performances are still worth experiencing, whether for their faded grand settings, the caviare and champagne in the intervals or the performers themselves.

CLUBS

Moscow's clubs and small restaurants come and go very quickly, so it's best to check the *Moscow Review*. **ARBAT ST** is where most of the clubs, cafés and street entertainers are. Try the **ARBAT BLUES CLUB** for live music.

CRISIS GENRE

22/1 PEREULOK OSTROVSKOGO

☎ (95) 243 8605

Small café-type bar and restaurant serving basic

NOTES FROM THE UNDERGROUND Spend the day going underground on the Moscow metro, which began construction in 1931. Many stations were designed by different people according to various themes; some boast chandeliers (**Kievskaya**), stained glass panels (**Novosloodskaya**), bronze statues (**Belorusskaya**), double staircases (**Sokol**), stainless steel columns and red marble with mosaics on the ceilings (**Mayakovskaya**), sculptures of Red Army soldiers and partisans (**Ploshchad Revolyutsii**), galleries (**Komsomolskaya**) or just simple columns and earth tones (**Kropotkinskaya**). Marvel at its efficiency (certainly in comparison to London's) and experience the long, long, crowded escalators that move rapidly.

GRAVEN IMAGES
Dead people are especially interesting in Moscow, where so many famous ones are buried. A day visiting Moscow's graves will give you a view of Moscow's history from a decidedly different angle. Start at **Lenin's mausoleum** on Red Square and then visit **Stalin's grave**, as well as the graves of various famous British spies who are buried in the **Kremlin wall**. Take a trip to **Novodevichy monastery** to see a beautiful, rambling cemetery with the graves of two of Russia's most celebrated writers – Chekhov and Gogol – as well as artists, poets and even disgraced Soviet leader Nikita Khrushchev. The next stop is **Vagankovskoye cemetery** near a 1906 metro station. Here many well-known Russians are buried, from Otari Kvantrishvili – an alleged Mafia godfather – to Vysotsky, the Russian Bob Dylan.

Russian food and reasonably priced drinks. Live acoustic music most nights of the week.

MAXIM MAXIMICH
15 KALANCHOVSKAYA ULITSA
☎ (95) 975 4536
This bar has live acoustic bands and a pleasant, relaxing atmosphere. Not the easiest place to find, but worth the effort. Serves food too.

HOTELS

BALTSCHUNG KEMPINSKI HOTEL
1 BALTSCHUNG ST
☎ (95) 230 6500
Part of the Kempinski group, a luxury hotel with all the latest facilities.

MARCO POLO PRESNAYA
9 SPIRIDONOVSKY PEREULOK
☎ (95) 202 0381
Very quiet, comfortable and traditional small hotel near Pushkin Square. Not grand but good, with a restaurant serving international cuisine.

METROPOL
1–4 TEATRALNY PROYEZD
☎ (95) 927 6000
A turn-of-the-century classic, now managed by Intercontinental. Efficient, comfortable and well decorated, with a nice old-fashioned ballroom and a gilded and marbled dining room, the **EVROPEISKY RESTAURANT**. **LE BISTRO** is an attractive alternative with simpler but equally good food. Finish the evening with a vodka in the **ARTISTS' BAR**.

SAVOY HOTEL
3 ULITSA ROZHDESVENKA
☎ (95) 929 8500
One of Moscow's best hotels. With only 80 rooms, it can be tough to get in – but worth trying. Franco–Russian cuisine in the elegant **LE SAVOY** restaurant (black tie preferred), and a British pub-style bar called the **HERMITAGE**.

RESTAURANTS

SEE ALSO HOTELS.

☻ CAFE MARGARITA
28 MALAYA BRONNAYA ULITSA
Located next to the beautiful Patriarch's Ponds, the café is popular with the Moscow art crowd as well as ex-pats. The live music can drown out conversation, but is always fun. Cheap and basic Russian food is served with lots of vodka.

☻ MAMA ZOYA'S
4 SECHENOVSKY PEREULOK
☎ (95) 201 7743
Moscow's best Georgian and most reasonably priced restaurant. Always very crowded, it has live Georgian music and a thoroughly Georgian atmosphere. Expect to queue for 20 minutes, but the delicious food and local red wine make it well worth the wait.

POMODORO
5 BOLSHOI GOLOVIN PEREULOK
☎ (095) 924 2931
An authentic Italian restaurant with good, but pricey food. A pleasant atmosphere near the centre.

Simon Sebag Montefiore's travel tips

There's always a chance on a journey, whether you're in Tuscany or Tehran, that you might stumble across some unforeseen and sinister situation. I have survived several hellish journeys, admittedly in some rather way-out places, but I now know that wherever you are and whoever you are with, it would be as well to learn a few basic tips, tried and tested by me. Travelling shouldn't be a life-or-death experience.

From the apocalypse of Grozny and Chechnya to the jungles of Nicaragua and the deserts of Mauritania; from the bedrooms of the Bristol in Paris and the Jacuzzis of Raffles in Singapore to the suites of the Carlyle in Manhattan – the first tip is to trust no one. Be utterly paranoid.

To put holidays from hell into perspective, on a recent adventure to Grozny I stayed in the Hotel Kafkaz (now a bombsite), which doubled up as the Presidential Guard's barracks (there were no proper hotels here). It was a mixture of Soviet Gothic and Spanish colonial, which might be termed "Stalin Hacienda". There was a malodorous gunman asleep on the reception desk, piles of ammo in the buffet, terrified babushkas warning me that it was too dangerous to stay and an insane gunman, who spent the whole night smashing on my bedroom door. Inside, my room teemed like a rodent menagerie, there was fresh blood all over the sheets and the ceiling, and the bathroom walls had collapsed. Outside, the gunmen, drunk and excited by the imminent war, skidded round and round in their Mercedes, shrieking and letting off bursts of fire into the sky. It was enough to drive any man crazy. And to top it off, my neighbours, bearded ruffians with bandoliers and rocket launchers, spent that and every other night shouting and throwing either their girlfriends or their rifles against the walls. This was about as close to hell as you can get.

So, if you're visiting such a place, rule one: book the hotel in advance so they can at least get your room ready. Second: always travel with a stock of Mars Bars in case the kitchen is out of order or the city under siege. Third: gun oil stains, so never leave designer clothes on or near ammunition dumps. Fourth: it is sensible to sleep in your clothes. Fifth: ignore it if frantic bloodsplattered women warn you the place is deadly; they are working for other travel agents or are simply jealous of your accommodation. And sixth: always enter into the spirit of a place. I, for example, went down and danced with the Chechen warriors on top of their tanks and BMWs. It seemed sensible and was good travelling *savoir faire*. Never forget that dancing, singing and sex are the international languages that will enable you to befriend even the most barbaric, brutish simpletons, so use them.

After settling into my hotel, I went up to the 10th floor of the Chechen Presidential Palace (now a ruin) where I encountered Dudayev's vice president. Western news agencies had reported that he had been killed in a motorcade bomb. I explained this and said I was glad he was still alive. Unfortunately, there was a mix-up in the translation. My 14-year-old interpreter had made a slight mistake; the vice president had got the impression that I thought he should be killed at once. He drew his pistol out of a glittery holster and raised it coolly to face level, while his bodyguards surrounded us. The gun was pushed between my lips. I could taste the cordite – rather like caviare with a dash of sulphur. Things were not going well in Grozny. It wasn't the time for jokes with poor punchlines. With some difficulty, I managed to persuade His Excellency that I meant no harm. It was my rendition of Village People's discothèque classic "YMCA", performed for his guards, and my recitation of the nobility of Chechen history that finally defused an almost fatal situation.

This illustrates that you must find a proper interpreter or else learn the language. But the lyrics and tunes of clichéed 1970s pop songs, by artists such as Engelbert Humperdinck and Elton John, can be life-savers too, if used wisely. By writing down the lyrics to "Space Oddity", I have both won permission for an aeroplane to take off and been given the chance to buy plane fuel. So it is worth learning a repertoire before you leave home. Warning: do not try and sing the Beatles. Every bandit and warlord knows all the words to the Beatles' songs. No one's going to keep you alive just so they can listen to you singing "Yesterday"; you will lose your head even faster than you'd bargained for.

Another vital tip is to learn a bit of history – the name of the national hero with a raised thumb will usually be enough. But you must talk about the country's history and its national hero in conjunction with some of the following words: nobility, culture, genius, honour, chivalry, civilization and heroism. I once saved myself from a lynching in a Transylvanian village by declaring that 13.2 per cent of the world's geniuses happened to be Romanian.

Always stop at a checkpoint. When you are asked into a policeman's hut for questioning, pretend that it's as great an honour as an invitation to Blenheim Palace. Remember that border guards get very bored, so entertain them with song 'n' dance routines and tell them how handsome, well endowed and brilliant they are. Inform them that you would give your right arm to wear such a dashing uniform – and *always* admire their gun by saying something like "My! What a beautiful gun."

Never forget to write down your passport number, its expiry date and place of issue inside the book you are reading, in case it is stolen. That way you retain a copy of all its most vital details. Do the same with your credit card numbers.

If you are going anywhere out of the ordinary, always carry the following medicines: antibiotics; a syringe; an antiseptic cream such as Fucidin; and obviously aspirin, painkillers and condoms. Condoms are vital for survival. In the desert, you can use them to keep sand out of your watch. KY Jelly doubles up as gun oil, so can be a life-saving gift to militiamen. Carry cigarettes, as they are useful as tips. Never wear jewellery or shorts if you are a girl. Never lie on your tummy or back in Muslim countries: it is a whorish insult. If you travel in the ex-USSR, never call a non-Russian (for example a Chechen or a Georgian) a Russian. This is an offence that they will gaily kill for.

If you are approached and offered either money, drugs, girls or boys, never take the bait; these lowlifes are usually police agents who will happily take your money and then double it by handing you over. And never, ever open your door at night: if they really want to come in, they will knock the door down.

Armed with these basic tenets, you should now be ready to take on any part of the world, bearing in mind that they might not be strictly necessary on your next visit to Cornwall.

STARLIGHT DINER

16 BOLSHAYA SADOVAYA
☎ (95) 290 9638
Russia's first authentic American diner complete with shiny aluminium exterior and 50s-style jukebox. Slightly overpriced but the meatloaf is worth any financial sacrifice.

TAGANKS BLUES BAR

15 ULITSA VERKHNAYA
RADISHCHEVSKAYA
☎ (95) 915 1004
Strange restaurant serving traditional Russian food and drink accompanied by a band, a magician, belly-dancer and traditional Russian songs. Reasonable prices.

U PIROSMANI

4 MOVODOVICHY PROYEZD
☎ (95) 247 1926
Popular Georgian restaurant with a wonderfully melancholic atmosphere. Delicious food and wine.

VILLA PEREDELKINO

1 CHOBOTOVSKAYA ALLEYA,
PEREDELKINO VILLAGE
☎ (95) 435 1478

An expensive restaurant in the village where Pasternak lived and is now buried. A 20-minute drive from Moscow, the restaurant serves very good Italian food.

THE SEYCHELLES

An archipelago of over 100 islands spread over 400,000 square yards of the Indian Ocean. The main island is **MAHÉ** (just 4 degrees off the equator). There are numerous Creole restaurants, craft shops, art galleries and a vibrant fruit and vegetable market in the capital town of **VICTORIA**. This island has 68 exceptional beaches, the most famous of which is **BEAU VALLON**. The best hotels include **NORTHOLME**, PO Box 333, Glacis, ☎ (248) 61222; fax (248) 61223, a 19-roomed hotel situated on a small headland overlooking a secluded beach; and **LE MERIDIEN FISHERMAN'S COVE**, Bel Ombre, PO Box 35, ☎ (248) 47252; fax (248) 47540, with rooms set in a tropical garden.

BIRD ISLAND

Thirty minutes by air from Mahé, this splendid 120-acre island is a haven for birds, as well as home to Esmeralda, the 150-year-old (male) giant tortoise. Privately owned, the island has one hotel, the **BIRD ISLAND LODGE**, PO Box 404, ☎ (248) 24925, with 25 thatched bungalows all facing the sea. The restaurant offers a Creole lunch and European-style dinner. Sports facilities include game fishing, snorkelling and tennis.

DENIS ISLAND

Just 25 minutes from Mahé, this is a must for game-fishing enthusiasts. Several record-breaking dogtooth tuna and bonito have been caught here. The **DENIS ISLAND LODGE**, PO Box 404, ☎ (248) 23392; fax (238) 24292, has 25 luxurious bungalows near the beach. The restaurant serves French cuisine with Creole specialities. Assorted activities such as snorkelling, windsurfing and tennis are available too.

PRASLIN

A mere 15 minutes by air from Mahé, or two and a half hours by boat, Praslin is the home of the unique coco-de-mer palm. Its secluded beaches and delightful small hotels make it a perfect choice for a few nights' stay. Try the wonderfully luxurious Relais & Château **CHÂTEAU DE FEUILLES**, ☎ (248) 233316, set in an old family mansion. It's also a good launching pad for trips into the Mai valley forests or to nearby uninhabited islands. **L'ARCHIPEL**, Anse Gouvernement, PO Box 586, ☎ (238) 32040/32242, is a small hotel built on a rising, landscaped site on the beach, where facilities include windsurfing, canoeing and deep-sea fishing. For further information contact the Seychelles Tourist Office in Mahé, ☎ (248) 25314; fax (248) 24035.

SINGAPORE

ARTS AND MUSEUMS

EMPRESS PLACE

1 EMPRESS PLACE, 0617
☎ 336 7633
A national monument beside the Singapore River near the spot where Sir Stamford Raffles first landed in 1889. It often holds one-off exhibitions from China and other displays you won't see elsewhere. There's also a good Chinese restaurant and café here.

BARS AND CAFES

TEA CHAPTER

9A-11A NEIL RD
☎ 226 1175
Beautiful traditional Chinese teahouse opened in 1989. Its rather eccentric noticeboards covered with personal messages make entertaining reading, while you sip one of many teas on offer.

CLUBS

CLUB 97

SPECIALIST SHOPPING CENTRE (BASEMENT), ORCHARD RD
☎ 733 0031
A fusion of high energy Canto Pop and a quiet piano lounge for members.

PAULANER BRAUHAUS

9 RAFFLES BOULEVARD, MILLENIA WALK
☎ 337 7123
A massive three-storey 20,000 sq ft of upmarket dining and entertainment. Come here to sample freshly baked German beer and to eat and dance.

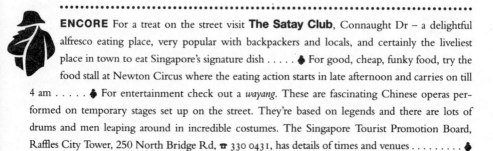

ENCORE For a treat on the street visit **The Satay Club**, Connaught Dr – a delightful alfresco eating place, very popular with backpackers and locals, and certainly the liveliest place in town to eat Singapore's signature dish . . . . . ♦ For good, cheap, funky food, try the food stall at Newton Circus where the eating action starts in late afternoon and carries on till 4 am . . . . . ♦ For entertainment check out a *wayang*. These are fascinating Chinese operas performed on temporary stages set up on the street. They're based on legends and there are lots of drums and men leaping around in incredible costumes. The Singapore Tourist Promotion Board, Raffles City Tower, 250 North Bridge Rd, ☎ 330 0431, has details of times and venues . . . . ♦

SINGAPORE is the one Asian city where you do not have to be afraid of eating at

the food stalls or "hawker centres" found throughout the city. Standards of hygiene, which are strictly regulated by the government, are no higher anywhere else in the world – it's not known as the Switzerland of the Far East for nothing. Here is one place you can try out many different kinds of dishes side-by-side with Singaporeans, who can be amazingly friendly to outsiders when they are gathered together to eat. At each stall you choose from up to 100 dishes: everything from satay (either Malay or Chinese styles) to curries and an array of vegetarian dishes. Some of the best are **Rasa Singapura**, on Tanglin Road near the tourist promotion board and the handicraft centre. **Newton Circus**, about a 10-minute walk from the Upper Orchard Rd hotel area, one of the biggest hawker centres, is open until about 2 am (not much happens here until after dark). Along **Queen Elizabeth Walk**, near the Singapore River, are stalls that specialize in different forms of satay, nicknamed "the Satay Club". In Chinatown, there's the multi-storey **Kreta Ayer** complex, on Trengganu Street a block north-east of Smith Street, and **Telok Ayer Market** between Chinatown and Clifford Pier. Also try **Cuppage Road Hawker Center**, a block north of Orchard Rd; **Geyland Serai**, a 20-minute taxi ride northeast of downtown, in a predominantly Indian section of Singapore; and the **Botanical Gardens Food Center**, a small complex across Cluny Rd from the gardens.

TOP TEN
400 ORCHARD RD, 4–35/36 ORCHARD TOWER
☎ 732 3077
Mega-popular with ex-pats and foreign visitors for its imported bands, great light show and four-tier bar. Cosmopolitan crowd. Happy hour 5–9 pm. Closes 3 am.

ZOUK DISCOTHEQUE
JIAK KIM STREET
☎ 738 2988
Housed in a single warehouse, up to 2,000 Zoukites will pack into this extremely popular disco on Wednesday nights, revelling in the high techno music.

HOTELS

GOODWOOD PARK
22 SCOTTS RD
☎ 737 7411
Grand old colonial building with a lovely terrace and several good eateries (see Restaurants). Rooms are gigantic, suites are mammoth and all are furnished in local style.

THE ORIENTAL
5 RAFFLES AVE, MARINA SQ, 0103
☎ 338 0066
This 21-storey pyramid-shaped hotel with fabulous outdoor pool (with piped underwater music) is among the best in Singapore. Understated elegance and the best service in Singapore. Great fitness centre.

RAFFLES
1 BEACH RD
☎ 337 8041
Some say a lot of the old Raffles disappeared when it was restored, but the rooms with their teak floors and 20s-style furnishings still hold much of that nostalgia for which Raffles is famous. "*I would think Raffles must be among the best hotels in the world. I was most impressed by the quality of service, the immaculate suites and the unhurried efficiency of all the staff*" is RAYMOND BLANC's considered opinion. Don't resist having a Singapore Sling in the infamous **LONG BAR**.

SHANGRI-LA
22 ORANGE GROVE RD, 0208
☎ 737 3644

Immaculate service, lavish rooms with sunken tubs and soft bathrobes, and lots of beautiful wood furniture. Very cosmopolitan. Excellent restaurants (see Restaurants).

RESTAURANTS

AZIZA'S
180 ALBERT ST, # 2–15
☎ 235 1130
In a row of picturesque 19C Peranaken (Straits Chinese) houses, this is one of the few restaurants in Singapore serving Malay food. The grilled Chicken Kasturi is a must. Closed Sun.

THE CHERRY GARDEN
AT THE ORiENTAL HOTEL (SEE HOTELS)
☎ 337 1886
A wooden-roofed pavilion building enclosing a beautiful courtyard. Some of the dishes are served in woven bamboo baskets.

GOODWOOD PARK
(SEE HOTELS)
☎ 737 7411
Something to please every taste. Splendid Chinese food at the **MIN JIANG** – fast service and great value too. A wonderful selection of fresh fish at the **GARDEN SEAFOOD RESTAURANT**. Eat Shanghainese served Western style in **CHIANG JIANG**. For good old continental steaks visit the **GORDON GRILL** and take coffee afterwards at the **CAFÉ L'ESPRESSO**. The highlight, however, is the **SHIMA** Japanese restaurant, offering bargain priced all-you-can-eat lunches.

GUAN HOE SOON
214 JOO CHIAT RD, KATONG
☎ 344 2761
Lies in suburban Katong and serves very unusual food indeed. This is classic Peranakan cuisine – the highly refined hybrid creation of well-to-do descendants of Chinese immigrants and their Malay wives. Here you may try ayam buah keluak (chicken in black-nut curry).

THE IMPERIAL HERBAL RESTAURANT
AT THE METROPOLE HOTEL, 41 SEAH ST
☎ 337 0491
This is the most interesting perhaps of all Singapore's foreigner-friendly restaurants. All the dishes are cooked with a number of different berries, flowers, roots, and tubers that are combined to balance yin and yang, build physical stamina, and treat all manner of ailments.

KINARA
57 BOAT QUAY
☎ 533 0142
Sophisticated North Indian food, including many vegetarian dishes. Beautifully designed interiors with wonderful murals. Many trendy bars line the quayside along Kinara – ideal for a pre- or post-prandial drink.

THE MOI KONG HAKKA RESTAURANT
22 MURRAY ST
☎ 221 7758
Serves the very best of a cuisine that originated from northern China. The food is mostly flavoured with fermented soybeans, rice wine, dried fish, and preserved mountain vegetables.

MUTHU'S CURRY RESTAURANT
76/78 RACE COURSE ROAD
☎ 293 7029
A Singapore institution where the food – fish-head curries (a delicious Singaporean delicacy) or meat – is served on banana leaves and eaten with your fingers. Popular with the locals.

PASTA FRESCA (4 OUTLETS)
BIK 833 BUKIT TIMAH RD; 30 BOAT QUAY; 350 ORCHARD RD; 77 UPPER E COAST RD ☎ 469 4920; 5326283; 735 0373; 2415560
Some good Northern Italian dishes, as well as an endless supply of spaghetti variations. Or, simply drop in for a quick cup of their aromatic espresso.

SHANGRI-LA
(SEE HOTELS)
☎ 737 3644
The **WATERFALL CAFÉ** in a delightful outdoor

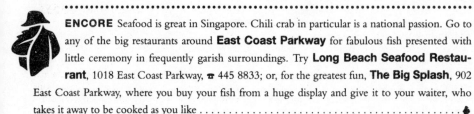

ENCORE Seafood is great in Singapore. Chili crab in particular is a national passion. Go to any of the big restaurants around **East Coast Parkway** for fabulous fish presented with little ceremony in frequently garish surroundings. Try **Long Beach Seafood Restaurant**, 1018 East Coast Parkway, ☎ 445 8833; or, for the greatest fun, **The Big Splash**, 902 East Coast Parkway, where you buy your fish from a huge display and give it to your waiter, who takes it away to be cooked as you like . . . . ♦

setting is great for Singaporean food – snacks are served all day. Continental food is served at the **LATOUR**, a deep pink dining room with huge batiks of tropical flowers. **SHANG PALACE** serves terrific Cantonese cuisine – they're well known for their dim sum lunches. The **NADAMAN**, on the 24th floor, has great views and serves superb meals in lacquer boxes. You can have a good buffet lunch or snacks throughout the day at the **COFFEE GARDEN**.

TEL SONG RESTAURANT

BLOCK 17, OUTRAM PARK
☎ 220 3544
This somewhat minimalist restaurant serves up the food favoured by the southern Chinese provinces of Guangdong and Fujian. Here you can find delicate, simply seasoned consommés and fish steamed with sour plums.

SHOPPING

Singapore is not the bargain-hunter's heaven that it once was but it's still pretty good for toys, cameras and electrical goods.

Most of it happens in **ORCHARD RD**: there's the massive **NGEE ANN CITY**, where all the top designer labels can be purchased – Gucci, Dunhill, YSL and others; the **PALAIS RENAISSANCE** centre, 390 Orchard Rd, which houses Ralph Lauren, Chanel and Karl Lagerfeld among others; the **PROMENADE**, 300 Orchard Rd, also jam-packed with designer gear, and **CENTREPOINT**, 176 Orchard Rd, which is where you can seek solace at the ubiquitous **M & S**.

For jewellery try the **LUCKY PLAZA** centre, 304 Orchard Rd, where there's a continuous price war between the many jewellers, including Cartier – be sure to haggle. Orchard Rd is still dominated by the luxurious giants of Asian retailing. **LANE CRAWFORD**, Hong Kong's favourite department store, is the latest arrival. Japan's **TAKASHIMAYA** inhabits an Art Deco-style palace of stone. You can't move far without bumping into a shopping mall; **RAFFLES CENTRE** offers comprehensive shopping, as does **MARINA SQUARE**, where you'll also find **TIMES BOOKS**, the best bookshop in Singapore.

HOLLAND VILLAGE is an ex-pat haunt, and a good place to look for unusual Asian items. You can almost always find something novel at **LIM'S ARTS & CRAFTS**, Holland Village Shopping Centre, Holland Rd. **TANGLIN SHOPPING CENTRE**, junction of Tanglin and Orchard Rds, is good for Oriental antiques

and carpets. It also houses **JUSTMENS**, Units 01–36, ☎ 737 4800, *the* tailor for the ex-pat and business community. Great tailoring can also be found at **ALLAN CHAI FASHION DESIGN**, 05–56 Peninsula Plaza, 110 N Bridge Rd, ☎ 338 4330. The **CHINA SILK HOUSE**, Tanglin Shopping Centre, is particularly good at tailoring for women – they also have a fantastic selection of fabrics. For electrical goods you can't do better than **COST PLUS ELECTRONICS**, 1–12 Scotts Shopping Centre, 6–8 Scotts Rd, where prices are as low as anywhere and the goods are guaranteed.

Finally, the latest additions to the Singapore shopping scene are the **SUNTEC CITY MALL** and the **MILLENIA WALK**. When fully completed in 1997, they will become Singapore's largest shopping and entertainment destination, housing a Virtual Reality Theme Park and a state-of-the-art cineplex.

SOUTH AFRICA
Cape Town

ART AND MUSEUMS

KOOPMANS DE WET HOUSE

35 STRAND ST
☎ (21) 242473
A beautifully restored example of an early 18C townhouse, with a fine collection of contemporary furniture.

SOUTH AFRICAN MUSEUM

GREY'S PASS RD, CITY CENTRE
☎ (21) 243330; fax (21) 246716
A natural history museum, the oldest and best in the country. Particularly strong in palaeontology and ethnography, it houses a planetarium where Northerners can unravel the mysteries of the Southern hemisphere's skies.

SOUTH AFRICAN NATIONAL GALLERY AND GARDENS

GOVERNMENT AVE, COMPANY GDNS
☎ (21) 451628; fax: (21) 461005
In a stunning setting with Table Mountain behind and the historic Company Gardens in front. A fine collection of mainly Western art, though fortunately the current acquisitions policy is now biased against "Eurocentrism" and towards local craftworks.

THE CAPE'S GRAPE

Wine has been grown around the Cape for 350 years. Those centuries of work in the vineyard and in the winery represent the development not only of a proud tradition but also of a fund of expertise unmatched, some contend, outside Europe. The Cape climate (Mediterranean, with widely varying rainfall) and soil (very diverse, from shales and granite to sandstone, and from sands to gravels) help produce wines of memorable quality from Old World cultivars or blends the foreign connoisseur will know well. South Africa's own noble grape, Pinotage (a cross between Pinot Noir and Cinsaut, or Hermitage), makes a fruity, full and complex red worth storing for a while, in a good cellar.

The vineyards themselves – about 250,000 acres – with their mountain backdrops and gracious homesteads in the Cape Dutch style are undoubtedly among the loveliest on earth. Take time off to taste Cape wines at the farm cellar door; spend at least a day touring four or five cellars; and be sure to send some home.

Among the most rewarding wineries are: **CAPE TOWN AREA**: Groot Constantia Estate, ☎ (21) 794 5128; fax (21) 794 1999, founded in 1685 and government-owned; **Buitenverwachting**, ☎ (21) 794 5190; fax (21) 794 1351; **Klein Constantia Estate**, ☎ (21) 794 5188; fax (21) 794 2464, with its magnificent maturation cellars inside a mountain. **STELLENBOSCH AREA**: **Kanonkop Estate**, ☎ (21) 884 4656/7; fax (21) 884 4719, the undisputed leading Pinotage producer; **Meerlust Estate**, ☎ (24) 43587/43275; fax (24) 43513, an outstanding Pinot Noir and Merlot farm, with tastings and sales by prior arrangement only; **Rust-en-Vrede Estate**, ☎ (21) 887 3153; fax (21) 887 8466, another excellent specialist red wine farm. Highly tradition-conscious; only three wine-makers in the last 100 years. **PAARL/FRANSCHOEK AREA**: **Nederburg**, ☎ (2211) 623104; fax (2211) 624887, possibly the country's most well-known label. Produces over 650,000 cases a year; **Boschendal Estate**, ☎ (2211) 41031; fax (2211) 41864, produces white wines as spectacular as its setting; **L'Ormarins Estate**, ☎ (2211) 41026; fax (2211) 41361, classic wines; **La Motte Estate**, ☎ (2212) 3119; fax (2212) 3446, a top Shiraz farm.

BARS AND CAFES

THE GECKO LOUNGE
29 LOOP ST
☎ (21) 419 8423; fax (21) 419 8423
Throbbing watering hole in the thick of downtown clubland. Live music on Wed, Fri and Sat.

MANENBERG'S JAZZ CAFE
ADDERLEY ST, CNR CHURCH STREET
☎ (21) 238595; fax (21) 238595
This is probably one of the best places to see Cape jazz talent, much of which is exceptional.

LA MED RESTAURANT AND BAR
GLEN COUNTRY CLUB, VICTORIA ROAD, CLIFTON
☎ (21) 438 5600; fax (21) 438 2018
A 20-minute drive from the centre of town. People come here more for the atmosphere and the fantastic sea views (its a great place to watch the sun go down) than the food. Not quiet, but great if you want that party atmosphere. Closed Mon in winter.

CLUBS

D-LITE
LOOP ST
☎ (21) 216038
Hip joint attracting all sorts of trendsetters. Squash yourself into the bar area and have a good pose or make for the dance area in the basement.

THE MAGIC LUSH ROOM
UPSTAIRS FROM CAFÉ DISTRICT SIX, DARLING ST
Super-cool dance space featuring ambient, trance, house and jungle sounds – indeed so cool, it doesn't appear to have a telephone.

HOTELS

THE BAY
CAMPS BAY
☎ (21) 438 4444; fax (21) 438 4455
Clean white lines, cool tiled floors, light, bright and airy – this is a refreshingly modern alternative in a town where it's almost obligatory for good hotels to double up as listed monuments. Every room enjoys a spectacular sea or mountain view.

THE CELLARS-HOHENHORT
PO BOX 270, CONSTANTIA 7848
☎ (21) 794 2137; fax (21) 764 2149
The 17C cellars of the former Klaasenbosch wine farm have been lovingly converted into this graceful hotel, set in nine acres of landscaped gardens. Noted restaurant and cellar, too.

MOUNT NELSON HOTEL
76 ORANGE ST, PO BOX 2608
☎ (21) 231000; fax (21) 247472
In the shadow of Table Mountain, the pale-pink "Nellie" has been a favourite of discerning travellers for nearly a century. It still retains its old colonial feel, exemplified by the wonderful afternoon tea.

MUSIC

THE NICO THEATRE
DF MALAN ST, THE FORESHORE
☎ (21) 217695; fax (21) 215448
The city's main performance venue, this enormous modern arts complex houses an opera house and several theatres, and hosts everything from Wagner to avant-garde gay musicals.

RESTAURANTS

SEE ALSO HOTELS.

BLUES RESTAURANT
THE PROMENADE, VICTORIA RD, CAMPS BAY
☎ (21) 438 2040; fax (21) 438 3238
Californian-style cuisine in a spacious, airy room overlooking one of the world's most pristinely beautiful beaches. Always packed, so book ahead.

BUITENVERWACHTING RESTAURANT
KLEIN CONSTANTIA RD, CONSTANTIA
☎ (21) 794 3522; fax (21) 794 1351
The name means "beyond expectation" and that's a fair description of this wonderful restaurant. The wine list is impressive. Closed Mon and in Aug. *"Set in one of the oldest and most beautiful vineyards of the Cape. Five full stars on all points"* – JOHN TOVEY.

CAFE PARADISO
110 KLOOF ST GARDENS
☎ (21) 238653; fax (21) 233042
Chef Freda van der Merwe dishes up exceptional Mediterranean-style cuisine in this relaxed and friendly café–brasserie, much loved by the local élite.

CONSTANTIA UITSIG
SPAANSCHEMAT RIVER RD, CONSTANTIA
☎ (21) 794 4480; fax (21) 794 7605
This wine farm restaurant offers fine Provençal cooking where fish and game are specialities. NED SHERRIN recommends that you *"try the carpaccio di pesce, wafer-thin slices of raw fish dressed in soya sauce, red vinegar, sesame oil, ginger and sea weed – the most memorable dish I have eaten this year."*

MORTON'S ON THE WHARF
V&A WATERFRONT
☎ (21) 418 3633; fax (21) 418 3637
One of the best bars and restaurants crowding this thriving – if somewhat touristy – dockside complex. Fine Cajun cooking and a cheery, bustling ambience.

PAVILION BISTRO
BMW PAVILION, GRANGER BAY BLVD, V&A WATERFRONT
☎ (21) 418 4210; fax (21) 418 4214
Another waterfront gem, all high-tech steel and chrome. Chef Else van der Nest (who trained under Marco Pierre White) cooks fabulously imaginative Mediterranean food.

Durban

CAFES

🕸 FUNKY'S
BAT CENTRE, SMALL CRAFTS
HARBOUR, VICTORIA EMBANKMENT
☎ (31) 373061
Hip watering-hole – despite the dubious name
– with live bands; the perfect place to watch
the sun set over Durban Bay. The attached
restaurant is very good value and serves particularly good curries.

CLUBS

PULSE
80 ST GEORGE'S ST
☎ (31) 304 2503
Dispensing the latest and best techno from foreign lands as well as trip, hop, club and trance.
Every Sat from 10 pm until late.

HOTELS

THE OYSTER BOX HOTEL
2 LIGHTHOUSE RD, UMHLANGA ROCKS
☎ (31) 561 2223; fax (31) 561 4072
Quiet and very comfortable, this is a superb
family-run hotel in an upmarket resort 9 miles
north of Durban. Right on the beach, and has
a good restaurant too, specializing in fresh
seafood and enormous steaks.

THE ROYAL HOTEL
267 SMITH ST
☎ (31) 304 0331; fax (31) 307 6884
Bland modern exterior, but large, luxurious
and exceptionally comfortable. Prides itself on
offering the classic "Last Outpost of the British
Empire" experience. The ULUNDI restaurant
specializes in fabulous curries. Has won the
country's prestigious Fedhasa award for Best
City Hotel five times since 1988.

SELBORNE COUNTRY LODGE AND GOLF COURSE
PO BOX 2, PENNINGTON 4184
☎ (323) 51133; fax (323) 51811

Just 40 minutes' drive south of Durban, this
lovely country house is decorated with
antiques and fine oil paintings, set in tropical
gardens which are a twitcher's delight. The
golf course is one of the best in the country.

RESTAURANTS

SEE ALSO HOTELS.

THE COLONY
FIRST FLOOR, THE OCEANIC, SOL
HARRIS CRESCENT
☎ (31) 368 2789; fax (31) 368 0393
A hot spot for power lunchers, who come for
the classic South African cuisine – warthog's a
speciality.

LA DOLCE VITA
DURDOC CENTRE, 460 SMITH ST
☎ (31) 301 8161; fax (31) 301 3347
Still widely regarded as the best and chicest
joint in town after 23 years. Chef/patron
Gianni Allegranzi prepares traditional Italian
cuisine with elegance and flair.

LE SAN GERAN RESTAURANT
31 ALIWAL ST, CENTRAL
☎ (31) 304 7509; fax (31) 305 4670
Eatery with a lively atmosphere in a lovely
pink, listed building. The Mauritian/Creole
cooking here is a firm favourite with locals and
visitors alike. Outstandingly delicious fish.

TWO MOON JUNCTION
45 WINDERMERE RD, MORNINGSIDE
☎ (31) 303 3078; fax (31) 303 1953
Buzzing, see-and-be-seen eatery with a picturesque courtyard, serving imaginative contemporary South African cuisine.

Johannesburg

ART AND MUSEUMS

EVERARD READ GALLERY
6 JELLICOE AVE, ROSEBANK
☎ (11) 788 4805; fax (11) 788 5914

ENCORE Africa's largest Asian community lives in **Durban** – for an authentic Eastern
experience, head for exotic Victoria Market in Grey St, which sells every kind of spice, from
cinnamon to fearsome mother-in-law curry power . . . . ♦

The best commercial gallery in Johannesburg. Hosts well thought-out shows covering a wide variety of work, from abstract landscapes to wildlife paintings to tribal art.

GERTRUDE POSEL GALLERY

SENATE HOUSE, UNIVERSITY OF THE WITWATERSRAND
☎ (11) 716 3632; fax (11) 716 8030
Houses the superb Standard Bank Foundation Collection of tribal art, including Xhosa and Zulu beadwork. Visits by appointment only.

BARS AND CAFES

BOB'S BAR

80 OP DIE BERGEN ST, FAIRVIEW
☎ (11) 624 1894
This cool café-bar with its retro-chic interior and displays of local art is a hangout for Jo'burg's hip and trendy. Also serves light meals.

KIPPIE'S

MARKET THEATRE AND PRECINCT, BREE ST, NEWTOWN
☎ (11) 834 4714; fax (11) 834 4714
Named after renowned black saxophonist Kippie Moroleng, this intimate bar is a showcase for the best performers on Jo'burg's township jazz scene.

LONG ISLAND ICED TEA BAR

SHOPS 1 AND 2, ILLOVO SQ, 3 RIVONIA RD, ILLOVO
☎ (11) 447 6272; fax (11) 447 6273
A young, modern and very trendy hangout, attracting lots of beautiful people.

PANDORA'S BOX

77 CARGO CORNER, TYRWHITT AVE, ROSEBANK
☎ (11) 447 3066; fax ☎ (11) 788 0891
Groovy club featuring a mix of techno, house and funk. Popular with young crowds.

PICASSO'S

ROSEBANK
☎ (11) 788 1213; fax ☎ (11) 788 9843
This divinely hip dive with its large, comfortable sofas has the wannabes flocking to marvel at the passing celebrity show.

STORYVILLE

KEYSTONE CORNER, KEYES AVE, ROSEBANK
☎ (11) 788 5569; fax ☎ (11) 788 5569
The mix of soul, funk and techno and the relaxed ambience attract the mainly over-25s.

HOTELS

THE PARK HYATT HOTEL

ROSEBANK
☎ (11) 280 1234; fax (11) 280 1238
Don't be put off by the prison-like exterior – inside, all is spaciousness, opulence and comfort.

KAROS INDABA HOTEL

PO BOX 67129, BRYANSTON
☎ (11) 465 1400; fax (11) 705 1709
Large, purpose-built hotel tucked away in one of the leafiest of Jo'burg's northern suburbs. Offers some of the best conference facilities in the country, as well as excellent sports facilities.

ⓦ LINFOURSON GUEST HOUSE

58 CURZON RD, BRYANSTON
☎ (11) 704 2575; fax (11) 704 2575
This upmarket guest house is outstanding. Five luxurious en suite rooms set in 3 acres of lush gardens, with tennis court, swimming pool and sauna; delightful, friendly service.

RESTAURANTS

BODEGA

ADMIRAL'S COURT, TYRWHITT MALL, 31 TYRWHITT AVE, ROSEBANK
☎ (11) 447 3210; fax (11) 447 3214
The best Italian food in Jo'burg. Cool, spacious and airy, with the menu written up on a blackboard.

CENTO

100 LONGEMAN DRIVE, KENSINGTON
☎ (11) 622 7270; fax (11) 622 6150
Not only do Al and Val Strick cook Mediterranean food with flair, their cellar contains the biggest stock of wines in Jo'burg.

GRAMADOELAS AT THE MARKET

MARKET THEATRE PRECINCT, WOLHUTTER ST, NEWTOWN
☎ (11) 838 6960; fax (11) 484 6359
A magnet for overseas visitors who come for the superb South African cuisine, including such delicacies as crocodile. Beautiful mock 18C decor.

ILE DE FRANCE

CRAMERVIEW SHOPPING CENTRE, 277 MAIN RD, BRYANSTON
☎ (11) 706 2837; fax (11) 706 2853
This large, airy space surrounded by windows is a rare oasis for local foodies, who go into

raptures over chef Marc Guebert's fine Provençal cooking.

LINGER LONGER
58 WIERDA RD W, WIERDA VALLEY W, SANDTON
☎ (11) 884 0465; fax (11) 884 0126
Despite the silly name, a luxuriously appointed restaurant serving really exceptional French food. Chef Walter Ulz is famed for his beautiful presentation, too.

SHOPPING

The best crafts plus an eclectically designed selection of china, silver and linen goods are to be found at CONGO JOE'S, ☎ (11) 726 4101; fax (11) 482 8173. ZEBRA CROSSING, 20a Rockey St, Bellevue, ☎ (11) 648 4548, and THE PAPER WORKSHOP, 1a Rockey St, Bellevue, ☎ (11) 648 03007, are both bursting with African treasures, too. Roam down the rest of Rockey St for clothes with a difference, cafés strong on wholefood, and an engaging mix of local funk and tat. The ORIENTAL PLAZA, at the corner of Main and Bree Sts, Fordsburg, is a traditional bazaar where bargain-hunters can find wonderful basketware, silver, bronze and copper crafts. Visit the multi-shop KWA DABGULAMANZI at 14 Diagonal St, City – they sell herbs and potions prescribed by a *sangoma* (traditional healer). If you feel like buying a few diamonds go to the SANDTON CITY shopping mall, ☎ (11) 783 7413.

THEATRE

THE MARKET THEATRE
MARKET THEATRE AND PRECINCT, BREE ST, NEWTOWN
☎ (11) 832 1641
One of South Africa's most famous arts complexes, and traditionally the best place to see contemporary black theatre with a cutting edge. Also houses a couple of trendy bars (see Bars and Cafés) and the renowned GRAMADOELAS restaurant (see Restaurants).

Port Elizabeth

HOTELS

LOVEMORE RETREAT
PO BOX 15818, EMERALD HILL, 6011
☎ (41) 361708/752; fax (41) 362304
There's a dismal lack of decent accommodation here so thank heaven for this luxurious coastal retreat on the outskirts of town. Offers a full range of health spa treatments; tranquil beach and nature walks too.

RESTAURANTS

THE SIR RUFANVE DONKIN ROOMS
5 GEORGE ST, CENTRAL
☎ (41) 555534; fax (41) 522229
Port Elizabeth's best restaurant is in an elegant 18C townhouse right in the city centre (the oldest and least depressing part of town). Good plain cooking, including fresh seafood.

Pretoria

DANCE

THE STATE THEATRE
CNR PRINSLOO AND CHURCH STS
☎ (12) 322 1665
An unappealing-looking modern complex which nonetheless showcases some of the best dance productions (as well as other performing arts) the country has to offer. Check local newspapers like *The Star* and *The Transvaaler* for listings.

HOTELS

MARVOL HOUSE
358 ARIES ST, WATERKLOOF RIDGE
☎ (12) 346 1774; fax (12) 346 1776
Small, very comfortable hotel in the white-washed-and-gabled Cape Dutch style. Set on a

ENCORE It may seem bizarre to treat the townships as a tourist attraction, but to truly appreciate the rapidly changing South Africa, you must visit them. One of the few ways to do it safely is on a guided tour. **Jimmy's Face to Face Tours**, ☎ (11) 331 6109, from central Jo'burg to Soweto are sensitively handled and highly informative . . . . ♣

ALL ABOARD Luxury travel by steam-hauled train in elegant turn-of-the-century style is the sort of romantic journey that has long held travellers' imaginations. **Rovos Rail**, PO Box 2837, Pretoria 0001, ☎ (12) 323 6052; fax (12) 323 0483, runs beautifully restored old trains on spectacular routes across the country. The most popular is from Cape Town to Pretoria and on up to Zimbabwe's Victoria Falls. A maximum of 46 passengers are attended by 16 staff; dressing for dinner is customary. Rovos definitely outstrips its older rival in the luxury rail travel stakes, the **Blue Train**, c/o Connex Travel, PO Box 1113, Johannesburg, ☎ (11) 774 4469, fax (11) 773 7643. It offers similar routes, but its 1970s decor and menus are now in need of an imaginative overhaul.

---

ridge, with two swimming pools, gym, Jacuzzi and sauna.

RESTAURANTS

GERARD MOERDYK

752 PARK ST, ARCADIA
☎ (12) 344 4856; fax (12) 344 4856
Old-fashioned, elegant restaurant with flounced silk curtains, antiques and artefacts, heavy tapestries and polished wooden floors. Serves superbly cooked traditional South African cuisine, such as springbok pie and ostrich.

LA MADELAINE

258 ESSELEN ST, SUNNYSIDE
☎ (12) 446076; fax (12) 341 5387
Sensational Provençal food. Simplicity is the watchword of Daniel Leusch's cooking, and it's won him many laurels. As a local magazine put it, "*There's no chi-chi, no gimmick, no theme, no pretence and no parking; yet no restaurant in the country has had more honours heaped upon it.*"

Rest of South Africa

FESTIVALS

STANDARD BANK NATIONAL ARTS FESTIVAL

GRANHAMSTOWN, EASTERN CAPE
☎ (461) 27115
The country's biggest and best arts jamboree is based on the Edinburgh model and combines a series of festivals, including a giant, chaotic fringe. Usually held during the first two weeks in July.

GAME RESERVES

LONDOLOZI

PO BOX 1211, SUNNINGHILL PARK
☎ (11) 803 8421; fax (11) 803 1810
A comfortable private reserve with an impressive conservation record on the borders of the Kruger National Park – thus sharing most of the "Big Five" animals. Accommodation is split into three camps (Main, Bush and Tree), each with luxury chalets. Excellent food, including fresh kudu and impala. One of PRESIDENT MANDELA's favourite retreats. JOHN CLEESE, CHRIS DE BURGH and MICHAEL HESELTINE have stayed here too. "*Fantastically well run and comfortable game lodge,*" DAVID GOWER.

··

"*SOUTH AFRICA IS OPENING UP TO TOURISM AND STILL ADAPTING TO CHANGE AND DEMAND, SO IT'S NOT YET UP TO SPEED, BUT ITS GREAT WILDLIFE PARKS ARE A MUST*" –
DAVID GOWER

··

MALA MALA

RATTRAY RESERVES, PO BOX 2575, RANDBURG
☎ (11) 789 2677
Less than 100 visitors are allowed into this 57,000-acre private reserve at any one time, so you're assured of undisturbed watching. Comfortable, and not far from Johannesburg.

HOTELS

AUBERGE DU QUARTIER FRANCAIS

16 HUGUENOT RD, FRANSCHHOEK
7690
☎ (2212) 2151; fax (2212) 3105
An exceptional country-house hotel just outside Cape Town. It's small and built round a garden courtyard with a pool. Well-placed for tours of the winelands, and the restaurant is highly acclaimed too.

THE GRAND ROCHE HOTEL

PO BOX 6038, PAARL 7622
☎ (2211) 632727; fax (2211) 632220
Simply the best hotel in South Africa. A superb setting in a vineyard, sumptuous accommodation, superb service. BOSMAN'S, the hotel restaurant, has classically trained staff, serving *haute cuisine* and a prize-winning cellar.

THE PALACE

THE LOST CITY, PO BOX 308, SUN CITY 0316
☎ (1465) 73000; fax (1465) 73111
Critics deplore its flamboyant, glitzy presence in one of the poorest regions of the country, but this is nonetheless a top-class hotel. It's set in an imported "tropical jungle" setting, complete with artificial beach and wave pool. Guests can take advantage of Sun City's entertainment facilities, a very good golfcourse and game viewing in the Pilanesberg National Park.

THE PLETTENBERG

PO BOX 719, PLETTENBERG BAY
☎ (4457) 32030
A grand hotel in the English country-house style. Very good food and service, and a pleasant, relaxing atmosphere. Amazing sea views.

ROGGELAND COUNTRY HOUSE

PO BOX 7210, PAARL NORTH
☎ (2211) 682501; fax (2211) 682113
A superb small (eight-bedroom) country-house hotel in the winelands. Located an hour from Cape Town, the ambience, the restaurant and the service have placed it firmly in the ranks of the 50 best country-house hotels in the world. The cuisine is South African regional.

TOURS

FLAMINGO FLIGHTS

BERTIE'S LANDING, THE WATERFRONT, CAPE TOWN
☎ (21) 790 1010
Flights round the Western Cape in a de Havilland Beaver Seaplane – great for fishing or waterskiing – or one-hour trips to beaches or the Winelands.

SOLITAIRE TOURS AND SAFARIS

PO BOX 957, NELSPRUIT 1200
☎ (1311) 24527; fax (1311) 27594
Excellent wildlife specialist company offering

●●

ENCORE For an exclusive bolthole in **Tanzania**, visit Sand Rivers Selous, in the Selous National Park, Africa's biggest game reserve. Just six thatched cottages, each with four-poster bed and power shower, set in 20,000 square miles beside the Rufiji river. Sand River Selous is the permanent lodge of one of East Africa's leading guides, Richard Bonham, who leads treks in search of the big five. You'll also bump into the odd crocodile, impala and hippo. For details contact Worldwide Journeys and Expeditions (see Travel Directory) . . . . . ♦ In **Zimbabwe** try the Iwaba Wildlife Estate, a private nature reserve (three hours' drive from Harare in central Zimbabwe). Renowned for its conservation work, this is one of the few places in the world where it is possible to see black and white rhinos on the same range. From its thatched rondavels in the bush, you can enjoy game-viewing by Landrover (and night drives), and game-walks followed by dinner under the stars when you can recover from your stirring encounters with the local wildlife. For details contact Abercrombie & Kent (see Travel Directory) . . . . . ♦ In **Zambia** escape to the completely romantic Tongabezi Lodge, run by old Etonians Ben Parker and Will Ruck Keene. Situated beside the Zambezi river, this is where VISCOUNT LINLEY chose to spend his honeymoon. Here you can drink Pimms and play croquet or watch wallowing hippos and the fabulous local bird life. And, of course, it's the perfect launch pad for a safari and a visit to nearby Victoria Falls . . . . ♦

tailor-made tours and safaris to the major parks and reserves, including the little-known and fascinating **KALAHARI GEMSBOK PARK**.

SPAIN
Barcelona

ART AND MUSEUMS

FUNDACIO ANTONI TAPIES
ARAGO 255
☎ (93) 487 0315
This foundation was inspired by one of the most important post-World War II Spanish artists, Antoni Tàpies. It now contains a permanent exhibition of Tàpies's work, as well as temporary exhibitions of like-minded artists.

FUNDACIO JOAN MIRO
PLAÇA NEPTUNO, PARC DE MONTJUÏC
☎ (93) 329 1908
Bauhaus-style museum on the heights of Montjuïc, overlooking Barcelona, built to house works by Catalan painter, graphic artist and designer Joan Miró, who died in 1983.

EL MUSEU D'ART CONTEMPORANI
PLAÇA DELS ÀNGELS 1
☎ (93) 412 0810
Spectacular new gallery recently opened off the Ramblas, containing Spanish and foreign paintings and sculptures from the last 40 years.

MUSEU PICASSO
CALLE MONTCADA 15-19
☎ (93) 319 6310
Splendid 15C palace in the Gothic Quarter now housing more than 900 paintings, drawings, engravings and ceramics by Barcelona's best-loved and best-known artist.

⊛ PARC GUELL
City park begun by brilliant but disturbing Catalan master Gaudí in 1900. Contains fine examples of his repertoire, including a giant decorative lizard and Gaudí's own house, now a small museum. A must see.

TEMPLE EXPIATORI DE LA SAGRADA FAMILIA
LA SAGRADA FAMILIA DISTRICT
Gaudí's project for 42 years from 1884. This church has three façades, Faith, Hope and Charity, each with four towers to represent the twelve apostles. The central tower, which was to have been 500 feet tall, was never built. A lift (or stairs) takes you to the top of the east tower for a breathtaking view. The church itself is a museum dedicated to Gaudí.

BARS AND CAFES

CAFE DE L'OPERA
RAMBLA 74
☎ (93) 317 7585
Probably the city's most popular café, not least because it's open long hours and is a great place for breakfast. It's situated on the Rambla, the city's longest and best promenade – but sit inside, not out.

EL DRY MARTINI
ARIBÁN 162
☎ (93) 217 5072
Fashionable cocktail bar boasting over 80 brands of gin.

ELS QUATRE GATS
MONTSIÓ 3
☎ (93) 302 4140
One-time celebrated hang-out of Picasso, Miró, Utrillo and other local artists.

EL XAMPANAYET
CALLE MONTCADA 22
☎ (93) 319 7003
One of Barcelona's thriving champagne bars, serving the ever popular cava as well as a wide variety of snacks – ideal refreshment following a visit to the Museu Picasso (see Art and Museums) down the road.

CLUBS

JIMMIZ
PL PIUS XII 4
☎ (93) 339 7108
Lively youth-oriented club complete with karaoke bar.

OLIVER Y HARDY
DIAGONAL 593
☎ (93) 419 3181
Next to the Barcelona Hilton (see Hotels), this is a restaurant, covered terrace, piano bar and disco all in one – for the older clubber.

TICKTACKTOE
ROGER DE LLURIA 40
☎ (93) 318 9770

Superbly designed and set in a former textile factory, it comprises a stylish restaurant, bar and nightclub.

TORRES DE AVILA
AVINGUDA MARQUÉS DE CAMILLAS 25
☎ (93) 424 9309
One of Barcelona's more eccentric clubs, both in decor and in clientele. Worth a visit.

VELVET
BALMES 161
☎ (93) 217 6714
Lively, theatrical club designed by Alfredo Arribas and Javier Mariscal. Barstools with buttock-cheek seats, and loos with strobe-lit urinals.

HOTELS

ARTS BARCELONA
MARINA 19–21
☎ (93) 221 1000
Luxury hotel overlooking the sea at Port Olímpic, with great views of the city and the mountains behind too.

BARCELONA HILTON
AVENIDA DIAGONAL 589–591
☎ (93) 410 7499
Better than your usual Hilton and located in Barcelona's business district. The fitness facilities which include a swimming pool, sauna and squash courts are among the best in town.

CLARIS
PAUL CLARIS 150
☎ (93) 487 6262

Sumptuous hotel housed in a late 19C mansion, in a great central location. Japanese water garden, excellent restaurant and swimming pool on the roof, plus a private museum of Egyptian sculpture on the second floor make this one of the city's finest hotels

CONDES DE BARCELONA
PASSEIG DE GRÀCIA 75
☎ (93) 487 3737
Book well in advance for this beautifully restored hotel, built in 1891. Unique features include the original pentagonal lobby, as well as rooms with terraces which overlook the sheltered gardens. Chic shopping nearby.

HOTEL COLON
AVENIDA CATEDRAL 7
☎ (93) 301 1404
A charming, old-fashioned hotel that used to be a favourite of Miró – the front rooms with balconies have a great view of the cathedral.

HOTEL MELIA
AVENIDA SARRIÀ 48–50
☎ (93) 410 6060
Bright, modern hotel in Barcelona's smarter part. The restaurant serves an excellent Sunday brunch, as well as both Catalan and international food.

HOTEL RITZ
GRAN VÍA 668
☎ (93) 318 5200
Luxurious institution built in 1919. Since then it has housed virtually every VIP that has passed through the city. The vast rooms feature an abundance of gilt and some rather hectic carpets. The Roman bath suites are fun. Excellent service.

ENCORE Escape the heat of the city and head out by metro to **Barceloneta Beach**, where you'll find a range of (mostly good-value) bars, restaurants and tapas bars in this fishing port. A surprisingly good restaurant, called the **Gato Negro Chiringuito**, is often set up on the beach. After midnight the whole waterfront area becomes particularly lively . . . . . ♠ The adjacent area, **Port Olímpic**, is where some of the most luxurious yachts are moored, having been lured in to port by the tapas bars and gleaming new buildings, marked by Barcelona's skyscraper, Hotel Arts (see Hotels) and a giant sculpture of a goldfish . . . . . ♠ Since the Olympic Games were held here, **Port Vell**, which means old harbour, has been completely redesigned. Now there is a series of bridges and piers containing a complex with shops, bars, restaurants, an IMAX 3D cinema and the biggest aquarium in Europe. There's also **Palau de Mar**, an old dock building converted to restaurants and terrace bars, with **Merendero de la Mari** being perhaps the best of these. . . . . ♠

"THE OLD 'GRAND' HOTELS DE
LUXE IN EUROPEAN CAPITALS ARE
BEING REPLACED BY SMALL
QUALITY HOTELS SINCE THE
CLIENTELE HAS RUINED THE
FORMER. THE SAME APPLIES
TO THE MOST FAMOUS
RESTAURANTS AS MORE CLIENTS
REQUEST KETCHUP WITH A
CHEESE SOUFFLÉ" –

CLAUS VON BULOW

LE MERIDIEN

RAMBLA 111
☎ (93) 318 6200
If you don't mind a bit of noise and enjoy
watching the world go by, choose a room on
the front overlooking La Rambla. Computers,
phones and faxes on demand. MADONNA and
MICHAEL JACKSON have both stayed here.

RESTAURANTS

SEE ALSO HOTELS.

AGUT D'AVIGNON

TRINITAT 3
☎ (93) 302 6034
Popular with businessmen and politicians.
Rustic-style restaurant serving rustic food
which includes a fine mix of Catalan, Basque
and French cuisine.

BELTXENEA

MALLORCA 275, ENTLO
☎ (93) 215 302
Wonderful long-established Basque restaurant.
Country-house atmosphere, with a series of
dining rooms, boasting log fires in winter. In
summer you can eat outside in the formal gardens. Formidable wine list.

LA DAMA

DIAGONAL 423–425
☎ (93) 202 0686
A beautiful conversion of a Moderniste house
designed by Manuel Sayrach, now an exclusive
restaurant in the capable hands of manager-
chef Joseph Bullich, formerly at Agut
d'Avignon. Great seafood.

ELDORADO PETIT

DOLORS MONSERDÀ 51
☎ (93) 204 5153
Traditional Spanish cuisine with a *nouvelle cuisine* touch. Very with it.

FLORIAN

CALLE BERTRAN I SERRA 20
☎ (93) 212 4627
Catalan food with a modern twist, particularly
good during the mushroom season.

NEICHEL

BELTRAN I ROZPIDE 16
☎ (93) 203 8408
This restaurant is the home of some of the best
(and most expensive) food in Barcelona –
thanks to Alsatian chef Jean Louis Neichel.

SET PORTES

PASSEIG ISABEL II 14
☎ (93) 319 3033
Traditional restaurant established in 1836 near
the old harbour, where you'll find the freshest
paella. Large and busy so book the day before
or be prepared to queue.

Madrid

Like Vienna, another landlocked Habsburg
capital, Madrid is very much a city of high culture. Madrid is also a city with a big appetite,
and eating is a favourite pastime. The day
begins with cups of thick and rich hot chocolate served with sugary doughnuts for breakfast, followed by mid-morning coffee, followed by lunch, followed by lengthy evening
drinks and snacks (Madrid has some of the best
and liveliest tapas bars in Spain) and finally
ending with a huge dinner eaten late, late at
night.

Foodies will be kept happy by the vast array
of Spanish olive oils, chocolates and spices for
sale here. In fact, you can shop very well
indeed in Madrid. All the international and
Spanish luxury names (like Loewe) have large
stores here. You can buy leather or arcane perfumes or antiques. You'll also find sophisticated children's clothes and toys and well-priced
acoustic guitars.

But the greatest thing about Madrid is what
there is to see. Nowhere in the world will you
find more or better works by Goya or
Velázquez. The quarter-mile around the
PLAZA CANOVAS DEL CASTILLO is home to
both the **PRADO** and the **THYSSEN-**

BORNEMISZA museums as well as two of Europe's great hotels, the RITZ and the PALACE. Less obvious treasures include the armoury at the PALACIO REAL (the King of Spain's official residence) with its encyclopaedic collection of suits of armour; the cafés around the PLAZA DE ORIENTE or the dramatic splendour of the PLAZA MAYOR. Energetic visitors will be well rewarded by a day trip to the forbidding palace of EL ESCORIAL or any of the wonderful cities around Madrid: AVILA (with its formidable Romanesque cathedral), SEGOVIA (home of the great double-decker Roman aqueduct) and TOLEDO (choked with tourists in high season but one of the fairy-tale sights of the world).

ART AND MUSEUMS

MUSEO DE ARTES MODERNAS REINA SOFIA
SANTA ISABEL 52
☎ (91) 467 5161
Spain's new modern art museum, now home to Picasso's *Guernica*, formerly at the Prado. Also contains works by Dali, Miró and Tàpies.

....

"EL PRADO IS THE
ABSOLUTE BEST IN THE WORLD"
– BEATRICE WELLES ON
MUSEO DEL PRADO

....

MUSEO DEL PRADO
PASEO DEL PRADO
☎ (91) 420 2836
The city's top attraction and one of Europe's largest museums. *Las Meninas* by Velázquez gets an entire room to itself, and rightly so (it inspired several paintings by Picasso). Along with works by El Greco and Goya, other features include a collection of 12C–19C Italian art and 15C–18C Dutch, French, Flemish and German art.

MUSEO THYSSEN-BORNEMISZA
PASEO DEL PRADO 8
☎ (91) 369 0151
The impressive $2 billion collection of Baron von Thyssen-Bornemisza was moved from Lugano to the beautifully restored 19C Palacio de Villahermosa a few years ago. The collection follows the course of Western art from 13C Italian works onwards. "*An absolutely wonderful way to spend the morning before popping*

across to the Ritz," declares DAVID SHILLING. The collection is due to remain here until 2002.

CLUBS

ARCHY
MARQUÉS DE RISCAL 11
☎ (91) 410 7343
Very fashionable club for late-night drinking. Reasonable food upstairs, packed disco downstairs.

BAGELUS
MARÍA DE MOLINA 25
☎ (91) 561 6100
Madrid's newest and trendiest club, with cabaret and theatre as well as a bar and disco spread over three floors of a converted embassy.

STELLA
ARLABAN 7
☎ (91) 522 4126
For insomniacs only – people only start arriving at 4 am. Brilliant music, from techno to 70s. Very trendy hangout.

THEATRIZ
HERMOSILLA 15
☎ (91) 577 5379
Bar/club/restaurant serving light food, plus a tiny, black-leather-padded disco.

HOTELS

HOTEL PALACE
PLAZA DE CORTES 7
☎ (91) 429 7551
A turn-of-the-century creation inspired by King Alfonso XIII. Charming *grande dame* hotel with a glorious glass-domed foyer and an impressive roll call of past guests. Popular bar among journalists and politicians, for late-evening drinks.

HOTEL RITZ
PLAZA DE LA LEALTAD 5
☎ (91) 521 2857
Superlative *belle-époque* hotel built at the instigation of King Alfonso XIII in 1906 to house royal guests for his wedding to Princess Eugénie, granddaughter of Queen Victoria. Come for an alfresco dinner under the palm trees or an aperitif in summer. Be sure to ask for a room overlooking the nearby Prado museum or the Castellana.

SANTA MAURO

CALLE ZURBANO 36, 28010

☎ (91) 319 6900

The old part of the hotel was once the Canadian embassy. Now it contains 12 characterful bedrooms, as well as the popular **BELAGUA** gourmet restaurant in the old wood-panelled library.

VILLA MAGNA

PASEO DE LA CASTELLANA 22, 28046

☎ (91) 576 7500

Newish hotel providing a neat hideaway for reclusive businessmen and celebs. Discreet service, lovely garden and good food. Good for afternoon tea.

THE WELLINGTON

VELÁZQUEZ 8, 28001

☎ (91) 575 4400

The place for bullfight aficionados. During the season, the pleasant bar is packed with fans.

RESTAURANTS

SEE ALSO HOTELS.

EL BOTIN

CUCHILLEROS 17

☎ (91) 366 4217

One of the world's oldest restaurants, established in 1725. Ernest Hemingway used to eat here, as NANCY REAGAN once did with the QUEEN OF SPAIN. Traditional Castilian food – the roast suckling pig is a highlight. Be sure to reserve a table in the wine cellar.

🐄 CASA PACO

PUERTA CERRADA 11

☎ (91) 366 3166

Still going strong. Paco Orales's son and daughter run the show now although his bull-fighting photos still adorn the walls. Best place for good, traditional Spanish food.

EL CENADOR DEL PRADO

CALLE DE PRADO 4

☎ (91) 429 1561

Extremely expensive, but the quality of food

brings Ministers and visiting dignitaries back again and again. Choose between the formal baroque salon or the more relaxed conservatory.

LA DORADA

ORENSE 64

☎ (91) 579 0383

As every Spaniard knows, seafood is often better and fresher in Madrid than it is on the coast, and this fab fish restaurant is no exception. Popular with the business community.

HORCHER

ALFONSO XII 6

☎ (91) 532 3596

A wide selection of game dishes available in this luxurious restaurant, adjacent to Madrid's famous Retiro Park, once the grounds of a Bourbon palace. Horcher's food is appropriately regal.

O'PAZO

CALLE REINA MERCEDES 20, 20020

☎ (91) 553 2333

Owned by a fish merchant, cuisine is predominantly northwest Spanish. "*The seafood is splendid. They're not afraid to be rough with it, and there's an authentic feel to the food*" – SIR PETER USTINOV.

PALACIO DE ANGLONA

CALLE SEGOVIA 13

☎ (91) 561 1079

Fashionable Spanish food for night-owls who like to have dinner at approximately 4 am.

VIRIDIANA

JUAN DE MENA 14

☎ (91) 531 5222

Trendy but relaxed gourmet restaurant with 60s decor. Choose from a variety of innovative dishes, such as sea bass with avocado and mango, or red onions stuffed with morcella (black pudding). Finish with a grapefruit sherbet accompanied by wine from the excellent list.

ZALACAIN

CALLE ALVAREZ DE BAENA 4

☎ (91) 315 9828

The finest restaurant in Spain. Grand and ele-

ENCORE For an authentic Madrileno flamenco show in Madrid, check out **Café de Chinitas**, Torija 7, ☎ (91) 559 5135, or **Corral de la Moreria**, Moreria 17, ☎ (91) 365 8446, where the best troupes perform. Down **Calle Huertas**, visit the turn-of-the-century wine and sherry bars, which offer a variety of chamber and guitar music . . . . ♦

MAKING LIGHT WORK
Forget the kitsch and glitz of the coast – for a truly cerebral holiday in southern Spain, join one of interior designer Charlotte Scott's wonderful painting holidays at Trasierra, Cazalla de la Sierra, 41370 Seville, ☎ (95) 488 4324. Charlotte hosts courses for budding artists in her beautifully renovated 16C country house, Trasierra, in the spectacular Sierra Morena mountains north of Seville. Trasierra is surrounded by olive and eucalyptus groves, with just five guest bedrooms, each with its own bathroom and sitting room. The studios and nursery – and even the swimming pool – are furnished with exquisite taste, using, whenever possible, using local artisans and local materials. Velázquez, Murillo and Zurbarán all revelled in the quality of light available in this part of Spain and here, and under Albany Wiseman's expert tuition, many people from all walks of life have come to hone their skills, including CLARE and DAVID ASTOR, THE DUCHESS OF ABERCORN and HARRIET WALTER. Wiseman's technique is said to have influenced the PRINCE OF WALES. All in all the emphasis is on relaxation for painters and non-painters alike.

gant, but cheap it ain't. "*Everything is made with extraordinary refinement; ranks with any of the great restaurants in any town. The service is very stylish, they know all the wonderful Spanish wines and they even warm the glasses*" – SIR PETER USTINOV.

Seville

CLUBS

Seville is the capital of flamenco and its ballroom equivalent, Sevillana. For strict flamenco performances, the best tablaos, or clubs, are LOS GALLOS, Plaza Santa Cruz 11, ☎ (95) 421 6981, or EL ARENAL, Rodo 7, ☎ (95) 421692.

ACADEMIA DE BAILE DE JUAN MORILLA
JESÚS DE GRAN PODER
☎ (95) 438 3559
The place to take flamenco lessons. They only speak Spanish so make sure you've understood those lessons first.

BARS AND CAFES

ABADES
CALLE ABADES 13
☎ (95) 422 5622
The most relaxed of all the bars, set in an old Sevillian house.

HOTELS

CASA DE CARMONA
PLAZA DE LASSO, CARMONA
☎ (95) 414 3300
"*Modern-day comforts in 16C surroundings, steeped in atmosphere and history*" – LADY WEINBERG.

HOTEL ALFONSO XIII
2 SAN FERNANDO, SEVILLE 41004
☎ (95) 422 8036
A sumptuous Mudejar-style palace, recently renovated, in the heart of Seville. "*In the warmest city in Spain, just a jump to Africa, the most incredible hotel, mind-blowing, like walking in a world of antiques,*" raves JOHN GOLD. Inside, the hotel is all marble, wood, stained glass and ceramics, which have been used to striking effect, in traditional Seville colours. It frequently becomes a temporary home to visiting royalty and celebrities.

RESTAURANTS

EGANA ORIGA
SAN FERNANDO 41
☎ (95) 422 7271
A light and breezy restaurant beside the elegant Murillo Gardens. Food is of the highest quality, reflecting the Basque origins of owner José Mari Egaña.

Rest of Spain

HOTELS

HACIENDA DE SAN RAFAEL
CARRETERA NACIONAL 4, KM NO 594,
CRUCE DE LAS CABEZAS, SEVILLE
☎ (95) 589 8014
Halfway between Jerez and Seville set among rolling sunflower fields, is an elegant, English-run Spanish house hotel which provides the perfect base for exploring Andalucía. Lovely Spanish tiled bedrooms filled with personal antiques and flowers from the garden.

HOTEL EL CORSARIO
OLD TOWN, IBIZA
☎ (971) 391953
Very beautiful, understated hotel offers exquisite bedrooms with old mahogany four-poster beds. Plus a spectacular restaurant terrace overlooking the whole of Ibiza town, and serving excellent food. Charming service.

HOTEL LA RESIDENCIA
DEYA, MAJORCA
☎ (971) 639370
Robert Graves lived in Deya for a while and to this day writers and artists still come here. The hotel consists of two 16C farmhouses; the dining room was once an olive mill, while olive and citrus groves attempt to keep the prying lenses of the paparazzi away from guests. Bedrooms are beautifully arranged, with old Majorcan furniture and big four-poster beds, and art, both modern and old. From the terrace there are great views of the cliffs and sea beyond. Delightful hotel, charming and relaxed. "*We go to La Residencia at least four times a year. I love the blue light of the mountains above Deya*" – says owner RICHARD BRANSON.

MARBELLA CLUB HOTEL
CARRETERA DE CÁDIZ, KM 178,
MARBELLA 29600
☎ (952) 282 2211
Founded by Prince Alfonso von Hohenlohe, the club now has a very loyal clientele. While the decor and size of the Andalusian-style bungalows vary, the lushness and beauty of the sub-tropical gardens does not. A little oasis.

EL PARADOR SAN MARCOS
PLAZA DE SAN MARCOS 7, LEÓN 24001
☎ (987) 237300
Beautiful hotel set in a 16C monastery with the world's grandest façade (built by de Badajoz, the architect of El Escorial). Rooms in the old section are filled with antiques and have oodles of character while the dining room overlooks the Bernesga River.

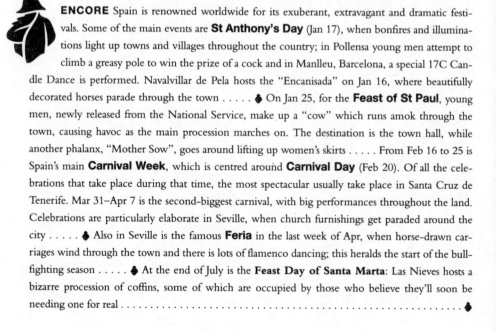

ENCORE Spain is renowned worldwide for its exuberant, extravagant and dramatic festivals. Some of the main events are **St Anthony's Day** (Jan 17), when bonfires and illuminations light up towns and villages throughout the country; in Pollensa young men attempt to climb a greasy pole to win the prize of a cock and in Manlleu, Barcelona, a special 17C Candle Dance is performed. Navalvillar de Pela hosts the "Encanisada" on Jan 16, where beautifully decorated horses parade through the town . . . . . ♦ On Jan 25, for the **Feast of St Paul**, young men, newly released from the National Service, make up a "cow" which runs amok through the town, causing havoc as the main procession marches on. The destination is the town hall, while another phalanx, "Mother Sow", goes around lifting up women's skirts . . . . . From Feb 16 to 25 is Spain's main **Carnival Week**, which is centred around **Carnival Day** (Feb 20). Of all the celebrations that take place during that time, the most spectacular usually take place in Santa Cruz de Tenerife. Mar 31–Apr 7 is the second-biggest carnival, with big performances throughout the land. Celebrations are particularly elaborate in Seville, when church furnishings get paraded around the city . . . . . ♦ Also in Seville is the famous **Feria** in the last week of Apr, when horse-drawn carriages wind through the town and there is lots of flamenco dancing; this heralds the start of the bullfighting season . . . . . ♦ At the end of July is the **Feast Day of Santa Marta**: Las Nieves hosts a bizarre procession of coffins, some of which are occupied by those who believe they'll soon be needing one for real . . . . ♦

EL PARADOR DE RONDA

PLAZA DE ESPAÑA, RONDA 29400,
☎ (5) 287 7500
The place to stay in Ronda, the home of bull-fighting and the subject of much of Ernest Hemingway's writing. The recently opened parador sits beside the magnificent 500 ft gorge (from which nuns were thrown during World War II). The building is a combination of a 17C town hall and a modern wing.

RESTAURANTS

SEE ALSO HOTELS.

⊛ ARZAK

ALTO DE MIRACRUZ 21, SAN SEBASTIÁN 20015
☎ (943) 28 5593
Juan Mari Arzak has done more to promote the food of Spain than any of his countrymen. This restaurant is small, cosy and good value, with a reputation that makes reservations essential. Almost exclusively fish.

SWEDEN
Stockholm

ART AND MUSEUMS

DROTTNINGHOLM PALACE

DROTTNINGHOLMS SLOTT
☎ (8) 759 0310
"Sweden's Versailles" is a 17C palace 5 miles west of the city which is still the official residence of the Swedish royal family. Features include the Chinese Pavilion and The Drottningholm Court Theatre is still Sweden's main opera house. The original 18C stage machinery is still in use, along with the antique instruments. The season lasts from May to Sept, and performances are well worth a visit. For tickets apply early to Drottningholms Opera, PO Box 27050, ☎ (8) 665 1100.

BARS AND CAFES

There are plenty of pubs and bars serving good food and lager at a reasonable price. Irish pubs are, oddly, a popular alternative and include the **BAGPIPER'S INN**, Rörstrandsgatan 21, ☎ (8)

311855; the **LIMERICK**, Tegnergatan 10, ☎ (8) 673 4398; and the **DUBLINER**, Birger Jarlspassagen, ☎ (8) 697 7707. For old-timers, try any one of the numerous piano bars: **RICHE**, ☎ (8) 611 8450; the **ANGLAIS BAR** at the Hotel Anglais, Humlegardsgatan 23, ☎ (8) 614 1600; or the **CLIPPER CLUB** at the First Hotel Reisen, Skeppsbron 12-14, ☎ (8) 223260. Or you can try the **OPERA CAFÉ**, which is *"right in the centre of one of the world's most beautiful cities, and combines functions as a restaurant, café, bar and nightclub"* according to JULIAN LLOYD WEBBER.

CLUBS

BORSEN

JAKOBSGATAN 6
☎ (8) 787 8500
The biggest nightclub in town, offering high-quality Swedish and international cabaret shows.

FASCHING

KUNGSGATAN 63
☎ (8) 216267
Stockholm's largest jazz club, attracting the best performers. Good atmosphere and very popular.

GALAXY

STRÖMSBURG (AN ISLET IN THE MIDDLE OF STRÖMMEN)
☎ (8) 215400
One of Stockholm's most popular clubs, which plays a wide variety of music including Swedish cult faves Abba. The outdoor bar and dining area are very popular in summer.

HOTELS

Contact "The Hotellcentralen", or Accommodation Booking Office, located in the main hall of the central station for direct personal booking on day of arrival, or telephone for advance bookings on ☎ (8) 240880, fax (8) 791 8666.

GRAND HOTEL

SÖDRA BLASIEHOLMSHAMNEN 8, PO BOX 16424, S-103 27
☎ (8) 679 3500; fax (8) 611 8686
Stockholm's grandest hotel, which opened in 1874. Facing the Royal Palace, it offers some of the best views of the town. The food is first-rate in both the French and Swedish restaurants.

HOTEL DIPLOMAT
STRANDVÄGEN 7C, BOX 14059, S–104 40
☎ (8) 663 5800; fax (8) 783 6634
A turn-of-the-century townhouse converted
in the 60s, this very elegant hotel has a magnificent view over Stockholm harbour. The
teahouse is popular for light meals.

LADY HAMILTON HOTEL
STORKYRKOBRINKEN 5, S–111 28
☎ (8) 234680; fax (8) 411 1148
Located right in the Old Town, it was initially
built as a private home in 1470 and was only
converted into a hotel in 1980. It has a beautiful collection of antiques, plus modern facilities including a pool and sauna.

SCANDIC CROWN HOTEL
GULGRÄND, BOX 15270, S–104 65
☎ (8) 702 2500; fax (8) 642 8358
Part of Sweden's main hotel group, this very
modern hotel is located on the increasingly
trendy south side of the city. Great facilities
with pool, sauna, solarium, two restaurants, a
bar and a good French eatery, **LA COURONNE
D'OR**.

MUSIC

KONSERTHUSET
HÖTORGET 8
☎ (8) 785 8182
Home of the Stockholm Philharmonic
Orchestra, whose main season runs from mid-
Sept to mid-May. Also offers lunchtime concerts
and, in summer, free concerts in several city
parks.

RESTAURANTS

BAKFICKAN
OPERAHUSET, JAKOBS TORG 2
☎ (8) 207745
Cheaper than the excellent Operakallaren (see

entry) and conveniently located at the back of
the Opera House. Its Swedish home cooking is
very popular at lunchtime.

DEN GYLDENE FREDEN
ÖSTERLÅNGGATAN 51
☎ (8) 109046
One-time haunt of Stockholm artists and
composers and now where, every Thurs, the
Swedish Academy meets for lunch. A tasty
combination of French and Swedish cuisine.

NILS EMIL
FOlKUNGAGATAN 122
☎ (8) 640 7209
Popular with the Swedish royal family and
famous for its traditional Swedish cuisine.
Delicious and unpretentious.

OPERAKALLAREN
OPERAHUSET, JAKOBS TORG 2
☎ (8) 411 1125
Located in the Opera House building, the best
in Stockholm and famous for its smörgasbord.
Book ahead if possible.

PAUL AND NORBERT
STRANDVÄGEN 9
☎ (8) 663 8183
Small and cosy French restaurant specializing
in game.

STALLMASTAREGARDEN
NORRTULL, NEAR HAGA
☎ (8) 610 1300
Beautiful old inn in the Haga park outside
Stockholm, serving a refined and delicate
combination of French and Swedish cuisine. In
summer meals are served in the courtyard
overlooking Brunnsviken Lake.

ULRIKSDALSVARDHUS
ULRIKSDALS SLOTTSPARK, SOLNA
☎ (8) 850815
19C country-inn restaurant set in a castle park
and well known for its lunchtime smörgasbord
and relaxing ambience.

ENCORE The **Stockholm Card** is the key to the sights of Stockholm. It gives you free
entrance to more than 60 places of interest, bus and boat tours and unlimited travel by bus,
underground and local trains. So does the **Göteborgskortet Card** within Gothenburg
which, in addition, offers free parking and reduced prices in selected shops and restaurants.
Cards for one, two or three days. Contact local tourist offices: for Stockholm, ☎ (8) 789 2495, fax
(8) 789 2491, and for Gothenburg ☎ (31) 100740, fax (31) 132184 . . . . ◆

Gothenburg

HOTELS

SHERATON HOTEL AND TOWERS
SÖDRA HAMNGATAN 59–65, PO BOX 288, S–401 24
☎ (31) 806000; fax (31) 159888
One of the most impressive hotels in Sweden it boasts a spectacular atrium lobby and several fine restaurants.

MUSIC

KONSERTHUSET
GÖTAPLATSEN
☎ (31) 167000
Built in 1935, and famed for its acoustics, the concert hall is home to the Gothenburg Symphony Orchestra under Sture Carlsson. Fine international performers also make the occasional guest appearance here.

RESTAURANTS

RAKAN
LORENSBERGSGATAN 16
☎ (31) 169839
Popular restaurant with unusual service: the tables are arranged around a long tank, and the house speciality, shrimp, arrives in a radio-controlled boat you navigate yourself.

SJOMAGASINET
KLIPPANS KULTURRESERVAT
☎ (31) 246510
Converted 18C shipping warehouse, offering great views of the port and very good fish specialities. Sit out on the terrace in summer.

SWITZERLAND
Basle

HOTELS

HOTEL DREI KÖNIGE
BLUMENRAIN 8, CH–4001,
☎ (61) 261 5252
Once an 11C coach stop and now one of the city's great landmarks. The building was expanded in 1835 and recently its opulent woodwork, paintings and furnishings have all been restored. Rooms overlooking the Rhine cost a little extra. The formal French restaurant has a heated terrace area so you can eat overlooking the river well into autumn.

RESTAURANTS

SEE ALSO HOTELS.

STUCKI
BRUDERHOLZALLEE 42,
☎ (61) 261 8222
Hans Stucki – ambitious, young and one of the finest chefs in the world – cooks modern classics. Usually necessary to book well in advance to get a table, either inside or alfresco in the charming gardens.

Geneva

HOTELS

BEAU-RIVAGE
QUAI DU MONT-BLANC 13, CH–1201
☎ (22) 731 0221
Beau-Rivage was a centre for European high society at the turn of the century. Set in a grand old Victorian palace where much of the original 1865 decor has recently been restored; velvet, parquet and frescoes abound, while each of the main rooms has retained fine old architectural details including the original fireplaces. Front rooms overlook the right bank of Lake Geneva as does the restaurant, LE CHAT BOTTE.

LE RICHEMOND
RUE ADHEMAR-FABRIS 8–10, CH–1211
☎ (22) 731 1400
Managed by the Armleder family for over a century, this hotel retains the opulence of its Victorian origins, with lots of scarlet, leather and gilt, without being overly grand. Flashy French cuisine in the resturant, LE GENTILHOMME (they get through 17 pounds of caviare a day). If you need to go anywhere, you can do it in style, as the hotel limousines consist of a selection of Rolls-Royces. The visitors' book gives a good overview of 20C culture: Colette, Miró, Walt Disney, Marc Chagall and, more recently, MICHAEL JACKSON are just a few of the names that appear.

RESTAURANTS

LE BÉARN
QUAI DE LA POSTE 4
☎ (22) 321 0028
Directed by young French chef Jean-Paul Godard, this small and elegant empire-style restaurant features predominantly modern, light and creative cuisine. The puddings are excellent too, as is the wine list featuring both French and Swiss vintages. Particularly popular with diplomats and politicians.

BRASSERIE LIPP
RUE DE LA CONFÉDÉRATION 8
☎ (22) 311 1011
Popular since its opening in 1986, the sister restaurant to the Left Bank brasserie in Paris is slick and synthetic-looking. Locals and foreigners come here for a quick but very good lunch. At night people queue up for the famous noise and animation along with pot-au-feu, platters of seafood and excellent beer.

LA PERLE DU LAC
RUE DU LAUSANNE 128
☎ (22) 731 7935
Set in one of the prettiest parts of Geneva, in a park-promenade beside a swan-populated lake. A grand wooden chalet with a summer terrace where you can have simple grilled meat dishes, fish and salads. Alternatively you can go for the more sophisticated panoramic restaurant, L'ORANGERIE which has views of the city and Mont Blanc.

Lausanne

HOTELS

BEAU-RIVAGE PALACE
CHEMIN DU BEAU-RIVAGES, CH–1000 OUCHY 6
☎ (21) 613 3333
Although there are many deluxe hotels in Switzerland, this gleaming *grande dame* is in a league of her own. The neo-classical structure has been seamlessly restored to its period opulence. The rooms vary, but the deluxe doubles overlooking the lake are some of the best in the country. Restaurants include the first-class LA ROTONDE; you can also eat outside in summer. "*Wonderful atmosphere and impeccable service, and a wine list from all over the world*" – ROBERTO GUCCI.

RESTAURANTS

SEE ALSO HOTELS.

GIRARDET
RUE D'YVERTON 1, CRISSIER, CH–1023
☎ (21) 634 0505
About 7 miles east of Lausanne, in a former town hall, is where you can track down Fredy Girardet, one of the best chefs in the world and named Chef of the Century by his Parisian peers. The waiting list for a table here is long: you must book at least a month in advance by phone, followed by a written confirmation and a large deposit. The classic French menu changes daily and features only the freshest ingredients. Make sure you allow the chef to advise you. Absolutely inspired food, hence the often hushed and reverent atmosphere.

LA GRAPPE D'OR
CHENEAU DE BOURG 3
☎ (21) 323 0760
Relaxed French restaurant serving imaginative modern cooking prepared to order by Bavarian chef Peter Baermann.

HOTEL RESTAURANT DE L'HERMITAGE
VUFFLENS-LE-CHÂTEAU
☎ (21) 802 2191
With a reputation beginning to rival Fredy Girardet, chef Bernard Ravet's double Michelin-starred restaurant offers an alternative at half the price. Housed in a cosy former winemaker's house surrounded by grand old trees, it's a very warm and welcoming restaurant with old beams and fireplaces you can sit beside with a glass of wine before dining. "*The chef is dedicated and his food is exquisite, up to the standard of Girardet. A restaurant to watch: it is going to be increasingly appreciated. They also have rooms so you can fully enjoy the evening*" – MARTIN SKAN.

Zürich

BARS AND CAFES

CONFISERIE SPRUNGLI
PARADEPLATZ
☎ (1) 221 1722
Landmark chocolatier and café for rich locals. They serve a good plain hot menu if you overdose on the sweet stuff.

HOTELS

BAUR AU LAC
TALSTRASSE 1, CH–8022
☎ (1) 221 1650
Highbrow father of Swiss hotels, it has less of the glitz and tackiness associated with hotels at this level. Looks out on to the lake and the manicured lawns of its own private park. In the summer meals are served in the glass pavilion beside the canal, and in winter in the RESTAURANT FRANÇAIS. The GRILL ROOM is a popular place for business lunches.

DOLDER GRAND HOTEL
KURHAUSSTRASSE 65
☎ (1) 251 6231
Sitting high on a hill above Zürich, this sprawling Victorian mansion offers unbeatable views of the city. The hotel, which is a picturesque mix of turrets, half timbers and mansard roofs, is reached by a funicular railway (free for guests). RESTAURANT LA ROTONDE serves excellent traditional French *haute cuisine*. Faultless facilities include a golfcourse with unique view, swimming pool complete with wave machine, and ice skating.

HOTEL WIDDER
RENNWEG 7, 8001
☎ (1) 224 2525
Situated in the middle of the town, just next to the famous 'Bahnhofstrasse', this sumptuous hotel has just been built at vast expense by The Union Bank of Switzerland. Each bedroom is overflowing with antique furniture and there is also a very good Jazz Club and bar.

RESTAURANTS

SEE ALSO HOTELS.

KÖNIGSTUHL
STUSSIHOFSTATT 3
☎ (1) 261 7618
Trendy and irreverent bar–bistro–restaurant complex, totally rebuilt from a traditional meeting hall. An oversized wooden throne (*Königstuhl*) and stylized gold banners decorate the entrance, along with jungle prints and swagged velvet. The cuisine is equally irreverent, with light suppers in the bistro downstairs and experimental international cuisine in the restaurant above, headed by chef Marc Zimmermann. In the summer meals are served on the sunny terrace.

Rest of Switzerland

ART AND MUSEUMS

FONDATION PIERRE GIANNADA
CH–1920, MARTIGNY
☎ (26) 22 3978
Large cultural centre featuring major art exhibitions, including, in recent years, the Modigliani retrospective in which previously unshown works from private collections were displayed. Also contains the popular Gallo–Roman museum.

HOTELS

LE MONTREUX PALACE HOTEL
GRANDE RUE 100, MONTREUX, CH–1820
☎ (21) 962 1212
Dominating the hillside above the Grande Rue and waterfront, this hotel is a colossal *belle-époque* folly full of stained glass, frescoes and flamboyant moulded stucco. A glassy shopping arcade and a pavilion across the street, accessible by tunnel, houses Switzerland's first HARRY'S NEW YORK BAR. The formal RESTAURANT DU CYGNE specializes in traditional Swiss food and seafood. Nice lakeside swimming pool.

RHEINHOTEL FISCHERZUNFT
RHEINQUAI 8, SCHAFFHAUSEN, CH–8200
☎ (53) 253281
A small hotel with nine individually decorated bedrooms, most of which have a great view over the Rhine. Also contains one of the country's best restaurants, run by French chef André Jaeger (who trained in Hong Kong) and his Chinese wife, Doreen.

MUSIC

FESTIVAL INTERNATIONAL DE MUSIQUE
MONTREUX TOURIST OFFICE, RUE DU THÉÂTRE, MONTREUX, CH–1820
☎ (21) 963 1212
Rather small and sedate classical music festival each Sept, featuring chamber music, philharmonic orchestras, recitals and 20C sounds which fill all the concert halls, churches and museums.

MONTREUX JAZZ FESTIVAL

MONTREUX TOURIST OFFICE, RUE DU
THÉÂTRE, MONTREUX, CH–1820
☎ (21) 963 1212
One of the world's most renowned rock and
jazz festivals, held every July. Big names – Elvis
Costello, Dizzie Gillespie – in the Casino hall.
Lesser-knowns tough it on the streets.

SKI RESORTS

CRANS

The resort of Crans-Montana is on a high
plateau, facing due south, where Mont Blanc
can be seen on a clear day. The resort offers
magnificent views over the Rhône Valley and,
because it is mostly south-facing, enjoys more
hours of sunshine than other Swiss resorts. For
non-skiers there's great shopping in the rue de
Golf. The best part of the region is the PLAINE
MORTE, a flat glacier a few miles long where
there is the best cross-country skiing for hundreds of miles. Experts should head for the
NATIONAL PISTE (site of the 1987 world
championships) or LA TOULA, where the
upper end is so steep it can't even be piste
bashed. One of the best hotels is AIDA
CASTEL, ☎ (27) 401111, oozing rustic chic,
with lots of terracotta and stucco, even though
it's set in a 60s-built resort. The new wing is
the best. The restaurant LA HOTTE serves
Italian fare, including a proper raclette made by
the fireside. The GRAND HOTEL DU GOLF, ☎
(27) 419758, is the true blueblood of Crans's
hotels. A genteel old resort built by English
golfers in 1908, it features 9- and 18-hole golf-
courses in summer.

GSTAAD

A charming village which consistently attracts
the jet set. It's famous less for the quality of its
pistes than for its glamorous hotels and clientele: PRINCE RAINIER et famille, ROGER MOORE,
THE BOUCHERONS and BULGARIS. It's at a point
where several valleys converge and in general
the climate is warmer than in many other ski
Alpine resorts. The best hotel is undoubtedly
the PALACE HOTEL, ☎ (30) 83131, a splendid,
burlesque-style fantasyland hotel standing
above the pine trees. It is also one of the most
expensive hotels in Switzerland, and hence in
the world – and one of the reasons that the
management will only accept cash. In contrast
the OLDEN HOTEL, ☎ (30) 343444, is a charming Victorian inn right in the centre of town.
Fresh, folksy and atmospheric, with state-of-

the-art bathrooms and a café serving great
food.

KLOSTERS

Small, smart, old-fashioned resort where
British royals go. Twinned with Davos, which
is Switzerland's second-largest resort (and
where you'll find the best skiing), it offers over
200 miles of piste and plenty of lifts, divided
equally among beginners, intermediates and
experts. The best and smartest place to stay is
the WALSERHOFF, ☎ (81) 691437, on the main
road in town. It has struck a clever balance
between old and new, and also serves great
food. The best restaurant is WYNEGG, ☎ (81)
691340. Cosy, slightly kitschy surroundings
with checked tablecloths and cuckoo clocks.
Also popular for a pint après-ski.

VERBIER

One of the top Swiss resorts for adventurous
skiing. About 5,000 ft up and right in the
middle of Switzerland's most famous transit
network, Téléverbier, which consists of a multitude of gondolas, cablecars and chairlifts
linking over 250 miles of piste and several
interlinking resorts. The ATTELAS and MONT
FORT sectors throw up a challenge to off-piste
experts and the black runs down to TORTIN
are thrilling. Good intermediate skiing down
the Lac de Vaux and on the opposite side of
the resort at SAVOLEYRES, but this is not really the place for beginners. The best hotels are
ROSALP, ☎ (26) 316323, a rustic hotel full of
honey-coloured pine, where you can also sample the great cooking of chef Roland Pierroz.
Go for the newer rooms, which have marble
baths, or the ones on the upper floors which
are cheaper and have better views. Smart
and comfortable. Or stay at RHODANIA,
☎ (26) 316121, built during the mid-60s but
chic inside. Lots of carved wood and a spectacular view.

ZERMATT

One of the world's most romantic ski resorts,
set just beneath the awe-inspiring Matterhorn
(14,500 ft high). Only horse-drawn sleighs and
electric taxis are allowed in town. The skiing is
very varied, and includes some of the best heli-
skiing in Europe. Non-skiers can take the
KLEIN MATTERHORN, a small train that creeps
up the mountain through an underground
tunnel. One aggravation is that the ski areas are
only connected at the bottom, which wastes
valuable skiing time. However, snow-making
machines mean that in Zermatt skiers are guaranteed 7,000 ft of vertical drop regardless of

ST MORITZ is the oldest, chic-est, and probably loopiest of Switzerland's resorts.

It is the original winter sports playground, established by the British, where the seriously sporty have access to some fairly decent skiing. Unusually for a country and people renowned for being very boring, St Moritz is full of colour and can at times be utterly surreal. There's the Cresta Run, for example, first established by the British and now dominated by Germans. Here grown men dress up in tweed plus-fours or latex bodystockings (depending on nationality) and thrust themselves down a manmade ice-shaft.

Around St Moritz there are three main ski areas – Corviglia, Corvatsch and Diavolezza-Laglap – and as the town is quite low in altitude you generally have to drive or take a funicular up to them. Oddities include the marquee/bar with a dance floor beside one of the cable car stations, halfway up a mountain. Here skiers kick off their skis, knock back the gluhwein and waltz in their boots. Another rather magical activity is the **Preda–Bergun toboggan run**. First you catch the evening train up to Preda, hire your toboggan and bomb down 3 miles of the old, winding road to Bergun. The smartest and most festive time to visit St Moritz is over Christmas and New Year, when the Cresta Run is in full swing. But the guestlists to the best clubs are invariably filled in advance – especially at New Year. Feb is the ultimate party month, and a bit more accessible, when Eurotrash turn up in droves to partake of cricket matches, horse-racing and polo. This is the time when families (many of whom have houses here) such as the AGNELLIS and the ROTHSCHILDS tip up.

The three main hotels are **Badrutt's Palace**, a pseudo-Gothic stone monster overlooking the lake, which in clientele and atmosphere feels more like an old people's home. Guests are ferried around in the hotel's Rolls-Royces. For skiers there are private skiing instructors, and for non-skiers the hotel regularly holds jewellery exhibitions and sales. The Palace also has its own evening hotspot, the **King's Club**. Further up there's the more appealing, pastel-coloured **Kulm Hotel**, owned by the Niarchos family (who also own the exclusive **Dracula Club** nearby). Here you can lunch in the famous **Sunny Bar**, favoured by the Cresta crowd, or have tea beside vast windows overlooking the mountains.

Of all the grand-scale hotels, the **Suvretta House** is the most discreet as well as the most family-oriented. It's slightly out of town in a smart residential area (nicknamed the Beverly Hills of St Moritz) and has unfettered Christmas card views of the mountains. It's a resort in itself with its own highly acclaimed ski school, ski lift, post office and several restaurants. As far as eating out is concerned, the best alpine restaurant is **La Marmite** on Corviglia, run by Reto Mathis, whose father Hartly was the first man to bring *haute cuisine* to the mountains. (Book ahead.) Immediately après-ski, everyone who's anyone traditionally heads for **Hanselmann's** in the town centre, the century-old coffee house serving chocolates and pastries to die for.

snowfall. The best place to stay is **MONT CERVIN**, ☎ (28) 668888, a sleek, urbane and luxurious but not grandiose hotel built in 1852. Best places to eat include **ELSIE'S BAR**, ☎ (28) 672431, a tiny log cabin which draws in an international crowd for cocktails and American-style light meals, as well as cheese dishes, oysters and snails. Great Irish coffee too. **FINDLERHOF**, ☎ (28) 672588, is a very stylish place filled with hip young people (often English and American). Stylish decor, great view and surprisingly good rösti and Käseschnitte (toasted cheese sandwiches).

THAILAND
Bangkok

ART AND MUSEUMS

GRAND PALACE
SANAMCHAI RD
☎ (2) 223 5172
Thailand's major landmark. The official residence of the king is the **CHAKRI MAHA PRASART** palace (built 1868–1910). To the left of the palace is the **AMARIN VINICHAI HALL** – note the glittering gold throne. Don't miss the small **EMERALD BUDDHA** (actually made of green jasper) which sits on the altar of the Wat Phra Kaeo, a traditional Thai monastery and the 160-ft long golden **RECLINING BUDDHA**. Don't wear shorts or T-shirts to visit these or any other religious sites in Thailand.

JIM THOMPSON'S HOUSE
6 SOI KASEMSAN 2, RAMA I RD
☎ (2) 215 0122
An incredible collection of Thai fine art and Southeast Asian furnishings. The houses were shifted from the ancient capital, Ayutthaya, by silk magnate Jim Thompson, who mysteriously disappeared in Malaysia in 1967.

CLUBS

Bangkok is one of the nightlife capitals of the world. While a lot of it is extremely seedy there is much for the sophisticate. Most of the nightlife will be found on **PATPONG I AND II**, packed with go-go bars, hostesses, massage parlours and every type of music. Alternatively, there's **SOI COWBOY**, off Soi 23 Sukhumvit

Rd, a more sedate version of Patpong with lively pub-style bars. And for something altogether more sober, **SILOM PLAZA** has many sophisticated café-bars which spill out on to the piazzas.

BLUES JAZZ
25 SUKHUMVIT RD 53
☎ (2) 258 7747
Listen to very talented jazz and blues musicians while sipping your drinks in the bar and waiting for a table in the rather good restaurant.

BROWN SUGAR
231–20 SARASIN RD
☎ (2) 250 0103
Lively bar split into several small rooms, attracting a lively crowd. Jazz and blues predominate.

HEMINGWAY BAR AND GRILL
SUKHUMVIT 55
☎ (2) 392 3599
Colonial-style old hunting lodge with an interesting collection of hunting and fishing trophies on display. Popular with Thais and expats who enjoy live jazz and country music.

OLD WEST SALOON
231/17 SOI SARASIN
☎ (2) 252 9510
Saloon bar re-creates the atmosphere of America's Wild West aided by swing doors and a great live band.

TAURUS
38/1 SUKHUMVIT 26
☎ (2) 261 3991–4
In with the local Thai in-crowd. Begin the evening to soft piano-playing in the restaurant then wind up in the disco.

HOTELS

HILTON INTERNATIONAL
2 WIRELESS RD
☎ (2) 253 0121
Set in 8 acres of landscaped gardens, complete with waterfalls, canals and bridges. Large, light bedrooms. Good nightclub, **JULIANA'S OF LONDON**, is attached. The award-winning **MA MAISON** restaurant serves continental food and **GENJI**, a Japanese restaurant serves good sushi and delicious Japanese breakfasts.

THE ORIENTAL
48 ORIENTAL AVE
☎ (2) 236 0400
For many years thought of as the world's best

• •

"EVERY HOTEL MANAGER IN THE WORLD SHOULD COME HERE TO LEARN WHY THE ORIENTAL CONTINUES TO BE THE BEST IN THE WORLD. SERVICE AND ATTENTION UNRIVALLED ANYWHERE" – KEN HOM ON THE ORIENTAL, BANGKOK

• •

hotel, this has been the resting place for practically every 20C dignitary or royal. Stay in one of several eponymous suites, such as the Noël Coward suite *"full of nostalgia with its dark green walls and four-poster cast-off Suez wooden beds, autographed happy snaps of the man himself, and first editions of Coward's works"* – JILL MULLENS. Or try the Graham Greene or the Somerset Maugham suite. Make sure you stay in the old part, rather than the modern wing, for a taste of the old colonial days. And don't leave without having had a top-to-toe session in the fabulous teakfloored spa. Helicopter as well as boat service available to the airport. The **AUTHOR'S LOUNGE** is great for a quick cup of tea and the **RIVERSIDE TERRACE** offers cocktails and a nightly barbecue. All the restaurants are firstrate (see Restaurants), with **LORD JIM'S** (fish), **LE NORMANDIE** (French), the **CHINA HOUSE** (Cantonese) and the **SALA RIM NAM** (Thai/Chinese). *"Unbeatable, old-fashioned class and luxury,"* says LADY HARDINGE.

THE REGENT
155 RAJADAMRI RD
☎ (2) 251 6127
More convenient than the Oriental for businessmen, and as good as the Oriental in many other respects. The lobby is amazing, with its hand-painted silk murals on walls and the bedrooms are luxurious. **LE CRISTAL** is a good restaurant, while Continental cuisine is served

at the informal **LA BRASSERIE**. The **REGENT GRILL**, a wonderfully designed French restaurant, has an outdoor terrace overlooking the incredible gardens.

SUKHOTAI
SATHRON TAI RD
☎ (2) 287 0222
Adrian Zecha's rarefied Bangkok hotel is still largely unknown by even the most privileged travellers. Full of marble and teak, it's a quintessentially minimalist hotel. And the food is totally exquisite, with some of the most delicate flavours that you'll find anywhere in Bangkok. Excellent service.

RESTAURANTS

SEE ALSO HOTELS.

LE BANYAN
SOI 8, 59 SUKHUMVIT RD
☎ (2) 253 5556
Imaginative French cooking from ex-Normandie chef Bruno Bishoff, with the odd traditional Thai spice thrown in. The lovely setting, in an old wooden Thai house with the silver duck press as its centrepiece in the dining room, provides added interest.

BUSSARACUM
35 SOI PIPAT 2, CONVENT RD
☎ (2) 235 8915
The place for traditional "Royal Thai" cooking. Beautifully presented dishes shaped like various birds. Great for fish too.

CALIFORNIA SEAFOOD GROTTO
PACHA U THI RD, SOI RAMKAMHAENG 39
☎ (2) 274 3959
The kind of food that Wolfgang Puck would cook if he lived in Bangkok, with all of those exotic local ingredients to juggle with. Fun, experimental cuisine that also works.

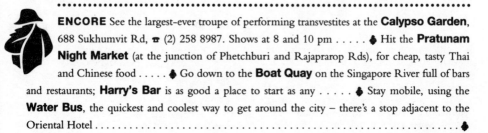

ENCORE See the largest-ever troupe of performing transvestites at the **Calypso Garden**, 688 Sukhumvit Rd, ☎ (2) 258 8987. Shows at 8 and 10 pm . . . . . ♦ Hit the **Pratunam Night Market** (at the junction of Phetchburi and Rajaprarop Rds), for cheap, tasty Thai and Chinese food . . . . . ♦ Go down to the **Boat Quay** on the Singapore River full of bars and restaurants; **Harry's Bar** is as good a place to start as any . . . . . ♦ Stay mobile, using the **Water Bus**, the quickest and coolest way to get around the city – there's a stop adjacent to the Oriental Hotel . . . . ♦

THE CHINA HOUSE

"A favourite restaurant of mine which features fine Cantonese cuisine prepared by four master chefs from Hong Kong" – ALAIN DUCASSE.

DYNASTY

AT THE CENTRAL PLAZA HOTEL, PHAHOLYOTHIN RD
☎ (2) 541 1234
Undoubtedly one of Thailand's best Chinese restaurants. Cantonese cooking *par excellence*. The house speciality is intriguingly named Monk Jump Over the Wall, comprising a mixture of delicacies ranging from shark's fin and abalone to deer sinew and dried turtle. Private dining rooms are available.

EL GORDO'S CANTINA

130/8 SILOM SOL 8, SILOM RD
☎ (2) 287 1415
Authentic Mexican cuisine and lively Mexican music played by a Filipino band. Relaxed and popular place for meeting and eating.

IMAGERIES

2 SUKHUMVIT 24, KLONGTON
☎ (2) 255 8835
Recently moved from Sukhumvit Soi 11, but retaining its unique art gallery-style decor, this popular restaurant produces Thai and European dishes to the highest standard at a reasonable price.. Do take advantage of its so-called music hall, where you can relax and listen to fine, live jazz and country.

LEMON GRASS

5/1 SOI, 24 SUKHUMVIT RD
☎ (2) 258 8637
Exquisite Thai food in an old Thai house decorated with Southeast Asian antiques and beautiful tapestries. Plenty of atmosphere in several small dining rooms and an outdoor dining area in the garden.

LORD JIM'S

AT THE ORIENTAL (SEE HOTELS)
☎ (2) 236 0400
Sit in a dining room done up as a 19C steamship stateroom and eat fabulous fish – particularly popular with the locals.

MAYFLOWER

DUSIT THANI HOTEL, RAMA IV RD
☎ (2) 233 1130
Fantastic Cantonese cooking in an aesthetically pleasing restaurant. The service is incredible – they even keep a record of what you had, ready for your next visit.

NATHONG

RATCHADAPISEK RD
☎ (2) 246 2160–1
The peaceful garden setting – together with its freshwater pond and fish – is as delightful as the food served. Very reasonably priced.

LE NORMANDIE

AT THE ORIENTAL (SEE HOTELS)
☎ (2) 236 0400
Perched at the top of the Oriental Hotel with fantastic views, Le Normandie offers classic French cuisine and great service. The French chefs import ingredients from home and some consider this to be some of the best French cuisine found anywhere in the world.

RA-CHA

13/2 MOO 3, RATANATIBETH RD, NONTHABURI
☎ (2) 585 8303
In an enchanting location in the bank of the Chao Phraya River, the Ra-Cha offers you a choice of air-conditioned comfort indoors or dining under the stars. Alternatively, have dinner while cruising down the river in a specially prepared boat.

ROYAL DRAGON RESTAURANT

35-222 BANGNA-TRAD
☎ (2) 398 0040–3
Possibly the largest restaurant in the world, it sits on a phenomenal 80-acre site and seats 5,000 people. Computer-run with hundreds of roller-skating, walkie-talkie-toting staff, a Thai and Chinese culture show theatre, music, dancing – and actually very good food.

SALA RIM NAM

AT THE ORIENTAL (SEE HOTELS)
☎ (2) 236 0400
"Take a boat across the river to the Sala Rim Nam – an absolutely wonderful Thai/Chinese restaurant which also has its own cooking school; ideal for wives who accompany their business executive husbands" – LADY HARDINGE. The hot salads are particularly recommended and there's often live Thai dancing in the evenings.

SANUKNUK

411/6 SUKHUMVIT SOI 55
☎ (2) 390 0166
Originally a drinking hole for Thailand's writers and artists, this place now offers a unique one-off menu with many of the traditional dishes originating from women from northern Thailand. Extremely lively, though somewhat eccentric.

SEAFOOD MARKET AND RESTAURANT

388 SUKHUMVIT RD

☎ (2) 276 1810

Push your shopping trolley around the market, choose the fish you want to eat from an amazing choice and then a waiter will come to your table and suggest how they can cook it. Great fun.

SPASSO

GRAND HYATT ERAWAN, RAJADAMRI RD

☎ (2) 254 1234

Sip cocktails and tuck into tasty clay-oven-baked pizzas and other Italian food while being entertained by an American band playing the blues.

SPICE MARKET

AT THE REGENT HOTEL (SEE HOTELS)

☎ (2) 251 6127

Spice Market looks like a well-stocked spice shop with sacks of spices and old racks holding earthenware jars. Here authentic recipes are served: lots of Thai curries and superb peppered foods.

TRADER VIC'S

AT THE ROYAL GARDEN RIVERSIDE, CHAROEN NAKORN RD

☎ (2) 476 0021–2, EXTN 1436

This elegantly decorated restaurant carries on the famous tradition of serving exotic cuisine from the South Pacific and Asia. Enjoy dishes from Hawaii, Tahiti and other parts of Polynesia while sipping imaginative cocktails such as The Potted Parrot and the Samoan Fog Cutter.

SHOPPING

For jewellery, try Princess Chailai's shop CHAILAI, Peninsula Plaza on Rajadamri Rd, which stocks northern Thailand pieces along with society dazzlers from Bulaad and Frank's. If you want something custom-made, try the A A COMPANY in the Siam Center.

For the best tailors try MARCO TAILOR, 430 Siam Sq, Soi 7, ☎ (2) 220689, where you can get a suit that might even rival Savile Row, very fast.

THE JIM THOMPSON THAI SILK COMPANY, 9 Surawong Rd, ☎ (2) 234 4900, is *the* place to buy silk by the yard – prices aren't cheap but the quality is fantastic. Fabulous dyes on all types of silk and ready-to-wear clothing; everything from marvellous pyjamas, cushions and purses to lipstick holders.

For designer wear, go to KAI GUERLAIN, 2–14 N Wireless Rd, ☎ (2) 253 2998. Alternatively, there's CHOISY, 9/25 Suriwongse Rd, ☎ (2) 233 7794, where you can buy Parisian-style clothing in exquisite Thai silk. Trendier gear is available on the 2nd floor of the CHARN ISALA TOWER, Rama V Rd, where you should look out for society dressmaker TEERAPHAN WANARAT, who does both day and evening wear.

Shopaholics should try the WORLD TRADE CENTER and the SIAM CENTER, which are full of little boutiques and shops. Thailand is terrific for fake designer goods, so try SILOM RD, where stalls are set up from the afternoon to late evening, or you can go to the GAYSORN area or the market in PATPONG.

Chic shoppers should definitely head for the REGENT AND ORIENTAL ARCADES and THANIYA PLAZA, between Silom and Suriwongse Rd near Patpong. LOTUS ARTS DE VIVRE in the Regent Arcade sells beautiful, but dizzyingly expensive Thai antiques, fabric and jewellery.

Fine ethnic crafts are sold at THAI HOME INDUSTRIES, 35 Oriental Ave. KRISHNA'S, 137–6–7 Sukhamvit Rd (between Soi 9 and 11), ☎ (2) 254 9944, has three floors of Oriental handicrafts, from elephant chairs to Burmese rugs to pottery. Also well respected, if a little more expensive, is PENG SENG, 942 Rama IV, ☎ (2) 234 1285.

All "antiques" can be checked for authenticity by the Fine Arts Department, ☎ (2) 233 0977.

Rest of Thailand

··

"SUN AND SEA BATHING IN THE
MEDITERRANEAN IS NOW SO
OVERCROWDED AND UNSANITARY
THAT ONE EITHER NEEDS THE
LUXURY OF A BOAT OR THE
OPTION OF NEW BEACHES IN
NORTH AMERICA, THE PACIFIC,
SOUTHEAST ASIA OR AFRICA" –

CLAUS VON BULOW

··

HOTELS

AMANPURI

PANSEA BEACH, PHUKET

☎ (76) 311394

The first of the Amanresorts (see Indonesia). The Amanpuri consists of 40 separate Thai temple-style suites set in 20 acres of coconut

Loyd Grossman on Scuba Diving

I began scuba-diving at the age of 10, gave it up by 20 and started again at 40ish, inspired by the fact that Phuket, one of my habitual destinations, is surrounded by superlative diving.

If you are not claustrophobic, didn't believe *Jaws*, swim reasonably well and are fit, you will be able to learn to scuba-dive on holiday. Thailand is as good a place as any to start, but you could also consider places like the Cayman Islands, Indonesia, Israel or Egypt. Britain offers some of the best wreck diving but the water is awfully cold.

Any destination that claims to offer even halfway decent diving will have diving schools and instructors available. Avoid anyone who offers to take untrained divers out to sea. Diving is safe, but things can go horribly wrong, and it is not a pursuit for the untrained and ill-prepared.

Most diving schools you come across will be affiliated to a big organization such as BSAC (British Sub Aqua Club) or PADI (Professional Association of Diving Instructors, an American organization). Both of these produce excellent diving manuals, and their courses are well thought out. Graduates of their schools are issued with a card that enables them to hire equipment and to dive around the world.

Even so, not all diving schools are created equal, so you must use your instinct to get a sense of how well run and businesslike the school you choose appears to be, and to judge whether the equipment is safe and in reasonable condition. Your hotel should be able to recommend a good local diving school.

Before you go away, do some homework by contacting BSAC or PADI for recommendations or by looking at advertisements in diving magazines, available from most newsagents. *Diver* is associated with BSAC, while PADI have some good magazines under their wing too; *Dive* is also excellent.

The basic course is a mixture of classroom lectures, bottom-of-the-swimming-pool work, written exams and, most excitingly, two open-water dives. Answer the questions, do your stuff at sea with some proficiency and within a week you will be a qualified diver (albeit a Novice, which means you must dive with a dive leader or instructor-level buddy until further qualified).

In Thailand, diving instructors tend to be nomadic Germans, Japanese or Australians. I am told that the mix is pretty much the same around the Far East but that you will find more British instructors around the Red Sea. It hardly matters, though, since the instruction is almost always in English.

You will not need to buy the whole aquanaut kit unless you are going to dive regularly throughout the year, but you should probably have your own mask and fins at least. You can dive wearing contact lenses, but if, like me, you wear glasses, you can get a mask with a prescription faceplate. It's better to arrange this *before* you go on holiday.

The rewards of scuba diving are immense and include a tremendous sense of freedom, thrilling encounters with weird and beautiful marine life, and citizenship – if only temporary – of a completely different world.

plantation, each with a private sun deck, sunken tub and beautifully crafted furniture made from local wood. Great pool, secluded beach, Thai and Italian restaurants. Hire the hotel's Chinese junk for picnic lunches or sunset booze cruises. Paradise.

BAAN TALING NGAM
295 MOO 3, TALING NGAM, KOH SAMUI, SURRATTHANI, 84140
☎ (42) 3019/022
Fabulous Mandarin resort on the northwestern coast of Koh Samui. Decorated in traditional Thai style with the most blissful service.

DUSIT RESORT AND POLO CLUB
1349 PETCHKASEM RD, CHA'AM, PECHBURI 76120, HUA HIN
☎ (32) 520009
Exclusive and luxurious, this hotel offers great rooms with private balconies overlooking the sea, swimming pool or cascading fountains. The restaurant offers a superb choice of Thai, Chinese and European food – the beef and pumpkin curry is highly recommended. The nearby bazaars in Hua Hin are fabulous, where you can find terrific fresh food with lots of duck. There's also a stunning gold statue 40 ft high on the beach.

TURKEY

Istanbul

Istanbul is best visited in spring or the beginning of summer, before it gets too hot. You can stay in one of several old palaces – now grand hotels – and visit the lively **GRAND BAZAAR**, exploring thousands of little shops, restaurants and cafés. Visit the magnificent mosque of **SANTA SOFIA**; the **TOPKAPI PALACE**, with its golden wonders; the **BLUE MOSQUE** (of Sultan Ahmet Camii), with its famous blue tiles and 260 stained-glass windows – and don't forget to have a look at the **HAREM** where the Sultan and his wives once lived.

HOTELS

The top hotels are located in the New Town, on the northern shore of the Golden Horn.

CIRAGAN PALACE HOTEL

CIRAGAN CAD 84, BESIKTAS

☎ (212) 258 3377

Istanbul's most expensive hotel, with superb rooms, Turkish baths, health spa, sauna and a glorious swimming pool. *"Endless views of mosques and the Bosphorus, chefs cheffing up all kinds of Turkish delights in the kitchen and a wildly romantic history, all cocooned in an elderly palace, make this the standout hostelry in Istanbul"* – JILL MULLENS

DIVAN

CUMHURIYET CAD 2, SISLI

☎ (212) 231 4100

Recently updated hotel with rooms that have terraces overlooking the Bosphorus. Good restaurant serving Turkish and international food, and a pub.

HYATT REGENCY

TASKISLA CAD, TAKSIM

☎ (212) 225 7000

This vast hotel is a tasteful, opulent affair. Views over the Bosphorus, muted tones within and thick, muffling, deep-pile carpets throughout.

PERA PALACE

MESRUTIYET CAD 98, TEPEBASI

☎ (212) 251 4560

19C palace built to accommodate guests arriving on the Orient Express, with a splendid view across the Golden Horn to the old town. Ataturk used to stay here (as did Greta Garbo and Agatha Christie) – his room still contains his personal belongings.

YESIL EV

KABASAKAL SOK 5, SULTANAHMET

☎ (212) 517 6785

An oasis of peace in the middle of hectic Istanbul, this 19C converted Turkish house, in its fabulous location next to the Blue Mosque, is decorated in traditional Ottoman style. The restaurant is set in a beautiful high-walled garden.

RESTAURANTS

BEBEK AMBASSADEURS

CEVDET PASA CAD 113, BEBEK

☎ (212) 263 3002

Good French and international cuisine while sitting on the terrace overlooking the sea.

BORSA LOKANTASI

YALIKOSKU CAD, YALIKOSKU HAN 60-62, EMINÖNÜ

☎ (212) 232 4200

Unpretentious restaurant serving some of the best food in Turkey.

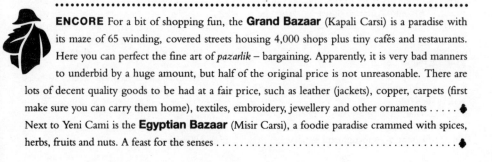

ENCORE For a bit of shopping fun, the **Grand Bazaar** (Kapali Carsi) is a paradise with its maze of 65 winding, covered streets housing 4,000 shops plus tiny cafés and restaurants. Here you can perfect the fine art of *pazarlik* – bargaining. Apparently, it is very bad manners to underbid by a huge amount, but half of the original price is not unreasonable. There are lots of decent quality goods to be had at a fair price, such as leather (jackets), copper, carpets (first make sure you can carry them home), textiles, embroidery, jewellery and other ornaments . . . . . ♦ Next to Yeni Cami is the **Egyptian Bazaar** (Misir Carsi), a foodie paradise crammed with spices, herbs, fruits and nuts. A feast for the senses . . . . ♦

COASTING ALONG For the sun seeker, Turkey is the ideal holiday destination, especially along the Aegean coast: not only is it the cheapest country in the Mediterranean, despite its gain in popularity over Greece, but also, according to JILL MULLENS, *"the Turkish coast is bliss. B-grade movie blue waters, pine trees, safe moorings, endless antiquities for shore jaunts and simple local food accompanied by wines which won't test your bank account. The only serpent in this yachting paradise is there's often not enough wind to satisfy keen skippers."* **Abercrombie & Kent** (see Travel Directory) offer very good tailormade or guided tours around Turkey, including cruises. You can choose to go bareboat but there are plenty of skippered and crewed boats available too.

GELIK
SAHIL YOLU, ATAKOY
☎ (212) 560 7284
This 19C villa is always packed with diners, which speaks for the high quality of food, especially the speciality Turkish meat dishes cooked in deep wells.

🐌 HACI SALIH
ANADOLU HAN 201, OFF ISTIKLAL CAD, BEYOGLU
☎ (212) 243 4528
A tiny, family-run restaurant with only ten tables and excellent traditional Turkish food worth queueing up for. Great lamb and vegetable dishes. Bring your own wine.

HANEDAN
CIGDEM SOK 27, BESIKTAS
☎ (212) 260 4854
All kinds of kebabs are served here and the setting is lively. Better than your average Istanbul kebab.

TUGRA
CIRAGAN CAD 84, BESIKTAS
☎ (212) 258 3377
Located in the historic Ciragan Palace, Tugra dishes up delicious old-style Ottoman recipes. Marble columns frame the view of the Bosphorus, and beautiful chandeliers hang from the high ceilings.

ULUS 29
AHMET ADNAN SAYGUN CAD, ULUS PARK
☎ (212) 265 6181
Seafood in an attractive park setting with a terrace overlooking both Bosphorus bridges.

VIETNAM
Hanoi

HOTELS

For a large capital, Hanoi still offers a relatively low standard of accommodation, but this is set to change. For character and charm, the venerable old **FRENCH PULLMAN METROPOLE HOTEL**, 15 Ngo Guyen, ☎ (4) 826 6919, is the best in downtown Hanoi, having been restored. Another grand relic of past eras is Hanoi's flagship luxury hotel, the Cuban-built, Soviet-style **THANG LOI HOTEL**, Yenphu, West Lake, ☎ (4) 826 8211, about 3 miles outside the city.

RESTAURANTS

For dancing, drinking and eating in an international atmosphere, the **PIANO BAR AND RESTAURANT**, 93 Phung Hung, ☎ (4) 825 9425, and **RESTAURANT 202**, 202 Pho Hue, ☎ (4) 825 9487, are popular. For a more authentic atmosphere and cuisine, the adventurous seek out the many tiny places – usually unsignposted and often just a few tables in a flat tucked away down a back alley.

Ho Chi Minh City

Ho Chi Minh City, on the west bank of the Saigon River, is far more vibrant than Hanoi,

---

A FISHY TAIL When in 1975 the North Vietnamese army took Ho Chi Minh City, or Saigon as it then was, the Continental Hotel was used to billet their troops. Simple country boys that they were, some soldiers bought live fish from the market which they stored in the lavatory – until one of their number, overcome by curiosity, pulled the chain. The fish disappeared in a flush and the enraged soldiers blasted the lavatory toilet to bits. It's probably not true, but all the toilets in the hotel do happen to be brand-spanking new.

---

with an intoxicating and energetic atmosphere imbued with the fledgling spirit of capitalism.

HOTELS

The wonderful old colonial **CONTINENTAL (HAI AU) HOTEL**, 132 Dong Khoi, ☎ (8) 829 4456, offers the most characterful and comfortable accommodation in the city. Sit in the lovely central courtyard garden with a cooling drink and soak up the unique ambience. It's the sort of hotel that fosters myth. Graham Greene used it as the backdrop for *The Quiet American*, many an ex-Vietnam War hack can describe the underside of its bar stools, and CATHERINE DENEUVE called it home while she was in town to make *Indochine*. Recently refurbished, the Continental is done out in French-colonial style – a cool limewash on the outside, with balconies, big windows, colonnades and, in the middle, a pretty courtyard garden. **DONG KHOI ST**, Vietnam's best souvenir market, is right on the doorstep, the travel agencies and airline offices are close and the bars of **HAI BA TRUNG ST** are within staggering distance. Despite the central location, it is one of the few hotels in Vietnam where you won't need earplugs at night. And while facilities are minimal, the staff are always helpful, despite the fact that the hotel enforces a no-tips policy – a minor miracle in a country where the dollar bill is the equivalent to three days' wages for a teacher.

Down the street, the **REX (BAN THANH) HOTEL**, 141 Nguyen Hue, ☎ (8) 829 2185, has stood as the city's *grande dame* since the time of the American occupation. The open-air rooftop restaurant, still decorated in a garish 60s style, is perfect for an incredibly cheap meal, and the view and atmosphere are fantastic – it'll doubtless be renovated soon, so visit beforehand. The **MAJESTIC (CUU LONG) HOTEL**, 1 Dong Khoi, ☎ (8) 829 5516 – once the chic-est of French hotels, where Graham Greene used to relax and write – still retains a shabby elegance and is another great place for an open-air meal with a view. The best hotel in terms of luxury and mod cons is the **NEW WORLD HOTEL**, 76 Le Lai Street, ☎ (8) 822 8888. This newly built hotel is complete with tennis courts, swimming pool and a fully equipped gym.

RESTAURANTS

LA BIBLIOTHÈQUE DE MADAM DAI, 84A Nguyen Du, ☎ (8) 8231 438, is perhaps the most popular restaurant, and the venerable **MAXIMS**, 13–17 Dong Khoi, ☎ (8) 8296 676, offers live music while you dine, plus there's dancing upstairs. For a taste of excellent home-style Vietnamese cuisine, try **THANH NIEN**, 135 Hai Bai Trung, ☎ (8) 8225 909, or wander down through the **BEN THANH MARKET** area, with its warren of local foodstalls and street kitchens, and sample such local delicacies as snake, bat and porcupine.

TRAVEL DIRECTORY

Best yachts . . . . . **CAMPER & NICHOLSONS**, 25 Bruton St, London W1X 7DB, ☎ (0171) 491 2950, is the oldest yachting company in the world, established in 1782. Today its network of offices throughout the world continues to sell, charter, manage and construct some of the most glamorous and famous yachts (motor and sail) ever.

Best holidays for families . . . . . **CLUB MED**, 106–110 Brompton Rd, London SW3, ☎ (0171) 225 1066, or ☎ (01455) 852249 for brochures, was set up over 45 years ago in France. It is now the world's largest all-inclusive holiday organization, with over 110 resorts worldwide covering sun, cruise and ski holidays; wonderful for families, and suitable for adults too. Children's facilities start from 4 months old, including childcare, and a vast range of sports with tuition.

Best of the Bosphorus . . . . . **SAVILE TOURS & TRAVEL**, Savile House, 6 Blenheim Terrace, St John's Wood, London NW8 OEB, ☎ (0171) 625 3001. Tailormade tours and itineraries from a collection of villas with pools, mini-cruises in the Med, mansions and former palaces of the sultans of Istanbul – well away from the crowded tourist beaches. Specializes in Turkey . . . . . **THE GREEK ISLANDS CLUB**, 66 High St, Walton on Thames, Surrey KT12 1BU, ☎ (01932) 229346, specializes in customized holidays to the most exclusive Greek properties.

Best train journeys . . . . . **ORIENT EXPRESS HOTELS**, Inc, Sea Containers House, 20 Upper Ground, London SE1 9PF 0171, ☎ (0171) 620 0003, established by James Sherwood in 1976, now oversees a series of luxurious trains. The Venice Simplon–Orient Express, with its 20s-style chic, travels between London, Venice, Prague and other major European cities. The Eastern & Oriental Express is the way the sybarite should see 1,200 miles of tropical landscape linking Singapore, Thailand and Malaysia. There's no shortage of space on either of the trains with en suite bathrooms and big fat armchairs by the windows. Don't forget to dress for dinner . . . . . The coolest way to see northern India is on board the **PALACE ON WHEELS**, c/o Greaves Travel, ☎ (0171) 487 5687. This train is fully air-conditioned and comprises rolling stock once owned by maharajahs. Meals are served by splendid liveried staff and evenings spent in the very best hotels.

Best of the wild . . . . . Originally founded as a safari company in Kenya, **ABERCROMBIE & KENT**, Sloane Square House, Holbein Pl, London SW1W 8NS, ☎ (0171) 730 9600, has now extended its repertoire from Andalucía to the Antarctic with offices throughout the world. However, A & K still offer some of the most exclusive, extensive and expensive safaris available . . . . . **ART OF TRAVEL LTD**, The Bakehouse, Bakery Pl, 119 Altenburg Gdns, London SW11 1JQ, ☎ (0171) 738 2038, also offers a wide variety of tailormade tours for individuals and groups in eastern and southern Africa and the Indian Ocean Islands. A great way to see Africa in style, using small, luxury tented camps and lodges which offer a range of activities including game drives, walking safaris, canoeing and horse riding . . . . . If you want to experience the most exclusive (and one of the most remote) natural parts of the world, **WORLDWIDE JOURNEYS AND EXPEDITIONS**, 8 Comeragh Rd, London W14 9HP, ☎ (0171) 381 8638, offers the best trips to the Galapagos islands. It also does tailor-made trips to other remote parts of the world while specializing in everything from safaris in Africa to treks in Nepal, Borneo and South America . . . . . **CAZENOVE & LLOYD**, Unit 1, 39 Tadema Rd, London SW10 0PY, ☎ (0171) 376 3746, offers safaris to eastern or southern Africa or to an island in the Indian Ocean. Though geared to the novice, any kind of holiday is put together for the independent traveller, and they'll arrange what you want to do rather than impose things on you. Good on the action holiday: walking or riding, canoeing and white-water rafting . . . . . The best fishing – from salmon and trout to saltwater, everywhere from Alaska to Cuba to Zanzibar – can be arranged by ROXTON BAILEY ROBINSON, 25 High St, Hungerford, Berks RG17 0NF, ☎ (01488) 683222.

Best of India . . . . . described as the kings of Indian travel (as well as Latin American), COX & KINGS TRAVEL LTD, 4th floor, Gordon House, 10 Greencoat Pl, London SW1P 1PH, ☎ (0171) 873 5000, organizes escorted and customized tours throughout India and the sub-continent with excellent local back-up in the places visited . . . . . If you want to head south, THE CAPE TRAVEL CO LTD, 18A Church Grove, Hampton Wick, Surrey KT1 4AL, ☎ (0181) 943 4067, specializes in Kerala, and other parts of southern India, including the Lakshadweep Islands. Offers hire of private old Keralan House, visits to Somatheeram, an ayurvedic health resort on a hillside of palm trees, and cruises on houseboats in the Keralan backwaters.

Best skiing . . . . . THE SKI COMPANY, Abercrombie & Kent Travel, Sloane Square House, Holbein Pl, London, SW1W 8NS, ☎ (0171) 730 9600 for the most luxurious and beautifully appointed chalets from Chamonix to Vail. Quite pricey but this always includes delicious four-course dinners, breakfast in bed, free babysitting, ski school for children, champagne and canapés before dinner with butler and cook service, as well as the use of a chauffeur-driven or self-drive car hire . . . . . For first-hand up-to-date knowledge of resorts throughout Europe, the United States and Canada, SKI SOLUTIONS, 84 Pembroke Rd, London W8 6NX, ☎ (0171) 602 2882, is a specialist agency (rather than tour operator). It aims to find your ideal holiday, along with the best and most luxurious accommodation in hotels and apartments, in over 100 ski resorts.

Best of the Caribbean. . . . . . CARIBBEAN CONNECTION, Concorde House, Forest St, Chester, ☎ (01244) 329556 for brochures, customizes the most exclusive holidays to the Caribbean. They'll send you to the best and most carefully vetted hotels and resorts, from Cobblers Cove, Barbados, to the Montpelier Plantation Inn, Nevis, to villas, private islands and yachts. They also offer the best rates and availability on Concorde . . . . . ELEGANT RESORTS, The Old Palace, Chester, CH1 1RB, ☎ (01244) 897999, still features smart holidays to the Caribbean but has also branched out. They have now applied the same formula to the Orient, the Indian Ocean and the South Pacific as well as various top hotels and resorts in Europe.

Best Mediterranean villas . . . . . CV TRAVEL, 43 Cadogan St, London SW3, ☎ (0171) 581 0851, is the original villa company with some of the smartest villas in the Med, from farmhouses to palaces in Majorca, Corfu, Paxos, Andalucía, Portugal, Corsica and the Tuscan and Umbrian hills.

Best of the exotic . . . . . STEPPES EAST, Castle Eaton, Swindon, SN6 6JU, ☎ (01285) 810267, creates the best tailormade itineraries to Russia, China, Central Asia, Bhutan, India and other destinations in the East, together with long weekends in Morocco or St Petersburg and holidays to some of the world's most exquisite resorts. Will suit the intrepid and enquiring traveller wanting to see the world's most interesting countries, museums and people . . . . . WESTERN & ORIENTAl, 56 Ledbury Rd, London W12 2AJ, ☎ (0171) 221 8677, headed by Studley Bruce Palling, specifically arranges holidays for the rich and famous, from a private island in Greece or the Indian Ocean to a Maharajah's tented camp.

Best musical holidays . . . . . TRAVEL FOR THE ARTS, 117 Regent's Park Rd, London NW1 8UR, ☎ (0171) 483 4466, arranges holidays to see the best orchestras and singers in the world's legendary opera houses, for ballet as well as opera lovers. Escorted tours for small groups and customized arrangements for individuals are offered, including tickets for highlights of the opera season and summer festivals such as Verona. Sightseeing and backstage tours can often be arranged too.

Best walking or cycling . . . . . ALTERNATIVE TRAVEL LTD, 69–71 Banbury Rd, Oxford OX2 6PE, ☎ (01865) 310399, takes the strain out of your cycling or walking holiday. They will tailor your programme to your requirements, complete with picnic lunches en route, servicing for your cycle and sending your luggage on ahead to the next hotel, all in some of the most picturesque parts of Europe . . . . . You'll be equally well cosseted by BUTTERFIELD & ROBINSON, Suite 300, 70 Bond St, Toronto, Canada, ☎ (416) 864 1354, who specialize in cultural walking and cycling holidays in Italy, France and now Africa.

INDEX

REPORT FORM

Courvoisier's Book of the Best is completely independent and regularly updated every two years. We accept no advertising or payment of any kind from establishments mentioned in this book. We would welcome your views on the current selection of entries and/or suggestions of any places you feel deserve to be included.

Please send your comments to:
Courvoisier's Book of the Best
Ebury Press
Random House
20 Vauxhall Bridge Road
London SW1V 2SA

PLACE NAME . . . .

ADDRESS . . . .

. . . .

TELEPHONE/FAX NUMBER . . . .

COMMENT . . . .

. . . .

PLACE NAME . . . .

ADDRESS . . . .

. . . .

TELEPHONE/FAX NUMBER . . . .

COMMENT . . . .

. . . .

PLACE NAME . . . .

ADDRESS . . . .

. . . .

TELEPHONE/FAX NUMBER . . . .

COMMENT . . . .

. . . .

CONTINUED OVERLEAF

PLACE NAME . . . .

ADDRESS . . . .

. . . .

TELEPHONE/FAX NUMBER . . . .

COMMENT . . . .

. . . .

PLACE NAME . . . .

ADDRESS . . . .

. . . .

TELEPHONE/FAX NUMBER . . . .

COMMENT . . . .

. . . .

PLACE NAME . . . .

ADDRESS . . . .

. . . .

TELEPHONE/FAX NUMBER . . . .

COMMENT . . . .

. . . .

PLACE NAME . . . .

ADDRESS . . . .

. . . .

TELEPHONE/FAX NUMBER . . . .

COMMENT . . . .

. . . .